The Coventry Leet Book:

OR

Mayor's Register,

CONTAINING THE RECORDS OF THE CITY

Court Leet

OR

View of Frankpledge,

A.D. 1420–1555,

WITH DIVERS OTHER MATTERS.

TRANSCRIBED AND EDITED BY

MARY DORMER HARRIS,

AUTHOR OF "LIFE IN AN OLD ENGLISH TOWN: A HISTORY OF COVENTRY COMPILED FROM OFFICIAL RECORDS."

PARTS III-IV

Original Series
138 and 146

LONDON:
1909, 1913

KRAUS REPRINT CO.
New York
1971

ADDITIONS AND ERRATA.

p. 628, note 1, for "the *Boke of Husbandrie* is sometimes attributed to him" read "the *Boke of Husbandrie*, sometimes attributed to him, appears to have been the work of his elder brother, John Fitzherbert, Lord of the Manor of Norbury from 1483 to 1531" (Sir Ernest Clarke).

p. 781, for "Joh. Warde, mercer" read "Joh. Waide, mercer."

The
Coventry Leet Book:
OR
Mayor's Register.

Early English Text Society.
Original Series, No. 138.
1909.

BERLIN: ASHER & CO., 13, UNTER DEN LINDEN.
NEW YORK: C. SCRIBNER & CO.; LEYPOLDT & HOLT.
PHILADELPHIA: J. B. LIPPINCOTT & CO.

The Coventry Leet Book:

OR

Mayor's Register,

CONTAINING THE RECORDS OF THE CITY

Court Leet

OR

View of Frankpledge,

A.D. 1420–1555,

WITH DIVERS OTHER MATTERS.

TRANSCRIBED AND EDITED BY

MARY DORMER HARRIS,

AUTHOR OF "LIFE IN AN OLD ENGLISH TOWN: A HISTORY OF COVENTRY COMPILED FROM OFFICIAL RECORDS."

PART III.

LONDON:
PUBLISHED FOR THE EARLY ENGLISH TEXT SOCIETY
BY KEGAN PAUL, TRENCH, TRÜBNER & CO., Ltd.,
DRYDEN HOUSE, 43 GERRARD STREET, SOHO, W.
AND BY HENRY FROWDE, OXFORD UNIVERSITY PRESS,
AMEN CORNER, E.C., AND IN NEW YORK.
1909.

OXFORD
UNIVERSITY PRESS

Great Clarendon Street, Oxford OX2 6DP
United Kingdom

Oxford University Press is a department of the University of Oxford.
It furthers the University's objective of excellence in research, scholarship,
and education by publishing worldwide. Oxford is a registered trade mark of
Oxford University Press in the UK and in certain other countries

© The Early English Text Society 1971

The moral rights of the authors have been asserted

Database right Oxford University Press (maker)

First Edition published in 1971

All rights reserved. No part of this publication may be reproduced,
stored in a retrieval system, or transmitted, in any form or by any means,
without the prior permission in writing of Oxford University Press,
or as expressly permitted by law, or under terms agreed with the appropriate
reprographics rights organization. Enquiries concerning reproduction
outside the scope of the above should be sent to the Rights Department,
Oxford University Press, at the address above

You must not circulate this book in any other form
and you must impose this same condition on any acquirer

Published in the United States of America by Oxford University Press
198 Madison Avenue, New York, NY 10016, United States of America

British Library Cataloguing in Publication Data
Data available

Library of Congress Cataloging in Publication Data
Data available

Original Series, 138, 146

ISBN 978-0-85-991885-5

FOREWORD.

To the historian of social life this—the third and concluding—portion of the Leet Book proper will be of the greatest interest. It is true that, unlike its immediate predecessor, Part III has few of those vivid personal touches concerning the doings and character of the citizens, or the movements of royal folk, such as gave so distinctive a feature to the episode of Laurence Saunders or the chronicles of the Wars of the Roses.[1] As a set-off to this deficiency, however, local historians and philologists will be inclined to attach great value to the frequent occurrence of familiar names and of rare words, special characteristics of the formal and business-like entries of which Part III mainly consists. On the whole, therefore, the matter of this issue is so instructive that, though the manner of it is rather precise like the lawyer's than discursive like the chronicler's, this volume must be regarded as of equal, though divergent, value with that of its predecessors.

It is impossible in these few words to deal with the economic questions which beset England between 1496 and 1555. They must wait for the more ample space of the Introduction in the concluding volume. But one salient problem for the town-dweller appears with startling frequency in this volume and cannot be quite passed over—it is the adjustment of the opposing claims of the monopolist craftsman within the town and the stranger at the gate, a matter further complicated by the intrusion of the town employer and consumer.[2] The stranger appeared as workman, craftsman, buyer and seller, and found his liberty restricted in every capacity. As a workman, possibly residing in a neighbouring village, he competed with the native craftsman, carpenter,[3] weaver[4] and fuller[5]; as a buyer he came into conflict with the native purchasers of raw material, yarn,[6]

---

[1] See, however, for survivals of this literary spirit Roger à Lee's election, pp. 619–21; Henry VII's death, pp. 625–6; and Walgrave and Whitley, pp. 626–7.
[2] See p. 795. [3] p. 807. [4] p. 661 *et passim*.
[5] p. 704. [6] p. 791.

vi Foreword.

malt,[1] hides[2] and tallow[3]; and as a seller with the native purveyors of victual.[4] The orders of Leet concerned with the making and unmaking of the craft of butchers, and with the admission and exclusion of the "Warwick" members of that calling, are among the most instructive entries later scribes have preserved for us.

Though the information we gather from these pages concerns men rather locally than nationally famous, circumstances have so combined to keep their memories fresh that the mere mention of many is a thing that adds interest to the record. Such are the names of Bond,[5] Ford,[6] Pisford,[7] Wheatley,[8] who, from the permanence of their charitable foundations—associated as they are with Tudor buildings of rare beauty—have gained at least a local immortality; while the memories of Wade,[9] Nethermyll,[10] Swyllyngton,[11] are likewise recalled by tomb or effigy in S. Michael's. The names of William Hopkyns,[12] Richard Sewall,[13] Edward Damporte[14]—or Davenport—strike a familiar chord by reason of our acquaintance with the doings of their better-known collaterals or descendants, a remark applying with particular propriety to William Shelley,[15]—not a Coventry man though he served as recorder of the city—whose family a later scion has made famous all over the world.

Another recorder sprang from the historic Warwickshire line of Throckmorton[16]; another, Antony Fitzherberde—or Fitzherbert[17]—a relative of the Willoughbys of Middleton, was famous as a legal writer; while a third, also with local connections, Edward Saunders,[18] is mentioned in the pages of the martyrologist, Foxe, and gains, through his brother Laurence, a certain interest. The author of the *Acts and Monuments of Martyrs*, whose wife's father and early patron was one Randall[19] of Coventry, refers also to other citizens, Christopher Waren[20]—or Warren—and Thomas Ryley,[21] in connection with Glover, the martyr, and to Richard Hopkyns.[22]

When we come to consider special words we note the unusual meaning, rare or early occurrence, of bowet,[23] strike,[24] forest iron,[25]

---

[1] p. 637. [2] pp. 585, 689 *et passim*. [3] p. 650.
[4] pp. 717, 780, 795, 803. [5] p. 588. [6] p. 582. [7] p. 600.
[8] p. 779. [9] Chris. Wade, p. 694. [10] p. 634. [11] p. 642.
[12] p. 598. [13] p. 724. [14] p. 796. [15] p. 635.
[16] p. 806. [17] p. 628. [18] p. 764.
[19] The name of William Randle occurs p. 721. Possibly this is Foxe's patron.
[20] p. 811. [21] *ib*. [22] *ib*. See also Astelyn, p. 694.
[23] p. 588. [24] p. 657. [25] p. 745.

Foreword. vii

piece-work,[1] and maystyme.[2] Botomes[3] has a Shakesperean interest. Among technicalities of the cloth trade we can only infer the meanings of bondyng[4] and dobbyn,[5] while wronghalf[6] eludes inquiry. The use of the words ardolf,[7] targes[8]—in connection with sport— and grand warrant[9] in this volume is, as far as I have been able to learn, unique.

Some miscellaneous matter, together with the introduction, glossary and index, will form a fourth volume.

[1] pp. 773, 792.   [2] p. 787.   [3] p. 796.   [4] p. 639.   [5] p. 640.
[6] ib.   [7] p. 719.   [8] p. 690.   [9] p. 684.

§ 81. Hen. Marler, Mayor, 1496.

MICHAELMAS LEET.

[1] ¶ [V. f. p. held on Thursday after Michaelmas, 12 Hen. VII.]   *"Couentre."* Oct. 6.

Ric. Lee, Joh. Gauge, Joh. Thrumpton, Ric. Braytoft, Will. Shore, Hen. Marler, Tho. Bailly, Will. Roweley, Tho. Chircheman, Rob. Grene, Joh. Padland, Will. Hopkyns, Ric. Smyth, Tho. Bonde, Will. Taillour, Will. fforth, Geff. Arthern, Tho. Padland, Joh. Gryme, Ed. Hulcote, Joh. Mathewe, Joh. Hadon, Rog. Mason, Joh. Stronge.   Jury.

[Edm. Barbour, Will. ffletcher, sherman.]   Sheriffs.

[Ordained] that no maner persone dwellyng within this Cite frohensfurth vexe, troble, assaute nor varie with eny his Neighbours withoute þe Citie in eny ffeire, market, or other place be measne of þe lawe feynyng matier ayenst hym or other wyse be which he myght take eny hurte in his persone, name or goodes, vppon peyn to lese at euery defalt C s. without pardon to þe vse of þe Condite to be apploied.   Orders of leet. Litigation forbidden, or 100s. fine.

At þis lete were Joh. Tedde & Hobley presented that they had bought & sold in gret hides contrarie to þe ordenaunces þeruppon made etc.[2]   The purchase of hides wholesale.

At þis lete was graunte to Will. Nashe þe Grey-fre[r]-ȝate & ij gardeyns duryng his life, vt [p]atet in filaciis.[3]   Grant of land to the common sergeant.

HEN. MARLER, MAYOR, 1496-7.

[4] ¶ [Election of a new mayor in Coventry on Saturday, Dec. 3. 12 Hen. VII. before Will. Roweley, formerly mayor of the said town and holding the place (loco (sic) tenenie) of the office of mayoralty of the said town,— that office being vacant by the death of Joh. Dove formerly mayor of the seid town, who died (diem suum clausit extremum) on Saturday Nov. 26 last preceding, and Ed. Barbour and Will. ffleccher, bailiffs of the said town.[5]]   *"Couentre."*

Joh. Gauge, Ric. Braytoft, Joh. Thrumpton, Will. Shore, Tho. Baylly, Rob. Colman, Ric. Lee, Tho. Churchman, Rob. Grene, Joh. Padland, Will. Hopkyns, Ric. Alen, Will. Tayllour, Joh. Gryme, Gal. Arthern, Tho. Maydford, Tho. Padland, Ed. Hulcote, Ric. Nores, Rob. Bowyer, Joh. Throughley, Tho. Grove, Joh. Whythed, Joh. Sissell.   Electors.

---

[1] leaf 278, back.   [2] v. p. 557.
[3] As in the files [of the Leet more fully] appears.
[4] leaf 279.   [5] "iuxta etc." follows.

§ 82. Will. Ford, Mayor, 1497.

[They elect H. Marler mayor until the next feast of the Purification. And this interval shall be accounted to him for a whole year, and for the remainder of his life he shall have as great privilege & liberty as he who has occupied the office for two years.]

Qui eligerunt (*sic*) Hen. Marler Maiorem, vsque festum Purificacionis B. Marie virginis tunc proximo sequens. Et tempus illud stabit sibi pro vno anno integro, et decetero durante vita sua habebit tam grande preuilegium & libertatem in omnibus sicut & ille qui officium illud per duos annos [1] integros in Ciuitate predicta preantea occupauit.

WILL. FORD OR FORTH, MAYOR, 1497.

¶ [[2] Election of officers.]

"Couentre." Jan. 25.

Will. Roweley, Joh. Gauge, Ric. Braytoft, Joh. Thrumpton, Will. Shore, Tho. Bailly, Rob. Colman, Ric. Lee, Tho. Chircheman, Rob. Grene, Joh. Padland, Ric. Alen, Will. Hopkyns, Joh. Gryme, Geff. Arthern, Tho. Maideford, Edw. Hulcote, Tho. Padland, Ric. Nores, Rob. Bowyer, Joh. Throughley, Tho. Grove, Joh. Whitehed, Joh. Sissell.

Officers.

[m. Will. fforth; cor. Rob. Topclyf; ch. Will. Bromley, Joh. Smyth, peauterer; w. Joh. Clerk, Grocer, Joh. Saunders, capper; mace, Hen. Walker; crier, Joh. Toures.]

SOLDIERS.

"xlviijti." Mar. 4, 1497.

Mem. that þe iiij^th day of March [12 Hen. VII] the Maire assemblyng his brether to þe nombre of xlviij because of a commaundement direct to them fro þe kynges grace be priue signet to be acertayned howe many persones fensibly arraied at þe kynges wages his grace shuld haue

There accompany the king on his voyage to Scotland

oute of þis Cite to attend vppon his grace in his viage roiall towardes Scotland, at which tyme was graunted xl able persone[s] with a Captaign then named, Tho. Maidtford,[3] to be fensibly arraied with jaketes & a standard to awayte vppon his grace at his wages, whech shuld be prepared at þe cost of Craftes in þis Cite as foloweth.

"40 souldiers set forth by Companys."

[Mercers and fishmongers 5 men; drapers and skinners 5 men; dyers and barbours 3 men; smiths and cooks 2 men; girdlers 1 man; weavers, bowyers and fletchers 2

---

[1] Marler had served previously, *v.* p. 503.   [2] leaf 280.
[3] The same man who was wounded at Bosworth, *v.* p. 532.

§ 82. *Will. Ford, Mayor. Taxes,* 1497.

men; whittawers, glovers and tanners 3 men; tailors and shearmen 3 men; corvisers 3 men; wiredrawers "with Humf. Belchier, Will. Ouerton, Ric. Crosseley & Wilkes" 1 man; wrights, pinners, tilers 1 man; bakers, millers, "with Joh. Pachet and Hen. Broune," 3 men; walkers and cappers 2 (?) men [1]; butchers 3 men; cardmakers, painters, saddlers and masons, "with Ropers, berebruers and Hen. Crosse," 2 men; "fforreyns" 2 men.]

THE FIFTEENTH.

[2] Mem. that at þe parliament holden at Westmynstre [Jan. 16, 12 Hen. VII] there was there graunted to þe kynges grace towardes his viage roiall into Scotland ij hole xv^{es} & a subsidy amountyng to þe somme of ij hole xv^{es}; þe first xv & þe half subsidy to be paiable þe last day of May then next folowyng; and the other xv & half subsidy to be paide the viij day of Nouembre then next folowyng, yf þe kynges grace went not into Scotland, & vppon oþer condicions as in the acte þerof made more pleynly appereth. The seid ij xv to be levied after the olde vsage & custome vsed to levie & pay xv^{es}. And to þe subsidy amountyng to þe somme of ij hole xv^{es} there shuld no persone pay onlesse he myght spend xx s. be ȝere ouer all charges, or els þat he be worth in goodes x marc' ouer all charges not accomptyng his plate nor houshold. Which first hole xv^{e} & þe half subsidye was paide at þe day assygned & þe other half subside was pardoned, & þe ij^{de} hole xv^{e} was paiable as appereth proximo folio.[3]

Here folowen the names of þe Collectours of þe first xv^{e} paiable þe last day of May anno xij° H. vij.

[For the names of wards,[4] hamlets[5] and sums[6] *v.* p. 406-7. The collectors' names are missing.]

1497.
Two fifteenths and a subsidy.
Half payable May 31;
half Nov. 8.

May 31, 1497.

---

[1] ij d. = 2d. in MS. ? a mistake. There are 39 men without any supplied by the walkers and cappers. [2] leaf 280, back.
[3] The first subsidy is given, leaf 280, back; the second (proximo folio) *i. e.* leaf 281.
[4] "Wel-strete" given instead of "Bischop-strete."
[5] "Asthull".and "Wodend" are not expressly named.
[6] On p. 407 Weston is assessed at 2s. Here "Weston iiij s. pro Boyes-waste" occurs; but a smear over the first two strokes of the iiij s. looks like an intended deletion. On leaf 281 it reads "Weston pro Boyswast iiij s." No total from wards or hamlets on leaf 280, back.

§ 82. Will. Ford, Mayor. Leet, 1497.

Nov. 8, 1497.

¹ Here followen the names of the Collectours² of a hole xv paiable³

[See above for names of wards, hamlets and sums. Total from the wards £50 0s. 8d. No total from hamlets.]

EASTER AND MICHAELMAS LEETS.

"Couentre."
Apr. 6.

⁴ ¶ [V. f. p. held before Will. fforth, m., Ed. Barbour, Will. ffleccher, b., on Thursday after the close of Easter, 12 Hen. VII.]

Jury.

Will. Roweley, Hen. Marler, Ric. Braitoft, Joh. Gauge, Tho. Baylly, Joh. Thrumpton, Will. Shore, Ric. Lee, Joh. Wygston, Tho. Chircheman, Rob. Grene, Joh. Padland, Tho. Bonde, Will. Taillour, Will. Hopkyns, Geff. Arthern, Tho. Maideford, Tho. Padland, Joh. Hadon, Edw. Hulcote, Ric. Jakson, Rob. Chambre, Will. Bromley, Joh. Saunders, Capper.

⁵ "ffor the Cundites."⁵
⁶ "No brewer to fetch water,

They woll & ordeyn that no bruer nor Malt maker nor oþer person frohensfurth fet eny watir at eny of þe Cundites within þis Cite to brue ne to stepe, but only for dressyng of mete & drynk, [or 20s. fine, half to the sheriffs, half to the cunduit at every default.] And þat prouision be made be Maister Maire & his Counceill that grates & lokkes be made to loke with all the Cundites in þe nyght, & persones named to kepe þe lokkes & to vnlok hit in þe mornyng; & to lok hit at certen tymes as can be thought resonable; and þat the Chamberleyns & wardeyns

nor no pipes for privat vses."

Informers to have 8d. reward.

with þe comien seriant within viij daies next suyng make serche yf eny suspirals⁷ be in eny house, garden or other grounde within þis Cite. & that knowen they furthwith to be closed & stopped & non such to be suffered hereafter in no wyse nor for no money; and that euery person that hereafter can espie or proue eny persone offend contrarie to þe premissez & woll shewe hit to Maister Maire, or þe alderman of his warde, haue for his so shewyng & provyng viij d. parte of þe seid forfeit etc.

¹ leaf 281. In both cases of the collection I have sacrificed chronology to subject matter. ² Not given.
³ Blank. ⁴ leaf 279. ⁵⁻⁵ Contemporary gloss.
⁶ Later hand. ⁷ = openings.

§ 82. Will. Ford, Mayor. Leet, 1497.

[Ordained] that þe ordenaunce before made þat no bochour shull sell his hides in gret sale shuld stand in effect & be executory;[1] and þat þe Tanners within þis Cite haue fre liberte to bye at all daies & tyme after þe hide is of þe bestes bak, so þat hit lye in þe market iij houres; and þat no straunger by no maner hides but on þe market daies, þat is to sey, Tewesday, Thursday & Seturday; and that frohensfurth nother on þe parte of þe Tanners, ne of þe bochours, ther be eny confederacy or priuate ordenaunce made amonges either of þe seid Craftes contrarie to þe ordenaunces afore made be lete, & which myght be hur[t]full to ether of þe seid Craftes, or contrarie to þe comien wele, [or 20s. fine for every default, half to the sheriffs, and half to the cunduit.]

"Betwixt Tanners & bochours ordinances."

Hides to lie three hours in the market.

[Ordained] that Buttur & Johan his doughter shuld fynde suerte of theire gode demeasnyng hereafter.

[2] *"ffor Buttour and his doughtour."* [2]

[Ordained] at þe pertiticion of þe hole ffeliship of smythes that no man shuld set vp within this Cite to occupie be hym-self vnto þe tyme he were agreed with þe maistre of þe Craft, & to pay for his fyn xx s., hit to be paide in iij ȝeres be even porcions.

[2] *"For þe Smythes."* [2]

[3] ¶ [V. f. p. held on Tuesday before S. Edward King and Confessor, 13 Hen. VII.]

"Couentre." Oct. 10.

Hen. Marler, Joh. Gauge, Ric. Braytoft, Joh. Thrumpton, Will. Shore, Ric. Coke, Tho. Bailly, Tho. Chircheman, Ric. Lee, Rob. Grene, Joh. Padland, Tho. Bonde, Ric. Smyth, Will. Taillour, Will. Hopkyns, Joh. Duddesbury, Geff. Arthern, Edw. Hulcote, Tho. Padland, Joh. Darlyng, Tho. Maidford, Ric. Jakson, Will. Bromley, Joh. Saunders.

Jury.

[Tho. Grene, vyntoner, Will. Deister, Grasyer.]

Sheriffs.

[Ordained] that all maner persones that hereaftur woll haue the belles to ryng after þe decesse of eny their frendes they shall pay for a pell ryngyng with all þe belles ij s., xx d. þerof to þe Chirchewark[5] & iiij d. to þe Clerkes; and yf he woll haue but iiij belles xvj d., xij d. to the Chirch & iiij d. to þe Clerkes. And as for iij belles euery person þat will haue them to paye but iiij d. to þe Clerkes.[6]

[2] *"For ryngyng of belles."* [2]

[4] *"2s. a peale 5 bells, xxd. a peale 4 bells."* [4]

---

[1] See p. 557. [2–2] Contemporary gloss.
[3] leaf 279, back. [4–4] In later hand. [5] *i. e.* repairs.
[6] The church affairs are evidently managed by the corporation.

§ 82. Will. Ford, Mayor. Leet, 1497.

[marginal: ² " For the Cundites." ²]

[Ordained] that euery persone inhabityng within þe wardes of þe Croschepyng, Smythford, Brodeʒate, Sponstrete, Erle-strete, & Bailly-lane hauyng & openyng a hall durre shall paye quarterly towardes the reparacion of þe Cundites j d.,[1] euery shop ob., euery Cotage ob., the first day of payement to be-gyn at þe fest of Cristmas nex[t] comyng. And who-so denyeth payement of þat he is taxed, he to be distreined be þe Gaderers þerto assigned for the double þat he is taxed; and þe seid Gaderes to haue euery of them for theire labour euery quarter iiij d.

[marginal: 1d. from every hall door.]

Here folowen the names of þe Gaderes thei assigned at þe seid lete :—

[marginal: Collectors of the rate.]

Croschepyng.   John Peyntour, Ric. Stevenson.
Erle-strete.   Hen. Hynde & Joh. Bradbury.
Brode-ʒate.   Joh. Clerk, Rog. Bromley.
Bailly-lane.   Ric. Shore, Ric. Garton.
Smythford.   Ric. Baron, Will. Alen.
Spon-strete.   Tho. Gates, Mores Smyth, Joh. Eyburn.

[marginal: ² " For þe Comien Ryver and stretes." ²]

[Ordained] that all maner persones hauvyng grounde adioynyng to þe Ryuers of þis Cite that they sufficiently let clense þe seid Ryuers before theire groundes betwix þis and þe fest of seynt Marten next comyng [or 6s. 8d. fine] þat to be levied oppon euery person not perfourmyng þe seid ordenaunce be þe comien seriant & Crier for the tyme beyng, and to þe vse of þe Cundite; and they to haue for their labour of euery vj s. viij d. forfetyd xij d. And after þe Ryuer is so clensed euery man frothensfurth to kepe hit clene before his grounde, vppon þe seid peyn. And that euery persone takyng eny persone vppon his grounde beryng eny filth into þe Ryver, or if he fynde hym [blotted and illeg.] þat he haue cast into þe ryuer, then such person that taketh such offender haue auctorite be þis present lete to distreign such offendour, or take plege; and þat distresse or plegge to kepe vnto þe tyme he haue made satisfacion towardes þe clensyng of þe seid Ryuer, that to be demed be þe alderman of þe warde where such defalt shall hap to fall. And that all open & comien places as be adioynyng to þe seid Ryuer be sufficiently

[marginal: The river to be cleansed, the fines to be levied by the common sergeant and the crier.]

[marginal: Informers may distrain upon offenders.]

---

[1] " d " repeated.   [2]—[2] Contemporary gloss.

§ 82. Will. Ford, Mayor. Conduits, 1497.

made with pale or otherwyse þat no person may cast dong into þe Ryuers in such places. And that euery person euery Saturday fro hensfurth for euer let swepe the stretes before their groundes, & the dong furthwith to ber away. *And yf eny person fayle eny Saturday in þat partie he to lose ij d. furthwith to be paide & gadered be þe comien seriant & Crier for the tyme beyng, which shall euery Sonday at afternoon & þe Munday go thurgh þe towne to ouerse that hit be kept continielly & wokely, the seid officers to haue j d. & þe oþer j d. to þe vse of þe Cundite. And yf eny person defendyng[1] refuse to pay ij d., & þat shewed to þe Maire for the tyme beyng be þe seid officers, then such person to paye iiij d., half to them and half to þe Cundite. And also hit is ordeyned þat the seid officers fayle not wokely to ouerse & execute duely & truly þe premissez, vppon þe peyn to lese iiij d. for euery woke, that to be levied be the swirdberer & þe Meirs seriant, half to themself & half to þe Cundite.

The streets to be swept on Saturdays

or 2d. fine,

or on refusing 4d.

The officers are not to fail to make a weekly collection.

THE MAYOR'S ACCOUNTS.

[2] Mem. that Will. fforth, Mayor of þe Citie of Couentre, the Wensday next before þe fest of þe Purificacion of our Lady, the xiij[th] ȝer of the reign of kyng Henre þe vij[th] at Couentre aforeseid before Joh. Wygston, the Maister of þe Trinite Gilde, Hen. Marler, Joh. Gauge, Ric. Braytoft, Joh. Thrumpton, Will. Shore, Tho. Bailly, R. Colman, Ric. Lee, Tho. Chircheman, Rob. Grene, & Joh. Padland in þe Counceill-house in seynt Marie hall shewed & made a cler accompt of such money as he had resceyued þat ȝere to þe vse of þe Cite.

ffirst, he resceyued of Hen. Colyns, Bochour, for a fyn xl s. Item, of money gadered of dyuers persons in þe wardes of þis Cite for þe reparacion of þe Cundites viij li. Item, of Bakers & Bochours & other þat offended contrarie to þe ordynaunces[3] of þis Cite at dyuers tymes xxxix s. viij d.

   Summa totalis resceyued xj li. xix s. viij d.

Of which somme was spent in lede & oder thynges

Jan. 31, 1498.
The mayor

received 40s. for a fine;
£8 0s. 0d. for the conduits;
fines £1 19s. 8d.
total £11 19s. 8d.

---

[1] denying.   [2] leaf 280, back.
[3] A stroke of "n" missing.

§ 83. *Tho. Bonde, Mayor*, 1498.

Payments
£10 0s. 0d.
Balance
£1 19s. 8d.

necessarie for rep*ara*cio*n* of þe Cund*ite*s as the seid Maire there & then shewed openly before his seid Brethern more at large x li. & so þ*er* rested vnspent xxxix s. viij d. Whićh som*m*e of money the seid Maire then & there let put into a bag & left hit in þe Counceill house in þe Maires Bowet[1] ther.

He thus departed quit.

Et sic quiet*us* recessit.

THO. BONDE, MAYOR, 1498.

"Couentre."
Jan. 25.

[2] ¶ [Election of officers.]

Joh. Wygeston, Hen. Marler, Joh. Gauge, Ric. Braytoft, Joh. Thrumpton, Will. Shore, Ric. Coke, Tho. Baylly, Rob. Colman, Ric. Lee, Tho. Churchman, Rob. Grene, Joh. Padland, Joh. Haddon, Will. Taillo*ur*, Tho. Maydeford, Tho. Padland, Ed. Hulcote, Will. Pysford, Joh. Dwall, Joh. Sissell, Joh. Smyth, Baker, Joh. Throughley, Ric. Nores.

Officers.

[m. Tho. Bonde ; cor. Rob. Topclyff ; ch. Hen. Perkyns, Dauid Chyrk, Coruis*er* ; w. Ric. ffoxale, Joh. Norton, Capper ; mace, Hen. Walker ; crier, Joh. Tours.]

THE BENEDICTINES' CHAPTER.

About July 2 the black monks hold a chapter here and go on procession.

[3] This ȝere the Chapt*ur* of blak monk*es* was kept at Couentre aboute þe visitacio*n* of our Lady. And many of the*m* cam on the Saturday at nyght, & some on þe Morowe & taried there vnto Wensday ; at which day t*h*ey had a gen*er*al p*ro*cession. And they came forth at þe south durre in þe Mynstere & toke their wey thurgh the newe bildyng downe þe Bailly-lane. And the Maire & his Brethern in their scarlet Clok*es* w*ith* all the Craft*es* in theire best araye stode vnder þe Elme in Seynt Mighell*es* Chirchȝard. And all þe pensels[4] of þe Cite before the*m* : whech pensels there went before the Crosse, & þe Maire w*ith* his Brethern & the Craft*es* stode styll till þe p*re*sident*es* cam whom the Maire toke be þe hand*es* & welcomed

The mayor and others stand under the elm,

and welcome them

---

[1] A box. Not given in this sense *N. E. D.*, which gives *bowet* = a lantern. But probably here the meaning is *box*, from F. *boite*, Mid. L. *boeta*.

[2] leaf 281. Another scribe, F.   [3] Scribe B.

[4] = streamers.

§ 83. *Tho. Bonde, Mayor. Black Monks*, 1498.

them to town, & so folowed þe procession ; which proces- *and join the procession.*
sion went down the Bailly-lane, & so forth as is vsuelly
vsed on[1] seynt George day ; & so into þe Priory ; & there
was a solempne sermon seyde, where the Maire there satte
betwixt both presidentes, & after sermon doon they
departed euery man to his loggyng & som with the Maire
to dyner, as dyuers of them did before. And so the
departed furth of þe Cite etc.

Be it had in mynde that ayenst their comyng the Maire *The mayor as clerk of the market makes a book of the price of victuals.*
satte as Clerk of þe market & made enquere of þe price of
all maner vitailles & made a boke þerof ; & set hit vp on
þe south durre in þe Mynster like as is doon when the
kynges grace or my lorde prynce cometh to þe Cite. And
ouer þat let make serch to þe aldermen in euery warde in
all þe hostries of þe Citie that horsemet & mannes-mete
shuld be accordyng to þe sisse sette, and þat they shuld
not sell hit to excessyue lucre.

RECEPTION OF PRINCE ARTHUR.

[2] Mem. that this ȝere the Wensday the xvij day of *Oct. 17.*
Octobre anno xiiij° Regis H. vij, prince Arthur, the ffirst
begoton son of kyng Henre the vij[th], then beyng of þe age
of xij ȝeres & more, cam first to Couentre & there lay in þe
priory fro Wensday unto þe Munday next suying, at which
tyme he removed toward London. Ayenst whos comyng
was þe Spon-strete-ȝate[3] garnysshed with the ix worthy[s],
and kyng Arthur then hauyng thus spech, as foloweth :—

[KING ARTHUR.] Hayle, prynce roiall, most amyable in *King Arthur promises that*
sight !
Whom the Court eternall, thurgh prudent gouernaunce,[4]
Hath chosen to be egall ons to me in myght,
To sprede our name, Arthur, & actes to auaunce,
And of meanys victorious to have such habundaunce,
That no fals treitour, ne cruell tirrant,
Shall in eny wyse make profer to your lande.

---

[1] MS. son.
[2] leaf 281, back. Printed Sharp, *Mysteries*, 154–7, and Hardin Craig (E.E.T.S.), 116–18. I have adopted the form of stanza of the latter.
[3] MS. ȝarte.   [4] A stroke of "n" too few.

§ 83. *Tho. Bonde, Mayor. Prince Arthur,* 1498.

And rebelles all falce quarels schall eschewe,

the favour of Pallas shall help to subdue enemies.

Thurgh þe fere of Pallas, that favoreth your lynage
And all outward Enmyes laboreth to subdue,
To make them to do to yewe as to me dyd homage.
Welcome therfore, the solace & comfort of my olde age,
Prince pereles, Arthur, Icome of noble progeny,
To me & to youre Chambre with all þis hole companye!

And at the turnyng into þe Croschepyng before Maister
Thrumpton's durre, stode þe barkers paiant well appareld,
in which was the Quene of Fortune with dyuers other
virgyns, whech quene has þis spech folowyng:—

Dame Fortune

[QUEEN OF FORTUNE.] I am dame Fortune, quene called,
　full expedient
To Emprours & princes, prelates, with other moo
As Cesar, Hectour, & Fabius, most excellent,
　Scipio, exalted Nausica, & Emilianus also,
　Valerius, also Marchus, with sapient Cicero.
E and noble men, breuely the truth to conclude, all
My favour verily had, as storys maketh rehersall;

With-oute whom, sithen non playnly can prospere,
　That in þis muitable lyfe as nowe procedyng,
I am come thurgh love. Trust me intiere
　To be with yewe & yours Evirmore enduryng,
　Prynce, most unto my pleasure of all þat ar nowe reyn-
　　yng;

bids him welcome.

Wherfore, my nowne hert & best beloved treasure,
Welcome to þis youre Chaumbre of whom ye be inheriture.

And the Crosse in the Croschepyng was garnysshed, &
wyne there rennyng, and angels sensyng & syngyng, with
Orgayns and othere Melody etc.[1] And at þe Cundyt, ther
was seynt George kyllyng the dragon, and seynt George
had this speche folowyng:—

---

[1] Sharp, p. 156, quotes *Chamberlains' Accounts*, made up anno 1499, It. pd. for settyng of the posts in þe Croschepyng, when þe king (*sic*) was here, in gret ij s; it. for takyng down of þe same posts a-geyn x d; it. for pavyng in þe Cros-chepyng ther as þe posts stode of viij yards viij d.

§ 83. *Tho. Bonde, Mayor. Prince Arthur,* 1498.

[SAINT GEORGE.] O most soue*r*aign lorde, be dy[vy]ne[1]   S. George
  p*r*ovision to be
The ruler of cruell Mars & kyng Insupe*r*able!
Ye reioyce my corage, trustyng hit to se,
  That named am George, you*r* patron fauorable;
  To whom ye ar & eue*r* shal be so acceptable,
That in felde, or Cite, whe*r*e-so-ever ye rayne
Shall I neue*r* fayle yewe, thus is my purpose playn.

To p*r*otect you*r* magnyficence myself I shall endevo*u*r,
  In all thynge*s* that yo*ur* highnes shall concerne,
M*o*re tenderly then I ʒit did ever;
  Kyng, duke, yerle, lorde, or also berne,[2]
  As ye be myn assistence in p*r*ocesse shall lerne,
Which thurgh yo*ur* vertue, most amorous knygh[t],
I owe to you*r* p*r*esence be due & very right.

Like-wyse as þis lady be grace I defended,   promises to preserve the prince, as he delivered the lady from the foul serpent.
  That thurgh myschaunce chosen was to dye,
ffro this foule se*r*pent whom I sore wonded;
  So ye in distresse p*r*eserve ever woll I
  ffro all parell and wyked veleny,
That shuld you*r* noble pe*r*sone in eny wyse distrayn,
Which welcome is to þis you*r* Chambre & to me right fayn.

  And this balet was song at þe Crosse: A ballad.
    Viuat le prynce Arthur.

Ryall p*r*ince Arthur, ⎫
Welcome nowe, tresur, ⎬ to þis you*r* cite!
W*ith* all oure hole Cur,[3] ⎭

Sithen in vertue der*e,* ⎫
Lorde, ye haue no per*e,* ⎬ as all we may see.
Of you*r* age tendr*e,* ⎭

Cunyng requyred, ⎫
All hath cont*r*ived, ⎬ you*r* intelligence.
And so receyued— ⎭

---

[1] Sharp suggests an omission, which does not appear in MS. Craig prints *divyne.*
[2] baron.   [3] From F. cœur = heart.

§ 83. *Tho. Bonde, Mayor.* Bristol, 1498.

That Yngland, all playn, ⎫
May nowe be right fayn ⎬ to their*e* extollence.
Yewe long to remayn, ⎭

Syng we þer foll all; ⎫
Also let us call ⎬ that he yewe defend!
God immortal   To God Immortall ⎭

defend the prince!
In this breve beyng ⎫
Youre astate supporting, ⎬ to yo*ur* lyfes yend!
And vertue ay spredyng, ⎭

THE PRINCE AND LOCAL DISPUTES.

Oct. 18.
A present to the prince.

[1] And vppon Thursday in þe mornyng the Maire with his Brethern cam vnto þe pri*nces* Chambr*e* and there p*resented* hym with a gilt Cup to þe value of x marc', & C marc' of gold therin, which was gadered in þe x wardes accordyng as þe xv^te is.

Oct. 19.
"Mayors complaint to prince Arthur of the prior,

And on þe Morowe the Maire pr*e*sented a bill to þe seid pr*ince* desiryng be þe same that he wold please to desire þe prio*ur* of Couentre to pay at his desire the Murage money which he had with-drawe*n* þe space of xx yere*s*: and also shewed his grace be the same bill howe the Citezenis of Couentre were trobled be there m*e*rchandisez in Bristoll,

& of Bristoll, Chester,[2] Worcester, & Gloster."

Glouc*estre*, & W*o*rc*estre* & c*o*mpelled to pay tholl & oþer customez contrarie to their libe*r*teez. Vppon which bill lettres went out to Bristoll, Glouc*estre* & Worcestre desiryng be the same þat the seid Citezenis of Couentre myght passe fre wi*th*out eny custome paying afte*r* their libe*r*te, or els they to apper at London crastino S. Martin*i*[3] þen next folowyng etc. And vppon þis þe prio*ur* & his Couent

A bond in £500

were bounde to my seid lord pr*ince* in v^c li. to abide þe awarde of my lord*es* of Lincoln & Couentre & oþer of þe Counceill of þe seid pr*ince* etc. and in like wyse the Maire & Co*mi*nalte bounde to þe seid pr*ince* in like some; þe tr*an*scr*i*pt of which obl*igacion* here ensueth. And the

as follows.   obligaci*o*ns both remaynen in þe kepyng of þe seid pr*ince*.

[Let all know by these pre-   Nouerint vniu*er*si per p*resentes*
sents that we Tho. Bande,   nos, Thoma*m* Bande, Maiorem Ciui-
mayor of the city of Coventry,   tat*is* Couentr*ie*, & eiusde*m* Communi-

[1] leaf 282.   [2] An error. See p. 549.   [3] The morrow of S. Martin.

§ 83. Tho. Bonde, Mayor. Murage, 1498.

and the community of the same, with unanimous consent and assent are held and firmly bound in £500 of legal English money to Arthur, Prince of Wales, Duke of Cornwall and Earl of Chester, the eldest son of the most illustrious Henry VII, King of England, France, and lord of Ireland, payable to the same prince or his attorney at All Saints (Nov. 1) next coming after the date of these presents; to make which payment well and faithfully we bind ourselves and our successors by these presents sealed with our common seal. Given on Oct. 21, 1498.]

tatem vnanimi[1] consensu & assensu teneri & firmiter obligari Arthuro, Illustrissimi Henrici septimi Regis Anglie & ffrancie & domini Hibernie primogenito, principi Wallie, duci Cornubie ac Comiti Cestrie in quingentis libris legalis monete Anglie soluendis eidem domino principi aut suo certo attornato in festo Omnium Sanctorum futuro post datam presencium; ad quam quidem solucionem bene & fideliter faciendam obligamus nos & successores nostros per presentes sigillo nostro communi sigillatas. Datum xxj° die Octobris a. r. r. Hen. septimi quartodecimo.

The condicion of þis obligacion is such that whereas certayn trauers is dependyng betwixt þe withinbounden Maire & Cominalte on the on partie and þe priour & Couent of þe Monasterie of our Lady within þe Cite of Couentre within-specified on þe oþer partie of & for the Murage of the same Citie yf the seid Maire & Cominalte stand, obeye, & perfourme thawarde, rule and Jugement of þe reuerent ffadirs in God William, Bisshop of Lincoln,[2] president of þe prynces Counceill, John, Bysshop of Chestre[3] & other of the same Counceill of in and vppon the said trauerse so that þe seid lord president, Bisshop of Chestre, & other as aforeseid make awarde in the same be þe fest of seynt Andrewe next comyng after the date hereof that then þis obligacion to be voide or els to stand in streng[t]h & vertue.[4]

Vppon which obligacion sealed Ric. Braytoft, & Ric. Coke, late Maire of þe seid Cite, & Joh. Boteler, styward,

A contròversy concerning the prior's murage having arisen,

both the prior and the mayor agree to abide by arbitration.

Judgment to be delivered Nov. 30.

Braytoft and others go to London

---

[1] One stroke of "m" is missing.
[2] William Smith, formerly Bishop of Chester.
[3] John Arundel; the bishops of Coventry and Lichfield were occasionally called by this title.
[4] On previous disputes about murage see above, p. 447 et passim.

§ 83. *Tho. Bonde, Mayor. Bristol*, 1498.

there were sent to London for the parte of þe seide Citie to sue for þe seid Cite in & for þe premissez; and they cam to London the Thursday þe ix^th day of Nouembre & continued there vnto þe first day of Decembre þen next folowyng; within which tyme, þat is to sey, the Wensday before þe fest of seynt Andrewe, the warde was made & gyffen vp be þe lordes betwixt þe priour & þe Cite in writyng accordyng as hereafter sueth the transcript þerof; which awarde is vnder þe seals of the seid Bisshops & the couent seall set to þat parte þat the town hath, & to þe oþer parte remaynyng with þe seid priour þe comien seal of þe Towne.

DISPUTE WITH] BRISTOL.

And as-for þe matier touchyng þe liberteez etc. ayenst Bristoll, Gloucestre & Worcestre þe seid Ric. Braytoft, Ric. Coke & Joh. Boteler, presented vnto þe lordes of þe princes Counceill iij seuerall billes, the tenures wherof hereafter suen :—

To þe Prynce.

In þe most humble wyse compleynyng shewen vnto your grace Tho. Bande, Maire of þe Cite of Couentre, Rog. Wode, Will. Barbour, shirrifs & Baillyfs of þe seid Cite, and the comiens of the same, that where they & all theire predecessours, fro þe tyme that no mannes mynde is, haue vsed to be fre, quyte & discharged be all the roialm of Ingland, as-well be lande as be water, within Citez, Boroughes, Townes and withoute, of all maner Toll, pontage, pykage, passage, pavage, stallage, murage, kayage and all oþer Imposicions, charges & seruitudes, whech libertez, priuileges & ffraunchisez the seid Maire, shirrifs, ballifs, and Cominalte, and all theire predecessours, and all Inhabitauntes in Couentre aforeseid, haue peasibly be all the seid tyme vsed and enioyed vnto þe tyme that the vj day of Aprill the xiij^th ȝere of þe reign of oure soueraign lorde, kyng Henre þe vij^th, and dyuers tymes afore Ric. Jakson and Ric. Pova of Couentre aforeseid, Merchauntes, and many oþer of the seid Cite of Couentre resortyng to þe Towne & havon of Bristol for wyn, wax & Iron and other Merchaundisez

§ 83. *Tho. Bonde, Mayor. Murage,* 1498.

to be had and bought there were be¹ late
Baillif of the seid Towne at Bristoll aforeseid at a place
there called the key wrongfully distreyned be their seid
Merchaundisez and compelled to paye for euery Ton tyght²
iiij d., ayenst all right and contrarie to their liberteez &
fraunchisez aforeseid ; whech in tymes past alwayes have
ben allowed them in the seid Towne of Bristoll : whereof
þe seid Maire, shirrifs, Baillifs & Comiens of þe Cite of
Couentre praye reformacion & remedy in þat partie. And
they woll euer pray to God for your grace.

margin: but now goods of merchants are distrained upon at "Bristolle" quay for toll.

And like billes, mutatis mutandis, were put In ayenst
Gloucestre & Worcestre. Howe-be-it in Gloucestre they
challenged there toll for passyng the streame etc.³ Vppon
which billes was this ordre taken be þe lordes & assent of
þe parties that ij of þe merchauntes of Couentre with a
lerned man shuld resorte to Bristoll, Gloucestre & Worcestre there to haue louyng communicacion betwixt them, &
þeruppon to take yend in þat partie yf they so coude, &
yf not then they to shew theire myndes to þe Recordours
of þe seid places, they to take yend yf they Coude, & yf
no then they to resorte vnto þe Counceill eft-sones etc.

margin: Toll at "Gloucester, Worcester."

margin: Two Coventry merchants and a learned man try to have loving communication with the towns in question.

THE PRIOR'S MURAGE.

⁴ To all Christien pepull to whome this present writyng
shall come, here or see, William by the grace of God
Bysshop of Lincolne, John by the same grace Bisshop of
Coventre and Lichefeld and other of⁵ the Counsell lerned
of Arthur first begoton sonne of kyng Henre the vij, Prince
of Wales (etc.), arbitrours indifferently chosen & named
bitwen Richard,⁶ Prior of the monastery of seynt Marye
in the Cite of Couentre & the Couent of the same on the
one partie and Thomas Bonde, Maire, & the Cominalte of
the same Citie on the other partie, witnessith that where-as
diuerse discordes and wariaunces were late moved & had
bitwen the seid parties of & vppon x li. of a yerely somme
which the seid Maire & Cominalte claymed of the seid

margin: "Couentre." "Murage paid by the priors land." The Bishops of Lincoln and of Coventry

---

¹ Blank.   ² = weight, v. *E. D. D.*
³ On the carriage of goods down the Severn v. *Rot. Parl.*, v. 569.
⁴ leaf 282, back.   Another scribe, F.
⁵ "of" repeated.   ⁶ Ric. Shaw.

§ 83. *Tho. Bonde, Mayor. Murage,* 1498.

priour & Couent for the Murage of the seid Citie; for the peasing therof the seid parties haue compromytted theym to abyde thawarde, ordinaunce & iugement of vs the said Bisshopes & Counsail lerned of the seid high & myghty Prince to awarde, ordeigne & deme of & vppon the ryght title & possession of the seid annuell somme of x li. and the arrerages of[1] the same, as by their seuerall obligacions theruppon made more pleynly appereth. And we the seid arbitrours takyng on vs the labour & payne to awarde, ordeigne & deme of & vppon the premissez, calling afore vs the said parties, hering & seing all their titles, answers & other their alegiaunces & their Evidences & proves, consernyng the same by good, long & gret deliberacion by thassent & also at the speciall request & desire of both the seid parties awarde, ordeigne & deme of & vppon the premissez in the maner & fourme folowyng:—

acting as arbitrators in the dispute about murage

That is to sey, furst we awarde, ordeigne & deme that from the daie of the date of this our present awarde forth the seid priour & Couent & their successours shall bere & paye ratabully with the Citesyns of the seid Citie to the forseid murage & making of the seid[1] walles abowte the seid Citie vnto such tyme as the same walles be fully made vp and accomplisshed; that is to sey, yerely x li. at the fest of All Sayntes, when the seid Citesyns & all other having londes & tenementes within the same Cite shall proporcionably be charged after the rate of the quantite of their seid londes & tenementes to the same murage; provided alwey that if any the seid Citisens or other personnes having londes & tenementes within the same be herafter ratid and assessed to a lesse somme of money than they now bee, that than the seid priour, Couent & their successours shal-be in like fourme lesse ratid & abatid of payment of the seid somme of x li., accordyng to the abatment ratabully of the seid Citizens & other persones for their londes & tenementes within the same Citie.

have decreed that the prior shall pay according to the rate of the other citizens for murage until the walls be made,

i. e. £10 a year,

Also we awarde (etc.) that the seid money thus assessed & gadered for the making of the walles of the seid towne shal-be duely apployde to the same vse & entent & to non other charges nor besynesse of the seid Cite; and that

which sum is to be used for murage,

[1] Deletions.

§ 83. *Tho. Bonde, Mayor. Murage*, 1498.

yerely ther shal-be a due accompte therof made afore certayn indifferent auditours, wherunto the seid priour & his Successours shal-be made pryvey, if they so desire.

Also we awarde (etc.) that the seid prior, Conuent, their successours nor their tenauntes shall not herafter be charged for the londes & tenementes of the seid priour & Conuent ouer the seid x li. be yere onles they purches any more londes & tenementes within the walles of the same Citie, and that the seid priour & Couent nor their successours shall not be charged nor chargeable to the payment of the seid x li. noo lenger but vnto such tyme as the seid Murage & walles aboute the seid Citie be accomplisshed & made, except & sauyd that the priour & Couent after the rate of their londes & tenementes their shal-be contributores with the seid Citesyns to[1] reparacion & amendyng of the same walles,[2] as other persones having londes & tenementes within the seid Citie shal-be charged, & that the seid money so assessed & gaderid shal-be duely imploied to the reparacion & amendyng of the same walles of the seid Cite, and auditours therupon to be sett,[3] as it is aboueseid, & þat þe seid priour & his successours be made privey to þe seid assessing & to the accomptes therof to be made, as it is abouesed.

until the work be accomplished, after which time the prior shall only be liable to charges for repairs.

and account thereof shall be rendered.

Also we awarde (etc.) þat þe seid Maire & Cominalte & their successours shall haue & reteigne yerely x li. of such sommes of money on the seid priour, Citezens & other hauyng londes & tenementes within the same Cite from the fest of Saint Michell tharchaungell last passed afore this oure awarde vnto thende of v yeres than next folowyng & noo lenger; which x li. so reteigned shall goo towarde the charge of the Chamberleyns of the seid Cite, which haue laied out in tymes passed more money to the making of the seid walles than they haue received for the same.

£10 to be retained yearly to pay up the chamberlains who have laid out more money than they received.

Also we awarde (etc.) that the seid Maire and Cominalte shall not herafter aske ner haue any arrerages of the seid yerely somme of x li. vnpaied by the seid priour afore the date of this oure awarde but l li., which l li. the priour and Couent shall paie to the seid Maire & Cominaltie to haue their good willes & favours, that is to sey, in the fest of the

The prior to pay £50 of arrears.

---

[1] MS. te.   [2] Deletions.   [3] or "seit."

§ 84. Will. Hopkyns, Mayor, 1499.

£10 at Candlemas;

£10 at Lammas; until it be paid up.

Purificacion of oure Lady next comyng aftur the date of this oure awarde x li., and at the fest of saint Petur called Ad-uincula then next ensuyng other x li., and so x li. yerely at the same festes vnto the seid 1 li. be fully contented & paied. In witnesse wherof both we the seid Arbitrours and the forseid parties to thies present indentures interchaungeable haue putte their Seales, that is to sey, the seid priour & Conuent the Comen Seale of their said howse, & the seid Maire & Cominaltie the Comen Seal of their seid Citie. Yeven the xxviijth day of Nouembre in the xiiijth yere of the reigne of the seid king.

Nov. 28. 1498.

MICHAELMAS LEET.

"Couentre."
Oct. 9. 1498.

¹[V. f. p. held before Tho. Bonde, m., Tho. Grene, Will. Deyster, b., on Tuesday after the octave of Michaelmas, 14 Hen. VII.]

Jury.

Joh. Wygeston, Joh. Gauge, Ric. Braytoft, Joh. Thrumpton, Will. Shore, Ric. Coke, Tho. Baylly, Rob. Colman, Ric. Lee, Will. Rowley, Tho. Chirchman, Rob. Grene, Joh. Padland, Will. ffoorth, Joh. Haddon, Ric. Smyth, Tho. Maydford, Joh. Gryme, Joh. Duddesbury, Galf. Ardern, Tho. Padland, Will. ffletcher, Ed. Hulcote, Will. Taillour.

Sheriffs.

[Rog. Wode, dyer, Will. Barbour, capper.]

WILL. HOPKYNS, MAYOR, 1499.

"Couentre."
Jan. 25.
Electors.

²[Election of officers.]

Tho. Chirchman, Hen. Marler, Ric. Braytoft, Will. Shore, Ric. Coke, Tho. Baylly, Rob. Colman, Ric. Lee, Joh. Wygeston, Will. Rowley, Rob. Grene, Joh. Padland, Will. Taillour, Galf. Ardern, Tho. Maydford, Edw. Hulcote, Edw. Barbour, Will. ffletcher, Ric. Hassale, Tho. Grove, Joh. Throughley, Joh. Syssell, Rog. Mason, Will. Wygeston.

[m. Will. Hopkyns; cor. Rob. Topclyff; steward, Joh. Boteler; ch. Edm. Deyster, Grasear, Will. Birdlyme; w. Nic. Burwey, Joh. Humfrey, dyer; mace, Hen. Walker; crier, Joh. Toures.]

¹ leaf 283.   ² leaf 283, back.

§ 85. Joh. Haddon, Mayor, 1500.

ATTORNEY.

[Monday, Aug. 19, 1499, before the mayor and others, Joh. Castell was admitted as attorney for the mayor and bailliffs in the Exchequer, taking the fee and wages due as of old. And he took the oath.]

Mem. quod die Lune xix die Augusti a. r. r. H. vij xiiij^{mo} apud Couentriam Coram prefato Maiore[1] ac Tho. Chirchman, Ric. Braytoft, Will. Roweley, Rob. Grene, Johannes Castell admissus fuit attornatus pro Maiore & Balliuis ville de Couentria in Curia domini Regis de Scakkario capiendo feodum & vadium ex antiquo debitum. Et juratus est.

JOH. HADDON, MAYOR, 1500.

[2][Election of officers.]

"Couentre."
Jan. 25.
Electors.

Rob. Grene, Hen. Marler, Ric. Braytoft, Joh. Thrumpton, Will. Shore, Ric. Coke, Tho. Bailly, Rob. Colman, Ric. Lee, Joh. Wygston, Will. Roweley, Tho. Chircheman, Joh. Padland, Tho. Bonde, Joh. Dwale, Will. Taillour, Tho. Maideford, Ric. Jakson, Ed. Barbour, Tho. Grene, Ric. Nores, Joh. Strong, Ric. Lansdale, Ric. Hassale.

[m. Joh. Hadon; cor. Rob. Topclyff; ch. Tho. Kervyn, Dauid Blakwall; w. Ric. Marler, Joh. Hardwen; mace, Hen. Peyntour; crier, Joh. Toures.]

Officers.

THE COUNCIL.

Hit is ordeyned at þis eleccion that the Maire kepe Counceill wokely ones in þe woke specially on þe Wensday, and that þe Maires seriant warne the Mares Brethern euery Tewesday to be at seynt Mari-hall at þe Counceill vppon þe Wensday without þe Maire commaunde þe contrarie, vppon peyn of þe seid seriant to lese at euery tyme he doth þe Contrarie iiij d.

"A Counceill to be held weekly on Wensday."

THE BRISTOL AFFAIR.

Mem. that þis in Estur terme was þe matier in variaunce betwixt þis Cite & Bristoll[3] as-touchyng kayage claymed

"Variaunce between Bristoll &

---

[1] "This mayor strove greatly against this town (sic) of our Lady." Annals quoted in Fretton, *Whitefriars* (*Proc. B'ham and Midl. Institute*), 10. There was an image of the Virgin kept in the Lady Tower by Whitefriars on the London Road.

[2] leaf 285. Scribe B. John Whitehed, Joh. Raynold bailiffs.

[3] See above, pp. 592 sqq.

§ 86. *Will. Pisford, Mayor*, 1501.

Couentry setled by indenture.

be þe Baillifs of Bristoll, determyned be þe Recordours of both places, as appereth be writyng indented vnder the comien seals of both Townes; wherof þe on partie sealed with þe comien seall of Bristoll remayneth in þe Tresorye in seynt Marie hall, & the copie þerof is regestred in the boke where þe Copie of þe Chartirs be registred, remaynyng with þe Styward etc.

WILL. PISFORD, MAYOR, 1501.

[1] I h s.

"Civitas Couentre." Jan. 25. Electors.

¶ [Election of officers.]

Joh. Padland, Hen. Marler, Ric. Braytoft, Joh. Thrumpton, Will. Shore, Ric. Coke, Tho. Bailly, Ric. Lee, Joh. Wygston, Will. Roweley, Tho. Chircheman, Rob. Grene, Will. fforth, Tho. Bonde, Will. Hopkyns, Geff. Ardern, Edw. Hulcote, Edw. Barbur, Will. Barbour, Ric. Nores, Joh. Sissell, Tho. Grove, Ric. Lansdale, Will. Burglen.

Officers.

[m. Will. Pisford;[2] cor. Rob. Topcliff; ch. Ric. Burwey, Tho. Turnour, Jun.; w. Tho. fforth, Nic. Heynes; mace, Hen. Peyntour " super suam bonam gesturam;" crier, Joh. Toures.]

"A common box."

Whech Will. Pisford in hys tyme be þe advyce of þe Counceill ordred a Comien box to be had in þis Cite, which he ordeyned of his cost, & let set hit in þe Counceill house in seynt Mary hall; in-to which boxe for a goode begynnyng Ric. Coke & Joh. Boteler, executors of þe testament of Sir Joh. Gilbert, late viker of both parish Churches in Couentre gaffe xl s; and ouer þat þe seid Joh. Boteler of such money as he had resceyued of printices .[3] To which box is made v keyes, the Maire for the tyme beyng to haue on of þeym, & þe iiij other to be in kepyng of iiij Comieners that haue not be in offices of wardeyn & chamberleyn, & they iiij to be Chosen be x comieners, they x to be Chosen be þe Meire &

The executors of the will of the " on Vicker of both parishes" give 40s.

Boteler more.

"5 keies" are made; to be in the keeping of 4 commons chosen by 10 others,

---

[1] leaf 286, back. The first time these symbolic letters appear here. Baillifs, Joh. Stronge, Ric. Hassale. Coventry is here described as " ciuitas siue villa."

[2] Part founder with Ford of the Grey Friars' hospital, which is still in existence. For Pisford's will, see Dugdale (1730), 184–5.

[3] Blank. Boteler as steward kept the book wherein the names of apprentices were entered. See above, p. 560.

§ 87. Ric. Jakson, Mayor, 1502.

his Counceill for the tyme beyng, þat is to sey in euery of þe x wardes in Couentre j to be named. And these ordrer (sic) to be kept frohensfurth for euer as often as eny of þe seid Comieners be called into office or happe to decesse or oþerwyse be remoued. And for þe begynnyng of þis ordre the seid Maire let Chose be þe advice of his Counceill þe x persones of þe x wardes in Couentre, that is to sey, Tho. Mosell, draper, Ric. Semyng, draper, Will. Wycam, draper, Hen. Grey, draper, Will. Banwell, Merser, Joh. Plesantyn, mercer, Tho. ffarman, smyth, Will. Brigges, Capper, Will. Huet, Baker, & Ric. Pova,[1] Mercer. Whech x let chose & name þes iiij persones folowyng to haue þe kepyng of þe keyes; to whech iiij persones þe seid Maire delyuered to euerych of theym a key, þat is to sey, Joh. Wodnet, dyer, Will. Carter, taillour, Will. Briggez, Capper, & Ric. Pova.

one from each of the respective wards.

RIC. JAKSON, MAYOR, 1502.

[2] I h s.

[Election of officers.]

Will. fforth, Hen. Marler, Ric. Braytoft, Will. Shore, Ric. Coke, Tho. Baylly, Ric. Lee, Joh. Wygston, Will. Roweley, Tho. Chircheman, Rob. Grene, Joh. Padland, Tho. Bande, Joh. Hadon, Will. Taillour, Gal. Ardern, Edw. Hulcote, Tho. Padland, Tho. Turnour, Rog. Wode, Ric. Nores, Joh. Sissell, Will Hardy, Tho. Grove.

[m. Ric. Jakson; cor. Rob. Topclyff; ch. Hum. Grene, Alan. Ruyley; w. Hugo Dawes, Ric. Dadynton, draper; mace, Hen. Peynter; crier, Joh. Toures.]

Jan. 25. Electors.

Officers.

RIC. COKE, MAYOR, 1503.

[3] I h s.

¶ [Election of officers.]

Tho. Band, Hen. Marler, Ric. Braytoft, Will. Shore, Tho. Baylly, Will. Roweley, Ric. Lee, Tho. Chircheman, Rob. Grene, Joh. Padland, Will. fforde, Joh. Haddon,

"Ciuitas Couentre." Jan. 25. Electors, 25 names.

---

[1] See above, p. 594.
[2] leaf 288, back. Ric. Lansdale, Joh. Saunders, bailiffs.
[3] leaf 290, back. Bailiffs, Joh. Hardewyn, Joh. Norton

§ 88. *Ric. Coke, Mayor*, 1503.

Tho. Padland, Will. Taillour, Rog. Chambre, Tho. Turnour, Will. Barbour, Ric. Hassall, Joh. Strong, Joh. Sissell, Tho. Grove, Will. Hardy, Ric. Nores, Tho. fforde, Nic. Heynes.

Officers. [m. Ric. Coke; cor. Rob. Topclyff; ch. Ric. Wilson, Will. Perkyns, Baker; [w.] Will. Barnwall, Will. Brigges, Capper; mace, Hen. Walker upon his good conduct; & Hugh Johnson crier, upon the condition that present and future sheriffs shall pay yearly to Joh. Toures, who before *Pension for the retiring crier taken from the new crier's fee.* this occupied the crier's office, during his life 13s. 4d. at the four terms of the year by equal portions, from the fee of the said Hugh or of any other occupier of the office during the said John's lifetime.]

THO. PADLAND, MAYOR, 1504.

¹ Ihs.

"Civitas Couentrs." ¶ [Election of officers.]
Jan. 25.
Electors. Joh. Hadon, Hen. Marler, Ric. Braytoft, Will. Shore, Tho. Bailly, Will. Roweley, Tho. Chircheman, Rob. Grene, Ric. Lee, Joh. Padlond, Tho. Bande, Will. Pysford, Tho. Turnour, Will. Taillour, Edw. Hulcote, Rog. Chambre, Joh. Strong, Ric. Hassale, Joh. Sissell, Ric. ffoxale, Tho. Grove, Will. Hardy, Humf. Grene, Tho. fforde.

Officers. [m. Tho. Padland; cor. Rob. Topcliff; ch. Tho. May, Grasiour, Tho. Estelen; w. Hen. Rogers, vyntener, Tho. Waren, dyer; mace, Hen. Peynter, crier, Hugh Johnson.]

THE TANNERS.

Nov. 21.
"John Bottelar, stuard, one of the Company of tanners, discharged of this keping of the Craft, ³paying a ffine." ³
² Mem. þat ² In the Counceill holden in Seynt Mary hall þe xxj^ti day of Nouembre [20 Hen. VII], there beyng present þe seid Maire, Hen. Marler, Ric. Coke, Ric. Braytoft, Will. Shore, Ric. Lee, Tho. Bailly, Tho. Chircheman, Joh. Padland, Tho. Bonde, Joh. Hadon, Ric. Jakson, in þe matier beyng in variance betwix þe ffeliship of þe Tanners & Joh. Boteler, which feliship had chosen þe seid Joh. Boteler for on of þe kepers of their Craft, which to

---

¹ leaf 292, back. Bailiffs, Joh. Clerk, Joh. Humfrey.
²—² Added later in another hand.
³—³ In the 17th-century hand usual in marginal annotations.

§ 89. Tho. Padland, Mayor, 1504.

take vppon hym þe seid Joh. Boteler refused,[1] & ther shewed[1] that he was discharged be þe hole Craft at þe tyme he was receyued into theire ffeliship of that charge & all othere charges, whils he liffed, concideryng þe office he had etc.; for which discharge he hath paide ȝerely xl d. & where the oþer of þe company paye but ij s. For which discorde to be appeised hit was ordred be þe seid Counceill at þat tyme that þe seid Joh. Boteler, concideryng þe charge he had dayly with þe officez of stywarship & Townclerk of þe Cite, that he shuld frohensfurth be discharged of Maistership & keper of þe seid Craft for euer and all oþer charges longyng to þe seid Craft, as offerynges,[2] assembleez & other metynges & charges sauyng only that he shall kepe & obserue all goode & resonable ordinancez made & to be made that shal-by (sic) godly & expedient for þe comien wele of þe seid Craft; ffor which discharge þe seid Joh. Boteler shall paye in hand vj s. viij d. & euery ȝere after whils he occupieth þe Craft ij s., & euery vij ȝere herafter whils he liffeth & occupieth þe Craft to pay vj s. viij d. in name of a ffyn for þe discharge aforerehersed etc.

JOH. DUDDESBURY, MAYOR, 1505.

[3] I h s.

[Election of officers.]

Will. Pysford, Hen. Marler, Ric. Coke, Ric. Braytoft, Ric. Lee, Tho. Bailly, Rob. Grene, Tho. Chircheman, Joh. Padland, Will. Shore, Will. ffoorde, Tho. Bonde, Joh. Hadon, Ric. Jakson, Tho. Wardelowe, Joh. Darlyng, Joh. Strong, Ric. Hassale, Joh. Hardwyn, Joh. Clerk, Will. Hardy, Ric. Nores, Tho. Groue, Th. ffoorde.

[m. Joh. Duddesbury, skynner; cor. Tho. Rastell; ch. Hen. Sampson, dier, Joh. Nix, Grasier; w. Joh. Hoton, mercer, Tho. Smyth, draper; mace, Hen. Peyntour; crier, Hugh Johnson. And the aforeseid Joh. Hoten died

"Civitas Couentrie." Jan. 25. Electors.

Officers.

---

[1] deletions. [2] i.e. at mass.
[3] leaf 294. Scribe B. Bailiffs, Ric. Marler, Ric. ffoxale. On the play of St. Crytyan or S. Christian played in the Little Park this year see Sharp, *Mysteries*, 10; Craig, *Two Corpus Christi Plays*, xxi.

§ 90. *Joh. Duddesbury, Mayor*, 1505.

within this year, and in his place Joh. Dixon was elected, which Joh. Dixon died also within the said year.[1]]

THO. WARDELOWE, MAYOR, 1506.

"Civitas Couentre." Jan. 25.

[2] ¶ [Election of officers.]

Ric. Jakson, Hen. Marler, Ric. Cooke, Tho. Baylly, Will. Shore, Rob. Colman, Rob. Grene, Joh. Padland, Will. ffoorde, Tho. Bande, Will. Pisford, Joh. Hadon, Joh. Strong, Joh. Darlyng, Rog. Chambre, Ric. Hassale, Joh. Hardwyn, Joh. Clerk, Ric. ffoxale, Ed. Hulcote, Ric. Nores, Tho. Warde, Rob. Dadyngton, Will. Banwell.

Officers.

[m. Tho. Wardelowe, Grasiour; cor. Tho. Rastell; ch. Joh. Payn, dier, Joh. Eyburn, Tanner; w. Ed. Hadley, Will. Wykam. And as to the election of a common sub-bailiff-at-mace & crier the election of them is referred to

Jan. 28.

the mayor and his council to be held on Wednesday next following. On which day the said Joh. Duddesbury, m., and his council, viz. Ric. Jakson, Hen. Marler, Ric. Cooke, Tho. Bailly, Tho. Chircheman, Joh. Padland, Rob. Grene, Will. ffoorde, Will. Pisford and Tho. Bande, elected and

Hen. Peyntour, mace, Ric. Freyby, crier.

named Hen. Peyntour common sub-bailiff on his good behaviour & Ric. ffreyby, crier.]

[And further at the same council they made an ordinance because hitherto the mayor for the time being at each court of the lord king held in the said city sat alone without the council of his brethren the aldermen; therefore it was ordained that for the future at each court to be held in the said city there shall sit with the said mayor at least two of his brethren as his councillors and coadjutors and assistants

Et vlterius ad eundem Consilium ordinauerunt pro eo quod Maior pro tempore existens preantea ad quamlibet Curiam domini Regis in dicta Ciuitate tenta[m], sedebat[3] solus sine concilio suorum confratrum 'alderman.' Ideo tunc ordinatum fuit quod decetero in futuro ad quamlibet Curiam tenendam in dicta Ciuitate sedebunt cum dicto Maiore duo ad minus de suis confratribus tanquam suis conciliariis & co-adiutaribus (sic) & sibi assistentibus vsque ad finem Curie predicte. Et adtunc & ibidem

---

[1] 1504 was a year of plague in London. The deaths of wardens within the year suggests an epidemic in Coventry.
[2] leaf 296. Bailiffs, not elsewhere named, Nic. Burwey, Joh. Smyth. Scribe B.
[3] "valde" deleted.

§ 91. *Tho. Wardelowe, Mayor*, 1506.

until the close of the said court. And then and there they appointed which of them shall begin and how they shall keep their turn for the future, that is to say on Tuesday next after Candlemas (Feb. 3) J. Duddesbury and R. Jakson, M.G. S. T., are assigned for that court; and for the next following R. Marler, R. Cooke. And for the third T. Bailly and R. Colman; and the fourth R. Lee and T. Churchman; and the fifth R. Green and J. Padland; and the sixth Will. Ford and T. Bonde; and the seventh J. Hadon and Will. Pisford. And thus to keep their turn for ever.]

limitauerunt qui eorum incipient & quomodo suum cursum imposterum[1] tenerent, videlicet ad proximam Curiam tenendam, videlicet die martis proximo post festum Purificacionis B. Marie proximo futurum, Joh. Duddesbury nunc Maior & Ric. Jakson, M.G.S.T., assignati sunt pro Curia illa : Et ad Curiam tunc proximo sequentem, Ric. Marler & Ric. Cooke ; Et ad terciam Curiam, Tho. Bailly & Rob. Colman ; Et ad iiij^{tam} Curiam Ric. Lee & Tho. Chirchman : Et ad quintam Rob. Grene & Joh. Padland : Et ad sextam Will. ffoorde & Tho. Bonde : Et ad septimam Joh. Hadon & Will. Pisford. Et sic custodiendo cursum eorum vsque in sempiternum.

ROB. GRENE, MAYOR, 1507.

[2] ¶ [Election of officers.]

Ric. Jakson, Hen. Marler, Ric. Cooke, Will. Shore, Tho. Baylly, Rob. Colman, Joh. Padland, Tho. Bonde, Joh. Haddon, Joh. Duddesbury, Edw. Hulcot, Rog. Chambur, Joh. Whithed, Joh. Darlyng, Ric. Hassall, Joh. Hardwyn, Joh. Humfrey, Ric. ffoxall, Ric. Nores, Joh. Syssell, Tho. Grove, Tho. Warde, Will. Hardy, Tho. fforth.

[m. Rob. Grene ; cor, Joh. Rastell ; ch. Tho. Kelyngworth, Will. Dawson ; w. Will. Wykam, Joh. Morse ; mace, Hen. Peynter.]

"Couentre." Jan. 25. Jury.

Officers.

[3][And as to the steward they wish to consider until Candlemas; at which day by the advice of the new mayor they elected J. Porter steward. And he took the oath.]

Et quoad senescallum volunt se aduisare vsque festum Purificacionis B. Marie etc. ; ad quem diem elegerunt (*sic*) per consilium noui Maioris Joh. Porter[4] esse[4] senescallum ; & juratus est etc.

---

[1] One stroke of "m" missing.   [2] leaf 297.
[3] Margin has "Joh. Porter chose steward."   [4] In a later hand.

§ 92. Rob. Grene, Mayor, 1507.

ORDERS OF COUNCIL.

"For elecion of the wardens."

Memorand*um* that it is agreed at this Elecc*i*on forasmoch as heretofore they haue vsed yerely to chose newe wardens so that the rep*ar*ac*i*ons of the Townesland was not repared for cause they were dysmyssed eu*er*y yere, so that the newe wardeyns were eu*er* to seke and eu*er*y man wold repare[1] at his pleasur :· And therfor hit is ordened þ*a*t from hensforth for eu*er* þ*a*t oon of the old wardeyns shall continue another yere, and a newe to be chosen to hym; so þ*a*t eu*er* oon of them shall contin*u*e ij yer*es*.

"Mr. Lee xl li. Mr. Churchman free from all offices."

Also for-asmoch as M*aister* Lee & M*aister* Churcheman han graunted to the vse of the Condit of this Citie to be apploid, the seid Lee xl li. and the seid M*aister* Churchman vj fowder[2] lede for þ*a*t cause, þ*a*t fro-hensfurth for eu*er* they shuld be discharged to be called or elect to eny office of Charge w*ith*in this Cite, which grauntes the have bounde them to p*er*forme & pay ; therfor at this elecc*i*on they haue discharged them and for the more suerty they haue graunted to them þ*a*t at the next lete hit shal-be confermed be auctorite of lete. And also M*aister* fforth by M*aister* Cooke in lyke wyse at that tyme graunted to the same vse xl li. to be p*ar*doned of the seid office vnto the next tyme þ*a*t his turne aftur his aunciente[3] shall come to hym etc.

Mr. Forth also excused office.

LEET.

"Couentre." Apr. 20.

[4] ¶ [V. f. p. held before Rob. Grene, m., Nic. Heynes, Will. Wigston, b., on Tuesday before S. George's day, 22 Hen. VII.]

Jury of 31.

Ric. Jakson, Hen. M*ar*ler, Ric. Cooke, Will. Shore, Tho. Baylly, Rob. Colman, Tho. Churcheman, Joh. Padland, Joh. Haddon, Will. Pysford, Joh. Duddesbury, Tho. Wardlowe, Tho. Turno*u*r, Joh. Darlyng, Edw. Hulcot, Rog. Chambur, Joh. Whithed, Joh. Saunders, Joh. Har-

---

[1] MS. rep*er*are.
[2] fother = a load ; a definite weight of lead : now usually 19½ cwt.
[3] MS. aunnciente. Evidently seniority played a great part in putting men in honourable places.
[4] leaf 297, back.

§ 92. *Rob. Grene, Mayor. Leet,* 1507.

wyn, Joh. Clerk, Joh. Humfrey, Ric. ffoxall, Joh. Smyth, Ric. Nores, Tho. Grove, Will. Dawson, Humf. Grene, Ric. Wylson, Hugo Dawes, Ed. Hadley, Tho. fforth.

Mem. [ordained] that the Craft & ffeliship of Bakers shal-be contributories & Charged from hensforth with the Craft & felishp of Smythes and to pay yerely to them toward theyre pagent at Corpus Christi tyde xiij s. iiij d. and so to contynewe from hensforth yerely etc. *"Bakers to Contribute 13s. 4d. yearly to the smiths pageant."*

[Ordained] for a Comien wele of this Citie that euery alderman of this Citie take with hym vj of the most discrete persons & of the most honest within their warde to serch and loke what euery man will gyffe towarde the makyng of the Condyte, and all such summys as shal-be graunted to certyfe Maister Maire & his brethern at a certen day. *"Conduit."*

["Ordened"] that the Maister of the Trinite yelde well & sufficiently make the broken paymentes of the Trinite Gylde grounde of this halfe the feist of Seint Michell tharchaungell next comyn at the Gyldes Cost. And yf it be not made be that day to make hit at his owen Cost immediatly [or 6s. 8d. at every default] and the Maister of Corporis Christi Gylde and the wardeyns[1] in lyke wyse. Also all other men that they make ther pavementes by the same day [or 6s. 8d. at every default.] *"Pavements to be Amended by occupyers oft Houses."*

[Ordained and agreed] that Maister Maire with iiij or vj of his brethern twyse a yere goo a-bowte the towne wall and se what fawtes be ther and se them mendyd by his discrecion etc. *"Repair the wall."*

[Ordained] that Ric. Nores, cardmaker, shall not from hensforth be sworn apon eny Jure or inpanelid of eny enquest, but to be therof vtterly discharged for his gret age & ffebulnesse from hensfforth for euer etc. R. Nores discharged from serving on juries.

[Ordained] that the ffelisship of Coruesers shal-be contributory & chargeable with the Craft of Tanners yerly from hensforth and to pay xiij s. iiij d. And to begyn theyre payment of the hole at Corpus Christi tyde next comyng, and so forth yerly at euery Corpus Christi tyde to pay xiij s. iiij d. etc. *"Tanners pageant."*

---

[1] Interesting presentment of city officials. Cf. pp. 293–6.

§ 92. *Rob. Grene, Mayor. Soldiers*, 1507.

"Bochers & whittawers to Repaire A pageant."

[Ordained and agreed] that from-hens-furth the feliship & Crafte of Bochers shal-be yerly contributorye to the felyship of whittawers toward there pagent at Corpus *Christ*i tyde xvj s. viij d. and so to conti*n*ue yerly forth lyke as they dydde afore etc.

SOLDIERS.

June 8, 1507.
"20 souldiers Retained ffor the King's seruis by indenture."

[1] This indenture made the viij day of June in the xxij^{ti} yere of the reigne of o*u*r soueraigne lord kyng Henry the vijth betwen Rob. Grene, Maire (etc.) on the oon pa*r*te & Joh. Richardson, weu*er*, Joh. Bradshawe, taillo*u*r, Will. Harre, plum*er*, Tho. Yate, taillo*u*r, Rauffe Tomson, carpent*er*, Miles Ale, tann*er*, Raufe Swetnam, carpent*er*, Joh. Braynsford, carpent*er*, Rauffe Craddock, taillo*u*r, Rob. Barton, Carver, Geo. Skelton, sherman, Rob. Hamond, coruis*er*, Hen. Snodon, sherman, Tho. Gyttyns, glover, Tho. Braynsford, sherman, Hugh ffelse, tann*er*, Wal. West, capp*er*, Will. Stevynson, weu*er*, Joh. Tylston, capp*er*, and Jas. Badeley, coruis*er*, sowdeers, appoyntid to do the king*es* grace ser*u*ice of warre, of the other p*ar*tye, Witnesseth that the seid sowdeyers above-namyd han p*r*omysed & g*r*auntid & by these p*r*esent*es* promisen & graunten to the seid Maire that they and eue*r*y of them shal-be at all-tymes redy & in a redynesse a-pon a dayes warnyng to doo the king*es* grace, o*u*r soue*r*aigne lord, ser*u*ice of warre at his g*r*aces wag*es* as well w*it*hin this his noble realme as elswhere, when-sume-eue*r* and as often as the case shall require, horsed & harnysed at the cost*es* & charg*es* of the seid Citie of Couentre. All which Couena*u*nt*es* well & truely to be p*er*formed & kept of the p*ar*te of the above-namyd sowdeers, the seid sowdyers bynde them, and eue*r*y of them by these p*r*esent*es*. And oue*r* that vppon payn of imp*r*isonment there to remayne at the kyng*es* pleas*ur*. In witnesse wherof to the oon p*ar*te of this Indenture with the seid Maire remanyng the abovenamyd sowdyers there sealls haue sette. At Couentre the day & yere above-seid.

[1] leaf 298. Scribe of C. type.

§ 92. Rob. Green, Mayor. Leet, 1507.

MICHAELMAS LEET.

[1][V. f. p. held on Tuesday after S. Dionisius' day, 23 Hen. VII.] — Oct. 12, 1507.

Ric. Jakson, Hen. Marler, Ric. Cooke, Ric. Lee, Tho. Churcheman, Joh. Padland, Will. fforth, Joh. Haddon, Will. Pysford, Joh. Duddesbury, Tho. Wardlowe, Ric. Hassall, Tho. Turnour, Joh. Strong, Ric. Smyth, Edw. Hulcote, Joh. Darlyng, Joh. Saunders, Rog. Chambur, Ric. ffoxall, Joh. Whithed. — Jury of 21.

[Tho. Grove, Hen. Rogers.] — Sheriffs.

Mem. that Joh. Bonde hath brought in at this day xx s. which his fader gaffe therto accordyng to the wyll of his seid ffader.[2] — Joh. Bond's father's will.

[3] Also it is ordeyned at this lete that on Joh. a Woode, mercer, let on-couere the Redde diche, which renneth throwgh his gardeyn to the grete noyaunce of his neighpours[4] . . . by-twene this and Cristenmas next comyng, apon the peyn to forfeyte xl s., the on half to the Chamberleyns of the Citee ant [5] the other half to the comen boxe etc. — "Clensing Red ditch."

[Ordained] that the Chamburleyns and Wardeyns of this Citee fromhensforth tweyes a yere, that is to seye at euery lete, bryng in a byll of all such ffawtes and noysoonces as be withyn there office, apon the payne of fforfetur of euery of them xx s., which shal-be receyvid of them apon their accompt, the on half to the Shirrefs, the other half to the comen boxe etc. — The chamberlains and wardens to bring in a bill of faults and nuisances.

THE PRINCESS'S MARRIAGE.

[6] A Copie of the obligacion wheryn the Citee of Couentre with other diuerse Citees stondith bounde for the mariage of my lady Marie to the duke of Burgoyne.[7]

---

[1] leaf 298, back. [2] The founder of Bablake Hospital.
[3] Scribe G.
[4] Evidently an omission ; supply "he must cover it again," or words to that effect.   [5] = and.
[6] leaf 301, back. This treaty was signed at Calais Dec. 21, 1507. Heavy penalties being attached to the breach of the engagement, the leading nobles and towns of England and Flanders were securities for the forfeitable sum.
[7] Mary (1496–1533) was betrothed to Charles, grandson of Maximilian, afterwards Charles V. The marriage never took place, the princess marrying (1) Louis XII, (2) Brandon, Duke of Suffolk.

§ 92. *Rob. Grene, Mayor. The Princess,* 1507.

[To all and sundry to whose knowledge the present letters shall come, We, the Earls of Arundel, Oxford, Northumberland, Surrey, Shrewsbury, Essex, Derby, Lords Herbert, Dacre, Berners, Mountjoy Darcy, Conyers, and Stafford, and also constables and communities of the cities, forts and towns of London, York, Coventry, Norwich, Exeter, Chester, Worcester, Bristol (etc.) [send] greeting.

[Whereas there is contained amongst other things in a certain treaty of the date Dec. 21, 1507, between the most illustrious, excellent and potent prince, our most dread lord Henry, by the grace of God King of England and France and lord of Ireland, on the one side, and the most sacred prince, Maximilian, by the favour of the divine mercy then King of the Romans but now elected as the ever august Emperor of the Romans, as well King of the Romans as

Vniuersis et singulis ad quorum noticias (sic) presentes litere peruenirent, Nos, Tho. Comes Arundellie,[1] Joh Comes Oxonie,[2] Hen. Comes Northumbrie,[3] Tho. Comes Surrey,[4] Geo Comes Salopie,[5] Hen. Comes Essexie, Tho. Comes Derbeie,[7] Carolus Somerset, dominus Harbart, Tho. ffyneux dominus Dacre,[8] Joh. Boucher, dominus Berneys,[9] Will. Blount, dominus Mountgoy,[10] Tho. Dercy, dominus Darcy, Will. Conyers, dominus Conyers, [11] et dominus Hen. Stafford, nec non Maiores, aldermannes, vicecomites, balliui, Constabularii et Communitates Ciuitatum, opidorum (sic) et villarum Londonie, Eboraci, Couentrie, Norwiche, Exonie, Chestre, Wigornie, Bristollie, Southampton, Boston, Hull and Newcastell, salutem.

Cum in quodam tractatu de data vicesimi primi diei Mensis Decembris A.D. Millesimo quingentesimo septimo inter Illustrissimum, excellentissimum et potentissimum principem, dominum nostrum metuendissimum Henricum D. G. Anglie & ffrancie Regem & dominum Hibernie ex vna parte, et sacratissimum principem Maximilianum, diuina fauente clemensia tunc Romanorum Regem nunc vero electum in Romanorum Imperatorem semper augustum etc, tam ut Regem Romanorum quam ut auum paternum et legittimum tutorem

---

[1] Tho. Fitz Alan.   [2] Joh. de Vere.   [3] Hen. Algernon Percy.
[4] Tho. Howard.   [5] Geo. Talbot.   [6] Hen. Bourchier.   [7] Tho. Stanley.
[8] Fienes.   [9] Bourchier, Lord Berners.   [10] Mountjoy.   [11] blank.

§ 92. *Rob. Grene, Mayor. The Princess*, 1507.

the paternal grandfather and lawful guardian, governour and administrator of the goods and person of the most illustrious and serene Charles, Prince, by the same grace, of Spain, both Sicilies and Jerusalem, and the same prince by the authority and express consent of the same King of the Romans as grandfather (etc.) aforesaid, Archdukes of Austria, Dukes of Burgundy, Brabant, etc. Counts of Hapsburg, Flanders, Artois, Lords of Slavonia, Mechlen, etc. and the most serene and far-famed Lady, Margaret[1] of Austria and Burgundy, dowager Duchess of Savoy, the most dear aunt of the Prince of Spain, on the other side, by their ambassadors therupon fully authorized, constituted and deputed, in order to have, contract and solemnize the marriage, with God's will, arranged, agreed on and concluded, between the aforesaid illustrious Prince of Spain and the most serene and famous lady, Lady Mary, most beloved daughter of our most dread lord, the said King of England etc. and by the said King of England, Emperor, Prince of Spain, and lady duchess by their distinct and separate letters patents, sealed

gubernatorem et administratorem corporis et bonorum Illustrissimi ac serenissimi principis Caroli, eadem gratia Hispanie, vtriusque Cicilie & Jerusalem, et eundem principem Hispanie, auctoritatem (sic) tamen et expresso consensu eiusdem Regis Romanorum, ut aui ac Tutoris, gubernatoris ac administratoris predicti, archiduces Austrie, duces Burgundie, Brabancie etc., Comites Hapsburgensis, fflandrie, Arthesie etc. dominos Sclauonie, Mechlenne, etc., ac serenissimam et preclarissimam dominam

Margaretam Austrie & Burgundie, viduam ducissam Sabaudir (sic), prefati principis Hispanie amitam carissimam, partibus (sic) ex altera, per oratores suos hinc inde sufficientes autorisatos, constitutos et deputatos pro matrimonio inter prefatum Illustrissimum principem Hispanie et serenissimam ac prec[l]arissimam dominam dominam Mariam, dicti Regis Anglie etc, domini nostri metuendissimi filiam carissimam, Deo dante, habendo, contrahendo & solemnisando nuper conuento, concordato & concluso Et per

dictos Anglie Regem et Imperatorem ac principem Hispanie et dominam ducissam per suas distinctas & separatas literas patentes magnis sigillis suis sigillatas et manibus suis subscriptas, confirmatas, ratificatas et approbatas, inter cetera contineatur

[1] Daughter of Maximilian and regent of the Netherlands. A marriage arranged between Henry VII and this princess was never accomplished.

with their great seals, subscribed with their own hands, confirmed, ratified, and approved, is contained that within 40 days from the time when the Prince of Spain shall have completed the fourteenth year of his age the aforenamed prince and the Lady Mary shall by word of mouth actually and in fact contract marriage, and duly celebrate the same in the place, manner and form specified in the said treaty;

[And that our most dread lord, the King of England aforesaid, shall take steps effectually that not only we, the above-named earls, barons and lords, by our valid and effectual letters patent, sealed with the seals of our arms, and subscribed with our hands, shall bind ourselves, our heirs and successors, and all and singular our goods, moveable and immovable, whether they be found by land or sea, but also that we the aforesaid mayors, aldermen, sheriffs, constables, and communities of cities and towns, both in our corporate capacity and as private persons, present and future, with provision that the corporate obligation shall not decrease the personal obligation, nor the contrary, by our authentic, valid and

quod prenominati princeps Hispanie et domina Maria infra quadraginta dies proximo et Inmediate sequentes

postquam dictus princeps Hispanie quartum decimum etatis sue annum perimpleuerit, Matrimonium per uerba inde presenti realiter et cum effectu contraherent[1] et Idem matrimonium in fac[i]e ecclesie debite solempnizarent locis, terminis, modisque et formis in dicto tractatu specificatis;

Quodque metuendissimus dominus noster Rex Anglie predictus curaret et realiter et cum effectu faceret quod non solum nos supranominati Comites, barones, et domini per literas nostras patentes validas et efficaces, sigillis armorum nostrorum sigillatas et manibus nostris subscriptas, obligeremus nos, heredes et successores nostros ac omnia & singula bona nostra mobilia et Immobilia presentia ac futura vbicunque per terram vel per mare fuerint reperta, verumeciam quod nos predicti Maiores, aldermani, vicecomites, balliui, constabularii ac Communitates Ciuitatum, opidorum et villarum predictarum, tanquam corpora et collegia ac eciam tanquam particulares persone que nunc sunt et pro tempore erunt, Ita quod obligacio corporis seu collegii non deroget obligacioni particulari, nec econtra, per literas nostras patentes & auctenticas, validas et efficaces, sigil-

[1] deletions.

§ 92. Rob. Grene, Mayor. The Princess, 1507.

effectual letters, sealed with our common seals, shall bind ourselves, our heirs and successors, and all our cities and towns and all and singular citizens and townsfolk for the time being, and our communities of the same, and all and every our goods, movable and immovable wherever they may be found, to the King of the Romans, now (etc.) and to the Prince of Spain, their heirs and successors, under the penalty of 50,000 golden crowns (over and above the sum of 250,000 in which the abovesaid our most dread lord, King of England, and the most illustrious and serene Prince Henry (etc.) son and heir of the same King of England, shall bind and oblige themselves to the aforesaid emperor as grandfather (etc.) and to the Prince of Spain, in the name of a penalty by virtue of the said treaty), that the said marriage between the aforenamed Prince of Spain and Lady Mary, when they shall have reached a marriageable age, shall be accomplished in the place (etc.) specified more fully in the said treaty;

[And that if it shall happen through the Lady Mary, or her parents, or any of them, or any one else, or by any occurrence, except it be on the Prince of

lis nostris Communibus sigillatas obligaremus nos, heredes et successores nostros, ac omnes Ciuitates, villas et opida nostra, omnesque et singulos Ciues et opidanos pro tempore existentes ac Communitates nostras eorumque, et nostra omnia et singula bona, mobilia et Immobilia presentia et futura vbicunque fuerint reperta, prefato tunc Regi Romanorum, nunc vero electo Romanorum Imperatori et principi Hispanie, heredibus et successoribus suis, sub pena quinquaginta Millium coronarum auri (preter et ultra summam ducentarum et quinquaginta Millium coronarum auri qua prefatus metuendissimus dominus noster Rex Anglie ac Illustrissimus et serenissimus princeps Henricus, princeps Wallie, dux Cornubie et Comes Cestrie etc. filius et heres eiusdem Regis Anglie, prefato Imperatori ut auo et Tutori predicto et principi Hispanie antedicto nomine pene virtute predicti tractatus sese obligarent et astringerent) quod dictum Matrimonium inter prenominatos

principem Hispanie et dominam Mariam cum ad maturam et legitimam nubendi etatem peruenerint locis, terminis, modisque et formis in dicto tractatu plenius specificatis debite perficientur (sic) et cum effectu;

Quodque si forte[1] per prefatam dominam Mariam, vel parentes suos vel eorum aliquem aut alium quemcunque, aut per quemcunque modum vel euentum preterquam per prefatum

---

Supply "steterit"; see below, p. 616.

Spain's part, or through his death or the death of either of the contracting parties (which God forfend) that the said marriage by word of mouth within forty days (etc.) shall not be contracted in the manner (etc.) and solemnised according to the rites of the Church, then and in that case we, the earls (etc.) aforesaid, our heirs and successors, shall be bound to pay to the aforesaid King of the Romans, and to the Prince of Spain, their heirs or successors, without delay or excuse the said sum of 50,000 gold crowns, and every part of it, as a penalty for the same breach of contract;

[And that it shall be lawful for the same king (etc.) and the Prince of Spain, their heirs (etc.) to levy and distrain upon, seize, possess and keep all and singular our goods movable and immovable of the said earls (etc.) mayors (etc.) our heirs (etc.) wheresoever by land or sea they may be found without challenge or resistance whatsoever:

[We, therefore, the earls

principem Hispanie, aut eius mortem, vel per mortem alterius contrahencium (quod Deus auertat)[1] quominus dictum matrimonium per uerba de presenti infra quadraginta dies post complimentum[2] quartumdecimum etatis eiusdem principis annum proximo et inmediate sequentes contrahatur modis, terminis, locis, ac formis in supradicto tractatu specificatis [et] in facie ecclesie solempnisetur, tunc & in eo casu nos Comites, barones, et domini, maiores, aldermanni, vicecomites, balliui, constabularii et Communitates predicti, nostrive heredes et successores, dictam summam quinquaginta Millium coronarum auri et quamlibet eius partem in penam eiusmodi repudiacionis dicto tunc Romanorum Regi, nunc vero electo Romanorum Imperatori, et principi heredibusve aut successoribus suis sine dilacione aut excusacione quacunque soluere tenerentur (sic);

Quodque eciam lic[er]et prefatis tunc Regi nunc vero (etc.) et principi Hispanie suisve heredibus et successoribus dictam summam quinquaginta millium coronarum auri et quamlibet eius partem de & super omnibus & singulis bonis mobilibus et Immobilibus nostris dictorum Comitum (etc.) Maiorum (etc.) heredumque (etc.) nostrorum vbicunque tam per terram quam per mare fuerint reperta sine contradiccione aut recistencia quacunque libere exigere, leuare, capere, possidere et detinere:

Nos igitur, Comites (etc.) necnon

---

[1] ? an omission. [2] *sic.* Read "completum," as below, p. 616.

§ 92. Rob. Grene, Mayor. The Princess, 1507.

(etc.) mayors (etc.) desiring to obey and please the foresaid our most dread lord not only in the premisses, but also in all other things wherein we can or should, and desiring a prosperous and happy ending for so holy an affair not only for us, but also for the benefit of peace of both sides, and an affair most advantageous for the realms, countries, lordships, and all their subjects and the whole commonwealth of the Christian religion, do bind and oblige, according to the tenor of these presents, as well ourselves, earls (etc.) our heirs (etc.) and all and singular our goods (etc.) and also ourselves, mayors (etc.) as well in our corporate and personal character (so that the obligation of corporate bodies shall not diminish the obligation of individuals, nor the contrary) our heirs (etc.) cities (etc.) our citizens for the time being, all and singular our goods

(etc.) to the aforesaid emperor (etc.) and Prince of Spain, their heirs (etc.) in 50,000 gold crowns in which the King of England (etc.) and the Prince of Wales (etc.) as is aforesaid, shall bind and oblige themselves in order that the said marriage between the aforesaid

Maiores, aldermanni, vicecomites, ball*iui* et Constabularii sup*r*adict*i*, cupientes p*r*efato d*omi*no n*ost*ro metuendissimo non solum in p*r*emissis veru*m* eciam in aliis o*m*nib*us* quib*us* possum*us*, vel debem*us*, obedire et complacere, Reiq*ue* tam sancte tam honorifice non nobis solum set et bono pac*is* vt*r*iusq*ue* parcium p*re*d*i*c*torum* ac Regnis, patriis, d*omi*niis & subdit*is* vniu*er*sis ac tocius religionis cristiane reipublice et vtili[ssi]me prosperum et felicem exitum etc., Non mediocrit*er* affectantes et desiderantes, tenore p*r*esencium [1] obligam*us* et astringim*us* tam nos Comites, Barones (etc.) heredes (etc.) n*ost*ros ac o*m*nia & sing*u*la bona n*ost*ra (etc.), quam eciam nos Maiores (etc.) et Com*mu*nitates tanq*uam* corpora et collegia et tanq*uam* p*ar*ticulares p*er*sonas que nu*n*c sunt et p*r*o temp*or*e erunt, Ita quod obligacio*n*es corpor*um* seu collegior*um* non derogent obligacio*n*ib*us* p*ar*ticularib*us* nec e cont*r*a, heredes (etc.) n*os*t*r*os, Ciuitates, villas et opida n*ost*ra, om*n*esq*ue* et singulos Ciues ac opidanos n*ost*r*os* p*r*o temp*or*e existen*tes* ac o*m*nia & sing*u*la bona n*ost*ra (etc.) vbicu*n*q*ue* fuerint rep*er*ta, p*r*efato Imp*er*atori vt auo et Tutori p*r*edicto et sup*r*anomi*n*ato p*r*incipi Hispan*ie* hered*ibus* (etc.) suis in quinquaginta Millib*us* coronar*um* auri qua p*r*efat*us* metuendissim*us* d*omi*nu*s* noster Rex Angl*ie* et p*r*efat*us* Illustrissim*us* et serenissim*us* p*r*inceps Wallie, ut p*r*edict*um* est, sese obligarent et

---

[1] leaf 302.

Prince of Spain and the Lady Mary when they come to a marriageable age shall be duly performed according to the said treaty.

[And if it shall happen through the Lady Mary's doing (etc.) or through any occur-

rence otherwise than on the Prince of Spain's part or by his death or by the natural death of either of the contracting parties (which God forbid) that this marriage (etc.) may not be celebrated, then and in that case we the aforesaid

earls (etc.) mayors (etc.) acknowledge that we will pay or cause to be paid to the afore-

said guardian and Prince of Spain the said sum of 50,000 crowns of gold (etc.), and we promise by these presents to

pay or cause it to be paid to the said emperor (etc.) and Prince of Spain or either of them (etc.) as a penalty for the same breach of engagement without any delay or excuse whatever.

[We will also and grant by

astringerent quod d*ictu*m matrimoni*um* inte*r* p*re*no*m*inatu*m* p*r*incipem Hispan*ie* et d*om*inam Mariam cu*m* ad legitima*m*[1] nubend*i* etatem p*er*uene*r*int i*ux*ta formam dict*i* t*r*actat*us* debite p*er*ficiet*ur*.

Et si forte stete*r*it pe*r* d*ict*am dom*in*am Mariam vel parentes suos vel eor*um* aliquem aut quemcu*n*que aliu*m* aut pe*r* quemcu*n*qu*e* modu*m* vel eventu*m* p*re*ter*qu*am pe*r* p*re*fatum p*r*incipem Hispan*ie* aut eius p*ar*tem vel pe*r* morte*m* naturalem alte*r*ius cont*r*ahenciu*m* (quod Deus a*ue*rtat) quominu*s* d*ictu*m mat*r*imoniu*m* per uerba de p*re*senti infra quadraginta dies post completum quartu*m*decimu*m* etat*is* eiusdem p*r*incipis annu*m* p*r*oxi*m*o sequente*s* modis (etc.) in p*re*d*ic*to t*r*actatu specificat*is* et conten*t*is et in facie eccl*e*sie debite solempnizet*ur*, Tunc et in eo casu nos p*r*ed*ic*ti Comites (etc.), Maiores (etc.) p*r*ed*ic*ti fatem*ur* et recognosim*us* Tutori p*r*edicto et p*r*efato p*r*incipi Hispan*ie* dictam su*m*mam quinquaginta Coronar*um* auri et quaml*ib*et eius p*ar*tem, Promittim*usque* per p*re*sentes quod eandem su*m*mam quinquaginta Milliu*m* Coronar*um* auri dicto Imperatori ut a*u*o (etc.) p*r*edicto et p*r*efato p*r*incipi Hispan*ie* vel eor*um* alte*r*i heredib*us*ve (etc.) in penam eiusmodi repudiacio*n*is sine dilacio*n*e aut excusacio*n*e quacu*n*que solu*e*mu*s* soluive faciemu*s*; Volum*us*que et pe*r* p*re*sentes concedim*us* p*ro* nobis d*ic*t*is* Comitib*us* (etc.) Maiorib*us* (etc.) heredib*us* (etc.) quod i*n*

---

[1] MS. has a stroke too many.

these presents for ourselves (etc.) our heirs (etc.) that in the case of the breach aforesaid

and the non-payment of the sum aforesaid it shall be lawful for the said emperor (etc.) and aforenamed Prince of Spain or their heirs (etc.) the said sum (etc.) to levy freely upon our

persons and goods (etc.), keep, possess and detain without challenge or resistance.

[We renounce expressly and as a legal compact under the names and qualities given above all and singular exceptions of law and fact and other defences and benefits of law and fact, and generally all appeals, pleas, challenges and benefits of laws and canons by which we may be aided against the premisses or any of them, or other exceptions or defences whatever whereby we may be protected, and in particular we renounce the exception of the non-payment of the penalty by the principal contractors or their kinsfolk at the espousals and matrimony, and (we renounce the benefit of) the law saying that a general renunciation is not binding unless a special one has preceded it.

[Provided that in case the

casu predicte repudacionis et non solucionis summe predicte licebit predicto Imperatori ut auo (etc.) et prenominati (sic) principi Hispanie suisve heredibus (etc.) dictam summam quinquaginta Millium Coronarum auri et quamlibet eius partem de & super personis, bonis mobilibus et Immobilibus nostris, heredibus (etc.) Communitatum, Ciuium, et opidorum nostrorum vbicunque (etc.) sine contradiccione aut resistencia quacunque libere exigere, leuare, capere, possidere et detinere.

Renunciamus in hac parte expresse et in vim pacti sub nominibus et qualitatibus quibus supra omnibus et singulis tam Juris quam facti excepcionibus et defencionibus aliisque Juris et facti beneficiis et generaliter omnium legum et canonicum (sic) appellacionibus, querelis, prouocacionibus et beneficiis quibus contra premissa seu ipsorum aliqua nos Juuare possemus seu alias quomodo-

libet[1] tueri et presertim excepcione pene non soluende per principales contrahentes vel eorum parentes in

sponsalibus et matrimoniis apposite ac Juridicenti generalem renunciacionem non valere nisi processerit specialis.

Prouiso tamen quod casu quo

---

[1] Contraction for -is follows.

said marriage between the aforesaid Prince of Spain and the Lady Mary is contracted and duly solemnised, or if it should happen that the aforesaid marriage be not contracted and solemnised by reason of failure on the part of the Prince of Spain (etc.) or his death or the death of either of the contracting parties (which God forfend) or otherwise than through the action of the Lady Mary and her side, or if the aforesaid sum of 50,000 gold crowns in these cases or in any of them has been fully paid, our present letters shall be quashed and be of no moment nor efficacy, and shall be restored to us in good faith by the abovesaid emperor, the Prince of Spain, or either of them, or their heirs (etc.), ambassadors, or proxies deputed to that end. In faith and testimony of all and singular we, the earls (etc.) have signed and sealed with the seals of our arms these our present letters patent, we indeed the mayors (etc.) have caused to be corroborated, and corroborated (the same) with the common seals of our cities and towns.

dictum matrimonium inter prefatum principem Hispanie et dominam Mariam contrahatur et debite solempnisetur, aut si per prefatum principem Hispanie vel parentes suos, vel eorum aliquem aut alium quemcunque aut per mortem alterius contrahencium (quod Deus auertat) per quemcunque alium modum vel euentum preterquam per prefatam dominam Mariam aut eius partem steterit quominus dictum matrimonium locis (etc.), ut prefatur, contrahatur et solempnizetur, vel si predicta summa quinquaginta millium coronarum auri in casibus predictis vel eorum aliquo plene fuerit soluta, presentes nostre litere tanquam casse et irrit[e] nulliusque momenti aut efficacie [et] nobis per prefatum Imperatorem, principem Hispanie vel eorum alterum, eorumve heredes et successores aut eorum oratores vel procuratores ad hoc deputatos bona fide restituantur. In quorum omnium et singulorum fidem et testimonium presentes literas nostras patentes nos Comites, barones[1] et domini predicti manibus nostris signauimus et sigillis armorum nostrorum sigillauimus, Nos uero Maiores, aldermanni, vicecomites, balliui, constabularii et Communitates Ciuitatum et opidorum predictorum sigillis Communibus nostris fecimus communiri et communiuimus.

---

[1] MS. barores.

§ 93. *Ric. Smyth, Mayor*, 1508.

RIC. SMYTH, MAYOR, 1508.

[1] ¶ [Election of officers.]

Joh. Duddesbury, Hen. Merler, Tho. Bayly, Ric. Lee, Joh. Padlonde, Tho. Churchman, Will. ffoorth, Joh. Haddon, Will. Pysford, Ric. Jakson, Tho. Wardelowe, Joh. Saunders, Joh. Derlyng, Joh. Clerk, Joh. Herdwen, Ric. Merler, Ric. ffoxhale, Will. Wygston, Rog. Chambur, Edw. Hulcote, Ric. Nores, Joh. Cysyll, Tho. fforth, Will. Banwell.

[m. Ric. Smyth; cor. Joh. Rastell; steward, Joh. Porter; ch. Tho. Hyll, Ric. Ryse; w. Will. Rokardyne, Hen. Wall; crier, Ric. ffereby; mace, Hen. Walker.]

Mem. it is agreed at this eleccion that the above-namyd Hen. Walker, comen seriaunt, shall kepe clene the Greyffrere yate, as well within as without, vnto a certeyn place callid the watryng-place; and in like-wyse the Cookstrete yate; and yf he do not to set in on his wages the carying a-way therof etc.

"Civitas Couentre." Jan. 25.

Officers.

The common sergeant to keep clean Grey-friar and Cook Street gates.

ROGER A LEE.

Mem. at this eleccion ther was on Rog. a Lee, Baker, elect & chosyn in-to the office of the Chamberleynship for the yere foloyng; which Roger, as sone as he herde he was chosen chamberleyn, came before Maister Meyre & his brethern, and shewid them he was not abull to occupy the seid Rome, and prayed them he myght be dischargid. Wheruppon ther was made ferther inquirre of hym whedir he were abull or noo. And ther it came to knolege afore them all that the seid Roger had with his wif, oon John Pachettes doughter, in redy money & plate xxx li., and also it was right well knowen that he hadde right largely of his owne, or els the seid Joh. Pachet wold not haue maried his doughter to hym; and also the seid Roger was for-boron and put of from the seid office by the space of iij yere afore at the instaunce of the seid Joh. Pachet; and so it was thought he was able y-nought for the rome,

[2] "Rog. a Lee chosen Chamberlaine."

"Refused" the office,

though the extent of his wife's dowry points to his being a man of substance,

and able to fill it,

---

[1] leaf 300. Scribe G. The mayor is described as "Maior Ciuitatis siue ville."
[2] The marginal annotations are here through lack of space written at the foot of the leaf.

§ 93. *Ric. Smyth, Mayor. Chamberlainship*, 1508.

if he wold. And þer he was louyngly entretid by dyuerse of my seid maisters, that is to sey, by Maister Rob. a Grene then Meire, Maister Will. ffoorth, Maister Joh. Haddon, Maister Will. Pysforde, Maister Ric. Jakson, to take the office appon hym, and they wold see he shuld haue no loose therby, but a forberyng a litell money for a tyme. Also they offerid hym to lene hym certeyn money tyll such tyme as he had gaderid it up a-geyn of the seid office, and so no loose to hym. Yet not-with-stondyng all thes offers he vtterly refusid the seid office and wold not take it uppon hym in no wyse.

in spite of persuasion and offers of a loan

he persists in his refusal.

Wheruppon Maister Meire & his brethern seyng his obstynacye and ffrowordnesse, commaundid hym in peyne of a C li. that he shuld not depart the Citee nor inbesell[1] noon of his goodes out þerof, and also to be foorthcomyng at all tymes afore Maister Meyre & his brethern when he shal-be send fore, apon the peyne afore rehersid, and answere to such thynges as shuld be leyed to his charge.

He is ordered on pain of £100 not to embezzle any of his goods.

And after apon Candilmas day next foloyng Maister Meyre with Maister Ric. Smyth, then newe elect meire, and my maisters, the aldermen, went in-to seynt Mary hall a-bowte ix of the clok, with such oþer officers as then & ther shuld be sworon, and take þer charge accordyng to the olde custome of the cite afore-tyme vsid. And then & þer in opyn audiance the seid Rog. a Lee was callid thryes solemply to com in and exercise the seid office of chamberleynship of the Citee which he was elect & chosyn in. And the seid Roger cam not but made defaute. And after that the seid Roger was callid a-yen thryes solemply to come and occupy the seid office apon peyn of C li.; and the seid Roger cam not, but eftsons made defaute. Wheruppon Maister Rob. a Grene, then beyng meyre, by the aduyse of my maisters, the aldermen, cawsid a newe eleccion of xxiiij accordyng to the olde custome; which xxiiij aforenamyd went into the counsell house and ther inmediatly chosyn Tho. Hyll afor-namyd to be an of the Chamberleyns in the stede of the seid Rog. a Lee.

Feb. 2. The officers come to S. Mary's Hall,

and Roger is solemnly summoned,

"caled 6 times. Refused: ffined 100 li.[2] (sic),

And then within a while after this new eleccion the

---

[1] = convey away secretly.
[2] This gloss is incorrect; Roger was only bound over in £100.

§ 93. Ric. Smyth, Mayor. Chamberlainship, 1508.

seid Rog. a Lee cam in-to the hall; and as sone as Maister Meyre saw hym he commaundid hym to warde, þer to remayn vnto such tyme as they wold be aduysed what punyshement he shuld haue for his mysdemener, and also for the parlous example that he hath shewid [1] to other in like cas so to do, which was neuer seyn afore. And after at the especiall instaunce of his freyndes the seid Roger was le⁊ to bayll to certayn of his ffrendes, which were bounde for hym to Maister Meyre in an obligacion of a C li. apon condicion that he shuld be foorth-comyng afore Maister Meyre & his brethern at eny tyme when he shalbe callid, and also to pay such fynes & mercimentes that shall hereafter be sett appon hym for his seid mysdemener & yl-example. And after the Wennysday the xxiiij day of May the xxiiij yere afore-rehersid at seynt Mary hall a-fore Maister Meire, Maister Duddesbury M.G.S.T.,[2] Maister Merler, Maister Grene, Maister Baylly, Maister Churcheman, Maister Padlonde, Maister Haddon, Maister Pysford, Maister Saunders, Maister Strong, Maister Hassall, Maister Hulcote, Maister Barbour, Maister Clerk, Maister ffoxhale, Maister Grove, Maister Rogers, Maister Heynes, the foreseid mater was spokyn of amonges them all; and there they were fully agreed that the seid Rog. a Lee for his mysdemener and also for the yll example that he had giffen to oder shuld pay for his ffyne xx li. of lawfull money to þe behoof & profet of the seid Citee, and yet not to be dischargid of the seid office for euer but to be at the plesure of Maister meyre & his brethern when they list to call hym to the seid office etc.

margin: and imprisoned."

margin: May 24, 1508.

margin: [3] "20 li. paid ffor Refusing to be Chamberlin, & yet Liable to serue when Again Elected."ᐟ "Roger Lee ffyned for Refusing to be Chamberleyn."[3]

LEETS.

[4] ¶ [V. f. p. held before Ric. Smyth, m., Tho. Grove, Hen. Rogers, b., on Tuesday after the feast of SS. Philip and James, 23 Hen. VII.]

Joh. Duddesbury, Hen. Merler, Rob. Grene, Tho. Baylly, Joh. Padlonde, Joh. Haddon, Will. Pysford, Ric. Jakscn, Tho. Wardlowe, Joh. Saunders, Joh. Strong, Ric.

margin: "Couentre." May 2.

margin: Electors.

---

[1] leaf 300, back. [2] "maister of Trinite gilde."
[3]—[3] These two glosses are in different hands; hence tautology.
[4] leaf 301.

§ 93. *Ric. Smyth, Mayor.* *Leet,* 1508.

Hassall, Edw. Hulcote, Joh. Derlyng, Rog. Chambur, Joh. Clerk, Ric. ffoxhall, Will. Wygston, Hugo Dawes, Tho. ffoorth, Joh. Mors, Will. Dawson, Tho. Kelyngworth, Ric. Ryse.

<small>Orders of leet. Tho. Empson elected joint recorder.</small>

ffirst, at this lete we amytt, elect, & chese M*aister* Tho. Empson to occupy and be in the office of Recordership in the Citee of Couentre ioyntly w*ith* M*aister* S*ir* Ric. Empson, his ffader; and he to occupy the seid office in the absens of his ffader as Recorder of the Citee etc.

<small>Draught-houses to be removed or 20*s*. fine;</small>

Item, [ordained] that the shirreffs goo & vewe the Co*m*en diche behynde the Pecok [1] in the Crosse-chepyng that gooth from M*aister* Hen. Merlers vnto the West-orcherd, and see that the draughtes be takyn a-wey betwene this and Midsom*er* next, apon [peyn] of eu*er*y man that hath eny draught there after Midsom*er* to leese xx s., and if the shirreff*es* see this not doon they to lese

<small>"Com*en* shores Clensed."</small>

for þ*er* nondoyng xx s. Also it is ordeyngned in like cas that no man haue eny draught*es* or oder noyaunc*es* in the Red-diche from Litell-pa*r*ke-strete to the Jurdenwell, nor no grat*es* except such as woll kepe out muk; and that the

<small>The Red-ditch not to be covered or 20*s*. fine.</small>

Cou*er* no place of the seid dich or gutter, which of olde tyme hath be kept opyn, in peyn of eu*er*y man doyng the cont*r*arie for eu*er*y defaute to forfeit xx s., wherof vj s. viij d. to the shirreff*es*, vj s. viij d. to þe Co*m*en boxe, and vj s. viij d. to the Chamberleyns. And if on Joh. a Woode, or the owner of the grounde, cast not opyn the Co*m*en diche as of olde tyme it hath be vsid by-twene this a[n]t Midsom*er* next to loose xx s. to be levyed in forme afore-rehersid etc.

<small>"Ride the bounds of the Countie."</small>

Also it is ordeyngned at this lete that M*aister* Meire & his brethern shall ryde the Circuyte of the ffraunchese by-tweene this and Michelmas next comyng.

<small>"Co*m*en serjant"</small>

[Ordained] at this lete that Hen. Peynter, co*m*en se*r*iaunt, shall make clene, and see boron a-wey all such muk as lieth w*ithout* the ffrere-yate to the Co*m*en noysaunce, as it was com*m*aundid hym at the last lete by-twene this & Whitsontyde next, uppon peyne of forfeture of his office; and that the seid Henr*e* eu*er*y Saturday wayte apon the

---

[1] This inn existed until comparatively recent times.

§ 93. *Ric. Smyth, Mayor. Leet*, 1508.

Chamburleyns to see þer werkmen payed, that the seid Chamburleyn shall pay for the Comen wele of the Cite, and also to wayte apon theym at all tymes requisite when they goo to gedir their murage money, apon peyn afore-rehersid.

to wait on þe Chamberlins."

[1] ¶ [V. f. p. held on Tuesday after S. Dionysius' day 24 Hen. VII.]

"Couentre." Oct. 10.

Joh. Duddesbury, Hen. Merler, Rob. Grene, Tho. Bayly, Tho. Churchman, Joh. Padlonde, Joh. Haddon, Ric. Jakson, Joh. Saunders, Tho. Turner, sen., Joh. Strong, Ric. Hassall, Rog. Sutton, Rog. Chambur, Ed. Hulcote, Joh. Whitehede, Ric. Merler, Ric. ffoxhall, Nic. Burwey, Will. Wygston, Hen. Wall, Ed. Hadley, Tho. Hyll, Ric. Ryse.

[Humf. Grene, Dyer, Hen. Perkyns, Grasyer.]

Sheriffs.

ffirst, [ordained] that all such officers as longyn to the breusters yelde [2] and the stresse-rolles, and also the shirrefs officers, that thei shall from-hensforth fynde sufficient suerty to the sherreffs for executyng there offices and also for there good attendaunce.

"Sergeantes to find suretys for their places & behauioris."

Also [ordained] that if eny straunger hereafter be disposid to dwell in this Citee, what craft so euer he be of, that he shall dwelle frely within the Citee xij monethes & a day without any assessement of the maister of the craft of the occupacion that he is, apon the peyn of xl s., but at his fre wyll.

"Strangers to be ffree."

[Ordained] that no boocher nor odur of the Citee suffre eny Mastyf dogges to goo at large after vij of the clok at nyght in the wynter and viij of the clok in somer; and in the morenyng vij a clok in wynter and v a clok in somer, [or 3s. 4d. fine at every default, "holf" to the common box.]

"Mastyffe Dogs."

[Ordained] that no man fromhensforth by eny barley or odur greyne at the Townes-ende or els-where, but in the comen Market, or at his own durre, apon peyn of euery quarter so bought to leese xx d., the on half to the Comen boxe, the other to the shirrefes.

Barley to be bought in the open market.

[1] leaf 304.
[2] The city officers apparently collected a quarterage from the victuallers, Corp. MSS. A. 3 (b), leaf 61. v. *supra*, p. 234, and Introduction.

§ 94. Ric. Marler, Mayor, 1509.

"Nota."
The price of shoes.
[illeg.]

[Ordained]¹ that M*aister* Meire for the tyme beyng shall call to hym vj or viij of his brether and se the reformac*i*on of the p*r*ice of shoon, botewes² and bot*es*; and also to reforme tanners³ as the case shall require etc.

[Ordained and enacted] that Tho. Warde, barker, from hensforth for dyue*r*se considerac*i*ons shall-be dischargid of the office of shirrefwyke of this Citee for eue*r*, payng for his ffyne x ma*r*ke to the makyng of the conduyte.

"Against laying muk in Cros-cheping."

Also it is ordeigned at this lete that noon of the inha*b*itaunt*es* of the Crosse-Chepyng ley eny muk or swepyng*es* in the ma*r*ket place ther tyll the ffriday at nyght for that it may be caried a-wey on the morow, apon the peyn of eue*r*y defaute iiij d., wherof the ffynder to haue for his laboure j d., and the residue to the co*m*en boxe.

"Sheriffes not levying þe amercementes."

[Agreed and ordained] that the shirrefes for the tyme beyng that if they levey not all the ame*r*ciement*es* that be assessed at the let*es* that they shall forfete as much money, and that to be leveyed of the shirrefes to the vse of the Co*m*en boxe for eue*r*y defaute etc.

RIC. MARLER, MAYOR, 1509.

*"Ciuitas Couentr*ie*."*
Jan. 25.

⁴ ¶ [Election of officers.]

Rob. a Grene, Hen. Merler, Tho. Bayly, Ric. Lee, Joh. Padlonde, Tho. Churchman, Joh. Haddon, Ric. Jakson, Joh. Duddesbury, Joh. Clerk, Joh. Hardwen, Ric. ffoxhale, Joh. Derlyng, Rog. Chambur, Edw. Hulcote, Joh. Humfrey, Nic. Heynes, Joh. Cesyle, Will. Wykam, Ric. Nores, Tho. Hyll, Will. Rocardyne, Hen. Wall, Ric. Ryse.

Officers.

[m. Ric. Merler; cor. Joh. Boteler; steward, Joh. Porter; ch. Tho. ffarman, Joh. Crampe; w. Joh. Bonde, Tho. Whyte; mace, Hen. Walker; crier, Ric. ffereby.]

EASTER LEET.

*"Couentr*e*."*
Apr. 17.

⁵ ¶ [V. f. p. held before Ric. Merler, m., Hum. Grene, Hen. Perkyns, b., on Tuesday after the close of Easter, 24 Hen. VII.]

---

¹ Leet spelled "let" here. ² = A short boot.
³ "as of" inserted in MS. ⁴ leaf 305.
⁵ leaf 305, back.

§ 94. Ric. Marler, Mayor. The King, 1509.

[1] Rob. Grene, Hen. Merler, Tho. Bayly, Tho. Churchman, Joh. Padlonde, Joh. Haddon, Will. Pysford, Ric. Jakson, Joh Duddesbury, Ric. Smyth, Will. Wygston, Joh. Clerk, Joh. Strong, Ric. Hassall, Joh. Saunders, Ed. Hulcote, Joh. Humfrey, Ric. ffoxhale, Nic. Burwey, Nic. Heynes, Tho. Grove, Hen. Rogers, Rog. Chambur, Joh. Whitehede.[1]

Jury.

[2] ffirst, [ordained] that the ffeliship and occupacion of Coruesers fromhensfurth shall pay & bere with the craft of Tanners toward ther charges xiij s. iiij d. in lyke wise as Maister Ric. Smyth did commaunde them when he was Meyre[3] tyll hit be better enquerid of etc.[2]

Order of leet. Corvisers and tanners' pageant.

CHRONICLE.

[4] Mem. that this yere dyed kuyng (sic) Henry the vij[th] the xxij day of April; and he graunted byfore his deth a generall pardon of all maner of hawte tresons, pety tresons, felonyes, Roberyes etc. And after his deth his son kuyng Henry the viij[th] ratyfied and confermid the same with more larger wordes for all maner of trespasses, brekyng of statutes, mysvsyng of offices with dyuerse oder articles doon before the xxiij day of April then begynnyng his Reyne etc. And the seid Henry the vij[th] dyed at Rychemount the day afore-rehersid and was brought to London in-to Pollys with many nobles of the Realme & grete nombre of torches and a grete nombre of peple both on horsbak & afote. And after iij dayes beyng in Polles he was brought to Westmynster; and ther he lieth & his quene Elizabeth with hym in a newe chapell which he causid to be made in his lyffe; on whoos saule Jhesu haue mercy. And his son kyng Henry the viij[th] was crownyd the same yere at Westmynster the Sonday next after Midsomer day. And the same yere ther was an heyre determyner[5] throw-out Ynglond; and ther came dyuerse

"King Henre VII died." Apr. 22. He granted a pardon which

his son ratified.

The late king lay in state at S. Paul's and

was buried at Westminster,

on whose soul Jesu have mercy! Henry VII is crowned July 1. An oyer and terminer held throughout the kingdom.

[1–1] Transposed. In the MS. the first order precedes the jury list.
[2–2] Transposed.   [3] i. e. in 1508.
[4] leaf 305. See for Henry VIII's charter of pardon Corp. MSS. B. 55.
[5] an eyre of justices of oyer and terminer = special courts held by commissioners to hear and determine certain causes.

§ 94. *Ric. Marler, Mayor. Whitley*, 1509.

com*m*yssione*r*s to this Citee of Couentre, that is to sey, M*aister* Joh. ffyssher, on of the Justic*es* of the co*m*en place, and M*aister* Guy Palmer, the king*es* seriaunt, Sir Ed. Ralegh, knyght,[1] Sim. Dygby of Colshull,[2] Ric. Hongerford,[3] esquyer. And the Meyre of Couentre was the cheef com*m*yssione*r* for the Citee, & was namyd by his name, Ric. Merler, Meyre of the Citee of Couentre, and he kept the chere thre dayes in the Jeyll halle contynually etc.

WHITLEY AGAIN.

June 10.
Laur. " Walgrave "
complains of wrong done by the commoners of Coventry in certain fields.

[4] M*em.* that the xth day of June this same yere ther cam on[5] Laur. Walgraue of Whitley afore M*aister* Meyre & his brethern & made a grete seyng to them that he had grete wrong in ce*r*teyn ffyld*es* a this half Whitley by the comens of Couentre, and that he wold compleyne fferther if he had no remedy theryn. Wheruppon M*aister* Meyre & his brethern let make a-semble at seynt Mary hall of the most honest co*m*myners of the Cite to the nombre of xlviij pe*r*sons or moo ; and ther the Meyre shewid them of the troubles mynde of the seid Laurence, & how he was disposid toward the Citee.

An assembly in S. Mary's Hall agrees
to support the corporation in any action.

And ther it was conducendid & agreed by all the hoole assemble at that tyme that the seid Laurence shuld be answerid to eny thyng that he wold ley to the charge of the Citee in-soo-much that eue*r*y man that was *p*er offered to bere ther pa*r*ties in money to defende his froward mynde & malice, and so was the answere gyffen to hym by M*aister* Meyre that he shuld be answerid to eny thyng that he wold sey or do.

Walgrave withdraws, and June 28

And then the seid Laurence aduysed hymself better and toke counsell of his ffrynd*es* and came ayen in-to the counsell howse a-fore M*aister* Meyre & his brethern the xxviij day of the same moneth and wit*h* feyre word*es*

---

[1] Of Farnborough, Warwickshire. *v.* Dugdale, 382.
[2] *v. ib.* p. 720.
[3] The Hungerfords held Woodcote near Warwick. Ric. Hungerford was also a lessee of the manor of Brailes, *ib.* 190, 397.
[4] leaf 306, back.
[5] It is difficult to distinguish this scribe's a from o. Is it on or an, answered or onswered, apon or opon ?

shewyng that he was on of the Citee, & that he wold be loth to make ony besynes w*ith* hit. And if it wold please M*aister* Meyre & his brethern to gif hym a ce*r*teyn money he wold bryng in the euidences of the same ffyld*es*, so that the Cite shuld be out of stryf for eue*r*. And it was answered to hym *p*at if he had eny such euydense or writyng if he brought them in he shuld haue the good love of the Citee, but as for eny other gif they know not wherfore; but if he wold doo so kyndly to bryng them in he shuld be kyndly dalt w*ith*all. And then he wold ned*es* know what he shuld haue. And he was answerid by M*aister* Meyre be-fore his brethern in the counsell howse that he shuld haue a potell of wyne, & if it were a galon it was well, & more he shuld not haue by pr*o*myse, but as they founde hym kynde so they wold loke appon hym. And if he list to bryng them yn thus he shuld haue good thanke, and if not then to kepe them and do his best. proposes to surrender his evidence for a consideration.

The mayor cannily offers only a pottle of wine—and thanks.

And then after the ixth day of July the seid Larence brought in ij boxys of euydens, amon*ges* the which ther was a tripa*r*tite exemplified vnder the kyn*ges* brode seall, the which he wold haue had a-geyn. And it was answerid him if he list to see hit if he came at euy tyme resonable he shuld see it w*ith* good wyll. And then w*ith* his feyre peynted word*es* and his insessaunt labour he hadde of M*aister* Meyre & his brethern at on[1] tyme & other to the some of ,[2] the which was more then eue*r* he dese*r*uyd or eue*r* woll etc.

After Jul. 9 Walgrave brings in his evidence

and gets something from the mayor therefor with fair painted words. "Variance About ffeild on this side Whitley ended."

MICHAELMAS LEET.

[[3] V. f. p. held on Tuesday after Michaelmas, 1 Hen. VIII.]

Rob. Grene, Tho. Churchman, Joh. Padlonde, Joh. Haddon, Will. Pysford, Ric. Jakson, Joh. Duddesbury, Ric. Smyth, Will. Wygston, Joh. Clerk, Tho. Turno*ur*, sen., Joh. Strong, Ric. Hassall, Joh. Saunders, Edw. Hulcote, Rog. Chambur, Joh. Whitehedde, Joh. Hardwen,

"Couentre." Oct. 2.

---

[1] See note 5 on p. 626. [2] Blank.
[3] leaf 306.

§ 95. *Joh. Saunders, Mayor,* 1510.

Joh. Humfrey, Nic. Heynes, Tho. Grove, Hen. Rogers, Tho. fforman, Joh. Cramp.

Sheriffs. [Tho. ffoorth, Will. Perkyns.]

Orders of leet.
"Bounds of County."
[Ordained] that certayn persons shall goo & see the Meres and boundes of the shire of Couentre; and there as lacketh eny merestones to set newe in all such p[l]aces. And the namys of them that be namyd to ryde heraftur foloyn, that is to sey, Maister Rob. Grene, Maister Joh. Padlonde, Maister Joh. Haddon, Maister Will. Pysford, Maister Ric. Jakson, Maister Ric. Smyth, Maister Tho. Turnour the elder, Maister Tho. Grove, Maister Joh. Boteler, Tho. ffarman, Joh. Cramp, Joh. Bonde, Tho. White; and they to ryde as sone as may be conuenyent, and, if it may be, on Thursday next etc.

The wall and ditch.
[Agreed] that Maister Meyre and certayn of his brethern by-twene thus & Saturday next comyng goo and vewe the Towne Wall; and to see the Comen noysaunȝses in the Towne dych, and make reformacion þerof by there discrecions etc.

THE RECORDER.

[Ant. ffitzherberde[1] was elected recorder of this city in the time of Ric. Merler about the end of his year.]

JOH. SAUNDERS, MAYOR, 1510.

"Cluitas Couentrie."
Jan. 25.
[2] ¶ [Election of officers.]

Ric. Smyth, Tho. Baylly, Ric. Lee, Tho. Churchman, Joh. Padlonde, Joh. Haddon, Will. Pysforde,[3] Ric. Jakson, Joh. Duddesbury, Joh. Hardwen, Joh. Clerk, Rog. Chambur, Edw. Hulcote, Joh. Derlyng, Joh. Whitehede, Joh. Humfrey, Nic. Heynes, Tho. Grove, Hen. Rogers, Tho. ffarman, Joh. Crampe, Ric. Nores, Hugh Dawes, Will. Wykam.

---

[1] Empson was executed after the death of Henry VII. Fitzherbert (1470–1528) was the author of numerous books on legal matters; and the *Boke of Husbandrie* is sometimes attributed to him, v. *Eng. Hist. Rev.* ix., p. 305. His wife was daughter of Sir Hen. Willoughby of Middleton (Mr. Stevenson) and Wyken, *see* Dugdale, 88.

[2] leaf 307. No mention of the recorder.

[3] See his will in Dugdale (1730), 184–5. He was associated with Ford in the foundation of Ford's or Greyfriars' Hospital, which is still standing.

§ 95. Joh. Saunders, Mayor. Leet, 1510.

[m. Joh. Saunders; cor. Joh. Boteler; steward, Joh. Porter; ch. Ric. Heryng,[1] grocer, Will. Tylet; w. Tho. Rowley, Ric. Kemsey; mace, Hen. Peynter; crier, Ric. ffereby.] *Officers.*

Mem. it is agreed at this eleccion that the Comen seriaunt shal-be sworon that he shall make a true accompt euery yere of all the vacande grounde a-bowte the Citee to Maister Meyre & his brethern when the Chamburleyns make theire accompt; and also he shall gif his due attendaunce apon the Chamburleyns, as well the olde as the newe, at all tymes to execute þer office without takyng eny thyng for his laboure but mete & drynk, in peyn of forfeture of his office. *"Comen seriant." "Comen seriant to waite on þe Chamberlins ffor his diett."*

EASTER AND MICHAELMAS LEETS.

[[2] V. f. p. held before Joh. Saunders, m., Tho. fforth, Will. Perkyns, b., on Thursday after the close of Easter, 1 Hen. VIII.] *"Couentre." Apr. 11.*

Ric. Smyth, Rob. Grene, Tho. Churchman, Joh. Padlande, Joh. Haddon, Will. Pysforde, Ric. Jakson, Joh. Duddesbury, Ric. Merler, Joh. Hardwen, Tho. Turnour, sen., Joh. Strong, Ric. Hassall, Joh. Clerk, Rog. Sutton, Rog. Chambur, Joh. Derlyng, Joh. Whitehede, Joh. Humfrey, Ric. ffoxhale, Tho. Grove, Nic. Heynes, Ed. Hulcote, Ric. Heryng.

ffirst, [ordained] that euery alderman in his warde as oft as he thynketh necessarie shall take too or thre Constabuls with him and make serche in his warde for all them that kepe mysrule in þer howses, and such as they fynde fawty to commyt them to warde or oder punyshement as they thynke is necessarie for them; and if they wyl-not mende by that, then to cause them to bannysh[3] the Citee. And also the seid alderman sholl gif knolege to þer londlorde or to his baylly if the londlorde be absent that they waren[4] all such suspect persons to departe from there tenure and to set there well-disposid persons etc. *"Aldermen search in their wards" and banish thence undesirables.*

[Agreed] that no inhabitaunt or Citezen within the

---

[1] Probably an ancestor of the Puritan divine, Julines Herring.
[2] leaf 308.   [3] = to be banished.   [4] = warn.

§ 95. *Joh. Saunders, Mayor. Leet,* 1510.

"For gre-h[un]des." Citee or the suborbes of the same kepe eny greunde[1] or grey bech[2] from this day forwarde, but if he may dispende xl s. by yere above all charges, apon [the peyn] to forfeite for the furst fawte xl d., the secunde vj s. viij d., and eue*ry* defawte after x s., this peyn to be leueyed by the sheriffes, the oon half to ther owne vse and the other half to the co*m*en boxe. And this to be executyd w*ith*out eny fauour accordyng to the act*es* of *par*lement etc.

"Coue*ntre*." Oct. 1.
[3] [V. f. p. held on Tuesday after Michaelmas, 2 Hen. VIII.]

Ric. Smyth, Rob. a Grene, Tho. Churchman, Joh. Padlonde, Joh. Haddon, Will. Pysford, Joh. Duddesbury, Ric. Merler, Joh. Hardwen, Joh. Strong, Ric. Hassall, Joh. Clerk, Edw. Hulcote, Joh. Whitehede, Rog. Chambur, Joh. Humfrey, Tho. Grove, Hen. Rogers, Hum. Grene, Hen. Perkyns, Will. Wykam, Ric. Heryng, Will. Tylet, Ric. Kemsey.

Sheriffs. [Tho. Waren, Dyer, Tho. Astleyn, Baker.]

Orders of Leet. "viij per-sones in euerie warde" to
[Ordained] that M*ais*ter Meyre that now ys shall eue*ry* weke on day in the weke shall let call afore hym viij *per*sons of substaunse w*ith*in a w*a*rde, shewyng to them for a substaunce or stok to be hadde w*ith*in this Citee for such c*er*tayn Charg*es* that casually shall come vnto the Citee; that it is thought eue*ry* warde shal-be com*m*enyd w*ith* by viij of the substaunce of such warde what enprowem*e*nt[4] myght be hadde in the Comen-ffe[5] or other opprowm*e*nt[6] or p*ro*fite myght ryse vnto the Co*m*en Weele of the Citee as haue be made afore-tyme, as of receyuyng of p*re*ntyses & such other; and to know the good mynd*es* of eue*ry* warde in the p*re*mysses; or if e*n*y other wyse wey myght be founde for the increse of such stok, as is afore-seid. And that the seid viij p*er*sons shall make relac*i*on to M*ais*ter Meyre of there mynd*es*; and that eue*ry* weke M*ais*ter Meyre let call viij p*er*sons vnto the tyme that all the x wardes be p*er*vsed.[7]

report to the mayor any scheme for the improvement of the city and the increase of s funds.

[1] ME. grehunde. [2] Female of grey-hound.
[3] leaf 308, back. [4] = improvement. [5] or ? Comensee.
[6] Approvement = profit, esp. profit arising from the enclosure of common lands.
[7] peruse = to go through in order.

JOH. STRONG, MAYOR, 1511.

[1] ¶ [Election of officers.]

Ric. Merler, Rob. a Grene, Tho. Churchman, Joh. Padlonde, Joh. Haddon, Will. Pysford, Joh. Duddesbury, Ric. Smyth, Rog. Chamber, Joh. Whitehede, Joh. Humfrey, Nic. Heynes, Hen. Rogers, Humf. Grene, Hen. Perkyns, Tho. fforth, Will. Perkyns, Ric. Heryng, Will. Tylet, Tho. Rowley, Nic. Kemsey, Ric. Nores, Will. Banwell, Will. Brygges.

m. Joh. Strong; rec. Ant. ffitzherberde; cor. Joh. Boteler; steward, Joh. Porter; ch. Nic. Hobson, Tho. Goppeshyll; w. Joh. Hopkyns, Tho. Burden; mace, Hen. Walker; crier, Ric. ffereby.

"Ciuitas Couentrie." Jan. 25.

Officers.

EASTER AND MICHAELMAS LEETS.

[2] ¶ [V. f. p. held before Joh. Strong, m., Tho. Waren, Tho. Astlyn, b., on Tuesday after the close of Easter, 3 Hen. VIII.]

"Ciuitas Couentrie." Apr. 29.

Ric. Merler, Rob. a Grene, Tho. Churchman, Joh. Padlonde, Joh. Haddon, Will. Pysforde, Joh. Duddesbury, Ric. Smyth, Joh. Saunders, Rog. Chambur, Ric. Hassall, Joh. Clerk, Joh. Whytehede, Humf. Grene, Hen. Perkyns, Tho. fforth, Will. Perkyns, Ric. Burwey, Nic. Hobson, Tho. Gopeshyll, Joh. Smyth, Ric. Nores, Ric. Heryng, Will. Brygges.

[Ordained] that where the Comen dyches & Comen gutters of the Citee byn gretely anoyed [3] with castyng of muke & ffilth in them and also in swepyng of ther fylth in-to the same by dyuerse yll-disposid persons, contrarie to all good rule of the Citee; therfore it is ordeyned (etc.) that euery persone that is fromhensforth takyn with eny such fawte shall pay for euery defaute ij d. to the Comen boxe and a peny to the constable for his fyndyng; and that euery persone fromhensforth after there swepyng bere a-wey the same, apon the same peyn.

Orders of Leet.

Filth in the river.

2d. fine.

[Ordained] that no man fromhensforth cast yn-to the

The river.

---

[1] leaf 309. New recorder mentioned as to be elected.
[2] leaf 309, back. There is an illegible heading to this page.
[3] annoy = to affect injuriously (*N. E. D.*).

§ 96. Joh. Strong, Mayor. Leet, 1511.

comen Ryuer eny muk or ffilth, or in eny other maner streite or stop the same with eny maner of thyng, he to lese fromhensforth for euery defaute xl d., iij s. to the comen box, & iiij d. to the constable that fyndeth it.

Fish water. [Ordained] that no man cast owte eny ffyshwater that ffysh hath ben watered yn after iiij of the Clok in the mornyng & afore ix of the clok at nyght, [or 2d. to the common box and 1d. to the constable that finds it.]

"No ffishmonger to buy butter to sell." [Ordained] that no ffyshmonger within this Citee by butter to sell but only for his owne howse, apon peyn to forfete for euery defawte iiij d. to the comen box and to the constable that fyndeth the defawte.[1]

Bakers, butchers and fishmongers not to sell candles. Also it is ordeyned that no baker, bocher, nor ffyshmonger, nor noen such vitaler make nor by eny candell to sell but onely for þer owne howses, apon the peyn of xx s. to the comen box; and the constable that fyndeth the defawte to haue of the same xij d.; and such stuf as they haue now to vtter hit by-twene this and Whitsonday next comyng, apon the same peyn; and also that no chaundler Wynter nor somer sell no candell a-bove a peny a pounde, apon the peyn afore-rehersid etc.

"The gaoler to Atend the mayor and to take no ffees for lodging in the Comon Goale." Also apon a byll of compleynt put in at this lete by my maisters, the Shirrefs, a-yenst the Jayler how he gaf not his attendaunce apon Maister Meyre and them as he ought to do, and it was seid by [2] hym that he toke larger fees of prisoners then he shuld do: where-fore it is ordeyned (etc.) that euery Jayler of this Citee fromhensforth shall gif his diligent attendaunce apon Maister Meyre as [? at] such tyme as oder officers doo, except it be for charge of prisoners; and also that he shall take no ffee of no man but such as come within the Jayle as prisoners; and also to take nothyng of eny prisoner for no chamber but only for his owne chamber, apon the peyn of lesyng of his office.

"Ciuitas Couentrie." Oct. 2. [3] ¶ [V. f. p. held before Joh. Strong, m., Tho. Waren, Tho. Astlyn, b., on Thursday after Michaelmas, 3 Hen. VIII.]

Ric. Merler, Rob. Grene, Tho. Churchman, Joh. Pad-

---

[1] ? How is the fine apportioned?   [2] = about, concerning.
[3] leaf 310, back.

§ 97. Ric. Hassall, Mayor, 1512.

londe, Joh. Haddon, Will. Pysford, Joh. Duddesbury, Ric. Smyth, Joh. Saunders, Rog. Chambur, Ric. Hassall, Joh. Whithede, Humf. Grene, Hen. Perkyns, Tho. fforth, Will. Perkyns, Joh. Smyth, Tho. Gopeshyll, Nic. Hobson, Joh. Hopkyns, Tho. Burdon, Ric. Kemsey, Will. Bregges, Ric. Herryng.

[Hugh Dawes, Draper, Tho. Turner, Grasyer.] *Sheriffs.*

[Ordained] that all such groundes, closys, lesues,[1] & pastures that the xlviij men which were chosen by the hoole body of the Citee to vewe all the comen ffyldes abowte the Citee, and byn agreed which may be takyn in at Lammas leuyng sufficient Comen[2]; that they shall be takyn in at Lammas & kept seuerall for the comen wele of the Citee; and the profete of that half yere comyng yerly to be apployed for the comen wele of the Citee; and that they shall soo be vsid accordyng to theyre agrement as long as the Comens be thus content, sauyng euery manys right. And he that vseth hym contrarie to this act or breketh eny parsell therof to forfeit for euery defaute vj s. viij d. to be payed to the comen box and gederid by them þat be lymyted to gedur the rent of the same groundes, prouyded allwey that it is agreed by the seid xlviij; & also by the xxiiij at this lete[3] that the Chamberleyns for the tyme beyng shall euery yere breke opyn at Lammas all the seid closis & pasturis recordyng it for þer Comen and then incontynent to be inclosid ayen *Orders of leet. By direction of "xlviij" men, chosen by the whole body of the city, a certain proportion of the "Comens" are to be "taken in"*

but pro formâ opened every Lammas day.

[Ordeyned] that no capper nor Sherman from this day forward flok,[4] myle or presse cappe or cloth, apon the peyn for euery defaute xx s. to be leueyd in forme foloyng, that is to sey, vj s. viij d. to the Meyre, vj s. viij d. to the Churchwardens, vj s. viij d. to the Comen box. *Cappers and shearmen not to mill cloth.*

RIC. HASSALL, MAYOR, 1512.

[5] ¶ [Election of officers.]

Joh. Saunders, Rob. a Grene, Tho. Churchman, Joh. Padlonde, Joh. Haddon, Will. Pysford, Joh. Duddesbury,

"Ciuitas Couentrie." Jan. 25.

---

[1] = meadows.
[2] This scheme must have arisen from a desire to improve the city finances. See above, p. 630.
[3] Supply "it is ordeyned," or words to that effect.
[4] Flock = to cover cloth with flock or wool dust, v. *N. E. D.*
[5] leaf 311.

§ 97. Ric. Hassall, Mayor. Leet, 1512.

Ric. Smyth, Ric. Merler, Ric. Hassall,[1] Tho. Grove, Joh. Clerk, Rog. Chambur, Joh. Whithede, Humf. Grene, Nic. Burwey, Nic. Heynes, Hen. Perkyns, Tho. fforth, Will. Perkyns, Will. Wykam, Nic. Hobson, Joh. Hopkyns, Tho. Burdon.

Officers. [m. Ric. Hassall; rec. Ant. ffitzherberde; cor. Joh. Boteler; steward, Joh. Porter; ch. Ric. Townesende, Rog. Walees; w. Jul. Nethyrmyll,[2] Tho. Dode; mace, Hen. Walker; crier, Ric. ffereby.]

EASTER LEET.

"Ciuitas Couentrie." Apr. 20.

[3] ¶ [V. f. p. held before Ric. Hassall, m., Hug. Dawes, Tho. Turner, b., on Tuesday before S. George's day, 3 Hen. VIII.]

Joh. Saunders, Rob. a Grene, Tho. Churchman, Joh. Padlonde, Joh. Haddon, Will. Pysford, Joh. Duddesbury, Ric. Smyth, Ric. Merler, Joh. Strong, Tho. Grove, Joh. Clerk, Rog. Chambur, Joh. Whitehede, Nic. Burwey, Nic. Heynes, Humf. Grene, Hen. Perkyns, Tho. fforth, Will. Perkyns, Tho. Astlyn, Ric. Townesende, Rog. Wales, Will. Tylet.

Orders of leet. Bakers not to be tallow-chandlers.

[Ordained and enacted] that all such bakers and euery othe[r] occupacion that were dischargid by leete to occupy or vse the occupacion of Talough-chaundelers that they shall forfeyt the peyn that was made therfore the last yere in Maister Stronges tyme then beyng meyre if they medle therwith.[4]

"Assiz off water."

[Ordained] that Will. Perkyns, Baker, shall mende thassise of his myll dame, callid Crowe-mylle,[5] and kepe the water there in a resonable course after the olde assise, by-twene this & Holy-rode day[6] next coming, [or 20s. fine.]

Sea-fish

[Ordained] that no persone within the Citee take up no sse ffysh by the pauyer nor by the seme,[7] but only take

---

[1] John S deleted. It is curious that the mayor's name should be among the electors.
[2] Died 1539, and buried in S. Michael's, where his tomb may be seen. The Christian name is here written Julinum.
[3] leaf 311, back.   [4] v. p. 632.
[5] Name perpetuated in Crow Lane.   [6] Sept. 14.
[7] = a load for a pack-horse, i. e. 8 bushels.

for there cuttyng if they cut eny viij d. for a seme [or 6s. 8d. fine each time]; and þat no mon nor woman cut no ffysh, but those persons here-writen, that is to sey, Tho. Hobbons, Joh. Colman, Joh. Alysaunder, Laur. Yrelonde, Joh. Halle, Joh. Leeke, Joh. Moseley, or els the ffysshers them-selff [or 6s. 8d. fine each time, half (the on half) to the common box and half to the sheriffs.] *(only to be cut by these persons.)*

[Ordained] that no man nor woman by eny ffresh-water-fysh in the market to sell ayen, but only the bryngers therof to sell it them-self, apon peyn of euery defaute xij d., and at the secunde defawte to pay the peyn and also goo to prison tyll he haue made fyn. Also that no ffysh-monger [buy] no more butter but such as shall serue themself, apon the peyn þat is lymyted in a lete afore this therof made.¹ *(Freshwater fish not to be bought to sell again.)* *("Fishmongers not to buy butter to sell.")*

THE RECORDER.

Mem. that in the ffest of the translacion of seynt Swythyn [4 Hen. VIII] Maister Antony ffitzherberde then Recorder of the Citee of Couentre cam unto Maister Ric. Hassall, [mayor] at seynt Mary hall and shewid to the seid Maister Meyre & his brethern that he had so grete besynesse by reason that he was seriaunt of the lawe that he cowde not nor myght not occupy the Rome of Recordership of the seid Citee as he was bounde to doo, and prayed them that they wold take a newe in his Rome, and shewed them on his consciens & honeste that he knew no man so mete for the rome as was on Will. Shelley,² a gentylman of good consciens and well lernyd in the lawe of the londe. Wheruppon the seid Maister Meyre & his brethern, heryng the good report of the seid Maister Will. Shelley and also hauyng diuerse lettres send to them, as well from the Kynges grace as from oder diuerse grete lordes, haue chosen the seid Will. Shelley to be theyre Recorder the same day afore rehersid. At which eleccion *(Jul. 15. Fitzherbert resigns the recordership, and recommends as his successor Will. Shelley, who is accordingly chosen.)*

---

¹ v. p. 632.
² This recordership not mentioned in *Dict. Nat. Biog.* Shelley (? 1480—? 1549) rose to be recorder of London and justice of the common pleas. The poet, Percy Bysshe Shelley, was descended from one of his brothers.

§ 98. *Joh. Hardwen, Mayor*, 1513.

these persons vnder-writen were at with all there full consent & agrement :—

Ric. Hassall, m., Joh. Saunders, Rob. a Grene, Tho. Churchman, Joh. Padlonde, Joh. Haddon, Joh. Duddesbury, Ric. Merler, Joh. Strong, Tho. Grove, [1]Hugh Dawes, Tho. Turner,[1] Joh. Clerk, Joh. Hardwen, Rog. Chambur, Joh. Whithede, Joh. Humfrey, Nic. Burwey, Nic. Heynes, Hen. Rogers, Humf. Grene, Hen. Perkyns, Tho. fforth, Will. Perkyns, Tho. Astlyn, Joh. Boteler, Joh. Porter, Ric. Townesende, Jul. Nethirmyll, Tho. Dodde, Tho. Smyth, Will. Banwell, Joh. Bonde, Will. Wykam, Tho. White, Tho. Hyll, Will. Dawson, Will. Kemsey.

MICHAELMAS LEET.

"Ciuitas Couentrie." Oct. 4.

[2] ¶ [V. f. p. held on Monday after Michaelmas, 4 Hen. VIII.]

Jury.

Joh. Saunders, Rob. a Grene, Tho. Churchman, Joh. Padlonde, Joh. Hadden, Joh. Duddesbury, Ric. Smyth, Ric. Merler, Joh. Strong, Tho. Grove, Joh. Clerk, Joh. Hardwen, Rog. Chambur, Joh. Whitehede, Joh. Humfrey, Nic. Burwey, Nic. Heynes, Will. Perkyns, Tho. Waren,[3] Hum. Grene,[4] Tho. Rowley, Will. Wykam, Ric. Townesende, Rog. Wales.

Sheriffs.

[Joh. Bonde, Draper, Tho. Smyth.]

Orders of leet. "Search of wooll."

[Ordained] that all maner of persons fromhensforth that bryng eny woll into the Citee to sell that it be sufficiently wounden, clene and merchanable for the Clothyer without eny ffylth or eny other defaute or disceite, apon the peyn of euery ston so founde fawty the owner to pay therfore ij d. to the Comen box; the faute to be tryed by the sercher, which is amytted [5] perfore; which at the tyme is Tho. Bakon; & he to haue for his labour by discrecion of Maister Meyre & his brethern.

JOH. HARDWEN, MAYOR, 1513.

¶ [Election of officers.]

"Ciuitas Couentrie." Jan. 25. Electors.

Rob. a Grene, Joh. Padlonde, Joh. Haddon, Will. Pysford, Joh. Duddesbury, Ric. Smyth, Joh. Saunders,

---

[1–1] Bracketed as vicecomites = sheriffs.   [2] leaf 312, back.
[3] "Ric. Townesende" deleted.   [4] "Tho. Waren" deleted.
[5] = admitted, placed in the position of.

§ 98. *Joh. Hardwen, Mayor. Leet*, 1513.

Joh. Strong, Joh. Humfrey, Joh. Whitehede, Nic. Burwey, Tho. fforth, Nic. Heynes, Hen. Rogers, Hen. Perkyns, Hugo Dawes, Tho. Turner, Will. Perkyns, Ric. Townesende, Rog. Wales, Jul. Nethyrmyll, Tho. Dodde, Will. Wykam, Tho. Rowley.

[m. Joh. Hardwen; rec. Will. Shelley; cor. Joh. Boteler; steward, Joh. Porter; ch. Tho. Banwell, Joh. Wylkes; w. Joh. Jette, Hug. White; mace, Hen. Walker; crier, Ric. ffereby. — Officers.

MICHAELMAS LEET.

[1] [V. f. p. held before Joh. Hardwen, m., Joh. Bonde, Tho. Smyth, b., on Tuesday after S. Dionysius' day, 5 Hen. VIII.] — "Ciuitas Couentrie." Oct. 11.

Rob. a Grene, Joh. Padlonde, Joh. Haddon, Will. Pysford, Joh. Duddesbury, Ric. Smyth, Ric. Merler, Joh. Saunder (*sic*), Joh. Strong, Joh. Clerk, Rog. Chamber, Tho. Grove, Joh. Whitehede, Nic. Burwey, Humf. Grene, Nic. Heynes, Hug. Dawes, Tho. Turner, Tho. Banwell, Hen. Perkyns, Joh. Wylkes, Joh. Jette, Hug. White, Tho. White.

[Tho. Rowley, Will. Wykam.] — Sheriffs.

[Enacted and ordained] that fromhensforth no bocher within the Citee sell any shippis hedes with thappurtenaunce to no maner of persone above a halpeny, apon peyn of euery sheppis hede sold a-boue a ob. to forfeit iiij d. — Sheeps' heads ½d. each.

[Enacted] that euery comen bruer within the Citee that hath vsid to bru when malt is of lowe pryse that they from-hensforth bru styll contynually when malt is of a grete pryce, vnder the peyn of euery weke that they so sese to lese euery weke vj s. viij d.; and that they sell no malt owte of the Towne when malt ryseth a-bove v s. the quarter, apon the same peyn; also that no maltmaker, that maketh malt to sell, if it fortune malt to ryse a-bove v s. that they sell no malt out of the Citee tyll it be knowen that the Citee be sufficiently seruyd, apon peyn of xx s. at euery defaute so provyd payed to the comen boxe etc. — Brewers to continue to brew when malt is dear; but none to be sold outside the city unless the city have enough when the price is more than 5s. a quarter.

Mem. apon a byll of compleynt put in at this day by

[1] leaf 313, back.

§ 99. *Tho. Grove, Mayor,* 1514.

"No Inholder to be a baker;

no baker to be an Inholder."

the Inholders ayenst bakers kepyng ynnes, it was agreed that the bakers kepe no hostryes accordyng to the olde rule of the Citee, nor no Inholder bake horsbrede within them, apon the peyn þeruppon lymyted etc.

THO. GROVE, MAYOR, 1514.

"Ciuitas Couentr*ie*."
Jan. 25.
Electors.

¶ [Election of officers.]

Joh. Saunders, Joh. Padlonde, Joh. Haddon, Will. Pysford, Joh. Duddesbury, Ric. Smyth, Ric. Merler, Joh. Strong, Ric. Hassall, Hen. Rogers, Joh. Whitehede, Nic. Heynes, Humf. Grene, Hen. P*er*kyns, Tho. fforth, Will. P*er*kyns, Tho. Waren, Hug. Dawes, Tho. Turn*er*, Joh. Bonde, Tho. Smyth, Tho. Banwell, Joh. Wylk*es*, Will. Banwell.

Officers.

[m. Tho. Grove; rec. Will. Shelley; cor. Joh. Boteler; steward, Joh. Porter; ch. Joh. Baker, Sherman, Joh. Smyth, Mason; w. Will. Towres, Drap*er*, Will. Shukborough, drap*er*; mace, Hen. Walker; crier, Ric. ffereby.]

EASTER AND MICHAELMAS LEETS.

"Ciuitas Couentr*ie*."
Apr. 27.

[1] ¶ [V. f. p. before Tho. Grove, m., Tho. Rowley, Will. Wykham, b., on Thursday after S. George's day, 6 Hen. VIII.]

Joh. Saunders, Rob. a Grene, Joh. Padlonde, Joh. Haddon, Will. Pysford, Joh. Duddesbury, Ric. Smyth, Ric. Merler, Joh. Strong, Ric. Hassall, Joh. Hardwen, Joh. Clerk, Rog. Chambur, Joh. Humfrey, Joh. Whitehede, Nic. Burwey, Humf. Grene, Tho. fforth, Will. P*er*kyns, Tho. Waren, Tho. Astlyn, Joh. Smyth, Joh. Baker, Joh. Hopkyns, dyer.

Orders of Leet. "Wev*er*s."

[Enacted] that where the ffeliship of the craft of weu*er*s haue put in at this lete a byll of compleynt a-yenst on Ric. Pastey, weu*er*, and Rob. Miles, weu*er*, which haue be founde fauty by þ*er* occupac*i*on,[2] that they fromhensforth shall worch no more in the Cite except they ffynde surety to the mast*er* of the occupac*i*on to be true in ther werkyng; and if they be founde fauty theire surete to

---

[1] leaf 314.
[2] This scribe's characteristic "o" is so like an "a" that I was almost tempted to write "accupacion."

§ 99. *Tho. Grove, Mayor. Weavers*, 1514.

make good for them & to satisfy the party greuyd his damages, apon peyn of euery defaute xx s., wherof vj s. viij d. to the Shirrefs, vj s. viij d. to þe comen boxe, vj s. viij d. to þe craft of weuers.

[Ordained] þat þer shal-be made ij serchers of the occupacion of weuers, & they to be sworen afore Maister Meyre & his brethern that they shall make true serch of all onlawfull slayes,[1] & þat þer be noen occupied but of a true pych,[2] þat [is] xiij quarters & a half or xiij at þe lest of brede, apon peyn of euery of them þat be founde fauty at eny tyme hereafter, when due serch is made, to pay for euery defaute xx s. in like maner afore-rehersid. *"Serchers for weauers."*

[Agreed] þat no weuer delyuer eny cloth þat he hath wouen to the owner nor to þe fuller tyll the serchers haue seen it whedir it be laufully wrough[t] or no, apon peyn of euery defaute xl d.; and if þer be eny varyance bytwene the weuer & þe owner for the werkemanship þerof, then the seid Serchers to be Juge by-twene them for þe werkmanship, and if þe owner woll not so doo then the weuer to compleyn to Maister Meyre & his brethern for his remedy: And the Serchers to haue of euery cloth þat is founde fauty ij d. for þer laboure. Also all such cloth [3]of þe Cite[3] that is put into the con[t]rey to weve þat it be brought vnto the forseid serchers or it be put to þe walkers that it may be seen whedir it be well wouen or not; and if þer be founde faute in þe weuer þat it kepe not they sley[4] & pych[4] as is above writen, then þe peyn to be leveyed apon the seid fauty cloth. Also þat the weuers sorte there yaron from coklyng,[5] bondyng[6] or pynrouyng,[7] apon the payn aforeseid. Mem. that ther is amytted to be serchers for this yere foloyng Joh. Locok & Will. Osgathorp. *Weavers to deliver no cloth to the owner until viewed by the searchers, who have for reward 2d. for each defective piece of cloth. Yarn to be even and of the same thickness.*

[Ordained] for the walkers that þer shal-be ij serchers *"Serchers for walkers."*

---

[1] A weaver's reed. "Its purpose is to keep the threads (ends) straight and in position, to act as guide for the shuttle, and to push the woven weft close against its predecessor." *E. D. D.* s. v. Slay.

[2] Pitch = ? breadth. It is now usual to speak of the depth of the weaver's reed. Quarter = 9 inches.

[3]—[3] Deleted.   [4] See above.   [5] = puckering.

[6] Is this connected with band = a fault in cloth caused by the shrinking of the defective weft, whereby tight strips appear? *N. E. D.* s. v. Band.

[7] Pinrow = a streak in cloth caused by mixed shades of weft. (*E. D. D.*)

§ 99. Tho. Grove, Mayor. Cloth, 1514.

chosen & sworen afore Maister Meyre & his brethern to make due serch þat non of the occupacion occupy Cardes, rought[1] tesels nor no nodur meane wherby eny cloth is hurted, nor wrong-half[2] no cloth but only vse dobyns[3] or smoth tesyls, apon peyn of euery defaute xxs. to be payed as a-fore is rehersid to þe Shirrefs, the comen box & the walkers.

Cloth to be properly dressed.

[Ordained] that the serchers make due serch apon þer othes that the cloth be truly burlyd & able cloth made or els to certifie the faute to Maister Meyre & his brethern; and that euery ffuller set his marke apon the cloth that he fullith, apon peyn of xl d.; and that no fuller delyuer his cloth by hym fullyd tyll the serchers haue sene it whedir it be truly wrought or no, apon the same peyn; and the serchers to haue for ther laboure for euery fauty cloth ij d., and if the owner woll not gif the ffuller for his labour as it is worth, then the party greuyd to compleyn to Maister Meyre & his brethern if þe serchers cannot agre them. Also þer be amytted serchers for the walkers Joh. Bradwell & Rauf Worsley.

Fullers.

[Agreed] that no walker take out no cloth aftir it is put into the stok[4] tyll it be fully stokkyd, [or 20s. fine]; and also that they put no cappis in the myll among the cloth [or 6s. 8d. fine]; and also that the Cappers myll no cappes on the Saterday after evunsong nor the Sonday tyll evunsong be don [or 6s. 8d. fine to the common box.]

Cappers not to work from Saturday evening till Sunday evening.

Spinners to receive 2½ lb. to a weight.

[Agreed] that euery clothmaker that putteth eny Woll to spynne that he put no more to the weight but ij lib. & dim.; and that they gif for the spynning of euery weight in redy money for the best v d. and the secunde iiij d.

"Ciuitas Couentrie." Oct. 5.

[5][V. f. p. held on Thursday after Michaelmas, 6 Hen. VIII.]

Joh. Saunders, Rob. a Grene, Joh. Haddon, Joh. Pad-

---

[1] = ? rough.
[2] Evidently some operation which involved turning cloth on the wrong side.
[3] This word, not to be found in dictionaries, is evidently connected with *dub* = to strike cloth with teazles in order to raise the nap (Glouc.), v. *E. D. D.* (Dr. Bradley).
[4] An instrument used in milling cloth. "When the cloth comes in the loom the threads may be counted; after it has been in the stocks it is much more difficult." v. *E. D. D.* s. v. Stock.
[5] leaf 314, back.

§ 100. Joh. Clerk, Mayor, 1515.

londe, Will. Pysforde, Joh. Duddesbury, Ric. Merler, Joh. Strong, Joh. Hardwen, Hen. Rogers, Joh. Clerk, Joh. Humfrey, Nic. Burwey, Nic. Heynes, Tho. fforth, Will. Perkyns, Tho. Waren, Tho. Astlyn, Hug. Dawes, Tho. Smyth, Joh. Baker, Joh. Smyth, Jul. Nethyrmyll, Joh. Hopkyns.

[Tho. Whyte, Ric. Burwey.] Sheriffs.

[Enacted] that such persons as byn assigned to gedir the rent of the ffyldes that be takyn in of the Comens that they shall come in with theire accompt by-twene this and the ffest of All halows day next comyng for the yeres that be past. The common fields.

[Ordained] that fromhensforth no maner of person that hath be prentyse at Tanners craft within þe Citee pay to the craft at his settyng up but vj s. viij d. ; and euery straunger of the same Craft to pay to the Craft no more but xx s., & it to be payed within thre yeres. Tanners' apprentices to pay but 6s. 8d. for freedom; strangers 20s.

Also that euery craft bryng in there boke afore Maister Meyre & his brethern, that all such fautes as be in them may be correctid & amendid by thaduise of Maister Meyre & his brethern ; and if there ffynes be to moch to moderate them after good consciens at such tyme as Maister Meyre commaundeth them etc. The crafts' fines to be moderated by the mayor and council.

JOH. CLERK, MAYOR, 1515.

¶ [Election of officers.] "Ciuitas Couentrie." Jan. 25.

Joh. Hardwen, Rob. a Grene, Joh. Padlonde, Joh. Haddon, Will. Pysforde, Joh. Duddesbury, Ric. Merler, Joh. Saunders, Joh. Strong, Ric. Hassall, Nic. Burwey, Nic. Heynes, Hum. Grene, Tho. fforth, Will. Perkyns, Tho. Waren, Tho. Astlyn, Hug. Dawes, Tho. Turner, Joh. Bonde, Tho. Smyth, Will. Wykam, Joh. Baker, Joh. Smyth.

[m. Joh. Clerk ; rec. Will. Shelley ; cor. Joh. Boteler ; steward, Joh. Porter ; ch. Tho. Lee, Ric. Westley ; w. Will. Cook, Ric. Povey ; mace, Hen. Walker ; crier, Ric. ffereby. Officers.

THE RECORDER.

[1] Mem. that the Munday next afore the ffest of seynt Valantyne the martyr [6 Hen. VIII] ther was assemble Feb. 12.

---

[1] leaf 316.

§ 100. *Joh. Clerk*, *Mayor*. *Recorder*, 1515.

at senynt (*sic*) Mary Hall afore M*aiste*r Joh. Clerk then Meyre and his brethern for the elecc*io*n and Chewsyng of a new Recorder of the Citee of Couentre in-so-m[o]ch as M*aiste*r Will. Shelley, then Recorder, hadde giffen them warnyng that he cowde not gif his attendance apon my seid maisters in that office as he ought to do. Wheruppon my seyde maisters callyng to them the worshipfull of the Cite, as well they that hadde byn Meyres and Shirrefs as other onest p*e*rsons, the day, yere & place afore rehersid, and went to a newe elecc*io*n; at whiche elecc*io*n these p*e*rsons whose namys ar underwriten were thoo that mad it.

*"Elecc*io*n of a Recorder."*

M*aiste*r Joh. Hardwen, M*aiste*r Joh. Padlonde, M*aiste*r Joh. Haddon, M*aiste*r Will. Pysford, M*aiste*r Joh. Duddesbury, M*aiste*r Ric. Merler, M*aiste*r Joh. Saunders, M*aiste*r Joh. Strong, M*aiste*r Ric. Hassall, M*aiste*r Tho. Grove, M*aiste*r Nic. Burwey, M*aiste*r Joh. Humfrey, M*aiste*r Tho. fforth, M*aiste*r Will. Perkyns, M*aiste*r Tho. Waren, M*aiste*r Tho. Astlyn, M*aiste*r Hug. Dawes, M*aiste*r Tho. Turner, M*aiste*r Tho. Smyth, M*aiste*r Will. Wykan, Joh. Porter, Tho. Lee, Ric. Westley, Julyns Nethermyll.

Swyllyngton elected.

Which chosen at that day Rauff Swyllyngton[1] Recorder of the Citee of Couentre for that yere foloyng; and how the seid Recorder and the M*aiste*r of the Trinite Gilde for the tyme beyng shall goo to-gedyr in assembles & metynge*s* and the Meyre to goo alone by hymself; also he is chosen on this condic*io*n to dwelle amonge*s* vs for the most p*a*rt of the yere, & in especiall the wynt*e*r season, and not to entre into the rome tyll after Est*u*r sessions be endid next comyng etc.

"The Recorder to be resident."

EASTER AND MICHAELMAS LEETS.

"Ciuitas Couentr*ie*." Apr. 17.

[2] ¶ [V. f. p. held before Joh. Clerk, m., Tho. White, Ric. Burwey, b., on Tuesday after the close of Easter, 6 Hen. VIII.]

Joh. Hardwen, Rob. Grene, Joh. Padlonde, Joh. Haddon, Will. Pysford, Joh. Duddesbury, Ric. Merler

---

[1] The effigies of Swyllington and his wife are in S. Michael's.
[2] leaf 315.

§ 100. *Joh. Clerk, Mayor. Leet,* 1515.   643

Joh. Saunders, Joh. Strong, Ric. Hassall, Tho. Grove, Nic. Burwey, Joh. Humfrey, Nic. Heynes, Hum. Grene, Tho. fforth, Tho. Waren, Tho. Astlyn, Hug. Dawes, Tho. Smyth, Will. Wykam, Tho. Lee, Ric. Westley, Tho. Banwell.

[Enacted] that ffromhensforth there shal-be a ffeliship of Taloughchaundelers among themself, and to be a ffeliship of them-self, and to haue a maister among them as oder craftes haue; and þat no ffyshmonger, sherman, nor no oder craft within the Cite occupy the seid craft, but only for his owne houshold, [or 20s. fine each time to the common box.] And that the seid Chaundelers serue the Cite sufficiently wynter & somer for a peny a pounde; and if eny defaute be prouyd ayenst any of them afore Maister Meyre for the tyme beyng to forfeite x s. to the comen boxe. *Order of leet.* "Chaundlers" to form a company. *Candles 1d. per lb.*

Also for-asmoch as afore this tyme at a lete holden at Couentre the Munday next after the Inuencion of the Holy Crosse [21 Ed. IV.] afore Ric. Colyns, then Miere of this Cite [1] etc., ther was diuerse & mony good ordynaunces made for reformacion of officers of the Cite as well for seriauntes as oder officers as the Jayler for the tyme beyng and what they shuld take for doyng ther offices, as more pleyntly (*sic*) apperith by the same lete. Howbeit as touchyng the Jaylers office it is not declarid certayn in euery thyng, what he shuld take for his ffee, wherfore mony of the kynges leage peple fynde them-self greuyd theryn. Wherfore it is enactid at this present letee (*sic*) that all such actes þat were made at the seid lete or eny lete heretofore for þe comen wele of this Citee þat they be stedfastly holden fromhensforth & kept and the breker of them to be punysshed accordyng to þer [2] demerites. And þat no Jayler fromhensforth take for his ffee of euery prisoner arestid by processe of the kynges Court here or from a-bove [3] but v d., that is to sey iiij d. for hym-self & a peny his vnder-keper. And if the mater wherfore eny prisoner is arestid be vndur the some of xl d. then the Jayler nor his seriaunt to take no thyng for þer *May 7, 1481.* "Jaylers' fee *is v d. upon Arest,*

---

[1] The leet records for that year are not given.
[2] "dere" deleted.   [3] A higher court.

§ 100. Joh. Clerk, Mayor. Jailer, 1515.

for fellony or misdemenor v d., and 2d. for his Irons."

fee. And if it fortune eny prisoner hereaftur to be commytted to the Jailer for treson, murdre, or felony then the Jayler to take of euery such prisoner when he is delyuered his ffee above-rehersid, and ouer & aboue þat ij d. for his Irons & no more ; & if he take more &[1] þat duly prosid[2]

"The gaoler."

to lose at the first faute xl d., and at the secunde to lese his office without eny favour. Also he shall take no double ffee of no prisoner except it be for grete & vrgent causes opynly knowen. Also þer hath be compleyntes made apon the Jayler that he hath takyn awey from the prisoners such money as hath byn gyffen to them in almys & conuertid it to his owne use. Wherfore it is enactid (etc.) that if it can be proved that if he or eny other Jayler after hym at eny tyme herafter doo soo that incontynent apon the prove therof the seid Jayler to forfeit it (sic) office without eny redempcion.

"Jaylers"

Also it hath be compleyned apon þe jailer þat where þe seriauntes haue arestid diuerse & mony, some for det & som for transgressions & delyuered them to þe Jayler safly to kepe till the next court day ; at which day þe prisoner is, & hath be, let goo ; and so the party not onswerid as they shuld be by the lawe to þe grete hurt & hyndraunce of þe pleyntyfs ; wherfore it is enactid at this lete þat if the seid Jayler, or eny oþer heraftur, haue not his prisoner redy at þe day of retorn of þe warent to answere the party

forfeit for estrayes."

pleyntyf that the seid Jayler and euery Jayler heraftur shall forfete for euery prisoner so departid xl d. for a

"For the gaoler."

mercyment, and þe secunde defaute vj s. viij d., and so euery court day doublid tyll he bryng hym in.

"The gaoler."[3] "Poor prisoners to be set to worke by the Jayler."

Also it is enactyd at this lete if it fortune eny Craftesman heraftur to be commytted to warde & in þe kepyng of the jayler for felony, transgression, det or suerty of the p[e]ace or oþer-wise, and may haue werke wherby he myght gete his lyuyng, that þe Jayler shall suffre hym or them to worch in þe day-tyme & such money as they gete to haue it them-self and the jayler for his suffraunce to haue of euery xij d. a peny & no more, apon peyn of euery defaute prouyd to forfet xij d.[4]

[1] and = than. [2] = proceed. [3] In another hand and ink.
[4] "Plus in dorso" (more at the back) follows.

§ 100. Joh. Clerk, Mayor. Leet, 1515.

[1] [Enacted] that no Jayler hereaftur shall take no ffee of no man, onlees he be commyttid to his warde, [or 40 d. fine at every default.] *"For the gaoler."*

[Ordained] that no capper in the Citee ffromhensforth flok[2] eny cappe and soo vtter it, apon the peyn to forfeit þer cappes so flockyd, and the seid cappes brent, and ouer that for euery cappe so founde fauty & brent to forfeit iiij d., that is to sey, j d. to the Shirrifs, a peny to the Sercher, and ij d. to the Comen boxe. And all such cappes that be nowe fflockid to sell noen of them but mende theym ageyn within vj dayes after this lete, vnder the peyn afore rehersyd; and that ther be chosen & sworen ij serchers therfore to serch the defautes & truly to present them etc. *Cappers forbidden to flock caps.*

[V. f. p. held on Tuesday after Michaelmas, 7 Hen. VIII.] *"Ciuitas Couentrie." Oct. 2.*

Joh. Hardwen, Rob. a Grene, Joh. Haddon, Will. Pysford, Joh. Duddesbury, Ric. Merler, Joh. Saunders, Joh. Strong, Ric. Hassall, Tho. Grove, Nic. Burwey, Joh. Humfrey, Nic. Heynes, Hum. Grene, Hen. Perkyns, Tho fforth, Tho. Waren, Hug. Dawes, Tho. Turner, Joh. Bonde, Tho. Smyth, Will. Wykam, Tho. Lee, Ric. Westley.

[Tho. Banwell, Hen. Wall.] *Sheriffs.*

[Enacted] that euery craft and occupacion of this Citee that is a ffeliship of them-self that they bryng in theire bokes of theire occupacion at such tyme as Maister Meyre commaundethe them, and such caues & rules as be onresonable to be reformyd by Maister Meire & his brethern, and euery occupacion to abide the same ordre, apon peyn to forfeit euery craft a C s. for brekyng of the same etc. And if eny craft or occupacion within the Cite make eny ordynaunce, Caue, or bylawe amonges them-self in þer occupacion or craft fromhensforth except Maister [Meyre] of the Cite for the tyme beyng & his brethern be made priuey therto and registrid in the Meyres boke; and they to see that the said ordynaunce, caue or bylawe stonde *"Masters off Companies to show their orders to the mayor vpon demand,* *& orders voyd iff not Asented vnto by [the] mayor & his brethern."*

---
[1] leaf 315, back.
[2] = to thicken prepared cloth by shaking powdered wool or cloth shearings over the same. *N. E. D.* s.v. Flock sb. and vb.

§ 100. *Joh. Clerk, Mayor. Leet*, 1515.

wit*h* the co*m*en weel of the Citee; and they so admyt hit or els to be voide, vnder the payn of eue*r*y such caue or bylawe otherwise occupied to forfeit for eue*r*y moneth so occupyyng xx s., the on half to the Co*m*en box and the other half at the plesure of M*aister* Meyre & his brethern. And all such imposic*i*ons & peynes as han be made afore-tyme amonge*s* eny craft cont*r*arie to good consciens and to the wele of the Citee be from hensforth voide & of noon effect.[1]

The chandlers

Also that no Taloughchaundeler wit*h*in the Citee or þe suburbys of the same sell eny candyll fromhensforth a-bove a peny a pounde, apon peyn of eue*r*y pounde solde a-bove that prise to forfeit xij d.; and that they sell no candyll in groce out of the Citee at a tyme above a dose*n* pounde, [or 20s. fine each time.] And that they see the Citee well & sufficiently s*e*ruyd, vnder the peyn of the hool body of the craft of a C s., the on half to the Co*m*en boxe, and the other half at the pleasure of M*aister* Meire and his brethern.

to serve the city sufficiently or pay 100*s*. fi*n*e.

"No men shall forstall eny fishe."

[Ordained] at this letee (*sic*) that no inhabitaunt wit*h*in the Citee lye by the wey by-twene this and the se-syde and by se-fysh comyng to the Citee, nor by it when it is comen into the Citee, but suffer the brynger therof & theire deputes to sell it. And the seid fysshers panyers to be pichid first in the m*ar*ket accordyng to the olde auncyent custome & not to be openyd ne set a-sale tyll M*aister* Meyre haue seen it as well oysters, musculs, as oder see ffysh, except they come oue*r* evun, apon the peyn of eue*r*y defaute of them that receyveth such ffysh into theire houses to forfeit for eue*r*y seme[2] vj s. viij d., and for eue*r*y seme that eny inhabitaunt lyeth by the wey & byeth it, or bieth it wit*h*in the Citee, to forfeit for eue*r*y seme x s., xl d. to the Shirrefs & vj s. viij d. to the Co*m*en boxe; and that no inhabitaunt wit*h*in the Citee make no contract nor bargeyn to by eny ffresh samon vnto tyme it be brought into the m*ar*ket nor then nodyr tyll M*aister* Meyre have seen it, and set the p*r*ise therof, apon peyn of imp*r*isonment & to make a fyne at þe Meyres co*m*maundment, and þ*a*t no saltffyshmen nor þ*er* wyfe*s*

"ffish to be viewed by the mayor before it be sold."

[1] See Introduction.   [2] "defaulte" deleted. Seme = load.

§ 101. *Joh. Humfrey, Mayor.* 1516.

medle with no sefysh, heryng, oysters nor musculs, apon the peyn afore-rehersed.

JOH. HUMFREY, MAYOR, 1516.

¹ ¶ [Election of officers.]

Tho. Grove, Joh. Haddon, Will. Pysford, Joh. Duddesbury, Ric. Smyth, Ric. Merler, Joh. Saunders, Joh. Strong, Ric. Hassall, Joh. Hardwen, Tho. Waren, Nic. Heynes, Humf. Grene, Hen. Perkyns, Tho. fforde, Hug. Dawes, Tho. Turner, Joh. Bonde, Tho. Smyth, Will. Wykam, Tho. Warde, Will. Banwell, Will. Brygges, Tho. Hyll.

[m. Joh. Humfrey; cor. Joh. Boteler; steward, Joh. Porter; ch. Joh. Hyll, Draper, Ric. Herres, grasyer; w. Tho. Toty, Tho. Spenser; mace, Hen. Walker; crier, Ric. ffereby.

"Ciuitas Couentrie." Jan. 25. Jury.

Officers.

EASTER AND MICHAELMAS LEETS.

² ¶ [V. f. p. held before Joh. Humfrey, m., Tho. Banwell, Hen. Wall, b., on Tuesday after S. Ambrose' day, 7 Hen. VIII.]

"Ciuitas Couentrie." Apr. 8.

Tho. Grove, Joh. Haddon, Will. Bysford [Pysford], Joh. Duddesbury, Ric. Smyth, Joh. Saunders, Ric. Hassall, Joh. Hardwen, Tho. Waren, Nic. Burwey, Nic. Heynes, Hum. Grene, Hen. Perkyns, Tho. Astlyn, Hug. Dawes, Tho. Turner, Joh. Bonde, Tho. Smyth, Will. Wykam, Joh. Hyll, draper, Ric. Harres, Joh. Eburne, Tho. Kelyngworth, Will. Towres.

Jury.

³ [Ordained] that all the inhabitauntes of this Citee be obedyent to the Meyre for the tyme beyng, and also if eny decree or good ordynaunce or prouysicion⁵ be made & assentyd by the Meyre & counsell of the Citee, or by the moost parte of them, in theire counsell-howse or chambre for the pollitique contynuaunce of good ordynaunces & rulys wythyn the Citee, that euery inhabitaunt, of what condicion or degree so-euer he be of, duly obey, oberue & kepe the same decree, ordynaunce, & prouysion, appon the

Orders of leet.
⁴ "Euery inhabitaunt shall obey the ordinauncez of the leetes, vpon paine as ffolloweth." ⁴

---

¹ leaf 316.
² leaf 316, back. Possibly a different scribe, though of similar type.
³ The offender is John Strong, see p. 649.
⁴—⁴ Different hands.   ⁵ *sic.* Read "provision."

§ 101. *Joh. Humfrey, Mayor. Leet*, 1516.

A late mayor's punishment;

peyn hereafter ensuyng :—that is to sey, if he haue be Meyre that from thensforth he be exempt & vtterly abiect from the Counsell of the Citee & the Company of theym in all theire comen processions, ffestes, and all other assembles & from weryng of his cloke or skerlet in theire companyes and further to make ffyne & soeffre enprisonment by discrecion of the Meire & the counsell or the more part of theym. And if he hath byn Shirreff then to be obiect (*sic*) & exempt from werryng skarrelet amonges his company in all Comen assembles, ffestes & processions, and ferther to be punysshed by ffyne & imprisonment as a-bove is rehersid. And if he bere neuer the office of Shirref then he to lese the ffredom & liberte of this Citee, and ouer that to be punyshed by ffyne & inprisonment as above is rehersid. Also it is ordeigened (etc.) that if ther be eny maner of persone or persons of the Citee that woll fauoure or comfort eny such mysdoers in theire obstinacie or frowarde mynde that they shal-be punyshed in maner as the odur[1] bee.

a late sheriff's;

the punishment of those of lower degree.

"Nota." Disobedience to this, £10 fine.

[Enacted] that if eny man woll presume to were his lyuere or doo contrarie to this ordynaunce that he shall leese & forfett at euery defawte xli. the on half to the crosse, the oder to the Comen boxe.

The river.

1469.

[Enacted] that all good actes & ordynaunces afore this tyme made for the comen wele of the Citee be fromhensforth duly & truly put in execucion, and that the act that was made the ix[th] yere of kyng E. the iiij[th] for the comen ryuer of Shirburn be put in execucion etc.[2]

No wool to be brought into the city on a Friday.

[Enacted] that no maner of persone bryng in to the Citee apon the ffryday eny wooll, woode or hurdels, apon the peyn of euery lode so brought to forfet xijd., accordyng to an act peruppon made the ix yere of E. iiij[ti] at Ester court,[3] and this to be cryed thre ffrydayes and then to stonde in effect.

Tallow-chandlers not to sell tallow by the dozen.

[Enacted] that no bocher of the Citee sell eny taloo out of the Citee to eny man of the countray [or 40d. each time to the common box]; nor no Talough chaundler sell no candyll out of the Towne by the dosen, but only by the pounde, [or 20s. each time to the common box.]

[1] MS. adur.   [2] *v.* p. 347.   [3] See p. 339.

§ 101. *Joh. Humfrey, Mayor. Contumacy,* 1516.

Also the act for bying of hides on the Satirday and no odur[1] day is affermyd that was made the xth yere of king Henry the vij[th].[1]

Hides.

[Enacted] that such decree as M*aister* Meire & his brethern made & toke w*ith* M*aister* Strong for such money as he was awarded to pay to the Citee, that is to sey x li. xij s. vjd., that he to bryng it to M*aister* Meyre or a sufficient gage therfore by the ffest of seynt George next comyng or els to be in the daunger of the above writon act & decre, & to ran in the penalte therof; and further to be punysshed by the [2] discrec*io*n of M*aister* Meyre & his brethern or the more p*ar*t of them; and if he bryng in a Gage and no money then w*ith*yn a moneth next after that the gage to be sold by the aduyse of M*aister* Meire & his brethern, and the ou*er*-pluys therof to be delyue*r*ed to the seid Joh. Strong.

Master Strong's contumacy and fine.

Apr. 23.

Me*n*. that this act made for M*aister* Strong is performed on his part and he amytted of the Counsell as he was a-fore; and thus agrement was fully concludid & made afore M*aister* Waren, Mayre, & his brethern, the Tuysday next after the ffest of seynt Hillare [11 Hen. VIII.] as apper*i*the more pleynly in the Counsell boke, to the wych boke the seid M*aister* Strong hath set to his honde.

Master Strong re-admitted.

Jan. 17, 1520.

[3] [V. f. p. held on Thursday after Michaelmas, 8 Hen. VIII.]

"Ciuitas Couentr*ie*." Oct. 2.

Tho. Grove, Rob. Grene, Joh. Haddon, Will. Pysford, Joh. Duddesbury, Ric. Smyth, Ric. Merler, Joh. Strong, Ric. Hassall, Joh. Hardwen, Joh. Clerk, Tho. Waren, Hen. Rogers, Hen. P*er*kyns, Tho. Astlyn, Hug. Dawes, Joh. Bonde, Tho. Smyth, Will. Wykam, Tho. Whyte, Ric. Burwey, Joh. Hyll, drape*r*, Tho. Dode, Will. Towres.]

Jury.

[Jul. Nethyrmyll, Drape*r*, Tho. Hyll, Drape*r*.]

Sheriffs.

[Enacted] that eu*er*y alderman in his warde shall present iiij or vj p*er*sons of the most honest p*er*sons of p*er* warde that hath boren no office to be constabuls for the yere and bryng in ther byll of there namys to M*aister* Meyre for the tyme beyng & to his brethern w*ith*in viij dayes next after the lete holden after Michelmasse yerely,

"For elecc*io*n of constables."

---

[1] See pp. 557–8, 665–6. [2] leaf 317.
[3] leaf 317, back.

§ 102. Hen. Rogers, Mayor. 1517.

and then M*aister* Meyre & his brethern to chewse out of eue*r*y warde as money of them as they thynk conuenyent for the warde to be constabuls þe*r*, and this to contynue for eue*r* etc.

Butchers and tallow;

[Ordained] that no bocher of the Citee sell eny talough wit*h*in the Citee by-twene this & the next lete a-bove ij s. ij d. þe stone and that they sell noon out of the Citee, apon the peyn of euery defaulte xx s., [half to the sheriffs and half to the common box]. And that no chaundeler sell candyll above peny ferthyng a pounde, and that it be good stuf, by-twene thus and the next lete; and that they sell noen out of the Citee by hool-sale to them that woll sell them ayen w*ith*out license of M*aister* Meyre for the tyme beyng, apon the peyn afore rehersid, wherof half to the co*m*en box & half to the Shirrefs; also that they sell to the pore peple halpenyworth and penworth after the pounde that they excede not in prise aboue peny q*uadrans* a lib.

chandlers and candles, 1¼d. per lb.

"*Swynstiez & hogges kepyng.*"

[Ordained] that the olde ordyna*u*nces for styes and kepyng of ho*gges* be renuyd & kept accordyng to the olde act, & lyke peyn as is afore made to be hadde and taken, and if the Shirrefs se not execuc*i*on hadde in eue*r*y defaute wit*h*in viij dayes next afte*r* the same faute to forfeit for eue*r*y defaute such summes of money as they shuld haue þerfor, and the co*m*en s*er*iau*n*t to leuy such ffyne as the Shirrefs shuld haue hadde if they hadde executid þe*r* office, and it to goo to the Co*m*en box etc.

The fines to be levied on neglectful sheriffs.

Attorney.

[Baldwin Porter "to occupy the hoole office of the attorneyship of the city" henceforth, and to have the whole fee.]

HEN. ROGERS, MAYOR, 1517.

"*Ciuitas Couentrie.*"
Jan. 25.

[¹ Election of officers.]

Joh. Clerk, Rob. a Grene, Joh. Haddon, Will. Pysford, Joh. Duddesbury, Ric. Smyth, Ric. Merler, Joh. Strong, Ric. Hassall, Joh. Hardwen, Tho. Grove, Tho. Smyth, Nic. Heynes, Hen. Pe*r*kyns, Tho. Astlyn, Hugo Dawes, Tho. Turno*u*r, Joh. Bonde, Tho. Rowley, Will. Wykam, Will. Banwell, Will. Dawson, Joh. Hyll, Ric. Harres.

¹ leaf 319.

§ 102. Hen. Rogers, Mayor. Leet, 1517.

[m. Hen. Rogers; rec. Rad. Swyllyngton; cor. Joh. Boteler; steward, Joh. Porter; ch. Joh. Locok, weu*er*, Step. Lynsey, Baker; w. Tho. Both, m*ercer*, Tho. Brewer, m*ercer*; mace, Hen. Walker; crier, Ric. ffereby.] Officers.

EASTER AND MICHAELMAS LEETS.

[1][V. f. p. held before Hen. Rogers, m., Jul. Nethyrmyll, Tho. Hyll, b., on Tuesday after S. Mark's day, 9 Hen. VIII.] "Ciuitas Couentr*ie*." Apr. 28.

Joh. Clerk, Rob. a Grene, Joh. Haddon, Will. Pysford, Joh. Duddesbury, Ric. Smyth, Ric. Merler, Joh. Strong, Ric. Hassall, Joh. Hardwen, Tho. Grove, Joh. Humfrey, Tho. Smyth, Nic. Burwey, Tho. Waren, Nic. Heynes, Hen. P*er*kyns, Tho. Astlyn, Hug. Dawes, Will. Wykam, Tho. Whyte, Ric. Burwey, Hen. Wall, Joh. Locok. Jury.

[Ordained] that no bocher, inha*b*itant within the Citee, sell no man*er* of taloo out of the Citee but only to the Chaundelers of the Citee, and the inha*b*itant*es* of the same [or 20s. fine, half to the sheriffs, half to the common box]. Also that no chaundeler inha*b*itant w*ith*in the Citee sell eny candyll out of the Citee by desons[2] or half desons to sech as shall sell them a-yeyn, apone the peyn afore-seyd. "Bochers" only to sell tallow to chaundlers.

[Ordained] that no ffyshmonger, baker, sherman nor noon oder p*er*son except he be a chaundeler make eny candyll to sale but only for his owne howse, [or 20s. fine, half to the sheriffs, half to the common box.]

[Ordained] that all such ffyshmongers as sellith salt ffysh shall take yn no panyers of see ffsyh into the howses [or 6s. 8d. fine] but suffre the[3] hit accordyng to the auncient custome to be set at the crosse, and that they by no ffresh codd*es* to salt to thentent to sell them ayeyn afore on of the Clok, so that the Citee may be ffirst s*er*ued, apon the same peyn. And that all such see-ffysh as cometh ou*er* evun that it be set in the m*ar*ket by vij of the clok, and that they voide *per* bord*es* & make sale *per*of by ij of the clok, apon the fforfeture of the same ffysh that "Ffisshe-mongers" to set out their boards by the Cross.

---

[1] leaf 319, back.
[2] Difficult to distinguish between this scribe's "e" and his "o"; "desons" might be "dosens."
[3] redundant.

§ 102. Hen. Rogers, Mayor. Leet, 1517.

is then left onsold. Also that no woman nor oder person cut eny see-ffysh þat cometh to the market but such as be assigned by maister Meyre & his brethern, apon peyn of euery defaute vj s. viij d.; and that no cutter of seeffysh by no panyer of sseffysh to his own vse to sell a-geyn, apon peyn of euery defaute vj s. viij d., half to the Shirefs & half to the comen boxe.[1]

"Vagabonds and beggars."

Also it is ordeyned at this lete that euery alderman of the Citee within his warde make due serch for vacaboundes & lusty beggers and cause them to voyde out of ther warde within a day & a nyght after proclamacion made, apon peyn of inprisonment accordyng to the statute theruppon made.

"Ciuitas Couentrie." Oct. 13.

[[2] V. f. p. held on the Translation of S. Edward, 9 Hen. VIII.]

Jury of 25.

Joh. Clerk, Rob. a Grene, Joh. Haddon, Will Pysford, Joh. Duddesbury, Ric. Smyth, Ric. Merler, Joh. Strong, Ric. Hassall, Joh. Hardwen, Tho. Grove, Joh. Humfrey, Tho. Smyth, Nic. Burwey, Tho. Waren, Hen. Perkyns, Tho. Astlyn, Hug. Dawes, Joh. Bonde, Will. Wykam, Tho. White, Ric. Burwey, Hen. Wall, Will. Banwell, Joh. Locok.

Sheriffs.

[Ric. Herynge, Mercer, Rog. Walles.]

"For vacabundes,[3] pauing streets, swynsties, sweeping streets,

[Ordained] that euery alderman in his warde see that ther be due correcion made accordyng to the lawe & the auncient ordynnaunces of leetes for the punyshment of myghty beggers, of vacaboundes, as well wemen as men, suspect alhowses & blynde ynnes, clensyng of the stretes & swepyng of the stretes in-to the giter, but see it be boron a-wey. Also that þer be no swynstyes occupied within

draughtes,

the walles of the Citee, nor draughtes apon the comen dykes of the Citee that longeth to the conveyance of the water of the Citee; also to see the pawmentes well pavid; also to suffre no onlawfull games to be vsid; also to se

Chymneys, & Thaked housez, wooden Chimneys."

the excersysyng of shotyng in long bowes; also to se þer be no wodyn chymneyes nor howses thakkyd with brome or strawe; and to see the Comen ryuer be well kept

---

[1] See above, p. 635.   [2] leaf 320, back.
[3] Some of the gloss is in the writing of one scribe and some in that of another.

§ 103. Nic. Burwey, Mayor. 1518.

accordyng to the auncientes ordynaunces þeruppon made; and also that they execute all oder good ordynaunces made for the welth of the Citee within þer warde, euery alderman apon the peyn so offendyng to pay for euery defaute presentid at eny sessions or lete vj s. viij d. to the comen boxe without eny ffauour.

[Ordained] that Ric. Burwey and all other hauyng draughtes, swynstyes, or eny oder anyaunce to the preiudice of the Redde-dych that they reforme them & pull them downe by-twene this and the ffest of seynt Martyn next comyng [or 6s. 8d. fine each time.] Ric. Burwey to do away with his nuisances.

[Ordained] that from hensforth the bokes of ij leetes euer next afore shall remayn in the counsell howse opynly on the shekyr,[1] that they may be seen euery Wennysday by the counsell of the Citee to see what is kept & what is brokyn & see it reformyd, and that they determyn those maters afore they entre into eny oþer. "þe booke of actes to be open." "Leetes."

[Ordained][2] that the ffeliship of rough-masons & dawbers ffromhensforth be no ffeliship nor craft of them-self, but only comen laborers as they were afore, and to take such wages as is lymyte them by the statutes þeruppon made, & no more, apon peyn of inprisonment; also that the make noon assemble, conuenticle or caue amonges them-self, apon the same peyn etc.[3] Dawbers and rough masons not to form a fellowship.

NIC. BURWEY, MAYOR, 1518.

[[4] Election of officers.]

Joh. Humfrey, Rob. a Grene, Joh. Haddon, Will. Pysforde, Joh. Duddesbury, Ric. Smyth, Joh. Strong, Ric. Hassall, Joh. Hardwen, Tho. Grove, Joh. Clerk, Joh. Bonde, Nic. Haynes, Hen. Perkins, Tho. Astlyn, Hug. Dawes, Tho. Rowley, Will. Wickam, Hen. Wall, Jul. Nethermyll, Joh. Locok, Step. Lynsey, Tho. Warde, Will. Banwell. "Ciuitas Couentrie." Jan. 25. Electors.

[m. Nic. Burwey; rec. Rad. Swyllyngton; cor. Joh. Boteler; steward, Joh. Porter; ch. Rob. Welsch, Draper, Rog. Dawber; w. Tho. Wilmer, Tho. Napton; mace, Hen. Walker; crier, Ric. ffyreby.] Officers.

---

[1] A counting board. [2] "at this letee" (sic) follows.
[3] See Introduction. [4] leaf 321, back. Scribe H.

§ 103. Nic. Burwey, Mayor. Crafts, 1518.

EASTER LEET.

"Civitas Couentrie." Apr. 20.

[1][V. f. p. held before Nic. Burwey, m., Ric. Herryng, Rog. Walles, b., on Tuesday before S. George's day, 9 Hen. VIII.]

Rob. a Grene, Joh. Haddon, Joh. Duddesbury, Ric. Smyth, Ric. Marler, Joh. Strong, Ric. Hassall, Joh. Hardwen, Tho. Grove, Joh. Bonde, Tho. Waren, Nic. Heynes, Hen. Perkyns, Tho. Astlyn, Hug. Dawes, Will. Wikam, Tho. White, Tho. Banwell, Hen. Wall, Tho. Hill, Jul. Nethermyll, Rob. Walshe, Rog. Dawber, Will. Banwell.

Orders of leet.

[2][Enacted] that no man nor men within this Cite, of what occupacion so euer he be of, swere or cause to be sworne vpon a boke eny maner of person for eny poynt in ther occupacion, in peyn to forfet C s. to be payd to the Comen boxe forth-with withouten eny pardon. [3]And they[3] schall punysshe Misdoers in their Occupacions by penaltes resonable; and if ther be eny man in any ffelowschip or craft that brekyth & wolle not obey & kepe such ordynaunces as hath ben made resonable for the good ordre & welth of the Craft, let hym pay such penaltes as hath ben therfor ordeyned of Olde tymes. And if he denye & woll not pay his penaltes accordyng to the ordynaunces to suffre hym the furst tyme, and then within iij or iiij dayes let the Maister aske hit of hym agayn with Record with hym; and if he deny it eftsones & wolde not pay it, lete the master of the Craft with iij or iiij of the honest men of [3] the Craft come to Master Meire & schow vnto hym the delyng of that person; and then Master Meire with sum of the Justices of the pease to sende for hym forthwyth & Comm[an]de hym to pay doble penaltes, if it be xij d. to pay ij s., and all other penaltes [in] like Maner [3] forth-with; or els to Comyt hym to warde ther to remayn till he haue paid the doble penalte, the on half ,[4] & the other half to the Craft; and also to desire the master to be good master to hym for that yere beyng, and after to be his good louer.

"No person to be sworne by masters off Crafts."

Offenders refusing to pay the accustomed fines

ordered by the mayor to pay double.

And also that all such penaltes taken of eny man for

---

[1] leaf 322.   [2] See p. 302.   [3-3] Deletions.   [4] Some omission here.

§ 103. *Nic. Burwey, Mayor. Crafts,* 1518.

brekyng of eny poynt of the ordenaunce of his occupacion, if it be aboue the price of a li. of waxe, the on half to be vpleyd to the comen boxe.

Part of a fine to go to the box.

Mem. that these ffynes ffolowyng to be for euery Occupacion to be had to the plesure of God after the abilite of the people that now ben, & no forther, to [? so] the Cite be encreased to more welthynes then it is now, hit is ordeyned (etc.) that euery prentyce of Mercers & Drapers Craftes that schal-be bounde¹ to the seid occupacions his ffrendes to pay for hym at the sealyng of his Indentures before some of the Mercers vj s. viij d. & non other ffyne, but to sue his prenteshode truly.

Mercers' apprentices to pay 6s. 8d. at the sealing of the indentures.

Also al other prentes of other Occupacion to pay at his settyng vp & openyng of his shoope vj s. viij d., and non other ffynes, but to pay to the Craft penaltes for mysdoyng contrary to the good ordenaunces of his Craft, and also ther quarterage & other thynges as afore-tymes hath ben vsed.

Others 6s. 8d. at setting up shop.

Also if eny person dwellyng within this Cite hath a good occupacion to lyve by & woll leve it & occupie with a-nother occupacion, then he to agre with the seid Occupacion that he wold be with-all.

"No medling with other trades then the trades they are made free vnto."

Also if ther be eny Craftesmen in the Countrey that hath not been prentise in this Cite that will com & enhabet here to Com & welcom & accordyng to the libertees of this Cite to dwell here well & honestly a hoole yere, & then to pay towardes the Charges of the seid Craft x s. in this maner, that is to sey v s. at the full ende of that yere, & other v s. within the next yere, and after that to pay after the good ordenaunce of the seid Craft as other men of the same Craft after his abbilite do pay, and non other ffyne etc.

"Prentisez." Country settlers to pay 10s.

² Also for the olde ffynes that ben paid, if he have ben prentise in the towne & hath payd all his ffynes, vj s. viij d. or more, to sese & pay no more ; & if he have not payd to the somme of vj s. viij d. to pay out to that some & no more.

Only 6s. 8d. required from apprentices ;

And if he haue not ben prentise in the Cite & haue payd to the some of x s. to sese & pay no more ; & if he

and 10s. from non-apprentices.

---

¹ The mark over "n" is like a*u*. ² leaf 322, back.

§ 103. *Nic. Burwey, Mayor. Cloth*, 1518.

haue not paid to the seid some of x s. to pay it out & no more, but to pay the penalte, if he deserue therto.

<small>Repayment of security money ordered.</small>

And if eny master of eny Craft haue Couenaunted & Charged hymself for eny man by the will of the partie for eny some of money, Then the seyd partie to pay the duyte[1] to the seid Maister, for he hath paed it for hym, and hit is due dett etc.

<small>"No cayue to be maid without thassent of Master Meire."</small>

["Ordened"] that no Jurnamen of what occupacion or Craft so-euer he be of within the Cite make or use amonge them-self eny Cayue or bylawe or assemblez or metynges at eny place by ther somner without licens of Master Meire & the Master of his occupacion, vpon peyne of xx s. for the first fawte, & for the seconde his bodie to prison ther to remayne to he wol-be justified by the Master of his occupacion & vj honest persones of that occupacion; & to bryng in ther booke when they be comaunded by Master Maire, the forfeiture to be paed, the oon half to the Comen boxe, & the other half to thoccupacion that they be of.

<small>"Against bowling"</small>

Also for a good & a Resonable consideracion it is enacted at this present lete that no Bowlyng be vsed at seynt Annys by the Charter house before vj of the Clok in the Mornyng nor after vj of the Clok in the Evenyng, but if they be honest persones that will make litell noyse, in the payne of hym that kepeth the place xij d. at euery defaute.

<small>by poore Craftsmen."</small>

Also that he suffre not pore Craftes-men to vse bowlyng ther dayly and wekely, levyng ther besynes at home that they shuld lyve by, in the payne to pay for euery persone so daily vsyng vj d., the oon half to hym that presenteth the trueth, & the other half to the Comen boxe.

<small>"Cloth makyng." In order to recover prosperity an inspection of cloth</small>

[2]AN ORDER FOR THE TRUE MAKINGE OF CLOTHE.[2]

Hit is to be had in mynde that for a trueth of Cloth-makyng to be had in this Cite as foloeth, if it myght be folowed & the execucion of the same to be don schortly, Or els the Cite wol-be so fer past that it wol-be past remedie to be recouered to eny welth or prosperite—hit is thought hit were good to haue ij weuers & ij walkers

<small>by 2 weavers and 2 walkers,</small>

---

[1] = debt.   [2-2] In another hand.

§ 103. *Nic. Burwey, Mayor.* *Cloth*, 1518.

sworn to make true se*r*che of the weue*r*s doyng & also of the walkers, & to p*r*esent the trueth : and also to be chosen vj Drape*r*s to be Maiste*r*s & oue*r*seers of the doyng of the serchers, That if some of them cannot a-lesou*r* to be at the se*r*chyng at the dayes of the se*r*chers yet some of these vj Maiste*r*s schall eu*er* be ther; and by-cause it were to great a besynes for the se*r*chers to go to eue*r*y manne*s* howse, hit is enacted (etc.) to haue a howse of the gilde or of some other mannes nyghe the Drape*r*y doore to be ordeyned¹ Well with p*er*ches to drawe oue*r* the Clothes when they be thykked, and also weighte*s* & ballaunce to wey the Cloth. And when it cometh frome the walkers, The walkers to bryng it to the se*r*chyng house, & to serche it & to se it oue*r* a perche ; and if it be good Cloth, as it owght to be, in brede & lengh, that the Cite may haue a preise by hit & no sklaunder, then to sett vpon hit the Olyvaunt² in lede, and of the Bak of the seall the lengh of the Cloth, by the which men schall perceyve & see it is true Couent*r*e Cloth : ffor of suertie ther is in London & other place*s* that sell false & vntrewe made Cloth, & name hit Couent*r*e Cloth, the which is a gret[er] slaunder to the Cite than hit dese*r*ueth by a gret p*a*rtie. And if ther be eny man that hath eny Cloth brought to the serch*y*ng house, what degre so eu*er* he be of, if it be not able for the worship of the Cite to be let passe, let hym pay for the se*r*che, & lett hym do his best with hit, but set not the Olyvaunt vpon it.

overlooked by 6 drapers,

is enjoined.

A house is to be provided;

and good cloth to bear

the seal with the city arms upon it,

to guard against ill-made material and

the slander that it brings to the city.

& this se*r*che to be made after this fo*u*rme, ³That is to sey ij dayes in the weke, Tewesday & Saturday, and if the serch*e*rs be there from viij of the Clok to a xj, and frome on to iiij of the Clok, and a Sealer to be ordeyned & sworne to stryke⁴ the Cloth & seale hit & wrete⁵ hit & fynde leed & to haue a peny for his labor ; and the sealles to be put in a Cofre with ij keys, the M*a*ister of the vj Drape*r*s to haue the on & the se*rr*chers the other ; and for

The searchers are to be present on Tuesdays and Saturdays from 8 till 11 (a.m.) and from 1 till 4 (p.m.),

---

¹ o*r*dain = to equip.
² The elephant and castle are the city arms.   ³ leaf 323.
⁴ The early meaning of this word was "to pass one's hand, or something flat over a surface to smooth it out." Practically the sense here seems to be = measure (Dr. Bradley).
⁵ = ? write, *i. e.* the length of the cloth to be put on the seal.

§ 103. *Nic. Burwey, Mayor. Cloth,* 1518.

and take 1d. for every cloth they examine.

the serche of euery cloth to the serchers to haue jd., and it is to be thought euery good man schal-be gladde of that payment.

The mayor and 2 others

And for the spynners [1] an ordinaunce to be hadde after this Manner: Maister Meyre to do so moch to take the labour vpon hym with ij of the vj Maysters on day & ij or iij another day, and to go & se euery mannes weight that vseth cloth-making, and that they be laufull of such weight as can be thought resonable for the pore folkes to lyue bye, & to lett non be occupied but it be sealed with an Olyvaunt in payn of xij d.; and if eny person denye of ffrowardnes & will not obey to this ordenaunce let not his wilfull Mynde be suffred, and also let not the towne seale [2] till he or sche be content to the ordenaunce therof made; and also to gyue the pore Spynners redy money, and if they will haue cloth or eny other Chaffur let theym when they haue their money bye hit & paye for hit; and when eny spynner is founde with a fawte, other lakyng of ther weyte or in false vsyng of their warke, so that the Clothmaker do perceyue verely it is don wilfully, and if it be such a fawte that it is worthy to be ponysshed openly, then bryng her & her warke to the alderman of the warde, & he to call to hym some of the oversears,[3] and to se the fawtes & to lett the person to be openly ponysshed, that all other may take ensample accordyng to her deseruyng. And these bygge beggers, that wil-not worke well to gete ther levyng, but lye in the feldes & breke hedges & stele mennys fruyte in somour, let theym be banysshed the town, Or els ponyssh theym so without fauour that they schal-be wery to byde therin.[4]

to examine the cloth-makers' weights, and seal them.

Clothmakers are commanded to pay spinners in ready money and not by truck wages.

The alderman of the ward

to punish a spinner for any serious fault.
Big beggars to be expelled

from the city.

Also Memorandum to wey the warke at the spynners howses in wole or yorn & this thynges performed & ffolowed:—Ther is a man [5] nyghe vnto this Cite that wole delyuer amonges pore Clothmakers the next Shear tyme ij C stone of goode woole as it cost, the Costes payd, & iiij C s. with it in redy money for bycause the spynners & the weuers schall haue redy money for their true labour,

Haddon's loan;

200 stone of wool and 400s. (£20) to be divided

---

[1] See above p. 243.   [2] An omission.   [3] Who are these?
[4] On vagabonds see Leonard, *Poor Relief*, and above *passim.*
[5] May be Joh. Haddon, see *Coventry Charities* (1733), p. 1.

§ 103. *Nic. Burwey, Mayor. Cloth*, 1518.

& to gyue theym as they may lyue, & to be delyuered to x men, to euery man xx^{ti} stone & xl s. in redy money to pay for the spynnyng & the weuyng. And they to pay hym ayen at iij dayes, that is to sey, at Alhallowetyde on parte, & at Candelmas or in Lent the second, & at Couentre ffeyre¹ the iijrd parte, so that he may haue all his money to bye newe wole. And if they can not sell their cloth to lyue by hit, he wole sometymes take hit of them for payment; so that they schall not labour to lese, and by Godes grace some other good men will do the same, so that the Cite schal-be better occupied by the love of Jhesus, Amen. *[among ten clothmakers, who are to repay him at certain seasons either in money or in unsaleable cloth.]*

Provided alwey that no officer, Constable nor other arest no cloth borne toward the serchyng house nor from the serchyng howse to the owners house in payn of a C s. to the comein boxe. *[Cloth not to be seized as distress when it is being borne to the searching-house.]*

[Enacted] for truth of Clothmakyng that no man nor woman within this Cite put no cloth to ony walker to full but if he will burle² it & wranghalf³ it within the Cite in peyn of vj s. viij d. to the comen boxe, ffor this entent folowyng, that is to sey, that the sherchers may se that hytt be well byrled & clenne & well & truly wranghalft³ and the serchars to se the same Cloth and to putt in ther burlyng marke. *[Cloth to be fulled within the city.]*

⁴ And also that the serchers may se the cloth when it is in byrlyng whether ther be eny fawte in the weuers doyng or not, and if the walker do not sende for the serchers to se whiles it is in byrlyng, if ther be eny fawte in the cloth when hit cometh to the serchyng howse to be leyd to the walkers Charge, but if the cloth be well byrled, & well thyked, & kyndely handeled, that it be not let kole with takyng out of the myll or hit be thoroly thykked, nor that it be not walked with Cappes, nor no ffloxe⁵ drawen out with sharpe handylles nor cardes, then the walker to haue for his trewe labour for a lo price cloth xl d., & for a myddle Cloth iiij s., & for a fyne cloth v s., & other verrye fyne clothes as the owner & he can agree. *[Cloth to be viewed by the searchers when it is being dressed, and not let to cool by taking out of the mill before it is thoroughly thicked. Fullers' charges.]*

---

¹ Corpus Christi.   ² = to dress cloth by removing knots.
³ See above, p. 640.
⁴ leaf 323, back. "Clothe making" in a later scribe's hand heads the page.   ⁵ Tufts of wool.

§ 103. *Nic. Burwey, Mayor. Cloth*, 1518.

Weavers'

Also that no weue*r* ley no cloth no longer then he may make hit good cloth of good breed in the peyn of vj s. viij d., and to dryve in all the wole that he hath to the seid cloth ; and the weue*r* doyng his wa*r*ke truly to haue for a cloth weuyng if it go betwene viij or ix C.[1], iiij s. in money, & if it go betwene ix & x C., iiij s. vj d., and if it go betwene x & a xj C., v s., & fferther afte*r* the hundred*es* as the owner & he can agre. Also that no weue*r* make no throms of any pese of cloth aboue the lengh of a quarter besyde the knot, in peyn to pay for eue*r*y defaute xl d., xij d. to eny man that fyndeth it, & p*r*esenteth it to M*aister* Maire, & ij s. iiij d. to the comen boxe.

charges ; for a cloth of 8 or 9 hundred 4*s*., 9 and 10 hundred 4*s*. 6*d*.

Long thrums.

Flocks not to be drawn with cards.

Also that ony walker that is founde with eny ffloxe draen of Clothes with card*es* or scharpe handill*es* for eue*r*y li. defauted so founde to pay xl d., except it poffe[2] of the myll, xx d. to eny man that fyndeth, & xx d. to the comen boxe.

"The mayor to search ffullers houses ffor fflocks and thrums."

Also that ther be ij s*er*chers chosen by M*aister* Mayre & the Councell, & to haue auctorite gyuen theym by this lete to go in-to eny weue*r* or walkers house as oft as they lyst to make labo*u*r to s*er*che for throms & ffloxe, & they to haue their p*a*rt of the penalte, as afore is rehe*r*sed, for so moch as they ffynde.

For preventing such search

3*s*. 4*d*.

And what man that lettyth theym to come in-to their howsez to se & make s*er*che for the seid Throms or floxe they to pay at eue*r*y faute xl d. to the comen boxe without ony p*a*rdon.

No yarn to be sold except by its original owner.

And that no Capper nor hatmaker nor no other p*er*son by no colored yarne of no p*er*son but if he knowe verely hit is thér owne, & that wole be knowen vppon the pric*es*, vpon the peyn of eue*r*y defaute xl d., xij d. to hym that fyndeth it & p*r*esenteth hit, and the rest to the comen boxe.

Drawing out of kerseys and broad cloth

Also ther is an-nother thyng to take hede to & to be ponysshed, ffor hit is open ffalshed, ffor ther is nether drede of God nor shame of the worlde,[3] that is the Draw-

---

[1] It is impossible that C=cwt. here. For wages see below, p. 689.
[2] = puff or fluff, that came off in the mill, and was blown about in the air ; probably the weaver might have the genuine fluff as a perquisite (Dr. Bradley).
[3] MS. wordle.

§ 103. *Nic. Burwey, Mayor. Cloth*, 1518.

eng out of kerseys [1] & brode Cloth to the gret dyssete of the werers & the high displesure of God; wherfor it is enacted at this lete that who-so-euer fyndeth such cloth so don to take recorde if he can with hym [2] that hit be troweth that he scheweth to Maister Mayre or the justices of the peas & he schall haue xx d. for his labour forth-with. And the doer of that vntrewe dede to pay vj s. viij d. to the comen box forth-with, Or els to go to prison accordyng to the kynges Comaundement.

displeasing towards God.

6s. 8d. fine.

Also no man nor woman put no cloth to wevyng in-to the countre but to ther own neighbours within this Cite, in the payn for euery cloth so put xl d. tyll the Cite be better inhabyt.[3]

No weaving in country.

Also [4] by-cause [4] tyme of this day is fare past & certein bylles cannot be fynysshed, hit is agreed & enacted that those billes with other necessarye to the comen-welth shal-be ordered & stabelysshed by the Mayre & his Councell vpon a Councell day.

The day being far spent, it is ordered that the Council finish the business.

Mem. that if the sheriffes do not geder their fforfeates made by the letes within on quarter of a yere next after they haue out their stretes delyuered them, Then the comen sargeant to geder theym to the vse of the comen boxe.

"Streites."

Item, that bowes be vsed & no koyttyng nor boollyng. If ther be eny person that se such comen Boollers or koytters to schewe it to the sheriffes & they schall haue part of the penalte that they schall pay, that is to sey, euery such Boollers or koytters at euery defaute vj d., j d. to the fynders, & ij d. to the comen boxe, & iij d. to the sheriffes at euery defalt; and if ther be eny officer or constable that seith & knoeth eny such boollers or koytters & dothe not present them to the sheriffes to pay to the comen boxe vj d.

"Against bowlers and Quoiters."

Item, that no person cast no [2] bowle in the stretes within this Cite, vpon the peyn at euery tyme so doyng vj d. to

Bowls.

---

[1] = a kind of coarse cloth woven from long wool and generally ribbed. v. *N.E.D.*
[2] Deletion.
[3] See the complaint of the clothiers of Worcester, Evesham, Droitwich, Kidderminster and Bromsgrove in Cunningham, *Eng. Industry*, I. 518.   [4] Repeated.

§ 103. *Nic. Burwey, Mayor. Leet*, 1518.

the comen boxe, Or els to be comytted then to warde till they haue payd hit etc.

"Towne diche" to be cleansed by Master Marler.

[1][Enacted] that if Maister Rychard Marler wolde do so moch as to cast [2] & clense eny part of the town dyke betwene the Well-strete yate & The Hill-strete yate, Or bytwene the Coke-strete yate & the Priore yate he to haue thuse of the same dyke, & the bankes of the same dyke to hym & his assignez so long as he or his assignez kepe the seid dyke so cast with depnes of water so hie as the broke will serue to bring in the water, and if he or his assignez suffre eny parte therof to fyll with mudde or Mukke, the Chamberleins to entre vpon that part, and the seid Richard & his assignez to lose the cost that they haue made theron.

"For officers to waite on the mayor,"

at 7 a.m. to accompany him to church,

[Enacted][3] that every officer that is belongyng to Maister Meyre of this Cite that they ben Redy every workday at the meyres place by vij of the clok in the mornyng to bryng Maister Meyre to church; & if he haue eny besynes to do whyll Maister Meyre is at church to shewe of his departyng to Maister Meire or to the sordeberer & to harkyn of his goyng frome church, & to bryng hym home to his house, & lyke wise to evensong or els to pay at every defaute j d.; and to be redy to bryng hym to

to Jesus mass and to the market.

Jhesus masse [4] on the ffriday & after to wayte vpon hym in the market till he go home to dynner in the payn of every defaut ij d. Also on Sondays & holidays to be at Maister Meires house before the last pele be all rongen to matens or evensong, in the same payn of ij d. And all the penaltes to be payd forthwith if he aske not lycens of Maister Meyre when he goeth from hym etc.

MICHAELMAS LEET.

"Ciuitas Couentrie." Oct. 12.

Jury of 25.

[5] ¶ [V. f. p. held on Tuesday after S. Dionysius' day, 10 Hen. VIII.]

Joh. Humfrey, Rob. Grene, Joh. Haddon, Joh. Duddesbury, Ric. Smyth, Ric. Merler, Ric. Hassall, Joh. Hardwen, Tho. Grove, Joh. Clerk, Hen. Rogers, Tho. Waren,

---

[1] leaf 324.   [2] To dig out.
[3] "at these present lete" follows.
[4] See above, p. 333.   [5] leaf 325.

§ 103. *Nic. Burwey, Mayor. Leet,* 1518.

Tho. Smyth, Nic. Heynes, Hen. Perkyns, Tho. Astlyn, Hug. Dawes, Will. Wykam, Tho. White, Ric. Burwey, Hen. Wall, Jul.[1] Nethermyll, Tho. Hill, Rob. Welsh, Rog. Dawber.

[Will. Dawson, skynner, Joh. Hykkes, grasier.] *Sheriffs.*

[Agreed] that the ffelyship of the Cappers schall elect & chese xij of the best of the occupacion, & they at assemble emong theym-self to chewse ij serchers & they to serche & present all the fautes that ben found among theym to Maister Meyre, and the seid serchers to be sworn afore Maister Meire to make treue serche accordyng to their othe, & then Maister Meyre to se due correccion therin etc. *"Searchers" for "Cappers."*

[Enacted] that ther schal-be made due serche of all maner of Tiles & bryk that cometh to town that the stuff be good & laufull, [vpon] peyn of forfeiture of all such fauty tile; & euery tiler that leyth eny such fawty tile vpon eny house within the Cite to forfeit for euery fawte so by hym leid xl d. without eny pardon to the comen boxe etc. *"Tiles & brek."*

[Ordained] that Ric. Saunders, Joh. Gely,[2] Will. Warde & Will. Dale schal-be serchers of the Brode-well & the comen broke from the Hill-myll vnto seint Johyns at euery faute they ffynde the Offender to pay xij d. wherof the serchers to haue iiij d., & viij d. to the comen boxe; & so from seint Johyns to the Priore-myll. *"For ouerseyng the Brode-well & Riuers."*

Item, ther be chosen serchers of the water ffrom the Spon brige down to Seint Johyns brige Tho. Reves, Tho. Coton, Gef. Clowes & Joh. Sutton, & they to serche & haue for their laboure as is aforeseid, & the remanent to the comen boxe.

["Ordeigned"] that no bocher sell eny of his tallowe aboue ij s. the ston [on] payn of euery defawte vj s. viij d. wherof half to the comen boxe. And no chaundeler sell no candell aboue peny fferthyng a pounde, vpon the same payn, wherof half to the comen boxe etc. Also a [blank]. *"Talowe."*

[3] Also at this lete ther was a bill put in by Maister Richard Marler which bill herafter foloeth :—

---

[1] A stroke too many for Julius and too few for Julinus.
[2] ? Goby.   [3] leaf 325, back.

§ 103. *Nic. Burwey, Mayor. Gates,* 1518.

Ric. Marler's petition about the cleansing of the ditch;

Sheweth vnto this worshipfull company at this present lete assembled Richard Marler, That where it was graunted to hym & to his assignez to haue thuse & profett of the town dyke, the which he let cast[1] & clense at his owne cost betwene the Priore yate & the Coke-strete yate —Plese it you to graunt hym in lyke man*er*, if he make the cost, to cast & clense eny other place of the town dyke, Or if eny other p*er*son of the Cite wele cast & clense eny p*ar*t of the dyke, vpon eny syde of the cyte he or they to haue thuse & p*ro*fett of the water, if eny be, so long as he or their assignez kepe the seid dyke with water accordyng to the first entent. Also wher the gate-house

the "Bishop-gate tower"

ou*er* the Bysshop yate is not well vsed, ffor the ffloure*s* ben broken & the bord*es* born awey & the walles broken,

and a tower at the New Rents

that within litell contynuance hit will dekay sore. And also ther is a Towre next the newe Rent that hath ben long mysused with kepyng of swyne therin, & the mook of theym cast out at a hole in-to the strete to the gret noyauns & enfecc*io*n of the people comyng that way— Pleaseth it you to graunt to the seid Ric. Marler & his assignez by v*er*tue of this p*re*sent lete to haue the seid yate-house for t*er*me of xl yeres, & he & his assignez schall kepe the seid yate-house clene, & with ffloryng & wallyng; and also to cleanse & kepe clene the seid Toure duryng the seid t*er*me. And if the seid Richard or his assignes do not p*er*forme the couena*un*t*es* before-seid within a q*u*art*er* of a yere aft*er* they haue warnyng, Then the Chamb*er*leins to re-entre into the seid gatehouse & Towre at their plesure. And for a knolege of the same

"set ffor 2 li. off Almonds per annum."

the seid Richard graunted to gyue to the Chamb*er*leins eu*er*y yere the first ffriday of Lent ij li. of almons etc. Which bill was graunted, agreed & confermed by all my seid Masters at this p*re*sent lete etc.

[2] M*em*. that the elecc*io*n of M*aister* Tho. Waren when he was chosen Meire shuld haue byn entrid here; where it is writen on the next leef a-fore as apperith there etc.[2]

---

[1] To clear out a ditch, throwing the soil out, v. *N. E. D.*
[2–2] Another scribe. For Warren's election see leaf 324, back. See below.

§ 104. *Tho. Waren, Mayor*, 1519.

THO. WAREN, MAYOR, 1519.

[¹ Election of officers.]   "Civitas Couentre." Jan. 25.

² Mem. that this eleccion shuld haue byn entrydde after the lete foloyng and not here.²

Tho. Grove, Rob. Grene, Joh. Haddon, Joh. Duddesbury, Ric. Smyth, Ric. Marler, Joh. Strong, Ric. Hassall, Joh. Hardwen, Joh. Clerk, Will. Wykam, Nic. Haynes, Hen. Parkyns, Tho. Astlyn, Hug. Dawes, Hen. Wall, Julinus Nethermyll, Tho. Hill, Ric. Herryng, Rog. Walles, Rob. Welsh, Rog. Dawber, Ric. Kemsey, Tho. Burdon.   *Electors.*

[m. Tho. Waren, Dier; rec. Rad. Swyllyngton; cor. Joh. Boteler; steward, Joh. Porter; ch. Tho. Sponne, whitawer, Ric. Wyther; w. Will. Coton, Mercer, Will. Smyth, Draper; mace, Will. Alyn; crier, Ric. ffereby.]   *Officers.*

³EASTER AND MICHAELMAS LEETS.

[V. f. p. held before Tho. Waren, m., Will. Dawson, Joh. Hykkes, b., on Thursday after the Invention of the Holy Cross, 11 Hen. VIII.]   "Ciuitas Couentrie." May 5.

Tho. Grove, Rob. Grene, Joh. Duddesbury, Ric. Marler, Joh. Strong, Ric. Hassall, Joh. Hardwyn, Nic. Burwey, Will. Wykam, Tho. Smyth, Tho. Astelyn, Hug. Dawes, Tho. White, Ric. Burwey, Tho. Banwell, Hen. Wall, Tho. Hill, Rog. Walles, Tho. Spon, Ric. Wether, Joh. Morse, Will. Banwell, Will. Coke, Ric. Towneshend.

ffirste, it is ordened at this lete that the Talough Chaundlers of this Cetie sell Candell betwen this and the ffeste of seynt John Baptiste next comyng for peny fferthyng the pounde, and after from thens to the ffeste of seynt Michell next ffolowyng for a peny a pounde, and no derer, apon peyn of euery defaute vj s. viij d., halff to the comen Box and halff to the shryffes.   *Tallow chandlers.*

Also it is agreid (etc.) that the Tanners of the Countrey haue ffree lybertie on the Saterday to by hydes after vij of the Clocke in the mornyng till the Markett be inded, and that no Bochers sell noo maner hide afore the same ower   "Tanners of the Contrey."

---

¹ leaf 324, back.
²–² In the same hand as the note above. See above, p. 664.
³ leaf 326. A beautiful hand of H type.

§ 104. *Tho. Waren, Mayor. Market,* 1519.

of vij of the Clocke to noon Tann*er*, nor to no fforen Tann*er* of the Countrey by-fore that ower eny hide [or 6s. 8d. fine, half (etc.).]

Also it is enacted that the Bochers do ley forth ther hydes eu*ery* Saterday by vj of the clooke in the mornyng, apon the same peyn.

"Ciuitas Couentr*ie*." Oct. 11.

[1] ¶ [V. f. p. held on Tuesday after S. Dionysius' day, 11 Hen. VIII.]

Tho. Grove, Rob. Grene, Joh. Duddesbury, Ric. Hassall, Joh. Hardwyn, Joh. Clerke, Joh. Humfrey, Will. Wykam, Joh. Bonde, Nic. Heynes, Hen. P*er*kyns, Tho. Astelyn, Hug. Dawes, Tho. Banwell, Hen. Wall, Tho. White, Jul. Nethermyll, Tho. Hyll, Ric. Herryng, Rog. Walles, Tho. Spon, Ric. Wether, Tho. Burdon, Ric. Kemsey.

Sheriffs.

[Tho. Dodde, Mercer, Joh. Crampe, baker.]

Orders of leet.

"For bying of Corne."

ffurste, it is enacted (etc.) that no inha*b*itaunt of this Cetie nor fforener by eny Corne, on the m*a*rket day or it com in-to the m*a*rkett place, but suffer it to com in-to the m*a*rkett; and the towne to haue libe*r*tie to by ffrom ix of the Cloke forward, and at xij of the Cloke the Countrey to begyn to bye and not till then, [or 6s. 8d. fine each time, half to the common box, half to the sheriffs.] And iff eny fforener or Townesman fforstall eny Corne w*ith*in the libe*r*tie of this Cetie of Couentre or it com into the m*a*rkett to fforffet the same peyne and in lyke man*er*.

"For sellyng of malt."

Also it is Enacted that no man sell eny malte out of the Towne when it is of the price of v s. and aboue, apon the peyne lymyted in the olde lete, that is to sey, to fforfett for eu*ery* quarter so sold vj s. viij d. [half (etc.).]

[No tallow chandler to sell candles between this and the next leet above 1¼d. per lb. "apon peyn aboue lymyted."]

Also it is enacted (etc.) that the act*e* of hunters [2] to be put in execucion.

"For pren-tise; to bee [3]

[Enacted] that no man w*ith*in the Cetie take no prentyse ffrom this day fforward but iff he bryng into the Comen Box iiij d. and to the Styward ij d. And the Master of

---

[1] leaf 326, back. [2] See p. 630. [3] MS. ber.

§ 105. *Joh. Bonde, Mayor*, 1520.

every Craft to present the prentyse afore M*aister* Meyre and he to see his indenture sealyd and his name entred in the Styward Boke.[1]

enseled before the mayor."

[2]JOH. BONDE, MAYOR, 1520.

¶ [Election of officers.]

Rob. Grene, Joh. Duddesbury, Ric. Marlar, Joh. Strong, Ric. Hassall, Tho. Grove, Joh. Clerke, Joh. Humfrey, Nic. Heynes, Tho. Astelyn, Hug. Dawes, Ric. Burwey, Tho. Banwell, Hen. Wall, Jul. Nethermyll, Tho. Hill, Ric. Herryng, Rog. Walles, Will. Dawson, Joh. Hykke*s*, Tho. Spone, Ric. Wether, Tho. Warde, Tho. Burdon.

[m. Joh. Bonde, Draper; rec. Rad. Swyllyngton; cor. Joh. Boteler; steward, Joh. Porter; ch. Hum. Moseley, Jas. Gilbert; w. Hen. Hinde, Mercer, Tho. Tressell; mace, Will. Alen; crier, Ric. ffereby.]

"Ciuitas Couentrie." Jan. 25.

Officers.

EASTER AND MICHAELMAS LEETS.

[3] ¶ [V. f. p. held before Joh. Bonde, m., Tho. Dodde, Joh. Cramp, b., on Thursday after S. George's day, 12 Hen. 8.]

"Ciuitas Couentrie." Apr. 26.

Tho. Waren, Rob. a Grene, Joh. Duddesbury, Joh. Strong, Ric. Hassall, Tho. Grove, Joh. Clerk, Joh. Humfrey, Tho. White, Tho. Smyth, Hen. Perkyns, Tho. Astleyn, Hug. Dawes, Hen. Wall, Tho. Banwell, Tho. Hyll, Ric. Heryng, Rog. Walles, Will. Dawson, Joh. Hykkes, Hum. Moseley, Jas. Gylbert, Will. Cook, Will. Towrys.

[Enacted and agreed] that all such good ordyna*u*nces as be made for the co*m*en-wele of the Citee afore-tyme that from-hensforth they be truly kept & executid accordyng to the true entent therof, and that the booke [4] that is newe made be takyn for an act & p*r*oclamyd at this lete etc.

The book of ordinances to be proclaimed.

[Enacted] that all such grauntes, p*r*omyses & Couenaunt*es* as M*aister* Meyre & his brethern han made wit*h* Joh. Mors, Weue*r*, touchyng the office of Shyrrywyke of

The shrievalty.

---

[1] See above, pp. 560 *sqq.*
[2] leaf 327.   [3] leaf 327, back. Scribe G.
[4] Is the existing MS. the "boke" referred to here?

§ 105. *Joh. Bonde, Mayor.* *Leet,* 1520.

the Citie that the seid John enjoy them ¹accordyng¹ to there promyse without fraude or craft etc.

Tallow.
[Enacted] that no taloo be solde by-twene this & the next lete a-bove ij s. the Stonne, apon the peyn of euery defaute vj s. viij d., wherof half to the comen boxe etc.

Chandlers.
Also that no Talochaundeler [sell] no candyll a-bove peny ferthyng the pounde, apon the same peyn, wherof half to the Comen boxe etc.

[Enacted] that no inhabitant of the Citee cast eny muk or ffilth without the town wall within xl fote therof, or make eny gardeyn or wodpleck ² with-in xl^{ti} fote therof [or 40d. fine each time, half to the sheriffs, and half to the common box.]

No garden for "40 ffoot within the Citty wall."

"Ciuitas Couentrie." Oct. 9, 1520.
³ ¶ [V. f. p. held on Tuesday, S. Dionysius' day, 12 Hen. VIII.]

Tho. Waren, Rob. a Grene, Joh. Duddesbury, Ric. Marler, Joh. Strong, Joh. Clerk, Joh. Humfrey, Tho. White, Tho. Smyth, Will. Wykam, Hen. Parkyns, Tho. Astlyn, Hugo Dawes, Tho. Banwell, Hen. Wall, Jul. Nethirmyll, Tho. Hyll, Ric. Heryng, Rog. Walles, Will. Dawson, Hum. Moseley, Jas. Gilbert, Ric. Kemsey, Ric. Toty.

Bailiffs and Sheriffs.
[Tho. Hervy, Ric. Ryse.]

[Whereupon T. Hervy was enjoined in full court that he should be here, *i. e.* in the Gild-hall at the next holding of the court on Monday next after S. Luke the Evangelist's day (Oct. 22) to take the oath for the exercise of his office, on pain of £100. On which day Tho. Hervy solemnly cited does not appear, but makes default. Therefore he forfeited the afore-said penalty, *i. e.* £100. And further the same

Et super hoc Iniunctum⁴ est eidem Thome Hervy in plena Curia quod sit hic scilicet in Guyhalda eiusdem Ciuitatis ad proximam Curiam ibidem tenendam, scilicet die Lune proximo post ffestum S. Luce euaungeliste ad recipiendum sacramentum suum pro officio illo exercendo sub pena Centum librarum etc. Ad quem quidem diem Lune predictus Tho. Hervy solempniter exactus non venit set defaltum facit. Ideo fforisfecit penam supradictam, videlicet Centum libras. Et ulterius preceptum est

---

¹⁻¹ repeated.
² *N. E. D.* s. v. pleck = a small piece or plot . . . a small enclosure.
³ leaf 328, back.   ⁴ A stroke of " n " wanting.

§ 105. *Joh. Bonde, Mayor. Leet,* 1520.

Tho. Hervy was ordered to be at the next court held in the aforesaid Gild-hall to take his oath, under the penalty of £200. On which day the said Tho. Hervy came in his proper person, but would not take the oath as it was commanded him. Therefore he forfeited the aforesaid penalty, *i. e.* £200.]

eidem Tho. Hervy quod sit hic ad proximam Curiam in Guyhalda predicta tenandam ad recipiendum sacramentum suum etc. sub pena ducentarum librarum etc. Ad quem diem hic venit predictus Tho. Hervy in propria persona sua, set noluit recipere [1] sacramentum suum, sicut ei preceptum fuit. Ideo forisfecit penam supradictam, videlicet ducentas libras etc.

[Enacted] that no inhabitant of the parisch of seynt Michel when þer course comyth to gyf the halycake that they make but on haly-cake, and that they put no more theryn but the Teyre [2] of thre stryke of whete, and noder to make cake nor bun beside the haly-cake, [or 20s. fine to the common box.] And the inhabitauntes of the Trinity parish to put no more in theire haly-cate but the teyre of too strike of whete, & noder bun nor cake moo, [or 20s. fine to the common box.]   "Holicak."

[Enacted that no tallow be sold above 2s. the "stonne," and no "candyll" above 1¼d. per lb.] And that their penyworth and halpurth be sold after the same prise & no derre, apon the peyn of euery defaute vj s. viij d. to the comen box without eny grace.   Tallow.

[Enacted] that Maister Meyre for the yere beyng fromhensforth shall haue the denominacion and to chose yerely on of the kepers of the occupacion of bochers, and the craft to name the oder keper accordyng as is vsid with the phelishippes of Bakers and ffyshmongers, and if the bochers wyll not a-gre to this Act the hole occupacion to lese at euery defaut C s. to the comen boxe.[4]   "Eleccion of the Maisters of the bochers." [3]

[Enacted] that the gates of the Citee shal-be shot euery nyght at viij of the clok and openyd at v of the clok in the mornyng, and thus to contynue as long as hit is thought necessarie therfore for the preseruacion of good rulee etc.   "Gaittes of the Citie."

---

[1] MS. reperire.
[2] Tare = allowance of an extra weight, cf. "tare and tret." *v.* N. E D. *s. v.* Cloff. Probably this limitation was on account of the dearth. For the holy cake see p. 417, 680.
[3] "Bochers" deleted follows.   [4] See Introduction.

THE CAPPERS.

[1] The Constitucions and Ordinances of the Craft of the Cappers within the Cite of Couentre Made and Confermyd by Maistre John Bonde, Maier of the same Cite, at the lete day the ixth day of Octobre [12 Hen. VIII.]

To meet on the feast of the Name of Jesus, Aug. 7. "for electing masters,"

In primis That all the hoole Company Mete togeder at a place assigned apon the day and ffeast of the In nomine Jhesu, and that same Day than and ther to chuse new kepers for that yer ffollowyng, vpon the payne to forfett v li. vnto the comyn box; and yf he or they so choson Refuse yt he to pay xl s., half to the comyn Box and half to the craft, except he can shew a Cause Reasonable afore

who are to be received by the mayor.

Maister Meyer and his brethern why he so doith, and the same Maister to be admytted by the Maier and his brethern; and what persone of the Craft that ys awey that day yf he haue had iij Daies warnyng to pay xij d. without it be a cause Reasonable; and when it so fortunes that the said Eleccion day fallys vpon Friday, Satterday, or Sonday the second Maisters deuour [2] to be defferrid tel the Tewysday next after.

"Accompt" made at Christmas.

Also That euery Maister after he ys dischargid Make his accompte vnto the new Maisters atte feast of the natyvety of our Lorde next followyng, vpon the payne of iij li. half to the maier & half to the Craft, without license of the newe kepers for the tyme beyng etc.

"Apprentices." Two allowed.

Also That no Man haue no moo prentises at wons but two, and that he take them no lesse yers than vij, and that [no] man kepe them in his hows past the space of on monethe but yf ther Indentures be sealid before the Maisters of the said Craft for the yer beyng; and for

Fines to be paid on their admission,

euery prentyz to be brought in iiij d. to the Craftes box, iiij d. to the Maisteres Box, and iiij d. to the comyn box.

and their names "enroled."

And the said Maisteres to se inmediatly ther names Entrid in the craftes bok, ther termys and ther covenauntes, so that the craft may perfetly knowe of ther departing, and to se for bothe parties that al covenauntes be suerly kept; and he or they that sealid any Indenturs

---

[1] leaf 329. Another scribe. See above, pp. 572 *sqq.*
[2] Is the second master not to pay his duty to the mayor when time fails?

§ 105. *Joh. Bonde, Mayor. Cappers*, 1520.

but in the presens of on of the kepers to lese at euery deffaut xl d. without the licens of the kepers.

Also [but] yf the said kepers Registur trewly the said Indenturs and Couenauntes after the Ordinaunces aboue namyd then they to forfet at euery deffaut vj s. viij d., half to the Meyer & half to the Craft. *Indentures to be "Registred."*

Also yt ys ordenyd that no man of the said Craft take noo prenty3 vnlesse than he haue a obligacion of hym and sufficient surtes boundon for hym to performe his couenauntes, and he or they to be boundon to hys Maister in the somme of v li. at the least, and who so doith the contrary to forfet to ther craft xl s. half to the Meier and half to the craft etc. *"Apprentices bound by obligation."*

Also yf any prentiz of the said Craft departe from his Maister hereafter by any mean, & exceipt it be by the visitacion of God, the said Maister to haue no moo prenty3 duryng the said termys, exceipt he delyuer the obligacion of his said prenty3, so gone awey, to the Maister of the said Craft, and they to take the advauntage therof to the vse of the said Craft; and that the Maister of the said prenty3 shall avowe al accions[1] to be takon in his owne name by the Maister of the said Craft for the yer beyng, and not a quyttance to make lesse than by the grement of the said Maistre, vpon the payne of C s. *In the case of "Departing of Apprentices," the bond to be delivered to the craft master for the craft's profit, no discharge being allowed whereby the original sum should be diminished.*

Also yf any prentiz of the said Craft complayne hym to the said Maister that he haue not his sufficient fyndyng accordyng to the customys of this Cyte, so prouyd at the first tyme the Maisters to gyf to the maister of the said prenti3 a monycion to se it be amendid, at the second faut a Reasonable fyne, and at the iij^de tyme the Maistres of ther power to take the said prentiz awey from hym and sett hym with another Man of the Craft wher he shal-be better orderyd, and his Maister to be clerly dischargid of hym. *"Abusing Apprentices." First complaint a warning; second, a fine; third, the apprentice to be removed.*

Also that no persone of the saide Craft Rebuke any of the Maisters for the yer beyng, vpon the payne to pay vj s. viij d. at euery deffaut, half to the Maier and half to the Craft, and if any persone of the Craft will not agre *"Opprobrious words to the masters,"*

---
[1] *i. e.* for the recovery of the money from the securities.

§ 105. *Joh. Bonde, Mayor. Cappers*, 1520.

that this forfect[1] shuld be paide he hym-self to pay xl d. without any grace.

or "Against bretheren off the ffellowship."

Also yf any persone of the said Craft Rayle on against another in the premysses of the Maisters for the yer beyng after they be commaundid by on of the Maisters to kepe syllence he or they to forfeet vj s. viij d., half to the Mayer and half to the craft.

"Attendance on the Mastur of the Crafte."

[2] Also That all Mene of the Craft be Redy to wayte vpon the [3] Craft [3] Maisters at suche tymes as they shal-be Reasonably warnyd by the somner for the worship of the Cyte or the welthe of the Craft, vpon the payn to lose at euery deffaute xl d., half to the Mayer and half to the craft.

"Consell disclosed to move dissention."

Also That no persone of the said Craft disclose nor vtter no thynges that ought of Right to be secretly kept amonges themselfes wherby any dyssension or debate myght Ryse theruppon, vppon the payne of euery deffaute so provid vj s. viij d., half to the Maier and half to the Craft.

Forbidden "to put forth the worke" to any whose fines are unpaid.

Also That no persone of the Craft put forthe no pece of warke to noo Man exceipt he haue paide his hoole fynes, or elles the Maisters gyf hym leve to work for suche causes as shal-be thought nedfull by the advise of ther brethern, vpon the payn to lose at euery dyffaut so prouyd x s., half to the Maier and half to the Craft.

"Cappes thycking."

Also It is Ordenyde that no man thyk nor presse noo Journeymens Cappes Exceipt they be old Cappes [or 6s. 8d. fine each time, half to the common box, and half to the craft.] And that no man put forthe nother spynnyng nor knyttyng vnto none of them that vsithe to spyn or knyttythe any Journeymens Cappes tell they be brought before the Maisteres of the Craft and agre be-fore thaym and to vse it no more, vpon the payn who-so dothe the Contrary to pay vj.s. viij d. half to the comyn box and half to the Craft. And that no man sett his Journeyman vpon no notherman's work aftur he know he mak Cappis of his owne tell he haue paid his fyne, vppon the payn to lose at euery dyffaut so prouyd x s. half to the Comyn box and half to the Craft. And that no man tak no new spynner nor knytters yf they haue wrought to any of the

Boycott of spinners who work for Journeymen.

[1] or "forfeet."   [2] leaf 329, back.   [3]—[3] deleted.

§ 105. *Joh. Bonde, Mayor. Cappers*, 1520.

craft before, but that they bryng hym a token from hym that they wrought withall before To know that she haue well & Trewly vsid her self or noo in good work and puttyng in her stuf, and who so dothe the Contrary to lose at euery diffaute xx d. without any grace etc.

Every spinner must furnish a character from a former master.

Also It ys Ordeyned that euery Maister once in hys yer to goo through the hole Cyte to euery Mans hows of the Craft and by ther Registers to call for euery prentise be [2]-fore thaym to know how the constitucions be kept, and what Maistur that fautes herin to pay xl s. without any grace, half to the Meyer and half to the Craft.

"Maiour[1] [to] go abrode to examin prentises."

Also That noon of the said Craft Make no Cappis but that they put sufficient stuf in them so that they may abide the workmanship, and that they make them not slyghtly to the sale and gret dissaite to the people [or 40d. fine each time, half to the mayor and half to the craft.]

"Cappes" to be well made.

Also That noo Maister nor Journeyman by no Manour of yern or Colloryde woll, vpon the payn of xx s., half to the comyn box and half to the Craft. And that no Journeyman worke no Cappis in ther own howsys,[3] but Exceipt yt shalbe lefull to the said Journeymen to ffreshe and scower old Bonettes in ther own howsys, [or 12d. fine each time, half to the mayor and half to the craft.]

"Yarne & woll."

Journeymen not to compete with their masters.

Also That euery Journeyman of the said Craft from Michelmas to Easter cum to ther worke at syx of the Cloke in the mornyng and worke vntyll vij of the Clok at nyght, and from Ester to Michelmas to cum at v of the Clok and work tell vij at nyght. And that noo Journeyman go from his Maister exceipt he gyf his Maister xiiij days warnyng, upon the payn of vj s. viij d. And that no Journeyman be set on worke without license of the Maister of the Craft, and he to se wheder he be a workman or nott etc.

"Journeymen to worke what hower." 6 a.m. till 7 p.m. in winter. 5 a.m. till 7 p.m. in summer.

Due notice.

Also That noo person of the Craft teche noo poyntes of the Craft to noo person save to hys prentiz and hys wyf [or 100 s. fine, half to the mayor and half to the craft.]

"Apprentises onely to be taught."

---

[1] A slip; read Maister.   [2] repeated.
[3] "but in ther owne howsys" follows.

674 § 105. *Joh. Bond, Mayor. Dearth*, 1520.

THE DEARTH. A CENSUS.

Oct. 10, 1520.

A view taken during a dearth of the amount of provisions and the number of inhabitants in the city.

[1] Memorand*um* That the xth day of Octobre and in the yer of the Raigne of Kyng Henry the Viijth,[2] then Maister Joh. Bonde beyng Maier of the Cite of Couentre, The price of all maner of Corne and graynes be-ganne to a-Ryse, wheruppon a veu was takon by the said Maier and his brethern what stores of all Maner of Corne, and what nombre of people was then whithin the said Cite, men, women and Childern, etc.

Nomber of people in eue*r*y warde.   The nomber of Greynes of all Maner of Cornes.

707 persons; malt, 454 qrs.; rye, 36½ strike; wheat, 17 qrs. 2 strike.

S*um*ma :

Erle-strete warde.
vij C and vij p*er*sones.   { In Malt, iiij liiij q*uarter*,
In Rie, xxxvj stryke di*m*.
In whete, xvij q*uarter* ij stryk.

[Smithford Street ward.]

406 persons; malt and barley, 220 qrs.; rye, 15 qrs. 2 strike; wheat, 2½ qrs.; "ott*es*," 27 qrs.; "pese," 7½ qrs.

Gosford Street ward.

875 persons; malt, 456 qrs.; "whet & Rye," 16 qrs.; peas, 1 qr.

Much [3] Park Street ward.

719 persons; malt, 287 [4] qrs.; wheat, 14½ qrs. 1 strike; peas, 7 qrs.

Bishop Street ward.

1018 persons; malt, 334 qrs.; wheat and rye, 26 qrs.; peas, 1 qr.

Bayly Lane ward.

459 persons; wheat, 1 qr. 6 strike; malt, 150 qrs. 3 strike; barley, 20 qrs.; rye, 19 qrs.; oats, 9 qrs. 2 strike; peas, 1 qr. 6 strike.

" Brodyate warde."

552 persons; wheat, 1 qr. 3·[5] strike; malt, 100 qrs.; rye, 1 qr. 5½ strike; oats, 2 qrs.

[1] leaf 330.   [2] Year omitted.   [3] MS. Miche.
[4] ij C iiij^{xx} vij.   [5] "vj" deleted.

§ 105. *Joh. Bond, Mayor. Dearth*, 1520.

Cross-Cheaping ward.

884 persons; wheat, 1½ qrs.; rye, 18 qrs.; malt, 180 qrs.

[1] Jordan Well ward.

354 persons; malt, 100 (v score) qrs.; wheat, none (null*um*); rye, 3 qrs.

Spon Street ward.

627 persons; malt, 198[2] qrs.; rye and wheat, 3 qrs. 7 strike.]

S*um*ma totalis of the numbre of the people then beying wi*th*in the Cyte, of men, women and Childern.	S*um*ma to*ta*lys. vj M^{li} vjC & j.	In Malt, ij M^{li} iij^{c} $\overset{xx}{v}$ & v q*uar*te*r*,[3] In Rye & } jC q*uar*ter, Mastlin } j stryk, In whet, xlvij q*uar*te*r*, In ot*tes*, xxxix q*uar*te*r*, ij stryk, In pese, xviij q*uar*te*r*, ij stryk.

6601 persons; malt, 2405 qrs. (two thousand three hundred five score and five); rye and maslin, 100 qrs. 1 strike; wheat, 47 qrs.; oats, 39 qrs., 2 strike;

peas, 18 qrs., 2 strike.

Also a veu by hym takon what supstance of malt was then brewede wi*th*in the Cyte wokly by the comyn brewers that brewed to sell and fyll furthe by the Sesters; the nombre of the comyn brewers in all the Cyte ys . . . . iij$\overset{xx}{..}$ viij

"Brewers."

68 brewers.

Item, they brewid wekly in malt vij$\overset{xx}{}$ vj q*uar*ter, j b*us*.

146 qrs. 1 bushel,

Mem. that ther was brought into this said Cyte the ffryday before Crystmas day in the yer of the said Joh. Bonde then beying mayer by his labo*ur* and his ffrendys to helpe to susteyne the Cyte wi*th* corne of all maner of greyne.

S*um*ma iiij$\overset{xx}{}$ & xvij q*uar*ter and vj stryke.

97 qrs. 6 strike.

Me*m*. that ther was at that tyme xliij bakers wi*th*in the Cyte, the wiche dyd bake wekly a-mongest all vj$\overset{xx}{}$ q*uar*ter of whet & xij besyd*es* pese and Rye.

43 bakers who bake 132 qrs. of wheat every week.

---

[1] leaf 330, back.   [2] j C iiij$\overset{xx}{}$ xviij.   [3] Queer arithmetic.

§ 106. *Will. Wicam, Mayor,* 1521.

WILL. WICAM, MAYOR, 1521.

"Cluitas Coventre." Jan. 25.
Electors.

[1] ¶ [Election of new officers [2] "secu*ndu*m antiquam Consuetudine*m* Ciuitatis predicte ffacta per"]
Tho. Waren, M.G.S.T., Rob. Grene, Joh. Duddesbure, Ric. Marler, Joh. Strong, Ric. Hassall, Joh. Clark, Joh. Humfrey, Jul. Nethermyll, Tho. Astlen, Hug. Dawes, Tho. Banwell, Hen. Wall, Tho. Hyll, Ryc. Herryng, Rog. Walles, Will. Dawson, Joh. Cramp, Hum. Molsley, Jas. Gylbert, Ric. Kemsey, Ric. Totte, Tho. Gordon, Ric. Harres.

Officers.

[m., Will. Wicam,[3] drape*r* ; rec. Rad. Swyllyngton; cor. Joh. Boteler; steward, Joh. Porte*r* ; ch. Hugo Lawton, Rob. Seny; w., Rog. Palmer, Will. Alynson ; mace, Will. Alen ; crier, Ric. ffereby.]

EASTER AND MICHAELMAS LEETS.

"Cluitas Couentr*e*." Apr. 16.

[4] ¶ [V. f. p. held before Will. Wicam, m., Will. Towers, Ric. Ryse, on Tuesday, Apr. 16, 12 Hen. VIII.]
Tho. Waren, Rob. a Grene, Joh. Duddesbury, Ric. Marler, Joh. Strong, Joh. Clerke, Joh. Humfrey, Tho. Whyte, b. Tho. Smyth,[5] a. Jul. Nethermyll,[5] Hen. Pe*r*kyns, Tho. Astlyn, Hugo Dawes, Ric. Borwey, Hen. Wall, Ric. Herryng, Rog. Walles, Will. Dawson, Joh. Hyke*s*, Hug. Lawton, Rob. Seyne, Ric. Kemsey, Will. Banwell, Will. Smyth, drape*r*.

Coroner.

[Who elect Rob. Grene jun. coroner within the said city of the county of Coventry and liberty of the same.]

Office compulsory.

[Enacted] att This p*r*esent lete whereas in a lete holde*n* in the Tyme of M*ai*ster Joh. Bonde[6] that no man off what degre he be of, that is electyd[7] to any offyce, do Refuse hit & no peyne thereon is lymytyd, therfore hyt is agreyd and enactyd att this lete that if any pe*r*son from hensforthe be electyd Meyer & he

---

[1] leaf 331, back; another scribe. There is a space left unfilled for an ornamental initial.
[2] = [An election] made according to the ancient custom of the city by (names follow). This phrase follows the stereotyped election formula on this occasion.
[3] "Maistru*m*" prefixed.   [4] leaf 332.
[5] The a. and b. preceding these clearly shows that there was a due order observed in the names.
[6] See above, p. 668–9.   [7] "is electe" occurs lower.

§ 106. *Will. Wicam, Mayor. Leet*, 1521.

then absent hym-selffe and Refuse hyt he to pay to the Comen box a hundrethe poundes[1]; [for refusal to act as "Scheryffe," a hundred marks, as "Master of ether of the yeldes," £40, as chamberlain or warden, £20.] Provydyd allwey that ther be no man Chargeyd Twysse in one offyce, onles then he be Intretyd and content therwythall.

"The Maiors £100. For eleccion of officers. The Sheriffes, 100 markes. Chamberlaine and warden, xx li. No man to be charged with on office twise."

Also hyt is enacted & agreyd that euery aldurman serche hys warde & se whiche be Impotent and nedy beggers and euery of them that be amyttyd to beg to haue a Token of ther bagge of the signe of the Olyfaunt, & all other that haue no bagge not to be suffered to dwell in the Cytte, and that thei departe the Cytte with-in a nyght and a daye.

Aldermen to search for beggars. Every deserving beggar to have the city arms on his bag.

[2] ¶ [V. f. p. held on Tuesday before S. Dionysius' day, 13 Hen. VIII.]

"Ciuitas Coventrie." Oct. 8, 1521.

[Magister Tho. Waren, Magister Rob. Grene, Magister Joh. Duddesbury, Magister Ric. Marler, Magister Joh. Stronge, Magister Joh. Clarke, Magister Joh. Humfrey, Magister Joh. Bonde, Magister Tho. Smyth, Magister Tho. Whyte, Magister Hen. Perkyns, Magister Tho. Astlen, Magister Hugo Dawes,[1] Magister Ric. Burwey, Magister Tho. Banwell, Magister Hen. Wall, Magister Ric. Herryng, Magister Rog. Walles, Magister Will. Dawson, Magister Joh. Hykkys, Magister Joh. Cramp, Hugo Lawton, Rob. Seny, Ric. Kemsey.]

[Tho. Gopesell, Joh. Eborne.]

Sheriffs.

[Agreed] att this lete that there be euery yere Choson iiij ale Tastores[1] in euery warde, and that hit be geven them in commaundement by the aldurman of the warde that ij of them shal-be Redy att all tyme or Tymes[1] when any brewer in the warde sendith ffor them to gooe to the bruers howse and tast ther ale, & se that it be abull; & that thei se that they bruers sell no ale but by a Mesure sealyd with the Comen seale, apon the peyne of vj d. att euery defavte; and also that the seyde ale Tasturs schall see that ther be no Typlers in there warde sell any alle by any Mesure les[3] then it be sealed with the seale in the

4 "Ale-tasters" in each ward

to visit every brewer.

Standard measures.

---

[1] This scribe uses very often for final "s" the sign that stands for final "es."   [2] leaf 332, back.   [3] = unless.

C. LEET BK.   X X

§ 106. *Will. Wicam, Mayor. Leet,* 1521.

Cytte vseyd, apon lyke peyne, whether hyt [be] Mesures of pewter or of wode.

"Brewers" not to sell ale when malt is above 20d. a sextary.

[Ordained] att this lete that no bruer within this Cytte or the fforrens of the same sell any ale owt of his dore so long as Mavlt is of the price of a nobull or[1] a-bowe[1] xx d. a sestur. And yf the price of Malte be vndur the price of a noboll then the seyd bruers to sell ther ale for xviij d. a sestur; and that thei sell xiiij galondes to the sestur [or 6s. 8d. fine, to be paid to the sheriffs, half to the sheriffs' use, and half to the common box.] And if the seyde Marciment be nott payyd to the seyd Scheryffes att the furst askyng, then att the secunde askyng thei to pay for euere soche defavte xiij s. iiij d. And for defavte of payment of the seyd xiij s. iiij d. thei to ly in prison by the Meyres commaundement, ther to remayne vntyll soche tyme that thei haue payde the same Merceament.

Penalties for breaking this ordinance.

"Brewers."

[2] Also that no bruer sell no ale vntyll the ale-Tasters haue alowyd the same ale to bee good and sufficient, apon the peyne of euery bruer doyng the contrarie to pay vj d. to be apployd to the vse aforeseyde.

"Ale tasters."

[Ordained] that and casse be [3] that any of the seyd iiij ale Tastores in euere warde with-in this Cytte be necligent or remysse in doyng his office, when hee or thei be required by any of the seyd bruers, thei to forfett for euery defavte vj d. to be aployyd to the vse of the Comen box and the Scheryffes, as is afore-seyde.

"Tiplers"

[to] sell by sealed measures."

[Ordained] that euery ynholder and Typler within this Cytte and the forrens of the same schall sell a quarte of the best ale ffor ob. & a potell for a peny, and a galon off ale for ij d., & so to sell aftur the Rate; and that no bruer, ynholder or Typler schall sell no alle but by Mysure of pewter or of woode seallyd with the sealle of the Cytte apoynteyd & ordenyd for the same, apon the payne of euere soche offender that dothe the contrary for the ffurst defaute xl d., and for the secunde defavte vj s. viij d., and for the thyrde defaute Imprisoment by the Meires Commaundement vntyll the seyd Mercymentes be contentyd & payyd, and to be apployd the one halffe to the vse of the Scheryffes, and the other halffe to the Comen box.

[1] repeated. [2] leaf 333. [3] = if it happen.

§ 107. *Tho. White, Mayor*, 1522.

Also hit is Made that no bocher of this Cytte sell ane Taloo a-bowe the price of xx d. a stone; and the Chaundelers to sell ther Candull aftur a j d. a pownde, apon the peyne for euere defavte iij s. iiij d. to be payyd and gethereyd to the vse a-foreseyd withowt any ffauore or pardon.

"Talow."

THO. WHITE, MAYOR, 1522.

[1] [Election of a new mayor, recorder, coroner, steward, chamberlains, wardens, new . . . (cetera desunt).]

"Ciuitas Coventrie."

EASTER AND MICHAELMAS LEETS.

[2] ¶ V. f. p. held before Tho. White, m., Tho. Gobsell, Tho. Eyburn, b., on Tuesday after the Invention of the Holy Cross, 14 Hen. VIII.]

"Ciuitas Coventrie." May 6.

Joh. Bonde, Rob. Grene, Joh. Duddesbury, Ric. Marler, Ric. Hassall, Joh. Clerke, Joh. Humfrey, Tho. Waren, Will. Wycam, Hen. Wall, Tho. Smyth, Jul. Nethermyll, Henri Perkyns, Tho. Astlyn, Tho. Herryng, Joh. Cramp, Joh. Hykkes, Will. Parker, Will. Banwell, Ric. Povey, Ric. Townnesend, Jac. Hobson, Tho. Wylmer, Tho. Napton.

Be hyt rememberyd that where hyt was inactyd at a lete in the tyme of Maister Borwey,[3] m., that euere person what Craft he bee of comeyng to Inabet within the Cytte schall pay to the Maister of his Craft att the ende of the ffurst yere of his inabetyng v s., and in the ende of the seconde yeer other v s., hit is nowe agreyd & inacted that the same acte schall stonde in strenkeyth & effecte, and ffarther that att the ende of the fforst yere the same persones schall put in sufficient suertes to the Maister of his or ther Crafte to paye the same v s. in the iiij [? ij] yere acordyng to the same acte.

Orders of leet. Stranger craftsmen's fines.

[Enacted] that the ten men Choson & heraftur to be Choson getherars for the Comen box schall receve ther rerttes yerly of the Comen Grownde last taken yn be-fore the feaste of the holy Rode.[4]

Rent gatherers of the common lands.

Also that the Tenauntes of all the same Comen Growndes

"Comon grounde"

---

[1] leaf 333, back. [2] leaf 334. [3] See above, p. 655.
[4] Sept. 14.

§ 107. *Tho. White, Mayor. Leet*, 1522.

to be sown with wheat. — last taken yn to be seuerall schall yerly plowe & sowe all or halffe the same Growndes or els to fforfet ther takes[1] & leses.

The holy cakes. — Also that no man of this Cytte schall by whete ffor the hale-cakes[2] in the Market before the ower of a-leven of the cloke, on-les hit be bowght by the Comen seriaunt of the Citte, apon peyne of euere defavte xl d.

"Fishemongers" not to sell (salted) fish until it be sufficiently soaked in water. — [Enacted] that all ffyshemongers as sone as thei, or anne of them, haue solde ther well-watur fysche thei schall vp ther bordes, & washe vp non to sell that daye nor vntyll hit be well waturyd, apon peyn of euere defawte xl d. Allso that no fyshemonger by no ffreyshe Code in the Market be-fore the ower of ij of the Cloke aftur-none, apon lyke peyne.

"Fish & ffishmongers." — Also that no maner of ffreshe sey ffyshe schal-be in the Market to sell aftur the ower of ij of the Cloke, apon peyn of fforfetur to the prisoners.

"Chambleyns. Chamberlins to haue Little Parke." — [3] [Enacted] that the Chamberlens of the Cittee schal-be restoreyd to the Lyttull Parke to ocupi hit as thei haue don in tymes past and the Scheryffes to be dischargeyd therof.

"Apparell for shireffes." — Hit is inacted that the Scheryffes of the Cytte, nowe choson & heraftur to be choson, schall were in ther gowndes nothor fforre of ffoyndes,[4] nor marturnes, nor no veluet in ther dwblettes nor jerkyns or partletes,[5] except he or thei be notyd and knowyn in this Cytte to be of the Substans of iij li.$\overset{c}{}$ & a-bowe, a-pon peyne of euere man so offendyng to fforfet xx[ti] markes to be leveyd by the Meyre to the vse of the Comen box.

"Apparell" for commoners. — Also that all Comeners within this Cytte vndur the degre of a Scheryffe schall where in ther gowndes ffeore of ffox, schankes[6] or lambe & none other fforres, & in ther Dublettes or Jakettes bott Chamlet,[7] Saten of Bryges[8] or wolsted, & none other sylkes, on-les he be notyd & knowyn

---

[1] Take = a holding.   [2] v. p. 417.   [3] leaf 334, back.
[4] Fur of the beech-marten. L. fagina = a beech tree. v. Stat. 6 Hen. VIII. c. 1 (*Soc. Eng.* III. 161.) for sumptuary laws.
[5] Partlet = collar, ruff, or habit-shirt.
[6] Fur of animals' legs.
[7] Originally an Eastern fabric, and at one time made up from the hair of the Angora goat.
[8] Bruges.

§ 107. *Tho. White, Mayor. Leet*, 1522.

to be of the valure & substauns¹ of a C li. & a-bowe, [or £10 fine to be levied as above.]

Item, that no seruant man or woman reteyneyd for wages within this Citte where veluet in ² eny other aparell apon them, apon the peyne of ffarfatur of the same aparell to the vse of the Comen box of the Cytte, & upon peyne of imprisoment. "Apparell" for servants.

Also wher-as in tymes past the scheryffes hathe byn Chargeyd with the payment of xx^ti markes to Maister Recorder of this Cytte ffor hys ffee, hyt [is] enactyd (etc.) that for the terme of this thre yere next Insuyng that the seyd scheryffes new electe & here-aftur to be electe duryng the seyd thre yeres to be dyschargeyd in condicion that the seyd scheryffes newe electe take ther office on them lovyngly withowt contradiccion. And also the seyd eleccion haue condecendyd & agreyd that the xx markes schal-be born in maner & forme folowyng, þat is to sey, the Maister of the Trinite Gilde schall paye vj li. xiij s. iiij d., Item, the Maister of the Corpus Christi Gylde viij markes, & Item, the wardens of the Citte for the tyme beyng v markes. "Payments by the Shireffes"

defrayed by the gilds and wardens.

Hyt is ordenyd & inacted att this Comen cownsell daye³ that Maister Meyer of this Cytte ffor the tyme beyng schall yerly ffrom hensfforth⁴   shall⁵ Chose & apoynt ij onest men of this Cytte to be serchers of all lether to be solde within this Cytte, & that they thynke & alowe to be sufficient tannyd to sett a seall, whiche shal-be ordenyd & delyuerd ffor the same ; & the seyd serchers schall haue for ther labores vj s. viij d., the one halfe of the Tanners & the other halffe of the cordeners,⁶ and for euery hyd by them seallyd beyng fownde insufficient thei to fforfet xij d. to the vse of the Comen box. "Searchers of Leather."

"Tanners."

⁷ ¶ [V. f. p. held on Tuesday after Michaelmas, 14 Hen. VIII.] "Ciuitas Couentrie." Sept. 30.

---

¹ A mark looking like "*au*" above the line occurs sometimes in conjunction with "un."
² (?) read "or." Apparel = (1) attire ; (2) trimming, embellishment.
³ Sic. The Common Council must by this time have transacted the business of the Leet, when it was thought needful.
⁴ Blank follows in MS.   ⁵ redundant.
⁶ Cordwainers, shoemakers.   ⁷ leaf 335.

§ 107. *Tho. White, Mayor. Leet*, 1522.

[M*agister* Joh. Bonde,[1] Rob. Grene, Joh. Duddesbury, Ric. Marler, Ric. Harssall, Joh. Clarke, Joh. Humfrey, Tho. Waren, Will. Wycam, Hen. Wall, Tho. Smyth, Jul. Nethermyll, Hen. Perkyns, Tho. Astlyn, Ric. Burwey, Tho. Banwell, Ric. Herryng, Rog. Walles, Will. Dawson, Joh. Hykkys, Joh. Crampp, Will. Towers, Ric. Ryse, [1]Will. Parker.]

Sheriffs.   [Ric. Wether, Will. Tyllet.]

"No Baker, Bocher, Vitteler to be on *the*[2] graunde Jurie."

[" Inactyd "] that ffrom-hensforthe that ther schall no baker, bocher nor no whyttelleer be on[3] of the xxiiij [4]electyd for the graunt Jure[4] att any lete to be holden within thys Cytte heraft*ur*.[5]

"Assise of bred."

[Ordained] that M*aister* Meyre [4]for the tyme beyng[4] schall geyffe the bakers ther assyse aftur the price of the best whete in the Market by-cavse þe xxiiij[6] wolde haue them kepe ther full syse.

"Bakers" not to diminish the weight of the ha'penny loaf.

Also that eu*er*e baker ffrom-hensfforth kepe his ffull syse, & yf he lake in the whyght of a havpeny whete loff, eu*er*y baker so offendyng to paye xij d. [7]And if he be fownde defectyve abowe that then he to paye aftur the Rate for his [8] defaute.

"Bakers"

[Agreed] att the seyd lete that if any of the seyd bakers offende too tymes that then M*aister* Meyer ffor the tyme beyng schall gyffe hym warnyng to bake no more vntyll he haue ffownde schvrty to kepe the assyse that M*aister* Meyer dothe gyff hym ffrom that day fforward, a-pon the peyne of xl s.

to furnish security to keep the assize.

"Bakers" to sell three loaves a penny.

[Ordained] that the bakers schall bake no horsse-bred but of good stuffe, and that they sell no more for a peny but[9] iij lovis & xiij to the desen, & that thei kepe ther assyse that M*aister* Meyre gyffeth them, apon peyne att the furst defavte ij s., & if he be fownde favte any other tyme then M*aister* Meyer for the tyme beyng to gyffe hym warnyng to bake no more in the peyne of xl s. vntyll he haue fownd suerte [10]to be bowndon in the some of xl s.[10] to kepe hys assyse from that day fforward.

"Bakers"

[Ordained] that and yf any baker [9]wit*h*in this Cytte[9]

---

[1] Every name with the exception of the last is preceded by M*agister*.
[2] A later hand. þ here written y.   [3] MS. om.
[4]–[4] Interlined.   [5] See *Life in an Old Engl. Town*, p. 106.
[6] The Leet Jury.   [7] See above, p. 385.   [8] deletions.
[9] repeated.   [10]–[10] interlined.

§ 107. *Tho. White, Mayor. Leet*, 1522.

from hensforth sell or gyffe[1] any horsse bred[2] aboue iij loue*s* for a penne &[2] xiij^{th} to the dosen, that then the seyd baker schall fforfet ffor eue*ry* defavte vj s. viij d. to [be] leueyd by the scheryfe*s* of the Cytte,[2] halffe to them[1] & halffe to the[2] vse of the[2] Comen box.

to sell horsebread, three loaves a penny.

[3][Ordained] that all bruers & Typlers order them-selffe to sell ther ale wi*th* sealyd Mesure*s* soche as byn ordenyd, apon the peyne of the ffurst defavte vj s. viij d. ; and iff thei be ffownde favte an-other tyme that then M*aister* Meier ffor the yere beyng schall Gyffe them warnyng to sell no more alle vntyll thei haue fownd suertes to obse*r*ue & kepe the seyd acte, apon the peyne of xl d. alffe (*sic*) to the sheryffys & halffe to the Comen box.

"Brewers" to use sealed measures,

and also to find surety to observe this ordinance.

Also lefull be hyt to eue*ry* bocher wi*th*in this Cytte to sley of eue*ry* mane*r* of kynd of fflesch resonabull ffor mannys mete as moche as hym lykyth, and as oft, & that no ca*u*e nor ordenaunce[4] be made among the bochers to the contrary, apon the peyne of C s., and that eue*ry* bocher that obeyth to any soche Caue or ordenaunce[4] by the Masturs or by the Crafte so made he to paye att eue*ry* defawte xx s., halffe to [the] sheryffe*s* and halffe to the Comen box.

"Bochers" to kill when they like

notwithstanding any cave to the contrary.

[Ordained] that no bruer in this Citte bruve any all wi*th* hoppis, [or 20s. fine each time, half to the sheriffs, half to the common box.]

"Brewers" not to use hops.

[Ordained] that and yff the Scheryffe*s* do not gether all the merseamente*s* that byn delyue*ry*d vnto them wi*th*-in vj weke*s* aftur the strete*s* delyue*r*yd to ther hande*s*, that then M*aister* Meyer for the yere beyng schall [take] the seyd strette*s* owt of the Scheryffe*s* hande*s* & delyue*r* them to the Comen se*r*geant & he to gether them to the vse of the Comen box.

*" Shireffe*s* to gather t*he* streets within 6 weekes, or else to be gathered by serjant."*

Also hyt is agreyd (etc.) that no shomaker nor Correer nor n*o* man ffor them schall by no Talo wi*th*in the Cytte, on-les he by hyt betwene the ffeaste*s* of Mydsom*er* & Lammas, apon peyne att eue*ry* defavte a C s. to be leveyd halffe to the scheryffe*s* & halffe to the Comen box.

"Shomakers for talow."

[5][Inacted] that [no] Tann*er* schall sell lether onles hit be

Tanners not to sell

---

[1] deletions follow. [2] interlined. [3] leaf 335, back.
[4] The mark over "n" here resembles a*u* redundant.
[5] See p. 681.

§ 108. *Jul. Nethermill, Mayor,* 1523.

"Lether" unless it be sealed.

sealyd with the sealle aforseyde, and ffor euere hyde otherwysse solde the seller to fforfet xl d. and the byer other xl d. to the vse of the Comen box.

"Corioures" not to curry unsealed leather.

Also that no Coreer within this Citte Core any lether but soche as is seallyd with the seyde seall, apon peyne of fforfet for euery hyde soo Tanneyd xl d.

JULINES NETHERMILL, MAYOR, 1523.
EASTER AND MICHAELMAS LEETS.

"Ciuitas Coventrie." Apr. 21.

[1] [V. f. p. before Jul. Nethermill, m., Ric. Wethers, Will. Tillett, b., Tuesday before S. George's day, 14 Hen. VIII.]

¶ Will. Wikame, Rob. Grene, Joh. Duddesbury, Ric. Hassall, Joh. Clerk, Joh. Humfrey, Tho. Waren, Joh. Bonde, Tho. Banwell, Tho. Smyth, Hen. Wall, Tho. Astelyn, Ric. Burwey, Ric. Herryng, Will. Towres, Tho. Dodd, Joh. Cramp, Tho. Gopsill, Joh. Eyburne, Geo. Philips, Will. Banwell, Ric. Povie, Tho. Napton, Tho. Wilmer.

"Error in Curia."

[Enacted] that whosoeuer frome-hensforth doith sue eny wrytt of Error [2] or Certiorari [3] to remove eny recorde or pleynt out of the kynges Court of this Cite shall pay for the allowaunce of the same writt [4] or Error or certiorari the feez afore-tyme accustumed, and ouer & besides the same vj s. viij d. to the shireffes of the seid Citie for the tyme beyng etc.

Fees for the writ.

"Graund warrant." [5]

[Enacted] that the shireffes of the Citie for the tyme beyng frome-hensfurth shall graunt no graund warraunt [5] to be executed upon eny Townesman of this Citie without license & assent of Maister Meire for the tyme beyng etc.

[6] *"No speciall Capias without mayor and sheriffs." [6]*

Only "bochers"

[Enacted] that no dweller within this Citie shall comenlie sell or retaill eny maner of flesshe for vitaill within this Citie oneles he be of the Crafte of bochers or elles

are allowed to sell meat,

---

[1] leaf 336, back. Scribe I. Marginal notes are now usually in this scribe's hand.

[2] A writ to procure the reversal of a judgment on the ground of error (*N. E. D.*).

[3] A writ from a superior to an inferior court to call up for trial the record of the latter upon the complaint of a party that he has not received justice or cannot have a fair trial there. The word *certiorari* (= to be certified) occurs in the writ. [4] (?) of.

[5] The term "grand warrant" is unknown to Sir F. Pollock and Prof. E. Jenks; the latter agrees to the suggestion that it may probably refer to the process of arrest on Capias, though the use of the word "grand" is unexplained. [6–6] A later hand.

§ 108. *Jul. Nethermill, Mayor. Candles*, 1523.

brother to the same, vpon peyne who doith the contrarie to forfeit for euery defaute x s; and that it shall be laufull for the shireffes of the seid Citie for the tyme beyng havyng knowlege & prove of the seid offendoures to arrest & imprisone theme in the comen gaoll vntill the haue payed the seyd forfeyture; and the same forfeiture to be distributed in thre partes, wherof oon to the Meire & the other twoo to the shireffes for the tyme beyng etc. under pain of fine and imprisonment.

Item, forasmoche as Jas. Hobson & Ric. Niclyn, Bochers, with other haue taken vpon theme to be bounde to the Maisters of the Citie & serue & fynde all the Citie sufficient Candle of the price of peny & farthyng the pounde & xiij li. to the dosyne for the space of vij yeires next ensuyng, it is therfor enacted at this lete that no persones (*sic*) or personez of the Crafte of bochers within this Citie shall bargeyn or sell eny Talowe to eny persone or persones within this Citie or without, but onelie to the seid Jas. Hobsone & Ric. Niclyne & other foure mene by the same James & Richard to be named & assigned, [or 40s. fine to be levied by the sheriffs, half to the use of the sheriffs and half to the common box.] "Candelles" to be supplied by six persons only at 1¼d. per lb.

[1] Item, where-as by auctorite of dyuers letes holden in tymes past within this Citie the Craftes of smythes & Goldsmythes be vnite & knyt together in one with dyuers other occupacions Joyntlie to be contributories to all fynes & imposicions amonges the seid occupacions to be payed & levied, and to be present at all assembles as mariages, burialles, or otherwise whatsoeuer they be, by theme accustomed to be kept & mayntened, as by ther priuate ordinaunces affirmed by the seid leetes [2] pleynlie it may appere; betwene whome of lait dyuers controuersies & debates haue Risen & bene moved for the nonperfourmaunce of the same to the greit Inquietnes of Maister Meire & the Counsell of the Citie & to the hurt & hynderaunce of the seid occupacions: It is therfor at this leet establisshed & enacted in avoidyng of like troublez hereafter to ensue that the seid Craft of Goldsmythes frome The "Smythes & Goldsmythes" have fallen to disputing among themselves. The goldsmiths are

---

[1] leaf 337.
[2] For inspection of craft rules by the officers and council see p. 32. No copy of the smiths' rules has hitherto appeared in the Leet Book; but see those of the cappers, pp. 572–4.

§ 109. Tho. Banwell, Mayor, 1524.

ordered to pay their fines as usual,

hensfurthe shall not onelie for ther partes pay all suche fynes & imposicions due & accustomed by theme or eny of theme to be levied & payed for brekyng of eny of the seid ordinaunces, but also they shall at all tymes herafter be present at all Mariages, burielles & other assembles whatsoever they be, likewise as eny of the other occupacions to theme vnite & knyt doo accustume theme to keip accordyng to ther seid ordinaunces maid & establisshed & affirmed, as is aforsaid, vpon the peyne to ryne[1] in the forfeyture of the penalties of the same, and also to abide further punyshement of Maister Meire & the Councell of the seid Citie etc.

and attend assemblies.

"Ciuitas Couentrie."

[[2] V. f. p. held before Jul. Nethermill, m., Ric. Wethers, Will. Tillett, b., (cetera desunt).]

THO. BANWELL, MAYOR, 1524.

"Ciuitas Couentrie." Jan. 25, 1524.

[[3] Election of officers.]

[Magister[4] Ric. Marler, Ric. Hassall, Joh. Clerke, Joh. Humfrey, Joh. Bonde, Will. Wicame, Tho. Astlelene, Tho. Wilmer, Hen. Perkyns, Ric. Burwey, Ric. Herryng, Rog. Wales, Will. Dawson, Joh. Hickes, Joh. Cramp, Will. Towres, Ric. Rise, Tho. Gopsill, Ric. Wethers, Will. Tillett, [5] Chr. Mereman, Geo. Philips, Tho. Ward, Joh. Hill.[5]]

Officers.

[m. Tho. Banwell,[6] draper; rec. Rad. Swillyngton; cor. Rob. Grene; steward, Baldw. Porter; ch. Rob. Kyrvyn, Tho. Gardenour; w. Hen. Kylby, Sim. Parker; mace, Will. Alene; crier, Rog. Fraby.]

LEETS.

"Ciuitas Couentrie." Apr. 12.

[7] [V. f. p. held before Tho. Banwell, m., Tho. Wilmer, Tho. Spenser, b., Apr. 12, 15 Hen. VIII.]

¶ Tho. White, Ric. Marler, Ric. Hassall, Joh. Humfrey, Tho. Waren, Joh. Bonde, Will. Wicame, Julynus Nethermill, Tho. Astelen, Tho. Smyth, Hen. Wall, Hen. Perkyns,

---

[1] ? = run, v. p. 170. [2] leaf 337, back.
[3] leaf 338. The usual formula employed at the election concludes with the words "secundum antiquam consuetudinem Ciuitatis predicte" = according to the ancient custom of the said city.
[4] Magister before all names till note 5. [5-5] Untitled.
[6] Magistrum prefixed. [7] leaf 338, back.

§ 109. *Tho. Banwell, Mayor. Leet,* 1524.

Ric. Heryng, Rog. Wales, Tho. Dodd, Joh. Crampe, Will. Dawson, Joh. Hickkes, Will. Towres, Ric. Rise, Tho. Gopsill, Ric. Wethers, Will. Tillett, Rob. Kirvin.

¹ In primis, it is enacted (etc.) that no begger of this Citie fromehensfurthe shall begge within the two parishe Churches of this Citie in the tyme of Goddes seruice vsed ther, vpon peyn to be punysshed by imprisonment of the stokkes by the space of a day & a nyght; and that ther shal-be on certeyn persone assigned by the Meire for the tyme beynge to viewe & execute yeirelie the seid acte. *"Beggers" forbidden to beg in the churches during service.*

Item, it is enacted that the acte concernyng Clothe-makyng maid in the tyme of Maister Burwey, Meire of this Citie, shall stande & be in effecte & duelie executed frome-hensfourthe accordyng to the tenour of the seid acte; and for thexecucion of the same acte ther be now elected, as serchers for true weyvyng, Will. Dale & Owyne Blakmere, weivers, and for true walkyng, Joh. Grene & Rauf Worseley, walkers. ²*"Anno Henry 8. 9 foll. 322."* ² *The previous act concerning "Clothmakyng" to be put into effect.*

Item, ther is elected Hen. Braynesforde, draper, to be sealer of Clothe with the seale of this Citie, and to haue for his ffee of euery clothe sealed j d. *A sealer appointed.*

Item, ther is elected Tho. Boithe as sercher of wolles sold within this Citie. *A searcher of wool.*

Item, it is enacted that euery Craftes-mane within this Citie shall fromehensfurthe take as meny prentises & Journemen as they woll accordyng to the liberties of this Citie, eny acte or caue tofore maid to the contrary not-withstandyng.³ *No limit to "prentises & Journemen."*

[Enacted] that all the Journemen of euery Crafte in this Citie shall brynge in & deliuer ther bokes of ther Caues & actes to Maister Meire at suche tyme as he woll appoynt or warne theme, vpon peyne of imprisonement.⁴ *"Journeymen" to bring in their rules.*

⁵[Enacted] that so longe as the Crafte of Shomakers fynde & keip ther preist they shall reteyne & keipe in ther handes to ther owne vse yeirelie the Marke of money, which thei were wont to pay yierelie by acte of leete to the Crafte of Tanners. Prouided alweyes that the seid *"Shomakers & Tanners."*

---

¹ On poor relief see *Victoria County Hist. Warw.*, II, pp. 164 *sqq.*
²⁻² See above, p. 656. A much later hand.
³ See the cappers' rules, p. 573.
⁴ See Introduction.   ⁵ leaf 339.

Craft of Shomakers shall pay vnto the seid Tanners at Corpus *Christ*i tide next ensuyng vj s. viij d.

"Ale wyves." [Enacted] that all the ale wyves & tiplers of this Citie shall sell ther ale by measures sealed, accordyng to the acte maid in the tyme of M*aiste*r Wikame,[1] Meire, [or 3s. 4d. fine each time to the sheriffs.]

*"Ciuitas Coventri*e.*"* Sept. 27.

[2][V. f. p. held on Tuesday before Michaelmas, 16 Hen. VIII.]

Jury.

¶ [M*agiste*r Tho. White,[3] Ric. Ma*r*ler, Ric. Hassall, Joh. Humfrey, Tho. Waren, Joh. Bonde, Will. Wicame, Jul. Nethermill, Tho. Astelen, Hen. Wall, Nic. Heynes, Hen. P*er*kyns, Ric. Herryng, Rog. Wales, Will. Dawson, Joh. Hick*es*, Tho. Dodd, Joh. Cramp, Will. Towres, Ric. Rice, Tho. Gopsill, Rob. Kyrvyn,[4] Tho. Gardeno*ur*,[4] Hum. Moseley.[4]

Sheriffs.

[Will. Smyth, Tho. Trussell.]

"Rauf Swillyngton, Recorder," who took oath to dwell in the city half the year,

Wher-as Rauff Swillyngton, Recorder of this Citie, tyme of his admission to the office of Recorder, p*r*omysed by his corp*or*all othe to be resident & demurraunt[5] w*ith*in this Citie, the on half of the yeir, or the moost pa*r*t therof,

except in times of plague,

except & savyng suche tymes as the greit sekenes[6] shulde reign within the Citie, and except such tymes as he shuld be conu*er*saunt at London. It is now ordeyned by auctorite of this lete by thadvice of the Meire, alderme*n* & the Co*m*ens of this Citie ther assembled, that forasmoche as the seid Rauf is nowe gen*er*all attou*r*ney to o*u*r soue*r*eig*n* lorde, the kynge,[7] be nowe by the seid auctorite

is released from this obligation.

exon*er*at, releassed, put at large & discharged of hi*s* seid othe hertofore maid in that behalf, and that the seid Rauf shal-be here at the ij gen*er*all Cessiones & great letes after Michelmas & Eister to be holden & ij dayes before & ij dayes after, or more or lesse, as the busynes for the Citie thene shall require, if the sekenes reign not in the Citie, or that he be occupied otherwise in the kyng*es* busynes.

Weavers to have "for

[8][Enacted] that the weivers of this Citie shall haue for

---

[1] *v.* p. 677.   [2] leaf 339, back.
[3] All names save the last three preceded by M*agiste*r.
[4] Untitled.   [5] = dwelling, abiding.
[6] The sweating sickness was very rife in 1517 ; the plague in 1521. See Traill, *Soc. England*, III, 145, 257.
[7] Supply "he."   [8] leaf 340.

§ 110. Nic. Heynes, Mayor, 1525.

the weyvyng of eue*r*y Cloithe, to the makyng wherof goithe & is putt iiij̽ & viij li. of woll or more to the nombre of iiij̽ li. & xvj, v s. for the weyvyng of eue*r*y such Clothe, and if the seid Cloithe conteyn aboue the seid nombr*e* Then the weyvyng to be payed for as the parties Cane agre, and if the Cloith conteyn vnder the seid nombr*e* then the oner to pay for weyvyng but iiij s. vj d. And if the Clothe be maid of restes or grene woll[1] then to pay as the p*ar*ties cane agree ; and the payment to b*e* maid in redie money & not in wares, as it is wont to be. And who refuseth thus to do & so p*r*oued befor M*aister* Meire to forfett for eue*r*y said defaut iij s. iiij d. to be levied by the s*er*chars of the seid Craft of weyvers, w*ith* an officer to theme appoynted by the seid Meire, to the vse of the com*e*n box.

[Enacted] that eue*r*y Clothier within this Citie shall pay for walkyng of eue*r*y Cloithe of Grene woll or midle woll iij s. iiij d., and for eue*r*y Cloith of fyne woll as the Clothier & the walker can agre, and that the Clothier do pay therfor in redie money & not in wares [or 3s. 4d. each time to the common box.]

[No country tanner to buy beast hides, raw or untanned, upon the market day or any other day before 12 o'clock,[2] or 6s. 8d. fine, to be levied on the butcher, or other person selling the same, to the common box.]

[Enacted] that if eny p*er*son of this Citie beyng no bocher do kyll eny beiff*es*, Mottons, veilles, porkett*es*, or lambes w*ith*in this Citie, [he] shall not retayll eny of the seid vitall by lesse porc*i*on then the half or the quarter [or 6s. 8d. fine each time to the common box.]

NIC. HEYNES, MAYOR, 1525.

[3][Election of officers before Tho. Banwell, m., Tho. Wilmer,[4] Tho. Spens*er*,[4] b., on the feast of the Conversion of S. Paul, 16 Hen. VIII . . . cetera desunt.]

Marginalia: weyvyng of Clothes," to which from 88 to 96 lbs. of wool go, 5s., — and for those of less weight, 4s. 6d. — The payment is to be in ready money, not truck wages. — Clothier to pay "for walkyng of Clothes" 3s. 4d. — "Tann*er*s." — Against "retaillyng of vitayll." — Jan. 25, 1525.

---

[1] Evidently wool of inferior quality : but whether discoloured or obtained from a poor fleece I do not know. For payments cf. p. 660.
[2] MS. "the owre of xii of the Cloke."   [3] leaf 341.
[4] These bailiffs' and sheriffs' names are put in error, see above, p. 688, and below, p. 690.

§ 110. Nic. Heynes, Mayor. Hunting, 1525.

EASTER LEETS.

"Ciuitas Couentrie."
Apr. 27.

[V. f. p. held before Nic. Heynes, m., Will. Smyth,[1] Tho. Trussell,[1] b., on Thursday after S. Mark's day, 17 Hen. VIII.]

[¶ Jul. Nethermyll, M*a*gister[2] Ric. M*a*rler, Ric. Hassall, Joh. Humfrey, Will. Wicame, Tho. Whit, Ric. Herryng, Tho. Smyth, Hen. Wall, Tho. Astelen, Hen. P*er*kyns, Rog. Wales, Will. Dawson, Joh. Hicke*s*, Tho. Dod, Will. Towres, Ric. Rise, Tho. Spens*er*, Tho. Gopsill, [3] Hen. Burne, Will. Ridyng, Cristofer Wadde, Tho. Burdon, Ric. Townesend.]

"For hunters & hawkers."

Wher-as in tyme past dyu*er*s & meny of the Inh*a*bit-ant*es* w*ith*in this Citie disposed to Idlenes not havyng xl s. of freholde by yeire inordinatlie haue vsed to hawke & to hunt, kepyng hauke*s*, greyhounde*s* & hounde*s*, spaniell*es*, ferette*s*, hey*es*,[4] Targes,[5] & other engennes, wherby all maner of fowles & beast*es* of waren & of chace be excessyvelie taken & distroyed, not feryng the penal-ties of dyu*er*s & meny good estatut*es* maid by auctorite of p*ar*liament for the punyshement of the same, wherby moche idlenes & pou*er*tie is greatelie encreassed w*ith*in this Citie. It is therfor establisshed (etc.) that no p*er*sone inh*a*bited w*ith*in this Citie ner the libe*r*tiez of the same fromehensfurth do p*re*sume to keip eny hauke*s*, grey-hounde*s*, or hounde*s*, ferette*s*, hayes, Targes or eny other engennes, ner do p*re*sume to hunt or to hauke w*ith* the same, oneles they may dispend xl s. of frehold by yeire, vpon the peyne to rone in suche penalties as be exp*re*ssed in the seid estatut*es* and that to pay for eu*er*y tyme so offendyng vj s. viij d. to be levied by the shireff*es*, the on half to ther owne vse and the other half to the Co*m*en box of the Citie etc.

The use of nets and other engines t (take game forbidden

except in the case of 40s. freeholders.

[6] Item, wher-as by auctoritie of lete holden w*ith*in this Citie in the tyme of M*ai*ster Burwey,[7] Meire of the same, it was ordeyned that it shuld be lawfull to the inh*a*bit-aunt*es* & apprentices of this Citie & to estraung*er*s to

"Prentices & other

---

[1] See p. 689, note 4. [2] Title repeated until note 3. [3] Untitled.
[4] A net used particularly to catch rabbits. *N. E. D. s. v.* hay.
[5] This word is unknown to Dr. Hen. Bradley and the compilers of the *New English Dictionary* in any sense connected with sport.
[6] leaf 342. [7] *v.* p. 655.

§ 110. Joh. Humfrey, Mayor. Leet, 1525. 691

inhabite & to sett vp ther craft or facultie in this Citie, what Craft or facultie so euer they were of, paying to the Maisters of the same Crafte x s. for fyne, that is to say, at the ende of the first yeire after ther settyng vp ther seid Crafte v s., and at the ende of the first yeire after that other v s. ; ffor-asmoche as it is now compleyned & enfourmed[1] at this lete that meney of the seid persons, so settyng vp ther craftes, do depart the Citie before thende of the seid first yeire, & before eny peny of the seid fyne of tene shelynges be payed in fourme aforseid : It is therfor enacted at this present lete that euery persone that haith beene full prentise within this Citie, & doithe[2] sett vp his occupacion or Craft within the same, shall pay frome-hensfurth at ther furst settyng vp ther seid Craft to the Maisters of the Craft iij s. iiij d., and at the ende of the first yeire of ther occupying other iij s. iiij d. And that euery estraunger that so shall sett vp his Craft within the seid Citie shall pay in like maner x s. to the Maisters of his Craft as befor is seyed.[3] And that euery persone that so herafter shall sett vp his occupacion within this Citie shall fynde ij sufficient suerties to be bounde vnto the Maister of the Craft for payment of the seid fyne. And that the same persone so settyng vp his Craft shall be obedient vnto all ordinaunces & estatutes of his occupacion etc.

settyng vp ther occupacions"

to pay their fines, half on setting up, and half at the end of the first year,

and to find security.

JOH. HUMFREY, MAYOR, 1525.
MICHAELMAS LEET.

[4] ¶ [V. f. p. held before Joh. Humfrey,[5] m., Will. Smyth, Tho. Trussell, b., on Tuesday after S. Dionysius' day, 17 Hen. VIII.]

"Ciuitas Couentrie." Oct. 10.

[Magister Jul. Nethermyll, Ric. Hassall,[6] Tho. Waren, Joh. Bonde, Will. Wicame, Will. Whit, Tho. Banwell, Ric. Herryng, Tho. Smyth, Hen. Wall, Tho. Astelen, Hen. Perkyns, Rog. Wales, Will. Dawsen, Joh. Hickes, Joh.

Jury.

---

[1] = to lay information or complaint. A curious impersonal use of the verb.
[2] Characteristic of this scribe.
[3] *i.e.* half at setting up, and half at the end of the first year.
[4] leaf 343, back.   [5] He served out Heynes' year. See p. 692.
[6] All save the last three are called " Magister."

§ 111. Hen. Wall, Mayor, 1526.

Cramp, Will. Towres, Tho. Gopsill, Ric. Wethers, Tho. Wylmer, Tho. Spenser, Will. Rydyng,[1] Tho. Burdon,[1] Humf. Moseley.[1]]

Sheriffs.
[Ric. Townesend, Skynner, Hugh Lawton, Capper.]

"For thelleccion of Constables."
[Enacted] that every alderman of this Citie yeirelie frome-hensfurth with-in iij or iiij [2]dayes[2] after Michelmas lett shall elect & chose onest & well ruled persones within his warde to be constables, and every of the seid aldermen to sertifie the names of the seid Constables vnto the Shireffes for the tyme beyng in wrytyng, and[3] the seid Shireffes to swere the same persones in the office of Constables etc.

"For thenclosyng of Comens."
[Enacted] that all such comen groundes as haue bene latelie inclosed about this Citie shall fromehensfurth bee Comen as they haue bene vsed in auncient tyme & no more to be enclosed, accordyng to the ententes & myndes of the xlviij Mene appoynted for the resonyng of the same so that the kynges grace & his Councell be contented to affirme the same.[4]

"For drying of malt."
[Enacted that no person dry any malt with straw within this city, or 20s. fine each time to be levied by the sheriffs to their own use.]

HEN. WALL, MAYOR, 1526.
EASTER AND MICHAELMAS LEETS.

"Ciuitas Couentrie." May 1.
[5][V. f. p. held before Hen. Wall, m., Ric. Townesende, Hugo Lawton, b., on Tuesday SS. Philip and James, 18 Hen. VIII.]

[Magister Tho. Banwell, Ric. Hassall,[6] Joh. Humfrey, Tho. Warene, Joh. Bonde, Will. Wicame, Tho. White, Tho. Smyth, Tho. Astelen, Ric. Herryng, Hen. Perkyns, Rog. Wales, Will. Dawson, Joh. Hickes, Will. Towres,

---

[1] Untitled.   [2-2] repeated.   [3] deletions follow.
[4] v. p. 679. The commons had been enclosed for corn sowing in time of dearth. This order was the sequel of a rising which took place on "Ill Lammas Day," when "the Commons of Coventre rose & pulled down the gates and hedges of the grounds inclosed; and they that were in the Cittie shutt the Newgate against the Chamberlains and their Company. The Mayor was almost smothered in the Throng; he held with the Commons, for which he was carried as prisoner to London : he was put out of his office, and Mr. John Humphery served out his year." Harl. MS. 6388.
[5] leaf 344, back.   [6] Magister prefixed. See p. 693, note 1.

§ 112. *Ric. Herryng, Mayor*, 1527.

Tho. Gopsill, Tho. Spenser,[1] Rob. Smyth, Ric. Ives, Will. Banwell, Tho. fforman, Will. Rogers, Rob. Kirvyn, Tho. Gardenour.]

[Enacted] that the Journemen of the Craft of Cappers within this Citie shall fromehensfurth keip ther owres & tymes in beyng at ther worke as is lymyt in an acte maid at a lete holden in the tyme of Maister Joh. Bonde, Meire,[2] vpon peyn to be abriged ther wages by ther Maisters accordyng to the tyme of ther absence. — *"Journemen of Cappers" to keep their appointed hours.*

[Enacted] that all Carvers within this Citie frome-hensfurth shal-be associat with the Craft of peyntoures, and that euery Carver shall pay yeirelie to the peyntoures towardes the Charges of ther pagiaunt xij d. without contradiction, vpon peyn for euery defaut to forfett vj s. viij d. to the seid Craft of peyntoures, and that the seid Carvers frome-hensfurth shal-be dismyssed & discharged frome the Craft of Carpenters, and that Richard Tenwynter shall pay suche arrerages to the Carpenters as he oweth theme for the xij d. which he shuld haue payed theme yierelie in tymes past.[3] [4] — *"Carvers to be associat with peynters."*

RIC. HERRYNG, MAYOR, 1527.

[5] [Election of officers.] — *"Ciuitas Couentrie." Jan. 25.*

[Magister Joh. Bonde, Ric. Marler,[6] Ric. Hassall, Joh. Humfrey, Will. Wicame, Jul. Nethermyll, Tho. Banwell, Rog. Wales, Hen. Perkyns, Will. Dawson, Joh. Hickes, Will. Towres, Ric. Rise, Tho. Wylmer, Tho. Spenser, Tho. Gopsill, Ric. Wethers, Will. Smyth, Ric. Townesend, Hugh Lawton, [7] Rob. Smyth, Ric. Ives, Tho. Warde, Tho. Burdon.[7]]

[m. [8] Ric. Heyryng, Mercer; rec. [8] Edm. Knyghteley; [9] cor. Rob. Grene; steward, Baldw. Porter; ch. Will. Herdie, Barbour, Ric. Sewall, jun., Grasier; w. Tho. Herryng, — *Officers.*

---

[1] This name and those that follow are untitled.
[2] 1520 *v.* p. 673.
[3] "Item" follows. The rest is wanting.
[4] An imperfect heading of the next Leet is on leaf 345.
[5] leaf 346. [6] Magister prefixed to names preceding note 7.
[7–7] Untitled.   [8] Magistrum prefixed.
[9] On the Knightleys of Fawsley *v.* Whitley, *Parl. Representation of Coventry*, p. 36.

§ 113. *Tho. Dodd, Mayor*, 1528.

draper, Will. Saunders, Capper; mace, Will. Alene; crier, Joh. Weyt.]

EASTER LEET.

"Ciuitas Couentrie." May 15.

¹[V. f. p. held before Ric. Herryng, m., Will. Banwell, Rog. Palmer, b., on Tuesday, May 15, 19 Hen. VIII.] [M*agister* Joh. Bonde,² Ric. M*a*rler, Joh. Humfrey, Tho. Waren, Tho. Gopsill,³ Will. Wycame, Jul. Nethermyll, Tho. Banwell, Hen. Wall, Hen. Wethers, Rog. Wales, Tho. Smyth, Tho. Astelen,⁴ Hen. P*er*kyns, Will. Dawson, Joh. Hick*es*, Will. Towres, Ric. Rice, Tho. Spens*er*, Will. Smyth, Ric. Townesend, Hugo Lawton, Will. Herdy,⁵ Ric. Sewall.⁵]

"For sellyng of hides."

[Enacted that no bocher of this Citie shall sell eny beast hides which they kill on the Thurresday or Fryday to eny tanner of the Contrey before the houre of ix of the Cloke on the Saturday, vpon peyn to forfett for eu*er*y hide so solde iij s. iiij d. to be levied by the Sheriff*es* by distres to ther owne vse.

*"Jo*ur*nemen of dyers"*

to be servants and not a fellowship.

[Enacted] also that the Jo*ur*nemen of diers of this Citie fromehensfurth shall make none assembles at weddyng*es*, brotherhodd*es* or buryell*es* ne make eny Caues among*es* theme, but shall vse themeselfe*s* as s*er*uaunt*es* & as no Craft or feliship, vpon peyn of Imp*r*esonement & to make suche fyne as shal-be assessed vpon theme by M*ai*ster Meire, & the justices of the peas of this Citie for the tyme beyng.

"Ciuitas Couentrie."

⁶[V. f. p. held . . .]⁷

THO. DODD, MAYOR, 1528.
EASTER AND MICHAELMAS LEETS.

"Ciuitas Couentrie." May 11.

⁸[V. f. p. held before Tho. Dodd, m., Chr. Wade,⁹ Rob. Kervyne, b., on Tuesday May 11, 20 Hen. VIII.]

---

¹ leaf 346, back.
² M*agister* prefixed to all names until note 5.
³ Deleted, but "stet" interlined.
⁴ A certain Richard Astelyn, haberdasher, was sent up to Queen Mary's Council in Nov. 1553 for seditious behaviour, see *Victoria County Hist. Warw.*, II, 33.
⁵ Untitled. ⁶ leaf 347, back.
⁷ Rest wanting. ⁸ leaf 349.
⁹ A defaced, early Renaissance tomb (c. 1550) now in the Mercers' Chapel of S. Michael's is traditionally known as "Wade's tomb."

§ 113. *Tho. Dodd, Mayor. Leets,* 1528.

[M*agister* Hen. Wall,[1] Joh. Humfrey, Tho. Warene, Joh. Bonde, Will. Wicame, Jul. Nethermyll, Tho. Banwell, Ric. Herryng, Will. Dawson, Tho. Smyth, Tho. Astelen, Rog. Wales, Hen. P*er*kyns, Joh. Crampe, Will. Towres, Ric. Rise, Tho. Gopsill, Ric. Wethers, Tho. Wilmer, Ric. Townesend, Hugo Lawton, Will. Banwell, Rog. Palmer, Tho. Enderby.]   *Jury.*

[2][E:acted] that for-asmoche as the Tanners of this Citie refuse to by hides of the bochers of this Citie of such reasonable price as the bochers of the Contre wolde, The seid bochers of this Citee frome-hensfurth shall haue ther libertie to sell ther hides to the Tanners of the Contrey, eny acte or actes heretofore to the contrarie maid not-wi*th*standyng.   *Orders of leet. "Hides to be sold to the Tanners of the contrey."*

[Enacted] that the Carpenters of this Citie shal-be restored to be a Crafte ageyne as-longe as they demeane themself well in ther seid Craft; and that the Caruers of this Citie frome-hensfurthe that haue not be p*r*enteses nor Maisters of the seid Carpenters Craft shal-be associat wi*th* the Craft of Peynters & not wi*th* the Carpenters.   *"Carpenters, Carvers & peynters."*

[Enacted] that eu*er*y p*er*sone havyng wydraughte*s*[3] in ther Gardens adioynyng to the Whit freers wall shall take downe the seid widraughte*s* befor the feist of Seynt John Baptist next comyng, vpon peyne of vj s. viij d. for eu*er*y widraught standyng ther after the seid feist, to be levied by the Shireffe*s*, to ther owne vse.   *"For widraughtes at the whit frer wall."*

[4][V. f. p. held on Oct. 22, 20 Hen. VIII.]

[M*ajister*[5] Ric. Heryng, Joh. Humfrey, Tho. Warene, Will. Wicame, Jul. Nethermyll, Hen. Wall, Will. Dawson, Tho. Smyth, Tho. Astelene, Rog. Wales, Joh. Hicke*s*, Joh. Cramp, Will. Towres, Ric. Rise, Tho. Gopsill, Ric. Wethers, Tho. Wilmer, Tho. Spens*er*, Will. Smyth, Ric. Townesend, Hugo Lawton, Will. Banwell, Rog. Palmer, [6] Tho. Enderby.   *"Ciuitas Couentr*i*e." Oct. 22. Jury.*

[Jas. Gilbert, Will. Coton.]   *Sheriffs.*

[Enacted] that no p*er*sone Inha*b*ited wi*th*in this Citie frome-hensfurth shall by eny Barley comyng towarde*s* this

---

[1] M*a*g*ister* prefixed to every name.   [2] See above, p. 694.
[3] = a gutter, sewer, sink.   *E.D.D.*   [4] leaf 349, back.
[5] Repeated before names until note 6.   [6] Untitled.

§ 114. *Tho. Astelene, Mayor*, 1529.

Citie to be solde before it come & be brought into the Citie, vpon peyn to forfeit for eu*er*y defaute fyue pound*es*; and that no p*er*sone aboueseid shall sell eny malt or other Greyne, but onelie to the co*m*en bruers or bakers of this Citie, vpon like peyn to be levied at eu*er*y defaut by the shereff*es* at the Meires comaundeme*n*t to ther owne vse.

"Bruers" to sell ale at 2*s*. a sextary,

and not above 3*d*. a gallon.

[Enacted] that no bruer or other inh*a*bitant of this Citee fromehensfurth shall sell eny ale w*ith*in this Citie by the Cester¹ aboue ij s.; and that they sell xiij galons to the Cester; and that they that sell ale by the galon or vnder sell not aboue the rait of iij d. a galone, [or 6s. 8d. fine each time to be levied by the sheriffs to their own use.]

THO. ASTELENE, MAYOR, 1529.

"Ciuitas Couentr*ie*."

²[Election of new officers ³by the underwritten citizens and burgesses.]

Electors.

M*agister* Ric. Herryng,⁴ Joh. Humfrey, Tho. Waren, Joh. Bonde, Will. Wicame, Julinus Nethermyll, Tho. Banwell, Hen. Wall, Tho. Wilmer, Joh. Hick*es*, Joh. Cramp, Will. Towres, Ric. Rice, Tho. Gopsill, Ric. Wethers, Tho. Spens*er*, Will. Smyth, Ric. Townesend, Hugo Lawton, Will. Banwell, Rob. Kyrvyn, Tho. Enderby,⁵ Ric. Sewall,⁵ Will. Norton.⁵]

Officers.

[m. ⁶ Tho. Astelene, Clothier; rec. Rog. Wigston; cor. Rob. Grene; steward, Baldw. Porter; ch. Ric. Niclyne, Gresier, Joh. Some*r*felde, Brewer; w. Cristofer Wharton, skynn*er*, Rob. Nicoll*es*, Gresier; mace, Will. Alene; crier, Joh. West.

[They chose J. Bonde and Will. Wicame to aid and assist the aforesaid mayor in assessing the prices of victuals for this year following.]

Item eligeru*n*t (*sic*) M*agistrum* Joh. Bonde & M*agistrum* Will. Wicame esse auxiliant*es* & assistent*es* p*re*fato Maiori in assessando p*re*cia victual*ium* p*ro* hoc anno sequ*en*te.

---

¹ = sextary.   ² leaf 350.
³ "p*er* Ciues & Burgens*es* subscript*os*"; these words follow the usual election formula.
⁴ M*agister* prefixed to these names as far as note 5.
⁵ Untitled.   ⁶ M*agistru*m prefixed.

§ 114. *Tho. Astelene, Mayor.* Leet, 1529.

[1] EASTER AND MICHAELMAS LEETS.

[V. f. p. held before Tho. Astelene, m., Jas. Gilbert, Will. Coton, b., Apr. 8, 20 Hen. VIII.] *"Ciuitas Couentrie." Apr. 8.*

[M*agister*[2] Ric. Herryng, Joh. Humfrey, Tho. Warene, Joh. Bonde, Will. Wicame, Jul. Nethermyll, Tho. Banwell, Hen. Wall, Tho. Dodd, Tho. Wilm*er*, Will. Dawson, Tho. Smyth, Rog. Wales, Joh. Hick*es*, Joh. Cramp, Will. Towres, Ric. Rise, Tho. Gopsill, Ric. Wethers, Tho. Spens*er*, Will. Smyth, Ric. Townesend, Hugo Lawton, Will. Banwell.]

[Enacted] that the Crafte of Capp*ers* of this Citie fromehensfurth shal-be [4] owners of the weyvers pagiaunt wit*h* all the implement*es* & app*ar*ell belongyng to the same pagiaunt ; and that the seid Craft of weyvers shall yeirelie fromehensfurth pay vnto the M*aister* of the seid Crafte of Capp*ers* vj s. viij d., and so the seid Craft of weyvers fromehensfurth to be clerlie discharged of ther seid pagiaunt & of ther name therof. *[3] "The Cappers to haue the weivers pagiaunt."*

[Enacted] that no p*er*sone wit*h*in this Citie shall bake or make eny spised Caks wit*h* butter to be sold wit*h*in this Citie, but onelie suche p*er*sones as shal-be therunto assigned vnder M*aister* Meires licens for the tyme beyng [or 3s. 4d. fine to be levied by the sheriffs to their own use.] *[3] "For bakyng of spiced cakes."*

[Ordained] that eu*er*y p*er*sone that hereafter shal-be founde or takyn Brekyng of hegges or cuttyng of mennes wood*es* or trees shal-be brought vnto the next stokk*es* wit*h*in this Citie & ther to continue by the space of ij day*es* wit*h* bred & water & non other sustina*u*nce, and if he or they be takyn the seconde tyme wit*h* like offence, then the same p*er*sone to be banysshed the Citie for eu*er*. *[3] "For brekyng of heggi*s* & cuttyng of wood*es*."*

[5] [Enacted] that it shal-be laufull for eu*er*y inhab*i*tant of this Citie to occupie the Craft of dying & settyng of wadd fromehensfurth w*i*t*h*out lett or inter*u*pc*i*on of the M*aister* or Journemen of the Craft of dyars & wadsett*ers* *[6] "For settyng of wadd."*

---

[1] leaf 350, back. [2] Prefixed throughout the list.
[3] In the same scribe's handwriting.
[4] MS. shabbe. [5] leaf 351.
[6] In the same hand. Set = prepare. Wadd = woad, a dye made from the plant *Isatis tinctoria*. For previous rules concerning dyers see p. 418.

§ 114. *Tho. Astelene, Mayor. Dyes,* 1529.

Every inhabitant may be a dyer, so that he does not inveigle away the servants of other men.

of this Citie, so that they seid person or persons so occupying the seid Craft of settyng of wadd do not enveigle or entice eny Journeman or prentice beyng reteyned in seruice with eny dier within this Citie out of his Maisters seruice without thassent of his Maister, vpon peyne of x s. to be leuied to thuse of the Condite if it be laufullie proved befor Maister Meire & the Justices of the peas;

And if they cannot get local journeymen to work for them then they may chose others.

and if in case eny such persone occupying the seid Craft of settyng of wadd cane geit¹ no² Journemen within this Citie to work with theme, Thene it shal-be laufull for theme, & euery of theme, to prouide theme, & euery of theme, seruauntes out of the Citie to worke with theme within the Citie without lett or enterupcion of the seid Maister or Journemen of diers.

"For makyng disceavable Coloures in Cloith."

[Enacted] that no person or persons inhabitant within this Citie shall fromehensfurth die or colour within this Citie eny woll or Cloith with the new or disceivable Coloures of Musters³ or Medleys⁴ latelie invented & begone in this Citie by a frenche-man, vpon peyne to forfett for euery Cloithe or porcions of woll so disceavablie died or coloured xx s., to be levied the on half therof to the shireffes of this Citie for the tyme beyng and the other half to the Maister keper of the Condite to be bestowed on the Condite.

The town seal to be removed from cloth dyed with musters.

And that the owners of all such Clothes as be now within this Citie & died with the seid disceavable Coloures & sealed with the towne seall shall within two dayes nowe next ensuying take of the seid seall frome the seid Clothes in avoydyng the gret sclander that myght happen to this Citie by reason of the premissez, vpon peyne to forfett for euery Cloith so sealed iij s. iiij d. to be leuyed & bestowed in fourme aforseid.

"Ciuitas Couentrie." Oct. 12, 1529. Jury.

⁵[V. f. p. held on Oct. 12, 21 Hen. VIII.]

[Magister Ric. Herryng,⁶ Joh. Humfrey, Tho. Waren, Will. Wicame, Hen. Wall, Tho. Wilmer, Tho. Smyth,⁶

---

¹ Indistinct. ² deletions.
³ *Muster*, short for musterdevillers. *N. E. D.* (see above, p. 283), but an example given seems to refer not to the material but to colours. 1549, Act 3 and 4 Edw. VI, c. 2, § 1, Russetes, Musters, Marbles, Grayes . . and such lyk colors.
⁴ = of a mixed colour. ⁵ leaf 351, back.
⁶⁻⁶ M*agister* prefixed to these names.

§ 114. *Tho. Astelene, Mayor. Leet,* 1529. 699

[1]Rog. Wales, Will. Dawson, Joh. Hickes, Joh. Cramp, Will. Towres, Ric. Rise, Tho. Gopsill, Ric. Wethers, Tho. Spenser, Will. Smyth, Ric. Townesend, Hugo Lawton, Will. Banwell,[1] Rob. Kirvyn,[2] Ric. Niclyne,[2] Joh. Somerland,[2] Joh. Jett.[2]]

[Rob. Seny, dier, Tho. Gardenour, Baker.] Sheriffs.

Item, wheras on Tho. Reives of Berkeswell, wekelie selleth Cowpers wares within this Citie beyng vnlawfull stuff & disceavablie maid havyng a shope at the Spicers Stoke,[3] wherin all his wares do lie; which Thomas beireth no maner of Charges with the Craft of Cowpers of this Citie; Wherfor it is enacted that the seid Reives shall not occupie eny shop within this Citie oneles he agre with the Cowpers of this Citie; and it is further prouided that the seid Cowpers shall not take for eny agrement or fyne of the seid Reives aboue ij s. a yeire etc. "Reives, Cowper," sells deceitfully made wares; and pays nothing to the coopers' craft; he is ordered to pay 2s. a year.

[Enacted] that no persone that occupieth the Craft of a Tiler within this Citie shall fromehensfurth occupie or vse the Crafte of a plomner or Soderyng, vpon the peyne to forfeit for euery defaut iij s. iiij d. "No Tyler to occupie the Craft of a plummer."

[Enacted] that the Craft of Cappers of this Citie shall pay yeirelie fromehensfurth to the Craft of Gurdelers xiij s. iiij d., and that the Craft of Walkers shal-be fromehensfurth discharged of all paymentes to the Craft & feliship of Girdelers & clerelie dismyssed frome the seid Craft; and that the seid Craft of Walkers shall pay yeirelie a Sevennyght before Corpus Christi day to the Crafte of Weyvers tene shelynges in Consideracion of ther gret Charges etc. "Cappers" pay to "Girdelers"; and "walkers" leave girdlers, and pay to "weyuers."

[4] ffor-asmoche as the Citizyns & Inhabitauntes of this Citie & also foreners & estraungers beyng pleyntiffes in accions personelles sued within the kynges Court in this Citie be by long tyme tracted[5] & delayed frome ther dettes & rightes by reason of the long & dilatorie course & custome of the same Court: for remedie & reformacion wherof Itt is enacted, ordeyned & establisshed (etc.) that if the "For sute of accions in the Courte." Remedy against protracted suits.

[1–1] Magister prefixed to these names.   [2] Untitled.
[3] To the south of Butcher Row, to which it runs at right angles.
[4] leaf 352.
[5] = drawn out, protracted. On the "tedious forbearance" of mediæval law see Pollock and Maitland, II, 591–2.

§ 115. *Will. Dawson, Mayor*, 1530.

defendaunt in eny acc*i*on p*er*sonell sued in this Co*ur*t do not appere vppon the first distresse s*er*ued & ret*ur*ned that thene he shall lesse the issues[1] ret*ur*ned and a Capias[2] awarded for his body ageynst the next Co*ur*t; and if the pleyntif in eny suche acc*i*on do not sue his distresse[3] before the defendaunt be foure Court dayes Called in the distresse roll that then the seid pleyntif shal-be non-suyt.

WILL. DAWSON, MAYOR, 1530.

"Ciuitas Co*u*entr*ie*."
Jan. 25.

[4] ¶ [Election of officers.]

[M*agister* Tho. Dodd,[5] Joh. Humfrey, Tho. Waren, Will. Wicame, Jul. Nethermyll, Tho. Banwell, Hen. Wall, Ric. Herryng, Joh. Cramp, Will. Towres, Tho. Gopsill, Tho. Wethers, Tho. Spens*er*, Will. Smyth, Ric. Townesend, Hugo Lawton, Will. Banwell, Rog. Palmer, Ric. Niclyn, Joh. Som*er*feld, Tho. Burdon,[6] Joh. Jett,[6] Joh. Saunders,[6] Geo. Philips.[6]]

Officers.

[Will. Dawson,[7] drap*er*; rec. Rog. Wigston,[8] cor. Rob. Grene; steward, Baldw. Porter; ch. Hug. Gregory, whittawer, Rad. Dale, Gresier; w. Ric. Ley, M*er*cer, Cuthbert Joyno*ur*, drap*er*; mace, Will. Alen; crier, Joh. West.]

DEATH OF THE MAYOR.

Apr. 7.

✝ M*em*. this meire supplied the rome of Meire frome the feist of the Purific*i*on of o*ur* ladie in the yeire aforseid vnto the vijth day of Aprile thene next folowyng, by which tyme he gou*er*ned this Citie well & worshipfull and then he dep*ar*ted this worlde.

On whose soul Jesus have mercy!

On whose soule Jhesu haue m*er*cy.

ROG. WALES, MAYOR, 1530.

Apr. 13.

[9] [Election of a new mayor and coroner on Wednesday, April 13, 21 Hen. VIII, before Rog. Wigston, rec., Rob.

---

[1] *i. e.* the profits of the distress seized by the sheriff in order to secure his appearance at court.
[2] A writ directing the officer to seize the person of the defendant.
[3] *i. e.* set the law in motion.
[4] leaf 352, back.   [5] M*agister* prefixed to all names until note 6.
[6] Untitled.   [7] Magister prefixed.
[8] The Wigstons were a Leicestershire family. Roger represented the city in parliament 1529–36. Whitley, *Representation of Coventry*, 37.   [9] leaf 353.

§ 115. *Rog. Wales, Mayor,* 1530.

Seny and Tho. Gardeno*ur*, b., by the citizens and burgesses underwritten.]

[M*agister* Tho. Dodd,[1] Joh. Humfrey, Joh. Bonde, Will. Wicame, Jul. Nethermyll, Tho. Banwell, Hen. Wall, Ric. Herryng, Tho. Astelen, Ric. Rise, Joh. Crampe, Will. Towres, Tho. Gopsill, Ric. Wethers, Tho. Spens*er*, Ric. Townesend, Hugo Lawton, Will. Banwell, Rog. Palmer, Rob. Kyrvyn, [2] Hug. Gregory, [2] Rad. Dale, [2] Ric. Ley, [2] Joh. Jett.]   *Electors.*

[m. Rog. Wales, Irenmong*er*, "until the next feast of the Conversion of S. Paul"; cor. Tho. Gregory] vsq*ue* p*roximam* letam hic post festum Pasche p*roximo* futur*um* tenend*am*, ea intenc*io*ne q*uo*d pred*ictus* Thomas exhibeat prefato nouo Maiori Juramen*tum* suu*m* quia Rob. Grene absentus est[3] etc.   *Officers. A temporary coroner is chosen to serve until the next leet to be held here after Easter for the purpose of tendering the oath to the new mayor because Rob. Grene is absent.*[3]

LEETS.

[4] [V. f. p. held before Rog. Wales, m., Rob. Seny, Tho. Gardeno*ur*, b., on Tuesday the Exaltation of the Holy Cross, 22 Hen. VIII.]   *Sept. 14.*

[M*agister* Tho. Dodd, [5] Joh. Humfrey, Joh. Bonde, Will. Wicame, Jul. Nethermyll, Tho. Banwell, Hen. Wall, Ric. Herryng, Tho. Astelen, Ric. Rise, Tho. Smyth, Joh. Cramp, Will. Towres, Tho. Gopsill, Ric. Wethers, Tho. Spens*er*, Will. Smyth, Ric. Townesend, Hug. Lawton, Will. Banwell, Rog. Palmer, Jas. Gilbert, Will. Coton, [6] Rad. Dale.]   *Jury.*

[Who elected Rob. Grene, gentleman, coroner, and Tho. Banwell and Ric. Herryng to aid and assist the aforesaid mayor in assessing the price of victuals.]

Qui Eligeru*n*t (*sic*) Rob. Grene, gen*erosum* in officium Coronat*oris* hu*ius* Ciui*tatis*: Et Tho. Banwell & Ric. Herryng esse assistent*es* & auxiliant*es* p*re*fato Maiori in assess*ando* p*re*cia victu*alium*.

Item, wher-as the Craft of Cappe*rs* of this Citie haue vsed to pay yeirelie vnto the Craft of Girdelers vj s. viij d. toward*es* ther pagiaunt: Itt is now enacted that the seid   *"A discharge of vj s. viij d. paid by the Cappe*rs* to the Girdelers."*

---

[1] M*agister* prefixed until note 2. [2] Untitled.
[3] The mayor had to take his oath before the coroner. Green was reinstated in his office at the ensuing leet.
[4] leaf 353, back.
[5] M*agister* prefixed to all names until the next note.
[6] Untitled.

§ 115. *Rog. Wales, Mayor. Leet*, 1530.

Craft of Cappers fromehensfurth for certeyn consideracions alleged shall not pay the seid vj s. viij d. in fourme aforseid.

"No Tyler to occupie the Craft of a plummer."

Item, it is enacted that no persone of this Citie occupieng or vsyng the Misterie & Craft of plummers shall fromehensfurth vse the Craft of a Tyler, ner no Tyler to vse the Craft of a plummer, vpon peyn to forfett for euery defaut contrarie to this present acte vj s. viij d. to be leuyed, immediatlie vpon the seid offence commytted, by the Shireffes for the tyme beyng; the on half of the same to ther owne vse, & the other half to the vse of the Maister or Maisters of the Craft to whome the seid offence is doon contrarie to this acte.

"For flokkyng of Cappes."

¹ Item, it is enacted that no persone or persones of the Crafte of Cappers of this Citie shall dresse eny Cappes with flokkes ² in desseit of the people, vpon peyn to forfett for euery Capp so disceavablie dressed & flokked xij d. to be leuyed by the Shireffes of the Citie for the tyme beyng, the on half to thuse of the seid Shireffes & the other half to thuse of the Maisterz of the seid Craft of Cappers.

"Carvers to be associat with peynters."

[Enacted] that such persones as fromehensfurth woll onelie vse & occupie the Craft of Carvers shal-be contributories ³ to the Craft ³ of peynters & not to the Craft of Carpenters.

"For the Redd-diche."

Item, it is also enacted that the Chamberleyns of this Citie for the tyme beyng fromehensfurth shall ouerse & commaunde euery man havyng eny landes or tenementes, Gardens or vake ⁴ groundes adioynyng on bothe sydes the Red-diche shall Cast,⁵ clense & make cleyne the seid diche so fare as ther grounde doith extend yeirelie before the feist of Pentecost, vpon peyne of euery defaut iij s. iiij d. to be leuyed by the Shireffes to ther owne vse; and further it is enacted that ther shal-be an able persone assigned by

It is to be cleansed every quarter.

Maister Meire & his brethern, which shall quarterlie clense the seid diche in all other places defectyue, & he to haue for his labour yeirelie iiij s. to be paid by the Chamberleyns for the tyme beyng.

¹ leaf 354. ² *i. e.* to powder with flock or cloth-shearings.
³—³ Repeated. ⁴ = vacant, unoccupied.
⁵ = to dig or clear out.

§ 115. *Rog. Wales, Mayor. Leet,* 1530.

[Enacted] that no persone shall occupie the Craft of a Chaundeler within this Citie but such as shal-be[1] admytted by Maister Meire for the tyme beyng & his brethern; and that no Craftesman or housholder of this Citie shall by eny more talow within this Citie then shall suffice or serue his housholde for his owne expensez, vpon peyn to forfeit vj s. viij d. to be levied by the Shireffes for the tyme beyng to ther owne vse; and also that Maister Meire for the tyme beying shall yeirelie elect & chose ij kepers which shall haue auctoritie to entre into euery chaundelers house & wey ther Candelles, to thentent the people be not disceaved, and to try whether the Stuff be good & laufull or not.

"Chaundelers."

"Mayor" to appoint two keepers "to weigh their Candles."[2]

[3] [Ordained] that euery persone that occupieth the Craft of Chaundeler within this Citie shal-be redie to come to the kepers of the seid occupacion at ther warnyng or commaundement at an houre appoynted at all commonicacions & metynges of the seid Craft for the Comen welth of this Citie, vpon peyne of xij d. for euery defaut to be leuyed to thuse of the seid Crafte.

"Chaundelers" to attend at the summons of the keepers of the craft.

[Ordained] that no Chaundeler ne fishemonger,[4] ner non other persone or persones for theme or in ther name, fromehensfurth shall Carie eny Candelles to be sold out of this Citie in eny Markett or faire, vpon peyne to forfett for euery defaut xx s., the on half therof to Maister Meire for the tyme beyng, & the other half to be divided betwene the Shireffes, & the kepers of the seid Craft of Chaunders (*sic*) for the yiere beyng, without eny further deley.

"Chaundelers" and fishmongers are forbidden to sell candles outside the city.

[Ordained] that no Chaundeler, ner other persone that maketh eny Candell to sell, shall by eny talowe, ner make eny bargeyne with eny bocher of this Citie for talowe betwene Guttyde[5] & Midsomer, but onelie of such price as shal-be lymytt by Maister Meire & his assistaunce & the kepers of the seid Craft of Chaundelers, vpon peyn of xiij s. iiij d. to be payed half therof to the shireffes for the tyme beyng & the other half to the kepers of the seid

"Chaundelers" between Good-tide and Midsummer to pay for tallow the price fixed by the mayor and keepers;

---

[1] MS. shabe.
[2] The gloss as written in the MS. is erroneous. The mayor did not personally weigh the candles. The handwriting is late.
[3] leaf 354, back.   [4] See p. 632.
[5] Good-tide Monday is the day before Shrove Tuesday.

§ 115. Rog. Wales, Mayor. Leet, 1530.

and between Lammas and Michaelmas the craft by the advice of the mayor and justices to fix the price of candles.

Craft; and that the kepers of the seid Craft of Chaundelers euery yeire betwene Lammas & Michelmas shall Call the Craft to-gither, & by the aduice of Maister Meire & the Justices of the peace shall sett such price of Talowe as shal-be thought thene moost convenient by ther discrecions for the eas of the Comenaltie; and that euery persone that selleth Candell & will not keip the price of Candell so lymyt & assessed shall forfett for euery defaut x s., that is to say, vj s. viij d. to the Shireffes & iij s. iiij d. to the kepers of the seid Craft; prouided alwey that if ther happen a gret Scarsenes of Talowe then the seid kepers by thaduise of Maister Meire & his assistence after Cristenmas shall sett another price of Candelles, so that the Citie may be serued better cheipe[1] then other townes herabout.

"Ciuitas Couentrie."

[2][V. f. p. held on Tuesday, Oct. 11, 22 Hen. VIII.]

Magister[3] Tho. Dodd, Joh. Humfrey, Joh. Bonde, Will. Wicame, Jul. Nethermyll, Tho. Banwell, Hen. Wall, Ric. Herryng, Tho. Astelen, Ric. Rise, Tho. Smyth, Tho. Wilmer, Joh. Cramp, Will. Towres, Tho. Gopsill, Ric. Wethers, Will. Smyth, Ric. Townesend, Hugo Lawton, Will. Banwell, Rog. Palmer, Chris. Wadd, Jas. Gilbert, Will. Coton.]

Sheriffs.

[Joh. Jett, Mercer, Sim. Parker, Grasier.]

"Rob. Perkyns" to continue his occupation of dyeing in spite of the craft of dyers.

[Ordained] for dyuers Consideracions that Rob. Perkyns shall haue fre libertie to worke in his occupacion of dyyng with Tho. Burdon without interupcion of eny persone of[4] or persones of the seid Craft of dyers & without daunger of eny penaltie of[4] or forfett by reason of eny acte or estatute hertofor to the contrarie maid.[5]

Resident craftsmen only to be employed

[Enacted] that no Citizene or inhabitaunt of this Citie after the feist of Cristenmas next comyng shall deliuer or cause to be deliuered eny Cappes or wollene Cloithe to be Thikked to eny walker but onelie suche as that be thene inhabited within this Citie or the Suburbes of the same,[6]

"for thykkyng of Cappes & Cloith."

---

[1] At a more reasonable price, more cheaply.
[2] leaf 355. Rog. Wigston, rec., is here first mentioned as one of those before whom the leet is held. Cf. p. 700.
[3] Magister prefixed before all names.   [4] Redundant.
[5] For troubles with the dyers v. supra, p. 698 et passim.
[6] For the competition of the country craftsmen see above, p. 661

§ 115. *Rog. Wales, Mayor. Sale*, 1530.

vpon peyne to forfett for euery such defaut vj s. viij d. to be leuyed by distresse, to the vse of the Citie & Shireffes for the tyme beyng egallie to be dyuyded.

[Enacted] that no Skynner of this Citie shall fromehensfurth dry eny Skynnes within the Litle Parke oneles he holde of the wardens of the Citie on of ther housez in the seid Litle Parke, [or 6s. 8d. fine each time] to be leuyed to thus[1] abouseid.

[2] [Enacted] that no Bocher or other inhabitaunt of this Citie shall sell eny talow to eny person dwellyng out of this Citie, vpon peyne to forfett for euery Stone so solde xx s. to be leuyed to thuse of the Citie; ner that no persone sell eny talowe to eny Cordener,[3] vpon like peyn etc.

Also that no bocher or other persone shall sell eny talowe aboue ij s. iiij d. the Stone, vpon peyn of vj s. viij d. for euery Stone sold to the contrarie to be leuyed as is aboueseid. And also that no Chaundler of this Citie sell eny Candelles aboue the price of j d. ob. the li., vpon peyn of iij s. iiij d. for euery pound so sold to be leuyed to thuse abouseid. And also that no persone doo enterup or lett eny estraunger to sell Candelles within this Citie vpon peyn of iij s. iiij d. to be levied as is aforseid.

Order "for drying skinnes in Litle Parke.

No butcher to sell "Talow" to non-residents,

nor above 2s. 4d. a stone;

no chandler to sell "Candelles" above 1½d. per lb.;

and no one to prevent strangers selling them.

RECORD OF THE SALE OF A HOUSE.

Mem. that the xx^ti day of Octobre in the xxij^ti yeire of the reign of kyng Henry the eight, before Maister Rog. Wales, Meier (etc.), Maister Will. Wicame, Maister Julyne Nethermyll & other aldermen in the Councell house of the seid Citie, on Philip Partriche & Anne his wif, doughter & heire vnto on Edw. Colett & Alice his wif, doughter to Ric. Cardemaker, which Philip & Anne the day & yeir aboueseid for a grement & anende (*sic*) with the Craft of Gurdelers of the Citie for a house in the Yorle-streit next vnto the Corner house of the Abbott of Combe haue received & hadd in recompense of ther cleyme & title in the seid house fyve nobles[4] & fyve shelyinges (*sic*) of money. & for the same money the

Oct. 20, 1531. Phil. Partriche and his wife

renounce their claim. to a house in Earl Street,

---

[1] *i. e.* the use.   [2] leaf 355, back.
[3] Cordwainer, shoemaker.   [4] A noble = 6s. 8d.

§ 116. *Ric. Rise, Mayor*, 1531.

and deliver their title deed to the mayor.

seid Philip & Anne also in the presens of the seid Maisters deliuered a deedd (*sic*), wherby they cleymed the seid house, to the seid Meir to be cancelled & adnulled. & so it was doon by the seid Meir immediatlie etc.

RIC. RISE, MAYOR, 1531.

Jan. 25. ¹[Election of officers.]

Electors. [Magister² Tho. Astelen, Joh. Humfrey, Will. Wycame, Jul. Nethermyll, Tho. Banwell, Hen. Wall, Ric. Herryng, Tho. Dodd, Will. Smyth, Tho. Smyth, Joh. Cramp, Will. Towres, Tho. Gopsill, Ric. Wethers, Tho. Spenser, Hugo Lawton, Will. Banwell, Rog. Palmer, Rob. Kervyn, Rob. Seny, Tho. Gardenour, ³Hugo Gregory, Rauf Dale, Tho. Brewer.]

Officers. [m. Ric. Rise, Mercer; rec. Rog. Wigston; cor. Rob. Grene; steward, Baldw. Porter; ch. Joh. Talont, Goldsmyth, Rad. Hopkyns, Taillour; w. Hug. Dalawey, Mercer, Hug. Blore; mace, Will. Alen; crier, Joh. Weytt.]

EASTER AND MICHAELMAS LEETS.

"Ciuitas Couentrie." ⁴ ¶ [V. f. p. held before Ric. Rise, m., Rog. Wigston,⁵ rec., Joh. Jett, Sym. Parker b., on Thursday Apr. 20, 22 Hen. VIII.]

⁶"Inquisitio" = the inquest. [Magister⁷ Tho. Astelen, Joh. Humfrey, Will. Wicame, Jul. Nethyrmyll, Tho. Banwell, Hen. Wall, Ric. Herryng, Rog. Wales, Will. Smyth, Tho. Smyth, Joh. Cramp, Will. Towres, Tho. Gopsill, Ric. Wethers, Tho. Spenser, Ric. Townesend, Hugo Lawton, Rog. Palmer, Chris. Wadd, Jas. Gilbert, Will. Coton, Rob. Seny, Tho. Gardenour, ⁸Rad. Hopkyns.]

Searchers [Enacted] that Joh. Grene & Rauf Worseley, weyuers,

---

¹ leaf 356. The first letter is highly ornamented. After the usual election formula there follows: "per Ciues & Burgenses dicte Ciuitatis quorum nomina subscripta existunt = by the citizens and burgesses of this said city whose names are underwritten.
² Maister precedes all names as far as note 3.   ³ Untitled.
⁴ leaf 356, back.
⁵ For the mention of the recorder's name see above, p. 704.
⁶ The marginal glosses appear to be in the same handwriting as the rest of the script.
⁷ Repeated before all names as far as note 8.   ⁸ Untitled.

§ 116. Ric. Rise, Mayor. Leet, 1531.

shal-be for this yeire serchers to se the acte maid at the last lete¹ concernyng Cloithe & Cappes to be thickked by walkers dwellyng within the Citie to be put in due execucion accordyng to the tenour of the same acte. *appointed for preventing the employment of non-resident fullers.*

Item, wher-as great defaut is thought in the seriauntes in warnynge the watche for that they warne nyghtlie meny, & verey fewe do watche, so that therby it is supposed that the seid seriauntes shuld [have] great geyn & advauntage, It is therfore enacted that the seriauntes fromehensforth shall not warne nyghtlie aboue the nomber of xxiiij persones to keip the watche, vpon peyne if they be proved to do the contrarie to leesse ther offices, or otherwise to be punysshed by the discrecion of Maister Meire for the tyme beyng. *²"The watche." 24 persons to be warned by the sergeants every night to keep watch.*

[Enacted] that no Clothier, Capper, nor no other inhabitaunte of this Citie shall fromehensfurthe deliuer to eny spynner or other workefolke aboue ij li. & a half of woll for a weight;³ And to pay redie money for the workemanship therof, & no wares, vitayll, nor other stuff,⁴ vpon peyn to forfeit for euery defaut vj s. viij d. to be levied by distresse or by the Meires commaundement to the vse of the Citie. And that all spynners & knytters do ther worke truelie & substanciallie, vpone peyn of imprisonment. *²"No weyght of worke to be aboue ij li. & di." No truck wages to be given to spinners.*

[V. f. p. held before Ric. Rice, m., Joh. Jett, Sym. Parker, b., on Tuesday, Oct. 10, 23 Hen. VIII.] *"Ciuitas Couentrie."*

[Magister⁵ Tho. Astelen, Joh. Humfrey, Will. Wycame, Jul. Nethermyll, Tho. Banwell, Hen. Wall, Ric. Herryng, Rog. Wales, Will. Smyth, Joh. Cramp, Will. Towres, Tho. Gopsill, Ric. Wethers, Tho. Spenser, Ric. Townesend, Hugo Lawton, Chris.⁶ Wadde, Rob. Kyrven, Will. Coten, Rob. Seny, Tho. Gardenour, ⁷Rad. Hopkyns, Rad. Dale, Tho. Brewer. *Jury.*

[Will. Marler, Mercer, Tho. Burdon.] *Sheriffs.*

⁸ Item, wher-as the Company, felishyp, & Craft of Cardmakers & Sadelers of this Citie meny yeires & of longe continuaunce haue hadd & yet haue the cheif rule, *²"Cardmakers, sadelers & Cappers to be vnyte together."*

---

¹ See p. 704.   ² Contemporary hand.
³ v. *supra*, p. 243 *et passim*.   ⁴ See above, p. 689.
⁵ Repeated before names until note 7.   ⁶ Xpoferus in MS.
⁷ Untitled.   ⁸ Craig, *op. cit.* 79–80, Sharp, *Mysteries*, 43–5.

§ 116. *Ric. Rise, Mayor. Cappers,* 1531.

The card-makers and saddlers, who have hitherto maintained a chapel, pageant and pageant-house,

gouernaunce, reparyng & meyntenaunce as-well of a Chappell within the parishe Churche of seynt Michelles in the seid Citie, named seynt Thomas Chappell,[1] & of the ornamentes, Juelles & lightes of the same, As also of a pagiaunt with the pagiaunt-house & pleyng geire with other appurtenaunces & apparells belongyng to the same pagiaunt. The Meyntenaunce & reparacion wherof haithe

find they are unable to bear so great a charge:

been & is yeirelie to the greit charge, cost, & expenses of the seid company & crafte, beyng now but a fewe persones in nomber & havyng but smale eyde of eny other Craft for the same. So that ther said Charge is & like to be more ponderouse & chargeable to theme then they may convenyentlie bere or susteyn in shorte tyme to come, oneles provision for a remedy may be spedilie hadd. In consideracion wherof & for-asmoch as the company, feliship, & Craft of Cappers within this Citie, now beyng in nomber meny welthy and honest persones, & have maid dyuers tymes sute & request unto the Meire & his brethern, the aldermen of this Citie, to have a certeyn place to theme assigned & lymyted, as dyuers other Craftes have, to sitt to-gether in ther seid parishe Churche to here ther dyvyne service & bere suche charges for the same as by Maister Meire & his brethern, the Aldermen,

it is therefore ordained that the cappers, a wealthy craft,

shal-be assigned: It is therfor by the Mediacion of Maister Richard Rice now Meire of this Citie & of his seid brethern, the aldermen, at this present lete assembled & by auctoritie of the same with the agrement, consent, & assent of all the seid parties, Companyes, & Craftes, enacted, ordeyned, & constituted that the seid company

shall be associated with them,

& Craft of Cappers frome-hensforthe shalbe associat, Joyned, & accompanyed with the seid Craftes of Cardemakers & Sadelers in the gouernaunce, reparyng, & meynteynyng, as well of & in the seid Chappell, named Seynt Thomas Chappell, & of the ornamentes & lightes of the same, As of & in the seid pagyaunt [2] [3] And pagiaunt house with the Implementes, appurtenaunces, pleaers, reherces,

---

[1] The chapel proper is in the south aisle. Over the south porch is a parvise. It is still called the Cappers' chapel, and the company still meet and eat there on the feast of S. Thomas of Canterbury.

[2] There follows "verte ffolium" = turn the leaf.

[3] leaf 357, back.

§ 116. *Ric. Rise, Mayor. Cappers*, 1531.

& pleyng geire accustumed, belongyng & necessarie to & for the same, after suche maner or better as it haithe been used & accustumed before tyme. And that euery housholder or Shop-keper of euery of the seid companyes and Craftes toward & for the charges and exspenses aboueseid shall not onelie pay yeirelie to the Maisters & kepers of the seid Craftes at such tyme & day as the seid Craftes shall appoynt xij d.; And upon Seynt Thomas day, named the Translacion of Seynt Thomas,[1] shall also offere yeirelie euery of theme j d. at the high Masse seid in the seid Chappell; But also the seid Maisters, company, & Craftes fromehensfurthe shall applie & bestowe to & vpon the seid reparacions & charges all the revenues, rentes, & profittes of all soche landes, houses, and tenementes as they or eny of theme now haue or herafter shall haue to the vse & behove of the seid companyes & craftes; And the viij s. of yerelie pencion which is yeirelie payed by the peynters & Caruers unto the seid charges shall yeirelie be payed & go to the same charges. And that the seid Maisters now electe & hereafter to be electe Maisters of the seid Craftes shall yeirelie, upon suche a day as the seid Maisters shall appoynt & agre, accompeny themeselfes to-gethers & bryng in & make a true & a full accompt euery of theme to the other of all ther seid receites, revenues, and profittes. And the seid charges & the charges of the kepyng of harnes belongyng to the seid Craftes with the weiryng of the same in the watches & other necessarie charges & busynes for the seid Craftes allowed, payed, & performed, the ouerpluse of the seid money of the seid revenues, profittes, & money shal-be bestowed & put in a box with two lockes & two keyes, the on key to remeyne with the Maister3 of the Craft of Cardmakers and Sadelers, And the other key to remeyn with the Maisters of the Craft of Cappers, sauelie to keip the seid money in the seid box untill they have nede to bestow it upon the seid Charges or otherwise, as they shall thynk convenyent; & the seid box to remeyn in the said Chappell fastoned with a cheyne.

Also it is enacted by the auctoritie and consent aforseid

and that each member of the united fellowship

shall pay 12d. a year towards expenses,

and 1d. at the offertory on S. Thomas's day,

the painters and carvers contributing 8s. a year between them.

Accounts are to be rendered annually,

and surplus funds to be kept in a box

in the chapel.

[1] Dec. 29.

§ 116. *Ric. Rise, Mayor. Pageants,* 1531.

<small>All these crafts are to sit lovingly and familiarly together during service time,

and walk two and two in processions,

taking turns in matters of precedence year by year.</small>

that the Maisters & compeny of the Craft of Cappers shall fromehensfurthe femyliarlie and louynglie accompeny & sitt togethers in the seid Chappell with the seid compeny and craft of Cardemakers & Sadelers to here ther divyne seruice, & also shall go togethers in ther processions & watches[1] too & too togethers. And that the seid compeny & craft of cardmakers & Sadelers shall haue the preemynence & ouerhande in ther sittynges & goyng together oon yeire, & the seid Craft & compeny of Cappers shall lykewyse haue the preemynence & ouerhande in ther sittyng & goyng the other yeire, and so to continew frome yeire to yeire lovynglie fromehensfurthe; so that the seid Cardemakers & sadelers shall not lack ther rome nor sittyng in the seid Chappell.

<small>[2] "The barbars to pay yeirelie vj s. viij d. to the Girdelers."</small>

[3] Item, it is enacted also that the Company & Craft of Barbars of this Citie shall yeirelie fromehensfurthe pay unto the Company & Craft of Gurdelers of this citie vj s. viij d. toward ther charges of the pagyant & processions at suche day & tyme as they were wont to pay the seid some vnto the Craft of Cardmakers, vpon peyn euery of theme to forfeit for ther defaut xij d. to be levyed by distresse to the vse of the Citie.

<small>"The walkers to pay yeirelie vj s. viij d. to the weyvers & the skynners to pay v s."</small>

Item, it is also enacted that the compeny & Craft of walkers of this citie shall yeirelie pay unto the company & Craft of weyvers vj s. viij d. towards the charges of ther pagyant at such day & tyme as it hathe be wont to be payed. And that the Company & Craft of Skynners shall likewise pay unto the seid Craft of weyvers yeirelie v s. towardes ther seid Charges.

<small>[2] "Bruers & alewyves."</small>

[Enacted] that all bruers that brue to sell shall sell ther ale after the rait of xviij d. the Cester, and threttene galons to the Cester:[4] And that euery ale-wiff & tipler sell & send furthe of ther house ther ale to theme that require it after the rait of a half-peny a quarte, vpon peyn to forfett for euery defaut iij s. iiij d. And that no bruer that this yeire doith ley downe or leive ther bruing shall [not] brue herafter eny more, vpon peyn to forfett xx s.

---

[1] On the riding of the watch on Midsummer Eve and S. Peter's night see above, p. 35 ; Sharp, *Mysteries*, pp. 174–206.
[2] Contemporary hand.   [3] leaf 358.
[4] This measure evidently varies, see above, p. 678.

WILL. SMYTH, MAYOR, 1532.

¹[Election of officers.]

[M*agister*² Rog. Wales, Joh. Humfrey, Joh. Bonde, Will. Wicame, Jul. Nethermyll, Tho. Banwell, Hen. Wall, Ric. Herryng, Tho. Dodd, Tho. Astelen, Tho. Smyth, Hugo Lawton, Joh. Cramp, Will. Towres, Tho. Gopsill, Tho. Spens*er*, Ric. Townesend, Rog. Palmer, Rob. Kyrvyn, Will. Coton, Tho. Gardeno*u*r, Sim. P*a*rker, ³Joh. Talont, Rad. Hopkyns.] Electors.

[m. Will. Smyth,⁴ drap*er*; rec. Rog. Wigston; cor. Rob. Grene; steward, Baldw. Porter; ch. Laur. Fane, fyshemong*er*, Tho. Keveit, sherman; w. Tho. Smyth, Jun., drap*er*, Tho. Riley, drap*er*; mace, Will. Alen; crier, Joh. Weyt.] Officers.

EASTER AND MICHAELMAS LEETS.

⁵[V. f. p. held before Will. Smyth, m., Will. M*a*rler, Tho. Burdon, b., on May 14, 24 Hen. VIII.] May 14.

[M*agister*⁶ Rog. Wales, Will. Wica*m*, Jul. Nethermyll, Tho. Banwell, Hen. Wall, Ric. Herryng, Tho. Astelen, Ric. Rise, Hugo Lawton, Tho. Smyth, Tho. Wilmer, Joh. Cram*p*e, Will. Towres, Tho. Gopsill, Ric. Wethers, Ric. Townesend, Chris. Wadd, Rob. Seny, Tho. Gardeno*u*r, ⁷Laur. ffane, Tho. Keveit, Will. Alyson, Joh. Foxall, Tho. Herryng.] "Inquis*itio*" = the inquest.

[Enacted] that all Bakers inha*b*ited wit*h*in this Citie fromehensfurth shall make all ther brede of good & true stuff of what Greyn so eu*er* it be, & that the keip the assise of the same truelie as it shal-be lymyt & assigned vnto theme by M*ai*ster Meire of the Citie: And that the seid Bakers ne eny of them sell eny of ther brede, nether horsebred ne other bred, aboue the rait of xiij penyworthe to the dose*n*. And also that they ne eny of theme sell eny horsebred to Innes or otherwise aboue the Rait of iij horseloues for a peny, vpon peyn to forfeit for eu*ery* Orders of leet.
⁸ "Bakers to kepe the Assize." ⁸

Horse bread to be sold at 3 loaves a penny.

---

¹ leaf 358, back.   ² Title prefixed to all names until note 3.
³ Untitled.   ⁴ Mag*iste*r prefixed.   ⁵ leaf 359.
⁶ Prefixed to all names as far as note 7.   ⁷ Untitled.
⁸ In different handwritings. Marginal annotations are henceforth usually in the same handwriting as the text is.

§ 117. *Will. Smyth, Mayor. Leet,* 1532.

offence contrarie to this acte vj s. viij d. to be levied by distresse of ther goodes, the on half therof to goo to the vse of the seid Meier, & the other half to the vse of the Shireffes for the tyme beyng etc.

"Constables" are not to be summoned "for wache,"

[Enacted] at the request & peticion of the Constables of this Citie that all Constables within the Citie & suburbes of the same shal-be discharged fromehensforth of the Comen watche in this Citie & also of all paymentes & charges of the same, so that the seid Constables &

but they must expel vagabonds.

every of theme in his ward endeyver theme-selfes diligentlie to avoyed out of the Citie all such vacabundes & myghtye beggers¹ as herafter shall resort & come into the Citie.

"Tanned lether."

[Enacted] that thre men of this Citie shal-be yeirelie fromehensforth Chosen & sworne at Eister lete by Maister Meire for the tyme beyng to be serchers of Tanned lether; which serchers shall haue auctoritie to allowe & disable Tanned lether, & to sett a seall appoynted for the same to every well tanned hide for the prove of the

"Searchers' fee 2d."

allowaunce of the same hide. And the seid serchers to haue for ther labour ij d. of every hide not well tanned, the same ij d. to be levyed by distres of the hides or other goodes of the offendoures etc.

³ " Lether not to be sold till serched & sealed." ³

²[Enacted] that no Tanner within this Citie carie eny lether tanned within the Citie out of the Citie to sell vntill it be serched, allowed & sealled by the serchers appoynted for the same, vpon peyn to forfett for euery hide solde & caried to sell contrarie to this acte vj s. viij d. to be levied in forme aforseid to thuse of the Meire & Shireffes for the tyme beyng.

Pavements between Grey-friar and Cheylesmore Gates to be repaired.

[Enacted] that every person havyng grounde, land or tenementes betwene seynt Fraunces yait⁴ & Chellesmore yait shall amend & make ther pavymentes ther befor ther growndes befor the feyst of seynt John Baptist next comyng, vpon peyn of x s.

"Peynters, Gurdelers, Cardmakers."

[Enacted] that the Craft of Peynters shall pay yeirelie fromehen[s]furth iiij s. of the viij s. that they wer wont to pay to a pagiaunt vnto the Craft of Gurdelers, &

---

¹ See above, p. 652.   ² leaf 359, back.
³⁻³ Different handwritings.   ⁴ Gray-friar Gate.

§ 117. *Will. Smyth, Mayor. Leet*, 1532.

the other iiij s. of the seid viij s. vnto the Craft of Cardemakers.

Wher-as dyuers & meny within this Citie as well vynteners, ale wyves & Tiples, as dyuers other inhabitantes of the same do vse & occupie measures & weightes vnlawfull & not sealled ne allowed by Maister Meire nor his officers to the great disceit & hurt of the Comen people of this Citie, And for reformacion therof It is enacted at this lete that no persone within this Citie sell eny wyne, ale or other stuff, ne vse eny weightes after the feist of seynt John Baptist next comyng by eny maner measures or weightes oneles they be sealled or allowed by Maister Meire, or by his officers, vpon peyn to forfeit the seid Measures or weightes not sealed nor allowed, as is aforesed, And that it shal-be laufull to the swardeberer or the Meires seriaunt to seas & take the same, wheresoeuer they fynde them to ther owne vse etc.

"Weightes & Mesures"

unlawful and unsealed

to be seized by the officers.

¹[V. f. p. held on Tuesday, Oct. 15, 24 Hen. VIII.]

"Ciuitas Couentrie."³ Oct. 15.

[Magister² Rog. Wales, Will. Wycam, Jul. Nethermyll, Hen. Wall, Ric. Herryng, Tho. Astelen, Ric. Rice, Hugo Lawton, Tho. Smyth, Tho. Wilmer, Joh. Cramp, Will. Towres, Tho. Gopsill, Ric. Wethers, Rog. Palmer, Rob. Kyrvyn, Rob. Seny, Tho. Gardenour, ⁴ Laur. Fane, Will. Norton, Tho. Herryng, Crist. Wharton, Will. Alyson, Rob. Smyth.]

[Joh. Saunders, Marcer, Will. Rogers, Gresier.⁵]

Sheriffs.

[Enacted] that the bakers of this Citie shall sell ther bred, as well mannes-bred as horse-bred, after the rait of xiiij to the dosyn as they haue be wont to doo notwithstandyng the acte maid the last lete to the contrarie,⁶ so that the seid bakers keip the true assise to theme gyven by Maister Meire for the tyme beying : And that the brewers of the Citie shall sell ther ale frome-hensfurth after the rait of xviij d. the Cester & xiij to the dosyne, vpon the peyn for euery Cester sold to the contrarie to

"Bakers" to sell 14 pennyworth to the dozen;

"& brewers" to sell ale at 18d. a sextary.

---

¹ leaf 360. ² Names preceded by Magister until note 3.
³ See note 3, p. 712.   ⁴ Untitled.
⁵ The usual formula followed by "& jur[ati sunt]" = and they were sworn.
⁶ See above, p. 711.

§ 118. *Hugo Lawton, Mayor*, 1533.

forfeit vj s. viij d. to be levyed by the Shereff*es* by distresse to ther owne vse.

"Candell." [Enacted] that no p*er*sone of this Citie shall sell eny Candell aboue the rait of j d. ob. the li., vpon peyn to forfeit for eu*er*y pounde j d. to be levied as is aforseid.

HUGO LAWTON, MAYOR, 1533.

"Ciuitas Couentr*ie*."
Jan. 25, 1533.

¹¶ [Election of new officers.]

[M*agister* ² Rog. Wales, Will. Wyca*m*, Jul. Nethermyll, Tho. Banwell, Hen. Wall, Ric. Herryng, Tho. Dodd, Tho. Astelen, Ric. Rise, Tho. Smyth, Rog. Palmer, Joh. Cramp, Will. Towres, Tho. Gopsill, Ric. Wethers, Tho. Spenser, Ric. Townesend, Cris. Wadd, Rob. Kyrvyn, Rob. Seny, Tho. Gardeno*ur*, Joh. Jett, Will. Ma*r*ler, Tho. Burdon.]

Officers. [m. Hugo Lawton,³ Capp*er*; rec. Rog. Wigston, "Armig*er*"; cor. Joh. Grene; steward, Baldw. Porter; ch.⁴ Joh. Moseley, Marcer, Will. Joyno*ur*, sen., Grasier; w. Cris. Waren, Drap*er*, Hen. Over, M*er*cer; mace, Will. Alen; crier, Joh. Weit.]

BUSINESS AND LEETS.

[They elected Masters Will. Wicam and Tho. Dodd, aldermen, to assist and help the aforesaid H. Lauton, newly elected mayor, in assessing the prices of victuals to be sold in the aforesaid city for the year following.]

Ite*m*, eligeru*n*t (*sic*) Mag*i*str*u*m Will. Wica*m*, drap*er*, & Mag*i*str*u*m Tho. Dodd, M*er*cer, ac Alderma*n*nos Ciui*tatis* pre*dict*e, ad assistand*um* & auxiliand*um* pred*i*ct*u*m (*sic*) Hugonem Láuton, m. nunc de nouo elec*tum* in assessando precia victual*ium* in Ciui*tate* pred*icta* vendend*orum* pro hoc anno seque*n*te etc.

¶ Me*m*. that it is enacted by the assemble & elecc*i*on aforseid that M*aister* Tho. Banwell, drap*er*, shall haue libe*r*tie to occupie the Craft of wadd-settyng⁵ wi*th* such seruaunt*es* as he cane geit to exercise the seid occupac*i*on, so that the seid Tho. Banwell do no acte ne thynge to enveagle or take away the seruaunt*es* or Jo*ur*nemen of

"M*aister* Banwell" may occupy the craft of wad-setting

so long as he does not enveigle away other men's servants.

---

¹ leaf 360, back.   ² Repeated before every name.
³ M*agister* precedes this name.
⁴ MS. mistakenly calls these wardens.   ⁵ See above, p. 704.

§ 118. *Hugo Lawton, Mayor. Butchers*, 1533.   715

the diers or wad-setters of this Citie, oneles the seid seruauntes or Journemen gyve laufull warnyng to deeparte frome their seid seruices accordyng to the order & custome of this Citie etc.

[1] [V. f. p. held before Hugo Lawton, m., Joh. Saunders, Will. Rogers, b., on May 6, 25 Hen. VIII.]

[2] Essonia ¶.

¶ [Magister [3] Rog. Wales, Jul. Nethermyll, Tho. Banwell, Hen. Wall, Tho. Asteleyn, Will. Smyth, Rog. Palmer, Tho. Smyth, Tho. Wilmer, Joh. Cramp, Will. Towres, Tho. Gopsill, Ric. Wethers, Ric. Townesend, Rob. Seny, Tho. Gardinour, Sym. Parker, Will. Marler, [4] Joh. Moseley, Will. Joynour, Will. Alyson, Will. Saunders, Tho. Napton, Hen. Hynde.]

[Enacted] that all inhabitauntes of this Citie fromehensfurth shal-be at libertie to bie & sell as moch barley & malt as they woll or cane within the Citie so that the Citie may be sufficientlie serued, And that they do not forstall nor regrate the Market within this Citie in that behalf, eny act of leet maid hertofore to the contrarie notwithstandyng.

¶ [Enacted] at this present leete that all the bochers & vitailloures within this Citie shall kill & sell wekelie within the Citie asmoche beiff as they woll; And that they shall make no dyvision of ther beiff so killed aboue the number of too of the seid bochers to a beiff; And that if eny of the seid bochers & vittailloures sell, or kill to sell, eny Mottons, veilles or porkes, & haue no beif to sell in manour & fourme aforseid That then the seid Motton, veill & porke & euery of theme shal-be forfeited & taken frome theme by the shireffes of this Citie for the tyme beyng; and to be ordered & dyvided by the discrecion of Maister Meire for the tyme beyng; And that this present acte shal-begyne & take effecte vpon Thurresday next before the Assencion day next ensuyng.

"Ciuitas Couentrie." May 6.

Essoins.

The sale of "barley & malt"[5] to be unrestricted.

The [5] "bochers" are [6] "not to Combine or stint themselues to what number of beasts they will kill,"[6]

under pain of forfeiture.

---

[1] leaf 361.
[2] From *essoniare* = to essoin, tender an excuse for non-appearance. The fact that no names follow shows that no one essoined himself, and that all were present.
[3] Prefixed up to note 4 to the names of the jury.   [4] Untitled.
[5] The scribe's contemporary gloss.   [6]–[6] Later hand.

§ 118. *Hugo Lawton, Mayor. The Queen,* 1533.

<small>1 "Craftes."
2 "All men to Associate to some one Craft, as the mayor shall Apoynt."[2]</small>

¶ [Enacted] that such persones as be not associat & assistant to eny Craft which is charged with eny pagiant of this Citie, as fishemongers, bowyers, flechers & suche other, shall now be associat & assistaunt to such craftes as Maister Meire shall assigne & apoynt theme.

<small>The 1 "brewers" to sell ale 14 gallons to a sextary.</small>

[3] [Enacted] that euery brewer that brewes to sell within this Citie shall sell xiiij galonse ale to the Cester,[4] And not above the price of xviij d. the Cester, vpone peyne to forfeit for euery defaut vj s. viij d. to be levied by distrese by the Shireffes to ther owne vse: And that all Tiplers of ale shall sell ther ale as well by farthyngworthers as otherwise, and not aboue the rait of iij d. the galon, vpone like peyn for euery defaut.

ANNE BOLEYN'S LETTER.

The Copie of a lettre deliuered to the Meire frome the quene.

To our trusti & wel-beloued the meire & his Bretherne of Couentre.

By the quene.

<small>Sept. 7, 1533.
2 "Prince borne."[2]
The queen announces her safe and happy delivery of a princess (afterwards Queen Elizabeth),</small>

Trustie & wel-beloued, we great yow well; And wheras it haith pleased the goodnes of almyghtie God of his infinite mercie & grace to send vnto vs at this tyme good spede in the deliueraunce & bryngyng furth of a princes to the great Joy, reioyce & singuler comfort of my good lord, vs, & of all his good & lovyng subgiettes of this his realme; for the which his inestimable benevolence so s[h]ewed vnto vs, we haue no litle cause to gyve high thankes, laude & preysyng vnto our seid maker, like as we doo most lowly, humbly, & with all the inwarde desire of our hert. And in-asmoch as we vndoubtidelie trust that this our[5] good spede is to your great pleasure, comforte & consolacion we therfore by these our lettres aduer-

<small>and asks for their prayers to God for the infant's preservation.</small>

tise yow therof, desyryng & hertelie prayng yow to gyve with vs vnto almyghtie God high thankes, glorie, laude & preysyng, And to prey for the good helth, prosperitie & continuell preseruacion of the seid princes accordynglie.

---

[1] The scribe's contemporary gloss. [2–2] Later hand.
[3] leaf 361, back. [4] See above, p. 713.
[5] deletions.

§ 119. *Rog. Palmer, Mayor*, 1534.

Yeven vnder *our* signet at my lordes Manou*r* of Grenewich the vij day of September in the xxvth yeire of my seid lordes Reigne.¹ — *From Greenwich.*

MICHAELMAS LEET.

²¶ [V. f. p. held on Oct. 7, 25 Hen. VIII.] — *"Ciuitas Couentrie." Oct. 7, 1533.*

Esson*ia*. ¶.

[M*agister*³ Rog. Wales, Jul. Nethermyll, Tho. Banwell, Ric. Herryng, Tho. Dodd, Tho. Asteleyn, Will. Smyth, Rog. Palmer, Tho. Smyth, Tho. Wilmer, Joh. Crampe, Will. Towres, Tho. Gopsill, Ric. Wethers, Tho. Spenser, Ric. Townesend, Rob. Kirvyn, Jas. Gilbert, Rob. Seny, Tho. Gardinou*r*, Joh. Jett, Will. Ma*r*ler, Tho. Burdon, ⁴Joh. Mosely, Will. Joynou*r*.} — *Jury of 25.*

¶ [" Magister" Tho. Brewer, Me*r*cer, " Magister" Geo. Philips, Cowper.⁵] — *Sheriffs.*

¶ [Enacted] for dyue*rs* consideraci*o*ns that all the bakers of Warwick & of the contrey, which bryng bred wekelie into this Citie to be sold on Wedensday & Fryday at the gaoll hall dore, shall from-hensfurth leave all such bredd as they cannot sell the seid dayes at iij Tiplers howsez at the seid gaole-hall dore or at on of theme: That is to say at Alexanders house, Ric. Cookes house, and at Alice Tiplers house, ther to be sold to the co*m*en people of the Citie when they come for it, And not to be sold in eny other place of the Citie, vpone peyn of eu*er*y of the seid bakers to forfeit all such bredd as they offer to be sold in eny other place. — *Orders of Leet. Country ⁶"bakers" to leave their unsold bread at certain houses to be sold to the common people.*

ROG. PALMER, MAYOR, 1534.

⁷¶ [Election of officers.] — *"Ciuitas Couentrie." Jan. 25. 25 electors.*

[M*agister*⁸ Will. Smyth, Jul. Nethermyll, Tho. Banwell, Hen. Wall, Ric. Herryng, Tho. Dodd, Tho. Asteleyn, Rog. Wales, Tho. Smyth, Joh. Cramp, Will. Towres, Tho.

---

¹ The original of this letter is preserved in the *Letter Book*, Corp. MS. A 79.
² leaf 362.   ³ Title prefixed to names until note 4.
⁴ Untitled.   ⁵ " & Jur[ati sunt] " = and they were sworn.
⁶ The scribe's contemporary gloss.   ⁷ leaf 362, back.
⁸ Title repeated until note 1 next page.

§ 119. *Rog. Palmer, Mayor. Leet,* 1534.

Gopsill, Ric. Wethers, Ric. Townesend, Jas. Gilbert, Will. Coton, Rob. Seny, Tho. Gardynour, Joh. Jett, Sym. Parker, Will. Marler, Tho. Burdon, [1]Joh. Moseley, Will. Jeynour, Cris. Waren.]

Officers.
¶ [m. Rog. Palmer, Mercer; rec. Rog. Wigston; cor. Rob. Grene; steward, Baldw. Porter; ch. Will. Stirropp, Joh. Nories; w. Ric. Humfrey, Mercer, Jas. Rogers, vintener; mace, Will. Alen; crier, Joh. Weit.[2]

EASTER AND MICHAELMAS LEETS.

"Ciuitas Couentrie."
[V. f. p. held before Rog. Palmer, m., Tho. Brewer, Geo. Philips, b., on Apr. 21, 25 Hen. VIII.]
[3]Essonia. ¶.

Jury.
[¶ Magister[4] Will. Smyth, Jul. Nethermyll, Tho. Banwell, Ric. Herryng, Tho. Dodd, Tho. Astelen, Rog. Wales, Hugh Lawton, Rob. Kirvyn, Tho. Smyth, Tho. Gopsill, Ric. Wethers, Ric. Townesend, Cris. Waid, Jas. Gilbert, Will. Coton, Tho. Gardynour, Sym. Parker, Joh. Saunders, Will. Rogers, [5]Will. Stirropp, Joh. Norres, Hugo Dalaway, Hugo Bloure.]

Orders of Leet.
[6]"Bochers" are forbidden to sell hides to foreigners before 11 o'clock on Fridays.

¶ [Enacted] that non of the Craft of Bochers within this Citie shall fromehensfurth sell eny of ther beastes hides to eny forener or foren Tanner vpon the Fryday within this Citie before the owre of xj of the Clocke before non, vpon peyn to forfeit for euery of the seid hides sold contrarie to the tenour of this acte iij s. iiij d. to be levied by the Shireffes by distrese to thuse of the seid Shireffes.

The sheriffs are to give the "seriauntes" but one livery suit a year instead of two.

¶ Also wher-as the Shireffes of this Citie haue been accustumed to geve to euery seriaunt of this Citie dyuers lyvereys in the yeire, In consideracion of the ease of ther great charges It is now enacted that the seid Shireffes frome-hensfurth shal-be charged to geve vnto euery of the seid seriauntes but onelie oon honest liuery of iiij yardes of brode cloith ageynst Cristenmas, and at Corpus Christitide suche sleves [and] Jackettes as they haue been wont to gyve vnto the seid seriauntes And no moo liuereys in the yeire. And at Whitsontide next the seid Shireffes shall

---

[1] Untitled. [2] "Et Jur[ati sunt]" = and they were sworn.
[3] leaf 363. [4] Title repeated as far as note 5.
[5] Untitled. [6] The scribe's own gloss.

§ 119. *Rog. Palmer, Mayor.* The Commons, 1534.

pay vnto euery of the seid seriauntes iij s. iiij d. in recompense of the lack of parte of ther seid lyuereyes to theme yevon at Cristenmas last past.

[1] ¶ [Enacted] that all & euery persone & persones, that haue eny housez or land adioynyng to the River of Shirburne within this Citie, shall befor Midsomer next comyng clense, make clene & scoure to the botome the seid River as fare as his or ther house or landes goith, vpone peyne to forfeit xx s. for euery defaute to be levied by the Shireffes of the Citie by distrese of the goodes of the owner of the seid landes, or of the goodes of the tenauntes of the seid landes, to the vse of the Meire, beilleffes & Cominaltie of the seid Citie.

Every one having house or land adjoining the "Shirburne"[2] to cleanse the river as far as their property extends or 20s. fine.

¶ Wher-as by auncient custome tyme owt of mynde the comen groundes aboute this Citie & within the liberties of the same, which owe to be opone & in comen at Lammas, & parte of theme at Michelmas, meny of theme haue been now of lait yeires by tolleracion & sufferaunce put into ardolf[3] & broken vp to soo corne vpone, and so gentillie & favourablie suffered for a tyme because of the great darthe & scarsenes of corne, which in fewe & lait yeires haith fallen in all parties of this Realme: And albeit so that now, thankes be to almyghtie God, Corne is comon to good plentie & to easie & reasonable price, Yet that notwithstandyng dyuers persones, regardyng more ther owne private profites then the seid aunciente custome & the comen welth & profite of the Citie, or the good & favourable sufferaunce of the gouernoures & hedes of the same, haue broken vpp, aerede[4] & soen moo of the seid groundes now latelie then euer were before, to the great hurte, preiudice & nocument[5] of all other the Citizens, dwellers, & inhabitauntes of the same, Not onelie in puttyng theme from ther recreacions & walkes, in Shotyng & other laudable & honest pastymes, but also in takyng awey the depasturyng of the mylche kie, Catell, & hakney horsez, which of necessitie the comeners & inhabitauntes of the

Order [2] "for Comen grounde plowed."[2]

More of the common land is under tillage in time of plenty than was permitted in time of dearth, to the hurt of the citizens in their deprivation of honest pleasures and

---

[1] leaf 363, back.   [2] The scribe's own gloss.
[3] In this form the word is neither in *N.E.D.* nor *E.D.D.* Dr. Hen. Bradley suggests the derivation from *seo erede healf* = the ploughed portion.   The word evidently signifies tillage.
[4] Ear = to plough.   [5] injury.

§ 119. Rog. Palmer, Mayor. The Commons, 1534.

<small>means of livelihood.</small>

Citie must & ought to haue, and without the which thei cannot well liff & meynteyn ther occupacions & menyall seruauntes, In Consideracion of the premissez and that the seid persones, which haue broken vpp & sowen the seid groundes, haue agreed & contented themselfes before Maister Meire & the Councell of the Citie no-more hereafter to breke vpp or heier[1] eny of the seid groundes, havyng libertie at this tyme to carie awey ther corne now sowen, It is enacted at this presente lete that no persone or persones hereafter of what estait or degre so-euer he or thei be, shall breike vpp, aier,[1] or sowe eny of the seid comen groundes accustumed to lie open at Lammas & Michelmas, vpon peyn to forfeit to the Citie for euery acre so broken vp & put in tillage xl s. except the especiall license opteyned & hadd of the Meire for the tyme beyng and his brethern & the comen Councell of the Citie. And that it shal-be leful to all theme that haue now sowen corne vpon the seid groundes to cary the same awey when it is ripe, be it before Lammas or after, without lett or interrupcion of eny persone or persones etc.

<small>Henceforward "none" are permitted "to plow"</small>

<small>without Licence off the mayor and his brethren and the Comon Councell."</small>

<small>"Ciuitas Couentrie." Oct. 8.</small>

[[2] V. f. p. held on Oct. 8, 26 Hen. VIII.]
Essonia.

<small>Jury of 26.</small>

[Magister[3] Will. Smyth, Jul. Nethermyll, Tho. Banwell, Tho. Astelen, Rog. Wales, Hugo Lawton, Rob. Kirvyn, Tho. Smyth, Tho. Wilmer, Joh. Crampe, Tho. Gopsill, Ric. Wethers, Ric. Townesend, Jas. Gilbert, Will. Coton, Rob. Seny, Tho. Gardynour, Joh. Saunders, Will. Rogers,[4] Joh. Norres, Ric. Humfrey, Cris. Waren, Tho. Smyth, Will. Norton, Tho. Keveit, Hug. Dalaway.

<small>Sheriffs.</small>

¶ [[5] Joh. Seill, draper, Hugo Gregorie, whittawer.]

<small>[6] "Seriauntes" are to have their usual liveries.</small>

¶ [Enacted] that all & euery seriaunt & officer of this Citie shall fromehensfurth haue & enyoye all such liuereyes & fees yeirelie as thei in tymes past haue hadd & been accustumed to haue, notwithstandyng an acte maide at the last leet to the contrarie.[7]

¶ [Enacted] that no persone of this Citie shall fromehensfurth cast eny dunge or muck into the River of

---

[1] Ear = to plough.   [2] leaf 364.
[3] The title precedes all names as far as note 4.   [4] Untitled.
[5] Magistros prefixed.   [6] The scribe's own gloss.
[7] See above, p. 718.

§ 120. Rob. Kyrvyn, Mayor, 1535.

Sherburne, Ner swepe the streit to convey the dunge or Mucke therof into the seid River, vpone peyne of eu*er*y housholder that so offendeth by hymself, his wyff, his s*er*ua*u*nt, or otherwise, for eu*er*y defaute xij d. to be levied by the Shire*ff*es of the Citie by distrese to ther owne vse of the goodes of the housholder etc.

The river
[1] *"Sher-burne" again!*

ROB. KYRVYN, MAYOR, 1535.

[[2] Election of officers.]

[M*agister*[3] Hugo Lawton, Jul. Nethermyll, Tho. Banwell, Ric. Herryng, Tho. Dodd, Tho. Astelen, Rog. Wales, Will. Smyth, Cris. Waid, Tho. Smyth, Joh. Cramp, Tho. Gopsill, Ric. Townesend, Jac. Gilbert, Will. Coton, Rob. Seny, Tho. Gardyno*u*r, Sym. P*a*rker, Will. Marler, Tho. Burdon, Will. Roge*r*s, Tho. Brewer, Geo. Philips, [4] Will. Stirr*c*pp, Joh. Norres.]

¶ [m. [5] Rob. Kirvyn, fishemonger; rec. Rog. Wigston; cor. Rob. Grene; steward, Baldw. Porter; ch. Edm. Damport, Will. Randle; w. Tho. Co*tes*, dier, Joh. Lawton, Cappe*r*; mace, Hen. Thirkell; crier, Joh. Weit.[6]]

"Ciuitas Couentrie."
Jan. 25.
25 electors.

New officers.

EASTER AND MICHAELMAS LEETS.

[7] ¶ [V. f. p. held before Rob. Kirvyne, m., Joh. Seill, Hugo Gregorie, b., on Apr. 20, 26 Hen. VIII.]

[M*agister*[8] Hugo Lawton, Jul. Nethermyll, Tho. Banwell, Ric. Herryng, Tho. Dodd, Tho. Astelen, Rog. Walles, Rog. Palmer, Cris. Waid, Tho. Smyth, Tho. Wilmer, Joh. Cramp, Ric. Townesend, Jas. Gilbert, Rob. Seny, Tho. Gardyno*u*r, Joh. Jett, Sym. P*a*rker, Tho. Burdon, Will. Rogers, Tho. Brewer, Geo. Philips, [9] Edm. Damport, Will. Randle.]

[Enacted] that the actes & ordinau*n*ces maid at a lete in the tyme of M*a*ister Burwey,[10] Meire of this Citie, for the true makyng of Cloith & seallyng of the same shal-be

"Ciuitas Couentrie."
Apr. 20, 1535.

Searchers to be chosen to seal *"Cloith."* [1]

---

[1] The scribe's own gloss.   [2] leaf 364, back.
[3] The title precedes the names up to note 4.
[4] Untitled.   [5] Magister prefixed.
[6] "Et jur[ati sunt"] = and they were sworn.   [7] leaf 365.
[8] Repeated before every name until note 9.
[9] Untitled.   [10] See above, p. 656.

§ 120. Rob. Kyrvyn, Mayor. Leet, 1535.

frome-hensfurth per*fou*rmed & kept, vpon the penalties & peynes lymyt in the same: And that too of the Craft of weyvers & too of the Craft of walkers shal-be yeirelie electe & sworne to be serchers & to make true reaport & presentement of eu*er*y defaute comytted in ther occupa-cions; And that also a sealer shal-be yeirelie electe & sworne to put a seall to such Cloith as shal-be truelie maid & to non other etc.

The price of "vitaill." [1]

[Enacted] that M*aister* Tho. Banwell & M*aister* Ric. Herryng, beyng assistaunce with M*aister* Meire in the order of vitaill & p*r*ices of the same, shall refou*r*me the order of the fishe M*ar*ket & all other vitulacio*n* accordyng to good order etc.

Orders concerning "talow" [1]

[Enacted] that the bochers of the Citie shall sell ther talow to the inha*b*itaunte*s* of the Citie for the p*r*ice of ij s. iiij d. the stone, vpo*n* peyn to forfeit for eu*er*y stone vj s. viij d. to the shireff*es* etc. And that the Chaundelers shall sell ther Candell after j d. ob. the li., and not to sell eny into the Contrey till the Citie be se*r*ued, vpon like peyn for eu*er*y defaute.

and "Candell" [1]

and· "ale wifes." [1]

Item, that the ale wives shall sell ther ale after xviij d. the Cester & xiiij galons to the Cester [2] [or 6s. 8d. at every default to the sheriffs' use].

"Ciuitas Couentrie."

[3] [V. f. p. held on Oct. 12, 27 Hen. VIII.]

[M*agister* [4] Hugo Lawton, Jul. Nethermyll, Tho. Banwell, Ric. Herryng, Tho. Dodd, Tho. Asteleyn, Rog. Wales, Will. Smyth, Rog. Palmer, Chris. Waid, Joh. Crampe, Ric. Townesend, Jas. Gilbert, Rob. Seny, Tho. Gardino*ur*, Joh. Jett, Sym. Pa*r*ker, Will. Rogers, Tho. Brewer, Geo. Philips, [5] Will. Randell, Will. Norton, Hugo Dalawey, Hen. Over.]

Sheriffs.

[Ric. Ley, M*er*cer, Cuthb. Joyno*ur*, dr*a*per.]

The union of "the gildes." [1]

¶ Me*m*. that xx[ti] of the Jure aboue-named [6] haue agreed that Corpus Ch*r*isti gilde shal-be annexed & vnyte vnto the Trinitie gilde & maid boithe on after suche ordyn-au*n*ce as the meire, recorder & the councell of the Citie

---

[1] The scribe's own gloss.   [2] See above, p. 713.
[3] leaf 365, back.
[4] Repeated before names until the next note.
[5] Untitled.   [6] They were not unanimous then.

§ 121. *Joh. Jett, Mayor*, 1536.

shall dyvyse, so that it may stand with the order of the lawe.[1]

[Enacted] that Candelles shal-be sold after the rait & price of j d. ob. the pounde, and talow after the rait of ij s. iiij d. the stone, vpon peyne for euery li. of Candell & euery stone of talow sold to the contrarie vj s. viij d.

<small>Order concerning 2 "candelles & talowe."</small>

[Enacted] that Alice Grene, Cakebaker, shall pay yierelie frome-hensfurth to the Craft of bakers xij d. toward ther charges.

<small>2 "Alice Grene, 3 Cakebaker."</small>

[Enacted] that non inhabitaunt of this Citie frome hensfurth shall put or deliuer eny Cloithe to eny walker to be walked or burled, but to such walkers or burlers as be inhabite within this Citie, vpon peyn who doithe the contrarie to forfeit for euery defaut vj s. viij d. to be levied by the comen seriaunt to thuse of the Cominalte of the Citie: And the said seriaunt to haue for his labour iiij d: And that the said walkers shall burle the same Cloithe within the said Citie, vpon like peyne for euery Cloithe burled to the contrarie to be levied in fourme aforseid.[4]

<small>No cloth to be fulled by 2 "walkers," who are not inhabitants of the city; offenders to pay 6s. 8d. to the use of the commonalty.</small>

[Enacted] that euery Alderman shall electe & apoynt ij honest men within euery ward to ouersee that noo man do cast eny fi[l]th in the rivers or swepe the stretes in tyme of reyne, and that thei that so doo shall forfeit for euery defaut xij d.

<small>Concerning 2 "the River: 3 none to sweep their streets into the Chanell in time off Raine."</small>

JOH. JETT, MAYOR, 1536.
EASTER AND MICHAELMAS LEETS.

[5][V. f. p. held before Joh. Jett, m., Ric. Ley, Cuthb. Joynour, b., on May 9, 28 Hen. VIII.]

<small>"Ciuitas Couentrie."</small>

[Magister [6]Will. Smyth, Jul. Nethermyll, Ric. Herryng, Tho. Dodd, Tho. Asteleyn, Rog. Wales, Hugo Lawton, Rog. Palmer, Tho. Smyth, Joh. Cramp, Ric. Townesend, Jac. Gilbert, Rob. Seny, Tho. Gardynour, Sym. Parker, Will. Marler, Tho. Burdon, Will. Rogers, Tho. Brewer,

<small>Jury.</small>

---

[1] Both gilds were suppressed in 1545. The corporation re-purchased the lands etc. of the gilds and chantries in 1552 for £1,315 1s. 8d. See Corp. MS. B. 75.
[2] The scribe's own gloss. [3] A later hand.
[4] See above, p. 661. [5] leaf 367.
[6] Repeated before names until note 1 next page.

§ 121. Joh. Jett, Mayor. Cloth, 1536.

Geo. Philips, Joh. Seill, Hugo Gregorie, [1]Joh. Clerk, Joh. Thomson.]

The act for making of 2 "Cloith" to stand.

¶ [Enacted] that the acte of leet latelie maid within this Citie for the serchyng & seallyng and also true makyng of wollen Cloith[3] shall stand still in force & effecte, and that euery Cloithe-maker of this Citie shall soeffer & allow his Cloithe to be serched & sealled by the officers admytted for the same, vpone peyn of euery defaut vj s. viij d. to be levied by the comen seriaunte etc.

2 "Cloith"

to be prepared by resident fullers.

[Enacted] that the walkers belongyng to this Citee shall burle ther Clothes of this Citie within the same Citie accordyng to the acte & ordinaunce therof maid at the last leet, vpon peynes mencioned in the same.[4]

The 2 "brewers" are ordered to brew when malt is dear, as well as when it is cheap.

Item, it is enacted that all suche inhabitauntes as now brue or intend to brue to sell within this Citie shall brue to sell now fromehensfurth as-well in the tyme of darthe of malte as in the tyme of cheip & plentie of malt, vpon peyne to forfeit for euery defaut v li. to be levied to the vse of the Meire, Cominaltie & Shireffes of this Citie equallie to be dyuyded amonges theme.

2 "Craftes."

5 "Euery ffreeman to hold off some Company."

[Enacted] that euery householder of this Citie, which is not associat to some Crafte, shal-be associat & bere with some Craft before Whitsontyde next, vpon peyne to be punysshed by the discrecion of the meire, etc.

"Ciuitas Couentrie." Jury.

¶ [6] [V. f. p. held on Oct. 10, 28 Hen. VIII.]

[Magister[7] Jul. Nethermyll, Tho. Banwell, Ric. Herryng, Tho. Dodd, Tho. Astelen, Rog. Wales, Hugo Lawton, Rog. Palmer, Rob. Kirvyn, Tho. Smyth, Joh. Cramp, Ric. Townesende, Cris. Waid, Jac. Gilbert, Rob. Seny, Tho. Gardynour, Sym. Parker, Will. Marler, Tho. Burdon, Joh. Saunders, Will. Rogers, Tho. Brewer, Joh. Seill, Hugo Gregorie.

Sheriffs.

[Joh. Talontes, Goldesmyth, Ric. Sewall,[8] Gresier.]

---

[1] Untitled.   [2] The scribe's own gloss.   [3] See above, p. 656.
[4] See above, p. 723.   [5] A later hand.
[6] leaf 367, back.   [7] Repeated before all names in this list.
[8] Undoubtedly of the family of Sewall or Sewell, which furnished two mayors to Coventry, William (in 1617) and Henry (in 1606), and has even now representatives in the Old and New World. For the wills of both William and Henry see 79 Byrd, 63 Barrington (Somerset House), and for much of the subsequent history of the family, and their emigration to America see *Midl. Antiquary*, iv. 157 *sqq.*, where the publications of the Massachusetts Hist. Soc. v. are quoted.

§ 122. Chris. Waid, Mayor, 1537.

[Ordained] that all the Brewers of this Citie, which brewe to sell, shall sell ther newe ale after the rait of xviij d. the Cester & xiiij galons to the Cester,[2] vpon peyn to forfeit for euery defaute to the Shireffes of the Citie vj s. viij d.

The price of "ale,"[1] wholesale

Item, that all reteyllers & tiplers of ale of this Citie shall sell ther ale by reteyll after the rait ensuyng, That is to say, the best stale ale dronke owt of the house for ij d. the galon, and within the house for iij d. the galon: And that the said Tiplers shall ordeyn & make ther pottes & measures after the raites aboueseid within x dayes next ensuyng this presente lete, vpone peyn to forfeit for euery defaute vj s. viij d. to the vse aforseid.

and retail.

Tiplers to make "pottes"[1] and measures according to the rate.

Item, that euery Alderman in his warde frome-hensfurth yeirelie shall electe ij able Altasters & swere the same truelie to execute that office.

"Aletasters."

Item, that the price of Talow & candell shal-be assessed by Maister Meire frome tyme to tyme etc.

"Candell."

CHRIS. WAID, MAYOR, 1537.

[3] ¶ [Election of officers.]

"Ciuitas Couentrie." 25 electors.

[Magister [4] Jul. Nethermyll, Ric. Herryng, Tho. Dodd, Tho. Astelen, Rog. Wales, Hugo Lawton, Rog. Palmer, Rob. Kyrvyn, Tho. Smyth, Joh. Cramp, Ric. Townesend, Tho. Spenser, Jac. Gilbert, Will. Marler, Tho. Burdon, Joh. Saunders, Will. Rogers, Tho. Brewer, Geo. Philips, Joh. Seill, Hugo Gregorie, Ric. Ley, Cuthbert Joynour, [5] Joh. Clerk, Joh. Tomson.]

[m. Magister Chris. Waid; rec. Rog. Wigston, armiger; cor. Rob. Grene [6] "sub condicione quod se inhabitet infra Comitatum Ciuitatis Couentrie citra festum S. Michaelis archangeli proximo"; steward, Baldw. Porter, generosus [7]; ch. Mauricius Gilbert, draper, Jac. Farmour, Roper [8]; w. Arth. Gudrich, Marcer, Joh. Bolat, draper; mace, Hen. Thirkell; crier, Joh. Wood.

---

[1] The scribe's own gloss.   [2] See above, p. 722.
[3] leaf 368.   [4] Repeated before names until note 5.
[5] Untitled.
[6] On condition that he shall dwell within the city before Michaelmas next.
[7] = gentleman.   [8] = rope-maker.

§ 122. Chris. Waid, Mayor. Leet, 1537.

EASTER AND MICHAELMAS LEETS.

"Ciuitas Couentrie." Apr. 24.

[1] ¶ [V. f. p. held before Chris. Waid, m., Joh. Talont*es*, Ric. Sewall, b., on Tuesday, Apr. 24, 29 Hen. VIII.]

Jury.

[M*agister*[2] Joh. Jett, Jul. Nethermyll, Tho. Banwell, Ric. Herryng, Tho. Dodd, Tho. Astelen, Rog. Wales, Hugo Lawton, Rog. Palmer, Rob. Kirvyn, Tho. Smyth, Ric. Townesend, Jac. Gilbert, Tho. Gardyno*ur*, Sym. P*a*rker, Joh. Saunders, Geo. Philips, Joh. Seill, Hugo Gregorie, Ric. Ley, Cuthb. Joyno*ur*, [3] Maur. Gilbert, Jac. Farmo*ur*, Tho. Napton.]

The "cappers" [4]

Item, wher-as the meire, Aldermen, Beilleff*es* & Comin-altie of this Citie by ther wrytyng indented & sealled with ther co*m*en seall haue g*r*aunted, given & dymysed vnto the M*a*isterez, kep*er*s, frate*r*nitie, & company of the

are to have the pageant, pageant-house and chapel formerly belonging to the cardmakers.

Craft of Cappe*r*s of this Citie the pagyaunt & pagyaunt-house, which was latelie surrendered & given vpp by wrytyng to theme by the ffrate*r*nitie & company of Cardemakers & sadelers, It is nowe enacted by auctoritie of this lete that the seid frate*r*nitie & company of Cappe*r*s shall enjoy the seid pagiaunt, pagiaunt-house & Chappell accordyng to the teno*ur* of the seid wrytyng indented etc.

"Ale-tasters & ale wives." [4]

Item, it is enacted (etc.) that eue*r*y Alderma*n* of this Citie in his warde shall electe & apoynt too ale-tasters in eue*r*y warde or moo if nede be ; And that eue*r*y Brewer that breweth to sell shall sell ther ale after the rait of xviij d. the Cester & xiiij galons to the Cester, vpon peyn of forfeyture of vj s. viij d. to the Shireff*es*, and that the seid brewer shall send to the seid ale-tasters & requyre theme to tast ther ale before thei sell or vtter the same, vpon peyn of iij s. iiij d. to be levied to the vse of the Shireff*es* by distres at eue*r*y suche defaut.

Candles 1¼d. a lb.

[5][Enacted] *that*[6] no ma*n* shall sell candell aboue j d. qua.[7] the lb., vpon peyn to be grevouslie amercied.

Tallow.

Item, *that*[6] no talow shal-be sold owt of this Citie by eny bocher of the same vntill the Citie be se*r*ued, vpon peyn of ij s. the Stone.

---

[1] leaf 368, back.
[2] Repeated before each name as far as note 3. [3] Untitled.
[4] The same or a contemporary handwriting. [5] leaf 369.
[6] "þ" is here written like "y." [7] = quadrans, a farthing.

§ 123. Will. Coten, Mayor, 1538.

Item, that the serchers of the weivers & serchers of walkers shall execute ther offices for the true makyng & ordryng of Cloith, vpon peyn of euery sercher to forfeit vj s. viij d. to the shireffes. *[Searchers of "Clothyng" to execute their office.]*

[1] [V. f. p. held on Tuesday, Oct. 16, 29 Hen. VIII.] *["Ciuitas Couentrie." Oct. 16. Jury of 25.]*
Magister [2] Joh. Jett, Tho. Banwell, Ric. Herryng, Tho. Dodd, Tho. Astelen, Rog. Wales, Hugo Lawton, Rog. Palmer, Tho. Smyth, Joh. Cramp, Tho. Wilmer, Ric. Townesend, Jac. Gilbert, Rob. Seny, Tho. Gardynour, Sym. Parker, Joh. Saunders, Will. Rogers, Tho. Brewer, Joh. Seill, Cuthb. Joynour, [3] Maur. Gilbert, Jac. Farmour, Art. Gudriche, Joh. Bowlat.]

[Hen. Over, mercer, Chris. Waren, draper.] *[Sheriffs.]*

[Enacted] that the hedd Maister of the Craft of walkers shal-be alwey inhabited within this Citie duryng the tyme of his office: And that on Tho. Glegg shal-be hedd Maister this yeire, and Alex. Howe of Stoneley the vnder Maister.[5] *[[4] "walkers."]*

Also it is enacted (etc.) that all brewers shall sell ther best ale after the rait of xviij d. the Cester, & not aboue, and xiiij galons to the Cester: And also that the tipelers shall sell ther ale owt of ther doores after the rait of ij d. ob. the galon, & within the dores after iij d. the galon, vpon peyn to forfeit for euery defaut vj s. viij d. to be levied by distresse by the Shireffes to ther own vse. *["Ale wifes." [6]]*

[7] Also it is enacted (etc.) that all men that haue eny draughtes vpon the Reed-diche shall put down & take away the same before the feast of All Seyntes next, vpon peyn to forfeit for euery draught xx s. to be leuyed as is aforseid. *["Reed [6] diche."]*

WILL. COTEN, MAYOR, 1538.
[8] [Election of officers.]

[Magister [9] Tho. Dodd, Tho. Astelen, Rog. Wales, Hugo Lawton, Rog. Palmer, Joh. Jett, Tho. Smyth, Joh. *["Ciuitas Couentrie." Electors.]*

---

[1] leaf 369, back.   [2] Repeated before all names as far as note 3.
[3] Untitled.   [4] The same or a contemporary handwriting.
[5] This looks as if a union had been made of resident and non-resident fullers. See for "foreign" fullers p. 723, *et passim.*
[6] The same handwriting.   [7] leaf 370.   [8] leaf 370, back.
[9] Repeated before each name as far as note 1, p. 728.

§ 123. Will. Coten, Mayor. Leet, 1538.

Cramp, Jac. Gilbert, Rob. Seny, Sym. Parker, Joh. Saunders, Tho. Brewer, Joh. Seill, Joh. Talontes, Ric. Sewall, Will. Marler, Will. Rogers, Ric. Ley, Georg[e] Philips, Cuthbert Joynour, [1] Maur. Gilbert, Jac. Fermour, Jac. Rogers.]

Officers.

[m. Magister Will. Coton, mercer; rec. Rog. Wigston, armiger; cor. Rob. Grene, "so that he shall dwell within the city before the feast of the Nativity of S. John Baptist next"; steward, Baldw. Porter; ch. Ric. Hurt, mercer, Tho. Wheteley, Cardemaker; w. Mart. Ridell, Tho. Diglyn; mace, Hen. Thirkyll; crier, Joh. Wood.]

LEET.

"Ciuitas Couentrie."

[2][V. f. p. held before Will. Coton, m., Hen. Over, Chris. Waren, b., on Thursday, May 10, 30 Hen. VIII.]

Jury of 27.

[Magister [3] Tho. Banwell, Tho. Dodd, Tho. Astelen, Rog. Wales, Hugo Lawton, Rog. Palmer, Rob. Kirvyn, Joh. Jett, Ric. Townesend, Tho. Smyth, Joh. Cramp, Tho. Wilmer, Tho. Spenser, Jac. Gilbert, Rob. Seny, Tho. Gardynour, Sym. Parker, Tho. Burdon, Joh. Saunders, Will. Rogers, Tho. Brewer, Geo. Philips, Joh. Seill, Ric. Ley, Cuthb. Joynour, Ric. Sewall, [4]Ric. Hurt.]

The "Redd-diche" [5]

["Ordeyned"] that all persones haivyng or vsyng eny draughtes or other anoyaunces vpon or nygh the Reedd-dyche, or eny sluses or other conveyaunces of water or filthe frome eny draughtes into the said Reed-diche, shall take vpp, remove & vtterlie adnull the same before the Assencion of our Lord God now next comyng, vpon peyn to forfeit for euery defaut xx s. to be levied by distresse by the shireffes, the on half therof to ther own vse, & the other half to the vse of the comen box; and that Joh. Borresley, Will. Wightman, Joh. Stele, & Ant. Giller shall haue the ouersight of the execucion of this acte. And that the Chamberleyns of the Citie immediatlie after the removyng & avoydyng of the said draughtes & anoy-aunces shall Scoure the said diche frome the Micheparke Streit vnto the Jourden Well etc. And that non inhabit-

is to be [6] "scowred by the Chamber-lins."

---

[1] Untitled. [2] leaf 371.
[3] Repeated before all names until note 4. [4] Untitled.
[5] In the same handwriting. [6] In later hand.

§ 123. *Will. Coten, Mayor. Commons*, 1538.

aunt of this Citie after the feast of the Assenc*i*on of o*ur* Lord God now next ensuyng shall cast eny filthe or other anoya*u*nce into the said diche, ner shall mak or sett eny drauughte*s* (*sic*) oue*r* or nygh the same diche, vpon peyn of xx s. to be levyed to the vse aforseid.

[Enacted] that no bocher, ner non other inha*b*itaunt of this Citie, shall sell eny talowe before the feast of Eister next aboue the p*r*ice of ij s. iiij d. the Stone, ner shall sell eny talow out of the Citie before the seid feast, vpon peyn to forfeit for eu*er*y Stone xx s. to the vse aforse*i*d.

²[Enacted] that no p*er*sone or pe*r*sones of this Citie frome-hensfurthe shall make or cause to be maid eny Capp or Cappes Spone or maid of Cloithe yarne, vpon peyn of forfeyture of the said Capp or cappes : and that it shal-be laufull to eu*er*y p*er*son of this Citie to seasse & take the same to his own vse : and that the makers of the same shall haue punysheme*n*t of ther bodyes by the pilorie, or otherwise, at the discrec*i*on of the Justice*s* of peace.

No filth to be cast into the "Red diche."

No butcher to sell any "talowe" before Easter above ij s. iiij d. the stone.

No ¹"Cappes" to be made of yarn.

COMMON LANDS.

Where-as the Meire, beilleff*es* & Com*i*naltie, Citi3ens & inha*b*itaunte*s* of the Citie of Couent*r*e, & ther p*r*edicess*o*u*r*es by title of p*r*escripc*i*on & by auncient tyme owt of mynde haue hadd & haue the yeirelie vsage & exercise of com*m*on of pastures wi*th* ther beaste*s* & catalle*s* frome Lammas day to Candelmasse day of & in certayne Closez & pastures lying & beying wi*th*in the circuit of the Shire, ffraunches & libe*r*ties of the said Citie, which Closez & pastures by the vsage of the said Com*m*on and by the yeireli*e* rydyng of the Chambe*r*leyns of the said Citie to clayme & make gappes & weyes to the same be well & p*er*fitelie knowen to the said Citi3ens, Com*m*oners & inha*b*itaunte*s* : And for-asmoche as it is noo well & p*er*fitelie knowen to the same Citi3ens & inha*b*itaunte*s* that the greatest nomber of theme take & haue no benefites, vsage, ner p*r*ofite of the said Comon of pasture, and that meny of those p*er*sones that do take the vsage,

¹"The commons about the Citie"

are well and perfectly known,

though the greater part of the inhabitants have no profit of the same ;

¹ In the same or a contemporary hand.   ² leaf 371, back.

§ 123. Will Coten, Mayor. Commons, 1538.

and those who have surcharge them,

benefite & profite of the said Common do mysvse & surcharge the same contrarie to the auncient orders & good custumes of the said Citie, ffor reformacion wherof & to thentent that a vniuersall profite & commoditie may come & be hadd to all the said Citizens & Cominalte of the said Common Closez, the said Cominalte by the license, assent & consent of Will. Coton, now beyng meire of the said Citie, & of his bretherne, the Aldermen of the same, haue

it is therefore ordained that 50 persons,

elected, named, admytted & chosen fiftie persones of the said Cominaltie, that is to say, in euery warde of the seid

5 in each ward,

Citie five discreit & credible persones to speke, conclude

be chosen to make a scheme for dealing with the same commons for the general profit.

& doo as thei shall thynk best & moost convenient for the reformacion of the premissez to the effect & intent aforseid: which fiftie persones haue not onelie by good deliberacion reasoned & debated the said matters amonges themselfes & with the said meire & aldermen, but also thei haue perused[1] & viewed all the said Closez to se howe meny of [2] theme may be permytted & soeffered to lie & be seuerall all the yeire for a reasonable rent to be payed yeirelie for the same to the vse & behove of all the said Cominaltie, leavyng sufficient common to the said Commoners in other of the said Common Closez.

"The acte." "Commen ground seuerall." Whereupon

And therupon for the good gouernaunce, rule & conseruacion of the said Cominaltie & commoners and for the vniuersall profit & commoditie of the same, the said Meire, Aldermen, & the said fiftie persones with the assent & consent as well of the said Cominaltie as of the enheritoures & freholders of the said Closez with other now assembled, haue concorded, concluded & agreed, And

it is enacted by Leet

also haue ordeyned, enacted & constituted by auctoritie of this presente lete, And by auctorite of the grauntes & liberties to the said Citie grauntedby the kyng our souereign lorde & diuers his progenytoures, concernyng the premisses in manour & fourme followyng: That is to

that the closes named by the fifty persons shall be several all times of the year, a reasonable rent being paid to the

say, that all suche of the said Closez & pastures as the said fiftie persones haue named, assigned & appoynted, & hereafter expressed & wrytten, shall lie & be seuerall at all tymes fromehensfurthe duryng all the said tyme of Common for suche a reasonable rent to be payed yierelie

[1] = gone over.   [2] leaf 372.

§ 123. *Will. Coten, Mayor. Commons,* 1538.

for the same to the vse of the said Cominaltie as the same fiftie persones haue lymyted & sett vpon the same Closez & pastures. *use of the community.*

ffurst, a Close called the Myree feild[1] by yeire	xxiij s. iiij d.	23s. 4d.
Item, the Peny feildes[2] in the holding of Maister Lawton by yeire	xv s.	15s. 0d.
Item, Maister Wales feild by yeire	vj s. viij d.	6s. 8d.
Item, Maisteres Clerkes feild by yeir	x s.	10s. 0d.
Item, the Corner feild & a medow at the ende of it in the holdyng of Joh. [3] Yerdeley by yeir	vj s. viij d.	6s. 8d.
Item, a feild next Maister Wales feild by yeire	viij s.	8s. 0d.
Item, the quarell feild by Horsall side by yeire	vj s. viij d.	6s. 8d.
Item, v feildes called Whaberleyes[4] by yeir	xl s.	"ij Closez." 40s. 0d.
Item, the Black Croft[5] by yeir	ij s.	2s. 0d.
Item, a feild next the Steppyng Stones by yeir.	xx d.	20d.
Item, a feild next to it by yeire	v s.	5s. 0d.
Item, Maister Merlers feild by yeire	iiij s.	4s. 0d.
Item, half the iiij li. feildes in the ij great feildes next Assho by yeire[6]	xxvj s. viij d.	26s. 8d.
Item, the Thistell-feild[6] & the Rie feild by yeire	xiij s. iiij d.	13s. 4d.
Item, the ij ouermoost of Botmans acre[7]	xiij s. iiij d.	13s. 4d.
Item, the Chilter-leyes[8] by yeire	xvj s.	16s. 0d.
Item, iij feildes of Maister Kebeelles by yeir	xv s.	15s. 0d.
[9] Item, the pytfeildes by yeire	v s.	5s. 0d.
Item, a medow at the ende of it	iiij s.	4s. 0d.
Item, the Holowe-wey-feild[10] by yeire	viij s.	8s. 0d.
Item, Pycardes Croft by yeire	iiij s.	4s. 0d.
Item, Barkers-leys[10] by yeire	xx s.	20s. 0d.
Item, the overmoost Shokemoore[11] by yeire	iiij s.	4s. 0d.
Item, the nethermoost Shokemore by yeire	v s.	5s. 0d.
Item, the Stripp beyonde the Steppyng Stones by yeir	ij s.	2s. 0d.

[1] See above, pp. 440, 576. [2] See p. 48.
[3] This scribe puts the same sign for I, Y, and very frequently J.
[4] See p. 50. [5] "Blake Orchard," p. 49.
[6] See Inclosure Award, 1860. [7] See pp. 4, 51.
[8] See p. 51. [9] leaf 372, back. [10] See Inclosure Award, 1860.
[11] See "Sugmore Croftes," p. 52.

§ 123. *Will. Coten, Mayor. Commons*, 1538.

5s. 0d.	Item, Ma*ister* Kirvynse feild by yeire. . . .	v s.
6s. 0d.	Item, the feild next it	vj s.
15s. 0d.	Item, a feild called Picardypere¹	xv s.
4s. 0d.	Item, the Wardense feild at Harnall-bridge by yeire	iiij s.
10s. 0d.	Item, ij feild*es* called Byllynge*s*feild*es* by yeire²	x s.
2s. 0d.	Item, a litell Croft next theme by yeir . . .	ij s.
15s. 0d.	Item, the Kynge*s*-feild*es* or Ludlowe-feildes at Gosford Grene by yeire³	xv s.
15s. 0d.	Item, the Quarell-feild ageynst the Charte*r*house by yeir	xv s.
23s. 4d.	Item, Barnes-feild*es*⁴ by yeir. . . . . . xxiij s. iiij d.	
5s. 0d.	Item, a medowe at Waryng*es* Milne	v s.
5s. 0d.	Item, a medowe & a litle Croft at the Milne in the holl by yeir	v s.
	Item, a medowe at Jeffreyes Milne⁵ & the orchard to it by yeir.	⁶
12d.	Item, the Goosse Croft⁷ at Radford by yeir . .	xij d.
26s. 8d.	Item, a Close called the Sholder of mutton⁷ with the house at the Hill Crosse . . . . xxvj s. viij d.	
£18 18s. 8d.	The Some of all the rents of the said Closez & pastures doith amount vnto. . . . . . xviij li. xviij s. viij d.	

⁸ " Peyne xx s."

The people are warned that the above-named pastures are to be held in severalty.

And it is also enacted by the auctoritie aforseid that all the said Citi*z*ens & inha*b*itaunt*es* frome-hensfurthe yeirelie duryng all the said tyme of Comon shall pe*r*mytt & soeffer all the said Closez & pastures before-wrytten to lie & be seue*r*all & enclosed to & for the vse & behove of suche & ⁹those pe*r*sones which at eny tyme hereafter shall take & haue theme, or eny of theme, in ferme accordyng to the tenou*r* & intent of this p*r*es*e*nte ordyna*u*nce, acte & constituc*i*on, So that the fermou*r*es of the same may peasiblie take & haue the herbage & profittes therof w*i*th*o*ut lett or distu*r*baunce of the said Co*m*inaltie, or eny of theme ; And that all suche Closes as shall lie

Certain ⁸ " pastures

---

¹ See p. 53.   ² See p. 46.
³ See p. 46. Traditionally called after Richard II because it was there that in 1397 the king forbade Mowbray and Bolingbroke to engage in combat.
⁴ ? Barons-fyld, see p. 350.   ⁵ (?) See " Geffrey feild," p. 11.
⁶ blank.   ⁷ See Inclosure Award, 1860.
⁸ In the same handwriting.   ⁹ leaf 373.

§ 123. *Will. Coten, Mayor. Commons*, 1538.

common to the said Citizense shal-be permytted & vsed to lie in pasture & not vsed in tillage & sowen with corne,[1] vpon peyne of euery of the said inhabitauntes wilfullie doyng or commaundyng eny acte to be doon to the contrarie to forfeit for euery suche defaute xx s., the same forfeyture to be levyed & taken of the said offendoures by attachement & imprisonement of ther bodies or distreynyng of ther goodes, vntill thei doo pay the said peyne & forfeyture vnto the meire of the seid Citie for the tyme beyng: And the same attachement or distresse to be doon by the said meire or by suche officers or constables as the said meire shall assigne & appoynt to & for the same: And the on half of the same forfeyture shal-be put in a Comen box to the vse & behove of the said Cominaltie, And the other half, or asmoche therof as the said meire shall thynk convenyent, shal-be payed to the farmour or farmoures of the pastures or Closez so tilled or sowen in recompense of ther losse & damages susteyned in that behalf, And the residue to be put in the said box to the comen vse aforseid.

margin: not to be sowen
on peyn of
xx s.",
half to the common box,
half to the farmers of the closes.

Also it is further enacted, ordeyned & constituted by auctoritie aforseid concernyng the premissez that the said Closez & pastures, lymytted & appoynted to be maid seuerall, shalbe lett & sett to farme by tene men of the said Cominaltie, That is to say of euery warde of the said Citie on man, which shall haue auctoritie & power to lett & sett to farme the said Closez & pastures for the terme & tyme of ix yeires or vnder & not aboue, frome the feast of Lammas next ensuyng this presente lete, takyng of the farmoures therof an obligacion to be maid in due fourme of the lawe, wherin thei shal-be bound to iij or iiij of the said tene men in a more some then the rent, to pay ther rent yeirelie at seynt Valentynes day accordyng to [2] the said bonde. And that thei shall till & sowe the same pastures & Closez so appoynted to be seuerall at ther pleasures, So that thei leave the same at thende of the seid ix yeires with grene sord of the age of

margin: "The order to lett & sett."
The closes are to be let by 10 men, 1 man from each ward,
on a 9 years' lease
at a yearly rent payable on S. Valentine's day.
"For payment of the Rentes."

---

[1] Apparently this refers to arable encroachments on the common lands, see pp. 719–20.
[2] leaf 373, back.

§ 123. *Will. Coten, Mayor. Commons*, 1538.

<small>The present freeholders are to be preferred before other possible tenants.</small>

two yeires at the leaste, And that those persones that have now in farme the free-holders parte of the said Closez shal-be preferred before other to haue in farme the said Cominalties parte[1] paying the rent in fourme aforseid.

<small>"The accompt" is to be presented on Mar. 26,</small>

And also that the said tene men or the servyvoures of theme shall yeierlie bryng in & make before the meire & aldermen of the said Citie for the tyme beyng ther accomptes & the money due & comyng of the said rentes vpon the morowe after the feast of the Annunciacion of our Ladie seynt Marie, if it be not Sonday or verey nigh Eister, And then the said accompt to be maid at suche day as the seid meire & Aldermen shall appoynt: At which accompt & payment of the said rent ther shal-be

<small>20s. being allowed for a breakfast or recreation after delivery of the accounts.</small>

deliuered & allowed to the seid x men xx s. of the said Rentes to be spent for a brekefast or a recreacion after the same Accompt maid at discrecion of the said meire & aldermen.

And the money that shall rise & come vpon the said Accomptes shall then be put into the said Comen box, and shal-be bestowed to the vniuersall profite, ease & commoditie of the said Cominaltie in manour & fourme

<small>[2] "To what vse the rentes shal-be apployed."</small>

folowyng, That is to say, ffor the generall & comen paymentes which hereafter shal-be & ought to be payed by the Cominaltie of the said Citie as fivetenes & suche other common charges.

<small>[2] "The box & keyes."</small>

And the said box shall alweyes remayne in the Treasoure-house in Seynt Marie hall, and be locked with v keyes, wherof ij keyes shall alweyes remeane in the custodie of the said meire & aldermen; and the residue of the said keyes shall alweyes remeane in the custodie of

<small>Any one of the ten dying is to be replaced,</small>

the said x men. And if eny of theme fortune to die then the said meire & Aldermen [3] to electe & chose other of the same warde to be in his or ther Steid for the receit of the said Rentes & makyng of the said Accomptes.

And after thende of the said leasse & terme of ix

---

[1] *i. e.* those that hold the land during the "several" season from Candlemas to Lammas are to have the first chance of renting the commonable rights during the season between Lammas and Candlemas.

[2] In the same handwriting.   [3] leaf 374.

§ 123. *Will. Coten, Mayor. Commons,* 1538.

yeires & at the last Accomptes of & for the said Rentes The said meire & Aldermen by the assent of the seid tene mene shall electe, name & chose other tene men, in euery warde oon, which shal-be then charged and shall haue like auctoritie to lett & sett the said Closez for other ix yeires as is before lymyted & assigned to the said first x men. And that euery of the said accomptauntes defectyue in his accompt, or payment of the said Rentes by hyme received, shal-be punysshed by impresonment by the commaundement of the seid meire as a disturbour & an enymy of the comen-welth of the said Citie vntill he haue maid due satisfaccion & recompense for his said offence.

and a fresh set to be chosen at the end of 9 years.

Defaulters to be punished.

Also it is further enacted, ordeyned & constituted by auctoritie aforseid that no Commoner, or inhabitauntes of the said Citie shall haue comen within the said liberties for or with eny other kyndes of Beasse or catall, or with eny mo beasse or catall then with two Milche kyen & on geldyng, or two geldynges & oon Mi[l]che cowe; except onelie the bochers of the said Citie, which vse vitulacion, who shall & may common euery of theme with fivtene sheipp ouer & besides the Stynt abouelymytted, vpon peyne of euery persone passyng or brekyng the said order & stynt to forfeit & pay for euery tyme so doyng xij d. to the vse of the Chamberleynse of the said Citie. And that the said Chamberleynse shall not lett ner sett the said commons, ner eny part of theme, ³ to farme, or give eny libertie or auctoritie to eny persone to breke the said stynt, vpon peyn to forfeit for euery tyme that thei so do xx s. to the comen box of the said Citie.

[1] "The stynt of Catall." [1]

[2] "2 melsh kine and one Guelding or two Gueldings and one melsh Cow. Butchers to haue 15 sheep [on the] Comons besides the said stint." [2]

The chamberlains are [1] *"not to lett the comons to farme."* [1]

The names of the tene men appoynted to lett & sett the said Closez & to gether the rentes of the same for the first ix yeires.

Gosford-stret warde: Joh. Bowlat, draper.
Much-parke-Streit warde: Will. Beilie, draper.
Jourden-well warde: Ric. Wightman, thelder.
Erle-streit warde: Tho. Enderby, barbour.
Beilie-lane warde: Rauf Hopkynse, Tayllour.

¹⁻¹ In the same hand as the text.   ²⁻² A later hand.
³ leaf 374, back.

§ 123. Will. Coten, Mayor. Commons, 1538.

Broid-[1]*Yait warde:* Joh. Clerke, Coriour.
Croschepyng warde: Hugh Dalawarr, mercer.
Smythford-stret warde: Rauf Dale, [1]Inholder.
Spone-stret warde: Jas. Farmour, Grasier.
Bisshop stret warde: Philipp Shirrerd, draper.

[2] The names of the fiftie men which haue viewed & appoynted owt the Closez & pastures before-wrytten to be seuerall & enclosed.

Gorforde (sic) Streit warde.

Joh. Bowlat, draper, Joh. Lawton, Capper, Tho. Sconse, Capper, Clement Temple, dier, Ric. Collynse, Shirman.

Myche-parke Streit warde.

Will. Ruddyng, Clothier, Tho. Keyvett, Sherman, Will. Beilie, draper, Owyn Blakemer, weyver, Joh. Nicolles, Sherman.

Jourden Well warde.

Joh. Hill, Capper, Ric. Wightman, thelder, Ric. Baguley, tayllour, Joh. Annesley, yoman, Joh. Borresley, Capper.

Erle-stret warde.

Joh. Chambers, Capper, Martyne Ridell, mercer, Will. Stirropp, flecher,[3] Tho. Seny, draper, Tho. Enderby, barbour.

Beilie lane warde.

Henrie Hynde, mercer, Rauf. Hopkynse, Taillour, Olyver Forest, poticarie, Joh. West, Goldesmyth, Joh. Grene, mercer.

[4] Broid Yait warde.

[5] Chris. Wharton, Skynner, Joh. Clerk, Coriour, Tho. Saunders, Capper, Mourice Appowell, draper, Tho. Diglyng, mercer.

Croschepyng warde.

Hugh Dalawarr, mercer, Jas. Rogers, vyntener, Guy Speke, Inholder, Tho. Saunders, bocher, Will. Vnderwood, Coruiser.

---

[1] This scribe's "Y," "I" and "J" are identical. [2] leaf 375.
[3] "Pet. Browne" deleted. [4] leaf 375, back. [5] Xpofer.

§ 124. *Sim. Parker, Mayor,* 1539.

Smythford Streit ward.

Arture Gudriche, mercer, Rauf Dale, Inholder, Tho. Cotes, dier, Tho. Busterd, Inholder, Tho. Morres, draper.

Spone-streit ward.

Jas. ffarmour, Gresier, Will. Norton, dier, Hugh Bloure, whittawer, Ric. Smyth, Sherman, Joh. Eyburn, Tanner.

Bisshop-stret ward.

Will. Kelyngworth, bocher, Joh. Wall, weyver, Tho. Owres, baker, Henrie Collynse, bocher, Philipp Shirrerd, draper.

MICHAELMAS LEET.

[¹ V. f. p. held on Oct. 8, 30 Hen. VIII.]   *"Ciuitas Couentrie."* Jury of 27.

[Magister² Tho. Banwell, Ric. Herryng, Tho. Dodd, Tho. Astelen, Rog. Wales, Hugo Lawton, Rog. Palmer, Rob. Kirwyn, Joh. Jett, Chris. Waid, Ric. Townesend, Tho. Smyth, Jas. Gilbert, Rob. Seny, Tho. Gardynour, Sym. Parker, Will. Marler, Tho. Burdon, Joh. Saunders, Will. Rogers, Tho. Brewer, Joh. Seill, Ric. Ley, Cuthb. Joynour, Joh. Talontes, Ric. Sewall, Tho. Smyth, draper.]

[Joh. Herford, Tanner, Hug. Bloure, whittawer.]   Sheriffs.

SIM. PARKER, MAYOR, 1539.

³[Election of officers.]   *"Ciuitas Couentrie."* Electors.

[Magister⁴ Tho. Banwell, Ric. Herryng, Tho. Dodd, Tho. Astelen, Rog. Wales, Hug. Lawton, Rog. Palmer, Rob. Kyrvyn, Joh. Jett, Chris. Waid, Tho. Gardynour, Tho. Burdon, Tho. Brewer, Geo. Philips, Ric. Ley, Cuth. Joynour, Joh. Talontes, Ric. Sewall, Her. Over, Chris. Waren, ⁵ Rad. Dale, Ric. Hurt, Tho. Diglyng, Maur. Ridell.]

[m. Magister Sym. Parker, Gresier⁶; rec. Rog. Wigston, armiger; cor. Rob. Grene; steward, Baldewinn Porter; ch. Tho. Saunders, sen., Gresier, Rob. Colman, Cowper; w. Ric. Warnour, barbour, Tho. Owres, baker; mace, Hen. Thirkell; crier, Joh. Wood.]   Officers.

---

¹ leaf 377.
² Repeated before each name, but perhaps deleted before the last.
³ leaf 377, back.   ⁴ Repeated before each name until note 5.
⁵ Untitled.   ⁶ Probably also a butcher, see p. 738.

§ 124. Sim. Parker, Mayor. Leet, 1539.

[And because the said S. Parker is a common victualler[1] they elected Master R. Herryng and Master C. Joynour to assist the said mayor in fixing the price of victuals.]

Et pro eo quod dictus Sim. Parker est communis victu[a]larius[1] eligerunt (sic) in assistentes dicti Maioris pro taxacione precii victualium Magistrum Ric. Herryng, & Magistrum Cuth. Joynour, et Jurati sunt.

EASTER AND MICHAELMAS LEETS.

"Ciuitas Couentrie." Apr. 22.

[2] ¶ [V. f. p. held before Sym. Parker, m., Joh. Herford, Hug. Bloure, b., on Tuesday, Apr. 22, 30 Hen. VIII.]

Jury of 25.

¶ [Magister[3] Ric. Herryng, Tho. Astelen, Rog. Wales, Hug. Lawton, Rog. Palmer, Chris. Waid, Tho. Gardynour, Ric. Townesend, Joh. Cramp, Jac. Gilbert, Rob. Seny, Joh. Saunders, Will. Rogers, Tho. Brewer, Geo. Philips, Cuth. Joynour, Joh. Talontes, Ric. Sewall, Hen. Over, Chris. Waren, [4]Tho. Saunders, Rob. Colman, Jac. Rogers, Ric. Niclyn, Hug. Dalawey.]

To no [5]"weyvers" shall work be given unless he belongs to the craft of weavers of the city, or 6s. 8d. fine.

[Enacted] that non inhabitaunte of this Citie fromehensfurthe shall put eny lynyn or wollen Yarne to be woven to eny weyver of the Citie or of the contrey oneles the same weyver be a brother admytted & associat with the weyuers of the Citie, vpon peyn to forfeit for euery tyme so offendyng vj s. viij d., the on half therof to be to the Shireffes for the tyme beyng, & the other half to the Masterz of the said Craft of weyvers, & to be levyed by way of distresse, etc.[6]

[7]"The comen."

[Enacted] that the Actes latelie maid for the order of the comen & of the comen groundes enclosed shall stand & bee in full strenght & duelie put in execution accordyng to the tenur of the same actes, etc.[8]

[Enacted] that fromehensfurthe the seriauntes that shall warne the comen watche of this Citie shall furst begyn to warne the said watche at seynt Margettes Chappell[9] & kepe the southe side of the Streit, and so to

Constables

---

[1] v. note 6, p. 737.   [2] leaf 378.
[3] Repeated before each name until note 4.
[4] Untitled.   [5] The same scribe's handwriting.
[6] See above, p. 723.   [7] The same handwriting.
[8] See above, p. 729.
[9] This chapel, with which was connected a hermitage (see above, p. 118), was afterwards converted into a tithe-barn. It stood outside Gosford Gate.

§ 124. *Sim. Parker, Mayor. Leet,* 1539.

go thorought the Citie in euery Streit as the holie Cake[1] goith. And that the Constable of the warde shall go euery nyght with the seriaunt to warne the watche & shall haue for his labour ij d. to warne the watche."

[2] [V. f. p. held on Oct. 7, 31 Hen. VIII.] "Ciuitas Couentrie." Oct. 6. Jury.

[Magister[3] Will. Coton, Tho. Banwell, Ric. Herryng, Rog. Wales, Hugo Lawton, Rog. Palmer, Joh. Jett, Tho. Gardynour, Ric. Townesend, Tho. Spenser, Jac. Gilbert, Rob. Seny, Tho. Burdon, Will. Rogers, Tho. Brewer, Geo. Philips, Ric. Ley, Cuth. Joynour, Joh. Talontes, Ric. Sewall, Chris. Waren, [4] Tho. [5] Saunders,[5] [6] Tho. Riley, [7] Tho. Owres.]

[Tho. Smyth, draper, Will. Colman, fisshemonger.] Sheriffs.

¶ [Decreed] that Edw. Smyth, seriaunt to the Shireffes, shal-be dismyssed & discharged of his office of seriauntshipp; And that Joh. Cragges, late put owt of the same office shal-be admytted to haue & occupie the seid office etc. [8] "Changing serjants."

¶ [Enacted] that no bocher or vitaillour frome-hensfurthe shall sell eny vitaill of fleshe within this Citie but onelie in the comon bocherie. And that no man shall sell or kyll eny fleshe within the Citie except he be brother with the bochers & admytted as oon of that felishipp, vpon peyn of xl s. to be levied by distresse to the vse of the Shireffes. No [9] "bochers" to sell flesh except in the Butchery.
All butchers to belong to the craft.

[10] [Enacted] that no man within this Citie shall sell eny talowe aboue the price of ij s. iiij d. the stone, ner convey no talowe to be sold owt of the town, vpon peyne to forfeit for euery defaut vj s. viij d. to the vse of the Shireffes to be levyed in forme aforseid. [9] "Talow" to be sold at 2s. 4d. the stone.

[Enacted] that no Inholder or alehouse-keper shall frome-hensfurth permytt or suffer eny person or persones of this Citie to sitt or be in ther housez at brekefastes or drynkynges at Matyns, high masse or evensong tymes on the Sondays or holydayes [or 3s. 4d. each time to the sheriffs.] [11] "For drynkyng in seruice tyme [11] [12] on saboth days."[12]

---

[1] See p. 669.   [2] leaf 378, back.
[3] Repeated before all names until note 4.
[4] "Magister" here deleted.
[5]—[5] Surname deleted. "S" follows.
[6] "Magister" here appears to be deleted.   [7] Untitled.
[8] In a later hand.   [9] The same handwriting.   [10] leaf 379.
[11]—[11] The same handwriting.   [12]—[12] In a later hand.

§ 125. *Tho. Gardynour, Mayor*, 1540.

THO. GARDYNOUR, MAYOR, 1540.

¶ [Election of officers.]

¶ [M*agister*[1] Hugo Lawton, Tho. Banwell, Ric. Herryng, Rog. Wales, Rog. Palmer, Joh. Jett, Will. Coton, Tho. Burdon, Joh. Cramp, Tho. Spens*er*, Jac. Gilbert, Rob. Seny, Joh. Saunders, Will. Rogers, Tho. Brewer, Geo. Philips, Ric. Ley, Joh. Talont*es*, Ric. Sewall, Chris. Waren, Joh. Herford, Hugo Bloure, [2] Tho. Saunders, Rob. Colma*n*.]

[m. Mag*ister* Tho. Gardyno*u*r, baker; Tho. Banwell and Chris. Waren are chosen to be the mayor's assistants in assessing the price of victuals, because the same Tho. Gardyno*u*r is a common baker; rec. Rog. Wigston; ch. Tho. Kyrvyn, fisshemong*er*, Hen. Godson, Coruis*er*; w. Ric. Giller, m*er*cer, Tho. Sconse, capp*er*; mace, Hen. Thirkyll; crier, Joh. Wood.]

EASTER LEET.

[3] ¶ [V. f. p. held before Tho. Gardyno*u*r, m., Tho. Smyth, Will. Colman, b., Apr. 13, 31 Hen. VIII.]

[M*agister*[4] Tho. Banwell, Ric. Herryng, Rog. Wales, Rog. Palmer, Joh. Jett, Will. Coton, Sym. Parker, Tho. Burdon, Ric. Townesend, Jac. Gilbert, Rob. Seny, Joh. Saunders, Will. Rogers, Tho. Brewer, Ric. Ley, Cuth. Joyno*u*r, Ri*c̊*. Sewall, Hen. Over, Chris. Waren, Hugo Bloure, [5] Tho. Kyrvyn, [6] Hen. Godson, Will. Norton & Tho. Keveit.]

[Enacted] that no baker of the Contrey bryngyng bred to this Citie to be sold shall deliu*er* or put to sale eny suche bred before it be weyed by the meire or his deputies: Ner that no Citiȝene here shall receive or by eny suche bred before it be weyd, vpon peyn of eu*er*y baker to forfeit ij s. And eu*er*y Citiȝen to forfeit xij d. for eu*er*y tyme offendyng.

¶ [Enacted] at this lett that no brewer of this Citie shall sell eny ale above xviij d. the Cester & xiiij galons to the Cester: And that no Tipler sell or vtter eny ale

---

[1] Repeated as far as note 2.   [2] Untitled.   [3] leaf 379, back.
[4] Repeated as far as note 6.   [5] "M*agister*" apparently deleted.
[6] Untitled.   [7] Gloss in different hands.

§ 125. *Tho. Gardynour, Mayor. Tenths and Fifteenths,* 1540. 741

within ther house aboue ij d. the galon, ner owt of ther house aboue j d. ob. the galon, vpon peyne for euery brewer to forfeit for euery defaut vj s. viij d., and euery Typler iij s. iiij d., to be levyed by the shireffes to ther own vse. *to be sold at 2d. a gallon within doors and 1½d. out of doors.*

¶ [Enacted that butchers are only to sell flesh in the Butchery or Market-place, or 20s. fine to be levied as aforesaid.] *The "bochers" to sell meat in the Butchery.*

TENTHS AND FIFTEENTHS.

"Ciuitas Couentrie."   [1] Recorda de xv.

[Particulars of the account of T. Gregorie and R. Walker, collectors of the first whole fifteenth and tenth of the four fifteenths and tenths granted to the lord king, Hen. VIII, from the laity in the 32nd year of his reign (1540), in the city of Coventry and the county of the same.]

¶ Particule Computi (*sic*) Thome Gregorie & Ricardi Walker, Collectorum prime integre xv^e & x^e quattuor (*sic*) xv^{arum} & x^{arum}, domino Regi Henrico octauo a laicis anno regni sui xxxij° concessarum in Ciuitate Couentrie & Comitatu eiusdem.[2]

[3] Deducciones.   [4] Remanentes clare.

¶ Gosford-streit Warde.	ij s.	[v li. xiiij s.][5]	2s.
Jourden-wel warde.	ij s. iiij d.	[xvij s. viij d.][5]	2s. 4d.
Miche-parke Streit ward.	ij s. iiij d.	[viij li. xvij s. viij d.][5]	2s. 4d.
Bailie-lane warde.	xx d.	[iij li. xviij s. viij d.][5]	1s. 8d.
Erle-streit ward.	ij s.	[vj li. xviij s.][5]	2s.
[6] Croschepyng [6] warde.	ij s. viij d.	[viij li. xvij s. iiij d.][5]	2s. 8d.
Broid Yait ward.	xx d.	[viij li. viij s. iiij d.][5]	1s. 8d.
Smythford-streit ward.	ij s. viij d.	[viij li. xvij s. iiij d.][5]	2s. 8d.
Spone Streit ward.	ij s. viij d.	[iiij li. xvij s. iiij d.][5]	2s. 8d.
Bishop-streit ward.	ij s. viij d.	[vj li. viij s. iiij d.][5]	2s. 8d.
Summa totalis 1 li.	Summa deduccionum xxij s. viij d.		Total £50. Deductions £1 2s. 8d.

The Shire or forrience of the same Citie.

		Remanentes clare.	
Stichall.	vj d.	xxiij s. x d.	6d.
Sow & Caloughdon.	iij d.	xv s. ix d.	3d.

[1] leaf 389.   [2] 32 Hen. VIII, c. 50.   [3] = deductions.
[4] = remaining clear.   [5] deleted.
[6]—[6] "Litle-parke-stret" deleted.

§ 125. Tho. Gardynour, Mayor. Leet, 1540.

7d.	Pynley, Biggyng, Stoke & Whitley.	vij d.	xxxj s. ij d.
5d.	Wykyn.	v d.	xxvj s. vij d.
5d.	Coundon & Radforde.	v d.	xxvj s. vij d.
	Shulton.	[1]	xvj d.
1s.	Ansty.	xij d.	xlix s. vj d.
10d.	ffolleshull	x d.	xlij s. x d.
1d.	Weston	j d.	xxiij d.
6d.	Exall	vj d.	xxxiij s. x d.
5d.	Keresley	v d.	xxvj s. ix d.

Total £14 0s. 1d.
Deductions 5s.

Summa totalis xiiij li. j d.   Summa deduccionum v s.

[And since deductions are not allowed, then let them be charged as follows.]   Et cum deducciones non allocentur tunc onerentur vt sequitur.

[Stichall, 24s. 4d.; Sowe, Caloughdon, 16s.; Pynley, Biggyng, Stoke and Whitley, 31s. 9d.; Wykyn, 27s.; Coundon and Radford, 27s.; Shulton, 16d.; Ansty, 50s. 6d.; ffolleshull, 43s. 8d.; Weston, 2s.; Exall, 34s. 4d.; Keresley, 27s. 2d.]

[Sum total of the fifteenth within the foreigns £14 5s. 1d., whence in deductions 5s.   Summa totalis xv^e infra forinsecos xiiij li. v s. j d., vnde in deduccionibus v s.

[Sum total of the fifteenth and tenth of the whole city and county £64 5s. 1d., whence in deductions 27s. 8d.]   Summa totalis xv^e & x^e tocius Ciuitatis & Comitatus lxiiij li. v s. j d., vnde in deduccionibus xxvij s. viij d.

MICHAELMAS LEET.

"Ciuitas Couentre."
Jury of 25.

[2][V. f. p. held on Oct. 12, 32 Hen. VIII.]

[Magister [3] Hugo Lawton, Tho. Banwell, Ric. Herryng, Rog. Wales, Rog. Palmer, Will. Coton, Sim. Perker, Tho. Spenser, Jac. Gilbert, Rob. Seny, Will. Rogers, Tho. Brewer, Geo. Philips, Cuth. Joynour, Ric. Sewall, Chris. Waren, Hugo Bloure, [4]Will. Norton, Tho. Owres, Joh. Lawton, Jac. ffarmour, Tho. Sconse, Ric. Warner, Will. Stirropp, Rob. Smith, sen., skynner.]

Sheriffs.   [Jac. Rogers, Mercer, Will. Saunders, capper.]

---

[1] blank. Cf. p. 407.   [2] Scribe J. leaf 380.
[3] Repeated as far as note 4.   [4] Untitled.

§ 125. *Tho. Gardynour, Mayor. Smiths,* 1540.

Item, it ys ordyned (etc.) that if eny bocher dwellyng & kepyng a shoppe owte of the bocherie do at any tyme herafter Carre ther fleshe or vyttell owte of ther howses in baskettes or bagges to be solde by them or ther seruauntes, that then it shal-be lefull for the Sheriffes of this Cetie & ther Officers and the Maisters of the Crafte of Bochers of the seid Cetie, and to euery of them, to sease and take from the seid Bocher or his seruaunte the seid fleshe & vittell to the vse & behove of the seid Sheriffes and ther Prisoners. [1]

[Enacted] that the felyships and craftes of the Pinners, Tylers and Cowpers shal-be by auctoritie of this lete one felyshyp and Crafte vnyt together as they have ben in tymes past etc. "Tilers, pinners & Coupers."

[2][Enacted] *that*[3] none inhabitante of thys Cetie shall sell eny Talowe above the price of ij s. vj d. the stone, vpon payne of euery persone doyng the contrarie for euery defawlte to forfett vj s. viij d. to thuse of the Sheriffes of thys Cetie for the tyme beyng. "Talowe."

[Enacted] þat none inhabitantes of this Cetie shall sell Candels above j d. ob. the pounde, [or 6*s.* 8*d.* to the sheriffs at every default.] "Candels."

[1] "Butchers not to carry their meat to sell."

THE RULES OF THE SMITHS.

Item, it is ordeyned that xij of the Eldest & discretest of the felishyp of Smythes in this Cetie euer on sancte Loys daye[5] shall chuse iij kepers for the yere, that is to wytt the hede-keper and his two brethern.[6] And in case they refuse to take ther office vpon them or eny of them the hede-keper to forrfytt to the seid Crafte xx s. in the name of a payn: And if eny of his brether refuse ther office to forfett x s., And so to goo quyte for that yere, And the seid xij[th] [7]to chose[7] other in ther stedes. [4]"Ordynaunces for the felishipp of Smythes."[4] "Refusing to serue master or warden to fforffeit [illeg.]."

Item, it is ordeyned that what person or persons of the

---

[1] Gloss in later hand with one exception throughout this leet's entries.
[2] leaf 380, back.   [3] "þ" is written like "y" by this scribe.
[4–4] Contemporary hand.
[5] Dec. 1. S. Eloy or Eligius was the patron of smiths.
[6] A later hand.   [7–7] Repeated.

§ 125. *Tho. Gardynour, Mayor. Smiths,* 1540.

"To be present at mariages or buriells."

sayde Craftes that will not com to the kepers for the yere beyng when they be send for for eny busynes commaunded by maister Meyre, or wyl-not be present at all Mariages, burialles or eny other lawfull assembles for the welthe of the seid Crafte, And to the worshup of the Cetie, to forfett vj d. in the name of a payn withoute a lawfull excuse.

"None to give euill Language to the master."

Item, what person or persons of the seid Crafte that rebell in the kepers presence, or speke eny opprobrius wordes wherby that Charitie myght be broken, nor wyl-not kepe silence at the kepers commaundement, to forfett iij s. iiij d.

The "watch on Midsomer nyght"

Item, what person or persons of the seid Crafte that wylnot go to the watches on Mydsomer nyght & seynte Petur nyght or brekethe the watche without a lawfull cause to forfytt for Midsomer nyght iij s. iiij d. in the

and S. Peter's night.

name of a payn, And for seynte Petur nyght xx d., withowte eny grace.[1]

"None to sue Another without Licence."

[2] Item, it is ordeyned that no brother of the seid Crafte shall sew one another in the lawe to the tyme be he haue asked license of the kepers for the tyme beyng to thentent that the kepers may agree them if they can, vpon payn of vj s. viij d. Provided alwayes that the kepers make an ende within the space of xiiij dayes of eny suche cause, or els to giffe licence.

"Clarke & somner."

Item, it is ordeyned ther shall no kepers for the yere beyng put in nor owte Preste, Clarke nor Somner without assent & consent of xij of the eldest & dyscretest of the seid Crafte, vpon payn of xl s. to be paid in the name of a payn, the one half to Maister Meyr for the tyme beyng, & the other halfe to the seid Craftes.

The "masters to be

Item, what person or persons of the seid Crafte that rebuketh the keper or eyther of his brother to forfett iij s. iiij d. Provided alwayes that if the kepers for the yere beyng do offende in ther office that then they to be

punished by xij of the fellowship."

punished by xij of the seyd Occupacion accordyng to consciens.

Item, it is ordeyned that ther shall no Smyth within

---

[1] See above, pp. 35, 710.
[2] leaf 381.

§ 125. *Tho. Gardynour, Mayor. Smiths*, 1540.

this Cetie shoo no horse with forest[1] shoyes nor forest[1] nailles in deceyvyng the kynges subiectes, vpon payn of iij s. iiij d. to be to the said Crafte in the name of a payn.

Item, it is ordeyned that ther shall no man of the said Crafte procure awaye his brother seruaunte nor set hym on worke to he knowe that the said seruaunte be lawfullie departed from his maister he wrought withall, vpon payn of iij s. iiij d.

Item, it was enacted at Michaelmas lete in the xvij yere of kyng Henrie the viij[th] that wher-as in the tyme of Maister Nicholas Burwey, late Maire of this Cetie,[3] emonges other thinges that euery craftes-man that setteth vp his Crafte within this Cetie, & hathe not ben prentes within the same, shuld paye to the saide Crafte of Smythes x s., that ys to saye, at thende of the fyrst yeir v s., And at thende of the second yere other v s. :

Item, it is nowe enacted (etc.) that the same fyne of x s. shal-be xiij s. iiij d. to be payed to the Maisters of the same Crafte of Smythes the fyrst daye of his setting vp vj s. viij d., and at the ende of the fyrst yere other vj s. viij d., vpon payn of forfiture to the said Crafte the doble value of the same fyne.

[4][Ordained] [5]that if any smythe offend in the said occupacion the offender to be punished by the xij men of the seid Crafte, and if eny suche person or persons be obstacle[6] and will-not be orderyd by the seid xij that then it shal-be lefull to the seid Maisters for the tyme

Against [2]"Shoeing with fforrest[1] Iron."[2]

Against "Inticing other men's seruants."

"x s. ffor making ffree."

"xiij[s] 4[d] to be paid to the maisters at setting vp."

"Smythes."

"All offences to be punished by 12 off the Company."

---

[1] This term seems to refer to iron from the Forest of Dean (see Fell, *Early Iron Industry of Furness*, pp. 232–3), and not as Rogers supposed to Sussex iron (see *Agric. and Prices*, v. 479). Yarrenton (*England's Improvement by Sea and Land*) speaks (1677) enthusiastically of "our forest iron," in which term he may include possibly that of Clay Hill in Shropshire, *ib.* p. 127. He also notes the fact that the Coldshore iron from Worcestershire, Staffordshire, Warwickshire and Derbyshire, which differed from Dean iron, was better fitted for the manufacture of nails and small commodities, *ib.* p. 58, 147.

[2–2] In a later hand.

[3] See p. 655. It was at the Easter leet of Burwey's mayoralty in 1518 (9 Hen. VIII) that this order was made. At the Easter leet of 1525 (17 Hen. VIII), in Heynes' mayoralty, the order was modified, *v.* p. 691.   [4] leaf 381, back.

[5] "at the seid lete it" follows ; the "it" is redundant.

[6] = obstinate.

§ 126. *Cuth. Joynour, Mayor,* 1541.

beyng to shewe ther names to M*aister* Meyre & the Justice of peax, and they to send for the seid offenders & cause them forw*i*th to paye doble penaltie, or els to comytt them to warde vnto suche tyme they wyll be orderyd by M*aister* Meyre & his brethern.

CUTHBERT JOYNOUR, MAYOR, 1541.

"Ciuitas Couentre."

¹¶ [Election of officers.]

Jury of 26.

[M*agister*² Sim. P*ar*ker, Tho. Banwell, Ric. Herryng, Rog. Wales, Hugo Lawton, Rog. Palmer, Joh. Jett, Will. Coton, Joh. Saunders, Tho. Spens*er*, Jac. Gilbert, Rob. Seny, Will. Rogers, Tho. Brewer, Geo. Philips, Ric. Ley, Joh. Talont*es*, Ric. Sewall, Hen. Over, Chris. Waren, Joh. Herforde, Hugo Blour, Tho. Smyth, Will. Colman, ³Tho. Kyrvyn, Hen. Godson.]

Officers.

[m. M*agister* Cuth. Joynou*r*, drap*er*; rec. Rog. Wigston, armig*er*; cor. Rob. Grene; steward, Baldw. Porter; ch. Rog. Adnet, grasier; Chris. Bromley, gyrdeler; w. Tho. Mores, drap*er*; Will. Beyley, jun., drap*er*; mace, Hen. Thyrkell; crier, Joh. Woode.]

LIBERTIES AND FRANCHISES.

⁴ Tituli libertat*um* & ffranches*i*arum Ciuitat*is* Couentr*ie*.⁵

[In parliament of Edward III held at Westminster on the Monday after S. Mathias' day (Mar. 2), in the 11th year (1337) it among other things is contained:

[Also it is accorded in full parliament by assent of all as well bishops, earls, barons and other nobles as commoners, that for the honour of our

In p*ar*liamento d*om*ini Edwardi tercii tent*o* apud W*e*stm*on*a*s*terium die Lune p*ro*xim*o* post festu*m* *s*ancti Mathei ap*o*st*o*li anno regni sui vndecimo inter alia sic c*on*tinet*ur*:

¶ Auxint est accorde in plene p*ar*liment p*ar* assent de toutz auxibien prelatz, Counties, Barons & auters (*sic*) g*r*antz come gentz de com*un*e

---

¹ leaf 382. ² Repeated until note 3.
³ Untitled. ⁴ leaf 382, back. Scribe of I type.
⁵ Titles of the liberties and franchises of the city of Coventry. See *Rot. Parl.* vi, 12a (Mr. E. F. Kirk). The Anglo-French document is copied in the Burton MS., leaf 56. I do not know why this entry occurs here.

§ 126. *Franchises*, 1467.

lord the king, and the country and for enforcing of the same and for that [there] was anciently a Duke of Cornwall, that our lord the king ought to make Sir Edward his son, Earl of Chester, Duke of Cornwall, and that the eldest sons of the Kings of England, that is to say, those who are next heirs to the kingdom, should be Dukes of Cornwall; and that the said county should be given to Sir Edward as a duchy, and that that county should always remain as a duchy to the eldest sons of the Kings of England, who are nearest heirs to the kingdom, without being given elsewhere.	que pour le honeur [de] nostre seigneur le Roy & de la terre, & a forcement dicele & pour ceo que aunceonement eistoit vn Duke de Cornewall, que le dit nostre seigneur le Roy deuoit faire monsieur Edward son fitz, Counte de Cestre, Duke de Cornewall, & ¹que les fitz eignes des Roies dengleterre cestasauoir ceux qui serront² heires proschenes due (*sic*) roialme³ feussent dukes de Cornewall. ⁴Et que la dite Counte soit done au sire Edwarde come en nom de duschee,⁴ & que cele Counte de Cornewall toutz-iours demoerye,⁵ come duschee a lez eignes fitz [des] Roies dengletere qui seront heires proscheins du Roialme sunce⁶ estre aillours done.

In the great roll, 7 Ed. IV, 1467.   In magno rotulo⁷ de anno vij° Regis Edwardi quarti.

[R. Onley and W. Baxster, sheriffs of this county from Michaelmas in the 6th year of Edward IV (1466), until the following Michaelmas, by virtue of the letters patent of Henry VI, formerly in fact and not of right, King of England, dated November 26, the 30th year of his reign (1451),⁸ and enrolled in the Memor-	¶ Rob. Onley & Will. Baxster, vice-comites huius Comitatus, A festo S. Michaelis Anno sexto Regis Edwardi quarti vsque festum S. Michaelis tunc proximo sequens, pretextu literarum patencium Henrici sexti, nuper de ffacto & non de Jure, Regis Anglie, quarum data est vicesimo sexto die Nouembris Anno regni sui xxx°,⁸ Et Irrotulatarum in me-

---

¹ This passage to the end of the Anglo-French document is to be found in Rot. Parl. IV, 140, abbreviated as R. P. Slight variations not noted.
² R. P. serroient.   ³ R. P. inserts d'Engleterre.   ⁴⁻⁴ Not in R. P.
⁵ R. P. demoreroit, Burton MS. demverye.   ⁶ R. P. sanz.
⁷ *i. e.* the Pipe Roll, no. 312, 7 Ed. IV.   sub tit. Ciuitas Couentrie, abbreviated as Pipe R. (Mr. E. F. Kirk). See also Burton MS., leaf 50-1.
⁸ Charter Roll 27-39 Hen. VI (30th year), mem. 24, no. 29 (Mr. E. F. Kirk).

§ 126. *Franchises*, 1467.

anda of the 24th year (really 33rd), viz. among the records of Hilary term on roll 32 ;[2] and as well by a certain act enacted and provided in the parliament of the said former king held in the 33rd year (1454–5) for the cities, boroughs and towns of the kingdom of England, and enrolled in the memoranda on the side of the king's remembrancer of the 34th [3] year (1455–6) of the said former king, viz. among the records of Trinity Term, roll 14, as by two several, similar acts had and provided in the parliament held at Westminster in the 1st and 3rd year of the present king, for the different cities, boroughs and towns of this kingdom of England, remaining in the custody of the king's remembrancer, and by the present lord king's writ enrolled among the Memoranda of the 7th year, Michaelmas term, roll 7 :—

[In which is contained among other things that the said former king, as aforesaid, by his letters patent, which the said present king has confirmed, granted to the mayor, bailiffs, and community of the city of Coventry, their heirs (etc.) that the city or town of Coventry

morandis de Anno xxiiij°,[1] videlicet inter Recorda de termino S. Hillarii Rotulo xxxij° ;[2] Ac tam per quemdam Actum in parliamento dicti nuper Regis apud Westmonasterium Anno regni sui xxxiij° tento pro Ciuitatibus, burgis & villis regni Anglie editum & provisum & irrotulatum in memorandis ex parte Rememoratoris Regis de Anno xxiiij° [*interlined* xxxiiij] [3] dicti nuper Regis, videlicet inter Recorda de termino S. Trinitatis Rotulo xiiij°, quam per duos seperales consimiles actus in parliamento [4] domini Regis nunc apud Westmonasterium Anno (*sic*) regni sui primo & tercio tento pro Ciuitatibus, burgis & villis huius regni Anglie separatim, habitos & prouisos & in custodia rememoratoris Regis remanentes, ac per brevem dicti domini Regis nunc Irrotulatum in memorandis de Anno septimo Termino S. Michaelis Rotulo vij° :—

In quo inter alia continetur quod dictus, vt premittitur, nuper Rex per predictas literas patentes, quas dictus dominus Rex nunc confirmauit, concesserit tunc Maiori, balliuis & Communitati Ciuitatis Couentrie & eorum heredibus & Successoribus quod Ciuitas siue villa de Couentria

---

[1] Read xxxiij.
[2] Memo. Roll, K. R. Hilary, 33 Hen. VI. Communia, roll 32 (Mr. E. F. Kirk).
[3] Pipe R. xxxiiij.   [4] Pipe R. parliamentis.

§ 126. *Franchises*, 1467.

with Radford, Keresley, Foleshill, Exhall, Ansty, Shilton, Calloughdon, Wyken, Henley le Woodend, Stoke, Bigging, Whitley, Pinley, Asthull, Horwell, Harnal, and Whoberley, hamlets of the city (etc.) aforesaid ... of the hamlets (etc.) and parcels aforesaid, which were within the county and of the county of Warwick, should be from the feast of S. Nicholas in the 30th year of the said former king's reign (Dec. 6, 1451) an entire county incorporated in itself, in name and deed, and distinct and separate from the said county of Warwick for ever, and not part of the said county of Warwick: and that the same county, so incorporate, distinct and separate from the county of Warwick should be named and called by name the county of the city of Coventry for ever.

[He willed also and granted for himself, his heirs (etc.) to the aforesaid mayor (etc.) for ever that the bailiffs of that city (etc.) who should be bailiffs on the morrow of the said feast of St. Nicholas, and the bailiffs of the same city

predicta cum Radforde, Keresley, Folkeshull, Ecleshall, Anesty, Shulton, Calwedon, Wykyn, Henley la Woodende, Stoke, Byggyng, Whitley, Pynley, Asthull, Horewell, Harnehall, Whaburley, hamlettos [1] Ciuitatis siue ville predicte [2] ... hamlettorum & parcellarum predictorum, qui infra Comitatum &

de Comitatu Warrwicensi existerint (*sic*), a festo S. Nicholai Anno

Regni dicti nuper Regis xxx°, essent vnus integer Comitatus per se corporatus in re & nomine, ac distinctus & separatus a dicto Comitatu Warrwicensi imperpetuum, & non parcella ipsius Comitatus Warrwicensis: Et quod idem Comitatus sic [3] corporatus a dicto Comitatu

Warrwicense distinctus & separatus Comitatus Ciuitatis Couentrie pro [4] perpetuo nominaretur, nuncuparetur, & appellaretur:

Vo[l]uerit etiam & concesserit pro se, heredibus & Successoribus suis prefatis Maiori, Balliuis & Communitati & Successoribus suis imperpetuum quod balliui Ciuitatis (etc.) illius,

qui in Crastino dicti festi S. Nicholai essent, & balliui eiusdem Ciuitatis

---

[1] Pipe R. hamlettis.
[2] An omission here. See p. 753-4. Supply "ac illa parcella de Sowe & illa parcella de Styuchall que sunt infra libertatem Ciuitatis, siue ville, illius & procinctus Ciuitatis, ville," ... and that part of Sow and that part of Stivichall which are within the liberty of that city or town, and the precinct of that city, town, ...
[3] MS. sit.   [4] leaf 383.

§ 126. *Franchises*, 1467.

(etc.) who for the time should be, to be elected from thenceforth in the manner and form used in the time of Edward III, during the time that they be bailiffs of the city should be sheriffs of the county of the city of Coventry from the aforesaid feast for ever:

[And that as well they who should be sheriffs of the aforesaid city from the said morrow of the feast of S. Nicholas as all others who should be sheriffs of the same city from thenceforth in all future times, should, after that they were sheriffs of the same city, duly take the oath before the mayor of the city (etc.) for the time being in the Gildhall, and not before any other or elsewhere, duly and faithfully to fulfil, exercise and perform the office of sheriff of the said county of the aforesaid city so long as they should be in the office of sheriff :

[And that the mayor of the said city (etc.) for the time being should certify into the chancery of the king and his heirs from time to time without delay the names of such sheriffs (etc.) thus sworn under his letters patent to be sealed with the seal of his office of mayoralty ; and that such

(etc.) modo & forma tempore Regis

E. tercii vsitatis extunc eligendi qui pro tempore essent, quemdiu (*sic*)

balliui Ciuitatis (etc.) illius extitissent, essent a predicto festo vicecomites dicti Comitatus Ciuitatis Couentrie imperpetuum :

Et quod tam ipsi qui vicecomites Ciuitatis predicte a[1] dicto Crastino S. Nicholai existerint (*sic*), quam omnes alii qui vicecomites eiusdem Ciuitatis extunc perpetuis futuris

temporibus essent, postquam vicecomites eiusdem Ciuitatis fuissent, Sacramentum suum coram Maiore Ciuitatis siue ville predicte pro tempore existente, & non coram aliquo

alio, in Guylhalda[2] eiusdem Ciuitatis, & non alibi, in forma debita prestarent ad officium vicecomitatus dicti Comitatus Ciuitatis predicte debite & fideliter faciendum, exercendum & exequendum quamdiu ipsi in officio vicecomi[ta]tus extitissent :

Et quod Maior dicte Ciuitatis (etc.) pro tempore existente[3] Nomina huiusmodi vicecomitum dicti Comitatus Ciuitatis predicte sic juratorum per literas suas patentes sigillo officii Maioratus illius sigillandas in Cancellariam Regis & heredum suorum de tempore in tempus indi-

---

[1] Pipe R. in. [2] Pipe R. Guyhalda. [3] Pipe R. existens.

§ 126. *Franchises*, 1467.

sheriffs of the city aforesaid who for the time should be should hold the king's county courts of the city from month to month on the Tuesday throughout the year for ever :

[And that they should have and use all kind of and such power, jurisdiction, authority and liberty and other things whatsoever belonging to the office of sheriffs in the same city (etc.) as any other his sheriffs or his heirs had and ought to have in their baillywicks within the kingdom of England, as is more fully contained in the said writ, rendering an account of farms and other dues, as below.

[The mayor and bailiffs and men of the town of Coventry, tenants of the manor of Cheylesmore, owe £50 a year for having the farm of the town from June 21, the first year of King Richard II (1378) to him and his successors for ever; paying thereof to the king the said £50 at the feasts of Easter and Michaelmas equally, as is contained in the first roll of this king, and in the 32nd roll of Hen. VI in Warwick and Leicester.

[The Prior and Convent of Coventry owe £88 6s. 8d. of

late certific[er]et ; quodque huiusmodi vicecomites Ciuitatis predicte qui pro tempore essent Comitatus Regis Ciuitatis predicte infra Ciuitatem illam de mense in mensem per diem Martis Annuatim tenerent imperpetuum :

Et quod haberent & exercerent omnimodas tales potestatem, jurisdicionem, auctoritatem & libertatem ac quecunque alia ad officia vicecomitatum pertinencia in eisdem Ciuitate siue villa, hamlettis, parcellis & procinctu eorundem quales & qualia aliqui alii vicecomites sui

& heredum[1] infra Regnum Anglie in balliuis suis haberent & habere deberent, prout in eodem breui plenius continetur, reddendo Compotum de firmis & aliis debitis, vt infra :—

Maior & balliui ac homines ville de Couentria, tenentes Manerii de Chelesmore, debent l li. per annum de firma ville predicte habenda a xxj°

die Junii anno primo Regis Ricardi secundi sibi & successoribus suis imperpetuum. Reddendo inde Regi

per annum dictas l li. ad festa Pasche & S. Michaelis equaliter, sicut continetur in rotulo primo huius Regis

& in Rotulo xxxij° H. vjⁱ in Warrwico & Leicestria.[2]

¶ Prior & Conuentus de Couentria debent iiij^{xx} viij li. vj s. viij d. de

---
[1] Pipe R. adds "suorum."
[2] The Burton MS. copy and Pipe R. add "et in Rotulo ij° Regis Ricardi ij^{di} et DCCC li. de annis preteritis, summa DCCC li."

§ 126. *Franchises*, 1467.

the rent of half the town of Coventry in the county of Warwick called Earl's-Part, which half indeed the same prior and convent hold a part in demesne and a part in service of the king as of his manor of Cheylesmore, being in the king's hand by service etc.

[Will. Loff of Coventry owes 12*d.* a year to the Exchequer of Michaelmas for retaining a certain house in Much-park Street; to have from December 10th in the end of the 15th year of King Edward [III], to the said William and his heirs, as it is contained in the 34th [4] roll in Warwick and Leicester and in the 16th roll of the said king Edward of which the sheriffs answer within.

[Rob. Haddeley owes 3*s.* 8*d.* a year for the custody of a messuage with appurtenances in the town of Coventry which formerly was of the Jews [5]

redditu medietatis ville de Couentria in Comitatu Warrwicensi vocate Erlespark [1]; quam quidem medietatem ijdem prior & Conventus tenent parcellam in dominico & parcellam in seruicio de Rege vt de dominico suo de Chelesmore in manu Regis existente per seruicium etc. [2]

¶ Will. Loff de Couentria debet xij d. per annum ad Scaccarium S. Michaelis pro quadam domo retinente [3] in Miche-parke-streit; habenda a decimo die Decembris Anno xv° Regis E. finiente eidem Willelmo & heredibus suis imperpetuum, sicut continetur in Rotulo xxxiiij° [4] in Warrwico & Leicestria & in Rotulo xvj° dicti Regis E. de quibus vicecomites respondent infra.

¶ Rob. Haddeley debet iij s. viij d. per annum in custodia vnius Mesuagii cum pertinenciis in villa de Couentria, quod quondam fuit Judeorum [5] ibidem, & quod Tho.

---

[1] Pipe R. Erlespart, *i. e.* the half of the town belonging anciently to the Earls of Chester. See Dugdale (1730), 1. 162, *Life in an Old English Town*, 60.

[2] The Pipe R. and MS. Burton add: "iiij viij li. vj s. viij d. per annum pro omnibus seruiciis a septimo die Augusti Anno x° Regis Ricardi secundi, quamdiu medietas dicte ville de Coventria et Dominicum de Cheylesmore in manibus Regis vel heredum suorum contigerit remanere; Solvendo dictum redditum ad terminos S. Michaelis et Pasche equaliter sicut Continetur in Rotulo Secundo, Et in Rotulis primo et sexto Henrici quarti, Et in Rotulo x° Regis Ricardi Secundi; Et Dxxx li. de annis preteritis. Summa DCxviij li. vj s. viij d. [£88 6*s.* 8*d.* for all services from Aug. 7 in the 10th year of King Richard while the half of the said town of Coventry and the demesne of Cheylesmore happen to remain in the hands of the king or of his heirs; paying the said rent at the terms of Michaelmas and Easter equally, as it is contained in the 2nd roll, and in the 1st and 6th rolls of Henry IV, and in the 10th roll of King Richard II; and £530 for the past years. Total £618 6*s.* 8*d.*] These lump sums evidently apply to the Prior's arrears of the term. See *Life in an Old English Town*, 127.

[3] Pipe R. retinenda.   [4] *i. e.* the Pipe Roll 34 Edw. III (Mr. E. F. Kirk).

[5] On the Jewess, Antera of Coventry, see Cole, *Doc. Illust. Eng. Hist.*, 309–19.

§ 126. *Franchises*, 1467.

there, and which Tho. Wildegrice lately held, which is extended at 18*d.* a year.

[To have from Michaelmas in the 1st year of this king until the end of 20 years; rendering unto the king 3*s.* 8*d.* a year at Easter and Michaelmas by equal portions by the hands of Joh. Haddeley of Coventry, grazier, and W. Stephens of London, baker, as is contained in the 2nd roll of this king and in the Originalia roll of the first year in the 64th roll, of which the sheriffs answer within.]

Wildegrice de Couentria nuper tenuit, quod ad decem & octo denarios extendantur (sic) per annum. Habendum a festo S. Michaelis archangeli Anno primo Regis huius vsque ad finem xx^{ti} Annorum. Reddendo inde Regi per annum iij s. viij d. ad festa Pasche & S. Michaelis per

equales porciones per manus Joh. Haddeley de Couentria, Grasier, & Will. Stephens de London, Baker, sicut continetur in rotulo secundo

Regis huius & in origine [1] de Anno primo Rotulo lxiiij°; de quibus vicecomites respondent infra.

[2] In memorandis Scaccarii de Anno vij° E. quarti, videlicet inter brevia directa Baronibus de Termino S. Michaelis Rotulo septimo ex parte Rememoratoris Regis inter alia continetur sic:— [3]

[The king to his treasurer and barons of the Exchequer, greeting. Whereas Henry VI, formerly in fact though not of right, King of England, granted by his letters patent,[4] which we have confirmed, to the mayor, bailiffs and community of the city of Coventry and their heirs and successors that the city (etc.) of Coventry aforesaid with Radford, Keresley, Foleshill, Exhall, Anstey, Shilton, Calloughdon, Wyken,

Rex Thesaurario & Baronibus suis de Scaccario, Salutem. Cum H. sextus nuper de facto & non de Jure Rex

Anglie per literas suas patentes quas confirmauimus concesserit Maiori,

balliuis & Communitati Ciuitatis Couentrie, & eorum heredibus & successoribus quod Ciuitas (etc.) de

Couentria predicta cum Radeforde, Keresley, ffolkeshull, Eccleshale, Anesty, Shulton, Calwedon, Wyken,

---

[1] *sic.* Pipe R. Originalia.   [2] leaf 383, back.
[3] In the Exchequer Memoranda of Ed. IV, among the writs directed to the Barons on Michaelmas term, roll 7, on the side of the king's remembrancer it is thus contained among other things, *i.e.* Memoranda Roll, K. R. Mich., 7 Edw. IV, Writs to the Barons, no. 7, abbreviated below as Mem. R. (Mr. E. F. Kirk).
[4] See p. 747, note 8 (Mr. E. F. Kirk).

§ 126. Franchises, 1467.

Henley le Woodend, Stoke, Biggyng, Whitley, Pinley, Asthull, Horwell, Harnal, and Whoburley, hamlets of the city (etc.) aforesaid, and that part of Sow, and that part of Stivichall, which are within the liberty of the city (etc.) and the precinct of that city, town, hamlets, and parts aforesaid, which were within the county and of the county of Warwick, from the feast of S. Nicholas in the 30th year of his reign should be an entire county incorporated (etc.), and distinct and separate from the said county of Warwick, and not part (etc.).

[And that the same county thus incorporated, distinct and separate from the said county of Warwick, should be for ever named, called, and called by name the county of the city of Coventry.

[He willed also that the mayor and bailiffs of the city (etc.) hereafter to be elected, should be elected at the same place, times, manner and form, as in the time of his progenitor, Edward, of famous memory, formerly King of England, the third after the Conquest, by virtue of his letters patent, or in the time of any other his progenitor,

Henley la Woodende, Stoke, Biggyng, Whiteley, Pynley, Asthull, Horewell, Harnehall, & Whaburley, hamlettes [1] Ciuitat*is* siue ville predicte, ac illa parcella de Sowe & illa parcella de Styuchall que sunt infra libertatem Ciuitat*is* (etc.) illius & procinctus Ciuitat*is*, ville, hamlettorum & parcellarum predictorum, qui infra Comitatum & de Comitatu Warrwicensi existerint (*sic*) a festo S. Nicholai a. r. sui. xxx° essent vnus integer Comitatus per se corporatus in re & nomine, ac distinctus & separatus a dicto Comitatu Warrwicensi imperpetuum, & non parcella ipsius Comitatus Warrwicensis :

Et quod idem Comitatus, sic corporatus, a dicto Comitatu Warrwicensi distinctus & separatus, Comitatus Ciuitat*is* Couentrie pro perpetuo nominaretur, nuncuparetur & appellaretur :

Voluerit eciam quod maiores & balliui Ciuitat*is* (etc.) illius ibidem imposterum eligendi eligerentur imperpetuum eisdem loco, temporibus, modo & forma, prout tempore inclite recordacionis E. nuper Regis Anglie tercii [2] post Conquestum, progenitoris sui, pretextu literarum suarum paten-

---
[1] Mem. R. hamlettis.
[2] Pat. Roll, 19 Edw. III, p. 3, m. 6 (3 Dec. 1345). (Mr. E. F. Kirk.)

§ 126. *Franchises*, 1467.

King of England, by virtue of his letters patent, or in any other manner or by any other means as they were wont to be elected or made, or any of them was wont to be elected or made.

[He willed also and granted for himself, his heirs (etc.) to the mayor, bailiffs and community for ever that the bailiffs of the city (etc.) who should be bailiffs on the morrow of the said [feast of] S. Nicholas, and the bailiffs of the city (etc.), to be chosen from thenceforth in manner and form aforesaid, who for the time should be, during the time that they were bailiffs of the city (etc.) should be from the aforesaid feast sheriffs of the said county of the city for ever.

[And also that they should be for ever bailiffs of the city (etc.) and do and perform there the offices of bailiffs, according to the form and effect of the franchises and liberties in the same city (etc.) theretofore used and accustomed by virtue of the grants of divers his progenitors and (?) ancestors notwithstanding his own grant.

[And that as well they who should be sheriffs of the said city on the said morrow of S. Nicholas, as all those who

cium, vel tempore alicuius alterius progenitoris sui Regis Anglie pretextu literarum suarum patencium, vel aliquo alio modo elegi (*sic*) seu fieri consueverunt, seu eorum aliquis elegi seu fieri consueuit :

Voluerit eciam & concesserit pro se, heredibus & successoribus suis, prefatis Maiori, balliuis & Communitati & Successoribus suis imperpetuum quod balliui Ciuitatis (etc.) illius, qui

in Crastino dicti [festi] S. Nicholai essent, & balliui eiusdem Ciuitatis (etc.) modo & forma predicta extunc

eligendi, qui pro tempore essent, quamdiu balliui Ciuitatis (etc.) illius extitissent, essent a predicto festo vicicomites (*sic*) dicti Comitatus Ciuitatis Couentrie imperpetuum :

Et eciam quod essent imperpetuum balliui Ciuitatis (etc.) illius & officia balliuorum ibidem facerent & exer-

cerent secundum formam & effectum franchesiarum & libertatum in eadem Ciuitate (etc.) pretextu concessionum diuersorum progenitorum & successorum [1] suorum consuetarum [et] ibidem ante hec tempora vsitatarum, concessione sua non-obstante :

Et quod tam ipsi qui vicicomites Ciuitatis predicte in dicto Crastino

S. Nicholai existerent, quam omnes

---

[1] Read "antecessorum."

should be thenceforth sheriffs of the same city in all future times, after that they were sheriffs of the said city, should take their oath in due form before the mayor of the city for the time being, and not before another, in the Gildhall, and not elsewhere, duly and faithfully to do, exercise and perform the office of sheriff of the said county of the city aforesaid as long as they should be in the office of sheriff :

[And that the mayor of the said city (etc.) for the time being should immediately certify from time to time into our chancery, or that of our heirs, by his letters patent sealed with the seal of the office of mayoralty of the city, the names of the same sheriffs thus sworn :

[And that the same sheriffs of the said city, who for the time shall be, should yearly hold our county courts of the said city within that city from month to month on the Tuesday throughout the year for ever :

[And that they should have and exercise all such power, jurisdiction, authority and liberty and all other things whatsoever belonging to the office of sheriff within the

alii qui vicicomites eiusdem Ciuitat*is* extunc p*er*petuis futur*is* tempori- b*us* essent, postqu*am* vicicomites eiusd*em* Ciuitat*is* fuissent, Sacr*a*-

*ment*u*m* suu*m* cora*m* Maiore Ciuitat*is* (etc.) p*re*dic*te* p*ro* tempo*re* existe*nte* & non cora*m* aliquo alio, in Guyhalda eiusd*em* Ciuitat*is* & non alibi, in forma debita p*re*starent ad officiu*m* vicicomitat*us* (*sic*) dicti Comi*tatus* Ciuitat*is* p*re*d*ic*te debite & fideliter faciend*um*, excerc*e*ndu*m* & exequend*um* quamdiu ipsi in officio vice*co*mitatus extitissent :

Et q*uod* Maior d*ic*te Ciuitat*is* (etc.) p*ro* tempo*re* existente[1] nomi*n*a huiusmodi [2] vicecomitu*m* d*ic*ti Comitat*us* Ciuitat*is* p*re*d*ic*te sic iurator*um*

p*er* l*ite*ras suas patentes sigillo officii Maioratus illius sigilland*as* in Cancellari*am* n*os*tram [3] (*sic*) & hered*um* n*os*tror*um* de tempo*re* in tempus indilate ce*r*tific[er]et :

Q*uod*qu*e* huiusmodi vicicomites Ciuitat*is* p*re*dic*te*, qui p*ro* tempo*re* essent, Com*itatus* n*os*tros [3] Ciuitat*is*

p*re*dic*te* infra Ciuitatem illam de mense in mensem p*er* diem Ma*r*tis Annuati*m* ten[er]ent imp*er*petuu*m* :

Et q*uod* h*ab*erent & exercerent o*mn*imod*as* tales potestatem, iurisdic-

cio*n*em, auctoritatem & libe*r*tatem ac quecu*m*que alia ad officia vicec*om*itat*us* p*er*tinenc*ia* in eisdem Ciuitate

---

[1] Mem. R. existens.   [2] leaf 384.
[3] Note change of person.

§ 126. *Franchises*, 1467.

said city (etc.), hamlets, and precinct of the same, as any other his sheriffs, or (those of) his heirs, within the kingdom of England should have and ought to have in their bailywicks.

[And that the same former king, his heirs (etc.) should after the same feast cause to be made and directed to the sheriffs of the city of Coventry for the time being all and every his and his heirs' writs, bills, warrants and mandates, which should be directed or executed concerning any cause, matter or thing, or any causes, matters or things whatever, arising within the city (etc.) after the said feast of S. Nicholas, and which ought to have been directed to the sheriff of Warwickshire by him to be served and executed if the said city (etc.), the hamlets (etc.) had not been made a whole county in itself,

[And that no other sheriff of his kingdom of England, or bailiff, or servant of any sheriff of the same his kingdom, save only his and his heirs' sheriffs of the city aforesaid, their bailiffs, officers or servants, should, after the aforesaid feast, enter into the same city, the parts and precincts aforesaid, or by any means or in

(etc.), hamlett*is* & p*ro*cinctu eor*un*dem, quales & qualia aliqui alii *vicecomites* sui & hered*um* suor*um* infra regn*um* Anglie, in balliuis suis ha*berent* & *habe*re deberent :

Et q*uo*d idem nup*er* Rex, heredes et successores sui, *om*nia & sing*ula* br*ev*ia, billas, p*rec*epta & manda[ta] sua¹ hered*um* & successor*um* suor*um*, que ex quacu*m*que causa, re, vel mat*er*ia, seu quibuscu*m*q*ue* causis, reb*us* vel mat*er*iis infra Ciuitatem (etc.) hamlett*os*, p*a*rcella*s* & p*ro*cinctu*m* predicta eme*r*gente vel eme*r*genti*bus* post d*ic*tum festum S. Nich*ol*ai essent dirigenda seu exequend*a*, & que vicic*omiti* Com*itatus* War*r*w*icensis* dirigi p*er* ips*um* s*er*uiri & exequi deberent, si iidem Ciuitas (etc.), hamletti, p*a*rcelle & p*ro*cinctus integer Com*itatus* p*er* se f*a*cti non fuissent, vicicomiti*bus* Ciuitat*is* de Couent*r*ia p*ro* tempo*re* exist*entibus* post idem festu*m* fieri & dirigi faceret & heredes (etc.) sui pred*ict*i fieri & dirigi face*r*ent :

Et q*uo*d nullus alius vicecomes regni sui Anglie, aut balli*u*us seu s*er*uiens alicuius vic*e*comit*is* eiusdem regni sui, nisi solomodo vic*e*comites sui & hered*um* suor*um* Ciuitat*is* predict*e* & eor*um* balli*u*i, Ministri, vel s*er*uientes, eand*em* Ciuitatem (etc.), hamlett*os* (etc.), post festu*m* p*re*d*ictum* aliqualiter ingrederet*ur* seu ingrederent*ur* ad quicq*uam* q*uo*d ad

¹ MS. inserts "&" here.

any wise perform or execute anything at all there which should or might pertain to the office of sheriff, neither to intermeddle in the same in any wise :

[And that all sheriffs of the said county and bailiffs of the said city (etc.), who after the feast aforesaid should be bailiffs and sheriffs, should make their several accounts of or for the issues of their office pertaining or which ought to pertain to the said former king, as aforesaid, or to his heirs, every year before the treasurer and barons of his Exchequer and of his heirs, or before the barons of the same Exchequer, and that they should for ever do all things whatsoever belonging to their offices, or either of them, or for the performance of their offices, or either of them, by their sufficient attorneys constituted by their letters patent directed unto the aforesaid barons :

[And that no sheriff of the same county or bailiff of the said city (etc.) should be in any wise compelled or bound to come personally out of the same county for the making of any accounts concerning anything belonging to their offices, or to that of either of them, or concerning any other thing for the performance of their

officium vicecomitatus pertineret, seu pertinere potuisset, ibidem quouismodo exercendum vel exequendum, nec se aliqualiter intromitteret in eisdem :

Et quod singuli vicicomites eiusdem Comitatus ac balliui Ciuitatis (etc.) predicte, qui post festum predictum vicecomites & balliui essent,

de siue pro exitibus officii sui eidem, vt premittitur, nuper Regi & heredibus suis pertinentibus vel pertinere

debentibus quolibet anno coram Thesaurario & Baronibus de Scaccario suo & heredum suorum vel coram baronibus de eodem Scaccario separatim computarent, & omnia quecumque ad officia sua seu eorum alterum

spectancia siue pro officiis suis, seu eorum altero, faciendis facere possit & possint imperpetuum per sufficientes attornatos suos, per literas suas patentes prefatis baronibus dirigendas, constituendos :

Et quod nullus vicecomes eiusdem Comitatus, aut balliuus Ciuitatis (etc.) predicte, extra eundem Comitatum ad

Computandum de aliquibus ad officia, seu ad officium alicuius eorum, spectantibus, seu ad aliquod aliud pro

officiis illis seu eorum aliquo faciendis, personaliter venire compellaretur

§ 126. Cuth. Joynour, Mayor. Leet, 1541.

offices or that of either of them, as in the letters and confirmation aforesaid more fully it is contained.

[We command you that ye neither molest nor grieve the same mayor, bailiffs and community contrary to the tenor of the letters and confirmation aforesaid. Witness ourself at Westminster, Oct. 28, in the 7th year of our reign (1467).]

(*sic*) seu teneretur quovismodo, prout in literis & confirmacione predictis plenius continetur.

Vobis mandamus quod ipsos Maiorem, balliuos & Communitates Ciuitatis predicte contra tenorem literarum & confirmacionis predictarum non molestetis in aliquo seu grauetis. Teste me ipso apud Westmonasterium xxviij° die Octobris anno regni nostri septimo.

PEMBERTON.

EASTER LEET.

[1] ¶ [V. f. p. held before Cuth. Joynour, m., Jac. Rogers, Will. Saunders, b., on May 3, 33 Hen. VIII.] — "Ciuitas Couentrie."

[Magister[2] Sym. Parker, Tho. Banwell, Ric. Herryng, Rog. Wales, Rog. Palmer, Joh. Jett, Will. Coton, Tho. Gardynour, Joh. Saunders, Ric. Townesend, Tho. Burdon, Jac. Gilbert, Rob. Seny, Tho. Brewer, Geo. Philips, Ric. Lee, Joh. Talontes, Hen. Over,[3] Chris. Waren, Hugo Blowre, Tho. Smyth, Will. Colman, [4]Chris. Bromeley, Rog. Adnet, Will. Norton.] — Jury of 25.

[Enacted] that the Millers of the Priorie Milne, the Bastell[6] Milne, & Whit-frere Milne shall pull vpp ther flode-gaites in tyme of great reyne, so that ther be no hurt doon in the Citie by floides by reason of Stoppyng the River at eny of the seid Milnes at eny tyme herafter vpon peyne to forfeit for eu[er]y defaut xx s. — [5]"Millers; floodgates to be pulled vp in time off flood."[5]

[Enacted] that no persone or persones at eny tyme herafter shall ley or cause to be leyed by his seruaunt or otherwise eny fi[l]the or dunge in the Churche-yardes of the Trinitie and seynt Michell, or eyther of theme, or at the Priorie Yait, vpon peyne to forfeit for euery defaut iij s. iiij d.; of which forfeyture the fynder or presenter of — [5]"Church yardes layne [? lay no] Ashes or muck."[5]

---

[1] leaf 385. [2] Repeated before all names until note [4].
[3] The Over family came from Cester Over. [4] Untitled.
[5]—[5] In different handwritings.
[6] The Bastell-gate lay between the Cook-street and Gosford gates. Bastell, or bastille = a small fortified tower.

§ 126. *Cuth. Joynour, Mayor. Commons,* 1541.

the defaut shall haue xij d. & the residue to be dyuyded betwen the shireff*es* & the c*om*en box.

_{1 " Millers not to keep swine or ducks." 1}

[Enacted] that the Millers of this Citie shall take for gryndyng of eu*ery* quarter of bredcorne to the bakers vij d. ; and that no Milner shall keip eny Swyne or duck*es*, vpon peyne to forfeit for eu*ery* defaut vj s. viij d.

THE COMMONS.

_{The mayor}

² ffor-asmoche as it is perceived & knowen by the c*om*inaltie of this Citie that w*ith* the Rent*es*, issues & profitt*es* of the c*om*en groundes & pastures about the Citie latelie taken in & maid seu*er*all by auctorite of lete in the tyme of M*aister* Will. Coton, lait meire of this Citie,³ Ther haith been dyu*ers* great charges & payment*es* susteyned & borne for the Citie sith that tyme, which wolde haue been in man*er* unportable saue onelie for the said Rent*es*. And for-asmoche also that it is thought by the c*om*inaltie of the said Citie that the said Rent*es* in tyme com*y*ng shall growe to great pro*f*it for the Citie, The same C*om*inaltie haue therfor maid petic*i*on & request at this lete to the Meire & councell of this Citie that ther myght be mo of the said ground*es*, Closez & pastures taken in & maid seu*er*all for the same vse, p*u*rpose & intent as the other Closez latelie taken in be ; vnto the which request the said Meire & councell did condiscend & agree. And thereupon ther were thre men appoynted in eu*ery* Warde of the Citie to viewe and ssee (*sic*) which of the said c*om*en Closes & ground*es* be moost meit to be taken in ; whose names hereafter ensue.

_{and council agree to a petition}

_{that more of "the c*om*en Closez" shall be taken in.}

_{The commons are to be inspected by three men from each ward,}

Gosforde Streit warde.

¶ Joh. Lawton, Cap*per*, Will. Colma*n*, Cowp*er*, Will. Androwes, Baker.

Miche-p*ar*ke-stret warde.

¶ Owen Blakemer, weiver, Joh. Stele, boclemaker, Will. Beilie, drap*er*.

Beilie-lane warde.

¶ Joh. Grene, m*er*cer, Rauf Hopkynse, Taillo*ur*, Edm. Damport, pewterer.

^{1—1} In different hands. ² leaf 385, back. ³ See p. 729.

§ 126. *Cuth. Joynour, Mayor. Commons*, 1541.

¹Broid Yait warde.

¶ Chris. Wharton, Skynner, Joh. Clerke, coriour, Tho. Diglyng, mercer.

Bisshop-stret warde.

¶ Tho. Owres, baker, Ph. Sherrerd, draper, Mores Gilbert, draper.

Jourden-well warde.

¶ Joh. Hill, Capper, Tho. Philips, Capper, Joh. Borresley, Capper.

Erle-stret ward.

¶ Nic. Hopson, draper, Tho. Napton, boclemaker, Will. Stirropp, flecher.

Smythford-stret warde.

¶ Joh. Sparkes, Sadeler, Art. Gudriche, mercer, Will. Atkynse, flecher.

Croschepyng ward.

¶ Will. Vnderwood, Coruiser, Hugh Dalaway, mercer, Guy Speke, Inholder.

Spone Streit ward.

¶ Joh. Eyburne, tanner, Joh. Stiward, dier, Tho. Amourson, Chaundeler.

¶ Which men for & in the name of the hole bodie of the Citie haue viewed & appoynted the Closez hereafter named & wrytten to be taken in & maid Seuerall for the vse aforseid for euer. *who select certain closes to be taken in.*

²ffurst, a Close without Grey-frere-yait called the litill Podyngcroft³ & the Towne wall of the yeirelie rent of x s. for the latter half-yeire & comen at Lammas . x s. 10s.

Item, thre fieldes without Grey-freer Yait, called the Crab-tre-feildes,⁴ beyng comen at Michelmas & of the yierelie rent for the latter half-yeire of . xxxviij s. viij d. "on of [illeg.] next the Buttes." 38s. 8d.

Item, another feild next theme called the Pit-feild beyng comen at Michelmas . . . . vj s. viij d. 6s. 8d.

Item, a feild of the kynges called the Strip⁵ lying next the said Pit-field & comen at Lammas . . iij s. iiij d. 3s. 4d.

---

¹ leaf 386.   ² leaf 386, back.   ³ See above, p. 4.
⁴ See p. 47.   ⁵ See p. 576.

§ 126. *Cuth. Joynour, Mayor. Commons*, 1541.

Hearsall. 6s. 8d.	Item, a litle Croft or Close lying on the southe side a litle Croft lying on the west side Somerlesbuttes, and a great broid Close lying next beyond the same, stretchyng westward towardes Hethsall, with a pike[1] at the west end thereof, beyng boithe the kynges groundes & comen at Lammas . . . . vj s viij d.
10s.	Item, a field of Tho. Bondes called the Rie-feild, lying without the Spone-ende on the northe side the wey ledyng frome Couentre to Allesley and comen at Lammas . x s.
4s.	Item, a feild next beyond that belongyng to the hospitall of seynt John Baptist in Couentre[2] & comen at Lammas . . . . iiij s.
3s. 4d.	Item, on of the kynges feildes lying next beyond the lane ledyng frome Allesley-wey into the iiij li. feildes.[3] iij s. iiij d.
2s. 6d.	Item, a feild next beyond that . . ij s. vj d.
8s.	Item, ij litill medowes of Tho. Bondes lying by the River vnder the iiij li. feildes . . . viij s.
10s.	[4] Item, thre feildes ther, parcell of the iiij li. feildes. x s.
6s. 8d.	Item, ij feildes of Maister Stronge[5] lying on the eist side the said feildes . . . . . vj s. viij d.
20s.	Item, a feild called the Rowe-of-okes-feild[5] with a litle feild at the south ende of the same feild . . xx s.
12s.	Item, iiij pyngilles[6] or Croftes called Ropers-feildes lying on the back side of Hill-streit & Spone Streit xij s.
6s.	Item, a close of Joh. Talontes at the Hill-streit ende lying at the back side of his barne ther . . vj s.
13s. 4d.	Item, a Close ther called Litle-Grauntpurs-feild[7] xiij s. iiij d.
8s.	Item, a Close next Radford callid the Nether-botmans-acre[8] . . . . viij s.

[1] A narrow pointed piece of land.
[2] Probably the field mentioned in 1495–6, when a dispute arose concerning common rights. See p. 570.
[3] For the Four-pound-fields see Poole, *Coventry* (Boundaries of S. Michael's parish in 1675 from Harl. MS. 6839, leaf 167), p. 176.
[4] leaf 387.
[5] Strong's Lammas is marked 172 and Row of Oaks 104b in a list of names of lands, which list is in possession of the Freemen's trustees.
[6] = paddocks, close. The word is of uncertain origin (*N.E.D.*).
[7] Crampy- (or Grampy) -feld, p. 51.
[8] See pp. 4, 38.

§ 126. *Cuth. Joynour, Mayor. Commons*, 1541.

Item, a feild next Radford *that* was Joh. ffoxalles	v s.	5s.
Item, a-nother Close ther of the kynges . . .	v s.	5s.
Item, a Close of the kynges next the land beyond seynt Nicholas Churche [1]	v s. vj d.	5s. 6d.
Item, a Close next beyond *that* belongyng to seynt Johns	ij s. vj d.	2s. 6d.
Item, a Close on the northe side seynt Nicholas Churche of dyuers menes Rentes	vj s. viij d.	6s. 8d.
Item, a Close called Seynt-Nicholas-leyes .	x s.	10s.
Item, a litle Croft of the Tanners . .	ij s. vj d.	2s. 6d.
Item, a Close buttyng on Radford vpon the eist side the towne	x s.	10s.
Item, all Closes & feildes betwen Radford & Bishops-yait lying on the west side the wey ledyng frome Couentre to Radford . . . . . [3]		[2]"Adnet-feild. Herryng wiffes feild."[2]
[4] Item, ij Closes called the Great Swannes Croft [5] & the Litle Swannes Croft lying *without* Bisshop Yait [6]	xx s.	20s.
Item, thre feildes *without* the Newe Yait [6] betwen Seynt Annes Grove [7] & Hulles Milne on the est side the wey ledyng frome Couentre to Whitley .	xxiij s. iiij d.	23s. 4d.
Item, a litle Garden pleke [8] nygh vnto Dilcockes Milne [9]	iiij d.	4d.
Item, a litle paroche or Croft belongyng to the Trinitie gild lying in the Charterhouse-leys nygh vnto the tayllour & Shirmans lodge [10]	xx d.	20d.

¶ All which Closes before-wrytten, It is enacted at this present lete by auctoritie of the same, shal-be taken in & maid seuerall foreuer after suche maner, forme & order as the Closes latelie taken in and maid seuerall in Master Cotons tyme, lait meire, be, and the Rentes, issues & profittes of the same to be vsed as the Rentes of the other Closes latelie taken in be accordyng to the acte thereof maid. — All which "Closez" are to be taken in.

¶ And further it is enacted (etc.) that no persone — No holder of the enclosed

---

[1] This church has long since disappeared.
[2-2] At the foot of the page, but connected by a line.
[3] Blank.   [4] leaf 387, back.   [5] See p. 46.
[6] This scribe's "Y" and "J" are identical in character.
[7] See p. 47.   [8] = plot.   [9] See p. 576.
[10] "Milne" deleted. This is the only mention I have found of any property here belonging to the Tailors' and shearmen's guild of S. George.

§ 126. *Cuth. Joynour, Mayor. Commons*, 1541.

lands to enjoy privileges of common.

havyng in farme eny groundes now takyne in & enclosed, or before enclosed, shall haue eny maner of catall goyng before the herd or otherwise vpon eny comen grounde of this Citie, vpon peyne to forfeit to the comen box vj s.

Only one close to be held in severalty by any farmer, except he be an inn keeper, then he may hold two.

viij d. for euery suche defaute; and that no persone shall haue in farme eny moo then oon of the said Closes, except he be an Inholder, who shall and may by auctoritie hereof occupie & haue two of the said Closez by the discrecion of the x men appoynted for the lettyng of the same, vpon peyne to forfeit yeirelie xl s. for euery Close hadd & taken contrarie to this acte to the vse aforseid, prouided alwey that euery persone hauyng eny of the least parcelles of the said groundes may haue & take on other Close by the discrecion of the said tene men.

The closes are forbidden to be let

¶ Also it is further enacted (etc.) that the x men at eny tyme appoynted to let and set the seid Closez shall not let or set the same but onelie to inhabitauntes of this

to strangers.

Citie, and shall soeffer no estraunger to occupie eny of the same, ner eny farmour to make eny assignee therin, vpon peyne to forfeit x li., that is to say, euery of theme xx s. for the vse of a[fore]seid.

THE RECORDER.

[1] "*Eleccio Recordatoris.*" Election of the recorder.

[Mem., that on May 17, in the above-said year, Edw. Saunders,[2] sergeant-at-law, was chosen recorder of this city. And he was sworn.]

A PROCLAMATION.

"*Proclamacio.*" To be remembered that on May 31, 1541, proclamations were made upon the soil and in the tenements written below by C.

[3] Memorandum quod vltimo die Maii [33 Hen. VIII] proclamaciones facte fuerunt super sola & in tenementis subscriptis per Cuth.

---

[1] leaf 388.
[2] Saunders became Chief-Justice in 1555, and, dying in 1576, was buried at Weston-under-Wetherley, Warwickshire, where his mutilated tomb remains. See Foxe, *Martyrs* (ed. Malham), 146, for letters from him to his brother, the martyr, Laur. Saunders, and for other letters see Corp. MSS. A. 79, leaf 63. It is possible, though unproven, that both the Chief-Justice and the martyr sprang from the family of the Saunders of Coventry.
[3] leaf 384, back.

§ 126. Cuth. Joynour, Mayor. Proclamation, 1541.

Joynour, mayor (etc.), J. Rogers and W. Saunders, bailiffs, and many others of the community of the said city, according to the form of the statute thereupon before published and provided.

Joynour, Maiorem Ciuitatis Couentrie, Jac. Rogers, & Will. Saunders, b., (etc.) ac plures alios de Communitate dicte Ciuitatis secundum formam Statuti [1] inde nuper editi & prouisi.

Jourden Well.

¶ Item, at a tenemente ther of Master [2]   Grey.
Item, at a tenement ther of Joh. Stronges.
Item, at a Tenement ther of Master Hugh Lawtons.

Gosford-streit.

¶ Item, at a tenement ther of Ric. Joyne[r]s set betwene the grounde of the Kynge of the on parte and the ground of Master Rog. Wales of the other part.

Miche-parke-stret.

¶ Item, at a tenement there that Joh. Herford holdeth ouer ageynst Hum. Reynoldes house.

Deed-lane.

¶ Item, at a house in a voied ground ther of Ric. Giller, mercer.

Litil-parke-stret.

¶ Item, at a tenement ther ouer ageynst the Deed-lane ende.

Smythford-stret.

¶ Item, at a house & a voied ground ther beneyth the Conducte next a house belongyng to seynt Johns of the west side.

West-orchard.

¶ Item, at dyuers Cotages ther of Joh. Colynse, dier.

Seynt Johns briges.

¶ Item, at a tenement ther of Jasper Owen, Esquier,

---

[1] Probably this was the act "For Reedifieng of Townes" (32 Hen. VIII, c. 18), 1540, in which the decayed condition of Coventry —among other towns—is mentioned.
[2] Blank.

§ 126. Cuth. Joynour, Mayor. Leet, 1541.

betwen a tenement of the wardens of thone side and the kynges ground of thother side.

Item, at a Tenement ther of Will. Jackesons.

Cooke-stret.

¶ Item, at a voied ground ther belongyng to seynt Johns wher dyuers tenementes late stoode.

Croscheping.

¶ Item, at a Corner house there of Jasper Owen ouer ageynst Bancroftes-lane.

MICHAELMAS LEET.

"Ciuitas Couentrie." Oct. 11, 1541. Jury of 25.

[1] ¶ [V. f. p. held on Oct. 11, 33 Hen. VIII.]

[Magister [2] Sim. Parker, Tho. Banwell, Ric. Herryng, Rog. Palmer, Joh. Jett, Will. Coton, Tho. Gardynour, Joh. Saunders, Ric. Townesend, Tho. Spenser, Tho. Burdon, Jac. Gilbert, Rob. Seny, Will. Rogers, Tho. Bower, Ric. Ley, Joh. Talontes, Ric. Sewall, Chr. Waren, Hugo Bloure, Tho. Smyth, [3] Chr. Bromeley, Rog. Adnet, Will. Norton, Ric. Humfrey.]

Sheriffs.

[Edw. Damport, pewterer, Ric. Niclyn, Grasier.]

Orders of leet.
[4] *"Charcolles to be sold by Lawfull sacks." [4]*

[Ordained] that euery alderman of this Citie in his ward shall prepare a fate [5] to meit Charcolles with before the feast of All Seyntes next to thentent to se whether the Coliars [6] sackes be laufull or not.

Ditches to be scoured out.

¶ [Enacted] that euery man which haith eny landes adyoynyng vnto the lane ledyng frome Hil-streit end vnto the Barkers-buttes shall sufficientlie score ther dyches ther before Candlemas next, vpon peyn of euery man which doith not to forfeit vj s. viiij d.

All "walkers" to dress cloth within the city.

¶ [Enacted] that all walkers belongyng to this Citie shall burle ther Clothes within the Citie, vpon peyne to forfeit for euery burled owt of the Citie xx s. And that no Clothier shall put eny Cloith to eny walker which woll not burle it in the Citie, on peyne to forfeit for euery defaut vj s. viij d.

---

[1] leaf 388.   [2] This precedes every name until note 3.
[3] Untitled.   [4]—[4] In different handwritings.
[5] A dry measure usually = 9 gallons, v. N.E.D. s.v. Fat.
[6] = charcoal-burners.

§ 127. *Chris. Waren, Mayor. Leets,* 1542.

CHRIS. WAREN, MAYOR, 1542.

LEETS.

¹ ¶ [V. f. p. held before Chris. Waren, m., Edw. Damport, Ric. Niclyne, b., on Apr. 25, 34 Hen. VIII.] — "Ciuitas Couentr*ie*."

[*Magister*² Tho. Gardynour, Tho. Banwell, Ric. Herryng, Rog. Palmer, Joh. Jett, Sym. Parker, Cuth. Joynour, Ric. Townesend, Tho. Burdon, Joh. Saunders, Tho. Spens*er*, Jac. Gilbert, Will. Rogers, Tho. Brewer, Geo. Philips, Ric. Ley, Joh. Talont*es*, ["Joh." erased] Ric. Sewell, Hugo Bloure, Will. Saunders, ³Owin Blakemer, Will. Vnderwood, Art. Goodrich, Will. Norton, Ric. Humfrey.] — Jury of 25.

¶ [Enacted] that all brekemak*ers*, which make breke to be sold in the Citie, shall make the same after the olde assise, that is to say, tene Inches longe, v ynches in breid, & twc Inches & dim. in thyckenes, vpon peyn to forfeit for eu*ery* hundred xij d. — Orders of leet. Concerning ⁴"breke." ⁵"Brick the Assise." ⁵

[Ordained] that eu*ery* p*er*son in this Citie shall sufficientlie make ther pavement*es* befor the feast of thassen*cio*n of o*u*r Lord next, vpon [peyn] to forfeit iij s. iiij d. — Concerning "pauement*es*." ⁵

It is also ordeyned that the feliship & Craft of Tilers shabbe (*sic*) associat w*ith* the Craft of Cowp*ers* & pynn*ers*. And that the Craft & company of Carpenters shal-be contributories to the said Craft*es* of Cowp*ers* & pynn*ers* after such [pro]porc*io*n & rate as thei haue been accustumed in tymes past.⁶ — "Craft*es* ⁴ ⁵ off Tilers and Coup*ers*." ⁵

⁷ ¶ [V. f. p. held Oct. 10, 34 Hen. VIII.] — "Ciuitas Couentr*ie*."

[M*a*gister⁸ Tho. Gardynour, Tho. Banwell, Rog. Palm*er*,⁹ Joh. Jett, Will. Coton, Sym. Pa*r*ker, Cuth. Joyno*u*r, Joh. Saunders, Tho. Spens*er*, Jac. Gilbert, Rob. Seny, Will. Rogers, Tho. Brewer, Geo. Philips, Ric. Ley, Ric. Sewall, Hugo Blour, Jac. Rogers, Will. Saunders, ¹⁰Owin

---

¹ lea: 388, back. Chr. Waren, who had represented the city in 1539 in Parliament, appears to have been a very zealous Roman Catholic. Rob. Glover, the martyr, accused him of seeking his (Glover's) death.

² Repeated before every name preceding note ³. ³ Untitled.

⁴ In the same handwriting. ⁵—⁵ In a later handwriting.

⁶ There follow the introductory words deleted about the recorder's election. See above, p. 764.

⁷ lea: 389, back.

⁸ Repeated before every name preceding note ¹⁰.

⁹ Father of the martyr, Julines Palmer. ¹⁰ Untitled.

§ 128. *Joh. Saunders, Mayor*, 1543.

Blakem*er*, Will. Vnderwood, Hen. Hynd, Will. Stirropp, Ric. Humfrey.]

Sheriffs.

[Art. Gudriche, m*er*cer, Tho. Keyvet, Clothier.]

Orders of leet. About "talowe."

[Enacted] that all talowe in this Citie shal-be sold after the rait of ij s. the Stone or vnder & not aboue, vpon peyne to forfeit for eue*ry* Stone sold to the cont*r*arie vj s. viij d.

"Candell to be sold at 1¼d. a lb."

It is also enacted that Candell shall-be sold after the rait of j d. q*ua*. the li. & not aboue, vpon peyne to forfeit for eue*ry* li. sold cont*r*arie iiij d.

JOH. SAUNDERS, MAYOR, 1543.

"Ciuitas Couent*rie*." Jan. 25.

¹¶ [Election of officers.]

[M*agister*² Cuth. Joyno*ur*, Tho. Banwell, Rog. Palmer, Joh. Jett, Will. Coton, Sym. P*a*rker, Tho. Gardyno*ur*, Ric. Ley, Ric. Townesend, Tho. Spens*er*, Jac. Gilbert, Rob. Seny, Will. Roge*rs*, Tho. Brewer, Ric. Sewell, Hugo Bloure, Jac. Roge*rs*, Will. Saunders, Edw. Damport, Ric. Niclyn, ³Owin Blakemer, Will. Vnderwood, Will. Norton, Ric. Humfrey.]

Officers.

¶ [m. ⁴Joh. Saunders, m*er*cer; rec. ⁴Edw. Saunders, serjeant-at-law; cor. Rob. Grene, "Gen*er*os*us*"; steward, Baldw. Porter, "gen*er*os*us*"; ch. Ric. Wightma*n*, Capper, Joh. Castell, b*o*cher; w. Tho. Beck, bedder, ⁵ Tho. Amo*ur*son, Chaundeler; mace, Hen. Thirkyll; crier, Rob. Swift.]

LEETS.

"Ciuitas Couent*rie*." Apr. 10, 1543.

⁶¶ [V. f. p. before Joh. Saunders, m., Art. Gudriche, Tho. Keyvet, b. Apr. 10, 34 Henry VIII.]

[M*agister*⁷ Cuth. Joyno*ur*, Joh. Jett, Will. Coton, Sym. P*a*rker, Tho. Gardyno*ur*, Ric. Ley, Ric. Townesend, Tho. Spens*er*, Jac. Gilbert, Will. Rogers, Geo. Philips, Joh. Talont*es*, Ric. Sewall, Joh. Herford, Hugo Blour, Tho. Smyth, Jac. Roge*rs*, Will. Saunders, Edw. Damport, Ric. Niclyn, ⁸ Ric. Wightman, Joh. Castell, Tho. Enderby, Tho. Dyglyn.]

---

¹ leaf 390. ² This precedes every name until note 3.
³ Untitled. ⁴–⁴ Preceded by "Magister." ⁵ = upholsterer.
⁶ leaf 390, back. ⁷ Repeated before each name until note ⁸.
⁸ Untitled.

§ 129. *Hen. Over, Mayor. Commons*, 1544.

[Enacted] that no bocher or other inhabitaunt of this Citie shall frome-hensfurthe haue or vse eny comen belongyng to this Citie with sheipp, vpon peyne to be distreyned by the Chamberleyns of the Citie for the tyme beyng, and to forfeit for euery Sheip found vpon the comen iiij d., half therof to be to the vse of the Chamberleyns, and the other half to the vse of the comen box, and to be leuyed by distres.

Orders of leet.
1 " The comen for Sheip taken away from butchers. 4d. A sheip forfeit." 1

[Enacted] that no persone hauyng in farme eny parcell of the comen Closez to the value of x s. shall haue eny maner of comen for eny beasse, vpon peyn to be distreyned etc. Prouidet alwey that it shal-be laufull to euery bocher to vse & haue ther comen for horsez & beassez accordyng to the former actes & vsages therof etc.²

None to enjoy privileges of " comen " when they already have common lands to the value of 10s. in farm, except butchers.

[³ V. f. p. held on Oct. 9, 35 Hen. VIII.]

[Magister⁴ Cuth. Joynour, Rog. Palmer, Joh. Jett, Will. Coton, Tho. Gardynour, Ric. Townesend, Tho. Spenser, Jac. Gilbert, ⁵Ric. Townesend, Tho. Spenser, Jac. Gilbert,⁵ Tho. Brewer, ⁶Geo. Philips,⁶ Joh. Talontes, Hugo Bloure, Jac. Rogers, Will. Saunders, Ric. Niclyn,⁷ Ric. Wightman, Joh. Castell, Tho. Amourson, Hen. Hynd, Chr. ? Whayton, Tho. Diglyn, Ric. Giller.]

"Ciuitas Couentrie." Oct. 9, 1543. Jury of 22.

[Tho. Enderby, waxchaundeler, Will. Joynour, Grasier.]

Sheriffs.

[Ordained] that talowe shal-be sold the rait of xxij d. the Stone & not aboue, vpon peyne to forfeit for euery Stone ij s., and that Candell shal-be sold after the rait of j d. qua. the li. & not aboue.

About " talow and Candell."

HEN. OVER, MAYOR, 1544.

⁸¶ [Election of officers.]

[Magister⁹ Chris. Waren, Rog. Palmer, Joh. Jett, Will. Coton, Sym. Parker, Tho. Gardynour, Geo. Philips, Ric. Townesend, Tho. Spenser, Jac. Gilbert, Rob. Seny, Will. Rogers, Tho. Brewer, Ric. Sewall, Hugo Bloure, Ric. Niclyn, Art. Goodrich, Tho. Keyvet, ¹⁰Ric. Wightman,

"Ciuitas Couentrie." Jan. 25. 25 Electors.

---

¹⁻¹ In different handwriting. ² See p. 735.
³ leaf 391. ⁴ Repeated before each name until note ⁷.
⁵⁻⁵ a repetition. ⁶⁻⁶ Deleted. ⁷ Untitled.
⁸ leaf 391, back.
⁹ Repeated before each name as far as note ¹⁰. ¹⁰ Untitled.

770   § 129. *Hen. Over. Mayor. Leets*, 1544.

Joh. Castell, Joh. Moseley, Ric. Giller, Tho. Diglyn, Will. Norton, Ric. Humfrey.]

Officers.   [m. Mag*ister* Hen. Over, alias dict*us* Waver,[1] m*er*cer; rec. Edw. Saunders, Sergeant-at-law; cor. Rob. Greene; ch. Joh. Hyndema*n*, ?alias[2] Joyno*ur*, Joh. Jeynard; w. Ric. Dodd, m*er*cer, Joh. West, goldesmyth; mace, Hen. Thirkyll; crier, Rob. Swyft.]

LEETS.

[3][V. f. p. before Hen. Over, m., Tho. Enderbie, Will.
May 6, 1544.   Joyno*ur*, b., on May 6, 36 Hen. VIII.]

Jury.   [M*agister*[4] Chris. Waren, Rog. Palmer, Joh. Jett, Will. Coton, Sim. P*ar*ker, Tho. Gardyno*ur*, Cuth. Joyno*ur*, Joh. Saunders, Geo. Philips, Ric. Townesend, Tho. Spens*er*, Jac. Gilbert, Will. Roge*r*s, Ric. Ley, J*oh*. Talont*es*, Ric. Sewall, Joh. Herford, Hugo Bloure, Tho. Smyth, Will. Saunders, Edw. Damport, Ric. Niclyn, Art. Goodrich, Tho. Keivet.]

[5] "Sheipp ffa[i]re; none to set penns aboue White-frier-lane end."[5]   [Enacted] that no p*er*sone frome-hensfurth shall sett eny fold or pene to sell sheipp in at the faire tyme in the Gosforde Streit aboue the White-frere-lane ende vpon peyne to forfeit x s.

The "bochers" are permitted to form as heretofore a craft;   [Enacted] that the bochers of this Citie shal-be restored & admytted to be a Craft & a felishipp together as they haue been in tymes past & to haue & vse all ther laudable vsages & customes as they haue doon. And that noon ap*r*entice of that Craft, or of eny other Craft wi*thi*n this Citie, Ner eny other p*er*sone shall sett vpp & vse ther Craft or occupac*i*on here vntill they haue s*er*ued ther holl ap*re*ntisshipp wi*th*out license of the Maist*e*rs of ther Craft & the felishipp of the same Craft, vpon peyne to be grevouslie punysshed by the discrecc*i*ons of the said Maist*er*s.

no butchers are to set up without having been "appr*en*ticez."

Brewers and "ale-wif*es*,"   Item, wher-as befor this tyme dyu*er*s good lawes &

---

[1] On this family, whose seat was at Cester Over, see Dugdale, 64–5. Hen. Over became possessed of the Charterhouse soon after the Dissolution; see Whitley, *Representation*, 38.
[2] MS. looks like "ald." For Joh. Joynour's name see below, p. 773.
[3] leaf 392.   [4] Repeated before every name.
[5–5] In different handwriting.

§ 129. *Hen. Over*, Mayor. *Leets*, 1544.

Statutes haue been ordeyned & maid at dyuers letes holden within this Citie ageynst the abuses of ale-brewers & tiplers of the same Citie, which former lawes & statuzes for lack of due execucion of the same be nothyng regarded nor obserued, and dyuers & meny of the said brewers & tiplers nothyng regarding the displeasure of God, the daunger of the lawes of the realme, ner the loue & charitie which thei ought to bere to ther neighbour, ne the comen-welthe of this Citie, for ther owne privat lucre & singuler availl, do comonlie euery market day forstall & regrait barley comyng to this Citie to be sold, and gredelie geit into ther handes [1] so great quantitie therof that therby the price of the same is moche aduaunced. And then after makyng the same in malt do brewe it & sell ther ale at excessive & vnreasonable prices to ther owne great aduauntage, By reason wherof the said brewers & tiplers be now encreased & multiplied to suche a great nomber that a great parte of thynhabitauntes of this Citie be nowe become brewers & tiplers of ale, & have forsaken ther occupacions & Craftes by the which in tymes past they haue opteyned & hadd a moche more welthy lyvyng then they now haue, Wherby almyghtie God is highlie displeased, the comen-Welthe of this Citie greatlie decayed, and vice, Idelnes, & other innumerable myscheves norisshed and encreased, And shall daylie more & more if spedie remedie be not therin prouided & hadd:

ffor reformacion whereof it is ordeyned, enacted & established (etc.) that noon inhabitaunt of this Citie shall frome & after the feast of Penticost now next ensuyng brewe or tiple eny ale within this Citie to sell but onelie suche person & persones as shal-be therunto appoynted, named & licensed by Maister Meyre & the Justices of the peace of this Citie for the tyme beyng, vpon peyne to forfeit xl s. for euery monthe that thei or eny of theme shall brewe or tiple contrarie to the tenour of this acte. The same forfeitur to be leuyed & taken by the Shireffes of the Citie & the vnderbeilleffes of the same for the tyme beyng by distresse or otherwise to ther owne vse.

nothing regarding the displeasure of God,

for their own private lucre forestall and regrate barley, and greedily get so much into their hands that the price rises.

There is an " Excessiue number of Ale-houses and decay of Trades," because many of the inhabitants of the city have forsaken their old callings and become brewers and tiplers, whereby God is displeased, and the common-wealth of the city decayed, and vice and idleness encreased.

It is ordained that after the feast of Pentecost no person is to brew nor sell ale without licence of the mayor and justices of the peace, under pain of 40s. fine.

[1] leaf 392, back.

§ 129. Hen. Over, Mayor. Measures, 1544.

Ale is not to be sold above 18d. the sextary, with 14 gallons to the sextary,

And that no brewer within this Citie after the said feast of Penticost shall sell eny ale aboue the price of xviij d. for on Cestur & xiiij galons to be in euery Cester, vpon peyne to forfeit for euery Cestur sold contrarie to this acte vj s. viij d. to be leuyed & taken in fourme aforseid & to the vse aforseid. And that no Tipler or other inhabitaunt of this Citie frome & after the said feast of Penticost shall sell eny ale within this Citie to be dronke within the house aboue ij d. the galon, & owt of the house aboue j d. ob. the galon, vpon peyne to forfeit for euery defaut vj s. viij d. to be leuyed & taken in fourme aforseid.

nor above 2d. a gallon within doors and 1½d. without.

And it is further ordeyned (etc.) that no Tipler or other inhabitaunt of this Citie frome & after the said feast shall sell or vtter eny ale but onelie by such pottes and measures as be laufull pyntes, quartes, pottelles & galons, & sealled according to the lawe, vpon peyne to forfeit for euery [1] defaut vj s. viij d. to be leuyed & taken to the vse & in fourme aforsed. And that also it shal-be laufull as-well for the Shireffes of the said Citie for the tyme beyng as for the swirdebeirer & meire seriaunt & euery of theme to take & breke all pottes & measures wherewith eny ale shal-be vttered & sold after the said feaste contrarie to the tenour of this acte. And to thentent that this acte may be put in execucion & take effecte it is further ordeyned (etc.) that all the articles & all the effecte of this acte shal-be yeirelie from hensfurthe declared & given in charge by the Recorder or Stiward of this Citie for the tyme beyng at euery quarter Cession & lete holden in this Citie, to the intent the offendoures therin may be enquyred of, knowen & punysshed accordynglie.

All measures are to be sealed,

the swordbearer and mayor's sergeant having liberty to seize and break all those that are defective.

All the articles of this act are to be given in charge by the recorder or steward at quarter sessions.

The "Milners" are "to be a ffelloshhip,"

[Ordained] that the Milners of this Citie shal-be fromehensfurthe be [2] a felishipp & a Craft or company amonges themselfes as the moost parte of the Craftes of this Citie be, and to make lawes, ordynaunces & constitucions in their booke for the comen-welthe of this Citie by the assent and allowaunce of the meire and his brethren for the tyme beyng. And that they shall yeirelie electe amongest

to make their own rules,

subject to the mayor's authority.

[1] leaf 393. [2] redundant.

§ 129. *Hen. Over, Mayor. Leets,* 1544.

themeselfes at ther day of assemble for that purpose two persones of the same Craft to be gardens and gouerners of the said felishipp & company; which gardens & gouerners shal-be alweyes obedyent to the meire & aldermen of the same Citie & to meynteign & cause the said ordynaunces & constitucions to be well & truelie perfourmed & kept. To the which Gardens & gouerners for the tyme beyng all the said felishipp within the said Citie & liberties of the same shall-be alweys obedyent & confourmable, as-well to meit at all assembles vpon a laufull monycion & warnyng, as to perfourme & keipp the said ordynaunces & constitucions. And that the said gardens shall take & receive as-well of theme that shall sett vpp & begyn to occupie the said Crafte as of theme that shal-be maid prentisez to the same Craft suche fynes & fees as the gardens & kepers of other faculties & Craftes within the said Citie vse moost comonlie to take accordyng to the kynges Statutes & lawes therof maid.

Two persons are to be yearly elected to be guardians,

to whom the fellowship shall be obedient,

and to whom fines and fees shall be paid.

[1] ¶ [V. f. p. held before Hen. Over, m., Tho. Enderbye, Will. Joynour, b., on Oct. 7, 36 Hen. VIII.]

"Ciuitas Couentrie."
Oct. 7, 1544.

[Magister[2] Chris. Waren, Rog. Palmer, Joh. Jett, Will. Coton, Sym. Parker, Tho. Gardynor, Cuth. Joynor, Joh. Saunders, Geo. Phillipes, Tho. Spenser, Jac. Gilbert, Rob. Seynye, Will. Rogers, Ric. Ley, Ric. Sewall, Joh. Harford, Hugo Bloure, Tho. Smythe, Jac. Rogers, Will. Sanders, Edw. Damport, Ric. Nyclyne, Art. Goodriche, Tho. Keyvet, [3] Joh. Joynoure, Joh. Jonarde, Joh. Moysley, Ric. Humfrey, Joh. Chambers.]

Jury of 29.

[Will Norton, draper, Ric. Hurte, mercer.]

Sheriffs.

[Ordained] at this leete that noo persone of the Crafte or felowshipe of Cappers[5] within the saide Citie shall fromhensforthe vse or occupye to putte forthe any worke callide peece-worke to any persone or persones of the same felowshype or Cratfe, except a laufull and a needefull cause shulde soo requyre, and that the same laufull or

The [4] "Cappers" are forbidden

to give out piece-work,

save for urgent reasons

---

[1] leaf 393, back. Scribe K.
[2] Repeated before all names until note 3.   [3] Untitled.
[4] In Scribe K.'s handwriting.
[5] For previous rules see pp. 572-4, 670-3.

§ 129. Hen. Over, Mayor. Cappers, 1544.

admitted by the head masters of the craft.

needefull cause shal-be openned and examyned before the heade maisters of the said Crafte for the tyme beinge and by theym admytted and allowed so to be soeffered and doon, vpon payne to forfayte for eue*r*y defaulte x s. to the vse of the said Crafte.

Searchers

to be chosen to make search for "Stolne yarne."

Also it is furthere enacted *tha*t there shal-be twoo sufficiente and honeste pe*r*sones of the saide Crafte admytted and sworne, who shall haue auctoritye to make Searche, as-well for suche peece-worke, as for suspecte and stollen yarne, as-well clothe yarne as cappe yarne, to thentent *tha*t noo disceyte be therin vsed, vpon like peyne for eue*r*y defaulte.

Only two "apprentyzes" to be kept, save that during the last year and a half of the term of apprenticeship one more is allowable.

Ite*m*, that noo pe*r*sone of the saide Crafte or felowshype shall from-hensforthe haue, reteygne or keepe in his house any moo prentizes but onely ij, excepte *tha*t it shal-be laufull for eue*r*y suche pe*r*sone to take oone prentyse more within oone yeare and a half before the last ende of the yeares and terme of his olde apprentyse, vpon like peyne for eue*r*y defaulte.

No "Jorneymen" to depart before the week's end without his master's leave,

Ite*m*, it is furthere enacted by the auctoritie of the same leete *tha*t noo Jorneyma*n* of the saide Crafte shall from-hensforthe vse to depa*r*te or goo forthe of his maisters worke or Servyce at any tyme before the weekes ende oneles he haue the licence and consente of his maister for the tyme beynge, and that he shall haue a laufull and needefull cause soo to doo, and the same laufull and needefull cause to be examyned and allowed before the maisters of the saide Crafte for the tyme beynge,

under penalty of 6d.

vpon payne to forfayte for eue*r*y suche defaulte vj d. to his maister for the tyme beynge. And if his saide m*aiste*r be remysse or neclygente in levyinge and takinge of the saide forfayture, that then it shal-be laufull for the m*aister*s of the saide Crafte for the tyme beinge to leavye and take the same forfayture to the vse of the saide Crafte.

Anything taken as "Distres or

[1] Ite*m*, it is furtheremore ordeyned (etc.) that non inha*b*itante of this Citie whiche at any tyme hereafter whiche [2] shall distrayne or take any goodes or Catalles as a

---

[1] leaf 394. [2] redundant.

§ 129. *Hen. Over, Mayor. Leet,* 1544.

distres or as a Streyve within this Citie or the liberties of the same shall from-hensforthe impounde, imparke, brynge or delyuer any suche distres or Strayve to any othere pounde thene to the Comon pounde of olde tyme belonginge to this Citye, that is to saye to the pounde of the Newe Yaite or to the Litle-parke, vnder the gouernaunce of the Chamberlaynes of the Citie for the tyme beynge, whiche shall keepe the same as a distres or Strayve accordinge to the order of the Comon lawe, vpon payne of euery inhabitaunte delyuerynge or ympoundinge any distres or Strayve contrarye to the tenor of this Acte to forfayte for euery defaulte vj s. viij d. to be levyed by distres by the Shreffes of the saide Citye for the tyme beyinge to theyre owne vse.

And also whereas thinhabitauntes of the Croscheapinge in tymes paste haue not onelie comonlye vsed to laye donge and other fylthe nighe vnto the Crosse [2] there to the great incomoditie of the marketh-place and to the great daunger of infection of the plage, but also haue vsed comonlye to swepe the pavymentes there, and thereby reasynge duste doo deface and corrupte the saide Crosse, It ys nowe enacted by auctoritye aforesaide that noon inhabitaunte of this Cytye shall from-hensfurthe ley any dunge or fylthe in the Croscheapinge, ner shall at any tyme Sweepe the pavymentes there excepte they Immediatly before the Swepe do caste and Sprynkle water vpon the saide pavymentes, vpon payne to forfaite for euery defaulte iij s. iiij d. to be levyd by distres by the Comon Sergyaunte, Cryer and Cloke-berer [3] of the saide Citye for tyme beinge to theyre owne vse.

Also whereas the highewayes lyinge nere vnto the Suburbes of this Citye been soore decayed and in great ruyne,[4] the occasion and pryncipall cause wherof is that

Strayves" to be taken to the common pound.

The penalty for wrongfully [1] *"Impoundyng"* [1] *is 6s. 8d.*

The inhabitants of Cross Cheaping lay filth near the Cross, heedless of the infection of the plague and the defacing of the Cross, the practice is forbidden and an order is laid down for the [1] *"watring"* [1] *of the* [1] *"streets before sweeping."* [1]

Evil state of highways.

[1–1] A later handwriting.

[2] This was the new cross built during the years 1541-3 by Sir Will. Holleys, Lord Mayor of London, who entrusted Over and Waren with money for the purpose.

[3] This combination in the present sense is not mentioned in the *N.E.D.* It refers to an official who bore the mayor's cloak.

[4] Dame Swyllington, widow of the recorder, bequeathed by her nuncupative will money to repair the bad roads in and near Stivichall and Coventry.—Whitley, *Representation,* 38.

§ 129. Hen. Over, Mayor. Weavers, 1544.

"For scouryng of dyches."
It is ordered that ditches bordering the highway shall be scoured by those having lands adjoining.

the ditches beinge nighe vnto the same highe-wayes be not Scoured and clensed, It is therfore ordeyned (etc.) that euerye inha*b*itaunte of this Citie occupyinge or holdinge any clooses, pastures, or othere groundes nyghe vnto anye of the saide highe-wayes, shall sufficientlye clense and scowre all ditches of his clooses, pastures, or other groundes lyinge nyghe vnto the saide highe-wayes before the feaste of Eister nexte, vpon payne of x s. to be levyed by distres by the Shireffes of the saide Citye for the tyme beinge to theyre owne vse, p*r*ouided alwaye that if eny pe*r*sone beynge tena*u*nte of any suche grounde, as haithe ditches lyinge nighe vnto any of the saide highe-wayes, do leaue the saide grounde at oure Laydye daye the Annu*n*ciac*i*on nexte ensuynge this leete That then the tenaunte, whiche shall nexte occupye the same grounde, shal-be bounden by vertue hereof to scoure and clense the saide ditches before Witsontyde nexte, vpon like payne.

"Clothyars & weyvers." The weavers do not make cloth of true breadth,

[1] Also whereas moche complaynte is maide by the clothyars of this Citye for that that (*sic*) the weyvers do not theyre duetye in weyvynge theyre clothes & warpinge theym of laufull breade accordinge to the actes of pa*r*liamente therof maide, for that that many of theym haue not lomes & Sleys [2] able & meete for the same to

to the great slander of the city: it is ordered that every weaver shall

the great Sclander & diffamacion of all the Clothyars of this Citye, It is therfore enacted by auctorytye aforsaide that euery weyvere of this Cytye, whiche hereafter shall take vpon hym to weyve any broode clothe, shall haue lomes and Sleys sufficiente and able to make the same

make his cloth 7 quarters (1¾ yds.) broad.

cloothe of laufull breade, that ys to saye, vij quarters within the lyst*es*,[3] and noon of the saide weyvers shall refuse to spole [4] the yarne of eue*r*y suche clothe if the owner therof soo will or commaunde hym, vpon payne to forfait for eue*r*y defaulte vj s. viij d. to the vse of the Shireffes aforesaide. And that eue*r*y clothear of this Citye

---

[1] leaf 394, back. [2] See p. 639.
[3] list = selvage, border of cloth; *within the lists* is usual in statements of measurement. See (1535) 27 Hen. VIII, c. 12, § 2, "Euery brode cloth shall conteine in breadth seuen quarters of a yarde within the listes" (*N.E.D.*).
[4] = to wind on reels.

§ 129. *Hen. Over, Mayor. Weavers*, 1544.

shall at his libertye weyve his owne clothes, so that he at his enterye and begynnynge paye vnto the occupacion of weyvers iij s. iiij d., and also be contributorye to the weyvers in theyre chardges, as other weyvers be, if he weyve any othere mannes clothes but oonelye his owne.

<small>Every clothier may weave his own cloth, if he pay to the weavers' charges.</small>

It is furthere enacted (etc.) that the Comon Sealler of Clothes within this Citye shall from hensforthe Seall noo clothes but suche as be sufficientlye and truelie maide within the liberties of this Citye, vpon payne to forfayte xx s. for euerye defaulte to be levyed in forme aforesaide to the vse of the Shireffes of the saide Citye for the tyme beinge.

<small>"The Comon Sealler of Clothes" shall not seal any cloth but such as is sufficiently made.</small>

Item, it is ffurthere inacted (etc.) that euerye inhabitante of this Cytie whiche nowe is or haithe been or that hereafter shal-be mayour, Shiref, Chamberlayne or wardeyn, and euery inholder, and all and euery other persone and persones, whiche take theym-selfes to be honeste Comyners, within this Cytye yerelie from-hensforthe from and after the feaste of All Saynctes vntill the feaste of the Purification of our Laydye shall cause a lanterne with a candle light to be sette or honge at his doore to gyve light into the Streyt euery night when the moone doethe not Shyne from suche tyme as daylight is paste vntill ix of the Clocke in the nyght, vpon payne to forfayte xij d. for euery defaulte to be levyed by distres by the Comon Sergyant and Cryer of this Citye to theyre owne vses. And that euery constable of this Citye within his warde shal-be chardged to se this acte executed and the offenders therin to be by theym presented and Shewed to the mayor of this Cytye for the tyme beynge, vpon payne to forfayte xij d. for euery defaulte of euerye of the saide Constables to be levyed by distres by the Comon Sergyant, Cryer and Clokeberer of this Citye to theyre owne vses.

<small>Late officers, innholders, and all honest commoners are to set up at their doors between All Saints' and Candlemas "Lanternes & light in the nyght."</small>

[Enacted] that noo clothyar of this Citye from-hensforthe shall delyuer to any Carder or Spynner above ij li. & a half cf woll for oone weight, vpon payne to forfayte xij d. for every weght to be levyed by distres by the Shireffes of the saide Citye for the tyme beinge to theyre owne vses.

<small>"Clothyars, Carders & Spynners."</small>

JOH. TALONTES, MAYOR, 1545.

¹ ¶ [Election of officers.]

[M*agister* ² Will. Coton, Sim. P*a*rker, Tho. Gardynor, Cuth. Joynor, Chris. Waren, Joh. Saunders, Will. Rogers, Tho. Spens*er*, Jac. Gilbert, Rob. Seynye, Geo. Phillipes, Ric. Ley, Ric. Sewall, Joh. Herforde, Hugo Blowre, Tho. Smythe, Edw. Damport, Ric. Nyclyne, Art. Goodriche, Tho. Keyvet, Tho. Enderbye, Will. Joynor, ³Joh. Hyndeman, Joh. Joynarde.]

¶ [m. M*agister* Joh. Talont*es*, goldesmythe; rec. Edw. Saunders, sergeant-at-law; cor. Rob. Greene, ⁴"sub condicione q*uo*d continue manebit infra Ciuitatem vel Com*itatum* eiusdem Ciuitatis;" steward, Baldw. Porter; ch. Will. Westeley, Capper, Tho. Phillipes, Capper; w. Phil. Sherrarde, drap*er*, Hugo Harvye, Capper; mace, Hen. Thyrkyll; crier, Rob. Swifte.

LEETS.

⁵ ¶ [V. f. p. held before Joh. Talont*es*, m., Will. Norton, Ric. Hurte, b., on Apr. 28, 37 Hen. VIII.]

[M*agister* ⁶ Joh. Jett, Will. Coton, Sym. P*a*rker, Tho. Gardyno*ur*, Cuth. Joyno*ur*, Chris. Waren, Joh. Saunders, Geo. Philips, Tho. Spens*er*, Jac. Gilb*er*t, Rob. Seny, Will. Rog*er*s, Ric. Ley, Ric. Sewall, Hugo Broure (*sic*), Will. Saunders, Ric. Niclyn, Art. Gudrich, Tho. Enderby, Will. Joyno*ur*, ⁷Will. Westley, Tho. Philips, Rad. Hopkyns, Tho. Wheteley, Joh. Joyno*ur*.]

[Enacted] that no Capp*er* shall haue eny mo p*r*enteses at ones then ij, savyng that he may on yeire & a half before thende of eny app*r*entisshipp take on other new p*r*entesse.⁸

Item, that the Shireff*es* of the Citie fromehensfurth shall haue the svme of x li. given theme owt of the

---

¹ leaf 395.   ² Repeated before every name until note 3.
³ Untitled.
⁴ = upon condition that he shall continually remain within the city or the county of the same city.
⁵ leaf 395, back.   Former scribe of I type.
⁶ Repeated before names until note 7.
⁷ Untitled.   ⁸ See above, p. 774.

§ 131. Joh. Herforde, Mayor, 1546.

.profittes of the comen groundes takyn in towardes ther charges, and that no shireff frome-hensfurthe shall pay any Rent for the gaoll-hall.

[Enacted] that the meir & Shireffes shall fromehensfurthe keipp ther drynkynges on Midsomer nyght & saynt Peters nyght[2] befor the watche & not after as haithe been vsed in tymes past.

[Enacted] that Maister meir for the tyme beying shall haue & correccion & punysshement of bakers and not the maister of the Craft of bakers, as he haith hadd in tymes past.

[3] [V. f. p. held on Oct. 4, 37 Hen. VIII.]

[Magister[4] Hen. Over, Will Coton, Sim. Parker, Tho. Gardynor, Cuth. Joynor, Cris. Waren, Joh. Saunders, Will. Rogers, Tho. Spenser, Jac. Gilbert, Geo. Philippes, Ric. Sewall, Hugo Blowre, Jac. Rogers, Will. Saunders, Ric. Nyclyne, Art. Goodriche, Tho. Keyvet, Will. Joynor, [5] Will. Westeley, Rad. Hopkyns, Tho. Morres, Tho. Amorsame, Joh. Weste, Hen. Hynde, Will. Vnderwoode, Owen Blakemere.]

["Magister" Tho. Rieley, draper, [5]Tho. Whaiteley, Irenmongere.][6]

Marginalia:
[1] "Shireffes x li. Alowed then toward their Charge and to pay no Rent ffor the Gaole."[1]
The Midsummer armed "Watche."
[1] The "bakers" are "not to punish any offenders, but the mayor."[1]
"Ciuitas Couentrie." Oct. 4. Jury of 27.
Sheriffs.

JOH. HERFORDE, MAYOR, 1546.

[7] ¶ [Election of officers.]

[Magister[8] Will. Coton, Sim. Parkere, Tho. Gardynor, Cuth. Joynor, Chr. Waren, Joh. Saunders, Hen. Over, Ric. Ley, Will. Rogers, Tho. Spenser, Hugo Blowre, Ric. Sewall, Art. Goodriche, Tho. Keyvet, Edw. Damport, Ric. Nyclyne, Will. Joynor, Will. Norton, Ric. Hurte,

Marginalia: "Ciuitas Couentrie." Jan. 25, 1546. 25 Electors.

---

[1]—[1] In different handwritings.
[2] See above, p. 35, and Sharp, *Mysteries*, pp. 174–206.
[3] leaf 396. Scribe K.
[4] Repeated before every name until note 5.   [5] Untitled.
[6] The "Dick Whittington" of Coventry, see Dugdale (1730), i. 194, *Life in an English Town*, 311. He came to the city "a poor boy in a white coat." He traded in Spanish iron, and a servant of his obtained by mistake a chest of ingots of silver in lieu of one of steel gads at a fair in Spain. Wheatley gave the money towards the foundation of the Bablake School, and other charities.
[7] leaf 396, back.
[8] Repeated before all names until note 1, p. 780.

§ 131. *Joh. Herforde, Mayor. Leets,* 1546.

Officers.

¹Tho. Philipes, Will. Westeley, Joh. Nethermyll, Tho. Owres, Tho. Amorsame, Joh. Weste.]
[m. "M*agiste*r" Joh. Herforde, lethereseller; ²M.G.S.T. and M.G.C.C. "M*agister*" Joh. Talontes, goldesmythe; rec. Edw. Saunders, sergeant-at-law; cor. Tho. Gregorye; steward, Baldw. Porter; ch. Tho. Seynye, Edm. Brownhill, drape*r*s; w. Tho. Bustarde, me*r*cer, Ric. Smythe, vyntenar; mace, Hen. Thirkyll'; crier, Rob. Swifte.]

EASTER AND MICHAELMAS LEETS.

"Ciuitas Couentrie." May 18, 1546.
Jury of 25.

³¶ [V. f. p. held before Joh. Herforde, m., Tho. Rieley, Tho. Whayteley, b., on May 18, 38 Hen. VIII.]
[M*agiste*r,⁴ Joh. Talont*es*, Sim. P*ar*ker, Tho. Gardynor, Cuth. Joynor, Chr. Waren, Joh. Saunders, Will. Rogers, Tho. Spens*er*, Jac. Gilbert, Geo. Philipes, Ric. Ley, Tho. Smythe, Will. Saunders, Edw. Damport, Art. Goodriche, Tho. Keyvet, Will. Norton, ⁵Edm. Brownehill, Tho. Seynye, Tho. Bustarde, Hen. Hynde, Will. Styrope, Ric. Warnar, Rob. Colman, Owin Blakemere.]

Orders of leet. "Corne set vp." ⁶

⁷¶ It is enacted that no housholder of this Citie shall receive eny strau*n*ge*r*s corne to keipp it in his house frome ma*r*ket day to m*ar*ket day, vpon payn to forfeit for eue*r*y default vj s. viij d.

Butchers forbidden to sell hides to foreign "Tanners" on Fridays.

¶ It*em*, that no bocher of this Citie frome-hensfurthe put eny slaughter hid*es* to sale to eny forene tann*er* on the Fryday, but vpon the Satu*r*day and on other dayes when thei put ther fleshe to sale, and then to no foren tann*er* before ix of the Clock, and in noon other place but at the Bull-ryng, vpon peyn of x s. for eu*er*y def*a*ult.

The "bochers off" the "cuntrey to sell flesh on Tuesday, Thursday and Saturdays."

¶ Also it is enacted that the bochers of the Citie shall p*er*mytt & soeffer all fore*n* bochers quietlie to sell ther vitayll in the Citie eue*r*y Tuesday, Thursday & Satu*r*day bryngyng ther hid*es* & talow w*ith* theme, vpon payn of xx s. for eue*r*y def*a*ult, and to be further punysshed by imp*r*isonm*en*t by discrec*cio*n of M*aiste*r meir.

¹ Untitled.
² "In officium Magis*tr*i gildar*um* S. Trinitat*is* et Corporis *Chr*isti in Ciuitate pred*ic*ta."
³ leaf 397. Scribe K.
⁴ Repeated before every name until note 5. ⁵ Untitled.
⁶ In different hands. ⁷ Former scribe of I type.

§ 132. *Jas. Rogers, Mayor*, 1547.

Item, it is enacted that the acte maid for pece-work & takyng of p*re*ntesez in M*aiste*r Overs yeire[1] shall stand in force. *"Cappers."*

[Leet held in the 38th year of the reign of Lord Henry VIII, by the grace of God, King of England, France and Ireland, Defender of the Faith, and Supreme Head of the English and Irish Church in this country.

[2] [V. f. p. held on Oct. 5, " a. r. *dom*ini Henrici octaui, Dei gr*aci*a Anglie, ffrancie, & Hibernie Regis, fidei defensoris, & in terra ecclesie Anglicane & Hibernice Supremi Capit*is*, tricesimo octauo."] *"Ciuitas Coventrie."*

[Magister[3] Joh. Talont*es*, Sim. P*a*rkere, Chris. Warene, Joh. Saunders, Hen. Over, Geo. Philippes, Jac. Gilbert, Jac. Rogers, Will. Saunders, Edw. Damport, Will. Norton, Ric. Hurte, [4]Tho. Seynye, Edm. Brownehill, Tho. Bustarde, Ric. Smythe, Chris. Bromeley, Tho. Owres, Hen. Hynde, Will. Styrope, Will. Westeley, Hugo Harvye, Joh. Bolat, Will. Forster, Phil. Sherarde.]

[Joh. Warde, m*er*cer, Tho. Amorsame, Chaundelar.] *Sheriffs.*

[5] [Enacted] that no p*er*sone after the feast of All Seynt*es* next ensuyng this leet shall keipp eny alehouse or Inne w*ith*out the walles of the Citie except suche as shal-be admytted & allowed so to do by M*aiste*r Meire & the Justices of peace, vpon peyne to forfeit for eue*r*y defa*ult* xl s. to be leuyed by distresse to the vse of the Shireff*es*.[6] *No "alehousez" are to be kept without license of the mayor and Justices.*

It*em*, also that Peter Typpyng & Joh. Walland shall not fr*o*me-hensforthe keipp eny ale-house or vitayllyng, ner lodge eny p*er*sones where thei now dwell, vpon like payn. *Typping and Walland are forbidden to keep an alehouse.*

JAS. ROGERS, MAYOR, 1547.
EASTER AND MICHAELMAS LEET.

[7] ¶ [V. f. p. held before Jas. Rogers, m., Joh. Wayde, Tho. Amorsame, b., on May 3, 1 Edw. VI.[8]] *"Ciuitas Coventrie."*

---

[1] See above, p. 774.   [2] leaf 398. Scribe K.
[3] Repeated before names until note 4.   [4] Untitled.
[5] Former scribe of I type.
[6] This act is in advance of contemporary legislation. "By the Statute of 5 and 6 Edw. VI, c. 25 (1552), the Justices of the Peace were authorised to select ... certain persons, who were alone to exercise the trade of keeping a common alehouse." v. Webb, *Liquor Licensing*, 5.   [7] leaf 399, back. Scribe K.
[8] The king's titles are repeated as above.

§ 132. *Jas. Rogers, Mayor.* *Leet,* 1547.

Jury.

[M*agister*¹ Joh.' Saunders, Tho. Gardynor, Cuth. Joynor, Chris. Warene, Hen. Overe, Joh. Talontes, Tho. Spens*er*, Jac. Gilbert, Geo. Phillipes, Ric. Ley, Ric. Sewall, Hugo Blowre, Edw. Damport, Ric. Nyclyne, Will. Saunders, Tho. Keyvet, Will. Joynor, Will. Norton, Ric. Hurte, ²Hen. Lynggham, Ric. Scotte, Joh. Chambers, Ric. Warnar, Will. Vnderwoode, Rad. Hopkyns.]

³ "Millers orders to be Aproued by the mayor, and his Councell." ³

⁴[Enacted] that the Milleries [? Milners] of this Citie shall frome-hensfurthe be vnyted together as a felishipp & company of themeselfes, and shall haue libertie to chose M*aisteres* & kepers of ther occupac*i*one for the good rule & order of the same, So that thei make orders but suche as M*aister* Meire & his councell shall allowe.⁵

⁶ "Constablez of Any persons vnder the degree off sheriffs." ⁶

¶ It is enacted that euery alderma*n* shall frome-hensfurth appoynt the moost discretest & substanciallest men in his ward Vnder the degre of a Shereff to be Constablez.

"Cowp*ers*."

⁷ It is also enacted that the Cowp*ers* of this Citie shall frome-hensfurthe be associat with the Tilers & pynners, and bere suche charges as thei haue doon in tymes past; And that the Cowp*ers* shal-be the hedd & cheffest of theim & stand charged w*ith* the pagyaunt.

"Walkers" are to be a company.

[Enacted] that the walkers of this Citie shall frome-hensfurthe be a felishipp & company of themeselfes, and haue libertie to electe & [c]hoose maisters of ther Company for the good order of the same, & meynteynyng of true clothyng.

The "bochers" and tanners.

Item, that no bocher of this Citie shall sell eny hyd*es* of beasse to eny forene Tanner before xij of the clock on the Fryday, vpon peyn to forfeit xx d. for euery hide sold contrarie, and after xij of the Clock to sell at ther pleasures, notwi*th*standyng eny former actes maid to the contrarie, the same to be levied to the vse of the shireffes.⁸

⁶ "Chamberleyns."

¶ *Item*, if any inha*b*itaunte of this Citie by hymself or by his deputie or s*er*uaunt do take frome the Chamberleyns of this Citie or ther s*er*ua*un*tes or frome eny other

---

¹ Repeated before all names until note 2.
² Untitled.   ³—³ In different hands.
⁴ Scribe of I type.
⁵ See above, pp. 772-3.   ⁶—⁶ In different handwritings.
⁷ leaf 400.   ⁸ See above, p. 780.

§ 132. *Jas. Rogers, Mayor. Leet*, 1547.

Citizene by wey of Rescue eny catall beyng laufullie taken as a distres for damage-fesaunt[1] in the Comons of this Citie, or otherwise, The same per*s*one or per*s*ones so offendyng shall forfeit for eue*r*y suche default iij s. iiij d. to the Chamber*l*eyns to be levyed by wey of distresse of the offend*o*u*r*es good*es* immediatlie after the p*r*ove of eue*r*y suche offence maid befor Ma*is*te*r* Meire of this Citie for the tyme beyng.

[2][V. f. p. held on the feast of S. Luke the Evangelist, 1 Edw. VI.]

[Magister[3] Joh. Saunders, Sim. Pa*r*kere, Tho. Gardyno*u*r, Cuth. Joyno*u*r, Chr. Warene, Hen. Over, Joh. Talontes, Joh. Herforde, Will. Rogers, Tho. Spense*r*, Jac. Gilbert, Geo. Philippes, Ric. Sewall, Hugo Blowre, Ric. Nyclyne, Will. Saunders, Tho. Keyvet, Will. Joyno*u*r, Will. Norton, Ric. Hurte, Tho. Rieley, Tho. Whaiteley, [4]Hen. Lyngham, Ric. Scotte, Joh. Fytherbert, Ric. Sparrye, Hen. Hynde, Will. Sterope, Ric. Smythe.]

¶ [Joh. Nethermyll, drape*r*, Will. Westeley, Capper.]

¶ To thentente it maye be knowen whethere there be moo people in this Citye of the poorest*e* sorte that muste bee sette on worke[5] then othere *that* be able to sette theym on worke It ys inacted (etc.) that eue*r*y alderman in his warde shall make a boke of the names of all thinh*a*bitauntes of his warde and whoo be the lordes and owners of theyre howses, wherin they dwell, of what age the inh*a*bitaunt*es* be and howe longe they have dwelled in the Citye, whethere they be maried or not, and what nombere of chylderne they haue, of what occupacion they be, and whethere they be able to sette theymselfes on worke or not; and the same booke to exhibette vnto Ma*is*te*r* Mayo*u*r and the Counsaill of this Cytie before the feaste of the Nativitye of oure Lorde God nexte.

[6]¶ Ite*m*, whoo be able to sette othere on worke and howe many they doo vse to sette on worke weekely and

---

[1] = doing damage, *i. e.* trespassing.
[2] leaf 403. Scribe K.
[3] Repeated before all names until note 4.   [4] Untitled.
[5] Cf. the census taken of the Warwick mendicants in 1586, v. Kemp, Joh. Fisher, pp. 165, *sqq.*
[6] leaf 403, back.

§ 132. *Jas. Rogers, Mayor, Work*, 1547.

the number of those they employ, and the workmen being in excess of employers' needs [? in that ward] they shall be set on by other masters.

whoo they be, and if it be perceyved that the pooreste sorte is the greateste nombere that then suche persones as haue the Cityes moneye in Stooke be ordered to sette thee pore[1] on worke, and if they be not able to sette theym all on worke that then they be appoynted to other, and that they shall not worke with any othere so longe as they that they be appointed vnto will sette theym on worke.

Masters unable to employ workmen shall give them warning, and inform the alderman, in order that fresh situations may be found.

¶ Item, if he that theye were appointed to worke with refuse theyre worke, or be not able to sette theym any longer at worke, he shall then give his laborer warnynge therof, and shall lykewise declare the same to the alderman, who vpon inquisition maide amongste his neyghtbors (*sic*) who lackethe any workemen shall apoynte hym a newe Maister other in that warde or ellis in an-other warde.

Idlers to be punished, and, if incorrigible, banished.

¶ This beyng doon if any be idle and doo not labour truelie & iustely that then the Alderman do pvnyshe hym, and if he doo not then amende, that then the alderman shall cause hym to be banyshed out of the Citye.

The deserving poor are to be relieved.

¶ Item, if any persone eythere for age, infirmytie or multitude of childerne, be not able by his labour to gette to susteyne his famylye that then the alderman se hym releved by the Comon almes of the Citye out of the Comon Cheiste.

"Aldermans charge."

¶ Item, that euery alderman in his warde and the Constables shall goo euery weke oones throughe-out his warde and looke vpon the people what they doo.

The "Consell" is to "syt" every month to consider these questions.

¶ Item, that the mayour and the Councell of the Citye shall sytte purposely oon day euery monethe to here whethere thies thingis be obserued or not, and devyse what may be bettur doon and more for the bettur mayntenaunce therof.

It is ordered that "wages" are "given" and to be paid in ready money, on pain of fine and imprisonment.

¶ Item, it is further enacted (etc.) that all men whiche sette any people on worke shall give like wages and paye it in reedye money and not in wares or vitayle, vpon payne to forfayte for euery defaulte vj s. viij d., the oone moytie therof to be to the Shireffes of the Citye for the

---

[1] Blotted. The "money in stook" probably refers to the loan to clothiers in 1518, see above, p. 658.

tyme beinge, and the othere moytye therof to be to hym or theym *that* shall presente and *p*rove the same defaulte before M*aiste*r Meyre for the tyme beinge by wittenes or otherwise, and the offender therin to be ymprysoned vntill suche tyme as he haue paide the same forfayture.

¹ ¶ [Enacted] that noo freeholder or other *per*sone or *per*sones shall from-hensfurthe take any *per*sone to be his tena*u*nte in this Citye oneles the same *per*sone be furste examyned before the mayo*u*r and the alderma*n* of the warde from whense he come and what labo*u*r he can doo; and if it be thought that the same *per*sone be not a *per*sone meyte to labor, that then noo *per*sone doo admytte hym as tena*u*nte to any howse within the Citye, vpon payne of xx s. to be payed in forme aforsaid to the vse aforesaid.

² "No stranger to inh*ab*ite without license." ²

¶ [Enacted] that eue*r*y alderman within his warde shall before the feaste of All Saynct*es* nexte make a booke of all the Innes, alehouses and other vitayllingehowses within his warde, and the same booke before the saide feaste to exhibet vnto M*aiste*r Mayo*u*r, and that then M*aiste*r Mayo*u*r w*i*th the saide alderman shall consulte togethere, and thervpon take an ordere what Innes, alehouses and other Suspecte houses as well in the Suburbes as other places maye be dismyssed, dissolued and dischardged, & what houses shall be admytted and aloued to remayne and contyneue. And this beynge doon noo *per*sone to take vpon hym after the saide feaste to kepe eyther Inne, alehouse or othere vytaylinge-house oneles he be licensed and admytted soo too doo by M*aiste*r Mayo*u*r for the tyme beynge by the consente of the alderman of his warde, vpon payne to forfayte xl s. for eue*r*ye monethe that he shall soo kepe or vse any suche Inne, alehouse or vytaylinge-house contrarye to this acte to be paide and taken in fo*u*rme aforsaid to the vse aboue-mencioned; ner *that* noo alehouse-kepere o*n* othere vytaillo*u*r, excepte inholders, shall from-hensforthe lodge any *per*sone or *per*sones in theyre houses, vpon payne to forfayte for eue*r*y defaulte vj s. viij d. to the vse aforesaid.

Every alderman to make a book containing a list of all inns and ²"alehousez,"

and the mayor and justices are to consider which alehouses can be suppressed, and which allowed to continue.

No one is to be permitted to keep an ale-house without licence of the mayor and aldermen of the ward.

¹ leaf 404. ²–² In handwriting of former scribe of I type.

§ 132. Jas. Rogers, Mayor. Inns, 1547.

It is ordered that "no laborer" is to be in the alehouse on the "workeday."

And forasmuche as it is daylye seen that they whiche be of the pooreste sorte doo sytte all daye in the halehouse drynkynge & playnge at the Cardes and tables and spende all that they can gett prodigally vpon themselfes to the highe displeasure of God and theyre owne ympouershynge, whereas if it were spente at home in theyre owne houses theyre wiffes and childerne shulde haue parte therof, It is therfore ordeyned (etc.) *that* noo laborer, Journeyman or prentyse vpon any worke daye shall from hensforthe resorte to any Inne, taverne, or alehouse to eate or drynke, vpon payne of ymprysonemente by the space of oone day and oone night.

It is ordered that "ale" shall be sold at 1d. a gallon.

¹ ¶ [Enacted] that noo brewer or Typpelar within this Cytye from and after the feaste of All Saynctes next ensuynge shall sell any of theyre best ale or beste beere aboue the pryce of a peny for euery galon, and that they shall not sell by any measures but by suche as be laufullye sealled, vpon payne to forfayte for euery defaulte iij s. iiij d. to be levyed in forme aforsaid to the vse aboue-mencioned.

Acts made at the last leet to stand.

¶ [Enacted] that all actes, Statutes & Ordenaunces maide & prouided at the laste leete shall stande and remayne from-hensfurthe in theyre full strengthes and effectes accordinge to the tenours and purportes of the same.

An order against excessive fines raised by "Impoundyng of Catall by the Chamberleyns."

¶ And forasmuche as dyuerse inhabitauntes, as well of the forence of this Cytye as Cytizense, be ofte and many tymes fore-greved ² and oppressed by reasone of vnreasonable fynes and executions taken by the Chamberlaynes for ympoundinge of Catall neclygentlye comynge vpon the Comons, and doynge litle or noo hurte vpon the same, to the great Sclandere of the Citye, It is therefore inacted by auctoritye aforesaide that the Chamberlaynes of the Citie nowe beinge and all other Chamberlaynes hereafter for the tyme beinge shall not take of any Cityzene or othere inhabitaunte within the liberties or Shyre of this

The fine for redemption of cattle fixed at

Citye for any Catall brought to theyre pounde or taken vpon the Comons, and not beynge wilfully putte thervpon, aboue the some or Somes of moneye hereafter mencioned, that is to saye, for the ympoundynge of any kyen or

---

¹ leaf 404, back.   ² i. e. very much grieved.

§ 132. Jas. Rogers, Mayor. Commons, 1547.

other kynde of beastes or Catall excepte Sheepe, but oonelie a penny for a beste and not above; And for euery Scoore of Sheepe iiij d. and not above; provided alwayes that Suckinge Calves, or suckinge pygges, or any other kynde of Catall Suckinge be not accompted for any nomber of Catall; provided also that they shall not ympounde any Swyne in maystyme [1] beynge lawfully rynghed by vertue of this Acte, or any custome here-before vsed; provided also that this acte or any thynge therin conteygned do not extende to dissolve and make voide any acte or actes heretofore maid for surchardginge or puttinge Catall vpon the Comons, but that the same actes and euery of theym maye stande and remayne in theyre full strengthes and effectes accordinge to the tenours and purportes of the same, any thynge herein conteigned to the contrarye notwithstondinge.

[marginal note: 1d. for a beast, and 4d. for 20 sheep, not counting the sucking young.]

[marginal note: No ringed swine are to be inpounded in time of mast, nor are these acts to invalidate those of former times.]

[2] ¶ [Enacted] that noon inhabitaunte of this Citye shall from-hensfurthe soeffere any woole to be bought and solde in theyre houses in any othere place but onelie in the comon woole-hall [3] of the saide Citye, ner shall sell any wollen yarne owt of the Citye whiche is sponnen in the Citye, vpon payne to forfayte for euery defaulte vj s. viij d., the oone moytie therof to be to the Comon Almes Cheste, and the othere moytye to hym or theym that shall presente and prove the same by wittenes or otherwise before Maister Mayour for the tyme beinge, and the offender therein to soeffer ymprysonemente vntill the said forfayture be paid in forme aforesaid.

[marginal note: "No wole to be sold but in the wolehale."]

¶ [Enacted] that noo boochere of this Citye shall fromhensfurthe sell any Talowe above iij s. iiij d. the stoon, ner shall Sell any owt of the Citye, vpon payne to forfayte for euery stoone iij s. iiij d., the oone half therof to the Shireffes of the Citye for the tyme beinge, and the othere half to hym or theym that shall presente and prove the same defaulte before Maister Mayour by wittenes or otherwise.

[marginal note: No "talow" to be sold above 3s. 4d. a stone.]

¶ [Enacted] that no Chaundelar of this Cytye shall

---

[1] In time of mast, i. e. when acorns, beech-nuts, etc., are plentiful. There is only one example (1682) in the *N.E.D.* for this word.
[2] leaf 405.   [3] See above, pp. 192, 567.

§ 133. *Tho. Kevet, Mayor,* 1548.

No "candell" to be sold out of the city to retailers.

from-hensforthe sell any Candell above ij d. the pounde, ner shall sell any out of the Cytye to any bager,[1] fyshere, or othere per*s*one whiche shall sell the same agayne for a geyne, vpon like payne for eue*r*y defaulte to the vse aforesaid, and all the same Candell so sold to be forfayted to the Shreyfe*s* of the sayd Citie for the tyme beinge.

THO. KEVET, MAYOR, 1548.

LEETS.

May 16, 1548.
Jury.

[2][V. f. p. held before Tho. Kevet, m., Joh. Nethermyll, Will. Westeley, b., on May 16, 2 Edw. VI.]

[M*agister*[3]] Sym. Parker, Tho. Gardynou*r*, Cuth. Joynou*r*, Chris. Waren, Joh. Saunders, Joh. Talonte*s*, Jac. Roger*s*, Tho. Spense*r*, Jac. Gilbert, Ric. Ley, Ric. Sewall, Ric. Niclyn, Will. Saunders, Will. Joynou*r*, Tho. Riley, Tho. Amou*r*same, [4]Mich. Robe*r*de*s*, Tho. ffoyden, Joh. Hill, Joh. Sneyd, Rad. Hopkyns, Hen. Hynd, Joh. Chambe*r*s, Will. Beylie.]

"Water."
"Cunduits."

¶ [Enacted] that no per*s*one shall fetche water at eny Condyt in this Citie for eny intent but onelie to dresse meit w*ith*, vpon peyn to forfeit iij s. iiij d. for eue*r*y def*a*ult, the on half therof to the Shireffe*s* and the other half to hyme or theme that shall p*r*esent the same.

*"Ciuitas Couentr*ie*."*
Jury of 28.

[5]¶ [V. f. p. held on Oct. 9, 2 Edw. VI.]

[M*agister*[6] Sim. Parker, Tho. Gardynou*r*, Cuth. Joynou*r*, Chris. Waren, Joh. Saunders, Hen. Over, Joh. Talonte*s*, Joh. Herford, Jac. Roger*s*, Will. Rogers, Tho. Spense*r*, Jac. Gilbe*r*t, Ric. Ley, Ric. Sewall, Edw. Damport, Ric. Niclyn, Will. Saunders, Will. Joynou*r*, Will. Norton, Ric. Hurt, Tho. Wheteley, Tho. Amou*r*same, [7]Mic. Robe*r*de*s*, Tho. Foydon, Joh. Hill, Joh. Sneyd, Her. Hynd, Rad. Hopkyns.]

Sheriffs.

[Hum. Reynolde*s*, drape*r*, Will. Beilie, drape*r*.]

Orders of leet.
[8] *"Closez within the Libertys of the Citty as well as without"* [8]

[Enacted] that all Closez & pastures, as-well w*ith*in the liberties of this Citie as w*ith*out, whiche in old tyme haue

---

[1] Badger = huckster, middleman.
[2] leaf 406. Former scribe of I type.
[3] Repeated before each name until note 4.   [4] Untitled.
[5] leaf 406, back. Former scribe of I type.
[6] Repeated before each name until note 7.
[7] Untitled.   [8]–[8] In different hands.

§ 134. *Will. Saunders, Mayor*, 1549.

been vsed to lie & be comon yeirelie frome Lamas vnto Candelmas and frome Michelmas vnto Candelmas, and of lait tyme haue been by vertue of sondry actes of leet maid & kept seuerall all the yeire, shal-be frome & after Lamas next comyng comon yeirelie frome Lamas to Candelmas, or frome Michelmas to Candelmas, as the same Closez & pastures & euery of theme haue been in old tymes past, eny acte, vse or custome to the contrarie notwithstandyng. And that no persone keipp vpon the comens aboue the old stynt, that is to say, ij meche kyen & a geldyng, or ij geldynges & oon mech Cowe, vpon peyn to forfeit to the Chamberleynes iij s. iiij d. for euery default.[2]

[3] ¶ [Enacted] that noon inhabitaunt of this citie shall frome-hensfurth convey or carie, or cause to be conveyed or caried, owt of this Citie eny wollen Yarne spone within this Citie to be sold in eny forene place, vpon peyn to forfeit for euery default xl s. to be levied by distresse vpon the offendoures by the Shireffes of the Citie to ther owne vse.

¶ [Enacted] that noon inhabitaunt of this citie shall haue or vse eny wollen weightes beyng aboue the weight of ij li. & dim., vpon peyn of forfeyture of iij s. iiij d. for euery default to be levyed as is aforseid.

WILL. SAUNDERS, MAYOR, 1549.

¶ [Election of Officers.]

[Magister][4] Sim. Parker, Tho. Gardynour, Cuth. Joynour, Joh. Saunders, Joh. Talontes, Jac. Rogers, Tho. Spenser, Jac. Gilbert, Ric. Ley, Ric. Sewall, Hugo Bloure, Will. Joynour, Will. Norton, Ric. Hurt, Joh. Waid, Tho. Amoursame, Joh. Nethermyll, Will. Westeley, Mic. Roberdes, [5]Tho. ffoydon, Rad. Hopkyns, Chr. Bromeley, Rob. Colman, Hen. Hynd, Joh. Chambers.]

[m. M*agister* Will. Saunders, Capper; rec. Edw. Saunders, sergeant-at-law; cor. Tho. Gregorie; steward, Baldw. Porter; ch. Joh. Eyburn, Tanner, Ric. Sewall, bocher; w. Rob. Walden, Capper, Joh. Saunders, bocher; Guid. Speke, mace; crier, Rob. Swyft.]

Marginalia:
- are henceforth to be common in time of common.
- [1] "Stynt of Catall. 2 Cows & 1 gelding, or 2 geldings, And 1 Cow."[1]
- "Wollen yarne" not to be sold outside the city.
- "Weyghtes."
- "Ciuitas Couentrie." Jan. 25, 1549.
- Officers.

[1-1] In different hands.   [2] See above, p. 729 *sqq.*   [3] leaf 407.
[4] Repeated before each name until note 5.   [5] Untitled.

§ 134. Will. Saunders, Mayor. Leets, 1549.

BUSINESS.

"Decret[um est]" = it is decreed.

The chamberlains are ordered to make two perches of the stone wall at the Little Park.

¶ Item, it is ordeyned & decreed this day by the said electours that the Cham[berleyns][1] now newlie chosen, and all ther Successoures beyng Chamberlayns of t[his][1] Citie shall make or cause to be maid at ther owne propre Costes (torn) two perches of the Stone Wall of the Litle Parke with stone, lyme & sand sufficientlie for defence & savegarde of the [2]kynges deers[2] of the Great Parke ther accordynglie as the Citie haith accustome[d][1] & been bound to doo, or-elles to pay to the councell of the Cit[ie][1] xl s. to be bestowed vpon the said Wall by ther (?) discedcione.[3]

EASTER AND MICHAELMAS LEETS.

"Ciuitas Couentrie." May 14, 1549.

Jury of 25.

[4][V. f. p. held before Will. Saunders, m., Humf. Reynoldes, Will. Beilie, b., on May 14, 3 Edw. VI.]

[Magister[5] Sim. Parker, Tho. Gardynour, Cuth. Joynour, Joh. Saunders, Her. Over, Joh. Talontes, Joh. Herford, Jac. Rogers, Tho. Keyvet, Tho. Spenser, Jac. Gilbert, Ric. Ley, Ric. Sewall, Edw. Damport, Ric. Niclyn, Will. Joynour, Ric. Hurt, Joh. Waid, Tho. Amoursame, Will. Westeley, [6]Ric. Sewall,[7] Rob. Walden, Joh. Saunders, Tho. Sconse, Hugo Hervie.]

Against inhabitants of the city bringing "foren sutes" against their neighbours.

¶ [Enacted] that no inhabitaunt of this Citie shall sue or vex eny his neyghbour beyng a Citizene here, in eny personall accion or sute vnder the some or value of xl s. without license of Maister Meire for the tyme beyng in eny Courte or place owt of this Citie, vpon peyne to forfeit for euery default xl s. to be levied vpon his goodes to the vse of the comen box of the Citie immediatlie vpon prove therof maid befor Maister Meire for the tyme beyng.

[8]"[f]elishipps, ffollowships. Euery man to enter into a ffellowship."[8]

¶ [Enacted] that noon inhabitaunt of this Citie shall frome & after the feast of seynt John Baptist next be in felishipp with eny other felishipp or company thene with

---

[1] torn.   [2-2] deleted.
[3] The handwriting is a careless scrawl here, and the edge of the page torn. *Discede* is given as a form of *decide* in *N.E.D.*
[4] leaf 407, back.
[5] Repeated before every name until note 6.   [6] Untitled
[7] (?) Son of Master Ric. Sewall, whose name occurs earlier in the lists.   [8-8] In different handwritings.

that company & Craft whosse occupacion & Craft he or his seruauntes doithe occupie & vse, vpon peyne to forfeit xl s. for euery monthe that he shall vse hymself contrarie to this acte, the ¹on moitie therof to be to Maister Meire for the tyme beyng, And the other moitie to the vse of the felishipp & Craft which shall in that behalf laufullie compleyne for the same forfeyture, to be levied of the offendoures goodes immediatlie after prove therof maid before Maister Meir for the tyme beyng.

¶ Item, wher-as in tymes past Maister Meire for the tyme being haithe vsed to keipp a watche on Midsomer nyght, and the Shireffes another watche on seynt Peters nyght, It is now enacted (etc.) that Maister Meire & the Shireffes shall frome-hensfurthe yoyntelie keipp onelie oon watche on Midsomer nyght at the indeferent costes & charges of Maister Meire & the Shereffes, That is, the meire to pay the on half & the Shireffes the other half.²

<small>Only one riding of the armed "watche" to be observed, viz. the Midsummer one.</small>

¶ Item, forasmoche as dyuers inhabitauntes of this Citie for ther owne priuat lucre & gayne do daylie engrosse & geit into ther handes great quantitie of wollen Yarne spone within this Citie and sell the same vnwrought in dyuers places in the Contrey to the great damage & hynderaunce of the comen-welthe of the Citie, It is therfore ordeyned (etc.) that no Citizene here frome-hensfurth shall sell eny wollen Yarne but to suche persones as shall make the same in Cloithe within this Citie, So that weyvers, walkers & Shermen of the Citie may haue the occupacion therof for meyntenaunce of the comen-we[l]the, vpon peyne to forfeit for euery default vj s. viij d. to be levyed vpon the goodes of the offendoures immediatlie after prove therof maid before Maister Meire for the tyme beyng, the on half wherof to be to hyme that shall first compleyn & declare the same, and the other half to the vse of the Citie. And if eny Clothier of this Citie hauyng Clothes maid within this Citie cannot haue & ³vtteraunce for the same in conuenyent tyme, Thene the same Clothier bryngyng his Clothes into seynt Marie Hall on the Wednesday before noon shall haue redy money for

<small>Certain citizens engross "wollen Yarne" to sell outside the city;

it is ordered that yarn shall only be sold to such as shall make cloth within Coventry.

Clothiers who cannot dispose of their cloth are to send it to Saint Mary's Hall on Wednesdays, when it shall be bought from them.</small>

---

¹ leaf 408.
² For the armed watch see Sharp's *Mysteries*, pp. 174 *sqq.*
³ = ? an.

§ 134. Will. Saunders, Mayor. Journeymen, 1549.

the same by prouysion of the Citie, so that the same Clothes be truelie wrought & maid.

"Cappers" are to have no more than three apprentices.

¹ ¶ [Enacted] that euery Capper of the Citie may haue thre [? two] prentises & no moo, vntill the yeires of the prentisez be expired within two yeires, and then to take another prentese to make vpp the nomber of three.¹ And that no persone of the Craft of Cappers shall put owt eny pece-woork,² but to suche of the same Craft as the maisters of the same Craft for the tyme beyng, with the assent & consent of xij of the moost auncient persones of that Craft, shall agree & consent vnto, or that the more part of the said maisters & xij persones shall agre & consent vnto.

No piecework to be put out except to such as the master of the craft and 12 ancient persons of the craft shall permit.

No "Journeymen" shall keep any quarterages or take fines from strangers coming to work.

¶ [Enacted] that no execucion or fyne shal-be takyn of eny Journeymen of eny occupacion within this Citie, ner no Journeymen ³ shall assemble or keipp eny quarterages or ⁴ take fynes of eny estraungers comyng to this Citie to worke, vpon the payne to be punysshed accordyng to the kynges actes of parliament in that [? behalf] latelie maid & prouided.

¶ Also that noon inhabitaunt of Litle-parke Stret or Cowe-lane shall frome-hensfurthe cast eny muke or dunge vnto Chelles[m]ore Courte,⁵ vpon peyn of iij s. iiij d. for euery default.

"Chelles-[m]ore."

No filth or "dung" to be cast into the churchyards.

¶ And likewise that no person cast eny filthe or dung about seynt Michelles Church-Yarde or the Trinitie Churche-Yard or the Sporn (sic) Yait vpon like payn.

6 "Sheipp. None to be kept by butchers vpon the Comons."⁶

¶ Also that no bocher or other inhabitaunte of this Citie shall frome & after Lamas next keipp eny Sheipp vpon the Comons of this Citie, vpon such paynes as be

---

¹ leaf 408, back. For rules about the Cappers' apprentices, see above, pp. 774, 778.
² The first instance of this combination in the *N.E.D.* is dated 1795.
³ A recent statute (2 & 3 Ed. VI, c. 15) forbade confederacies to raise prices of work, and also permitted free working by masons, carpenters, etc., in corporate towns. For Journeymen's Guilds see above, pp. 91 *sqq.*, 653, 687, 694; *Life in an Old English Town*, p. 97; *Victoria County Hist. Warw.* II, pp. 153-6; for London Journeymen, see Unwin, *Gilds of London*, pp. 224 *sqq.*
⁴ "keipp" deleted.
⁵ Probably the old residence of the Earl of Chester's children, subsequently a royal palace, see *Life in an Old English Town*, p. 129.   ⁶—⁶ In different hands.

§ 134. *Will. Saunders, Mayor. Millers*, 1549.

lymyted in the acte of let in that case latelie maid etc.[1]

[2] ¶ [V. f. p. held on Oct. 15, 3 Edw. VI.]

[M*agister*[3] Sim. P*a*rker, Tho. Gardyno*u*r, Cuth. Joyno*u*r, Chr. Waren, Joh. Saunders, Her. Over, Joh. Talon*tes*, Joh. Herford, Jac. Roge*r*s, Tho. Spens*er*, Ric. Sewall, Edw. Damport, Ric. Niclyn, Will. Joyno*u*r, Will. Norton, Ric. Hurt, Tho. Whetely, Tho. Amo*u*rsame, Joh. Nethermyll, Will. Westeley, Joh. Eyburn, Ric. Sewall, [4] Joh. Saunders, Tho. Sconse.]

[Rob. Colma*n*, Cowp*er*, Joh. Thomson, Carpenter.]

¶ [Enacted] that all the bakers of this Citie shall grynd all ther Corne w*ith* the Millers of this Citie, and not with forene Millers, and shall pay for eu*er*y quarter of corne gryndyng viij d., vpon peyn to forfeit for eu*er*y default doyng the contrarie iij s. iiij d. And that the Millers shall se*r*ue the said bakers truelie & honestelie in gryndyng & se*r*ue no foreners wherby the bakers of the Citie myght be delayed or disapoynted, vpon like peyn.

¶ Also it is enacted that the shireff*es* of the Citie shall frome-hensfurthe pay the Recorders ffee so longe as they pay no fee-farme [5] for the Citie to the kyng etc.

¶ [Enacted] that Ric. Tanner, bitter,[6] shall se*r*ue the fisshemonge*r*s & other the inhabitaun*tes* of the Croschepyng ward [7] after the Rait of thre bitt*es* for a peny, And all other to be se*r*ued after the rait of v bitt*es* [8] for ij d., vpon peyn of xx s.

¶ Also that M*aiste*r Meir for the tyme beyng shall yeirelie appoynt ij p*er*sones of the felishipp of Cardemakers & swere theme to make dylygent serche in the

"Ciuitas Couen*trie*." Oct. 15, 1549.

Sheriffs.

The "bakers" of the city are to employ resident "Millers" in preference to outsiders.

The "Recorder's" fee.

The bittur to serve the fishmongers at the rate of 3 bittes for a penny.

[9] "Cardemakers. The mayor to Apoynt searchers yearly and to swear them." [9]

---

[1] See above, p. 769.   [2] leaf 409.
[3] Repeated before every name until note 4.   [4] Untitled.
[5] The fee-farm of £50 a year was frequently in arrears, v. Madox, *Firma Burgi*, 217. In the reign of Edw. VI there was such poverty in the city that the citizens declared to the Earl of Warwick that one or two persons were yearly ruined by the fee-farm payments, see vol. of Correspondence, Corp. MS. A. 79, leaf 63.
[6] = water-carrier. See Gloss.
[7] Those who lived near the conduit could be supplied at a cheaper rate.
[8] v. *E. E. D.* In Worcester leather bags filled with water and borne on horses were called "byttes."
[9–9] In different hands.

§ 135. *Ric. Niclyn, Mayor*, 1550.

seid occupac*io*n for ill wares, and appoynt them a ma*r*ke wherw*ith* to ma*r*ke all lawfull wares. And that no pe*r*sone after Alhalowtide next shall put to sale or carie owt of the Citie eny Card*es*[1] before they be allowed & ma*r*ked, vpon peyn of iij s. iiij d., the half therof to be to the shereff*es* & the other half to hyme that shall first fynd the same.

RIC. NICLYN, MAYOR, 1550.

*"Ciuitas Coventr*ie*."*
Jan. 25.

[2] ¶ [Election of officers.]

[M*agister*[3] Sim. P*a*rker, Tho. Gardyno*ur*, Cuth. Joyno*ur*, Chr. Wa*r*en, Joh. Saunders, Her. Over, Joh. Talont*es*, Joh. Herford, Jac. Roge*r*s, Tho. Keyvet, Tho. Spens*er*, Ric. Ley, Ric. Sewall, Will. Norton, Ric. Hurt, Tho. Wheteley, Tho. Amo*ur*same, Joh. Nethermyll, Will. Westeley, [4] Joh. Eyburne, Ric. Sewall, Joh. Saunders, Rob. Walden, Joh. Chambe*r*s.]

Officers.

[m. "M*agister*" Ric. Niclyn, Grasier; rec. Edw. Saunders, sergeant-at-law; cor. Tho. Gregorie; steward, Baldw. Porter; ch. Ric. Kylby, me*r*cer, Roland Wilde, Smyth; w. Nic. Hobson, drap*er*, Joh. Sandebroke, drap*er*; mace, Guy Speke; crier, Rob. Swyft.]

[And they are sworn. And because the aforesaid R. Niclyn is a common butcher and victualler they elect C. Waren, draper, Joh. Herforde, tanner, to assist the said mayor in assessing the price of victuals according to the form of the statute.]

Et Jur*ati* exist*unt* etc. Et p*r*o eo qu*od* p*r*ed*ictus* Ric. Niclyn est com*mun*is carnif*ex* & victu[a]lar*ius*, eligeru*nt* Chris. Waren, drap*er*, Joh. Herforde, tann*er*, assistent*es* dict*um* Maior*em* (*sic*) in assessand*o* p*re*cia victual*ium* sec*un*d*um* forma*m* statuti etc.

LEETS.

*"Ciuitas Coventr*ie*."*
Apr. 9.

[5][V. f. p. held before Ric. Niclyne m., Rob. Colma*n*, Joh. Tomson, b., on Apr. 9, 4 Edw. VI.]

Jury of 25.

[M*agister*[6] Sim. Pa*r*ker, Tho. Gardyno*ur*, Cuth. Joyno*ur*, Chr. Waren, Joh. Saunders, Hen. Over, Joh. Talont*es*, Joh. Herford, Jac. Rogers, Tho. Keivet, Will.

---

[1] *i. e.* combs for combing wool. See above, p. 182, for previous troubles about ill-wrought cards.   [2] leaf 409, back.
[3] Repeated before every name until note 4.   [4] Untitled.
[5] leaf 410.   [6] Repeated before all names as far as note 1, p. 795.

§ 135. Ric. Niclyn, Mayor. Leet, 1550.

Saunders, Will. Rogers, Tho. Spenser, Ric. Ley, Ric. Sewall, Edw. Damport, Will. Joynour, Will. Norton, Ric. Hurt, Tho. Wheteley, Tho. Amoursame, Will. Westeley, Humf. Reynoldes, [1]Ric. Kylby, Rol. Wilde.]

[Ordained] that all suche inhabitauntes as occupie the facultie & Craft of dying of Cloythe & no [? in] wadsettyng in houses of ther owne shal-be frome-hensfurthe contributories to the Craft of diers & wadsetters, And to pay yeirelie euery of theme xvj d. after the rait of iiij d. a quarter.[2]

Also that no inhabitaunte of this Citie shall fromehensfurthe forestall or by in-groose eny butter, egges, Cheise, or eny other kynd of vitaill to thyntent to sell it ageyne [or 20 s. fine at every default] and to soeffer imprisonement at will of Maister Meire etc.

Also it is further enacted at the peticion & request of the comoners [4] of this Citie that the bochers & vitaylloures of the Contrey shall fromehensfurthe haue fre libertie & be allowed to sell ther vitayll within this Citie euery weike on the Wedensday & Fryday. So that the said bochers do brynge with theme ther hides & talowe & sell the same also with ther vitayll in suche place as shal-be appoynted at reasonable prises.[4]

Also it is further enacted that noon inhabitaunt of this Citie shall frome-hensfurthe shall [5] keip within this Citie eny greyhoundes, houndes, spanyelles, ferettes or nettes, or hunt duckes in other mennes waters, except he may dispend xl s. by yeir in landes within this Citie, vpon payne to forfeit iij s. iiij d. for euery default to be levied by the shireffes of the Citie by distresse to ther owne vse.

[6] ¶ [V. f. p. held on Oct. 14, 4 Edw. VI.]

[7] Tho. Gardynour, Joh. Saunders, Cuth. Joynour, Hen. Over, Joh. Talontes, Joh. Herford, Jac. Rogers, Tho. Keyvet, Will. Saunders, Tho. Spenser, Ric. Sewall, Will. Joynour, Will. Norton, Ric. Hurt, Tho. Wheteley, Tho. Amoursame, Joh. Nethermyll, Will. Westeley, Humf.

---

[1] Untitled. [2] See for previous orders about dyers pp. 704, 714.
[3-3] In different hands.
[4] Evidently the consumers were anxious for free trade.
[5] Redundant. [6] leaf 410, back.
[7] No title prefixed to any of these names.

Marginalia:
- Orders of leet. All "diers" to contribute to the craft
- 4d. a quarter.
- Against [3] "huesters" and "Regrators."[3]
- The [3] "foren bochers to sell fflesh on Wenesdays and ffridays,"[3]
- and also tallow and hides.
- An act "for hunters."
- "Ciuitas Couentrie." Oct. 14. Jury.

§ 136. Edw. Damporte, Mayor, 1551.

Reynold*es*, Ric. Kylby, Rol. Wild, Nic. Hobson, Her. Hynd, Ric. Sewall.

Sheriffs. [Ric. Giller, *m*ercer, Hugh Hervie, Capper.]

1 "Cloth*i*ars of this Citie." [Enacted] for the quyetnes of the Clothiers & weyvers of this Citie that all men frome-hensfurthe shal-be at libe*r*tie to put furthe ther yarne to the weyvers in Spyndell*es*,² botom*es*,³ or Skeynes, as the weyver & thei cane agre, eny acte or cussetome to the cont*r*arie not-wit*h*standyng.

EDW. DAMPORTE, MAYOR, 1551.

⁴ ¶ [Election of officers.]

"Ciuitas Couentr*ie*." Jan. 25, 1551. 25 Electors. [Magister⁵ Tho. Gardyno*u*r, Cuth. Joyno*u*r, Chr. Waren, Joh. Saunders, Hen. Over, Joh. Tallont*es*, Joh. Herforde, Jac. Rogers, Tho. Keyvet, Will. Saunders, Ric. Ley, Ric. Shewell, Will. Norton, Tho. Wheyteley, Joh. Waide, Tho. Amo*u*rsone, Joh. Nethermyll, Will. Westeley, Humf. Reynold*es*, Will. Baylie, Joh. Tomsone, ⁶ Ric. Kylbye, Rol. Wylde, Hen. Hynde, Rad. Hopkyn*s*.]

Officers. ¶ [m. M*a*gis*te*r⁷ Edw. Damporte, pewterer; rec. Edw. Saunders, sergeant-at-law; cor. Tho. Gregorie; steward, Baldew. Porter; ch. Tho. Taylli*ou*r, graysyer, Ric. Hopkyns, drap*e*r; mace, Guy Speyke; crier, Rob. Swyfte.]

LEETS.

"Ciuitas Couentr*ie*." Apr. 21, 1551. ⁸ ¶ [V. f. p. held before Edw. Damporte, m., Ric. Giller, Hugo Harvye, b., on Apr. 21, 5 Edw. VI.]

⁶ Tho. Gardyner, Cuth. Joyno*u*r, Chr. Waren, Joh.

---

¹ Scribe K.
² = a certain quantity of yarn, in Northamptonshire (v. *E.D.D.*) four hanks.
³ = a clew or nucleus on which to wind thread; also a skein or ball of thread (*N.E.D.*). Cf. Shakespeare's use of the word as a verb. *Two Gentlemen of Verona*, III. ii. 53, "As you vnwinde her loue from him . . . You must prouide to bottome it on me" (*ibid.*).
⁴ leaf 411. Scribe K.
⁵ Repeated before every name until note 6.   ⁶ Untitled.
⁷ The Damporte (or Davenport) family settled in Coventry about 1500. The most celebrated members of the family were Joh. Davenport, Puritan, who went to New England in 1644, and Christopher, a Franciscan friar, his brother, and chaplain to Queen Catherine of Braganza.
⁸ leaf 411, back.

§ 136. *Edw. Damporte, Mayor. Leet,* 1551.

Saunders, Hen. Over, Joh. Tallontes, Joh. Harforde, Will. Saunders, Ric. Nyckelyn, Ric. Ley, Ric. Sewall, Will. Joynour, Will. Norton, Ric. Hurte, Tho. Wheyteley, Will. Westeley, Will. Baylye, Joh. Tomsone, Ric. Hawten, Tho. Taylour, Hen. Hynde, Ric. Scotte, Ric. Warnour, Joh. Sneyde.

Inprimis it is ordeingned and inacted at this presente leete and by the aucthoritye of the same at the requeste and desyre of the Comynaltye of this Citie that the Bochers beinge Inhabitauntes of this Citie from hensforthe shal-be all at libertye and haue libertye to sell theyre ffleshe and vitayle at all dayes and tymes in the weeke excepte Soundayes, and at what place so euer or any of theym will wythin the saide Citye, And shal-be noo occupacion or felowshipe as in tymes paste they haue been. [1 "Flesh & Victuals."1]

[Ordained] that the Boochers of the Countrey shall haue like libertye to sell theyre vitayle within the seide Citie at reasonable prices at all dayes and tymes in the weeke (excepte Soundayes), So that they sell theyre hydes, Skynnes and talowe belonginge to the same within the saide Citie, and do not kyll theyre vitayle within the walles of the saide Citie.² ["Bochers" of the country are to be permitted to sell meat every day except Sunday, so that they also sell tallow and hides.]

[Ordained] that noo vyntenere of this Citie shall sell any Gasconigne³ wyne wythin the saide Citie by retayle from-hensforthe aboue the rate and price of xij d. the galon, vpon payne to forfayte for euerye defaulte x s., The oone halfe whereof to be to the Shireyffes of the Citie for the tyme beinge to theyre owne vses, and the other halfe to the vse of the fyrste taker and presenter of the same, to be levied by distres of the goodes of the offendours by the Shyreyffes of the saide Citie for the tyme beinge. And the offendours therein to be furthere punyshed by ymprysonmente at the discrecion of Maister Mayour of the saide Citie and his bretherne. ["Vynteners" to sell wine from Gascony at 12d. a gallon; on pain of 10s. fine] [and imprisonment.]

⁴[Ordained] that the ale-sellers and typlers of this Citie shall from-hensforthe sell theyre ale of the best Sourte not aboue the Rate and price of iiij d. the galon, [The "ale sellers" to sell ale at 4d. a gallon.]

---

¹⁻¹ In a much later hand.   ² See above, p. 795.
³ See above, p. 24.   ⁴ leaf 412.

§ 136. *Edw. Damporte, Mayor. Leets,* 1551.

vpon payne to forfayte for eue*r*ye defaulte vj s. viij d. to be levied in fourme aforesaid to the vses aforesaide.

[Marginal: ¹ "The M*a*rket. Stalles; none to be set between Broadgate and the Cu*n*duit."¹]

[Ordained] that noo man of this Citie dwellinge betweene the Bradeyaite and the Condythe in the Croscheapinge in the same Citie shall from-hensforthe pe*r*mytte or Soeffer any Stawles or boordes to sell any manore of ware vpon to be sette att theyre doores wythout the Eysynges² of theyre howses, nor soeffer any boorde or Stawle to stande in the Streete there, vpon payne to forfayte for eue*r*y defaulte iij s. iiij d. to be levied in fourme aforesaide to the vses aforesaide.

[Marginal: ¹ "The m*a*rket. Fysh [and] tanned leather to stand below the Cheeping Conduit."¹]

[Ordained] that all the fyshemounge*r*s and Sellers of tanned leethere, whiche shall sell any fyshe or tanned lethere within this Citie, shall from-hensforthe stande beneythe the Condeythe in the Croscheapinge in the saide Citie to sell theyre wares, vpon payne to forfayte for eue*r*y defaulte vj s. viij d. to be levied (etc.).

[Marginal: The millers, wrights and "Tylers" are no longer to be a fellowship.]

³[Enacted] that the mylners, wrigh*tes* and Tilers within this Citie shall from-hensforthe be noo Crafte, feloweshipe, nor companye nor haue any suche assembles and meetinges as they haue hadde in tymes paste.

[Marginal: The sale of "Hurdellz" without the New Gate.]

[Enacted] that noo man shall sell any hordelles or Sparres from-hensfurthe in any other place of this Citie, but oonelie vpon the hurdell hill wythout the Newe-yaite beinge the place accustomed for the same, as they haue been in tymes paste, vpon payne to forfayte for eue*r*y defaulte vj s. viij d. to be levied in forme aforesaide to the vses aforesaide.

[Marginal: "Ciuitas Couentr*ie*." Oct. 13. 1551. Jury of 23.]

⁴ ¶ [V. f. p. on Oct. 13, 5 Edw. VI.]

Tho. Gardyno*u*r, Cuth. Joyno*u*r, Chr. Waren, Joh. Saunders, Hen. Over, Joh. Tallon*tes*, Tho. Keyvet, Ric. Nyckelyn, Ric. Sewall, Will. Joyno*u*r, Will. Norton, Ric. Hurte, Will. Westeley, Rob. Colman, Joh. Tomsone, Ric. Hawton, Tho. Tailllo*u*r, Hen. Hynde, Tho. Owres, Rad. Hopkyns, Joh. Sneyde, Tho. Saunders, Joh. Parker.

[Marginal: Sheriffs.]

[Ric. Smythe, vyntener, Tho. Saunders, Graysyer.⁵]

---

¹ In different hands.   ² = eaves.
³ Cf. the making and unmaking of the butchers' craft, pp. 739, 770, 797, 803; for the millers' see above, p. 782.
⁴ leaf 412, back.
⁵ "et Jurat[i sunt]" = and they were sworn.

§ 136. *Edw. Damporte, Mayor. Bakers,* 1551.

[Ordained] that noone of the inhabitauntes of this Citie from-hensforthe shall by any barley within this Citie or liberties of the same but onelye to serve theyre owne howses with, and to be brewed and occupied in the same, vpon payne to forfayte for euery defaulte xx s., the oone halfe whereof to be to the vse of the Mayour and Comynaltie of the saide Citie, and the other halfe to be to the vse of the Shyreyffes of the saide Citie for the tyme beinge to be levyed by distres of the goodes of the offendours by the Shireyffes of the saide Citie for the tyme beinge to the vses aforesaide.

[1 " Byers of barly " 1 to make purchase of the grain for their own use only.]

[Enacted] that noone inhabitaunte of this Citie shall from-hensfourthe make any malte within the saide Citie for any persone or persones of the Countrey of theyre barlye of the Countrey vpon payne to forfayte for euery defaulte xx s. to be levied in fourme aforesaide to the vses aforesaid.

No inhabitants are to be "maltemakers to forenners."

2 [Ordained] that the Maisters of the Bakers of this Citie for the tyme beinge that shall wayte vpon Maister Mayour of this Citie to waye breade shall at all tymes from-hensfourthe wey to Maister Mayour as-well Warwicke breade as the breade of the Bakers of this Citie accordynge to the true Syse,³ vpon payne to forfayte for euerye defaulte xij d. to be levied in fourme aforesaide to the vses aforesaide. And also it is ffurther ordeingned (etc.) that the saide Bakers of Warwicke shall come to this Citie wyth theyre breade but oonelie twyse in oone weeke, that is to saye, but vpon the Wednesdaye and the Fridaye accordinge to the olde aunciente order and Custome of the saide Citie, and yf any Citizen do hereafter receave any breade of the saide Bakers of Warwike ᶜany breade⁴ vpon any other dayes then heretofore in this presente acte be lymitted & apointed, that then euerye suche offendour in the saide premisses shall forfaite and loose for euery defaulte xij d. to be levied in fourme aforesaide to the vses aforesaide.⁵

"To wey Warwicke breade."

"The bakers of Warwicke ij dayes in the weeke and noo moore."

Item, it is ffurthere ordeingned and inacted at this present leete and by the aucthoritye of the same that

---

¹⁻¹ Marginal notes are in the hands of this same scribe.
² lea⁻ 413. ³ = assize. ⁴⁻⁴ redundant. ⁵ See p. 717.

§ 137. Ric. Hurte, Mayor, 1552.

"No man to receave any fysshers horses ladon" with fish.

noone inholder or other persone within this Citie shall from-hensforthe receave into theyre howses any of the fyshe-sellers horses repayringe to this Citie ladon with fyshe, but shall suffere theym to vnloode theyre horses at the fyshe boordes in the markethe place, vpon payne to forfayte for euerye defaulte xx s. to be levied in fourme aforesaide to the vses aforesaide.

"To Scowre the River of Shirbourne.

[Ordained] at this presente and by the aucthoritye of this presente leete that all the inhabitauntes that dwell within this Citie and haue gardeyns and groundes adioynynge to the River of Shyrbourne from Saunte Johns bridge to the Sponne brooke in the Puddinge-Crofte shall Clense and Scowre the same euery man his porcion before the feaste of All Sainctes nexte, vpon payne euerye man to forfayte for euery defaulte vj s. viij d.,

No man to caste any donge into the River of Shyrbourne."

and noo persone or persones at any tyme hereafter to caste any donge or fylthe into the saide River, vpon like payne to be levyed in fourme aforesaid to the vses aforesaide.

RIC. HURTE, MAYOR, 1552.

"Ciuitas Coventrie." Jan. 25, 1552. 25 Electors.

¹ ¶ [Election of officers.]

Tho. Gardynour, Cuth. Joynour, Joh. Saunders, Hen. Over, Joh. Tallontes, Joh. Harforde, Jac. Rogers, Tho. Keyvet, Will. Saunders, Ric. Nyckelyn, Ric. Ley, Tho. Wheyteley, Ric. Sewall, Joh. Waide, Tho. Amoursame, Will. Westeley, Humf. Reynoldes, Will Bailye, Joh. Tomsone, Ric. Giller, Hugo Harvie, Tho. Taillour, Hen. Hynde, Rad. Hopkyns, Thos. Owres.

Officers.

[m. Ric. Hurte, mercer; rec. Edw. Saunders, sergeant-at-law; cor. Tho. Gregorye; steward, Baldw. Porter; ch. Joh. Rooper, whittawer, Chr. Tylinge, weyver; w. Math. Robbeson, mercer; Edw. Pell, draper; mace, Guy Speke : crier, Rob. Swyfte.]

LEETS.

May 10, 1552.

² [V. f. p. held before Ric. Hurte, mayor, Ric. Smythe, Tho. Saunders, b., on May 10, 6 Edw. VI.]

---

¹ leaf 413, back. ² leaf 414.

§ 137. *Ric. Hurte, Mayor. Inns*, 1552.

Tho. Gardynour, Cuth. Joynour, Joh. Saunders, Tho. Keyvet, Will. Saunders, Ric. Nyckelyn, Edw. Damporte, Ric. Ley, Ric. Sewall, Will. Hyndeman, Will. Norton, Will. Westeley, Will. Baylye, Rob. Colman, Joh. Tomsone, Ric. Giller, Hugo Harvye, Joh. Rooper, Chr. Tylynge, Edw. Pell, Joh. Sneide, Ric. Sewall, jun., Tho. Kirvyne, Tho. Owres, Joh. Saunders, Ric. Scotte. *Jury of 26.*

[Enacted] that all the Comon brewers within this Citie whiche shall hereafter brewe ale and beare to sell within the same Citie shall from-hensfourthe sell theyre ale and beere after the rate and price of twoo shillinges the Sestur, and shall sell fouretene Galons to the Sestur, and not above that price, vpon payne of euery brewere to forfaite for euery Sestour solde contrarye to the tenour of this acte iij s. iiij d. to be levied by wey of distres of the goodes of the offendours, the oone halfe whereof to be to vse of the Comynaltye and Comon box of the saide Citie, and the other halfe to the vse of the Shireyffes of the Citie for the tyme beinge, for levyinge and distraynynge for the same. *The brewers which brew* [1] *"Ale and bear"* [1] *to sell at the rate of 2s. a sextary.*

fforasmuche as by the excessiue nomber of ale-wives and Typlers of this Citie, and especiallye of suche as vse boothe to brewe and typle ale or beere, encreasinge dailye more and moore, all kyndes of vicesses be noryshed and the Comon-welthe of this Citie muche ympayred, for reformacion whereof it is ordeigned and inacted at this presente leete and by the aucthoritie of the same that noon inhabitaunte of this Citie from & after the feaste of Penthecoste nexte, whiche shall take vpon hym or theym to brewe any ale or beare, shall sell any of the same ale or beere by retayle. And likewyse that noo typpelar, whiche after the saide feaste of Penthecoste, whiche shal-be aucthorized by Maister Mayour, and the Justices of peace of this Citie, accordinge to the kinges acte of parliamente in that case laitelie maide and provided, to vse typpelinge of ale or beere, except the Inneholders [2] of *The excessive number of "Alewyves" leads to the increase of vice, and the decay of the commonwealth; it is ordered that those who brew ale and beer shall not sell it by retail, and that those licensed to sell by retail, except the innholders*

[1–1] In a later hand.
[2] See above, p. 771. This order maintains a difference between innholders, where people are lodged, and an ale house, where ale is supplied to any one. See Webb, *Liquor Licensing*, 5.

§ 137. *Ric. Hurte, Mayor. Sessions*, 1552.

of the city, shall not brew.

this Citie, shall brewe any ale or beere, vpon payne to Suffer ymprisonemente at the will and pleasure of Maister Mayour and the Justices of peace of this Citie, and to forfaite for euerye weeke vsynge the same contrarye to this acte xx s. to be levied of the goodes and Catalles of the offendours to the vses aforesaide in forme aforesaide.

The Justices of the peace and the officers of the law, insomuch as the

[1] Whereas the Justices of peace in mooste Counties of this Realme do vse to holde theyre ffowre generall quarter Cessions yerelie on iiij certayne dayes by reasone whereof not onelie the saide Justices, but also all other the kynges Baylives, officers, mynisters & Jurours in euerye Shyre, settinge aparte all other theyre affayres for that tyme, maye the bettur determyne withe theym-selfes at thoose dayes to keepe theyre apparaunces and to serue the kinge accordinge to thayre dueties. And forasmuche as the Justices of peace in this Citie and Countye vse noo

Quarter "Cessions" are not held on any fixed days, are often absent

certayne dayes to holde theyre iiij generall quarter Cessions, as-well the saide Justices and Shireyffes of the saide Citie, as also the Constables bothe of the Citie and Countye, and other Jurours of the same, geave litle or noo regarde or respecte thereunto, So that many tymes when those Cessions be apointed to be holden and kept, as-well the Justices as Constables and other the kinges officers, and likewise the Jurours, be forthe of the Citie and Shyre

from the city, it is therefore enacted for the better direction of their affairs and administration of justice

abowte theyre owne necessarye busynes, and so the kinge vnserued, where-as yf the Cessions were vsed to be holden at certayne dayes they might muche the bettur directe and order theym-selfes accordinge to theyre dueties to keepe the same dayes : Wherfore and for the bettur mynistracion of Justice it is ordeingned (etc.) that the Justices of peace of this Citie and Shyre shall from-hensforthe

that Quarter Sessions be held at four specified dates.

holde and keepe theyre iiij generall quarter Cessions yerelie vpon the iiij dayes hereafter mencioned, That is to saye, Moundaye Sevennyght nexte after Trynitye Sondaye, Mondaye nexte after Michelmas daye, Mondaye nexte after the Epiphanie of oure Lorde God, and Moundaye next after Lowe Soundaye, certainlye without any alteracion or changinge of any of the saide dayes.

[1] leaf 414, back.

§ 137. Ric. Hurte, Mayor. Leets, 1552.

[Ordained] that the Bochers of this Citie shall from-hensforthe be admitted and alowed agayne to be a Crafte and Companye as they haue been in tymes paste,[2] So that they woll be boundeyn by recognizaunce sufficiently to serve the people and inhabitauntes of this Citie with goode, laufull, hoolesome and sufficient vytaile at all tymes. *(The [1]"butchers Alowed to be a Company Againe."[1])*

And also it is ordeingned (etc.) that the Boochers of the Country shall from-hensforthe be vtterlye excluded from this Citye and not to haue any suche libertye to sell theyre meate and vytaile here as they haue hadde in tymes paste. *([3]"laudabile factum"[3] = a praiseworthy deed. Country butchers to be excluded from the city.)*

[4][V. f. p. held on Oct. 4, 6 Edw. VI.]
Essonia.[5] *("Civitas Couentrie." Oct. 4, 1552.)*

Tho. Gardynour, Cuth. Joynour, Hen. Over, Joh. Tallantes, Joh. Hereford, Jac. Rogers, Tho. Keyvet, Will. Saunders, Ric. Nyclyne, Ric. Ley, Ric. Sewall, Will. Hyndeman, Tho. Wheately, Joh. Wayde, Tho. Amorson, Joh. Nethermyll, Will. Westeley, Humf. Reynoldes, Will. Baylye, Joh. Thomson, Ric. Gyller, Joh. Roper, Cris. Tylynge, Edw. Pell, Math. Robson. *(Jury of 25.)*

¶ [Joh. ffitzherbert, mercer, Ric. Wightman, capper.] *(Sheriffs.)*

¶ Item, yt ys ordeyned and enacted at thys present leete by the aucthorytie of the same that noon inhabitaunte of thys Cytye shall haue or vse any Swyne Styes in the Subbarbes of thys Citie beynge within lx foote of any highe weye, or noyonse vnto the kinges leige people, vppon peyne to forfaicte vj s. viij d. to the vse of the Shyreffes of the sayd cytye for the tyme beinge to be leved by dystres etc. *(No "Swyne Styes" in the suburbs within 60 feet of the highway.)*

¶ [Enacted] That non inhabitante of thys Cytye shall permytt & Suffer any blockes, tymber, or other purpresture to be leyd vndur ther walles or any other place in the streites of the Citie ouer & aboue the space of oon weeke, vppon peyne to forfeicte for euery defalte vj s. viij d. *("Blockes, tymber & purpresture in the streites.")*

[1-1] In a later hand.   [2] See above, p. 798 and note.
[3] A hand of (probably) later date. On the exclusiveness of towns see Introduction.
[4] Scribe L; leaf 417. The last page was numbered 414. I do not perceive that any leaves are missing from the MS. The marginal notes are in the hand of Scribe L also.
[5] = Essions. See above, p. 715.

§ 137. *Ric. Hurte, Mayor. Leet,* 1552.

to the vse aforesayd, and besydes that lose & forfeyte the sayde blockes, tymber & other purpresture to any Constable, seriaunte, or other officer of the Citie that wyll sease & take the same.

"Pavementes" from the house-front to the gutter to kept in order by each citizen.

[1] ¶ [Enacted] that every inhabitauntes of thys citie shall sufficentlye repayre & amend ther pavementes in the streetes of the Citie Lyenge before ther howses from ther howse to the Channell before the feaste of Easter next, vpon peyne to forfeyte for every defalte vj s. viij d., to be leveyd of the goodes of the offenders by dystres to the vse of the Shyreffes of the sayd cytye for the tyme beinge.

¶ [Enacted] That for the better admynystracion & execucion of iustice & the trewe levyenge of all fynes & amerceamentes hence-furthe, That the two Seriauntes of the Citie called the Subbaylyfes shall haue the Colleccion and gatherynge of all thissues, fines and amercymentes hence-furthe Risinge & comynge of all Indictementes, presentmentes at any Cessions, Leetes or otherwise within thys Cytye, and shall make accompte of the same vnto Maister Maiour & Shyreffes of the citie for the tyme beinge at suche tyme as they shal-be thervnto called, savinge suche Resonable allowance for ther peynes therin as by Maister Maiour & the councell of the sayd citie shal-be thought good.

"Colleccion & gathering of Amercimentes."

[2] "No Sweepinge of the streites in time of Raine."[2]

¶ [Enacted] that no person within thys Citie shall from-hencefurthe Swepe ther streites in any Reyne time wher-by to pester[3] the Ryver with fylthe & mucke, vppon peyne to forfeicte for every defalte ij s., the oon half therof to the presentour of the same & the other to the shyrefes of the Cytye etc.

"Tallowe"

¶ [Enacted] That ther shal-be sold no tallowe from hence-furthe from or owte of the Cytye to any stranger vntell the feaste of Easter next comynge, neyther yt shal be sold to any Cytizin within the sayd cytye above fyve shyllinges & foure pence the stonne, and that Candle for the same tyme shall not be sold aboue iij d. the pound,[4] vppon the peyne for the Sellinge of every stonne of tallowe contrarye

5s. 4d. a stone, " & Candle " 3d. per lb.

[1] leaf 417, back.   [2-2] In different hands   [3] = obstruct.
[4] The steady rise in prices is to be attributed to the debasement of the coinage.

§ 138. *Will. Joynour, Mayor*, 1553.

to thys acte iij s. iiijd., & for every pound of candle xij d. to be levyed by dystres to the vse of the sayd Shyrefes.

[1] ¶ [Enacted] that noon inhabitaunte of thys Citie shall from hencefurthe caste any stoones, Raymell,[2] or other fylthe or purpresture, vppon the Grey-freer dunghyll or neere vnto the same, Excepte good mucke or dunge or cleane yearthe, vppon peyne to forfeicte for every defalte vj s. viij d. to be leved by dystres by the shyreffes of the Cytye for the tyme beinge of the goodes & Cattalles of the offenders to ther owne vse. "Greyfreer dongehyll."

¶ Item, yt ys allso enacted by aucthorytye aforesayd that the barbors of thys Citie shal-be dyscharged of ther pencion of vj s. viij d. that they were heretofore Charged yerelye to paye to the gyrdelers of the same Cytye.[3] The "barbors" pension.

¶ [Enacted] That no bruer of thys Cytye shall sell ther best ale but after the raite of xiiij[ten] gallons the Cester, & the typler to sell the same after iij d. the gallon, & ij d. ale for xx d. the Cester, vpon peyne of xx s. etc. The price of "Ale."

¶ [Enacted] That all actes & ordynaunces mayd at the last leete for the preseruacion & meyntenaunce of the Coemwelthe (Commonwealth) of thys Cytye shall stand and remayne in ther strengthe & forces according to theen[ten]tes and trewe meanynge of the same. The "old actes ratified."

WILL. JOYNOUR, MAYOR, 1553.

¶ [Election of Officers.]

[Names of electors all missing.]

"Cinitas Couentrie." Jan. 25.

| Who elect Master Will. Joyner mayor of this city for the year following. . . . | ¶ Qui Eligunt in officium Maioris huius Civitatis Magistrum Will. Joyner, gresyer, pro hoc Anno sequente. . . . |

LEETS.

[4] ¶ [V. f. p. held before Will. Joynour, m., Joh. ffitzherbert, Ric. Wightman, b., on Apr. 25, 7 Edw. VI.[5]] "Ciuitas Coventrie." Apr. 25, 1553.

---

[1] leaf 418. [2] = builder's rubbish.
[3] See above, p. 710. The yearly pension was to go towards the pageant.
[4] leaf 418, back.
[5] By a curious slip Edw. VI. is here described as "Regina."

§ 138. *Will. Joynour, Mayor. Leet₁* 1553.

¶ Esson*ia*.

Tho. Gardener, Cuth. Joyno*u*r, Chr. Waren, Joh. Saunders, Hen. Over, Joh. Tallont*es*, Jac. Rogers, Tho. Keivet, Will. Saunders, Ric. Nyclyn, Edw. Damport, Ric. Hurte, Ric. Ley, Will. Norton, Tho. Amorsam, Will. Beylie, Rob. Colmon, Joh. Thompson, Hugo Harvye, Tho. Saunders, Hen. Deves, Hen. Collins, Joh. Bollet, Ric. Wano*u*r [? Warnour], Hen. Lyngham, Tho. Tayler.

"*Ciuitas Coventrie.*"
Oct. 1, 1553.
Jury of 25.

[V. f. p. held on Oct. 10, 1 Mary.[1]]

¶ Esson*ia*.

[Tho. Gardene*r*, Cuth. Joyno*u*r, Chr. Waren, Hen. Over, Joh. Tallont*es*, Joh. Harford, Jac. Rogers, Tho. Keivet, Will. Saunders, Ric. Nyclyn, Ric. Hurte, Ric. Sewall, Will. Norton, Tho. Amorsam, Will. Westeley, Will. Baylye, Joh. Thompson, Ric. Gyller, Ric. Smy[t]he, Joh. Saunders, Hen. Devyas, Hen. Collyns, Joh. Pa*r*ker, Joh. Hyndma*n*, Ric. Sewall.

Sheriffs and recorder elected.

¶ [Tho. Dudley, "*generosus*," Tho. Kyrvyn, merc*er*.]
And they elected to the office of recorder of this city Joh. Throgmorton, Esq.

*Et eliger*unt *in offici*um *Record-*atoris *huius Ci*u*itatis* Joh. Throgmorton[2] *armi*ger*um.*

[3] "Carpenters a Company."[3]

[4][Ordained] [5] that the Companye of Carpenters wi*th*in thys Cytye shal-be admytted and allowed as an occupac*i*on & fellowshippe as in tymes past they haue bynne.

The wages of "Carpenters" 8*d*. a day, between Feb. 2 and Nov. 1;

[Enacted] that no m*aiste*r Carpenter or sawyer shall take for hys wag*es* from Candlemas to Allholuntyd aboue viij d. a daye, And for a yornyma*n* or a Suffycyent s*e*rvaunte not aboue vj d. a daye; And also that no m*aiste*r Tyler or Roughe Masson durynge the sayd tyme shall take aboue vij d. a daye, & for ther Suffycyent s*e*rvaunte not aboue v d. a daye; And no dawber durynge

of "Tylers & Massons" 7*d*. a day;

of "Dawbers"

---

[1] For the Queen's titles v. p. 781.
[2] Of the famous family of Throcknmorton of Coughton, Warwick, John Throckmorton was son of Sir George, father of Francis, the conspirator, brother of Sir Nicholas, the diplomatist, and uncle to Job, of Martin Marprelate fame. Both John and Nicholas were implicated in Wyatt's rebellion, but John, though condemned to death, was released and restored to Queen Mary's favour. In 1566 he was knighted by Elizabeth. Towards the close of his life he was accused before the Star Chamber of maladministration in his post of Justice of Chester, and declared guilty. He died in 1580.
[3-3] In different hands.   [4] leaf 419.
[5] "thaucthorite" occurs here.

§ 138. *Will. Joynour, Mayor. Carpenters*, 1553.

the sayd tyme shall take aboue vj d. a daye, nor hys servaunte aboue v d.; nor no Coem̄ (common) laborer durynge the sayd terme aboue v d. a daye.¹

6d. a day;
"& Coem (common) labor" 5d. a day.

[Enacted] that [no] maister Carpenter [&] maister sawyer shall take from Hallontyde vntell Candlemas aboue vj d. for a dayes wages, & for hys servant not aboue v d. a day; And that no tyler nor Roughe Masson shall take durynge the sayd tyme aboue vj d. a daye, and hys man not aboue iiij d. a day; And no dawber duryng the sayd tyme shall take aboue v d. a daye, & hys man not aboue iiij d.; & no Coem (common) laborer durynge the sayd time aboue iiij d. a daye.

² "Rates & wages" ² for winter. Carpenter, tiler, and mason,

6d. a day;

dawber, 5d.;

labourer, 4d.

[Enacted] that the Carpenters of thys Cytye shall permitt & suffer all Carpenters of the Countrey to worke in the Cytye takynge of euery suche carpenters wages of the countrey j d. a wycke, the same to be taken & Receyved of thandes of hym that settythe the sayd forren carpenter aworke. And these orders to be obserued vpon peyn of Impresonment at the discrecion of Maister Meyre & Justices of peace of thys Cytye.³

The "forren Carpenters" may work in the city, but their employers are to take 1d. a week from each one's wages (?) to be paid to the carpenters' craft.

[Enacted] that no person within thys Cyty of what degree so-euer he be shall geve to any of the sayd personnes aboue the wages aforesayd, vpon peyne to forfeycte for euery defalte vj s. viij d., & Lykewise the taker iij s. iiij d., to be Leveyd to the vse of the Shyrryfes of thys Cytye.

"*Nota pena.*"
None to give workmen higher wages than according to the established rates.

[Enacted] That all Carpenters, Massons, tylers, dawbers, & allso all kynd of laborers within thys Cytye Lackynge worke shall assemble themselves at fyve of the clocke in the mornynge in the somer tyme with ther tooles in ther handes at the Broide-yate accordinge as in tymes paste they haue donne to thentente suche as lacke workemen may fynd them ther, and that non of them be found idell at whome or in any ale house, vpon peyne of Impresonment.

The "assemblyng of workemen at *the* Broid-yate" for hire.

⁴[Enacted] that the foren bochers shall haue Libertie to brynge victuell in-to thys Cytye wickely on the

The "foren bochers" are to be admitted on Fridays.

---
¹ Cf. the wages of the year 1421 on p. 21, and note the rise that has taken place during the intervening period.
²⁻² In a later hand. ³ Cf. the previous order, p. 792.
⁴ leaf 419, back.

§ 138. Will. Joynour, Mayor. Inns, 1553.

Fryday & to sell the same in two place*s*, that ys to seye, in the Fleete-streite & Jordan-well, and on non other daye*s*.[1]

Order concerning the "kyllinge of fleshe."

[Enacted] that non inha*b*itaunte of thys Cytye other then a bocher shall kyll any kynd of fleshe to sell, vpon peyne of iij s. iiij d. for eue*r*y defalte.

All "bruers" to sell ale at 2s. the sextary, and "typlers" at 2d. the gallon.

[Enacted] That eue*r*y bruer in thys Cytye after the fyrst daye of Maye next shall sell ther ale after xiiij gallons to the Cestre, & after the Raite of ij s. the Cestre & not aboue; and the typler to sell yt after the raite of ij d. the gallon, vpon peyne of eue*r*y bruer or typler offendinge to the Contrarye to forfeicte for eue*r*y defalte vj s. viij d. to be levyed by distres etc., the oon half therof to the shyrrefe*s*, xx d. thereof to the Co*m*em[2] boxe, & xx d. thereof to the p*r*esenter, and bysyde*s* that to suffer imp*r*eson*m*ent etc., & that all typlers aforesayd shall sell ther ale owte of ther howses at the p*r*ises aforesayd, that ys to sey, ij d. the gallon.

Keepers of "ale-howses" are forbidden to permit inhabitants to drink in their houses except on a market day in a stranger's company.

[Enacted] That no typler within thys Cytye shall not suffer any inha*b*itaunte of the Cytye to have Resorte into ther howses to eate and drynke vnles yt be on the ma*r*ket daye & feyre tyme in the Compayny of an honeste stranger,[3] vpon peyne to forfeicte for eue*r*y defalte x s., wherof iij s. iiij d. to the p*r*esenter, iij s. iiij d. to the shyrryfe*s*, & iij s. iiij d. to the Coem̄ (common) boxe to be Leveyd by distres etc.

"Inholders" are forbidden to permit labourers to drink or play in their inns.

[Enacted] That no Inholder within thys Cytye shall not pe*r*mytt or suffer any handy-Crafte*s*-man, laborer, yornyman or aprentyzes of thys Cytye to haue Resorte or to be convu*r*saunte in hys howse to eate or drynke or pleye vnles yt be in Company of a strange*r* and then not to pleye, vpon peyne of x s. for eue*r*y defalte, wherof iij s. iiij d. to the shyrryfe*s*, iij s. iiij d. to the coem̄ box, & iij s. iiij d. to the p*r*esento*u*r etc.

Ordered that 4"no brewer [is] to ffeitch water at the Conduits."4

[Enacted] That no coem̄ (common) bruer nor maltemaker w*ith*-in thys Cyte shall not from-hence-furthe fetche eny water at the Condytte*s* wherw*ith* to brewe or

---

[1] See above, p. 803. [2] *i. e.* common.
[3] In obedience most likely to the time-honoured custom of drinking over the conclusion of a bargain. For other restrictions see above, p. 786.
4—4 In different hands.

§ 139. *Will. Norton, Mayor*, 1554.

to make malte, vppon peyne to forfeycte for euery defalte xx s., wherof vj s. viij d. to be to the shyrryfes, vj s. viij d. to the presenters of the defalte, & vj s. viij d. to the coem̄ (common) boxe, towardes the reparacions of the Condyttes, to be Leveyd by distres etc. ymedyatly after the prophe [1] of the offence before Maister Meyer etc.[2]

WILL. NORTON, MAYOR, 1554.

LEETS.

[3][V. f. p. held before Will. Norton, m., Tho. Dudley, Tho. Kyrvyn, b., on Apr. 24, 1 Mary.[4]

Essonia.

Tho. Gardener, Cutheb. Joyner, Chr. Waren, Joh. Tallantes, Joh. Hareford, Jac. Rogers, Ric. Nyclyn, Ric. Hurte, Will. Joyner, Ric. Ley, Ric. Sewell, Tho. Wheateley, Tho. Amorson, Joh. Nethermyll, Will. Westeley, Will. Baylye, Ric. Gillar, Ric. Smythe, Tho. Saunders, Ric. Wightman, Oliuer Lynd, ffran. Wayd, Will. Smalewood, Nic. Hopkins.

[Enacted] That no ale-bruer nor bere-bruer within thys Cytye shall from and after the feaste of Penticoste next sell any ale or bere aboue the prece of ij s. the Cester, & euery Cester to conteign xiiij galones, vppon peine to forfeicte for euery Cester x s., the same forfeicture to be Levied & taken of the goodes of the offenders by the shyrryfes of the Cytye for the tyme beinge to ther owne vse ymedyatly after profe therof mayd by wytnes or otherweyes before the Mayer of the sayd Cytye for the tyme beinge.

"Ciuitas Couentrie." Apr. 4, 1554.

Jury.

The "ale-bruers & bere-bruers" to sell ale at 2s. the sextary.

---

[1] = proof.
[2] On Nov. 20 of this year the mayor sent up to the Council Baldwin Clere, weaver, Joh. Careles, weaver, Tho. Wylcockes, fishmonger, and Ric. Astelyn, haberdasher, for "lewd and seditious behaviour on All Hallow Day last past." Careles died in the King's Bench prison in 1556. Astelyn was a member of a leading family in the city.—*Vict. County Hist. Warw.*, II. 33. He was probably soon released, as a Ric. Aslyn and one Francis are mentioned as being interviewed by an emissary of Suffolk in the January of the succeeding year, when an attempt was made to seize Coventry for the Protestants.—*ib.* 442-3.   [3] leaf 420.

[4] For the Queen's titles, v. above, p. 781. The night of the 29-30 January in this year was marked by much disturbance, and an abortive attempt on the part of the Duke of Suffolk's—the Protestant—party to seize the city.

§ 139. Will. Norton, Mayor. Ale, 1554.

Every "Typler" to sell no ale above 3d. the gallon,

And that no typler of thys Cytye from-hence-furthe shall sell eny ale or bere, aboue the Raite of iij d. the galon, vppon peyne to forfeicte for euery defalte iij s. iiij d. to be Levyed and taken of the goodes of the offenders in forme aforesayd to the vse aforesayd: And allso that no typler of this Cytye shall from and after the feaste of the Natiuitie of seynt John Baptiste next comynge sell eny ale or beare by eny other measures then by pyntes, quartes, pottells or galons beinge sealed[1] by the officer assigned for the same, vppon peyne to forfeicte for euery defalte vj s. viij d. to be levyed and taken in forme aforesayd to the vse aforesayd. And that yt shal-be laufull to euery person & persones seinge or findinge eny ale or beare sold by eny other mesures then as ys aforesayd, or by mesures not sealed to breake the same or to sease & take them to hys & theyr owne vse.

and by measures duly tested and sealed.

"Seasure of measures or breakinge of the same," if they are unlawful ones, is allowable. The "handy-craftesmen."

[Enacted] that the acte mayd at the laste Leete concernynge daylye wages of Massons, Carpenters, tylers, & other Laborers & handy-craftesmen shall stand and remayne in full strength and effecte in all poyntes accordinge to the tenour and purporte of the same acte: And that all other actes mayd for preseruacion of the coem̄welthe[2] of thys Cytye shall stand & remayne in their forces accordinge to the purporte of the same.

A "confirmacion of old actes."

Against "breakinge of headges."

[3][Enacted] that no person take vppon them to breake eny headges of Lammas pastures or other aboute thys Cytye, or carye awey eny headge-wood of the same, vppon peyne of ympresonment & to forfeicte for euery defaulte iij s. iiij d.

Against laying any filth near the "yates or barres of thys Cytye."

Allso that no person lay eny dunge or fylthe nighe or abowte the gates or the barres of thys Cytye, vppon peyne to forfeicte for euery defalte vj s. viij d. And that all suche persones that haue of laite leyd eny dunge or fylthe nighe vnto the sayd gaites or barres shall take & carry awey the same before Wytsontyde next, vppon the same peyne.

Allso yt ys further enacted (etc.) That no person or

---

[1] See Shakespeare, *Taming of the Shrew*, Introd. ii.
  . . . "and rail upon the hostess of the house,
  And say you would present her at the Leet,
  Because she brought stone-jugs and no sealed quarts."

[2] *i. e.* commonwealth.   [3] leaf 420, back.

§ 140. *Tho. Ryley, Mayor,* 1555.

persones of thys Cytye shall from hence-furthe ley or water eny hempe or flax in the Ryver of Shyrborne, vppon peyne to forfeicte for euery tyme so doinge xl shyllinges. *Against laying "hempe & flaxe" in the river.*

It is allso enacted by aucthorytie aforesayd That all the bochers of thys Cytye shall ley furthe in the streetes ther hydes to be sold, vppon the Frydaye before seven of the clocke in the mornynge, & no daye ells in the wycke, nor shall not sell eny hyde to eny tanner or eny other man before nyne of the clocke of the same Frydaye, vppon peyne to forfeicte for euery hyde & offence vj s. viij d. to be Levyed of ther goodes by wey of dystres, & the oon half of all the forfeictures to the fynder or presenter of the same, & the other half to the shyrryfes of thys City for the tyme being. *An order for "sellinge of hides" on Fridays only, and after 9 o'clock.*

Allso that no Chaundeler of thys Cytye shall sell eny tallowe to the corvicer nor to the Curriour, but shall converte the same tallowe to Candle-makinge, vppon peyne to forfeicte vj s. viij d., the half therof to the vse of the Shyrryfes etc., and the other half to the vse of the fyrste fynder of the same. *Every "Chaundeler" to make his tallow into candles.*

THOMAS RYLEY, MAYOR, 1555.
EASTER LEET.

[1][V. f. p. held before Tho. Ryley,[2] m., Ric. Hopkins,[3] Will. Hindeman, b., May 14, 1 & 2 Philip & Mary.] *"Ciuitas Couentrie." May 14, 1555.*

Essonia.

Tho. Gardener, Cuth. Joyner, Chr. Waren, Hen. Over, Joh. Tallantes, Joh. Hereford, Jac. Rogers, Tho. Kevet, Ric. Nyclyn, Will. Norton, Ric. Hurte, Will. Joyner,

---

[1] leaf 422.

[2] This mayor must have had Protestant leanings, as he sent to warn John Glover of his intended arrest. John escaped, but his brother Robert—the martyr—was taken. On the other hand, Christopher Waren, at whose house the captive Duke of Suffolk lodged, was a Catholic partisan. Foxe, *Martyrs,* VII. 393.

[3] Probably of the Hopkins' family of Palace Yard, Coventry. The sheriff was imprisoned this year in the Fleet, being "accused," says Foxe, "of matter pertaining to religion." He appears to have sent to a thief in prison, ready to be hanged, "a certain English book of Scripture for his spiritual comfort." After his release from prison he and his family went to Basle, where he lived until after Mary's death, being "a comfortable reliever of other English exiles." A letter to him from the martyr, John Bradford, is given in Foxe. See *Martyrs,* VII. 249-50.

§ 140. *Tho. Ryley, Mayor. Leet,* 1555.

Ric. Ley, Ric. Shewell, Tho. Wheateley, Tho. Amorsame, Will. Westeley, Will. Beyly, Joh. Thompson, Ric. Giller, Hugo Harvye, Tho. Saunders, Ric. Wightman, Tho. Dudley, Tho. Kervyn, Joh. Gosselyn, Tho. Syde, Will. Smalewood.

An order against "dryenge of malte."

[Enacted] that non inhabitant of thys Cyty shall fromhence-furthe after the feaste of All Seynctes next drye any mallte with strawe or furres within the walles of thys Cytye, vppon peyne to forfeicte for euery defalte xl s. to the vse of the shyrryfes to be Levyed by distresse etc.

No brewer, malt-maker and fishmonger to take from the "Condyte" any "water."

Item, no Coem̄ (common) bruer, no malt-maker or fisshemonger shall from-hence-furthe fetche eny water at the coundictes within thys Cytye to thentente therwith to make malt, brewe, or water fysshe,[1] [or 20s. fine each time, levied in the form and applied to the use above-written.]

The "Constables" are to enforce this act.

And that euerye constable shall endevour hymself to se the execucion of thys acte, vppon peyne of vj s. viij d.

No one to eat or drink in an alehouse during "seruyce tyme" on the Sabbath.

Allso that no ale-howse keeper or other vytayler in thys Cytye soeffer 'eny inhabitauntes of the Cytye to eate or drynke in ther howses in seruice tyme on the Sabott daye, vpon peyne to forfeite for euerye defalte xx s., vt supra.

Against "admytinge of estrangers" without they are examined before the mayor or an alderman and pronounced satisfactory.

Item, that non inhabitaunte of thys Cytye do admytt eny stranger to inhabite within thys Cytye Excepte the same estranger be fyrste brought to [? by] the Constable of the ward wher he shall inhabite before Maister Meyre or the alderman of the ward and by them examynyed & tryed whether he be a man meite to inhabite ther or not, vppon peyne to forfeicte xl s. vt supra.[2] And yf eny Constable do soeffer eny such to inhabite by the space of a moneythe that then he for hys necligens to forfeicte for euerye defalte vj s. viij d.

"Edwardes, bocher," to pay his fine to the fellowship.

[Enacted] that Joh. Edwardes, bocher, shall paye to the Maister of the fellowshippe of bochers for a fyne of liij s. iiij d.,[3] and all other paymentes quarterlye for hys brotherwod as other bochers doo.

[Enacted] that asewell the meyre & shyrryfes for the tyme beinge, as all other that haue bynne meyres &

---

[1] This probably applies particularly to the soaking of stockfish in water.
[2] See above, p. 785.   [3] A very high fine.

§ 140. *Tho. Ryley, Mayor. Watch,* 1555.

shyrryfes, & ther wyfes shall were ther scarlet gownes vppon principall dayes & dayes accustomed accordinge to the auncyent vse, vppon peyne of xx s.

[1] Allso that euery alderman shall were euery Sondaye & other principall dayes a velvet typpet vpon peyne of x s.

Allso that the shyrryfes for the tyme beinge shall at all tymes when they be owte of ther howses [3] shall haue ther sergeantes with ther maces to goo before them & ther yomen after them, vppon peyne to forfeicte for euery defalte xx s.

Allso that euery alderman & shyrryf beinge able to Ride shall accompanye Maister Meyre & ryde with hym in the watche on Mydsomer nyght in ther scarlet, & euery of them to haue a man weytinge vppon hym with torche-light, vppon peyne of xx s.[4]

"Skarlet gownes."

Every [2] "alderman to wear tippets vpon payne of x s." [2]

[2] "Shyrryfes serjants to bear ther maces before them."

"Mydsomer night."

[1] leaf 422, back. [2] In different hands.
[3] Deletions follow. [4] See Sharp, *Mysteries,* pp. 174, *sqq.*

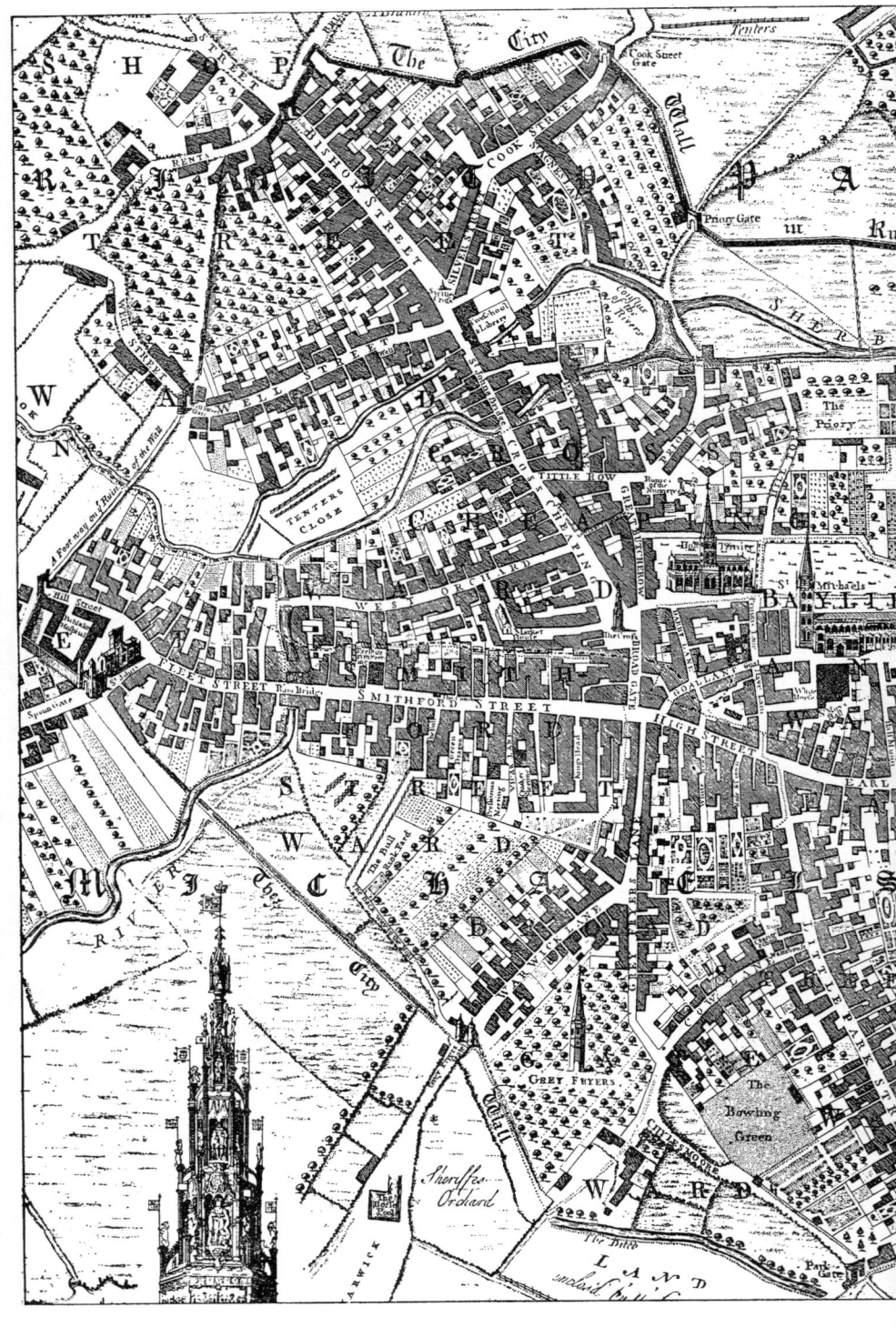

The Coventry Leet Book:
OR
Mayor's Register.

Early English Text Society.
Original Series, No. 146.
1913.

BERLIN: A. ASHER & CO., 17, BEHRENSTRASSE, W. 8.
NEW YORK: C. SCRIBNER & CO., LEYPOLDT & HOLT.
PHILADELPHIA: J. B. LIPPINCOTT CO.

The Coventry Leet Book:

OR

Mayor's Register,

CONTAINING THE RECORDS OF THE CITY

Court Leet

OR

View of Frankpledge,

A.D. 1420–1555,

WITH DIVERS OTHER MATTERS.

TRANSCRIBED AND EDITED BY

MARY DORMER HARRIS,

AUTHOR OF "LIFE IN AN OLD ENGLISH TOWN: A HISTORY OF COVENTRY
COMPILED FROM OFFICIAL RECORDS."

PART IV.

LONDON:
PUBLISHED FOR THE EARLY ENGLISH TEXT SOCIETY
BY KEGAN PAUL, TRENCH, TRÜBNER & CO., LTD.,
BROADWAY HOUSE, LUDGATE HILL, E.C.
AND BY HUMPHREY MILFORD, OXFORD UNIVERSITY PRESS,
AMEN CORNER, E.C., AND IN NEW YORK.
1913.

Price Ten Shillings.

Original Series, No. 146.

EDITOR'S PREFACE

Now that my laborious task is ended I have only to thank those who made its accomplishment possible by so generously giving their time to inform my ignorance, correct my faulty Latin and Anglo-French, and suggest textual emendations. Mr. W. H. Stevenson supervised the proofs of vols. i, ii, and the early portion of vol. iii; the late Mr. R. E. G. Kirk also overlooked the greater part of the proofs, and after his death Mr. E. F. Kirk most kindly continued his father's work, and also supplied me with several notes and transcripts from the Record Office. In addition to giving important help by overlooking the Glossary, Dr. H. Bradley supplied most valuable notes on the derivation of the words "Leet" and "Coventry," and Mr. G. J. Turner and others on "Forest Iron" and "Grand Warrant." Mr. William Page kindly allowed me to use in the Notes and Introduction some material to which I had access while working on Warwickshire for the *Victoria County Histories*, and in various ways I am greatly indebted to the kindness of Mr. S. O. Addy, Mr. Geo. Buchannan, and the late Miss Toulmin Smith, while thanks are no less due to several correspondents who put their knowledge at my disposal. Dr. Furnivall, who first encouraged me to undertake the transcription, and readily gave all the help in his power, is now, like some others I have named, beyond the reach of any expression of gratitude, but I am glad that before his death he personally as well as the Early English Text Society received the thanks of the Coventry Corporation for the publication of this valuable historical and literary document.

I ought to add that the full and careful name-index of this volume is the work of Miss Jessie Hayllar.

[NOTE ON THE DERIVATION OF COVENTRY KINDLY SUPPLIED BY DR. HENRY BRADLEY.]

THE form *Cofantrēo*, though of late occurrence (Chronicle C., an. 1053), is, there can be little doubt, genuinely old, so that the ending = tree. In most of the place-names ending in *trēo-*, the first element is the genitive of a personal name—the name of the man by whom, or in commemoration of whom, the tree was planted. I should feel sure that this was so in the present instance, but I find no example of Cofa as a personal name. There were several persons named *Cufa*, and if the *u* was short this might be a variant of Cofa.

The word *cofa* (genitive *cofan*) in Old English meant chamber, cell, cave. It may have had other specific senses that we do not know of; but one would expect *Coftrēo* and not *Cofantrēo* if this word were the first element of the name. The word-stem, not the genitive, is normally used in place-name compounds, except before a noun denoting either a possession or an essential part or appurtenance of something. If *cofa* denoted some kind of building or establishment that had a "tree" as a regular appurtenance—*e. g.* as a sort of sign-post to show its whereabouts—a "genitival compound" might be possible.

On the whole, I think that the hypothesis of origin from a personal name, Cofa, is, in the present state of our knowledge, more probable than any other.

There are one or two instances in which names in *-treō* apparently contain the name of a river or stream, but I do not know Cofa or Cofe as a river-name.

CONTENTS

INTRODUCTION

CHAPTER I

THE MANUSCRIPT

	PAGE
Previous workers at the *Leet Book*—Sharp, Reader, Wright—Paper of the MS.—"Black Book,"—"Mayor's Register"—Redactions of Scribes A and B—Other Scribes	ix

CHAPTER II

THE LEET AND COUNCILS

Earliest use of the word "leet"—The three Coventry courts—Early history of the Coventry manors—The Tripartite—Business of leets—Presentments—Framing of by-laws—Bills—The Twenty-four jurats—Electoral jury of Twenty-four—The Forty-eight—The Common Council xvii

CHAPTER III

ORDERS OF LEET

The leet at Coventry—The nucleus of municipal activity—By-laws on sanitation—Morality—Treatment of the poor—The School—Relations with the Church—The holy cake—Resistance of the crafts—The gild of the Nativity—Proceedings in courts Christian—The barbers—The dyers—The victualling crafts and foreign competition—The position of women xxvii

CHAPTER IV

THE LEET BOOK AS CHRONICLE

Localization of the crafts—The commons—Laurence Saunders—Sixteenth-century enclosures—Finance—Military service and fortifications—Historical Allusions, Henry V and Hornby—Gloucester and the Lollards—The pageants—Edward IV and Edward Prince of Wales—Elizabeth—James I—Shakespeare and the *Leet Book* . . . xlii

TEXT	1
APPENDIX A	845
GLOSSARY	847
ADDITIONAL NOTES	853
ERRATA	859
NAME INDEX	861
PLACE INDEX	917
SUBJECT INDEX	924

KEY TO ABBREVIATIONS, ETC.

a. r. r.	= anno regni regis, the year of the king's reign.
b.	= bailiff.
Burton MS.	= Humphrey Burton's MS., Free Library, Coventry.
ch.	= chamberlains.
cor.	= coroner.
Corp. MSS.	= MSS. in possession of the Coventry Corporation. Catalogued by J. C. Jeaffresson for Hist. MSS. Comm. 1896.
E. D. D.	= English Dialect Dictionary (Clarendon Press).
m.	= mayor.
mace	= sergeant-at-mace, sub-bailiff.
M. E.	= Middle English.
M. G. C. C.	= Magister Gilde Corporis Christi, master of the Corpus Christi Gild.
M. G. S. T.	= Magister Gilde Sancte Trinitatis, master of the Trinity Gild.
N. E. D.	= New English Dictionary (Clarendon Press).
V. f. p.	= Visum franci plegii, view of frankpledge, or leet.
w.	= wardens.
" "	in the margin denotes marginal annotations in MS.
(etc.)	in the text denotes the omission from the transcription of some oft-repeated formula, e. g. maior (etc.) = maior civitatis Coventrie, the mayor of the city of Coventry, etc., without brackets, however, is a copy of the MS.
[ ]	in the English text denotes an abbreviated rendering of a customary formula, e. g. [Ordained] = Hit was ordeyned by auctorite of this present lete.
[ ]	also denotes a translation from the Latin. MS. abbreviations and contractions are represented in the transcript by italics.

INTRODUCTION

CHAPTER I

THE MANUSCRIPT

Previous workers at the *Leet Book*—Sharp, Reader, Wright—Paper of the MS.—"Black Book," "Mayor's Register"—Redactions of Scribes A and B—Other scribes.

THE Coventry *Leet Book*, though unnoticed by Dugdale, has on occasion furnished material from the seventeenth century onwards to both lawyer and antiquary, the former regarding it as a valuable authority in matters of ancient custom and prescriptive right,[1] and the latter as a storehouse of information concerning the local religious drama and ancient buildings of the city. Never before has the volume been copied in its entirety, though in the seventeenth century Humphrey Burton, town clerk, grandfather of Humphrey Wanley of Harleian fame, made some extracts from it,[2] and his example was followed in the early nineteenth century by William Reader.[3] Both these fragmentary transcripts, however, remain in MS. The researches of Thomas Sharp, a contemporary of Reader, crystallized into book form. His *Dissertation on the Pageants or Dramatic Mysteries anciently performed at Coventry* (1825), together with the *Presentation in the Temple, a Pageant, . . . represented by the . . . Weavers in Coventry* (1836), remained until

---

[1] See below. p. xiii, for Sewell's request in 1611 for the "Black Book." A note on the flyleaf of the MS. shows that it was also consulted in the case of the Mayor of Coventry *v.* Lythall and others in 1842. See for particulars of case, Poole, *Coventry*, pp. 99 sqq.

[2] Burton was interested in collecting material bearing upon the claim of the Princes of Wales, as lords of the Manor of Cheylesmore, to an annual rent for the Earl's-Half of Coventry, payable by the corporation, as successors of the Prior and Convent after the Dissolution, see below, pp. 751-2. The extracts from the *Leet Book* are few. Of *Burton's Book* (Corp. MSS. A 34) two transcripts are in the Free Library.

[3] Reader MSS. Free Library, Coventry. A collection of extraordinary value and width of range.

x   *Introduction.*

1902, when they were superseded by the more modern scholarship of Dr. Hardin Craig's *Two Coventry Corpus Christi Plays*, the only authority on this subject; and both these works and Sharp's monographs on various buildings of the city, which it is convenient to call by the collective name of the *Antiquities of Coventry*, since they were reissued under that title in 1871, contain citations from the *Leet Book*, bearing on the subject of the churches, St. Mary Hall, the Free School, or the pageants and processions which in pre-Shakespearean days brought such fame to the city.[1]

The credit of calling attention to the *Leet Book's* existence belongs, however, not to Sharp but to James Wright, whose *Historia Histrionica; an Historical Account of the English Stage, showing the ancient Use, Improvement and Perfection of Dramatick Representation in this Nation*, was published in 1699, and who either saw the actual manuscript or a transcript of certain verses found therein, since he cites these, giving the correct folio for reference.[2] "But it is notorious," he says, "that in former times there was hardly ever any Solemn Reception of Princes or Noble Persons, but Pageants . . . were part of the Entertainment. On which there were Speeches by one or more Persons in the nature of Scenes; and be sure one of the Speakers must be some Saint of the same Name with the Party to whom the Honour is intended. For instance, there is an ancient Manuscript at Coventry, call'd the *Old Leet Book*, wherein is set down in a very particular manner (fo. 168) the Reception of Queen *Margaret*, Wife of H. 6, who came to Coventry (and, I think, with her, her young son, Prince *Edward*) on the Feast of the Exaltation of the Holy Cross; 35 H. 6

---

[1] Sharp's citations from the *Leet Book* concerning the crafts and their pageants found in the *Mysteries* and the *Weavers' Pageant*, together with fresh material from the MS., occur on pp. 72-81 of Craig's *Corpus Christi Plays*. So well has the ground been worked that I have been able to detect only one omission, namely, an order of leet (see below, p. 805) concerning the barbers' contribution to the girdlers. For the "Pageants on Special Occasions" taken from the *Leet Book*, see Craig, *op. cit.*, 109-18; Sharp, *Mysteries*, 145-57; see below, pp. 286-92, 391-3, 589-92. The principal citations in Sharp's *Antiquities* are Henry VI's visit to St. Michael's (*op. cit.*, 17; for a longer quotation see Sharp's (Anon.), *Epitome of the Country of Warwick*, 237-9, the section from "Reseavinge the King" to "Godde save the Kyng," see below, pp. 263-6); the preaching of Grace, the hermit (*Antiq.*, 204-5; see below, pp. 96-7); and the outburst of Laurence Saunders, with the specimens of "civic poetry" written by his followers (*Antiq.*, 234-6, see below, pp. 556-7, 566-7, 577-8). Both Reader and Sharp contributed to the *Gentlemen's Magazine*, the latter usually over the signature Σ; among this Coventry material are one or two citations from the *Leet Book*.

[2] Wright, *Hist. Histr.*, 20.

The Manuscript.

(1456)." Of the "pageants and speeches made for her welcome," Wright "observes" and quotes but "two or three in the Old English," namely the verses put in the mouths of the characters personating St. Edward, St. John Evangelist, and St. Margaret.[1]

Nothing, however, appeared until of late years[2] in print to show the immense value of the great bulk of the volume to the student of economics and of municipal institutions, and yet the book should take a high place among collections of town records, by reason of the variety and richness of its fifteenth-century material. The massive volume,[3] with ancient binding of boards and leather, containing some 436 numbered, and at the beginning and end divers unnumbered leaves, is well preserved, though the boards appear through the corners of the rubbed calf, and certain pages have undergone probably intentional mutilation.[4] The paper on which the book is written is of two kinds, which here and there intermingle, though as a general rule the earlier paper, bearing the older script, is found in the middle of the volume, and the later kind, used by later scribes, at its extremities, as if so placed by the binder to enlarge the original volume.[5] The earlier paper, probably of Milanese origin, has the watermark, which occurs as early as the thirteen nineties in the Florentine archives, showing the finely drawn letter M surmounted by a cross;[6] while the second, watermarked with the crescent rounded off by the moon's penumbra, containing the maker's initials, F. M., surmounted by a cross *pommée*, came most likely from the workshops of early sixteenth-

---

[1] See below, pp. 287–8, 292. Wright further alludes to the pageant of welcome to Prince Edward, *ib.* 391–3.

[2] In the article on "Laurence Saunders, Citizen of Coventry," in *Eng. Hist. Rev.*, ix. 633–51, and the paper on "Craft Guilds of Coventry," read before the Society of Antiquaries on Nov. 21, 1895 (*Proc. S. A.* 2 S., xvi. 15), afterwards reprinted in the present editor's *Life in an Old English Town*, and the *Story of Coventry*. These last-mentioned books contain very full and numerous citations from the *Leet Book*. See also *Jrnl. Brit. Arch. Ass. N. S.*, vol. xvi, pt. II, 65–70.

[3] The covers measure $16\frac{1}{2}$ in. × $11\frac{1}{2}$ in., and the book is $4\frac{3}{4}$ in. thick from cover to cover. There are remains of clasps, and the leather bears impressions of seals with the Lamb and the legend "Ecce Agnus Dei."

[4] See below, pp. 352, 354, 358.

[5] The later paper occurs on unnumbered leaves and up to leaf 38, and from leaf 349 to the volume's end, and also sporadically in the intermediate portion, which is, however, chiefly made up of the later specimen. See below, p. xv, for the association of this later paper with a particular scribe.

[6] I take it to be identical with the mark figured in Briquet, *Les Filigranes*, no. 8352. The mark is $3\frac{3}{8}$ in. from the top of the cross to the far point of the M, and the width of the M is $1\frac{5}{8}$ in.

century Genoa.[1] Parchment end-papers, spoils, maybe, of a monastic choir, bearing music written in square and diamond notation with ligatures, and words taken from the "Agnus Dei" of some forgotten Mass, line the inner side of the cover; it is the work of some late fourteenth or fifteenth century composer, perhaps Dunstable, flower of musicians of that day.[2]

"Qui tollis peccata mundi," it runs, "miserere nobis . . . [suscipe] deprecacionem nostram, qui sedis ad dexteram patris, . . . quoniam tu solus sanctus, tu solus dominus, tu solus altissimus, Jhesu Christe, cum sancto spiritu in Gloria Dei patris, Agnus Dei, qui tollis peccata mundi, dona nobis pacem."

The great bulk of this volume, and incomparably the more important part, is occupied by the record of mayoral elections and court sittings between 1421 and 1555, expressed in the formulæ consecrated by ancient usage, together with the names of those present and the account of business done. These are interspersed with memoranda on matters innumerable, mainly arranged with due regard to chronology. The less valuable portion consists of slight memoranda, entered with small regard for dates by later scribes on spare pages at the book's beginning and end, treating of matters as far apart in time as 1279-80 and 1622.[3] Certain passages may have been composed out of hand,[4] but the majority of entries are copies of letters, accounts, indentures, and documents of endless variety, while the chief source of the annual sequence of by-laws can be traced to the back files of the court-leet, which met twice a year to frame ordinances, grounded on petitions or bills presented by the folk of the city. As far as we may judge, the copyist followed his original closely,[5] though now and then he chose to summarize rather than transcribe in full, referring the reader to his authority in some such phrase as "as it appeareth in the book

---

[1] Though this nearly resembles Briquet, no. 5263 (occurring in the Genoese State Archives, 1536), the initials differ; but the *Leet Book* watermark initials do occur in an example of a different type (Genoa, 1522-3), Briquet, *op. cit.*, no. 10746. The mark is $2\frac{5}{16}$ in. long, and the circle $1\frac{7}{16}$ in. in diameter.

[2] Dr. Lea Southgate, to whom I am indebted for this information, assures me that neither he, nor any of the high authorities to whom a photograph of the music was shown, knew this mass. The fragment is therefore unique.

[3] See pp. 1-2, 7-19, 815-41.

[4] *Ib.* 332, where the sudden use of the 1st person indicates that the mayor probably wrote or dictated the passage.

[5] *e. g.* the Survey of the Commons, pp. 45-53, when compared with Corp. MS. E 7, exhibits only very trifling variations; most of the originals, however, have perished.

The Manuscript.

of recognizance," or "the book of council;"[1] or in the case of a leet entry, "ut in filaciis plenius apparet,"—as it appeareth in the files more at large.[2]

It is natural that a book on so large a scale, drawn from so many sources, should present many problems; and, indeed, the how and the when of its compilation is something of a mystery, and its early name a matter of some doubt. In the seventeenth century Humphrey Burton and James Wright knew the volume as the *Leet Book* or *Old Leet Book*,[3] but there is testimony that at one time the name *Black Book* was in regular use. Thus in 1622 an agreement between the council-house and the common council was ordered to be entered "into the black booke, which is kept in the said councell-house," and accordingly the agreement is found in the *Leet Book's* pages.[4] Another allusion shows that the record had begun to assume legal importance. In 1611 Henry Sewell, who went up to London on business concerned with a dispute between the city and the Prince of Wales's council, advised the sending up of divers court rolls "with the black booke to shewe vnto the princes Cownsell our Auncyent Custome & vsage of our election, which, as I take it, hath been from þe first yeare of Henry þe sixth,"[5] a statement which shows Sewell to have been by one year in error, since the entries of mayoral elections in the *Leet Book* begin in the last year of Henry V. The name, however, occurs as early as 1480, when Laurence Saunders declared that he never "noysed" any pasture to be common, "but such as he vnderstandes owen to be Comen be the blak boke of this Citie, which specifieth þe cerțente of comen,"[6] an obvious allusion to the survey of the common lands entered in 1423, in Peyto's mayoral year.[7]

The appellation, *Black Book*, is not, however, the one which was earliest in use. The name of *Register* or *Mayor's Register* is that with which the records first make us familiar. The *Leet Book* was

---

[1] p. 577.
[2] See p. 83 for a reference to the endorsements of certain bills put to the leet for uncopied ordinances. The miscellaneous papers belonging to each mayoral year appear to have been kept in bags. The "mayor's bag" is frequently mentioned.
[3] There is a second *Leet Book* begun in 30 Elizabeth, Corp. MSS. A 3 (b).
[4] See below, pp. 835-7.
[5] Vol. of Correspondence, Corp. MSS. A 79, leaf 110.
[6] See below, p. 464.
[7] *Ib*. 45-54. The present *Leet Book* entry must be a copy of the actual entry referred to by Saunders, since it contains an allusion to events of 1491; see p. 83.

either known in its early days as the "Mayor's Register," or more accurately the *Mayor's Register* was a predecessor of the *Leet Book*, into whose pages the earlier volume was copied at a later date, probably in 1520, when there is mention of a "booke that is newe made,"[1] a date that tallies well with the style of handwriting peculiar to the first portion of the MS. Regular entries begin— in this early sixteenth-century hand [2]—with the chronicle of events and transcript of leet ordinaunces in the 1421 mayoralty of John Leeder,[3] and in the opening pages occurs the earliest mention of a volume wherein the orders of the Coventry Court Leet should be copied for their better preservation. At a "hall" or meeting of the council under the presidency of this mayor, it was laid down:— "Þat all good ordynaunce of the leetys be sought up and wryton in a regestre, that they may be of record foreuermore, be ouersight of the recorder, for worschip and honesty of this Cite."[4] The book was evidently purchased—for in John Leeder's accounts, made up two years later, the item occurs, "isto libro, vocato le Registre, vijs.," for that book called the Register, 7s.[5] and the record forthwith begun. The book soon acquired particular importance, and documents other than those concerned with strictly municipal business were copied therein to secure their permanent preservation. Thus in 1430 the company of wiredrawers having entered into a covenant before the mayor and others to maintain "a devout thyng callyd the new Canape" over the altar in S. Michael's church, desired that the indenture thereupon made should be "registred in a boke callyd the meyres Regestur in saynt Mary Hall,"[6] and accordingly the entry is found in the *Leet Book's* pages. But for this lack of chronological correspondence between the style of handwriting and the date of these entries, coupled with Scribe A's interpolation in his copy of the 1423 Survey of the Commons of references to enclosures which took place in 1469 and 1491,[7] we might conclude that we have in the *Leet Book* the actual *Mayor's*

---

[1] See below, p. 667. The leet of 1520 laid down that all "good ordynaunces as be made for the comen-wele of the Citee-afore-tyme . . . from-hensforth . . . be truly kept and executid accordyng to the true entent thereof, *and the booke that is newe made be takyn for an act* and proclamyd at this lete."

[2] Scribe A, who incidentally refers, while apparently copying matter connected with the year 1423, to events occurring in 1469 and 1491 ; see pp. 47, 53.

[3] *Ib.* 21. The insertion of leet rules passed under Esterton's mayoralty, 1420 (*ib.* 20-1), or transactions of earlier time (pp. 2-6, 19-20) are evidently by the way.

[4] *Ib.* 33. [5] *Ib.* 57, "isto" is wrongly rendered "this."
[6] *Ib.* 132. [7] *Ib.* 47, 53.

Register of the wiredrawers' indenture, the volume whereof we may trace the inception in the order of 1421, a supposition all the more credible at the outset since no other MS. of this character survives. It is, however, impossible that any portion of the *Leet Book* in the handwriting of Scribe A, which appears *consistently* in all entries from 1421–5 and *intermittently* among later ones until 1445, should be identical with the *Mayor's Register*, though there is every probability that the former MS. contains a copy of the latter within its pages; indeed, it is possible that parts of the actual MS. of the *Register* not in the handwriting of Scribe A may have been incorporated in the *Leet Book* at the "newe" making of the manuscript mentioned in 1520.[1] We may imagine that at this redaction—the redaction of Scribe A—a great portion of the original volume, called indifferently the *Mayor's Register* or the *Black Book*, written on thick and glossy Italian paper and watermarked with the M and cross, was preserved, being here and there interleaved with crescent-marked Genoa paper, while on additional leaves of this latter make at the book's front Scribe A copied afresh the 1421–5 entries from the old MS.—adding also entries on the interleaved portions—and that his originals were thereafter destroyed. Additions of this paper at the book's end were left blank, to be filled as the years went on by a succession of later scribes.

It is clear that besides Scribe A another redactor has worked over the highly composite material, wherein characteristic hands disappear and reappear in somewhat bewildering fashion. Scribe B also shows commendable zeal in recovering for transcription documents of a bygone generation, and entering the copies in due place on blank spaces and back leaves, a practice making for completeness, but also confusion of calligraphy. This scribe's recension, which is earlier and more important than the new making of 1520, dates from the town-clerkship (1480[2]–1507) of John Boteler, beyond doubt, since a signed letter of his occurs elsewhere,[3] the scribe in question. Evidence of handwriting is notoriously untrustworthy, and we can only hazard what Boteler— no mean chronicler—found ready to hand in the *Leet Book*, and what he added with his own pen.

---

[1] See below, p. 645, for the order (1515) that craft by-laws are to be "registred in the Meyres boke."
[2] *Ib.* 474, but the writing begins in 1474.
[3] Letter-book A. 79, f. 52, back.

Apparently before his day the *Leet Book* records consisted of entries of orders of leet up to the year 1425, with divers other municipal matters, but that after 1425 the orders of leet were omitted,[1] though a set of scribes with slightly differing characteristics, whom I have called—somewhat inadequately [2]—types of B, and others called D and E continued to enter a chronicle of events, official elections, lists of names of collectors of fifteenths, and of the king's creditors within the city, with the method of procedure at royal visits.[3] This had continued until about 1475. Boteler's contribution to our historical knowledge consists not only in his very full and interesting continuation of the chronicle and official record during the years of his town-clerkship,[4] but in his recovery and transcription of the back orders of leet from 1425, an addition of immense importance to the historical value of the volume before us. In this latter task he appears to have been assisted by Scribe C,[5] an illiterate writer, of curious orthography, with whose handwriting his own mingles oddly, C sometimes entering the names of the leet jury, and B the orders of leet. Considerations of space often drove Boteler to practise a minute hand, especially in enlarging D's record; for that careless and illiterate scribe bequeathed a most ungenerous legacy of space to his successor.

Additions falling outside the ordinary character of the *Leet Book* are those made at its beginning and end by Scribe Z, otherwise Thomas Banester, town clerk in 1581, who sometimes concluded his entries with a flourishing monogram T.B., and there are subsequent entries by even later scribes.[6]

[1] See, however, pp. 117-19, leaf 47, for an exception to this rule, a leaf of leet entries, *without names of the jury* in the hand of a B type (chronicle) scribe.
[2] They differ from B and should have been put in a letter class apart.
[3] See below, pp. 262-3.
[4] See especially the Saunders and Prior Deram affairs in 1480, pp. 430 sqq.
[5] It is, of course, possible that C's entries took place before Boteler's time.
[6] See pp. 1-2, 7-19, 815-41. There is more definite information about the scribes in Appendix A. This reconstruction of the compilation of the *Leet Book* can only be of the most tentative character.

CHAPTER II

THE LEET AND COUNCILS

Earliest use of the word "leet"—The three Coventry courts—Early history of the Coventry manors—The Tripartite—Business of leets—Presentments—Framing of by-laws—Bills—The Twenty-four Jurats—Electoral jury of Twenty-four—The Forty-eight—The Common Council.

IN the earliest instances discoverable of the use of the word "leta" = leet, it denotes an area; "leta de Stanlei" or "de Brinkelow" appear as divisions of Knightlow Hundred [1]; later the term came to be applied to a court of justice administering the affairs of a certain district; "the Court-leet," says Prof. Vinogradoff, "is at bottom a portion of the Hundred Court in private hands." [2] Three of these courts are mentioned in these pages: the leet of the city, that of the prior of Coventry, and that of the tenants of the royal manor of Cheylesmore. Of the affairs of the first-named court the *Leet Book* was designed to furnish an enduring record; with the second, relic of the manorial jurisdiction of the Earls of Chester, the city officials came into conflict in 1464 [3]; to the third, allusion is made in 1480 when Prior Deram accused the citizens of laying their filth and builders' rubbish by his orchard wall, an accusation [4] the mayor countered by attributing the offence to the prior's tenants, who as such were amenable to Deram's jurisdiction and not to that of the leet of the city. "The seid offence," he said, ". . . is don be . . . the inhabitantez on that partie of the seid Priour, calde the Priours-parte, wherein he hath his Court of lete [5] and poiar to enquer

---

[1] Dugdale, *Warw.* (1656), 2. This occurs in a taxation roll of 1335.

[2] *Eng. Soc. in the Eleventh Century*, 97. See Dr. Bradley's explanation of the word, Part I. x. The Danish word *lægd* may be defined as a "division of the country for military conscription" (Round, *Feudal England*, 101).

[3] See below, p. 325. The steward of Cheylesmore is accused of "arting," *i. e.* inciting inhabitants of the city without the purview of this manor to sue in this court.

[4] *Ib.* 462.

[5] This franchise, which included "a great quarter of the city," passed to the Hales family after the Dissolution, and by 1573 the corporation had bought it, together with the Priory site, water-mill and dye-house, for £400: Fretton, *Bened. Mon.* (*Trans. B'ham. and Midl. Inst.* 1876), 14. The Coventry court of the Priory estate seems to have been held in the church, see Corp. MSS. C 20. There are two membranes of a frankpledge roll (*ib.* E 5) of the prior's various manors giving transactions of his court in Oct. 1380; Wasperton court includes also Honington: Southam includes Caldecote, Radbourne; Pakington includes

of all maner annusauncez ther don and hadd, and so of right the offenders owe to be punysshed there, and nott be the lete on the parte of the Maire and Cominalte."

This passage strikes the keynote of the city's early history, the two-fold manorial and parochial division of Coventry dating from the foundation of the monastery in the eleventh century. Elsewhere I have told of the rivalry between the lay manor, the Earl's-half or Chester fee, and the clerical manor, the Prior's-half[1]; of the prior's purchase of manorial rights over the Earl's-half in 1249, and the consequent subordination to clerical masters of the tenants of the lay estate; of the aid given to the Earl's-men by Isabella, widow of Edward II; of their rebellion and withdrawal from the prior's courts; and of their ultimate triumph in 1345 with the incorporation of the city. One result of this ancient quarrel between the queen, representative of the Cheylesmore—or Chester—interest and the Earl's-men on one side and the prior on the other persisted down to the days of the *Leet Book* record. A fruitful source of commotion in 1384[2] and at subsequent dates was the enclosure of certain common pastures by the Trinity gild. The gild avowed that the several rights of these fields were granted in compensation for the annual payment of £10 to the prior, due by the terms of the Tripartite[3] from the whole community but discharged by the brotherhood. The promised payment of this sum, a feature of the threefold composition drawn up in 1355 between Isabella, the prior, and lastly the Earl's-men in their corporate capacity of mayor, bailiffs and community, was an acknowledgment of the prior's surrender of leet and other franchises in the Earl's-half to the queen, who in her turn conveyed them to the corporation. By the Tripartite also the queen surrendered—with certain reservations

---

Snypston (Leicester); Potter's Marston includes Granborough, Southam; Scraptoft (Leic.); Sowe includes Stivichall, Sowe, Binley; Packwood; Coventry (Oct. 27); Coundon (same day); a court (date missing) includes Marston, Napton, Shuckborough, Hardwick. The offences punished are the ordinary ones of nuisances, obstructions, effusions of blood and infractions of the assizes of bread and ale. In the Wasperton-Honington court a fine of 5s. "leyrwite" is marked over against the name of a "nativa."

[1] M. D. Harris, *Life in an Old English Town*, 59 sqq., *Story of Coventry* (Mediæval Town Series), 56 sqq.

[2] See below, pp. 2-4, and for similar contracts cf. Tawney, *Agrar. Problem in Sixteenth Century*, p. 181.

[3] See pp. 2, 444, 454, also Burton MSS. ff. 98-103. In the Tripartite the prior claimed view of frankpledge or leet, portmanmote, fair, sherrif's tourn, gallows, assize of bread and ale, infangthief, waif, stray, free warren, pillory, tumbril, cuck-stool, and all that appertained to a leet or view of frankpledge.

The Leet and Councils.

—the exercise of leet jurisdiction within her manor of Cheylesmore, an area including several villages and townships, later co-extensive with the shire of the city.[1] In this manner did the corporation become possessed not only of the city leet franchises, but also of those within the surrounding villages, for which with other benefits they covenanted to pay £50 a year to the queen, a payment they thereafter continued to the queen's successors, Dukes of Cornwall and Princes of Wales. The fact that Isabella retained her suit of court from divers Cheylesmore tenants accounts for the separate existence of the courts leets and baron of the royal manor, and the rivalry which in 1464 sprang up between these and the courts of the city.

A court leet is primarily a court of justice. As such it appeared at Norwich in the thirteenth, at Manchester and Southampton in the sixteenth century; it had well-defined powers; it could execute summary criminal justice on the hand-having, back-bearing thief; it could punish those who baked or brewed contrary to the assize of bread or the assize of ale [2]; it received from the capital pledges [3] presentments of minor offences such as assaults with effusion of blood, and of nuisances redounding to the injury of the king's liege subjects. No witnesses were called; the criminal need not even be present; the presentment was enough; and the verdict could not be traversed, unless, through a writ of *Certiorari*,[4] the matter was transferred to a higher court. Payment of fines inflicted were enforced by actions of debt or levy of distress.[5] The court usually met at Easter and Michaelmas,[6] the lord's steward or—in this case where the lord's place was filled by an urban corporation—the mayor and bailiffs occupying the position of president.[7] Like the

---

[1] On the transformation of certain neighbouring villages and the city itself into a county, see pp. 748–9. It was a natural development of the Tripartite. On the similar grant to Norwich, which involved that city in lawsuits, see Hudson, *Rec. Norwich*, I. lxxx–i.

[2] A certain definite price was laid down by authorities varying with the price of grain.

[3] Heads of tithings wherein all males were enrolled in bodies of nominally twelve persons.

[4] See p. 684 and note.

[5] *Ib.* 296, 804; Hearnshaw, *Leet Jurisdiction*, 139.

[6] The bailiffs of Coventry were elected at the Michaelmas leet, whereas the new officials under the corporation, the mayor, chamberlains, and others were elected on St. Paul's day (Jan. 25). Thus it appears that the holding of the leet is older than the incorporation. Constables were also chosen at the leet.

[7] Curiously on one occasion the justices of the peace are associated with the mayor as presiding officials; see below, p. 36.

gemot of the ancient township the leet's functions included the framing of by-laws, so these in no wise contravened the law of the land.

Information about the police and judicial procedure of the Coventry leet is scanty and hard to come by. "Inquiry is made at every leet holden within the city," said the mayor and his brethren in 1480, "concerning the stoppers of the common river,"[1] an assertion implying a certain amount of normal leet activity at the sittings of the court. Several presentments of nuisances are recorded, and in one instance the amount of the amercement laid on a particular offender;[2] other presentments point out the existence of uncovered drains,[3] broken pavements,[4] use of conduit water for brewing,[5] stoppage of floodgates,[6] waterpipes,[7] and so forth[8]; others the violation of trade rules by a wholesale traffic in hides, or faulty workmanship,[9] or breach of the regulation which forbade citizens to sue in courts outside the city.[10] These presentments took the form of bills, and in 1507 the chamberlains and wardens were ordered to bring in at every leet a bill "of all such faults and nuisances as be within their office."[11] Forfeitures for breach of leet ordinances furnished some of the incomings of the mayor,[12] and these were "affeered" or assessed by four worshipful persons selected by him for the office.[13]

The aspect of the Coventry leet, whereof the fullest record remains, is not, however, judicial, but legislative. The framing of by-laws, inherent, so sixteenth-century legists declared, in the court leet, is but a small step from making inquiries under countless heads concerning breaches of already existing law.[14] In Coventry the leet by-laws were grounded on bills presented to the mayor four days before the assembly of the court, by any individual or group of

[1] See below, p. 455.
[2] *Ib.* 105. The bill was put up by the commons of the Cross Cheaping Ward; the offender, John Stafford, who had interfered with the conduit, was amerced 40*d*.
[3] *Ib.* 609. [4] *Ib.* 607. [5] *Ib.* 548. [6] *Ib.* 196. [7] *Ib.* 190.
[8] See also *ib.* 622. On one occasion (*ib.* 186) the mayor was ordered to take with him the worthy men of the leet and make sight of the Red Ditch within a short time, so that its defects might be amended.
[9] *Ib.* 581, 638.
[10] *Ib.* 194. See also Bateson, *Rec. Leicester*, II. xxxv.
[11] See below, p. 609. [12] *Ib.* 187.
[13] *Ib.* 186. The process of amercement was threefold: the jurors present; the president declares the offenders at mercy; the affeerors assess the fine (Hearnshaw, *op. cit.* 135).
[14] *Ib.* 64. The inquiries can be classed under ninety heads.

The Leet and Councils.

men who laboured under a grievance or desired to amend in some way or other the practices of their fellow-citizens. "Allso hit is ordenyd," the *Leet Book* runs, "þat all maner men that will sew here aftur remedy for to haue by ordynaunce of the lete generall or specyall þat they mak hur bylles, and delyuer hem to the maiour iiij dayes before every lete, þat the maiour may tak afor the lete the generall councell of this cite xxiiij to comyn of the maters conteyned in hur bylles for the mor spede of the day of the lete and that no byllez aftur the forsaid day be receuyd."[1] In spite of a little vagueness in the order—we are ignorant of the significance of the distinction between a general and special ordinance of leet, and are unable to fix with any certainty the meaning of the "general council of this city"—it makes clear the fact that the mayor and twenty-four councillors [2] overlooked leet petitions before the day of assembly, thereby controlling to a great extent the legislation of the court. Bills were said to be "endorsed"[3] with the decision of the leet upon their contents, such endorsements representing, no doubt, the ordinances whereof the bulk of the *Leet Book* is composed. Occasionally a bill would be rejected or "respited"; "que petitio respectuatur," the endorsement of the prior's petition to have lands in severalty, recalls the stereotyped "le roi s'avisera" of parliament.[4]

The headings of the bills preserved are very various :—

"As Maire, Ballyfs, Chamburlens, and autres bonez gentez del enquest"[5] is the exordium of the Trinity gild bill in 1384; "to you worshipfull and Reuerent masturs and souerens of this wurthy cite"[6] is the beginning of the petition for a reward; "to the worshipfull astates, mair and his peres of the cite of Couentre,"[7] "to you fullwurshipfull Meir, Recordour, bayles and to all your discrete counsell,"[8] "to the reuerent Meire of the Cite of Couentre and to halle the wurthy men of the same,"[9] "to all the wurthy men of this present lete,"[10] these addresses, so different in form, argue that the power behind the leet lay with a wider body than the presiding officers. The term "bones gentz del enquest," which occurs in 1384, refers without doubt to the twenty-four "honest and lawful" elected

---

[1] See pp. 30–1.
[2] Cf. p. 32, where the mayor, recorder, and bailiffs are to take eight or twelve of the general council to consider craft rules.
[3] *Ib.* 105, 115–16.
[4] *Ib.* 115. The petition for aldermen (*ib.* 258) is passed over in silence. The leet records were "filed" (*ib.* 194).
[5] *Ib.* 3.   [6] *Ib.* 36.   [7] *Ib.* 105.
[8] *Ib.* 115.   [9] *Ib.* 181.   [10] *Ib.* 257.

jurats,[1] by whose "common assent"[2] all ordinances of the court were passed, and whose names immediately follow the record of the date and place of the sessions and the names of the presiding officers. What legislative powers—if any—the suitors of the court, the general body of the commons, possessed is not clear, but it seems probable that there was a certain attendance of people outside the strictly official class during this part of the proceeding.[3]

Later testimony goes to prove—contemporary evidence failing—that this body of twenty-four jurats was not *elected* as we understand the word, but selected by the mayor (alone or in concert with his council) with due regard to seniority from among members of the official class. According to Elizabethan practice the mayor could not impanel a leet jury without the consent and agreement of his brethren of the council-house,[4] while in making a return of the names of those who were to elect officers for the ensuing year he was to select such as had previously held office "as they shall be in ancientie," the validity of any omission to be reserved for the council's decision.[5] Neither the leet jury nor the electoral twenty-four were absolutely permanent bodies: they differ slightly from election to election and from leet to leet;[6] yet inasmuch as the great majority of the names correspond, and are arranged each year in

---

[1] They present the bills "per sacramentum," p. 3.

[2] Per commune assensum proborum et legalium hominum ad hanc letam electorum," *ib.* 4, 19, 36.

[3] "Be the avise of all the wurthy of the seid lete [the Twenty-four] and all oder apon the same lete beeng" (*ib.* 116). See also *ib.* 688, where "commons" are mentioned in this connection.

[4] *First Council Book*, Corp. MSS. A 14 (a), leaf 867, back. Prof. Hearnshaw (*op. cit.*, 191) suggests that in normal cases the town clerk "drew up the panel, placing first the officials in descending order ('there was a regular and recognized succession of offices,' *ib.* 190), and then filling up with other burgesses; that he next handed his proposed panel to the sheriff, who made such modifications as he thought fit, and that finally the sheriff laid the revised list 'pro forma' before the assembly for confirmation."

[5] *Second Leet Book*, Corp. MSS. A 3 (b), f. 23 (42 Eliz., Apr. 8, 1600). Perhaps in earlier days something of discretion had been left to the mayor in this respect, but by the sixteenth century the aldermanic clique of the council-house had become omnipotent.

[6] Taking at random (pp. 302, 304, 305) the Michaelmas and Easter Leet juries of 1457-8, and the intermediate (Jan. 1458) electoral twenty-four, we find thirty-five names in all, of which the three bodies were successively formed: sixteen names from the electoral twenty-four are identical with those of the Michaelmas Jury, while twenty-one names from the Easter Jury occur in one or other of the two former bodies. The only name I cannot trace as a previous official's is Joh. Honyburn's (*ib.* 304); but he was a man of substance, and had subscribed towards the purchase of a charter, *ib.* 221. See also *ib.* 642 for an electoral twenty-four composed of "late mayors and sheriffs" with "other honest persons."

much the same order as the last, the list being invariably headed by the master of the Trinity gild and the justices of the peace,[1] they can have differed little from the close permanent bodies of twenty-four, such as were evolved during the fourteenth and fifteenth centuries at Leicester, Norwich,[2] and many other towns of England.

Thus at the outset we perceive a near connection between the leet jury of twenty-four and the "discreet council," the "mayor and his peers," the "masters and sovereigns" of the city. Bodies of the quasi-sacred number of twelve,[3] and multiples of twelve, *i.e.* twenty-four and forty-eight, occur with surprising uniformity in English town government, and by the fifteenth century had become mostly close, permanent councils, executive, deliberative, legislative, independent of the will of the community. In Leicester the Twenty-four appears as early as 1225; by 1489 a council of this number had made itself supreme; the gradual evolution of a permanent body of twenty-four aldermen in Norwich is shown in a series of documents extending from the end of the thirteenth century until 1417. York[4] possessed a body of twenty-four in the fourteenth century, as well as one of twelve and another of forty-eight; and Worcester[5] in the succeeding century was ruled by two councils, one containing twenty-four and another forty-eight members. At Coventry numbers were less hard and fast; late officers[6] seem to have formed a class from which the mayor summoned his council, the administrative, deliberative and legislative bodies which controlled the government of the city. In many towns it is easy to mark off one council from another, to speak in definite terms of the

---

[1] The position of the justices of the peace is curious. In 1420 (p. 21) they put forth a "rate of wages" with the assent of the leet; in 1421 (*ib.* 36) they appear in connection with the mayor as presidents; the mayor's name being followed by that of J. Weston, A. Hiton and his fellows (socii) the Lord King's justices of Coventry, though Hiton's name heads the jury, and Weston (recorder) is not named thereon. In 1422 (*ib.* 42) the names of six jurymen head a list of thirty, *not* twenty-four; some of the six are undoubtedly justices.

[2] Bateson, *op. cit.*, I. 34, II. xlvi–viii; Hudson, *op. cit.*, xxxv–lxx.

[3] The judicial reforms of Henry II helped to stereotype twelve as a jury number. For the Twelve in Coventry and their connection with the incorporation of the city, see below, p. xxv. The twelve "lawmen" of Lincoln formed probably the borough jury (Birch, *Charters of Lincoln*, viii).

[4] Sellers, *Mem. Bk.*, 39.

[5] Toulmin Smith, *Eng. Gilds*, 376–409.

[6] Late mayors seem to have been *ex-officio* members of the council; see below, p. 648, where an offending mayor is to be cast out of the council of the city; but this penalty is not attached to other officers.

Assembly,[1] Common Council, the Twelve, Twenty-four or Forty-eight. In Coventry various councils seem on occasions to blend into one another; their constitution lacks definiteness; the town government long maintained something of the elasticity of earlier times; not until we approach the days of James I's charter of 1621 does the governing body of the city assume that rigid formal shape which lasted during the period of municipal decadence until the passing of the Municipal Corporation Act in 1835.

Besides the Twenty-four, the electoral jury and the jury of leet, two other bodies appear to be of great importance in the constitution of the city; first, the mayor's council, with a nucleus of the executive and a few permanent members, forerunner of the grand council of aldermen under the charter of 1621, at one time merging into the Forty-eight,[2] and again shrinking into a quorum of the mayor and six aldermen;[3] and secondly, a larger body of varying numbers, representative of the ten wards[4] summoned by the mayor to express the popular will concerning the common lands,[5] or money matters,[6] or to witness grants made under the common seal,[7] and consisting of late officials coupled sometimes with commoners who had never borne municipal office.[8] Of these the first council represented the governing body, the second the power of the community over the executive; but the distinction is somewhat hard to maintain, since the presence of officials and the summons of the mayor played a great part in the formation of both bodies; moreover, each can be identified with the Forty-eight, the number of the expanded mayor's

---

[1] This word seldom occurs in the *Leet Book*, e. g. p. 626.
[2] See below, p. xxv.
[3] See p. 517. The numbers of this smaller body vary, *e. g.* twelve in 1503 (*ib.* 602), eleven in 1506 (*ib.* 604). This reveals the state of affairs after the creation of aldermen, first mentioned in 1477 (*ib.* 420); before the numbers had been rather higher, *e g.* fourteen in 1426 (*ib.* 102), fifteen in 1427 (*ib.* 109). Occasionally the numbers even exceed forty-eight (*ib.* 206). Late mayors were *ex-officio* members of the council (*ib.* 648). The mayor's council seems to have the power of making by-laws, *ib.* 22. See also *ib.* 35, "ordenyd by no lete, nor be counsell of the maiour and his peerys."
[4] Cf. the common council of London, where, in 1384, the members were elected by wards (*Letter-Book* H, 227). In Coventry, however, the usual rule was that they should not be elected by the wardsmen, but selected by the mayor.
[5] See below, pp. 3–4, 351, 513.
[6] *Ib.* 60, 62, 119, 174. See also *ib.* 150, when five, six or seven are summoned from each ward to take council about the measures.
[7] *Ib.* 40. A smaller council had been at first summoned.
[8] *Ib.* 244. "These worthy men and also commoners . . . ordained." The representative principle came into force in the sixteenth century (*ib.* 633, 730).

The Leet and Councils.

council in 1423,[1] and of the common council in 1477.[2] It seems as if the mayor's council might have its ancestry in the Twelve[3] lawmen or jurats who meet us at the gain of the Incorporation Charter, though at other times its numbers recall the Twenty-four[4] and—on special occasions—the Forty-eight. While the common council having control over divers matters touching the community tends to supersede in the sixteenth century the large, irregular assemblies of the Wards.[5] A difficulty arises with regard to the "general council," whereto reference is made in the so-called proclamation of John Leeder;[6] what precise interpretation can be placed on the words it is impossible to determine; probably this council consisted of such as had borne office, and were therefore liable to receive the summons of the mayor, who was the pivot on which seems to revolve the whole constitution of the city.

The common council of Coventry, though roughly speaking it inherited the powers of the Forty-eight commoners, whom the leet of 1422 ordered the mayor to summon "from every ward a certain" to hear accounts and witness grants made under the common seal,[7] must be identified as far as *personnel* is concerned rather with the official Forty-eight,[8] first heard of at the mayor's election in the following year. This second Forty-eight is something of an anomaly; a double Twenty-four,[9] it consisted—in its inception at least—half of the electoral jury and half of the mayor's nominees, strengthening the ruling body on its legislative side, and in no wise representing the controlling power of the

---

[1] See p. 44.   [2] *Ib.* 421.
[3] The mayor-lists (Corp. MSS. A 37, 43, 48 *et passim*) usually begin with the names of the twelve men who purchased the liberties in 1345.
[4] See p. 572.
[5] Perhaps there were occasionally summoned (see p. 626) "the most honest commoners of the city to the number of 48 persons or more."
[6] This proclamation is written in Scribe A's hand, which is a hundred years later than John Leeder's time, and is probably later than 1450, since the order forbidding the carrying of weapons except in the case of a knight or squire, (p. 29) recalls a Privy Council ordinance of that year (Bateson, *op. cit.*, II. xxxv; Rymer, *Fœdera,* xi, 262. A similar set of ordinances at Leicester and Worcester belong to 1467 (see Bateson, *op. cit.*, II. 287). For the general council see above, pp. 31, 32.
[7] See below, p. 42.
[8] *Ib.* 44, 68-9. The members of the Forty-eight clearly were drawn from the official class; so also were the majority of those who formed the common council of 1477. *Ib.* p. 421.
[9] On the first nomination (p. 44) the council is oddly arranged in companies of 11 (12 with the mayor) and 36. The number was not restricted to 48 absolutely; the expression "48 and more" occurs (*ib.* 258); nor was the nomination of permanent character, cf. the lists on p. 44 and pp. 67-8.

community. Whether it was intended to act as a counterpoise to less officially constituted bodies, such as the obscure and apparently short-lived assembly of the Forty-eight commoners,[1] or to the " hall " of the wardsmen, it is impossible to say, nor is it easy to trace its development throughout the sixteenth century, by reason of the gap in the leet records in the latter half of this period. At first, however, its business was legislative; the electoral Twenty-four of 1423 laid down as the special function of the Forty-eight that its members should "ordain and put in good rule all manner of good ordinances that are profitable to the said city";[2] after 1445 this body transacted business through a quorum of twelve persons;[3] in 1477, however, when a new constitution had come into force,[4] the Forty-eight was revived as a common council whose ordinances appear to have had the same validity as those of the leet.[5] Later, in the early seventeenth century, we find the Forty-eight apparently split into two bodies[6] again, and at warfare the one with the other, the omnipotent self-elected council-house of the mayor and aldermen evidently seeking to deprive the common council, then consisting of twenty-five members, of all initiative and proper control in the administration of the affairs of the city. After a short struggle the inferior council, utterly worsted in the conflict,

---

[1] In York in the fourteenth century a body of Forty-eight was drawn from the artificers or crafts, Sellers, *op. cit.* v. ix. At Worcester the Forty-eight were commoners, Toulmin Smith, *op. cit.* p. 386. At Coventry the forty-eight auditors were occasionally summoned, see below, pp. 54, 65, 66, though it is not distinctly said that the mayor summoned commoners; later the practice of summoning forty-eight auditors appears to have died out, though the evidence is not conclusive, *ib.* 114, 116. See also *ib.* 633, where it is said that a company of forty-eight was chosen by the whole body of the city to view the common fields.

[2] See below, p. 44.

[3] The members of the Forty-eight were the most sufficient men "at home" on any given occasion; disobedience to their ordinances was punished by a fine of 7s. 6d., *ib.* 157, 421, 520. The position of the Forty-eight was probably strengthened by the charter, dated July 7, 23 Hen. VI, which contained a proviso allowing the mayor, bailiffs, and commonalty to amend, correct, make, ordain or add to any custom. Cf. the letter of Richard III, *ib.* 523, for a further confirmation of this. See also Hudson, *op. cit.* liv–v.

[4] There seems to be no new charter about this time, but a royal letter is addressed to the "mayor, *aldermen*, sheriffs, and *common council,*" see p. 420. See also p. 421 for the "common council."

[5] See p. 681, where the business under a leet heading is continued "at this common council day." On another occasion (*ib.* 661) it was agreed that the mayors' council should dispose of overstanding leet legislative business. Earlier we find the leet asked to confirm the ordinances of the Forty-eight, *ib.* 258.

[6] In reality into two bodies of Thirty-one (electoral jury) and Twenty-five (common council), *ib.* 836.

sank, by the terms of James I's charter of 1621, into a mere advisory committee and thereafter into nullity, no common council having been summoned by the executive, say the Municipal Commissioners of 1835, for over two hundred years.[1]

CHAPTER III

ORDERS OF LEET

The leet at Coventry the nucleus of municipal activity—By-laws on sanitation—Morality—Treatment of the poor—The school—Relations with the Church—The holy cake—Resistance of the crafts—The gild of the Nativity—Proceedings in courts Christian—The barbers—The dyers—The victualling crafts and foreign competition—The position of women.

IT was the court leet of Coventry, not as in some other towns the assembly,[2] the common hall[3] or the meeting of the gild merchant,[4] which became in the fifteenth century the centre for the legislative activity, which is so marked a characteristic of urban life at this period. Some of these by-laws—such as those forbidding the bearing of weapons, more than three day's exposure of meat, the indulgence in sport, gaming, or too costly apparel—were but the echo of legislation in parliament or of ordinances passed by the Privy Council.[5] More often the orders of leet were the outcome of local needs, representing the nice adjustment of various

---

[1] *Report of the Municipal Commissioners* (Meridew, Coventry), p. 11. See below, pp. 835–7, and *Second Leet Book*, Corp. MSS. A 3 (b) ff. 37, 51, for details of this struggle between 1605 and 1617. The common council in 1605 were elected by the mayor and his brethren, the bailiffs and "a certain number of the commonalty (thereunto called)," at the great leet—the Michaelmas leet, which, as this record shows, then elected all officials—members being removable by the mayor and his brethren with the common council's consent. The council had a certain amount of control over the disposal of the city lands; took part in the election of the mayor; and one of their members had the key of the chest containing the common seal. Some of these powers were subsequently curtailed, even before the 1621 charter, by the provision whereof the common council became entirely dependent on the council-house, which body appointed and could remove the members.

[2] For the assembly (congregatio) at Northampton, see *Northampton Rec.* I. 241 *et passim*.

[3] Bateson, *op. cit.* II. 287 sqq.

[4] Toulmin Smith, *op. cit.* pp. 376–409 (Worcester). The gild was a centre of burghal activity in the towns of mesne lords, where the borough courts were not under the control of the burgesses: see Gross, *Gild-merchant*, 1. 62, 90.

[5] Bateson, *op. cit.* II. xxxiv. See also below, pp. 630, 690.

local interests, and touching every department of a citizen's life, his food, his work, his conduct. The order against bearing of weapons, hard to enforce in those troublous times, aimed at ensuring the preservation of the peace,[1] and the frequently repeated provisions to ensure a clean river,[2] an unobstructed water-supply[3] and the proper disposal of refuse,[4] even if they failed sometimes of their object, at least indicate a desire for wholesome surroundings. Streets were to be lighted at night-time[5] and watch duly kept;[6] pavements[7] and wells[8] to be repaired when necessary; while there were provisions made to guard against outbreaks of fire,[9] and obstruction in the streets.[10]

Several orders of leet touch the question of morality; any one entertaining a woman of ill-fame and refusing to put her away on due warning should lose, so the order ran, 20s. at each default, half to the church and half to the bailiffs:[11] while a late mayor "slandered in the sins of avowtre, fornication or usury" and refusing to amend his ways, was to be deprived of his cloak and council, and never rise to be master of the Trinity gild.[12] It was a fear, no doubt, that single women living alone might betake themselves to ill-ways of livelihood, which caused the leet to issue such stringent orders that they should go to service,[13] or take a chamber with "an honest person," who would answer for their good behaviour; while the orders against daily and weekly bowling by poor craftsmen "leaving their business at home that they should live by,"[14] or against the habits of the poorest sort, who, according to an order of 1547, "do sit all day in the ale-house drinking and playing at the cards and tables, and spend all they can get prodigally upon

---

[1] See below, pp. 28, 29. [2] *Ib.* 720–1 *et passim.* [3] *Ib.* 105.
[4] The chief place for disposing of refuse was outside the gates, particularly at the Grey-friar gate, the "town's-end," *ib.* 191, 425; see *ib.* 552 for the weekly coming of the refuse cart and the quarterly rate. Cf. *ib.* 194, 234, 389, 555 *et passim.* There were two great sewers, one from Much Park Street, by Grey-friar Lane to Jordan Well, and another from the "Peacock" in Broad-gate to West-Orchard.
[5] *Ib.* 234, 777.
[6] *Ib.* 253, 707, cf. the case of Chester quoted Sellers, *op. cit.* xiii.
[7] *Ib.* 767. [8] *Ib.* 201.
[9] It was ordered that houses were not to be thatched with straw, see below, p. 389; for provision of fire-buckets, *ib.* 549.
[10] Order against ducks going in the streets, *ib.* 27, cf. Bateson, *op. cit.* II. 292. See also below, p. 803; and for slaughtering of cattle, *ib.* 32.
[11] *Ib.* 219–20, 278, 279, 545, 552.
[12] *Ib.* 544. [13] *Ib.* 545, 568.
[14] *Ib.* 656. For encouragement of archery, and regulations against "koyttyng and boollyng" see *ib.* 661, 572.

themselves to the high displeasure of God and their own impoverishing, whereas if it were spent at home in their own houses their wives and children should have part thereof," [1] display a zeal for the moral and economic welfare of the people, that would provoke great resentment nowadays were it embodied in legislation.

A section of orders of leet deal with another important social question, the case of the wandering and impotent poor. Enclosures, the decay of tillage, so marked in the midland districts, and the disbandment of bodies of retainers by the nobility after the Wars of the Roses were mainly answerable for the Tudor problem of the sturdy beggar. The policy of the leet with regard to vagabonds, who first made their appearance, as far as Coventry was concerned, under Edward IV, as a political rather than a social inconvenience,[2] was simply that of expulsion;[3] "vagabonds and beggars" "mighty in body" must void the city, the order ran, within three days after the proclamation of this ordinance.[4] Nevertheless the practice obtained of discriminating between these, and the "impotent and needy," the latter being suffered to ask alms, and to have, in testimony of this permission, "a token of their bag of the sign of the Elephant," *i.e.* the arms of the city.[5] Meanwhile every effort was made both by public authority and private charity to combat two special factors of poverty, dearth and unemployment, by ploughing up the commons and sowing them with corn,[6] by loans to manufacturers,[7] the purchase of unsaleable cloth;[8] and in 1547 —by means of a census taken by the aldermen of all the inhabitants of every ward, their families, length of residence and capacity for labour—to find employment for the workless; the incorrigibly idle, it was decreed, should suffer banishment, but those burdened by age, impotency or "a multitude of children" should be relieved out of the town chest.[9]

---

[1] See below, pp. 786, 808. The restrictions with regard to licensing at Coventry were in advance of the legislation of the day, *ib.* 771, 781.
[2] *Ib.* 374.
[3] For search made for "hazarders, dicers and carders," see *ib.* 538–9.
[4] *Ib.* 568, 652, 658; constables are ordered to search for and "avoid" out of the city all "vagabonds and mighty beggars," *ib.* 712.
[5] *Ib.* 677. This custom of giving a special licence to beg was adopted in Coventry rather than Norwich, where it followed on the legislation of 22 H. VIII, c. 12. See Tingey, *Norwich Rec.* II. xcviii.
[6] See below, pp. 630, 719.   [7] *Ib.* 658–9.   [8] *Ib.* 791.
[9] *Ib.* pp. 783–4: Cf. the census taken in 1520 (*ib.* 674–5), when corn was dear. See also Tingey, *Norwich Rec.* II. xcvii. for the provision of a stock of wheat by the aldermen of that city during dearth.
This was 12 years after a collection in churches for the poor was made

The orders of leet[1] reveal the existence of a town grammar school—probably supported by the Trinity gild[2]—as early as 1425, and the rivalry that had sprung up between this and the Priory grammar school fourteen years later. Earlier than this it would seem that Coventry teachers had fallen under suspicion of Lollard sympathies[3] and the heads of the Priory school, founded as early as 1303, may well have "grudged" and "moved" at the desire of the townsfolk to "put" their children "to a teacher of grammar" free from monastic control. How the dispute ended is not revealed, but the complaint of Prior Deram in 1480 and the long-standing quarrel over the non-payment of murage dues, show that relations between the convent and the city often lacked harmony during the period covered by the *Leet Book* record.[4] In other matters besides the instruction of youth the secular power in Coventry encroached upon the province usually reserved for the exercise of ecclesiastical authority; hence church affairs appear to a great extent under secular control. The mayor appointed the hermit occupying S. Margaret's hermitage on Gosford Green;[5] the leet ordered the churchwardens[6] to present their accounts after due warning under a heavy penalty in like manner as municipal officers.[7]

In continental towns the erection of a belfry (*berefridus*) was a symbol of communal independence, and at Coventry the leet regulated the ringing of church bells.[8] Ordinances passed by the same authority frequently refer to the holy cake whereof the provision was a parochial obligation, infraction of these orders being punished by the levy of a monetary fine devoted to lay uses.[9] The

---

compulsory by 27 H. VIII, c. 25. In order to prevent immigration of the unfit, every newcomer had to be examined by the mayor and alderman of the ward as to his capacity before he was allowed to take a house in the city.

[1] See below, pp. 101, 118, 190, also Mr. Leach in *Vict. County Hist. Warw.*, II. 318–19.
[2] The salary of the schoolmaster of Bablake was paid by the Trinity gild at the Reformation, Leach, *op. cit.* II. 320.
[3] Abram, *Eng. Life and Manners in later Middle Ages*, 206; a commission addressed to the prior and mayor ordering the arrest of all offenders against an act forbidding Lollard teachers. For Will Grene, "Skole maister," see above, p. 177. [4] See pp. 443 sqq. 595–8. [5] *Ib.* 118, 227.
[6] See for other allusions to the churchwardens, *ib.* 110, "church–reeves of S. Michael's," and *ib.* 446.
[7] *Ib.* 296. The penalty was 40s. payable half to the mayor and half to the church; cf. the fines against morality, *ib.* 220.
[8] *Ib.* 335, 338, 585.
[9] *Ib.* 417, 669, 680, 739.

Orders of Leet.   xxxi

holy cake (*panis benedictus*),[1] distributed after the mass to those who had not communicated, " and cut according for every man's degree "[2] by the deacons or clerks, was furnished by every householder of both parishes in turn, the "course" beginning, says the *Leet Book* in 1539, "at Seynt Margettes Chappell" beyond Gosford-gate, and keeping "the south side of the street" in like manner as the obligation of watch and ward.[3] Of other ecclesiastical matters the court leet took cognizance, insisting that the priests supported by the crafts should perform their duty of repeating mass on work-days as well as holy-days, "in encreasing of divine service daily to be sungen in the parish churches" of the city.[4]

The conflict between ecclesiastical and secular powers—not nearly so marked a feature in Coventry in the fifteenth as in the preceding century—is involved in some small degree in the great struggle between the corporation and the crafts, so characteristic of the industrial history of the city during the *Leet Book* period. Abundant evidence is forthcoming of the control exercised by the corporation over the iron and wool-working, victualling and other crafts in whose hands the trade and industry of the city lay ; their rules were inspected ;[5] their fines regulated ;[6] their charges fixed ;[7] their work examined ;[8] their combinations crushed.[9] The leet in

[1] Cf. Littlehales, *Rec. London City Church*, II. lx, 35, 247, 328 ; *Ch. Accounts S. Edmund and S. Thomas, Sarum.* xviii. Addy, *Church and Manor*, 288–92.
[2] See W. Legg, *Book of the Parish Clerk*, 57–63, and Sharp, *op. cit.* 122–4 for the "Office of the Deacon" in Trinity Church.
[3] See below, pp. 738–9. Cf. the elaborate directions at Stanford in the Vale, Berkshire, Legg, *op. cit.* 96–7.
[4] See below, pp. 544–5. A curious point is the ownership of the cardmakers' (later cappers') chapel of S. Thomas in S. Michael's, see *ib.* pp. 707–10, Sharp, *op. cit.* 30–1 Addy, *op. cit.* 428–9. In the dispute between the prior and Corporation (see below, pp. 446–7, 460–1,) the former asserts that the "new building" of S. Michael's is upon the churchyard, and erected without his license, as rector, whereas the latter affirm that it was erected on the highway. This "new building" was very probably the cardmakers' chapel, which, according to a fairly reliable list of mayors or annals in the possession of Mr. Eynon, was "founded out of the ground" by this fellowship in 1465.
[5] See below, pp. 29, 32 ; cf. *ib.* 170, 222. In 1515 craft by-laws were ordered to be registered in the "Mayor's book" [? the *Leet Book*], *ib.* 645. The rules entered in the *Leet Book* are the barbers', cappers' (2) and smiths', *ib.* 224–6, 572–4, 670–3, 743–6.   [6] *Ib.* 654–5.
[7] For cooks and halfpenny pies, see *ib.* 111 ; the mayor and six or eight of his brethren are to "see reformation of the price of shoes, botewes and boots," *ib.* 624.
[8] For searching of tiles, see *ib.* 188 ; of leather, *ib.* 277, 712 ; of pewter-ware, *ib.* 554 ; of the cloth of weavers and fullers, *ib.* 639, 656–7 ; of candles, *ib.* 703 ; of cardmakers' wares, *ib.* 793–4.
[9] See Corp. MSS. B, 35, 38, 47, and *Story of Coventry*, pp. 228–9, for the patents suppressing new *gilds* ; for the fullers and tailors' gild, see below, p. xxxii.

1435, for example, observing the evils which sprang from the union of several processes undergone by iron in the workshops of a few capitalist masters, entirely revolutionized the organization of that industry by limiting to two the branches of the work in which any employer of labour might engage, a specimen of the drastic remedies employed by mediaeval local authorities, such as now-a-days no similar body would have the power or hardihood to administer.[1] But if the corporation was despotic the crafts were rebellious, and when occasion served made every possible effort to throw off the yoke. Thus the persistence of the fullers and tailors, founders of the Nativity gild,[2] the unmanageableness of the dyers, whereof the first evidence appears in 1415[3] when they took for their own use "the flower of the woad," the insubordination of the bakers,[4] who in 1484 rather than comply with the mayor's order departed *en masse* and took sanctuary at Baginton, leaving the city "destitute of bread," the prolonged struggle of the native butchers to exclude "foreign" competition,[5] all furnish evidence of the defiant attitude of the crafts towards the corporation, or the pertinacity they displayed in pursuit of their own interests irrespective of the well-being of the community.

It is not always possible to disentangle the various trade[6] and labour problems in mediæval industry; each craft, each set of workmen, had their distinct grievances, which added to the general unrest: but on some points workmen and minor craftsmen were at one; they wished to better their economic position and to give it solidarity by combination—hence, in spite of prohibitive patents

---

[1] See below, pp. 180 sqq. The leet, finding that the smiths who had all the branches of the iron trade in their hands passed on badly-wrought material, decreed that only smiths and brakemen should work together, and girdlemen and cardmakers. This instance is well worth study as showing the beginnings of the capitalist system. For a preliminary attempt to regulate this craft, see *ib.* 115.

[2] See below, p. xxxiii, and also below, p. 234, where the crafts are separated by order of leet.

[3] *Rot. Parl.*, iv, 75. See for the fullers, tailors and dyers, Harris, *Story of Coventry*, 219–21. In 1533 the leet evidently made to thrust on the dyers' craft unwelcome members, one a draper, *ib.* 704, 714.

[4] *Ib.* 519.   [5] *Ib.* 803.

[6] In the case of minor craftsmen of the woollen industry, trade rivalries with the drapers concerning the ways of dealing directly with the public in the sale of cloth may have stirred up discontent. The powerfulness of the drapers is shown by the fact that in the list of craftsmen providing armour in 1449-50 out of 59 drapers 16 had been municipal officers, including 6 mayors and 6 bailiffs; this compares with 7 out of 37 dyers with 1 mayor and 2 bailiffs, 2 out of 57 weavers with 1 bailiff, and none at all out of 64 tailors and shearmen or 27 fullers. See below, pp. 246 sqq.

Orders of Leet. xxxiii

obtained by the town rulers,[1] the formation and, after compulsory dissolution, the re-formation of gilds during this period; hence, also, the attempt to give to craft unions particular sanctity and effectiveness—since oath-breach was an offence punishable at ecclesiastical law—by requiring from all members an oath to obey the rules of the fellowship.

The pertinacity with which the minor craftsmen strove to maintain their existence as a licensed body-corporate can be illustrated by the action of the fullers and tailors, a combination that meets us in the *Leet Book* in 1448.[2]

Licensed in 1384, the gild was composed, according to the testimony of a commission of inquiry held soon after its incorporation, of labourers, inferior artificers and strangers, and was founded, says the same authority, to resist the mayor and other officials and not for welfare of souls.

Suppressed at this time, it re-appeared *possibly* under the guise of the journeymen fraternities of S. Anne and of S. George,[3] which, in spite of patents prohibiting the creation of fresh gilds, arose in 1406, 1414 and 1425, and *certainly* after the suppression of these, as the Gild of the Nativity of the fullers and tailors in 1439; and though the crafts were severed nine years later by order of leet the gild persisted, outlasting the Reformation, and holding land and buildings, including the chapel of S. George beyond Gosford Gate.[4]

The activity of the gild of S. George, whose members are officially described, in language suspiciously resembling that in the case of the fraternity of the Nativity, as journeymen, servants of tailors and other artificers,[5] finds its counterpart in 1424 in the strike of the journeymen weavers, wherein questions of wages, the employment of outsiders, with other matters touching the journeymen's funds, wherewith they maintained a church light, were in dispute. The terms of the arbitration show how successfully the workmen maintained their position.[6] It appears, however, less secure in the sixteenth century, when further testimony is forth-

---

[1] Corp. MSS. B. 35, 38, 47. See for a fuller account of these labour troubles my article in *Victoria County Hist. Warw.*, II. 154–5.
[2] See below, p. 234.
[3] Corp. MSS. B. 40, 41, 43, and *Vict. County Hist.*, ut supra. There is much misdating in the catalogue of Coventry MSS. on this point.
[4] Corp. MSS. B. 63. Green, *Town Life in the Fifteenth Cent.*, II. 208.
[5] Cf. the insubordination of the "yoman taillours" of London in 1415, Sharpe, *Letter-Book*, I. 136–7; and of the bakers in 1441, *ib.* K. 263–6.
[6] See below, pp. 91 sqq.

coming concerning labour combinations. In 1518 journeymen of every calling were forbidden by leet to make any assembly or by-law without licence of the mayor and the master of each of their several occupations, and commanded to give in their books of rules for the mayor's inspection.[1] Ten years later the dyers' journeymen were compelled to " use themselves as servants, and as no craft or fellowship." [2] That some sort of organization with a common fund persisted among the journeymen is evident from the order of 1549, which forbade them to collect quarterages or take fines from strangers coming into the city to work,[3] an order evidently prompted by recent parliamentary legislation.

The contumacy of other crafts, who took higher rank than mere journeymen, is shown by the treatment of "blacklegs" among the barbers and the dyers. The attempt of the former craft to strengthen their position by an appeal to the spiritual court—" the official of the Bishop of Chester "—is set forth in a pardon granted in 1396 to Robert Drayton, barber, of Coventry, evidently a leader among that craft in their endeavour to raise their prices and obtain some cessation of labour on feast-days—wherein they differed from the barbers of London, who would feel, said the Archbishop of Canterbury, more than any spiritual penalty the prohibition of Sunday shaving.[4] The pardon relates how Drayton assembled in the twelfth year of the king's reign with other barbers in unlawful assemblies, conspiring with them that no barber should shave any stranger, workman or servant, on feast-days, " making the cost of that art so much dearer to the damage of the whole people," and because John Wilnhall shaved strangers, workmen or servants on ordinary feast-days, Drayton and others maliciously harassed him at Coventry before the official of the Bishop of Chester, and threatened him " with mutilation of his members." [5] That the practice of making appeal to the bishop's court continued in the fifteenth century is shown by an order of leet passed in 1457 where complaint is made that " discord . . . falleth . . . amongst divers

---

[1] See below, pp. 656, 687. [2] *Ib.* 694.
[3] *Ib.* 792 and note. [4] Sharpe, *Letter-Book*, I. 115-6.
[5] *Cal. Pat. R.*, 1391-6, p. 720. I am indebted for the permission to use this reference to the kindness of Mr. William Page, editor of the *Victoria County Histories*, as I saw it among the material collected for Coventry by the workers on the *V.C.H.* staff. For references to Sunday shaving, see below, pp. 185, 226. Cf. the ordinance for Sunday observance on the part of the fletchers (arrow-makers), *ib.* 547 ; for innholders, *ib.* 739.

crafts because ... divers masters ... sue in spiritual court divers people of their craft, affirming that they have broken their oaths made in breaking divers their rules ... which rules oft times be unreasonable and the punishment ... over excess." [1]

Worse perhaps than the barbers' treatment of Wilnhall was that meted out to Thomas de Fenby and other dyers by the leaders of that craft about the middle of the fifteenth century. The complainants averred that John Egynton and William Warde had assembled them as members of their trade and compelled them to swear to divers things "contrary to law and their conscience" concerning the purchase of woad and dyeing of cloth,[2] and that moreover the said John and William "had hired Welshmen and Irishmen to waylay and kill the complainants on their way to neighbouring markets."[2] The leet of 1473 complains bitterly of an "unlawful ordinance" made by the dyers ... that none should colour ne dye but under a certain form among themselves ordained upon certain pains ... ordained by surety of writing and oaths unlawful in that behalf, "assessing the fine of any master of craft suing or troubling in any law any person for non-performing of any such ordinance" at the excessive sum of £10.[3] The dyers' craft continually troubled the peace of the corporation; they produced a most noteworthy rebel in the person of Laurence Saunders; and there seems to have been a determined effort during the years 1529–1533 to break down their monopoly, maybe to bring their organization to nought, by allowing outsiders to practise the art in the craft's despite.[4]

If labour and the wool-working crafts were hard to govern, so were the victuallers, and yet conditions of mediæval transport—when a temporary dislocation of trade meant dearth—made the disinterested regulation of the food supply a matter of the highest import. The precepts of the leet were excellent, and the court frequently busied itself with the misdeeds of the victualling crafts and the attempt to enforce law and ordinance in their despite,

---

[1] See below, pp. 302–3. In 1518 heavy penalties were laid on those causing any person to be sworn "on a book" for any point of their occupation, *ib.* 654.
[2] The points at issue were (1) that no one should buy any woad until it had been viewed and appraised by 6 men, chosen by Egynton and Warde; (2) no dyer should make any "grene" at less than 6s. a piece, nor put any cloth into woad at less than 5d. or 4d. See Hewitt, *Industries* in *Vict. County Hist. Warw.*, II. 252.
[3] See below, pp. 418–9.   [4] *Ib.* pp. 697, 704, 714.

xxxvi   *Introduction.*

Yet there were times when prices fixed and ordinances enrolled were without avail. Thus, in 1473, a great outcry arose that traders sold ale, wine and fish otherwise than the mayor appointed, "and in manner destitucion the city of malice of wines and victual ... because they may not utter it after their own consents and prices."[1]

How far administration usually fell short of legislation it is difficult to say, but there is no doubt about the thoroughness of legislation. There was a fixed price set on common necessaries such as bread and ale,[2] and a proper inspection of victuallers' goods brought into the city—strangers' bread was viewed by the mayor or his nominees before sale, and also strangers' fish[3]—and every precaution taken to prevent the raising of the cost of food to the consumer by the common mediæval practice of regratery.[4] To guard against the collusive pre-emption of fish the mayor assigned stranger fishmongers a place of lodging, forbidding them to be "osted" or "inned" at the house of a native brother of the craft;[5] while the custom of allowing bystanders to share in a bargain of salt-fish was evidently intended to prevent one dealer buying more than his proper share of food-stuff.[6]

Occasionally the leet set a price on victuals; thus in 1445 the court enjoined the cooks to sell a good goose no dearer than 4*d*., a pig for 7*d*., and a pig's head or quarter at 1*d*;[7] while every disposition to create profit out of a conflux of people to the city was nipped in the bud; thus in 1498 the mayor, in his capacity of clerk of the market on the occasion of the assembly of the Benedictine chapter, made enquiry concerning the price of all manner of victuals, "and made a book thereof, and set it up on the south door of the minster," the *Leet-Book* says, "like as is done when the king's grace or my lord prince cometh to the city."[8]

In order to increase the power of the civic authorities over the victuallers the mayor appointed one of the masters of the

[1] See below, pp. 386–7.
[2] By the Assize of Bread (51 Hen. III, c. 1), the price of bread was fixed in relation to the price of grain. See below, pp. 24, 385, 518–9, 799; and for regulations concerning ale-tasters and the sale of wine, *ib*. 191, 797.
[3] See pp. 646, 740.
[4] *Ib*. 25, 197, 623, 780, 795. A forestaller buys up provisions on the way to market, a regrater when they are in the market, but the terms are loosely employed of all who attempt to "corner" goods.
[5] *Ib*. 33.   [6] *Ib*. 193. Cf. the rule among the butchers, *ib*. 338.
[7] *Ib*. 223.   [8] *Ib*. 589.

Orders of Leet. xxxvii

bakers', the fishmongers', and (after 1520) the butchers' crafts respectively, the company being in every case allowed to select the other.[1] That it was sometimes necessary to suppress entirely a refractory craft is manifest from the chequered career of the butchers' fellowship in the sixteenth century.

Nevertheless, the power of the victuallers—and especially of this craft—is writ large over later leet legislation, which appears to have concerned itself less than formerly with the now unprosperous woollen industry, and more and more with the crucial question of the butcher's, tanner's and chandler's trades, the admission of free food and raw material. The dislike to "foreign" purveyors of foodstuffs, so marked in York and London,[2] was shared by the butchers of Coventry, and the impossibility of reconciling the protectionist aspirations of this craft with the consumer's desire for cheap and plentiful meat, is responsible for much of the vacillation of the by-laws on this point. Moreover, if the butcher wished to close the meat-market to the stranger, he was a free-trader when it came to the question of the sale of his waste material, hence the complexities of the matter are further shown in the tanners' and chandlers' demands for the exclusion of the "foreign" purchasers of hides and tallow.

"It is ordained," runs an order of 1497, illustrating the normal leet policy of restricting, as far as possible, the "foreign" manufacturer's purchase to the denizen's leavings, ". . . . that the tanners within this city have free liberty to buy at all days and time after the hide is off the beast's back, so that it lie in the market three hours; and that no stranger buy no manner hides but on the market days, that is to say, Tuesday, Thursday and Saturday."[3] In 1527 the foreigner's hours were further restricted; he was not allowed to make purchases until after nine o'clock on the Saturday morning,[4] a provision which, as it naturally tended, by removing

---

[1] See below, p. 669.

[2] Any attempt of the York butchers to exclude others from outside the city from the Thursday market was to be punished, say the butchers' rules in 1425, by loss of the franchise and imprisonment, Seller, *op. cit.* 57-8. See also Sharpe, *Letter-Book*, L. 100 (1471). The bakers of London are said to "make presentments . . . from envy . . . of foreign bakers, and make no presentments touching bakers residing within the liberty of the city."

[3] See below, p. 585. There also appear ordinances against wholesale purchase, *ib.* 557, 581.

[4] *Ib.* 694. There had been orders evidently more favourable to country tanners, *ib.* 665-6.

competition, to lower the price of hides, met with strong opposition from the butchers' fellowship. "It is enacted," says an order of leet passed in the following year, "that forasmuch as the tanners of this city refuse to buy hides of the butchers of this city of such reasonable price as the butchers [? tanners] of the country would, the said butchers of this city from hensforth shall have their liberty to sell their hides to the tanners of the country, any act or acts heretofore to the contrary made notwithstanding."[1] This policy was, however, reversed a few years later, and restrictions again set up,[2] changes which, no doubt, represent the predominance of one or other of the crafts, the waxing or waning of the influence of the butchers or tanners in the councils of the city. Similar vicissitudes attended the policy of the butchers in other directions. In 1520 the mayor was ordered to choose one keeper of the craft, any resistance to this order being punishable by a fine of 100s.;[3] the sale of meat by retail was, however, limited to members of the craft in 1523.[4] Evidently an unrecorded dissolution of this company took place, for in 1554 the butchers were again permitted to form a fellowship,[5] none but late apprentices of the craft being allowed to set up the occupation without the master's licence. Two years later, however, it was ordered that the city butchers should "permit and suffer" strangers "quietly to sell their victual" . . . every Tuesday, Thursday and Saturday, bringing their hides and tallow with them,[6] a privilege, which at the "petition and request of the commoners of the city" was soon after extended to Wednesday and Friday,[7] and in the next year (1551) to every day except Sunday, the butchers' fellowship being quashed, and the trade open to all of that occupation who were inhabitants.[8] Next year, however, some turn of Fortune's wheel brought about an entire reversal of this free trade policy. The butchers' guild re-appeared, and the country traders lost for the time being all liberty of sale within the city, an order some protectionist friend of the city butchers glossed in the margin of the MS. "laudabile factum";[9] its stringency, however, was a little relaxed next year, foreigners being permitted to sell on Fridays in two places in the city.[10]

Another set of townsfolk, allied to the victuallers, also struggling to maintain the monopoly incident to a craft organization, were

[1] See below, p. 695. [2] *Ib.* 718, 780, 782. [3] *Ib.* 669.
[4] *Ib.* 685. [5] *Ib.* 770. [6] *Ib.* 780.
[7] *Ib.* 795. [8] *Ib.* 797. [9] *Ib.* 803. [10] *Ib.* 808.

the chandlers, and the price of tallow, and consequently of candles,[1] and the butchers' sale of the raw material into the country away from the local craftsmen,[2] were matters greatly agitating the leet in the sixteenth century. At first the occupation seems to have been common to other craftsmen, bakers, butchers, fishmongers, and even shearmen, but in 1515 a fellowship of tallow-chandlers was formed, and folk of other occupations excluded from the practice of the calling.[3] The organization proving unsatisfactory from the point of view of the consumer, the leet of 1523 granted to two butchers and their four nominees a seven years' monopoly of the purchase of tallow in return for the guaranteed provision of sufficient candles at a given price.[4] How this arrangement worked is not revealed, but in 1530 the leet revived the fellowship, under the control of the mayor, who admitted such as he approved to practise the calling, appointed the two keepers of the craft with "authority to enter into every chandler's house and weigh their candles to the intent the people be not deceived. The mayor, also acting jointly with his assistants and the keepers of the craft, fixed for the nonce the price of tallow, the keepers having instruction to assemble the craft every year between Lammas and Michaelmas and by the advice of Master Mayor and the justices of the peace" to "set such price of tallow as shall be thought then most convenient . . . for the ease of the commonalty."[5] It is significant of the instant effect of gild organization—exclusion of the competing foreigner—that at the very next assembly of the leet it was necessary to pass an order against such as "do interupt or let any estranger to sell candles within this city."[6]

Not only were hides, malt and tallow sold out of the city to furnish work and trade for "foreigners," but many, so the *Leet Book* records, covetously engrossed yarn and sold it unwrought in divers places in the country while the city looms lay idle.[7] Thus the decay of agriculture, already in part responsible for the influx of country beggars, accounts also for the spread of handicrafts in rural

---

[1] See p. 400. The so-called Statute of Winchester entered in the *Leet Book* (*ib.* 395 sqq.) and in the *Liber Custumarum* of Northampton (*Rec. North.*, 1. 344–9) is no part of the celebrated statute of Edward I.
[2] *Ib.* 650, 651, 787 *et passim.* Cf. the sale of malt into the country by brewers, *ib.* 637, 666.
[3] *Ib.* 632, 643.   [4] *Ib.* 685.   [5] *Ib.* 703–4.   [6] *Ib.* 705.
[7] See below, pp. 789, 791. No doubt this was the sin of the capitalist clothier (see for the clothiers' and the weavers' company, *ib.* 776–7); for the prohibition against giving work to country weavers and fullers see *ib.* 661, 723 *et passim*.

districts, where the workers, free from the charges and strict supervision imposed by city and craft, seriously competed with members of urban organizations.[1] Occasionally country craftsmen joined a city gild; thus the fullers' company in 1537 included apparently both residents and non-residents,[2] while in 1539 the Leet forbade the putting out of linen or woollen yarn to be woven to any weaver of the city *or country* unless he were "a brother admitted and associate with the weavers of the city."[3] All provisions, however, to arrest the decay of the woollen industry proved unavailing, and the city never until these latter days rose to the height of prosperity it had enjoyed under the Plantagenets.[4]

There was not only a strong prejudice against the occasional foreign dealer, but the crafts manifested an equally strong distaste to foreign settlers, and the growth of ale-houses in the sixteenth and seventeenth centuries furnished excuse in 1622 for closing as far as possible to the stranger the profitable callings of brewer, maltster, or victualler.[5] More than a hundred years before, the leet had attempted to fix the fines taken by the crafts on the admission of new members of their calling at a reasonable sum " to the pleasure of God after the ability of the people that now be . . . so the city be encreased to more wealthiness than it is now."[6] The jealousy of the new-comer was, however, persistent, and the oligarchic government which, it appears, had become a feature of the craft constitutions in the sixteenth century, may perhaps have accentuated the tendency towards exclusiveness. In some cases it appears that the direction of affairs lay with a small inner body rather than with the whole membership of the calling; thus the masters of the cappers with twelve of the "most ancient" of the craft in 1549 regulated the putting out of piece-work, while, according to the

---

[1] There seems to have been no complaint of the *spinners* against the country folk; but that was woman's work, and probably paid for by the Coventry clothiers as low as possible; see, for the spinners' complaints against truck wages and false weights, p. 658 *et passim*.

[2] See p. 727.

[3] *Ib.* 738. See for precautions about the cappers' work going to residents, *ib.* 704-5, and for bakers and millers, *ib.* 793.

[4] For the decay of Coventry see Lamond, *Commonweal of the Realm of England*, 16, 19.

[5] On the exclusion of stranger victuallers see pp. 837-9. The question of the admission fines of strangers and apprentices I have treated of in a previous work. See Harris, *Story of Coventry*, pp. 224-8.

[6] See p. 655, also p. 623.

Orders of Leet.

rules of 1540, twelve of the "eldest and discretest" of the smiths were to choose the keepers for the ensuing year.[1]

There is no evidence to show what part women played in the trade organizations of the city beyond making the customary contributions towards the common funds of their craft[2]; but the whole subject of woman's industrial life receives but scanty treatment in civic records;[3] in Coventry they found employment as cutters of fish,[4] candle-makers,[5] knitters and spinners,[6] suffering much in the last occupation from their employers' oppression and trickery; but the career of the most remarkable of Coventry women merchants, Margery Russell, who flourished c. 1413,[7] and is mentioned in no less than three documents of the period, falls outside the *Leet Book* record.[8] Women were members of the Trinity and Corpus Christi gilds, and there is evidence that they could be admitted to the city freedom.[9] Incidentally the placing of Lady Abergavenny on the commission for raising a loan for Henry VI is a tribute to the administrative capacity of high-born women,[10] while the mention of the "mayoress and her sisters" implies an official recognition of the wives of the fathers of the city.[11]

---

[1] See below, pp. 743, 792.
[2] See the order concerning the payment of Alice Greene, cake-baker to the bakers' craft, p. 723.
[3] See, however, Sharpe, *Letter Book*, L. p. xxx–xxxii.
[4] See below, p. 652.   [5] *Ib.* p. 555.
[6] *Ib.* pp. 271, 658, 673, *et passim*. The complaints of truck wages and of false weights of wool are of frequent occurrence.
[7] Note kindly supplied by Miss Abram.
[8] Abram, *Eng. Life and Manners in the Middle Ages*, p. 36. This woman obtained letters of marque, which empowered her to seize goods of Spanish merchants, to recoup herself for the merchandise worth £800 of which she had been robbed by men of Santander.
[9] The *Council Book* (Corp. MSS. A. 14 (*a*)) contains an entry dated Jan. 26 Eliz., wherein Margaret Robertes is declared a freewoman of the city.
[10] See below, p. 123.   [11] *Ib.* p. 405.

CHAPTER IV

THE LEET BOOK AS CHRONICLE

Localization of the crafts—The commons—Laurence Saunders—Sixteenth-century enclosures—Finance—Military service and fortifications—Historical allusions—Henry V and Hornby—Gloucester and the Lollards—The Pageants—Edward IV and Edward Prince of Wales—Elizabeth—James I—Shakespeare and the *Leet Book*.

THE entry in the *Leet Book* of so much miscellaneous matter over and above the records of the Leet, throws light not only on the daily life of the citizen, but also on national affairs at a dark period of our history, when the torch of monastic learning was well-nigh burnt out, and that of the secular historian scarcely kindled; a time of war and trouble, when it chanced that the military position of Coventry gave the city a place of great importance in the annals of the kingdom.

Most of these supplementary entries fall under one or other of the following heads: name-lists, records of boundaries and commons, accounts, often including military items, letters and chronicle matter. Some of the entries are jejune in the extreme, but even name-lists and land-surveys will furnish food for reflection to the social historian and economist. Thus the record of those who furnished armour in 1449–50 enables us to gauge the wealth and municipal influence of the various crafts [1]; and a somewhat laborious comparison of this list with contemporary ones naming ward by ward those who lent money for the king's necessities shows that there was little localization of particular callings but rather an intermixture of trades in most parts of the city [2]; while the record of parish landmarks copied from the rental of Brother William

[1] In the list of craftsmen providing armour in 1449–50, out of 38 mercers 13 had held official positions, including 2 late mayors and 4 late bailiffs; 16 out of 59 drapers, with 6 mayors and 6 bailiffs; 7 out of 37 dyers, with 1 mayor and 2 bailiffs; 2 out of 24 girdlers had occupied inferior posts; 2 out of 57 weavers, with 1 bailiff; 2 out of 20 wiredrawers, with 1 bailiff; 2 out of 20 whittawers, with 1 mayor and 1 bailiff; none out of 64 tailors and shearmen, or out of 27 fullers, 39 corvysers, 49 smiths, or any of the minor crafts, except the pinners and tilers, who furnished 1 chamberlain or warden. See below, pages 246 sqq.

[2] The drapers were mainly located in Earl Street near the Drapery, the butchers in Cross Cheaping near the Butchery and Bull-ring. It is not easy to estimate the comparative wealth of the wards; Earl, Bishop and Much Park Streets appear among more wealthy, Broadgate, and Bayly Lane among less wealthy, districts.

Haloughton, monk of Coventry,[1] preserves not only an interesting enumeration of the prior's feudal and ecclesiastical rights, but enshrines an allusion to the liability of his villein tenants to take part in the great boon-work of hay-making at Finford, a feudal exaction from which the Coventry men had freed themselves as early as the reign of Henry III.[2]

With the survey of 1423[3] we enter upon a subject that bulks large in Coventry history at this period. Much *Leet Book* space is devoted to questions concerning the common, Lammas and Michaelmas, lands, their extent, and the complaints of their surcharging and enclosure, which culminated towards the close of the fifteenth century in the classic dispute between the city and Briscow[4] and the career of the rebel, Laurence Saunders.[5] No doubt powerful private people encroached on the commons,[6] and the temptation to convert areas of land bearing common rights into several holdings for public purposes[7] seems to have been found irresistible by the rulers of the city, though the temporary convenience of these proceedings was more than discounted by the suspicion and irritation they were ultimately sure to arouse among the common people.[8] The sixteenth century saw the official adoption on the plea of dearth and heavy charges of a further scheme of enclosure, which probably helped to confuse landmarks and imperil the continued existence of grazing rights. In 1511 a representative body of forty-eight selected and set apart a number of fields to be kept several all times of the year, and let on lease, the leet decreeing that the corresponding rent should be paid to the common box, that is, devoted to objects of public utility.[9] The policy thus initiated,

---

[1] See below, pp. 7 sqq.
[2] *Ib.* 10–11, 14, and *Victoria County Hist. Warw.*, II. 144–5.
[3] See below, pp. 45 sqq. On the surcharging and enclosure of the commons see *ib.* 191, 340, 348, 730.
[4] On Briscow s case (*Year Book*, 15 Edw. IV) see Hall, *Profits à Prendre*, 159 sqq., and below, pp. 349–50, 376 sqq.; Harris, *Story of Coventry*, 174–81.
[5] See below, pp. 430 sqq., *et passim*, *Story of Coventry*, 181 sqq.
[6] See the case of Briscow's father, below, p. 350.
[7] On the case of enclosures to recompense the Trinity gild and prior see pp. 2–6, 19–20, 46, 350–2, 439, 513–14.
[8] An enclosure showing what vigilance was required for the preservation of common rights is recorded in 1628 (Sharp, *Mysteries*, 12). The poor people that year rose and pulled down an enclosure that had been set apart for maintenance of the pageants, though these had been long discontinued.
[9] See below, pp. 633, 679. In 1541 (*ib.* 760) it was said that there had been "divers great charges and payments, . . . which would have been in manner unportable save only for the said rents."

persisted, though with notable re-actions, as is testified by the order of leet passed in 1525 after the riot on "Ill Lammas day," enjoining that lands lately enclosed should be laid open, no longer to be enclosed,[1] yet the example was so contagious that in spite of this order the complaint arose in 1534 that there was more land under tillage in time of plenty than had been formerly permitted in time of dearth, and unauthorized conversions of pasture to arable depriving the commonalty of grazing rights was forbidden.[2] The years 1538[3] and 1541,[4] however, saw a reversion to the practice of letting out the commons on lease, and an extension of the enclosed area, but in 1548[5] the year wherein a commission was appointed to inquire into enclosures in the Midlands, this policy was abandoned, the closes thrown open and the old stint regulations revived.

There is no doubt that the tendency to enclosures was accelerated by the financial strain of which there was such continual complaint in the sixteenth century. *Leet Book* scribes only deal by the way with money matters; and throw little light on the financial relations between the Trinity gild and the corporation, though it is clear the gild frequently advanced money at the city's need.[6] The fraternity, as we have seen, also paid the £10 annual ferm to the prior, but the bailiffs—later sheriffs—of whose finances no leet record remains, appear to have discharged, from the profits of various courts, the annual ferm of £50 due to the royal Exchequer.[7] The bulk of the money, however, filling the city "chamber" or treasury issued from amortized houses and lands,[8] whereof the wardens (*custodes camere*), whose office was probably created just before the *Leet Book* period opens, when a considerable amount of property was made over to the community,[9] gathered the rents, while the chamberlains, or treasurers proper, devoted

---

[1] See below, p. 692.   [2] *Ib.* 719–30.   [3] *Ib.* 729 sqq.
[4] *Ib.* 760 sqq.   [5] *Ib.* 788–9, cf. Lamond, *Common Weal*, xi.
[6] See below, p. 370, for money levied from the chamber and the gild; for the Corpus Christi gild, see *ib.* 198, 532. It is not clear why the mayor received certain items from the gilds (*ib.* 514, 515), nor why (*ib.* 503) he delivered the balance of his account to the master of the Trinity Gild; another mayor (*ib.* 532) delivered it to his successor.
[7] *Ib.* 62, 751.
[8] *Ib.* 66. Some of this town property was vested in the corporation for the purpose of founding obits for the donors; see receipts "for the souls of" divers persons, *ib.* 67.
[9] The mayor, bailiffs, and chamberlains are mentioned in 1384; but there is no reference to wardens. *ib.* p. 3. For amortization of property see below, p. 61, and Corp. MSS. B. 39.

themselves to the collection of murage, a rate levied on lands and moveables for the building and maintenance of the town-wall.[1] The administration of the central fund accruing from the balance over expenses of the wardens' rents, the chamberlain's murage, or any tallage [2] laid for a special purpose on the wards of the city together with certain fines of the leet, seems to have lain with the mayor, and the few existing specimens of mayoral accounts show to what heterogeneous uses the city funds were applied; thus among the items of expenditure are reckoned not only the entertainment of royalty,[3] the retaining of soldiers,[4] the repairs of the conduit,[5] but also the carriage of venison from Fulbroke,[6] the "seassyng" of the commons at a riot,[7] and a gallon of sweet wine for the prior and convent to drink [8] over a bargain with the recorder. A reserve fund was created to meet the incidence of rates and taxation when, in 1501, William Pisford initiated the practice of keeping a common box to which certain leet fines came to be allotted as well as rents of common lands enclosed and kept in severalty. Since the clavers of this box—in addition to the mayor, who held one of the keys—were appointed in a roundabout fashion from among those who had never borne office, control over this fund was to some extent vested in the commonalty jointly with the chief official of the city.[9]

Besides the occasional levy for such public works as the repair of the conduit, rates were laid on every household, hall-door and cottage-door, for the minstrels' quarterage [10] and the maintenance of the cart for the collection of refuse;[11] but probably of all municipal payments it was the murage which weighed most heavily on the citizens. Though the work of erecting the great three miles' mural circuit, begun in 1356, is said by the mayor-lists to have occupied but forty years, there are continual allusions to wall-building during the *Leet Book* period, and frequent reparations entailed a constant burden.[12] Moreover by an agreement with

---

[1] See below, pp. 59, 65, 108, 118, 119.
[2] These tallages were gathered throughout the wards like the fifteenths, *ib.* 66.
[3] *Ib.* 292.   [4] *Ib.* 501.   [5] *Ib.* 587-8.
[6] *Ib.* 503.   [7] *Ib.*   [8] *Ib.* 515.
[9] *Ib.* 600-1.   [10] *Ib.* 59.   [11] *Ib.* 21.
[12] *Ib.* 56, 136, and for the fortifications, *ib.* 261. The walls are said to have enclosed an area second to none in the Midlands; they were about 9 feet thick, and furnished with 32 towers and 12 gates.

Prior Shotswell in 1462 the original plan for the line of defence was abandoned, and the enclosed area enlarged to embrace certain convent property,[1] so that it would seem that in 1498[2] the work of walling was still incomplete, and the chamberlain's outgoings often exceeded their incomings, since at one period the prior and convent for twenty years refused to contribute towards the murage rate. In view of the great cost the fortifications involved, it is no wonder that the corporation was glad to be relieved of the burden of the upkeep of any particular building; thus when in the peaceful times of the Tudors the Bishop-street gate-house had fallen into a deplorable state of decay, the leet in 1518 consented to the lease of it—on an undertaking about repairs—to Richard Marler for forty years.[3]

Besides maintaining the fortifications the citizens were perforce obliged to make extensive preparations for sieges, to furnish arms and armour,[4] ammunition[5] and, on the receipt of the king's privy seal, tallage the wards to provide wages for soldiers during the civil wars. It was a time when constitutional precedent went by the board, and soldiers were waged at the city's cost, not at that of the king.[6] A hundred men were arrayed for Lancaster—though they took no actual part in the battle of S. Albans—in 1455,[7] and forty promised in 1460;[8] but the next year York was in power, and £100 gathered in the wards provided the hire of those accompanying the Earl of March to London after the second battle of S. Albans,[9] while £80 was collected for 100 soldiers that fought at Towton.[10] Military items crowd the records of the troubled years 1469–71, when money flowed like water for the pay of soldiers whose wages rose from the normal rate of 6*d.* to 12*d.* a day.[11] We seem to catch even in the discreet entries of the *Leet Book* an undertone of complaint at Edward's levies

---

[1] See pp. 447, 463. [2] *Ib.* 592 sqq.
[3] *Ib.* 664; cf. the letting off of Bablake gate in 1439 to the Trinity gild (*ib.* 188), and of the latrines and West Orchard bridge to Will. Pere (*ib.* 194).
[4] See below, pp. 244 sqq. There still exists a sallet in S. Mary's Hall, from the time of the Wars of the Roses: see Starkie Gardener, *Armour in England*, 58.
[5] See, for the provision of guns and gunpowder, below, pp. 262, 345.
[6] Stubbs, *Const. Hist.*, III, 255–6. According to the form of Commission of Array in use under Henry IV, soldiers outside their own counties were paid by the king except in case of invasion.
[7] See below, p. 283. [8] *Ib.* 310.
[9] *Ib.* p. 313–4. [10] *Ib.* 315.
[11] *Ib.* 343, 354, 355, 356, 362–3, 366.

for the Scotch war in 1481, when after some difficulty 100 men were raised in the Prince of Wales's name, and these after being prepared, kept together, and in some cases boarded by the leading men of the city for nearly two months, were ultimately discharged without going to the wars.[1] It was probably the remembrance of such inconveniences as led the mayor next year to offer £20 to the Prince of Wales in lieu of sending men for Gloucester's expedition against the Scots.[2] Under Henry VII the crafts—not the wards— provided for the equipment of forty men to accompany the king to Scotland,[3] at the royal wages. That the citizens soon forgot their warlike habits is evident from the apology tendered by the Commissioners for the mustering of horsemen in 1584 to the Privy Council. The citizens of Coventry, we are told, " wanted sufficient riders for their horses by reason their servants have rather been brought up in following their occupations than in riding of horses," an omission the writers humbly beseech their lordships to pardon.[4] We are irresistibly reminded of Falstaff's "cankers of a calm world and a long peace.[5] Six years later the famous name of Sir Thomas Lucy is associated with Sir Fulk Greville's and Sir John Harrington's on the commission for the Warwickshire musters, a fact no doubt remembered by Shakespeare when he despatched Sir John Falstaff " to fill up the muster book " at Justice Shallow's house.[6]

In other ways than the provision of soldiers the Coventry men ministered to the royal needs.[7] Henry IV obtained a loan of £300 in 1400,[8] whereof £163 remained unpaid in 1423. Henry V borrowed 200 marks " to the sege of Harflete " in Laurence Cook's first mayoral year, 1415, and fourteen years later by the instrumentality of the same mayor, repayment was made of at least half the sum,[9] the part proceeds of jewels handed over in satisfaction of royal debts. The cadets of the Lancastrian house, Bedford [10] and Gloucester, were also borrowers; and security for the loans of the latter might not be gotten without great labour;[11] while—to come

---

[1] See below, pp. 474 sqq. On Edward's unconstitutional manner of levying military service, see Stubbs, *op. cit.* III., 281, 286.
[2] *Ib.* 505.   [3] *Ib.* 582-3. Cf. the indenture, *ib.* 608.
[4] *Ib.* 832. For musters see *ib.* 830, note.   [5] 1 *Hen. IV*, iv, 2.
[6] 2 *Hen. IV*, iii, 2.   [7] See below, pp. 37, 60-1.
[8] In Will. Whitchurch's year. This is given incorrectly in my note (p. 61, note 1) as 1399. The chronological confusion of the mayor-lists frequently makes the assigning of a date to a particular mayor a matter of great difficulty.
[9] See pp. 61, 121.   [10] *Ib.* 121.   [11] *Ib.* 86.

to Yorkist times—Clarence left his jewels in pledge for a 300 marks' loan from the citizens.¹ The Earls of Warwick were also among those whom the townsfolk "eased" with a sum of money in their necessities; Richard Beauchamp obtained 100 marks from the wealthiest sort in 1444; and the "lord Richard Nevyle," who borrowed the same sum in 1471, can have been no other than the Kingmaker.² These loans were usually met by a collection according to a regular assessment throughout the wards; but wealthy men occasionally banded together to furnish the required sum; thus, in 1429, 23 marks was gathered from 28 citizens in amounts varying from 40s. to 3s. 4d. towards Talbot's ransom, after the hero of a hundred fights had been taken prisoner at Patay.³

Not only Talbot, but countless characters, whose deeds Shakespear and other chronicle playwrights have made household words, appear in the *Leet Book*. Prince Henry borrowed money from the citizens in Mayor Hornby's year, 1412, thus recalling the local variant of the Gascoigne story which credits the mayor with the arrest of the prince in the priory of Coventry.⁴ Nine years later Henry, as king, with his queen,⁵ Katherine of Valois, visited the the city, while the names of Bedford and Gloucester,⁶ recalling the beginning of a hopeless struggle abroad and disunion at home with suppression of Lollardy, constantly recur in the *Leet Book*, where also is noted the devotion paid to S. Michael by the gentle, luckless son of the hero of Agincourt,⁷ and the pageants of welcome to those phantom-like figures of woe, Margaret of Anjou and Edward, the elder of the "little Princes in the Tower."⁸ Some of the entries add to our scanty knowledge of this period of dynastic strife. Thus, the bailiff of Durham is named as one who suffered after

¹ See p. 381. ² *Ib.* 207, 364. ³ *Ib.* 119–20.
⁴ See pp. 42, 61. The matter is fully treated in the present editor's *Story of Coventry*, 105–6, and a letter in the *Athenæum*, no. 4437. The story is based on an entry in the mayor-lists; a possible explanation of its origin is that the prince was concerned in some arrest—as he certainly was in one in 1403—and that the present entry is a corrupt copy of an original entry in a lost MS. recording that fact.
⁵ See p. 34.
⁶ *Ib.* 111–12, 121, 137–8, 151–2. Gloucester's zeal for orthodoxy may have made him dreaded in a Lollard neighbourhood. For Lollardy in Coventry see *Cal. Pat. R.* Hen. IV, Ap. 28, 1407 (note kindly supplied by Miss Abram), Dormer Harris, *Story of Coventry*, 98–100; and for the connection of Coventry with Jack Sharpe's rebellion see *Proc. Privy Council*, iv, 89.
⁷ See pp. 263–6.
⁸ *Ib.* 287–92, 391–3. For the welcome to another early dying Prince of Wales, Arthur, see *ib.* 589–92.

The Leet Book as Chronicle.

the 1469 rebellion of the Lancastrian Nevilles,[1] and the journey of Warwick, Clarence and the Bastard Falconbridge to Coventry on their way from the west country towards Nottingham, where Edward lay in the autumn of 1470, appears in no other chronicle.[2] Apparently the Kingmaker, whose army before he reached the city had swelled to the number of 30,000 men, on hearing of Edward's flight from Lynn to Flanders, turned aside and went to London.[3] Of the trouble that befell the city, the confiscation of the franchises after Barnet and Tewkesbury, the *Leet Book* tells us little,[4] but there is clear evidence of the chief features of later Yorkist rule, the growing interference with city affairs on the part of the Prince's Council,[5] and the desire of Edward IV firmly to establish his dynasty.[6] After the mention of Bosworth—the field of King Richard[7]—little chronicle matter is recorded beyond an allusion to Henry VII's death,[8] but a long entry concerning the contemplated marriage of Princess Mary, later wife of Louis XII of France,[9] and transcripts of letters from Anne Boleyn,[10] Elizabeth[11] and James I[12] recall the names of those of the great world beyond the city gates.

Over and above its historical and literary interest the *Leet Book* has a distinct Shakespearean value as showing the manner of life among Warwickshire townsfolk for some four or five generations before the poet's birth. The connection between Stratford and Coventry seems to have been close both in Shakespeare's time and before his day; thus a Coventry notary held a court at Stratford, and the smaller town's measures were tested by the Coventry standard;[13] while in the times before the gilds were suppressed

---

[1] See below, p. 346. Mr. C. Kingsford informs me that the Warkworth and Croyland chronicles mention no bailiff of Durham in this connection.
[2] So I am informed by Prof. Oman.
[3] See below, pp. 358–9. [4] *Ib.* 381.
[5] This interference seems at first to have been resented, cf. the assertion of the mayor that he and his brethren could settle any variance about the pastures, *ib.* 433. The Prince's Council was probably appointed in 1471. See Skeel, *Council in the Marches of Wales*, 22. This book says nothing of the Coventry connection of Prince Edward.
[6] Cf. the oath to Prince Edward, 394.
[7] *Ib.* 531. [8] *Ib.* 625–6. [9] *Ib.* 609–18.
[10] *Ib.* p. 716. [11] *Ib.* 819–21, 833. [12] *Ib.* 834–5.
[13] These points are illustrated in the entries from the Stratford chamberlains' accounts, kindly supplied by Mr. Richard Savage. I do not understand why Coventry men should have been excluded from the fair.

1591-2.—Charges leyd out at Coventre.—A strike cost xij^d, the Sealinge xij^d, the cutting ij^d, his horse hier xij^d his charges for his horse and him selfe x^d . . . . iiij^s

Introduction.

each town furnished the other with brethren of its local society. Thus in 1533 Thomas Dycson and William Smythe of Stratford were brethren of the Coventry Corpus Christi gild,[1] and Thomas Maidford, who fought at Bosworth, and served as captain of Coventry's soldiers,[2] with Laurence Saunders and many more, belonged to the Stratford fraternity of the Holy Cross.[3]

Incidentally this study of fifteenth/sixteenth century civic life, showing something of its opportunities, its pageantry, its dramatic uncertainties, its abounding wealth of local tradition, should help to dispel the difficulty some scholars feel in reconciling Shakespeare's provincial upbringing with the acquaintance his works display of law, life and books. The townspeople are here shown keeping "leets and law days,"[4] assessing fines by "affeerors,"[5] and punish-

1596-7.—Paid to Abraham Sturley, (High Bailiff) for iij days Jurny for Thomas Vigers to serve Mr. Vnderhill at banbury at Coventry and at his oune house by Coventry . . . . iiij^s
1601-2.
It. pd ffor sendinge or brason mesueres to Coventree to have them tried . . . . xvj^d
It. pd to John Hudson ffor Carrienge the strike to Coventree . . xxij^d
It. pd ffor a standard strike at Coventree . . . . . x^s
It. pd ffor a horsse hiree to Coventree . . . . . xij^d
1603-4.
Paid to Rich. Whyting for his horse to Coventrie September 1° . xij$_d$
Paid to iiij men that did keep out of the Towne Coventriemen, for iij days at the great fair . . . . xj^s iiij^d
Paid to two watchmen that kept out Coventrie men, the Thursday after the first fair Octob. v° . . . . vj^d
1608-9.
Paid to a messenger that went to Coventrie for a Notarie . . xij^d
Paid for wax . . . . ij^d
Gyven to the Notarie when he came to keep a Courte . . . x^s
1611-12.
Payd to Mr. Bird of Coventry as to several tymes for keeping of 2 coortes . . . . j^{li} 0^s 0$_d$

[1] Corp. MSS. A. 6, ff. 303, 303, *dorso*.
[2] See below, pp. 532, 582. The nearness of Bosworth Field to the Shakespeare country makes it possible that the assertion that John Shakespeare's "parentes and late antecessors were for theire valeant and faithfull service advanced and rewarded" by Henry VII (S. Lee, *Shakespeare*, 196) was not altogether mere flummery on the part of Elizabethan heralds.
[3] Bloom, *Register of the Guild of the Holy Cross, Stratford*. [4] *Othello*, III, iii.
[5] For the Coventry "affeerors" see below, pp. 185-6. John Shakespeare was appointed in 1559 affeeror of Stratford court leet. Hence Shakespeare's allusion is not particularly recondite. The following note from the Stratford court records has been kindly supplied by Mr. Wellstood:—
Stratford Burgus. Visus Franci plegü cum curia et sessione pacis, 6 Oct., 1 Eliz.

affurares
{ Ric. Bydyll
Lewes ap Willim
John Whelar
John Shakspeyr

The Leet Book as Chronicle.

ing such ale-wives as "brought their customers stone-jugs and no seal'd quarts."[1] The talk is of "musters" and lawsuits, of enclosures, of lands "common" and "several," of sheep and "pasture," "pounds" and "pinfolds."[2] The city itself is ill-drained, it is true, with methods of disposing of refuse which recall Falstaff's famous comparison of himself when tossed from the buck-basket into the water as "a barrow of butcher's offal."[3] Yet in spite of defective sanitation the people are not dead to things of the mind; they have schools; they can relish a classical allusion;[4] even the "commonalty" can turn out a squib in verse;[5] they can boast of the acquaintance of bookish men, Rastell[6] and Grafton,[7] printers, John Hales[8] and Sir Thomas More;[9] and the library of a citizen, one Captain Cox,[10] ale-conner and mason, is famous all over the world. They love the arts, especially the drama, and albeit "rude mechanicals"[11] have played before kings and presented the "Nine Worthies" "when once a queen long dead was young."[12]

---

[1] *Taming of the Shrew*, Ind. ii. For Lord Campbell's extraordinary commentary on this passage see Robertson, *Baconian Heresy*, 61-2. For the Coventry measures see below, pp. 25, 134, 169, 401, 810.

[2] Shakespeare's frequent plays of words on "common" and "several" lands (Cf. *Love's L. Lost*, II, i, Sonnet 137) is an example of the engrossing character—especially to a Warwickshire man—of the subject of enclosures. Cf. also the dialogue on overcharging, "pound" and "pinfold" *Two Gent. of Verona*, I, i.

[3] See below, pp. 43, 389. *Merry Wives*, III, v. On Falstaff and Coventry see *Athenæum*, no. 4330. The existence of a dunghill (*sterquinarium*) before John Shakespeare's door in 1552 could, of course, be paralleled in Coventry.

[4] The welcome given to Margaret is mediæval in tone, but the Queen o Fortune's speech in the pageant for Prince Arthur is full of classical allusions, see p. 590.

[5] *Ib.* 567, 577-8.

[6] John Rastell was coroner in 1505, *ib.* 603; and Thomas Rastell, who married Thomas More's sister Elizabeth, was coroner in 1507-8, *ib.* 605, 619. He printed works of Fitzherbert, once recorder of Coventry, and the *Hundred Merry Tales;* and is sometimes credited with the composition of an interlude, *The Four Elements*. Is it possible that Rastell had anything to do with the play of *S. Christian* performed in the Little Park in 1505, or with the "interlude" at the Priory 1505-6?

[7] Richard Grafton, chronicler and printer, M.P. for Coventry in 1562-3. [Mr. Page of the *Victoria County History* has kindly allowed me to use this reference.]

[8] Probable author of the *Common Weal of the Realm of England*.

[9] On More's connection with Coventry see Nichols, *Bibl. Top. Brit.*, IV, no. XVII, p. 41. He—or a namesake—was also member of the Corpus Christi Gild, Corp. MSS. A. 6 leaf 291. "De Sur Thomas Moore ijs." (1530).

[10] See *Laneham's Letter* in Gascoigne's *Princely Pleasures of Kenilworth Castle*.

[11] *Mid. N. Dream*, III, ii.

[12] *L. L. L.*, V, ii. Cf. the "Nine Conquerors" as performed before Margaret of Anjou, see below, pp. 289-91. Other Coventry performances were S. Christian's Play, see *Story of Coventry*, 296, and S. Catherine's play, Sharp,

It is always worth noting that Shakespeare grew up in a district having for commercial centre a city whose inhabitants had greatly occupied themselves in acting for nearly 200 years. The fact that from the height of his great professional achievement in days when the local art was dying he spoke slightingly of the ranting delivery of the old-time actor [1] and of the ludicrous player's shifts of unlettered craftsmen, does not in the least detract from the importance of the local secular and religious plays in carrying down a dramatic tradition and preparing the way for the people's reception of a national drama that has become famous throughout the world.

Mysteries, 9. Even the monks had a mumming or "interludium," see *Compotus of Br. Rob. Colman, pittancer of the Priory*, 1505-6. Birmingham Free Library MSS. Warw. 168235.

[1] "It out-herods Herod," *Ham.* III, ii. Herod has a fine occasion for rant in the Coventry play of the tailors and shearmen.

§ 141. Stivichall, 1563.

FRAGMENT OF A DEED CONCERNING STIVICHALL, 1563.

[. . . of Tho. Essex, Esq., formerly of Vitalis de ffolkeshull (Foleshill), formerly of R. Marescall, formerly of John de Shulton or Hen. de Shulton, formerly of John de Honington, formerly of Will. de Lecestre, and lately of Will. Babtharpe. And also the homage and knight service of the lord of Baginton from a certain meadow there called Bridgemeadowe. And also the homage, service, and the chief rent of two [?] groats from the tenement there of Rob. Turnor formerly (etc.) with the suit of the tenants aforesaid to the great court there and the heriots of all the aforesaid [tenants] descending in fee, reliefs, escheats, wardships, marriages, views of frankpledge there, chattels waived, estrays, chattels of felons and fugitives, and the

. . . [1]Thome Essex,[2] ar*migeris*, quondam Vicalis (*sic*, read Vitalis) de ffolkeshull, quondam R. Marescalli, quondam Joha*nn*is de Shulton, siue Henrici de Shulton, quonda*m* Joha*nn*is de Honington, quondam Will*elm*i de Lecestr*e*, ac nuper Will*elm*i Babtharpe, necnon homa*gium* et servic*ium* militare d*om*ini de Bathekinton de quodam *prato* ib*ide*m vocat*o* Bridgemeadowe, necnon homa*gium*, servic*ium*, et redd*itum* Capital*e* duar*um* dragm[arum][3] de tenement*o* ib*ide*m Roberti Turnor quondam Steph*an*i de Liston, quondam Wu*al*te*r*i de Canley, ac nup*er* Will*elm*i Norres c*um* sect*a* tenenc*ium* pre*d*ictor*um* ad magnu*m* (*sic*) Curi*am* ib*ide*m ac heriett*is* omni*um* pre*d*ictor*um* in feodo decendenc*ium*, Releviis, escaet*is*, wardis, maritagiis, visu ffranci pleg*ii* ib*ide*m, Cattall*i* waviat*is*, extrahur*is*, Cattall*is* felon*um* et fugitiuor*um*, ac fines (*sic*), exit*ibus*,

---

[1] leaf 430. There is a great deal of difficulty about this fragment; it is the copy of a scrivener's copy of an original I cannot trace. Scribe Z. See p. 2.
[2] Tho. Essex was the husband of Dame Swillington, see above, p. 642.
[3] This word is very clearly written, but as the copy of a copy its form is not above suspicion. I am inclined to think that the scribe wrote "dragm*arum*" for "drachm*arum*," instead of "grossorum," a groat (grossus), worth 4*d*., being equal to a dram (drachma), ⅛ of an oz. in weight. This view is further strengthened by a reference—to which I am indebted to the kindness of Mr. Page, editor of the *Victoria County History*, and to Mr. E. F. Kirk—to the same property, where R. Turner's rent is given as 8*d*. "ac de et in annual*i* redditu octo denariorum de quo*libet* tenemento Roberti Turnor ib*ide*m" (Inq. p. m. Chancery, ser. II, Eliz., vol. 175, no. 105). This inquest was taken on the death of Tho. Gregory, Feb. 1, 18 Eliz. Another deed (Close Roll, Chancery, 14 Eliz., p. 27) introduces however a complication, as here in the quit claim between Edward, son of Tho. Fisher, and Arthur Gregory, Turner's rent is given as two shillings, "necnon de et in homagio, *ser*vicio et capitali redditu dnor*um* solidor*um* de ten*emen*to Roberti Turnor," (Mr. E. F. Kirk). Possibly here the word "grossorum" has been miscopied 'solidorum."

§ 141. *Stivichall,* 1563.

fines, issues, and amercements of all the aforesaid tenants, with other franchises and jurisdictions according to the tenor of charters and divers letters patent made to the aforesaid bishop and his predecessors, all and singular which things formerly belonged to the bishopric or church of Coventry, Lichfield and Chester, and were part of the ancient revenues of the same, and which I, the aforesaid Thomas, purchased in fee by charter of the aforesaid bishop dated Feb. 20, 1 Edw. VI (1547), and by confirmation of the said chapter dated April 15 in the abovesaid year of the aforesaid king.

[To have and to hold the said lordship and all and singular the premises with the appurtenances to the aforesaid Thomas and Arthur and the heirs of the same Arthur for ever. And also I, the aforesaid Thomas, and my heirs will warrant and defend for ever by these presents all and singular the premises with the appurtenances to the aforesaid Thomas and Arthur and the heirs of the aforesaid Arthur against me and my heirs.

[Know ye moreover that I the aforesaid Thomas in my

et amerciament*is* om*n*ium tenenc*ium* pred*ictorum,* ac aliis ffrancheciis et Jurisdicc*ionibus* secu*n*d*u*m tenores Cartar*um* et diue*r*sar*um* L*itt*erar*um* patenc*ium* p*re*fato E*pis*copo et predecessor*ibus* suis factor*um* (*sic*). Que om*n*ia *e*t singula Ep*is*copatie (*sic*) siue Eccle*s*ie Coven*tr*e*n*si Litch*f*eld*ensi* et Ce*st*re*n*si dud*um* spectabant et p*ar*cella antiquar*u*m Revencionu*m* eiusdem existebant Et que ego prefatus Thomas[1] p*er*quisiui in feodo per Ca[r]ta*m* p*r*efati E*pis*cop*i* data*m* xx° ffebr*uarii* a*n*no p*r*imo Reg*is* Edwardi Sexti Et pe*r* confirmacio*n*em dicti Cap*itu*li data*m* xv° Aprilis a*n*no p*r*ed*ic*ti Reg*is* sup*r*ad*i*cto.

H*a*bend*um* et tenend*um* p*r*ed*ictum* domi*n*ium ac om*n*ia et sing*u*la p*re*missa c*u*m p*er*tine*n*tiis p*r*e[s]atis Thome et Arthuro et hered*ibus* ip*s*ius Arthuri imp*er*petu*um.* Et ego vero p*r*ed*ictus* Thomas et here*d*es mei om*n*ia et sing*u*la premi*s*sa c*um* p*er*tinen*tiis* p*r*efati*s* Thome[2] et Arthuro[2] et hered*ibus* ip*s*ius Arthuri contra me et heredes meos warrantizabim*us* et imp*er*petu*u*m defendem*us* per p*re*sentes. Sciatis insup*er* me p*r*efatu*m* Thomam in p*ro*pria p*er*sona mea de-

---

[1] *i. e.* Fisher.
[2] *i. e.* Gregory. The last male descendant of this family, lords of the manor of Stivichall, died in 1909.

§ 141. *Stivichall*, 1574.

own person have delivered full and peaceable possession and seisin with all and singular the premises with the appurtenances according to the tenor, force, form and effect of this my present indented Charter.

[In witness whereof to this my present Charter I have affixed my seal of arms to these presents. Dated the last day of July the fifth year of the reign of the lady Elizabeth (etc.), 1563.]

liberasse plenam et pacificam possessionem et seisinam et omnibus et singulis premissis cum pertinentiis Secundum tenorem, vim, formam et effectum huius presentis carte mee Indentate.

In cuius rei testimonium huic presente Carte mee Indentate sigillum meum ad arma presentibus apposui. Datum vltimo die Julii anno regni domine Elizabethe, dei gratia Anglie ffrancie et Hibernie Regine, fide[i] defensoris etc., Quinto.

A true Coppie of the deed varying never a Lettre. A copy varying never a letter!

This deede was ingrossed by John More, servant to Lambert Thomas, scrivener, in fflete-street the 7 daye of ffebruarye 1574 to be newe sealled by Thomas Hawkyns alias ffisher[1] of the Towne of Warrwick, esquier.

Verte & vide plus.   *Turn and see further.*

THE COPYING OF THIS DEED, 1574.

[2] A true and perfect note of the order, maner & forme of the doing and writing of the originall of this Coppie as followeth with the discripcion of the persones.   *How the copy was made.*

Memorandum that the vijth of ffebruary anno domini 1574 one Arthure Gregory and one Edmund Gregory (thone being in a gowne muche like an vtterbarrester, & thother being E. G. in a Cloke) came to the shopp of one Lambert Thomas, scrivener, in fflet-strete, and asked of the same Lambert for one that could write a perfect & a faire secretarye hand; the which Lambert said, "Go to my man, & see his hand." The which they did, & liked well of the hand. And said, "I gave a deed to be ingrossed with speed, and yt must be done very secretly in a Close studdie or parlour & not in the open shopp in

---
[1] Of the Priory, Warwick. See Colville, *Worthies of Warwickshire*, pp 287-91.
[2] leaf 430, back.

§ 142. *Bablake School*, 1563.

<small>and returning in two days</small>
<small>receive it from his hand.</small>

any wyse"; And so lefte his Coppie there (the said Barrester). And so done, poynted a tyme to come for yt two days aftur. And so they bothe came for yt to the said Lambert, & yt was done according to their request; & so they receivid yt by the handes of the said John More, the engrosser of yt, and paid the said Lambert ij s. vj d. or ij s. iiij d. for the engrossing of the same, & gave the wryter for his paynes iiij d., & called for his Coppie & had yt also.

<small>Nevertheless the engrosser had previously revealed the existence of the deed to Mr. Turner, and given him a true copy</small>

<small>for a ryal.</small>

<small>The above copy is the one made by the engrosser,</small>

<small>who signs his name, avouching his account as true.</small>

This ys the true Coppie of the deed verbatim, And I, the said Moore, being in a parlour doyng the same Master Turner comes in about a recognizans for Master Essex. And I said vnto hym, "Master Turner, here ys a deid that maketh mencion of your manour of Stychall." And Master Turner was verye desierous to se yt, (and sawe yt) & went to the said Lambert & desiered hym to have a true Coppie of yt, & he promised hym a Ryoll[1] for yt, the which Coppie I wrote by my Masters comaundement. And this ys a true Coppie of the same deid and true wordes & doinges by the said Gregories aboutes the same.

Per me, Joh. Moore, shriuener predicti Lamberti Thomas.

Per me, Walterum Meredithe, shriuener predicti Lamberti Thomas.

BEQUEST TO BABLAKE SCHOOL.

<small>Will of W. Locker, of London, Jul. 16, 1563.</small>

[2] A note taken out [of] the will & testament of Will. Locker, Citizen & Plommer of London, which will is dated the xvjth daye of July, 1563, in the third[3] yere of her ma^{ties} Raigne, Elizabethe Regine.

<small>The testator's executors</small>

Item, I ordayne & make Wolston. Dixsey & Tho. Walkeden my full & whole executors, & they to paye my dettes & receive all my dettes due & owing to me, & to see my funeralls in & by all thinges discharged; To whome I give all my Landes in Warwickshier, being x li.

<small>are to pay from the proceeds of his Warwick-</small>

---

[1] Ryal (or rose-noble), first coined in Edward IV's time, was worth about 10s. See Kenyon, *Gold Coins*, pp. 57–8.
[2] leaf ix.
[3] July 1563 occurs in the fifth year of Elizabeth.

§ 143. *Tho. Ryley, Mayor. Prices,* 1564.

by yere, paying out of the same x s. by the yere at two termes or feastes vsuall vnto the hospitall of pore Children in Coventre. And they with the same Landes to paye my dettes & discharge my funeralls, & the overplus to be & remayne to their owne vses for & towardes keping of my house in Thistellworthe[1] & the mayntayning of the same in reparacions vntill suche tyme as my Children shall come to their Landes. & then my said executors to surrendur vpp my said Landes truly vnto them without fraud or guyle. And this I Charge them with as they trust to be saved, So that they may quietly enter on the same Landes to them by me before given, & they to have the said overplus of the same x li. Landes to their owne vses for ever.

shire lands 10s. a year to Bablake School,

the surplus to be used for the maintenance of the testator's children.

THO. RYLEY, MAYOR, 1564.
MICHAELMAS LEET.

[2][V. f. p. held before Tho. Ryley, m., Tho. Wyght, Sim. Cotone, b., on Oct. 12, 6 Eliz.]

Oct. 12, 1564.

Mayster Tho. Ryley, Draper, beinge maior of the cytie of Coventre, Anno 1564. In the beginninge of this yere one Stryke of wheate was at Eighte Shillinges and one Strike of rye at Sixe Shillinges, but in the ende of the same yere a strike of wheate was at fourtene pence And a strike of Rye at tenne pence.

JOH. HARFORD, MAYOR, 1569.
THE MAYOR'S CRIME.

[3]Elizabeth R. By the Queene.

Trusty and wel-beloved, we grete you well. We perceive by Lettres written from you vnto our right trustie & right wel-beloved Cosen & Councellour, the Earle of Leicester, whereof he hathe made Report vnto vs, the late mischance happened vnto the maiour of that our Cittie of Coventre being Charged with the deathe of one of our subiectes of our said Cittie for the which he is Comitted

The queen,

on being informed by the Earl of Leicester, that the mayor is charged with having caused the death of one of her subjects,

---

[1] Isleworth.
[2] On a loose leaf beautifully written. See Dugdale, I. 149.
[3] leaf 423. The original of this letter is in the collection of letters Corp. MSS. A. 79, leaf 32. See Dugdale, I. 150. Scribe M.

§ 144. Joh. Harford, Mayor. His crime, 1569.

wishes him to be tried by ordinary course of law,

to ward, And like as we fynd it reasonable that his Cause be tried & ordered by the ordinarye course of Justice, & the lawes of our Realme, without any particuler regard of persones or other privat respect, so do we not thinke convenient that our said Cittie shold Remayne without a head & governour till the accustomed tyme of the eleccion of newe maiour there, which as we be given to vndurstand is not vntill the monethe of November, we lett you therefore witt our pleasure and Comaundement is that

and commands the officers of the city to deprive him of his office and elect another mayor in his stead.

vppon the Receipt of these our lettres, and by aucthoritie of the same, you shall forthwith proceede as well to the deprivacion of the said maiour from his maioraltie, as also to the eleccion of another in his steed to occupie the place of maiour of our said Cittie, vntill you shall at your accustomed ordinary tyme make Choice of a newe, in suche wise as by your Charters you might & ought to do, if the said former maiour weare either dead or otherwise found vnable to execute his said Charge.

This command, however, must not be held to prejudice the said mayor's cause.

Whereby or by any other thing contayned in these our Lettres we meane not to preiudicate[1] the cause of the said late maiour, or that any hold or advantage shold thereby be taken to enforce any matter agaynst hym, or that he shold be otherwise dealt withall in this matter, wherewith he is Charged, then may stand with the ordinary Course of our Lawes, and the due & vpright administracion of Justice, without any maner of parcialitie, or other indirect dealing.

And when your ordinary tyme for the Choice of a newe maiour shal-be come you maye consider whether it shal-be fitt to continewe the persone that you shall nowe Chose in-steed of hym that is to be deprived, or to make choice of a newe, and to do therein as you shall fynd most necessary for the Comon-weale of the said Cittie.

The queen desires to be certified of the proceedings in the trial.

If by order of lawe the fact[2] of your maiour shall deserve deathe, our meaning is that before any execucion be therefore done, you shold certifie vs of your proceadinges in the triall.

---

[1] = to judge (adversely) beforehand.
[2] = deed.

§ 145. *Joh. Myles, Mayor. Bounds*, 1581.

Yeoven vnd*ur* o*ur* Signet at o*ur* towne of Southampton, the viij[th] daye of September the xj[th] yere of o*ur* Raygne.

Southampton, Sept. 8, 1569.

To o*ur* trustie & wel-beloved the Recorder, and aldermen of o*ur* Cittie of Coventre.

The Queenes L*ett*res for the deprivac*i*on of M*aster* Joh. Harford,[1] Maio*ur*.

METES AND BOUNDS, 1581.

[2] A speciall S*ur*vey of the bound*es* & meares, w*hich* devide the Libe*r*tie & Countie of the Cittie of Coventre from the Countie of Warr*wick*, taken the xxvj[th] & xxvij[th] dayes of September 1581 in the xxiij[th] yere of the Raign of o*ur* soue*r*aigne Ladye, Queene Elizabeth, by certen Maiores, Shreiff*es*, Chamberlayns, wardens, & other yong men specially appoynted by Joh. Myles, Maior of the said Citie, to Ryde & S*ur*vey the same, whose names hereafter followe, (that is to saye) Hen. Kervyn, Ric. Barker, Raffe Bowne, Rob. Letherbarrowe, Edw. Burrowes and Tho. Saunders, Late Maiors; Will. Eborne, Hen. Breers & Joh. Rogerson, Late Shreiff*es*; Tho. Graveno*ur*, then one of the Chamberlayns for that yere; & Will. Parker, then one of the wardens; Joh. Bowne, Pet. Willmer, Jas. Rogers, Ric. Saunders, (yonge men appoynted); Joh. Amerson, bayliff of the Citie, & Tho. Banest*ur*, Clarke of the fyle there,[3] w*i*th dyue*rs* others of eue*r*ie Townshipp somm*une* w*i*thin the forrens appoynted by speciall p*r*ecept for that p*ur*pose.

"Civitas Coventrie." A survey is taken on Sept. 26-27, 1581, by certain town officials and other young men specially appointed to the same, of the metes and bounds of the city.

Which S*ur*vey agreeth w*i*th the old record as followethe. [For possible monogram which follows see p. 2.[4]]

ffirst, beginning at Bynley Bridge, Leaving the bridge

The boundary line starts at "Bynley Bridge" and thence

---

[1] One day the mayor, walking outside the town with his greyhounds, encountered one Will. Heley, an embroiderer, accompanied by his spaniel. The animals fell to fighting, and Heley so enraged the mayor by beating the greyhounds off his dog that the latter hit the former so heavily with a stick that he died in a fortnight. Harford was expelled from the council of the city, and compromised with Heley's wife for pardon. Whitley, *Representation*, 56.

[2] leaf v. Scribe Z. See p. 7. For other metes and bounds see above, pp. 7 *sqq.*, and Poole, *Coventry*, pp. 175 *sqq.*

[3] = town-clerk.   [4] The monogram should read T. B. (not as wrongly given p. 2, T. G. D.), *i.e.* Tho. Banestur. See Bateson, *Leicester*, III. 320.

§ 145. *Joh. Myles, Mayor. Bounds*, 1581.

goes to "Wynhall-bridge," thence to "Bagington-milne,"

on the Lefte hand & so following the broke on the left hand vnto Wynhall-bridge,[1] leaving that bridge also & the water on the left hand, & so following that water vnto Baggington-mylne, including the mylne wheele, & all the buylding*es* on this side the whele w*i*thin the Countie of the Citie of Coventr*e*, & so following that wat*u*r throughe the midle arche of the further bridge; and

and by "Marden Siche"

from thence by the said Ryver vnto a corner called Marden Siche[2] betwene Stichall & ffynham ffeild*es*, and from thence turning vp by the said Syche, leaving the

to a mere-stone and to "Cock-lane"

sitche vppon the Left hand vntill you come to the further end of Grangepeece,[3] where standethe a mear-stone. Then

and a mere-stone. From Daniel-field it goes some way to

turne vp to the lanes end, called Cock-lane,[4] where standethe also a mear-ston.

Then leave Daniell-feild on yo*u*r Left hand, & followe the lane still till you come to the corner of the Close

a mere-stone,

there, and so followe the hedge on the Left hand till you come to the Grene Lane, & there standeth a meare-ston.

thence to "Babthorp-wast" and another stone, thence by the "Quenes Crosse" some way to another stone, thence to "Hower-hyron"

& so Crosse oue*r* to the corner of Babethorp-wast vnto another stone there sett, & so oue*r*thwart the heathe vnto a place where somtyme stode a Crosse, called the Quenes Crosse[5] in the highe-waye that leadethe from Coventre toward*es* Kyllyngworthe, & so crossing that waye to the corner of Cannoll Close to another stone ther sett. & so leaving the said Close on the left hand vnto Hower-

and "Call-ers Lane" and another stone, and on to another stone, thence to "Nightin-gale-lane" and another stone.

hyron, & so following the hedge still on the Left hand vntill you come to a lanes end, called Callers Lane, & there standethe another meare-ston. & so Crosse the waye & leave the hedge on the left hand vnto another stone there sett. & so followe the hedge still by the meare-stones till you come to Nightingale Lane end to

Thence the line goes to "Horwell streame"

another [6]stone there sett.

Then followe the hedge still on the Lefte hand vntill you come to a litle River there, called Horwell streame, and so by that River or streame, Leaving yt on the Left

---

[1] See Poole, *Coventry*, p. 175.   [2] See above, p. 12.
[3] *Ibid.*   [4] Given erroneously as Cork-lane, p. 12.
[5] See Poole, *Coventry*, p. 176.
[6] leaf v, back. Nightingale Lane is mentioned in the account of Stivichall Manor, Inq. p. m. Chancery, ser. II, Eliz., vol. 175, no. 105 (Victoria County History MSS. references). See also Poole, *op. cit.* p. 176.

§ 145. *Joh. Myles, Mayor. Bounds*, 1581.

hand, vntill you come to the well called Horwell,[1] & ther ys another mere-stone ssett. & so leaving the said well on the right hand & go betwene the well & the hedge, Leaving the hedge on the Left hand, vnto the corner of the Lane to another stone there sett. & so crosse by the said Lane to another stone. & so by the mear-stones ther sett till you come to a place there, called the Wrastling-place, leaving yt vppon the right hand, & from thence crosse ouer the heathe, called Hersall, by certen mer-stones there standing till you come to a lane, called Guphill-lane, & so downe that lane till you come to thend thereof in the kinges highewaye, leading from Coventre to Alseley, where standethe another meare-stone, & where somtyme stode a payre of gallowes, & so turning by the stone bridge there into a feild, called Stepping-ston-feild, leaving the broke on the left hand. & so following the same ouer the more & Broke-feild, & so ouer the broke into the Nether-hill-feild, where at the Corner neare the broke ys another mear-ston sett. & a litle higher at the next corner ys another stone.

& so following the hedge & ditche on the left hand vnto another stone there sett. & so still vp to the corner of Ouer-hill-feild to another stone there sett. & so turne vp by the meare-stones to Barkers-grove, & there at the gate going out of the Lane into a close on the left hand ys a meare-stone sett.

And so by Barkers Butes, leaving the hedge on the left hand till you come to a meare-ston standing in the Lane end that leadethe toward Coundulne. & so forward still leaving Priors-feild on the Left hand vntill you come to another Lane that leadeth towardes the Mote-house, where standethe another stone, Leaving that lane on the left hand, & so to the lane that leadethe from Coventre to the Mote-house, & ther standethe another stone.

And from thence crossing ouerthwart the waye after the hedge on the left hand vnto the kynges highe-waye that leadethe from Coventre towardes Corley, and so holding that way still by ditches & hedges on the left

Marginalia: and "Horwell" and another stone, and by various stones to the "Wrastling-place" and "Hersall" and by certain stones to "Guphill-lane," and thence to another stone where the gallows stood, thence to "Stepping-ston-feild" and thence to another stone, and thence to the next corner where stands another stone. And the line goes by hedge and ditch to another stone, and thence to "Hill-feild" and another by the stones to "Barkers-grove," and another stone, and by "Barkers-buttes" to a mere-stone, and thence for some way to another stone, thence to the Moat-house and yet another stone, thence some way

---

[1] This is spelled "Whorewel" in Poole, *op. cit.* 176.

§ 145. *Joh. Myles, Mayor. Bounds,* 1581.

to the place where "Corley gallowes" once stood, and another stone.

hand by Counden-wast, & so forward till you come to a grene where som-tyme stode a gallowes, called Corley gallowes,[1] & there standethe another meare-stone.

Thence the line goes past another stone and from "Theiffe-stake-hedge" to "Theiffe-stake pittes" where there is another stone,

Then Crosse ouerthwart the king*es* highewaye there to another stone there standing in the hedge. & so into the Close somtyme the Priors of Coventre, Leaving the hedge, called Theiffestake-hedge on the left hand vntill you come to Theiffe-stake-pittes[2] at a corner of a grove there [3] where standethe another stone in the verie Corner of the dytche. & so followe the dytche of the grove on the Left hand, leaving the grove on the right hand, vntill you come into

and past another,

a lane, & there is another stone. Then turne vpp that lane a litle on the left hand till you come to a stone

and thence some way to "Heyne-lane" and "Corley-grove, now called Newland-parke," and another stone,

standing at another Lanes end on the right hand, called Heyne Lane.[2] And so downe that lane vntill you come to Newland-parke[2] corner, somtyme called Corley-grove, & ther agaynst the lane end leading towardes Astleye standethe another stone, & another in the ditche right agaynst yt. & so fallowe the dytche on the left hand

thence to the Park pale and another stone,

vnto the corner of the hedge agaynst the parke pale, & there in the ditche standethe another meare-stone. Then follow that ditche leaving the parke or grove on the

and thence some way to the "Old-broke," where there is another stone;

right hand till you come to the corner of the hedge to the broke there Runing, called the Old-broke, & ther standethe another meare-stone.

and so from another stone,

& so followe the broke a litle waye & you shall come to another stone there sett. & so fallowe the broke into

by the brook

another woodground, leaving the broke on the left hand

to another

vntill you come to a stone there sett. & so following

to "Smer-cote," by the meres and stones to a place where the flood-gates once stood.

the broke still throughe a meadowe in Smercot[4] by the meares and stones there sett in the old sytche till you come to a place where sometyme the flowdyates of Smer-cote-mylne stode, leaving yt vppon the right hand.

The line passes thence some way to "Kewe-ditche" and a mere-stone to "Birche-feild or Margeries ffeild"

& so from thence turning by the ditche there, called Kewe-ditche[5] by the meare-stones vnto a feild of the Master of S. Jones, sometyme called the Birch-feild, otherwise called Margeries ffeild, & so vp a thorowe[6]

---

[1] See above, p. 15.   [2] *Ibid.*   [3] leaf vi.
[4] See p. 16.   [5] *Ibid.*
[6] = a public way. See "through," s. v. *E. D. D.*

§ 145. *Joh. Myles, Mayor. Bounds,* 1581.

betwene two Land*es* in the middes of the feild by certain meare-stones there sett till you come to the hadlond, then turne on the right hand by the thorowe[1] of the hadland a litle waye to another stone there sett.

Then Crosse ou*er* on the Left hand by certen stones there sett till you come to the lane, called Bawdye-lane, crossing over to the further syde of the said lane to a stone there sett in the ditche. & so following that ditche on the left hand to the next corner to a stone there sett. & so followe that ditche still till you come to another turning in the said lane, & there is another stone sett. There leave the lane & go ou*er* into a Close on the left hand following the hedge & ditche on the left hand till you come to another lane, & so Crosse ou*er* the lane to the further ditche of the same, & so vnto Lufaye-greene,[2] & so followinge the ditche, called Rowe-ditche, vnto Catcrofte-lane,[3] & so fo[llo]wing the said ditche on the left hand vnto Bedworthe-heathe vnto a stone there set. & so Crossing the heathe to another stone there sett. & so to the gate Leading to Bedworthe [4]Pa*r*sonage[2] to another stone there sett. & so downe the Lane leaving the Pa*r*sonage on the Left hand vntill you come to a stone ther sett on the left hand of the said Lane. Then Crosse the Lane to another stone there sett. Then followe the ditche on the right hand, called the Rowe-ditche, betwene Exall & Bedworthe vntill you come to a yate, called Howe-yate,[2] standing in Bedworthe-waye to a stone there sett. Crossing the Lane & following the Dytche & hedge there on the left hand till you come to Weston-heye, & so forward vntill you come to Preist-wood end[2] & to a stone there sett. & from thence by the ditche betwene the heye & Sydnall-wood[2] to a corner of a feild there, called Boyes-wast, where is another stone sett.

& so following the ditche on the right hand, including Boyes-wast-meadowe wi*th*in the libe*r*ties of Coventre, till you come to Bulkington-waye to a stone there sett. Then turning downe the ditche on the right hand a litle waye

by two lands and certain mere-stones to another stone,

thence some way to "Bawdy-lane" and a stone,

thence to another stone,

thence some way to "Lufay-greene," and following "Rowe-ditche" to "Catcroft-lane"

and another stone, and another and so to the "Parsonage gate of Bedworthe" and another stone, thence some way past another stone, and another

to "Howe-yate" and another stone,

thence to "Weston-hey" and by another stone,

to "Boyes-wast" and another stone.

The boundary goes on past

"Bulkington-waye" and another stone,

---

[1] = way, road.   [2] See p. 16.   [3] *Ibid.*
[4] leaf vi, back.

§ 145. *Joh. Myles, Mayor. Bounds,* 1581.

by "Sisley-hole" and "Hyndwell" and another stone, thence some way to "Barwangle-parke" and another stone.

Thence the boundary line goes to "Cancard-lane" and a stone, and "Chappell-feild" and in the lane another stone.

Thence the boundary line goes on to "Leicester-waye" and "Shilton Crosse"

by "Old-forlong" and the boundaries between the furlong to another stone. "Horlen," and thence to a stone set in "Tutbury-waye" to another stone at "Hagthorne," thence the line goes on including "two tenementes in Shilton within the libertie" and returning to two more stones, and down the headland to another and thence "Dunstall & Dunstall-hill" and another stone and by the hedge to another, and thence to another,

into the sitche there, called Sisley-hole, & so turning to the Bridge & vnder the bridge vp the sitche to Hyndwell to a stone ther sett. & so holding the said sitche ouer the pasture or wood ground ther, called Barnacle or Barwangle-parke vnto a Corner of the said parke, somtyme called Barnakle-yate, vnto a stone there sett.

& so following the ditche on the left hand vntill you come to a lane ther, called Cancard-lane to a stone ther sett. Then Crosse ouer the lane holding the ditche by the feild there, called the Chappell-feild, leaving the feild on the Left hand till you come to the Lane goyng into the towne to a stone there sett.

Then Crosse the lane to another stone there sett, following the ditche & hedge vnder Barnacle Leaving yt on the Left hand vntill you come to Leicestur-waye, & so following the lane by the meare-stones vnto Shilton Crosse. & from thence returning back agane downe by the other syde of the Lane vnto a forlong of the Crosse-holt there, called Old-forlong, including the forlong within the libertie of Coventre, & from thence decending by the meares there made betwene the said forlong & Shilton-feild vnto a stone there sett in a place called Horlen.

& so goynge by Horlen vnto a stone sett in Tutburie-waye. & so by Tutburie-waye vnto a stone ther sett in a place, called Hagthorne, & from thence to another stone sett in Hagthorne[1] waye, & so by that waye into Shilton Towne to two tenementes there, one in the tenure of Joh. Lyllye & thother in the tenure of Tho. Coke, including bothe those tenementes. And then retorning back agayne the same waye towardes Hagthorne to two stones there sett. & from thence downe the hade-waye betwene the feildes to a stone there sett. And from thence desending on the left hand downe the balke by Dunstall vnto a stone there sett at the hedge, called Dunstall-hill, & so turning by the hedge on the right hand to another stone at the corner sett. And so desending leaving the hedge & ditche on the right hand vnto the sitche to a stone there sett. & so after the sitche & Leaving the hedge &

---

[1] leaf vii. Repeated "weye."

§ 145. *Joh. Myles, Mayor. Bounds*, 1581.

the broke, called Washebroke, on the right hand till you come to the corner of the hedge to a stone there sett at the nether end of Clark*es*-peice. And so leaving the hedge still on the right hand to the vpper corner of the hedge at the vpper end of Clark*es*-peice to a stone ther sett.

& so turning by the hedge corner on the right hand after the hades[1] to another stone there sett at the nether end of Hanging. And so turning vp a balke there on the left hand betwene the feild*es* vnto two stones standing close together at the vpper end of Hanging, and so after the hades[1] Like a quit*es* cast[2] to two other stones there standing together, & so desending downe a balke on the left hand betwene the feild*es* by Turk-furlong vnto the corner of the hedge of Turk ffurlong. & so into Shilton Asmedowe to a stone at the corner of the hedge there sett. & so following the hedge on the right hand to the next corner of the hedge to another stone there sett. & so leaving the hedge still on the right hand to two stones in the corner vnder Turk-forlong.

And so leaving the hedge still by Broche Leys to a stone there sett. And so to the sitche betwene Asmedowe & Happisford-feild to a stone ther sett. & so following the siche on the left hand till you come to the broke, called Long-forde, to a stone there sett. & so leaving the broke on the left hand till you come to the gate going into Combe-pastures, called Anstie-stakes.

& so following the broke on the left hand vntill [3] you come to the Corner of the hedge at Humfrey-holme to a stone there sett. & so leaving the hedge on the left hand betwene Sowe-feild & Anstie to a stone there. & so leaving the hedge still on the left hand to the hadewaye, called Crowe-nest, to another stone there sett. & so to another stone about a quit*es* cast of standing at thend of Radma*n* Rowe, & so desending by the hedge on the left hand to another stone there sett at Radman-wall, & so

Marginalia: leaving the "Washebroke" the line travels to another, and yet another at "Clark*es*-peice." Another stone is set at "Hanging," thence the line goes some way to two more stones, and thence by "Turk-forlong" to "Shilton Asmedowe" and another stone, thence some way to another. The line passes on to "Brocheleys" and a stone, and so on to "Happisford-feild" and another stone, thence to "Long-ford" and another, and "Anstie-stakes." Thence the line passes to "Humfrey-holme," and thence to a stone, thence to "Crowe-nest" and another stone, and another at "Radman Rowe," and another at "Radman-wall,"

---

[1] A strip of unploughed land forming a boundary line. *N. E. D.* s. v. Hade.
[2] *i. e.* a quoit's cast, or, as we now say "a stone's throw."
[3] leaf vii, back.

§ 145. *Joh. Myles, Mayor. Bounds,* 1581.

and thence to another,

and another,

and another, and yet another at " Sowemeare."

At " Sowewast " is another stone,

and at the close corner another,

and the line follows the ditch to another, and the hedge to another, thence to " Woodlane " and another stone, again to another in the ditch, thence to " Shortcroft " and another stone. The line goes " Sitcheford " and a stone to " Heytell " and thence to a stone, and by the ditch to another,

and another,

thence to " Sowebroke,"

" Sowebridge " and " Sowetowne."

The line passes to a cottage, [2] *" now in the tenure of Condale,"* [2] *and to various other tenements.*

downe to another stone there sett in the corner of the sitche. And so assending by the sitche on the Left hand to another stone, and so to the Corner of the sitche to another stone. Then Crosse the sitche & leave yt on the right hand to a ston standing neare the gate, called Sowemeare. & so vpp by the said ditche still on the right hand by the meare-stones till you com to the corner of Sowe-wast to a meare-stone there sett. & so turning by Sowe-feild on the left hand, and including Sowe-wast, to a stone ther sett, neare to the Close corner, & so leaving the Close on the right hand to another stone there sett. & so following the ditche on the right hand still to another stone. & so after the hedge still by the meare stones to the gate betwene the feild*es* to a stone there sett. & so still forward by the said ditche till you come to the lane, called Wood-lane, to a stone there sett. & so Crosse the Lane to another stone there sett in the ditche. & so following the ditche on the left hand into a Close, called Shortt-croft to a stone there sett.

& so turning into the feild, called Sitcheforde, to a stone there sett, following the ditche by a close, called Heytell, leaving yt on the right hand till you come to the sitche vnto a stone there sett. & so following the sitche leaving yt on the right hand to a stone there sett in the feild called Sitcheford. & so following the sitche still to the gate going into Wiken-feild to a stone there sett. & so following the sytche [1] still on the right hand to Sowebroke to the nether corner of the feild, callyd Sitcheford, and so over the broke and leaping yt on the Left hand to Sowe Bridge. And so into Sowe towne vnto the Lodge Close, includinge all that Close. And so to a ten*ement* sometyme the Duke of Norfolk*es*, & nowe the Lo: Barkeleys, & nowe in the holding of Will. Wale.

And so to a Cottage of Joh. Petoes adioyning to the same, Late in the holding of one Joh. Cromcote & nowe in the holding of Ric. Woodward. And so to another ten*ement* of the same Joh. Petoe, somtyme in the holding of Will. Wilmer, and nowe in the tenure of Tho. Drught.

---

[1] leaf viii. [2]–[2] In a later hand.

§ 145. Joh. Myles, Mayor. Bounds, 1581.

And so to another tenement of the Lo: Barkley adioyning to the same somtyme in the holding of Margaret Quynton and nowe in the tenure of Agnes Jackson. And from thence to a tenement of the said Joh. Petoe which Will. Wilmer sometyme heild, & nowe yt is in the tenure of the said Will. Wale.

And from thence to a tenement of the said Joh. Petoe with iij quarterns[1] of Land, which one Tho. Sandes sometyme heild, & nowe in the holding of Tho. Lapworthe. And so to a Close called Cowles-grownd, with iij quarterns of Land, whereon somtyme was a tenement, & yt was the Priors of Arburie, & nowe Mr. Andersons, & is nowe in the holding of Rob. Ratlyffe. And so from thence to a Close of Mr. Petoes, where sometyme was a Cottage in the holding of one Hutchyns & nowe in the holding of Tho. Lapworthe & yt extendeth to Sowe-broke.

And so to another peice of grounde adioyning to the same where sometyme was a messuage of the Lord Barkeley, with halfe a yardland, which one Robynson, parker of Calloughdone, heild. And so to the Preistes house with a garden of the same, and so to Sowe Bridge agayne leaving the broke & the mylne on the right hand, including yt within the Countie of Coventre. And so following the River still till you come to Hongerley-corner to a stone there sett.

& so following the ditche [2] Leaving Hongerley on the right hand till you come to Combe-broke to a stone there sett. Then turne into Hungerley-meadowe, Leaving Combe-broke on the Left hand vnder the Coningre[3] till you come to Sowe-broke, leaving the broke on the left hand till you come to Bynley-milne Dame vnto the flodyates there. And then leaving them & the broke on the left hand, and so following the same water to Bynley Bridge where you began and there an end.[4]

unto "Sowe-mylne"

and a stone at "Hongerley" corner.

The line passes to a stone at "Combe-broke," then passes under the "Coningree" to "Sowe-broke" and "Bynley-mylne-dam",

and follows the water to "Binley-bridge" where the boundary line ends.

---

[1] quartern = one fourth of a virgate, generally reckoned as 8 acres. [2] leaf viii, back. [3] = rabbit-warren.
[4] Monogram follows as above.

§ 146. *The Musters*, 1584.

TROOPS, 1584.

[1] A Coppie of the Counsells Letters for the mustering horses.[2]

The Council writes to Sir Fulke Greville and others approving of the addition of divers citizens of Coventry to the commission for mustering horse within the county of the city.

After our right hartie Comendacions: We have receceivid (*sic*) your Lettre of the xij[th] of this present, & for answer therevnto have thought good to signifie vnto you that we Like verie well that in the vewing & mustering of the horsemen within the Citie & Countie of Coventre Hen. Breres, nowe maior, Ric. Smythe, Raffe Bowne & Ric. Barker, Aldermen, sholde ioyne with you, And so by vertue of her ma[ties] Comission, directed vnto vs in that behalfe, depute & aucthorize bothe you & them Joyntly to procede in the said service according to the Instruccions heretofore sent vnto you. And so requier you to make your certificat accordingly, whereof we praye you that there be no default, and so bydd you farewell.

Oatlandes,[3] Sept. 20, 1584.

ffrom Otelandes,[3] the xx[th] of September, 1584.

Your Loving ffrendes,

W. Burley,   G. Sheresbury,[4]   A. Warwick,
R. Leicester,   Howard,   James Croft,
Chr. Hatton,   Fra. Walsyngham.

To our very Lovinge frendes Sir ffulk Grevill,[5] knight, Geo. Digby,[6] and Edw. Bowghton,[7] Esquires.

The Certificate of the Muster of horses for the Citie & Countie of Coventre taken at Coventre the second daye of October, Anno 1584.

---

[1] leaf 423, back.
[2] The organization of the militia was promoted in Elizabethan times by the periodic holding of musters about every three years, carried on through the medium of commissions addressed to the nobility and gentry of every county. See *Dom. State Papers* (1547–80), pp. xiii.–xiv. The certificates transmitted from the Warwickshire commissioners to the Privy Council form the most complete specimen of their kind.
[3] In Surrey, one mile N.W. of Walton-on-Thames. Hen. VIII. built a palace here.
[4] George Talbot, sixth Earl of Shrewsbury.
[5] Fulke Greville, first Lord Broke, 1554–1628.
[6] Of the Coleshill Digbys, and father of John, Earl of Bristol.
[7] Of Causton, near Rugby. He is said to have built this mansion from materials obtained from the White Friars, Coventry.

§ 146. *The Musters*, 1584.

Lighte horses.

The Citie of Coventrie.	The Counte of Coventre.	
Hen. Breres, maior,[1] Tho. Niccolls and Ric. Barker. } 1.	Cha. Hales, gent., Humf. Baker, Arth. Gregory,[3] } 1.	*The city and county of Coventry respectively*
Ric. Smyth, Edw. Burrowes. } 1.	Joh. Hales, gent. 1.	
Edw. Damport, Hen. Kervyn and Ralfe Bowne. } 1.	Joh. Nethermyll, gent.[4] Joh. Horne and Anthony Randle. } 1.	
Raffe Joyner, Tho. Saunders,[2] Joh. Myles and Gilb. Diglen. } 1.	Rob. Turner, gent.,[5] Baldwyn Hill. } 1. Summa iiij. Summa totalis viij.	*furnish four horses, total eight.*

Summa iiij.

Hen. Breers, maior.	Sir ffulk Grivell, knight.	"Commissioners."
Ric. Smythe,	Geo. Digbye,	
Ric. Barker,	Edw. Boughton.	
Raffe Bowne.		

[1] Member for Coventry in the Parliaments of 1586, 1587, 1588, 1601 and 1604.

[2] Member in 1586, 1587, 1592 and 1601.

[3] See above, p. 815. For the suit in the Star Chamber between the Mayor and Community of Coventry on the one hand, and Arthur and Edm. Gregory on the other, see *Star Chamber Proceedings* (P.R.O.), Ble. 59, no. 13. 23 Eliz. ; Ble. 48, no. 7. 24 Eliz. ; Ble. 69, no. 30. 25 Eliz. Only the Interrogatories and Depositions have been found ; the Bill and Answer are apparently missing (Mr. E. F. Kirk). The Gregorys were accused of forgery of a Court roll, counterfeiting of hands, falsifying an ancient Register-Book, forging of blanks and divers other misdemeanours ; but the charge was dismissed on the ground of insufficient proof, a misdemeanour of Arthur not being within the power of the Star-chamber to deal with. Edm. Gregory was allowed and paid his costs (Corp. MSS. A 79, fol. **77).

[4] For Jul. Nethyrmyll see p. 634.

[5] See pp. 815, 818.

§ 146. *The Musters*, 1584.

[1] The Copie of the *Lettre* of answer to the *Lordes* of the Counsell.

The mayor and his brethren inform the Council that they have taken the muster of horsemen;

Our duties most humblie Remembred: Whereas we received your honorable Letters dated the xx[th] of September Last past, whereby you deputed vs to take the view and muster of horsemen in the Countie of the Cittie of Coventre, yt maye please your honors to be advertised that we have performed the said service accordingly, and have here-enclosed sent a certificat of suche persons as were there Charged, and of their seuerall charges, which were verie well furnished in all poyntes,

and apologise humbly for the lack of sufficient riders,

saving that the Citizens of Coventre wanted sufficient Ryders for their horses by reason their servantes have rather byn brought vpp in following their occupacions

owing to want of practice on the part of the citizens.

then in Ryding of horses, which want we humblye desier your Lordshipes to pardon, The rather for that this is the first tyme that they have bene so Charged and the warning so shorte as they could not well be provided of men to serve for that purpose. We have likewise taken notes of the names and furniture of the Ryders with the Coullors, Stature, markes and furniture of their horses. And so most humbly take our Leave. At Coventre

Oct. 9, 1584.

the ix[th] daye October Anno 1584.

Your LLordshipes most humblie to Comand
Hen. Breres, maior,
Ric. Smythe,   ffulke Grivell,
Ric. Barker,   Geo. Digby,
Raffe Bowne,   Edw. Boughton.

To the Right honorable our singler good Lordes, The arles of Warwick & Leicester, and to the honorable Sir Christopher Hatton, knight, vice-Chamberlayne to her ma[tie].

[1] leaf 424.

§ 147. *The Musters*, 1590.

ANOTHER MUSTER, 1590.

[1] Elizabeth R.

Trustie & wel-beloved, we greet you well : Whereas we have thought it meet to be perfectlie informed of the strengthe & forces of this our Realme, And therefore have given Comaundement to our privie Counsell to write their Lettres vnto our Lieutenantes of the seuerall Counties to muster as well the horsmen as fotemen that have ben reduced into bandes and companies within the Counties vndur their lieutenantes nowe before the winter dothe approche; and to send hither perfect Certificattes & muster Roles of the nomber of the said fotemen & horsmen by the middest of October next ensuing to be shewed vnto vs. These shal-be to will & aucthorice you, or any two of you, by vertue of theise our Lettres to take the vewe & musters of the horsmen & fotemen within the Countie of Warrwick and them to put in good araye for our servis by all suche meane & by suche direccions as you shall receave by Lettres vndur the handes of any syx of our privie Counsell. And we do Likewise by thes presents authorice you & the maiour of the Cittie of Coventre to take the vieu & muster of all those hable men that are within the said Cittie & liberties thereof, as well horsmen as fotemen in some convenient place within the Liberties of the said Cittie. And these our lettres shal-be your sufficient warrant for your procedinges in that behalfe.

Given vndur our signet at our Castle of Wyndsor the xvj[th] daye of September in the the xxxij[th] yere of our Raign.

> To our trustie and wel-beloved Sir ffoulk Grevile, Sir Tho. Lucie [2] & Sir Joh. Harrington,[3] knightes.

The queen directs Sir Fulke Greville and others

to muster horse and foot

within the shire of Warwick,

and the county of the city of Coventry.

Sept. 16, 1590.

---

[1] leaf 424, back. See for the original the correspondence volumes Corp. MSS. A. 79, leaf 76.

[2] See Mrs. Stopes' *Warwickshire Contemporaries of Shakespeare*, pp. 23-41.

[3] John, first Lord Harrington, sometime recorder of Coventry and tutor to Elizabeth, afterwards Queen of Bohemia.

§ 148. *The Sacrament*, 1611.

KING JAMES AND THE SACRAMENT, 1611.

[1] James R.

The king, James I, being informed

Trusty and well-beloued, we greet you well. We haue beene informed of a thing continued among you in that our Cytie of Couentry whereof we intend a presente reformacion according to that which is by law established in this our Churche of England, and Commaunded and, as we take yt, in all places els of this our Kingdom observed, as we ourself in our person doe carefully perform yt, although we doubt not but that yow and the whole world are assured that we detest both Idolatry and Supersticion as much as any whosoeuer.

that the citizens refuse to kneel when receiving the Sacrament, but sit or stand during its celebration, having charged the bishop to bring about conformity in this matter,

The said disorder noted with you is that you refuse to receiue the blessed Sacraments of the body and blood of Christ kneeling, but receiue it for the most parte standing or sitting. We haue hereof giuen especiall Charge to our servant, the Bishop of that diocese, to see this abuse reformed; Yet of our princly favor towardes you, and for that we find in our said servant, your Bishop,[2] a desire to affect this by good means and gentle persuasions rather then by legall proceedinges against any, we haue thought

admonishes the archdeacon of his dislike of this laxity,

good first to signifie our pleasure and to admonish you of our dislike hereof, presuming that the same shall so worke with you that there shall not need any other means to draw you to that which duty and piety doe binde you to.

We therefore hereby signifie vnto you that we hould yt an vnsufferable disorder in a well settled Church and State that any perticuler society or Cytie professedly and publickly (especially in a religious accion) should doe the contrary of that which the ordinances of that Church and State doe Commaund, and that we are

which he will no longer tolerate,

resolued by noe means to giue so much as the least way to any pretence of prescription or indulgence heretofore afforded to patronize such an enormity, but doe require of you both by your example and by all such authority as any way is Committed vnto you, and otherwise that you

---

[1] leaf 525, back. Scribe N. See for original Corp. MSS. A 79, leaf 35; see also *ibid*, leaf 97, for further correspondence.
[2] Ric. Neyle.

§ 148. *The Sacrament,* 1611.

endevour to bring all our Subiectes of that Cytie to the performance of that which in this Case both you and they are by our ecclesiasticall laws Commaunded as you tender our good opinion of your goverment in your places, or respect our displeasure for the Contrary.

And we doe allso hereby Charge you, Doctor Hinton, the Vicar of the parish Church of St Michaell within that our Cytie of Couentry and Archdeacon there, that you both in your own person obserue the Canons of our Church in that Case established for the receiuing of the said holy Communion kneeling; and likewise that you doe see the same to be performed by others, that both in private by conference, and in publique by exhortacion in preaching, you endeavour to draw all of your Cure and Jurisdicion to perform this duty which law justly enioyneth, and we upon so good a ground require of them. Hereof we require you not to faile as you tender our displeasure for the not doing thereof.

and charges him

to observe the canons in his own person, and insist on their observance by the citizens, urging them both privately and publicly to obey this injunction

on pain of his majesty's displeasure.

Given under our Signet at our Pallace of Westminster the fourth day of ffebruary in the eight yere of our raigne of Great Brittain, ffrance, and Ireland.

Feb. 4, 1611.

The superscription of the lettre.

To our trusty and well-beloued the Maior, Aldermen and Sheriues and other our Officers and louing Subiectes of our Cytie of Couentry, And To Doctor Hinton, [1] Archdeacon of Couentry and vicar of the Parish Church of St Michaell in our said Cytie.[2]

THE COMMON COUNCIL, 1617.

[3] The Confirmacion of the Common Councell.

Whereas there hath beene some matters of controuersie had & moved betweene the Maior and Aldermen & others of the Councell-house of this Citie of Coventrey and the Bailiffes & them of the Common Councell of the said Citie:

Whereas matters of controversy having arisen between divers members of the corporation

---

[1] Vicar of S. Michael's from 1583 to 1623. He was a sometime University preacher, and a liberal and charitable divine. A brass tablet in S. Michael's commemorates his first wife, who died in 1594.
[2] This letter has been printed by Dugdale and Sharp. See *Warwickshire,* (1730) I. p. 151, and *Antiquities,* p. 18.
[3] leaf 432. Scribe O.

§ 149. *The Council,* 1617.

it is agreed for pacifying these contentions that 25 citizens shall compose the common council, and that on the death of one of them, or his removal to the House of the mayor and aldermen, the jury of the next Court Leet shall choose another in his room.

It is now for pacifieng of all matters by theire mutuall consent*es* agreed in manner and forme following; That there shall from tyme to tyme be and contynue ffyve and Twentie Citizens and ffreemen of the said Citie of the Common Councell of the said Citie, as now they be, and that if any of them dye or be removed or called into the Councell House of the Maior and Aldermen of the said Citie,[1] That then there shall at the next Leete then following be chosen so many more of the ffreemen and Citizens of the said Citie, as shall make vp the nomber of ffyve and Twentie as aforesaid; The same choise to be made by the Jury of the Court Leete (as other Officers of the said Citie be).

At every Leet 31 citizens are to be returned upon the jury according to an act made in 1600.

And that from tyme to tyme henceforward there shal-be at everie Leete One and Thirtie Citizens and ffreemen of the said City impannelled and returned vpon the said Jury according to a former acte of Leete made in the Two and fourtieth yeare of the raigne of the late Queene Elizabeth of famous memorie.

And further the bailiffs and 6 of the said common council (which 6 are to be chosen by the said council) are to have a voice with the mayor and aldermen in letting or selling lands belonging to the city,

And it is further agreed that from henceforward there shal-be from tyme to tyme the Bailiff*es* of the said Citie for the tyme being, and Sixe of the Com*m*on Councell for the tyme being, w*h*ich shall have voyce w*i*th them in the said Councell-house of the Maior and Aldermen as they of the said Councell-house have in setting, letting, selling and buying of the land*es*, Tythes and Hereditament*es* of or belonging to the said Citie, The said Six to be chosen from tyme to tyme by the said Com*m*on Councell.

Provided alwayes that the said Six shall not have any voices with the letting, setting, or disposing of such land*es*, Tenement*es* and hereditament*es*, w*h*ich are conveyed by ffeoffment to other persons vpon trust, but the same shal-

such men being chosen as have no interest in the particular lands under consideration.

be disposed of according to the don*ou*rs intent. And it is agreed that the said Sixe persons shal-be such[2] as the matter wherin they shall have theire voyces shall not in any sorte concerne themselves or any of theire kindred.[3]

And it is further agreed from tyme to tyme that fower

---

[1] The existence of this Council House and the distinct body, the Common Council, received legal confirmation in the charter of 19 James I. [2] leaf 432, back.
[3] See above, p. 73, for the witnessing of indentures made under the common seal.

§ 150. *Strangers*, 1622.

of the Common Councell for the tyme being shall from tyme to tyme be present at the taking of the Accomptes belonging or concerning the Citie,[1] the same to be from tyme to tyme chosen by the said Common Councell of the said Citie. And they of the said Common Councell shall from tyme to tyme be acquainted with all the landes, Tenementes and Hereditamentes, which have or shal-be given to any charitable vses for the good of the said Citie, or poore of the said Citie, or for any other good vses concerning the said Citie, and to what charitable vses the same be given.

And it is likewise agreed that the Maior of the said Citie for the tyme being shall subscribe his name to every lease, which hereafter shall be made and the keyes of the Chest where the Common Seale lyeth[2] shal-be at all tymes kept as now they be.

And it is lastly agreed that when any landes, Tenementes or hereditamentes shal-be sett, sold, bought or lett, that the same shal-be first viewed by two or fower of the said Councell House of the Maior and Aldermen, and two or fower of the said Common Councell, before the same shal-be sett, sold, bought or lett, and not before such a viewe to be had and made.

In witnes whereof and for confirmacion of this agreement it is agreed by all the said parties that this agreement shal-be entred into the black booke,[3] which is kept in the said Councell-house, and the Maior, Aldermen and other of the said Councell-house have for theire part deliuerd to the said Bailiffes and Common Councell this Coppie thereof vnder the Common Seale of the said Citie. Dated the xiijth daie of September, 1617.

Samuell Myles, Maior.

Margin notes: Also 4 of the common council are to be present at making of the accounts. and the common council is to be informed of the disposal of land for charitable uses. The mayor is to subscribe his name to every lease; and the keys of the chest where the common seal is kept are to be where they now are. Any lands, etc., to be let or sold are to be viewed by two or four of the council of the mayor and aldermen, and two or four of the common council. This agreement is to be entered in the Black Book. Sept. 13, 1617.

STRANGERS, 1622.

[4] An act against Straungers.

Where at the last Leete houlden in this Citie the eight daie of October last there was then revived an Act of Leete towching fforrenors and Strangers vsing the Trades and meanes of ffreemen in the said Citie made

Margin: An act passed

---

[1] See above, p. 65. [2] See above, p. 73, *et passim.*
[3] See Introduction. [4] leaf 434. Scribe P.

§ 150. *Strangers*, 1622.

Apr. 23, 1616,

in these words:
The exercising of trades—particularly malting—by strangers,

the three and twentieth daie of Aprill in the fowerteenth yeare of the raigne of o*u*r Soveraigne Lord king James of England, ffrance and Ireland in hæc Verba :—

[1] Forasmuch as by daily experience it is found too manifest in this Citie that the exercising of the Trades of Maulting, brewing and victualing by manie Straungers, fforreyners in this Citie and Suburbs thereof (not being ffreemen) hath beene a great hinderance and damage to many of the poore Citizens, ffreemen of this Citie, vsing the same Trades in tyme of theire older age and decay of theire other Trades (manie of them having spent a good part of theire estates in the necessarie charg of the support and maintena*u*nce of the State of this Citie by office

who have borne nothing of the charge of the city's maintenance,

and otherwise—whereof the said fforreyner beareth no burthen). And where also some of the same fforreyners having great stock*es* do greedily ingrosse vp great quantities of barley for maulting, to the preiudice of all in

is hurtful especially to poor maltsters, and whereas undesirable strangers have obtained the freedom of the city by insufficient security, eventually having to be supported at the public charge,

generall, and more especially to the great damage of the poore Citizens vsing the same Trade of maulting: And where further it is founde by like experience that manie fforreyners having litle or verie small abilitie have obtayned theire ffreedome of this Citie by weake sureties for theire not charging this Citie by themselves, theire wyves or Children, which hath often after falne out to the generall Charg of this Citie (of all which inconveniences manie of the Com*in*altye of this Citie have often Complained for redresse) : And forasmuch as everie Citie, Towne Corporate and bodie politique hath vsed and ought to preferr theire owne Citizens and ffreemen before Straungers, and to provide by good act*es* and ordinances (not repugnant to the lawes) for the Conservac*i*on and better maintena*u*nce of them and theire said Cities, Townes Corporate and bodies politique to the vttermoste of thei[r] powers :—

it is enacted

It is therefore (and for the repressing of the excessive number of Maultsters, Brewers, and Victualers in this Citie) the excessive number whereof is against the law, Enacted at and by the authoritie of this Leete that from

that from Act. 8 [1622]

and after the said eight daie of October no fforreyner or

[1] For original order see *Leet Book* II, Corp. MSS. A 3 (b), leaf 83.

§ 150. *Strangers*, 1622.

Strang[er] shal-be admitted, made or sworne a ffreeman of this Citie vntil he have put in very good suerties for his not charging of this Citie by himself, wyfe or Children, and vntill he have the allowance thereof by Mr. Maior of this Citie (for the time being) and tenn of the Justices of the peace of the same: *(no one is to be admitted a freeman unless he has substantial people for sureties, and has the permission of the mayor and ten justices of the peace.)*

And also it is Enacted at and by the authoritie of this Leete that no fforreyner or Straunger (not being a ffreeman of this Citie and inhabiting in this Citie or Suburbs thereof) shall from and after the said eight daie of October without the consent and [1] Allowance of the said Maior and Tenn Justices) vse or exercise the said Trades of Maulting, Brewing, or victualling, or anie of them, within this Citie or Suburbs thereof, vpon paine that everie fforreyner so vsing or exercising the same Trades, or anie of them shall forfeite for every moneth he or they shall so vse or exercise the same ffyve pound*es* of lawfull money of England, to be levied by waie of distresse To vse of the Maior, Bailiff*es* and Co*min*altie of this Citie. *(Neither is any stranger to be a maltster without the consent of the mayor and ten J.Ps., on pain of £5 for every month that he has carried on this occupation.)*

ffor the better performance and accomplishment of which said Act, Wee the now Maior and Justices of the peace of the said Citie (whose names are subscribed) do hereby agree and promise that we, nor any of vs, shall or will at anie tyme or tymes hereafter by anie manner of wayes or meanes whatsoever directly or indirectly licence, authorise, allow, or tollerate any fforryner or Straunger whatsoever (contrary to the purport true intent and meanyng of the said Act of Leete) to vse, occupie, exercise, or enioy any the said Trades or meanes of Maulsters, Brewers, or victualers, or any of them within the said Citie or Suburbs thereof. *(The mayor and justices, whose names are underwritten, undertake to do nothing in contravention of this act,)*

In testimonie whereof we have herevnto put o*ur* hand*es* the ffyfteenth daie of October, Anno d*o*m*i*ni 1622, Annoq*ue* regni d*o*m*i*ni n*os*tri Jacobi reg*is* nunc Angl*ie* vicesimo. And it is further agreed that all succeeding Justices of the peace of this Citie (for the time being) shall (at theire entrance into that office) subscribe to this order. *(to which all succeeding justices must subscribe.)*

[1] leaf 434, back.

§ 151. *The School,* 1622.

[1] Joh. Pixley, major, Tho. Potter, maior elect, Hen. Sewall, Ric. Butler, Chr. Davenport, Will. Hancock, Hen. Smyth, Joh. Herringe, Joh. Barker, Sam. Myles, Hum. Smallwod, Mat. Collyns, Hen. Dauenport.[1]

DONATION TO THE SCHOOL, 1622.

A council held Dec. 18, 1622.

[2] [A council held there Dec. 18, 1622, before Tho. Potter, m., Hen. Sewall,[3] Ric. Butler, Chr. Davenport, Hen. Smyth, Joh. Herring, Sam. Myles, Will Sewall,[3] Humf. Smallwood, Isaac Walden, Joh. Pixley, Jac. Illedg.]

"Mr Chr. Dauenport,"

Whereas Mr. Chr. Dauenport (one of the Bretheren of this house) hath for many yeres heretofore at his owne charges mainteined and kept one Schoole-maister in the Schoole of this Citie for the educating and bringing vp of such poore Children of this Citie whose Parentes are not able to paie for theire learning, bookes, and thinges thereto apperteyning. And whereas it hath pleased God to put into the minde of the said Mr. Dauenport to establish the same good and charitable worke, so that it might be continued.

having maintained a schoolmaster at the school for the educating of poor children,

is minded to place his charitable work on a substantial footing: and accordingly has made over to the mayor, bailiffs and commonalty a bond, or Statute Merchant,

And where also the said Mr. Chr. Dauenport heretofore lent and delivered vnto Joh. Hammond (now deceased late of the said Citie doctor in Physicke) the summ of two hundred poundes of lawfull money of England, for the securitie of which money the said Mr. Dr. Hammond stood bounden to the said Mr. Dauenport in the summ of fower hundred poundes. The said Mr. Dauenport at the tyme of the delivery of the said money intending that the benefit thereof coming should be for the performance of the said charitable guift. And where since the said Dr. Hammond dyed, and the said Statut Merchaunt forfeited for none-payment of the money, which the said Mr. Dauenport was inforced to put in suyt by way of extent,[4] wherevpon divers landes, Tenementes, and hereditamentes (late the said Joh. Hammondes) were extended according

in £400 (being granted as security by one Dr. Hammond for a loan of £200 made to him by Davenport) together with lands, tenements, etc.,

the property of Hammond, seized into Davenport's

[1–1] All these names are in the hands of the different signatories.
[2] leaf 436. Scribe Q. See Dugdale, I. 151.
[3] See above, p. 724.
[4] Or writ of extent, *i.e.* seizure of lands, etc., for non-payment of debt.

§ 151. *The School*, 1622.

to law. The said Mr. Chr. Dauenport (desiring to see the setling and establishment of the said charitable guift in his life tyme) this present Counsell-house daie is contented and pleased to graunt and assigne over vnto the Maiour, Bailiffes and Cominaltie of the saide Citie of Coventrey and to theire Successours and assignes the said obligacion of Statut Merchaunt and all his estate, right, title and interest therein, and all the landes, Tenementes and hereditamentes extended by vertue of the same. To thend that the said Maior, Bailiffes and Cominaltye shall by sufficient conveyance in the law, assure and convey Twentie Markes per annum to be paid at fower vsuall feastes in the yeare to the said Mr. Christo. Dauenport during his naturall life, and after his decease the like yearely summ of Twentie Markes to performe and supply the said good and charitable guift in such manner as the said Mr. Christo. Dauenport in and by his last will and Testament in writing shall limit and appoint for the purposes aforesaid.

It is this daie agreed that yf any suite be had against the said Mr. Dauenport concerning his assignement of the said Statut that this house shall beare the charg therof.

Memorandum that in December 1625 Mr. Chr. Dauenport paid ten Shillinges for **Wyne** (parcell of his guift) as appereth by Mr. Wheatleys accompt.[1]

Marginalia: hands by reason of his creditor's non-payment of the debt. The arrangement is that the mayor, bailiffs, etc., shall pay Davenport 20 marks a year during his life and after his decease to employ the said sum in the performance of such charitable work as Davenport by his last will and testament shall determine. Dec. 1625 Mr. Davenport paid 10s. for wine.

§ 7 JOHN ESTERTON, MAYOR, 1422.

[2] [Gosford Ward.]	[Earl-street Ward.]
Joh. Wellford.	Will. Swan.
Bened. Marchall.	Will. Colas.
Joh. Style.	Joh. ffranklen.
Joh. Baker.	Joh. Euerdon.

---

[1] *Coventry Charities* (1733), p. 67. The Davenport trust arising from land called Black Orchard and administered by the drapers' fellowship was to be expended in (1) the salary of a schoolmaster to teach poor children to write and read £10 a year ; (2) to the city bailiff in seeing the poor children furnished with books 10/- a year ; (3) to the mayor and his brethren for their care 10/- a year ; the residue was to be spent in books, paper, ink, hose and shoes for the poor children.

[2] leaf 10. See p. 43 for sums collected.

§ 7. *Joh. Esterton, Mayor,* 1422.

[Jurden Well Ward.]
Rob. Defford.
Joh. Abram.
Joh. Cressy.
Joh. Lysturley.

[Much Park Ward.]
Rob. Pynnok.
Will. Bryde.
Will. ȝate.
Joh. Lee, smyth.

[1] [Bailly and Hay Lanes Ward.]
Joh. Ronton.
Joh. Harborgh, jun.
Will. Brooke.
Joh. Benett, wird[rawer].

[Broad gate.]
Will. Marchall.
Joh. Malory.
Rog. Cokkes.
Rob. Saxton.

[Smithford Ward.]
Tho. Carter.
Godef. Barbour.
Ric. Sadeler.
Joh. Tate.

[Cross cheaping Ward.]
Joh. Deyster.
Sun. Est.
Mat. White.[2]
Will. Pratte.

[Spon Ward.]
Will. Byneley.
Joh. White.
Joh. Lychfeld, mercer.
Joh. Stylle, deyster.

[Bishop-street Ward.]
Joh. Mongomery.
Ric. Marche.
Rog. Lesyngham.
Will. Bate.

§ 59. RIC. BRAYTOFT, MAYOR, 1474.
MICHALMAS LEET.

"Couentre." [3] ¶ [V. f. p. held on Thursday after Michaelmas, 14 Ed. IV.]

Will. Stafford, Ric. Braytoft, sen., Tho. Bradmedowe, Joh. Ruyton, Joh. Gauge, Will. Saunders, Joh. Thrumpton, Rob. Atterton, Rob. Onley, Tho. Ingram, Tho. Dove, Ric. Colyns, Joh. Hotton, Joh. Hadley, Rob. Blubere, Will. Baxster, Will. Thistulton, Joh. Assheburn, Hen. Marler, Will. Taillour, Bower, Will. Cramp, Tho. Bagot, Joh. Grove, Ric. Pulton.

Bailiffs. [Will. Shore, Will. Marchall.]

"Mayor & triers to Assiz the water at mills."
"water markes at milnes."

[Ordained] that the Meir with vj of his Brethern with assisers & triours shall goo to euery Mylle a-bowte this Cite, and se that they be assyseid & made accordyng as hit haith ben afore-tyme, and to vndurstond who is defec-

---
[1] leaf 10, back.   [2] "Joh. Lye, mercer," deleted.
[3] leaf 219. For the Easter Leet see p. 389. Scribe C.

§ 59. *Ric. Braytoft, Mayor,* 1474.

tyue, [and] to make & leve the peyne therof afore-tyme assest, and who doo they contrary heraftur shall fforfett xx s. at euery defaute.

Also for by-Cause þat ouer grett nombre of peopull of this Cite yerely at openyng & ouerseyng of the Comiem of this Cite not desyred nor appoynted by the Meir, Shirreffes or Chaumb[e]rleyns of this Cite by their own actorite taken on them to ryde with the seid Chaumb[e]rlens ofte tymes in excesse nounmbre & vnruly to full Ill example; & like to enduce ryott rather then good rule, hit is therffor ordeyned at this leete þat any persone of this Cite other then shall heraftur ȝerely to be appoynted by the Meir, Shirrefes et Chaummburlens of this Cite, take on hem to Com or be at the openyng of the fforseid Coimem [or 6s. 8d. fine and 3 days imprisonment at every default]; and that this ordennaunce be proclamed at euery lete-day as other ordenaunces ben. _{"Chamberlayn; none to Ride or be at opening Lamas but such as are Apoynted."}

[1] Also hit is ordeneyd to remembre to newe extende the murage of this Cite, and to extend men for their goodez as well as for lyvelod, accordyng to the Chartre of þis Cite; which newe Cessyng Ignorantly be longe tyme hayth ben differed. _{Murage.}

Also the Bondes and lymyttes of this Cite touchyng the shir theroff wold be redy for remembraunce, and the bondes of the lete from the bondys off the priours lete wold be knowe, and the Bondes of interest of Cheylesmore, which in maner byn so out of mynde that they be forgoton. _{"bounds of Leets."}

[Ordained] that no person of this Cite wey eny woll to be wrought, but the same woll be weyed be weyghtes enselad other at the Kynges escheker or by the Meyres officers of this Cite, and that noy person of this Cite put gret weyght to be wrought for the li : or weyght but only accordyng to the lawe, and to the Rule of this Cite [or pay a fine of 6d. or more at the mayor's discression]. Also yf eny person havyng no wyghtes enseleaded woll haue weyghtes enselaled (*sic*) com to the meires Officers, and the shall haue hem without eny fee of fyne to be paied to they officers in that behalf. _{Weights.}

[1] leaf 219, back.

APPENDIX A

SCRIBES.

THE only difficulties lie with scribes A, B, B types, C, Z, who are not always contemporary with their entries.[1] After the year 1465, when D appears, difficulties lessen considerably; and the scribes may be roughly taken as contemporary with the events they record; with the exception of B's and C's back leet entries, and even these need not be more than twenty to forty years out. As Z's early entries are in Latin, no English linguistic difficulty arises; but historians of the English language should be warned that portions of the text which, either in the footnotes or in this Appendix are given as copied from entries in the writing of A, B, or C, reproduce the word-forms usual in the late fifteenth or early sixteenth centuries. As in the case of B and C, these are entries of leet-proceedings, there is little difficulty in detaching them from the rest of the material. The lack of chronological correspondence in A's case is the more disappointing because it casts doubt on the age of the code of urban ordinances I have called the "Proclamation of John Leeder," which though given in the MS. among the ordinances of 1421 is in general form allied to the similar codes of Leicester and Worcester, which are dated 1467.

I.

MS.	PRINTED COPY.	DATE.	SCRIBE.	PAPERMARK.
i. 1–32.	pp. 2–6, 19–99, 101.	1414, 1421–5.	A.	Crescent.
ii. 33–7.	blank.			
iii. 38–50, back.	pp. 99–122.[2]	1425–9.	B types,[3] B.[4]	M. "
iv. 51.	blank.			
v. 52–8.	pp. 122–30, 131–2, 132–6.	1430.	A.	Crescent.
vi. 59–60, back.	pp. 130–1, 132, 137–8.	1430–1.	C,[4] B types.[3]	M.
vii. 61–7, back.	pp. 138–51.	1431–4.	A.	Crescent.
viii. 68–81, back.	pp. 151–69.	1434.	B,[4] B types.[3]	M.
ix. 82.	pp. 170–1.	1434.	A.	Crescent.
x. 83–107, back.	pp. 171–202.	1435–43.	B,[3] B types,[4] C.[4]	
xi. 108–16, 117–21.	pp. 202–16, blank.	1444.	A.	M.

---

[1] See above, pp. xv–xvi; and for watermarks, *ib.* xi–xii. It should be noted that some scribes of B type are early, probably contemporary. [2] Omit p. 101.
[3] Chronicle, mayoral elections. [4] Leet entries.

846   *Appendix A.*

II.

MS.	PRINTED COPY.	DATE.	SCRIBE.	PAPERMARK.
i. 122–99, back.	pp. 217–332.	1445–64.	Types of B,[1] B,[2] C,[2] D.[3]	M.
ii. 200–14, back.	pp. 332–372.	1465–71.	D,[1] B,[2] C.[2]	M.
iii. 215–227.	pp. 372–416.	1472–4.	E,[1] B,[2] C.[2]	M.
iv. 227, back–298, back.	pp. 416–609.	1474–1507.	B,[1] C, F.	M.

III.

MS.	PRINTED COPY.	DATE.	SCRIBE.	PAPERMARK.
300–422, back.	pp. 609–813.	1507–55.	G, H, I, K, L.	M. Crescent[4]

IV.

MS.	PRINTED COPY.	DATE.	SCRIBE.	PAPERMARK.
i. i, ii–iv, v–viii, 1–2, 7–19.	pp. 821–9.	1251–2, 1410–11, 1581.	Z.	Crescent.
ii. 423–36, back.	pp. 815–21, 831–41.	1563–1622.	Z, O, P, Q.	

The following is a description of the various scribes—

A, later copyist of leet ordinances and chronicle from 1414–44; writes—with one exception—on crescent-marked paper; date c. 1520.

B, later copyist of leet ordinances from 1426–74, and thenceforward contemporary recorder of both leet and chronicle entries to 1506;[5] to be identified with John Boteler; date c. 1480–1506.

B types.[6] Chronicle entries 1426–65. Probably in some instances contemporary, but may be as late as c. 1480–1520.

C, later copyist of leet ordinances from 1430–1507; date probably contemporary with scribe B.

D, contemporary copyist of chronicle entries, 1463–71.

E, contemporary copyist of chronicle entries, 1472–74.

F inserts a few entries in Boteler's town-clerkship, see p. 581 (mayor's election). Probably a contemporary scribe.

G, H, I, J, K, L, sixteenth century scribes. Entries are contemporary.

Z, Elizabethan scribe. Tho. Banester, town clerk. His thirteenth and fifteenth century entries (pp. 1–2, 7–19) not contemporary.

O, P, Q, Elizabethan and Stuart scribes entries are contemporary.

[1] Mayoral and chronicle entries.   [2] Leet entries.
[3] See p. 321.   [4] Paper changes leaf 349, p. 694.
[5] Another scribe seems to have worked under Boteler, in a hand so nearly resembling his that I can hardly detect a difference.
[6] Some of these also occur in the Chartulary, Corp. MSS. A. 2.

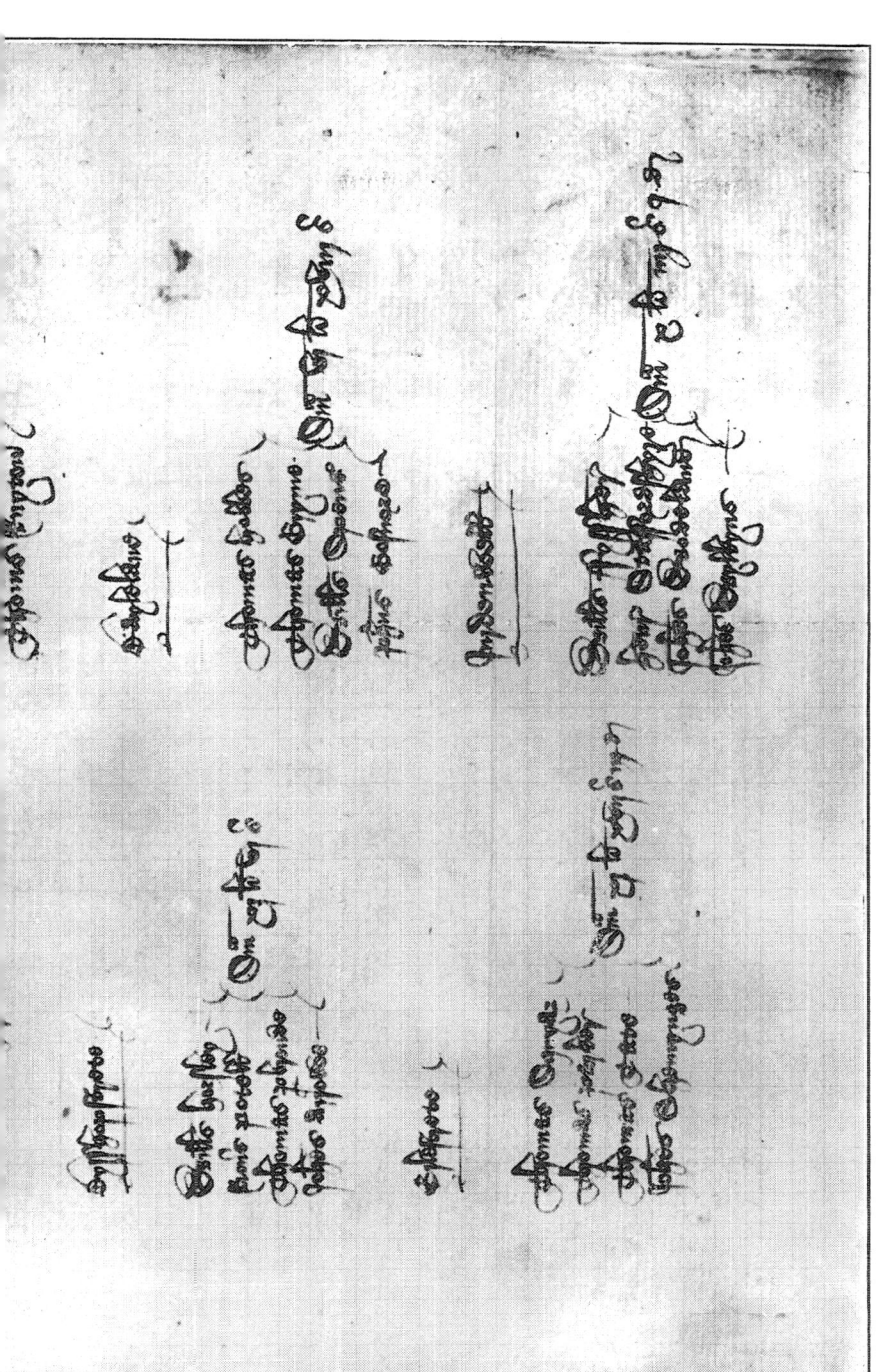

COLLECTION OF £100 FOR THE EARL OF MARCH, 1461.
(Leet Book, leaf 185; see pp. 313-14. The scribe is one of the B type.)

GLOSSARY

The words to which only the number of the page is affixed have been explained in footnotes.

acertayn, 484.
afered, 186, assessed. Affeer (late L. *afforare* = to fix the market value), to fix the amount of an amercement. (N.E.D.)
after-clappys, 577.
aier, 720.
algarbe, 24, a Spanish wine; (N.E.D., s.v. Algarde).
almery, 151, aumbry, cupboard, Med. L. *almarium*, altered from *armarium*, L. *arma*, tools; in the form *almery* corruptly confused with *almonry* as if a place for alms. (N.E.D.)
amytted, 636.
anoyed, 631.
aparell, 681.
approwements, 454.
ardolf, 719. See Part III. vii.
arretted, 455.
artyng, 326.
attaine, 294.
averye, 473.
avowrey, 124 (? -rez). See *Errata*.
avowtery, 118, adultery, O.F. *avouterie*.

bagger, 26, bager, 788; badger, a hawker.
bannysh, 629.
barer, 262, a barrier, forming the entrance to a city, originally of post, rail, or chain.
bastard, 24, a sweet Spanish wine. Shakespeare, 1 *Hen. iv.* ii. iv. "Score a pint of bastard in the Half-moon."
bates, 114.
bede-ale, 27, bid-ale or entertainment for the benefit of any one, to which a general invitation is given. (N.E.D.)
bendes, 283, scarves. "Et in xj uln*is* et dim. panni rub*ri*, iiij uln*is* j qr. panni alb*i* empt*is* pro lez bend*es* pro homi*n*ibus homin*um* armat*orum* . . . equitant*ium* cum dicto domino Rege ad castra de Alnewyk." Davies, *York Records*, 22.
berne, 591.
beter de Quyrnes, 307.
(1) bitter, 166, 201, 483, 793, bitters, 201, 570, (2) bits, bitt*es*, bitt*ez*, 277, 555, 793, (1) a water-carrier, (2) a water-bucket, possibly of leather (see p. 549).
"Also the sayd dekyn schall worden a barrell . . . a gayne the byttar bryng water for the awtars and the fautte," MS. (1462) in Trinity Church, Coventry, see W. Legg, *Clerk's Book* of 1549, 58. See also *Bytte*, E.D.D. for the Worcester custom of carrying water in a leather bag. Thoresby (*Letter to Ray* (1703), in Skeat, *Repr. Gloss.*, B. 17) gives "Bytte, a bottle or flagon, ab A.S. *bytt, uter, dolium*," as a Warwickshire word. See *Errata*.
bladys, 192.
blake of lyre, 204.
bolkys, 27; bulkes, 58. See Part I. ix–x.
bondyng, 639.
borwes, 557.
botewes, boteux, 503, 624.
bowet, 588.
brakeman, 181, 182 and note. "The brakeman drew these bars (*i.e.* the iron bars which had first been converted into convenient size by the smith) through a coarse wortle (plate) by means of a hand-lever or brake, from which the term 'breaking down,' still in use to-day, has been derived." See *Notes on Early Wiredrawing Practice* by P. Longmuir and J. Kenworthy, in *Engineering*, Apr. 18, 1913, an article to

848 Glossary.

which I am greatly indebted for information. See below *gurdelmen, middlemen, wirtelmaker.*
breth, 397, brews.
brethon, 25, brewing. O.E. *bryƀen.*
brym, 26, a brymmyng, 398 (of a sow), desiring the boar.
bultre, 23, the state of having been boulted or sifted. O.F. *buleter*, cf. Ital. *buratto*, a meal sieve, a fine transparent cloth, fr. *bura*, a kind of cloth, hence also *bureau*, which is lined with a particular kind of cloth. (N.E.D.)
burle, 659, burlyd, 640.
bygge, 472.

Cantell, 396.
Capias, 296, 700, a writ commanding an officer to take the body of, i.e. arrest, the person named therein.
Cast, 662, 702.
caue, 29, 645, cayue, 656, a "warning" by-law, or ordinance. Not in N.E.D.
Cayage, 550, quayage.
ceducious, 330.
Certiorari, 684.
Cestron, 25, Cestre, 530, Cester, 696, *et passim*, a liquid measure, not (see p. 530 note), here the sixth part of a gallon, but evidently a dozen gallons, with thirteen or fourteen to the dozen; L. *sextarium*. O.E. *sester*.
Chamlet, 680.
chesse, 191.
chiertees, 407.
clothyng, 487.
Cokett, 23, bread slightly inferior to wastell, possibly so-called because it was stamped with a seal (cocket). (N.E.D.)
coklyng, 639.
Coliars, 766.
comien, 190.
colted in, 259.
conable, 295; couenable, 75.
condescended, 490.
consuet, 58.
contenue, 340, contynue 535.
continuance, 34. In order to compel the attendance of a defendant at the court it might be necessary to go through several processes, including the issue of the writ *capias ad respondendum;* after such appearance had been made "a day was continually given and entered upon the record for the parties to appear on from time to time, as the exigence of the case required. The giving of this day is called the *continuance*, because thereby the proceedings are continued from one adjournment to another." Blackstone, *Commentaries*, III. 326.
cordeners, 681, Cordener, 705.
costrelli*s*, 272.
countre, 146.
Countre-poise, 63, an equal weight. Cf. *Plumpton Correspondence*, 21 (quoted by Gay in *R. Hist. Soc. Trans.*, new series, xiv. 260). "I have a counterpais wheith of the wheight stone that the wooll was weyed with."
coverted, 538.
Crache, 28, a cratch, rack or crib.
Cur, 591.

dalt, 498.
demened, 225.
demurraunt, 688.
dobyns, 640.
draff, 24, draffe, 385.
dragm[arum], 815.

eire, 455.
enbrase, 372, embracerye, 373.
encrease, 24, profit.
enormilies, 538.
enprowement, 630.
Essonia, 715.
experimently, 536.
extinted, 328
extrahu*ras*, 8, stray, tame beasts found wandering within the precincts of the manor; if unclaimed after due proclamation at the expiration of a year and a day they became the property of the lord.
Eysynges, 798.

fact, 820.
farithe foul, 181; to fare foul = to come to grief.
fate, 766.
fectyff, 398.

fensible, 539.
feying, 234, cleansing.
Fieri facias, 296, a writ directing the sheriff to take and sell a debtor's goods in execution of a judgment.
flok, *vb.* 633, 645 ; ffloxe, sb. 659, 660.
forbeng, 283 ; forbur, 250.
foreara, 145, headland ; "forera" Bateson, *op. cit.* 1. 392.
fowder, 606.
ffoyndes, 680.

gadir, 398.
garbelid, 400.
Goddardes, 531.
gooth, 399.
grene, 689, (of wool) probably unwashed, *i.e.* with yolk in. It might also refer to skin wool, *i. e.* wool removed from the skin of slaughtered animals, as to-day reference is still made to "green skins." The first suggestion is more likely to be the correct one (Prof. A. F. R. Barker).
greunde, 630.
gurdell, 181, girdull, 184 ; girdulmen, 181, gurdelmen, 183 ; gurdeldraweng, *ib.* The authorities quoted under *brakeman* (*q.v.*) say the girdleman annealed the wire ; and that the middleman "represented the cleaner, who removed the scale and prepared the wire after annealing for further manipulation." Now annealing and cleaning may well have been part of the business, but the combination *gurdel-drawing* implies that actual drawing of wire through, or by means of, a "gurdel" was the work of this craft of "gurdlemen," while the fact that "gurdelmen" and "middlemen" are mentioned (p. 182, 183) each time in connection with other wiredrawing crafts *but not together* [cf. also "middelyng," p. 184, mentioned together with wiredrawing, *while all reference to any "girdling" process is omitted*] seems to imply that "girdlemen" and "middlemen" were but different names for the same occupation, and that the process of "middelyng" and* fashioning the wire "atte gurdel"

were one. What a "gurdel" actually was can only be conjectured. A *girdle* or *gridle* is a circular iron plate on which cakes are cooked ; a *gird* is a hoop for a barrel. It seems at anyrate possible that a "gurdel" was a draw-plate intended for wire of a "middle" size, thinner than that fashioned by the wortle of the "brakeman," but not so thin as it became after the manipulation of the card wiredrawer. The instrument may have been the forerunner of the *barrels* employed by the *rippers* [who seem to correspond to the girdlemen, just as the *overhousemen* do to the cardwiredrawers] described in Ray's "Manner of the Wire-Work at Tintern in Monmouthshire." (Skeat, *Reprinted Gloss.*, B. 15, pp. 16-17). These barrels were furnished with hooks to which tongs were attached ; the tongs were fastened to the wire by the workmen, and, the hooks being forced back by the action of a wheel, drew the wire through the holes of a plate. The various processes of the Tintern manufacture reduced the iron bars (1) into rods "about the bigness of one's little finger," (2) after the operations of the rippers —to the size "as of a great pack thread." The third process of the small wiredrawers, or *overhousemen*, is not given in detail. It may be noted that at Coventre (p. 183) two kinds of wire, *i. e.* "Cardwyre" and "mystermannes wyre," are mentioned, the latter representing in all probability the material of ordinary commerce, and the former the thinner kind reserved for cards for combing wool.
gysarnez, 28.

haburions, 244.
hades, 827.
hakmen, 185.
holy cake, 417. See Introduction, xxx-xxxi.
handilles, 660.
(1) hangers, 272 ; (2) hangres, 188.
hanked, 257.

850   *Glossary.*

haut grece, 300.
hayls, 289.
hendley, 289.
here syve, 25 ; hair sieve, a sieve with the bottom of hair ; ale under the hair-sieve = newly-strained or new ale. Bateson, *op. cit.* III., 22.
hernes, 400.
heye, 510.
hidels, 26.
hopes, 334.

Imaginacions, 331.
importable, 476 ; unbearable.
inbesell, 620.
issues, 326, 700.

jakkes, 244.

kerseys, 661.
kyddes, 22, 552.

labour, 353.
laches, 417, 568.
laten, 151, 554, a hard mixed metal much resembling brass.
lemitre, 75, probably *limité*, assigned, appointed.
les then, 677.
lesow, 350 ; lesues, 633.
lesse, 187.
leyde, 313.
listes, 776.
lomes, 223.
lorymere, 250, bitmaker, from O.F. *loremier* from *lorain*, L. *loram*, thong.
loued, 491.
lowpes, 107.

mache-collyd, 142.
mainpurnable, 293.
marshallsy, 24, the court of the marshallesea of the king's household which was presided over by the Lord Steward and the Earl Marshall. One of the officers of the household, the clerk of the market, went round the country to test weights and measures. See Sellers, *op. cit.* 141, note. Coventry obtained the right of exemption from these visits of inspection when the mayor was made the clerk of the market in 1451, *Life in an Old Eng. Town*, 158.

maystyme, 787.
menused, 348.
medled, 554.
Medleys, 698.
Mese, 255.
Middlemen, 182, Middelyng, 184. See above *gurdel*, also below *Errata*.
missa de Jhesus (*sic*), 333.
Mure, 461.
Musturdevylers, 283 ; Musters, 698. See also Davies, *York Rec.*, 12–13.
Mystermannes wyre, 183, the wire of ordinary commerce ; misterman, craftsman, O.F. *mestier*, mod. F. *métier*.

neuid, 401.
Notary impereall, 59. *Notarii Apostolici et Imperiales* (Du Cange). Notarius vel Tabellio ab Imperatore, vel Papa, vel ab eo, cui speciali privilegio indultum erat, ordinatus posset, ubique etiam in Francia vel Anglia seu Hispania, non solum in terris eis specialiter subjectis, suo officio uti et instrumenta conficere. (Mr. Addy.) It is not clear why a "notary imperial" should not have been allowed to practise in Coventry court.
noysyng, 519.

obles, 392.
Olyvaunt, 657. See *Additional Notes*.
opprowment, 630.
ordeyned, 657.
Osey, 24, a sweet wine from Alsace. O.F. *Aussay*.
ourthewarde, 257.
owe, 455.

paaste, 29, 209, dough.
partletes, 680.
passynger, 22 ; passenger, 102.
paynemaynes, 300.
pelettes, 363.
pensels, 588.
perquisita, 171, fr. Lat. *perquirere*, to acquire, purchase ; here there has been a transference of meaning from "purchase" to "pursuit" or "prosecution."
pester, 804.
pervsed, 630.

Glossary.

plee reale, 274; plee riales, 224. See *Courts of Coventry* in *Additional Notes*.
pleke, 763.
plete, 268, plead.
poffe, 660.
preiudicate, 820.
prest, 529.
pretentyng, 476.
prikk*is*, 338.
prosid, 644.
purpensed, 475.
pych, 639.
pyngilles, 762.
pynrouyng, 639.

Queyre*s* anamelynges, 204.
quites cast, 827.

Ramell, 447, 462, Raymell, 805.
Rasyd, 396. "Rasyd strike," a level measure See below *strikis*.
recetted, 538.
recountre, 475.
refuse, 59.
rekou*eres*, 296, recoveries (of a debt, or money due).
Renovell, 521.
Rent sek, 444.
Replevye, 438.
required, 409.
reteigndour, 394, a token of retainder-ship. (N.E.D.)
revelisshen, 576.
romeney, 24, a sweet wine of Greek origin. Med. L. *romania* from the proper name *Romania*, used to designate Greece. (N.E.D., s. v. *rumney*.)
Rovers, 338.
Roper, 725.
rought tesels, 640, ? rough. Rough teasels probably means teasels of bad quality, not properly selected.
rydde, 430.
ryne, 686.
Ryoll, 818.

salettes, 244.
schaftmond, 399.
schankes, 680.
Schether, 89.
Scire facias, 34, 295, 296, a form of writ requiring the sheriff to "do to wit " the person named therein to come before the Court to "show cause" why execution should not be taken against him. (See N.E.D.)
Scrowes, 304, scrolls, records.
sege houses, 194, privies, latrines.
seliones, 145, ridges or narrow strips of land between two furrows. Anglo-Lat. *selion-em*, mod. Fr. *sillon*. (N.E.D.)
Seme, 634.
Semytyll, 279, a half-baked tile. This is not mentioned in the N.E.D., which however gives from Philemon Holland's *Pliny*, semi-brick, a half-baked brick (*L. semilater*).
sett out, 461.
settyng of wadd, 697.
seynsyng, 392.
skecons, 200.
slayes, 639.
sonde, 392.
Spayr, 261, spayre, *ib.*, spay, 121, spyre = ? sp[e]yre, 254, Spayers, 257, 258, Spayes, Spay[r]es, 258, spayre, 260. See *Spay* and *Spayre* in N.E.D.
spole, 776.
stresse-rolle, 169–70, a list of people whose goods were liable to distraint to compel their appearance in court.
(1) strik*is*, 334 *et passim*; (2) stryke, 396;
(1) a measure of corn, varying in amount (See *Friar John Bredon* in *Additional Notes*), so called because the grain was "struck" or smoothed level with the brim of the measure;
(2) a smooth piece of wood with which the surplus grain was so levelled; cf. *stryke*, vb., to smooth out, hence to measure, transferred from corn to cloth, p. 657. (See *strike* sb. E.D.D. and cf. *strickle*, O.E. *stricel*.)
stulpes, 252. There were "Stulpes" on the Southwark side of London Bridge, where the way could be barred by a chain.
surcuydance, 476.
suspiralles, 105, suspirals, 549, evidently openings in water-pipes giving access to the water before it reached the conduit. O.F. *souspiral*, L. *suspiraculum*.

Sussemy, 25. *i. e.* measly, Fr. sursemé; cf. porcos superseminatos, Hudson, *op. cit.* I. 359.

swan penne, 108. A pipe the size of a swan's quill seems ridiculously small.

sygh, 300.

tabull, 136.
takes, 680. Still in local use.
targes, 690. ? Scribal error for *trapes* (traps).
Teyre, 669.
þat one, 82.
Thrommes, 400.
thorowe, 825.
thymeler, 79, ? thimble-maker. Not in N.E D.
tracted, 699.
tree, 549.

vpholders, 191. An "upholder" is a broker, auctioneer, who holds up for sale, but see note to the passage.
vake, 702.
vayvium, 8, waif, stolen goods or cattle, of which the owner is unknown, abandoned by the thief in his flight from the hue and cry.

walker, 87.
waren, 629
warrant, grand, 684.
waturlad, 28, an artificial watercourse. (N.E.D., s.v. *lead.*)
weyued, 303.
wilfuly, 116.
wirtilmaker, 142, writelmaker, 160, a maker of wortles, drawplates of stone or iron, used in wire-making, see *brakeman.*
wodpleck, 668.
wrete, 657.
wronghalf, 640, wranghalft, 659.
wydraughtes, 695.

ADDITIONAL NOTES

Coventry Names.

Brother Holoughton's survey of "Metes and Bounds" (pp. 7-19) records many untraceable place-names; some, however, still survive, or can be found on the old 1-inch Ordnance Map. Sandipit-lane (p. 8) is now Sandy Lane; Steplefield (*ib.*) on the boundary between Radford and Coventry, is the site of the Corporation Electric Light Works. Hullane (p. 9) is now Coundon Lane; Pokebroke (*ib.*) is the northern branch of the Sherbourne; while "Northebrocke" (*ib.*) bounds Northfield Farm. "Browne's-lane" (*ib.*) still survives; "Holynfast" (*ib.*) is represented by Hollyfast Farm, "Merdonsiche" (p. 12) by Martyn Gutter, a small ditch on the south boundary of Stivichall parish, and "Grange-lane" (*ib.*) by Green Lane, near Stivichall Grange. "Heyne-lane" (p. 15)—modern Hen Lane—divides Keresley from Corley, while Newland House Farm preserves the memory of "Nova Terra" (*ib.*), and Breach Brook and Breach Oak that of the "Bryches" (*ib.*). "Corley broke," "Litle-heathe" (Bedworth), and "Catcroft-lane" (p. 16) still remain, and though "Sydnallwood (*ib.*) is gone, Sydnall Lane remains on the east boundary of Exhall, with Sydnall Field adjoining, the locality of the present Exhall Colliery. Weston-heye is part of Weston-in-Arden; "Wybylyns-broke" (p. 17)—the modern Wyblyns Brook—and "Lady Lane" (*ib.*) may still be found, while Endemer water (p. 18) is probably represented by Springfield Brook, and Locardes-lane (*ib.*) by Lockhurst Lane.[1] (For this information I am indebted to a letter from Ald. W. Andrews of Coventry in 1904.)

Other names, such as Wolpitlediat (p. 19), where the Cheylesmore Court Leet was held, appear to have vanished, though once a king's highway which formed part of the boundary of Foleshill parish led to it. For a wolfpit, which occurs not unfrequently in early descriptions of boundaries, and may mean either an artificial pit-fall, or a hole in the ground haunted by wolves, see Napier and Stevenson, *Crawford Charters*, 53. "Styffordeshale," another unremembered place-name (pp. 452, 513) is mentioned as lying in the fields of Stoke (Corp. MSS. C. (B) *Dateless Deeds*, bdle. 43), while Catesby-lane (p. 361), an unidentified street, recalls the city's connection with a famous Warwickshire family, who may have gained a footing in Coventry during the quarrel between Queen Isabel and the prior and convent (see *Ancient Deeds*, A. 10715, quoted by permission of the editor of the *Victoria County Histories*).

The Coventry Courts.

The local jurisdiction of the Coventry officials was administered in the following courts: (1) The Portmanmote (pp. 322, 548), otherwise the court of Coventry, or the court of the city of Coventry (*ib.* 34, 59, 325), the

[1] Corp. MSS. C. 126.

court of the mayor and bailiffs (*ib.* 59), the fortnight court (*ib.* 294), or the king's court (*ib.* 194, 223, 575, 606, 643, 684, 699), which originally derived its powers from Ranulf's charter (*ib.* 323) ; (2) the county court of the city sheriffs (*ib.* 274), which came into existence after the charter of 1451 ; (3) the coroner's court of Statute Merchant (*ib.* 275), which derived its authority from the incorporation charter of Edward III ; and (4) the Sessions of the Peace (*ib.* 224, 802), which came into being with the creation of Justices of the Peace for the city in the first year of Richard II. Portmanmote, to which resort was had as late as 1834 for the recovery of small debts (*Report Munic. Com.* 19), took cognizance of pleas concerning land, and civil suits for damage (pleas real and personal, *ib.* 244, 274, 325, 790) and suits could be removed from outside courts by an appeal of the city officers, who had return of writs. (Cf. *Trinity Church* MSS. 34, where the appeal of the mayor and bailiffs to "have their court" in a matter which the suitors had brought before the King's Bench in 1393 is allowed.) Apparently the Portmanmote had civil jurisdiction only,[1] felonies being dealt with before the Justices of the Peace at Quarter Sessions, and perhaps to some extent after 1451 by the bailiffs—as sheriffs—in the county court, though the exclusion of the sheriff of Warwickshire from interference in Coventry affairs did not extend to the Justices assigned by Royal Commission (*ib.* 98–9, 625) for Sessions of Gaol Delivery, and Oyer and Terminer, though the mayor (*ib.* 626) might be associated with these on the commission.

Friar John Bredon and the Standard Measures.

The Patent Rolls, dated May 16, 1441 (*Cal. Pat. R.*, 1436–41, p. 545) record a pardon granted to Brother John Bredon (see above pp. 97, 228), friar minor, Professor of Theology, who on Friday the first week in Lent, 18 Hen. VI. (1440) had been indicted before the keepers of the peace, and the justices of Oyer and Terminer in Warwickshire of having plotted to disturb the people of Coventry, and proclaimed in the market-place that he had been to the parliament at Reading and had obtained licence of the King and council that the burgesses of Coventry should use bushels larger by a gallon in the standard bushel of the Exchequer, and measure all corn with it contrary to the Statute of Measures, "and of having caused riotous gatherings against the mayor and bailiffs . . . to the danger of the people and the subversion of the Statute of Measures." The mayor-lists record that in 1434 "the small strike came in," *i.e.*, the standard measures, evidently differing from the local ones were adopted (see above p. 151) to be temporarily cast aside in 1439, a season of great dearth, through the instrumentality of Frer Bredon (Harl. MSS. 6388.)

Knights of the Shire.

Knights, p. 107, *i.e.* knights of the Shire. Coventry returned no burgesses between 1354 and 1452 (Whitley, *Representation*, 17.) As th citizens, however, after the charter of 1451, ceased to attend the county court of Warwickshire, where knights where elected, the city's rights as a borough were revived ; and thenceforth one or two members were

---

[1] See, however, the complaint about the acquiting of felons (p. 548), where the Portmanmote is mentioned. As the mayor was a Justice of the Peace and as he came to be supported in the king's court by aldermen (*ib.* 605) who were in many cases justices, it may have been difficult in practice to separate civil and criminal jurisdiction.

returned. The freeholders of the city of the county of Coventry outside the city boundary do not appear to have shared in the election of members, and in 1835 the Commissioners of Municipal Corporations noted that these were an unenfranchised class, having votes neither for the county of Warwick nor the city of Coventry.

MINSTRELS.

Mynstrelles of the kynges, p. 121. See Davies, *York Records*, 13–15 n.

THE CANOPY OVER THE SACRAMENT AND THE WIREDRAWERS.

The Canopy over the Sacrament which the wiredrawers supported (pp. 131–2) would be made of rich stuff, and be of the conical shape seen in illuminated MSS. of the period (see *Egerton MSS.* 1070, f. 54 *b*, and *Essex Review*, xxi, 230.) The weavers of Mainz obtained in 1099 special privileges from the Archbishop in return for support of part of the church fabric. (Keutgen, *Aemter und Zünfte*, 174. (Prof. Unwin.)

GARTON'S OBIT.

Will Cross's Charter, pp. 144–6. See for the reversion of this house, pp. 267–8, and for the heir-at-law's claim to it through the "Courtesy of England," Part III, Foreword vii. Garton's Obit was celebrated by the mayor, bailiffs and commonalty, Sharp, *Antiq.* 43.

THE VICTUALLERS.

Breusters ylde, 234 cf. p. 623. Bakers, brewers innholders, ale-house-keepers, tiplers and victuallers paid 3*d*. a quarter, which was collected by the city officers (*Leet Book* (B) leaf 61), cf. the "ale-silver of the city of London (Sharpe, *Letter Book L.*, 164, 170), and the "Cannemol" paid in Leicester (Bateson, *op. cit.* I. 207). In London "ale-silver" was the mayor's perquisite; in Coventry (*Report of Mun. Comm.*, 11) a custom prevailed that the mayor should receive certain fines of victuallers not being freemen, but this may have sprung from the order against strangers entered in the *Leet Book* in 1622 (pp. 837–9).

CHILDREN OF ISRAEL.

See p. 392. These were the Holy Innocents from the *Tailors and Shearmen's Play*.

STATUTE OF WINCHESTER.

See pp. 395–401. This is no part of the famous statute of Edward I. These entries also appear in the *Liber Custumarum* of Northampton, see *Northampton Rec.* I, 344–9.

CLARENCE'S JEWELS.

See pp. 381–2, 420. The transcript of the lost document relating to Clarence's jewels, dated on the vigil of S. Andrew, 17 Edw. IV. (Nov. 29, 1477) at Warwick is given in Featherston, *Coventry Charters* (1871), pp. 23–4, and takes the form of an indenture between Sir Tho. Vaughan, Sir Tho. Piers and Ric. Croftes on the one part, and the mayor, John Seman, and his brethren, on the other, wherein although the coronall of "goold full garnysshed whit diamants, rubyes, safers, balies [sic.?] and perls" had been forfeit for years past for non-payment of the debt, it is delivered up to the first-named parties acting on behalf of the king, £100 of the debt of 300 marks (£200) being remitted by the creditors of the duke.

JOHN FRENCH, ALCHEMIST.

See p. 422. On the various treatises on alchemy composed for Edward IV, and the licence given by him to two merchants to make gold and silver from mercury, see Stratford, *Edward IV.*, 263-4.

THE GODIVA LEGEND.

"Dame goode Eve made it free," 567. The Godiva legend from the point of view of the folk-lorist, is treated of in Hartland, *Science of Fairy Tales*, 71-92. There are other stories where—as Mr. Hartland reminds me—the Dido element of land-measuring also enters (see Maxwell-Lyte, *Dunster and its Lords*, 19), which recall certain features of the Godiva legend, as related by the chroniclers. In the Dunster account the lady, Joan de Mohun, won from her husband for the people as much common land as she could walk round barefoot in a day. In the Otmoor tale a nameless benefactress gave as much land as she could ride round while an oat-sheaf was burning for a common to the inhabitants (Dunkin, *Oxfordshire*, 120, note); while it is by crawling round a stretch of land while a torch (some accounts say a billet of wood) was burning that Isabel or Mabel, the dying wife of Sir Roger de Titchbourne, won from her churlish lord the wherewithal to establish a yearly dole for the poor for ever (Woodward and Wilks, *Hampshire*, II, 17 ; Chambers, *Book of Days*, I, 167. See also Dormer Harris, *Story of Coventry*, 19 sqq.)

Whether the figure of "Lady Godiva" figured in the "Show Fair" procession earlier than 1678, the year in which her presence is first recorded, is uncertain, but it is certainly clear from the craft records that there was a procession on the fair day as early as the fifteenth century, and that the armed guard, minstrels and other attendants accompanied the mayor when he went to proclaim the fair. Thus from the Mercers' Accounts (1590) we learn that 2s. was paid to 6 men for bearing harness on the Fair Day ; in 1485 the cappers paid 2d. to two harness men at the fair ; the butchers in 1562 paid 2s. 8d. "for harnessing 8 men on Fair Friday," and the smiths in 1466 paid "to two with jakks to attend on the mayor 4d. (*Reader MSS.* vol. 16.)

Item, for iiij men on fere Freydaye beryng harnes, viijd. (Drapers' MSS. 1534, in possession of the Drapers' Company, Coventry.)

Though the chroniclers differ as to the motive which prompted Godiva's action, local accounts all agree that she thereby made the city toll-free except for horses, possibly excluded from this exemption, says one version (Corp. MSS. A. 43, quoted by Hartland), because the horse, whereon Godiva rode, neighed, thus attracting the attention of the traditional peeper. It is not absolutely clear what this toll for horses originally was, who had to pay it, or who were exempt even from this payment. It appears in documents of later date as a market-toll on saleable horses due to the prior, in whose "Half" of the city the market originally was, and in whose tenants' parish church—that of the Trinity—the commemorative window mentioned by Dugdale was set up. Thus in the Tripartite of 1355 (Dugdale, *Warw.* I. 163, Burton MSS., ff. 98-103) it is laid down that the Friday market for timber, horse, oxen, kine and other beasts shall be held as of old in the Prior's-half in Bishop Street and Cook Street, the prior to take toll *for horses sold there only* and for no other thing saleable. Earlier the horse-toll would seem to be a payment from which the holders of certain burgage tenements [? in the Prior's-half] were freed. Thus, it appears, says Dugdale (*Warw.* I. 162) in an abstract of an inquisition taken under Edward I, "the whole town was then exempt from Toll, excepting for Horses, whereof the Burgers were only freed; but that the said Burgers had Toll of Horses for their own tenants there inhabiting." If Dugdale's abstract be correct we gather that while burgesses were free from this payment, their undertenants were not so exempt, but paid the toll—or some commutation of it—not to the prior, but to the intermediate (burgess) landlords. The supposition that the owners of certain burgage holdings were free of horse-toll is borne out by an early undated conveyance (*Ancient Deeds*, A. 8700 (P.R.O.) quoted by permission of the editor of the *Victoria County Histories*) wherein Will. de Weston in transferring to Martin Colbront a messuage in "Waste Garden" expressly says that Martin is to be free of horse-toll—" de tolneto equorum" (cf. the conveyance of a house of Brackley where liberty of buying and selling in the court of the earl in the town is included in the warranty, *Godstow Reg.*, 195, a reference kindly supplied by Dr. Andrew Clark.) This custom of horse-toll seems peculiar to Coventry, as it can scarcely be identical with the not uncommon incident of villein tenure, payment to the lord on the sale of a colt, but the subject is very obscure.

THE COVENTRY ELEPHANT.

For the "Olivaunt," see p. 657. The charge of the elephant and castle, adopted first on the seal and then copied on the city arms, probably owed its popularity to the tales in the "Bestiaries," which represent the elephant as slaying the dragon in defence of its young (cf. Pliny, *Hist. Nat.* viii. 11) or falling defenceless because hunters have sawn down a tree, against which it leant in sleep. See Romilly Allen, *Early Christian Symbolism*, 378-9, Collins, *Symbolism of Animals in Church Architecture*, 41-2). The devotion paid to S. Michael and S. George in Coventry, and the existence of the tree which gave its name to Coventry, would account for the adoption of an animal having associations, admitting of symbolic interpretations, with a dragon and a tree. Early Coventry seals show an elephant and castle with trees on the obverse, and S. Michael in combat with the dragon bearing a shield charged with S. George's cross on the reverse. The devotion to S. Michael seems to make it probable that the Archangel Militant figured in the Coventry Pageants. Was the "copper chain" worth 2*s.* 4*d.*, the only piece of pageant stuff belonging to the mercers on record used for the binding of Satan? The figure of the chained Satan appears on a misericord in S. Michael's church.

MUSTERS.

See pp. 830-3. The Coventry *Letter Books* (Corp. MSS. A. 79) show how "topical" the subject of musters was at the time Shakespeare's *Henry IV* was written. On June 5, 1597 (*ib.* leaf 83) the Privy Council wrote reproaching the mayor and his brethren for their overmuch nice and curious construction of their liberties—the citizens were evidently making difficulties because the mayor's name was not included in the commission of musters—and complaining that the county commissioners could get no assistance in the city for the accomplishment of the queen's service. Soon after the sheriff, Rob. Burgoyne, and the county justices

Sir Fulk Greville, Sir Thomas Lucy and Richard Verney in a letter dated Nov. 8, 1597 (*ib.* 84), informed the mayor that the amount of the Coventry contribution towards 100 soldiers lately sent to Tilbury Camp was £25 3s. 7½d, the assessment for the whole county being £377 13s. 4d., whereat the Coventry authorities grumbled sorely. In a letter, dated Nov. 12. 1597 (*ib.* 85), to other members of the corporation then in London—their "very loving friends," Mr. Hen. Kervyn and Mr. Tho. Saunders, aldermen of Coventry "at one Mr. Trologes house near S. Clement's church without Temple Bar"—Joh. Rogerson, Hen. Sewall, Hen. Smallwood, Hen. Gravenor, and Rob. Letherbarrow declare that they "utterly mislike" the fact that the justices have apportioned and set down their contributions. They beg their correspondents to have conference with Sir John Harrington, "now at parliament," and to make some means to acquaint the Earl of Essex herewith," using their utmost endeavours to obtain the city's discharge of the contribution, which they —the Coventry authorities—have no warrant to levy.

Whether Essex was induced to intervene does not appear in the correspondence, but in their reply to the justices, dated Nov. 30, 1597 (leaf 86), the city rulers complain of the proportion of the assessment, calculated after the rate of the fifteenth part of the county's contribution, whereas, they declare, they are not the thirtieth part. These payments, they urge, are not of duty, and only of late years yielded unto at the Privy Council's direction upon the necessity of present service, the mayor being on the commission; moreover without speciall commission from her Majesty, naming the mayor and others of the city, they have no power, they allege, to array men. "And furthermore," the letter continues, "You knowe that our Cyttie ys verie poore, by reson of this longe derthe ; And we are gretelie Charged dailie w*i*the poste-horses, and w*i*the her Ma*jes*tes Cariage and other extraordinarie char*g*es for Irelande "—a burden to which the county was less liable, all which reasons for a generous treatment are stressed by the city rulers.

Poverty is again pleaded next year in a letter praying for the good offices of Rob. Beale, clerk to the Privy Council, in this matter (Sept. 1, 1598, leaf 87). A levy of £400 is required for the poor, "so great is our oppression" with poor people, they urge, "beside the daily service to her Majesty being the thoroughfare towards Ireland with post-horses and carriages." They have been called on to bear "a reasonable proportion" with Warwickshire when called on to levy men, but shrewdly opine that they and the Warwickshire justices will differ about the extent of this reasonable proportion.

ERRATA

p. 2, "T.G.D." *read* "T.B."
p. 12, "Corks lane" *read* "Cocks lane."
p. 52, Note [1], "v. Corp. MS. C. 158," *read* "Sharp, *Antiq.*, 81-2."
pp. 8, 18, 53, "Ouenettesford," *read* "Quenettesford."
p. 61, Note [1], "in the years 1399" . . . *read* "in the years 1400" . . .
p. 69, Headline, "The Council," transfer to the top of the third paragraph.
p. 73, Note [3], "Tho. Kemp," *read* "Joh. Kemp."
p. 83, Marginal note, "Other ordinances transcribed," *read* "Other ordinances transacted."
p. 118, "xls. ye yere," *read* "xls. þe yere."
p. 124, "and that avowrey, and send it by a trusty messenger," *read* "state the amount which you are confident of being able to send."
p. 129, Note [1], omit.
p. 142, Note [2], omit.
p. 182, Note [2], omit. See *Glossary*, s. v. Middlemen.
p. 201, Note [4], omit. See *Glossary*, s. v. Bitters.
p. 322, Note [1], "rural jurisdiction," *read* "rival jurisdiction."
p. 324, Note [1], "meddle with the liberties," *read* "meddle within the liberties."
p. 346, "Lord Richard Herbert," "Lord John Woodville," "Lord Humfrey Neville," *read* "Sir Richard Herbert," "Sir John Woodville," "Sir Humfrey Neville."
p. 358, Marginal note, "land at Exeter," *read* "land at Exmouth."
p. 396, Note [2], omit. See *Glossary*, s. v. strikis.
p. 399, Note [2], and p. 793, Note [8], "E.E.D." *read* "E.D.D."
p. 412, Note [5], "of every man of every position," *read*, "of every man of any position."
p. 530, Note [2], omit. See *Glossary*, s.v. cester.
p. 534, "M¹ iiijc ix," *read* M¹ iiijc iiij ix " (*i.e.* 1489).
p. 830, Note [5], "Fulke Greville, first Lord Broke (1554-1628)," *read* "Fulke Greville, knight (d. 1606)."

NAME INDEX

Abell, Joh., 211, 236, 266, 316, 317.
—— Margareta, 165.
—— Tho., 154, 162, 179, 213, 242.
Abery, Joh., 328, 329.
Abowte, Joh., 164.
Abraham, Hen., 87.
—— Will., 87, 211. *See also* Abram.
Abram, Hen., 78, 79, 87.
—— Johanna, 180.
—— Joh., 37, 45, 78, 87, 125, 153, 162, 842.
—— Tho., 239.
—— Will., 78, 125, 154, 160, 164, 177, 184, 237.
Acaws, Joh., 165.
Acton, Joh., 366, 546.
—— Ric., 42, 44.
Adam, Ric., 125, 153, 162, 179.
Adbaster, Will., 248.
Adcok, Steph., 319.
—— Will., 316.
Adderbury, Joh., 165.
Adley, Joh., 156.
Adlyngton, Nic., 319.
—— Ric., 165.
Adnet, Rog., 746, 759, 766.
Adson, Will., 352.
Agar, Rob., 248.
Alansonne, Will., 249.
Alde, Ric., Aldee, 248, 256, 284, 285, 293, 304, 305, 307, 310, 312, 316, 317, 320, 521, 332, 333, 335, 336, 337, 339, 343, 344, 347, 364.
Alderews, —, Allerwas, Alderwes, Alderwas, 371.
—— Joh., 213, 219, 237, 251, 256, 366, 377.
Aldreskole, Joh., 212.
Ale, Joh., 352.
—— Miles, 608. *See also* Lee.
Aledus, Joh., 319.
Alerton, Mat., Allerton, 128, 168.
Alestre, Har., Allestre, 352, 360, 365, 371, 377.
Alexander, —, Alysaunder, Alyssandur, Alisawndre, 717.

Alexander, Joh., 635.
—— Rob., 351, 377.
Allen, —, Alleyn, Alen, Aleyn, Alyn, 546.
—— Joh., 120, 126, 156, 168, 177, 352, 366, 377, 478, 483, 518, 530, 534, 540.
—— Ric., 178, 201, 204, 207, 213, 217, 218, 221, 222, 226, 228, 229, 230, 231, 232, 233, 235, 242, 245, 246, 253, 256, 259, 267, 318, 337, 344, 352, 357, 359, 360, 362, 363, 365, 372, 376, 379, 385, 387, 389, 416, 423, 424, 435, 443, 481, 482, 485, 503, 514, 520, 532, 544, 547, 552, 553, 557, 570, 578, 579, 581, 582.
—— Rob., 514.
—— Tho., 155, 168, 175, 214, 241, 249, 318, 351, 368.
—— Will., 586, 665, 667, 676, 686, 694, 696, 700, 706, 711, 714, 718.
Allerwas. *See* Alderews.
Allesley, Christian, 79, Allysley, Christiana, 88.
—— Giles (Egid.), 20, 22, 36, 37, 39, 40, 44, 60, 62, 68, 71. 80, 84, 85, 89, 98, 99, 102, 109, 110, 113, 114, 116, 117, 122, 127, 131, 132, 134, 137, 138, 143, 150, 151, 154, 157, 159, 164, 169, 171, 172, 177, 185, 187, 188, 191, 194, 211.
—— Joh., 20, 22, 39, 41, 51, 82, 90.
—— Tho., 246.
—— Will., 39, 41, 79, 82, 88, 90, 129, 165, 174.
Allwold, Ric., Alwold, Alwode, 209, 219, 222, 238.
Alot, Rad., Alott, 39, 41, 42, 45, 60, 76, 78, 87.
Alrestre, Ric., 167.
Alspath, Gerard de, 1.
Alynson, Will., 676. *See also* Alyson.
Alys, Joh., 167.
—— Will., 129.
Alyson, Will., 236, 711, 713, 715.

Name Index.

Alythe, Joh., 366, 371.
Aman. *See* Man.
Amersen, Joh., 821.
Amourson, Tho., Amorsame, Amoursame, 761, 768, 769, 779, 780, 781, 788, 789, 790, 793, 794, 795, 796, 800, 803, 806, 809, 812.
Anabull, Joh., Anabuls, 254.
—— Ric., 160, 209.
Anderson, ——, 829.
Andrew, Joh., Androwe, Andreux, 5, 237.
—— Margare, 238.
—— Rob., 366, 546.
Andrewes, Joh., Androwes, 483.
—— Nic., 480.
—— Will., 760.
Andseld, Will., 161.
Anedam, Joh., 242.
Annesley, Alicia, 163.
—— Joh., 736.
Aphowell, Hugh, Appowell, 479.
—— Mour., 736.
Appulby, Joh., Appelby, Appalby, 81, 90, 128, 155, 168, 176, 213, 228, 241, 242, 246, 266, 286.
Archer, Joh., Archar, 39, 46, 80, 88, 127, 164, 177, 240.
—— Rob., 162, 180.
—— Tho., 165.
—— Will., 177.
Ardale, Joh., 365.
Ardern, Gal. [Geof.] Artherun, Arthern, Ardourne, Ardurn, 337, 345, 351, 360, 365, 368, 370, 377, 390, 419, 423, 424, 431, 435, 443, 473, 482, 485, 513, 516, 518, 520, 521, 522, 528, 532, 533, 534, 540, 542, 543, 544, 552, 553, 557, 563, 567, 571, 579, 581, 582, 584, 585, 598, 600, 601.
—— Joh., 212, 219, 238, 249, 266, 285, 286, 314, 317, 318.
Argent, Joh., 285.
Arglas, Rob., 161.
Arnold, Will., 242, 248, 266, 365.
Arrowe, Joh., Arowe, Arewe, 241, 248, 285, 313, 318, 329, 330, 337, 343, 352, 354, 363.
—— Will., 336.
Artage, Joh., 421, 483.
Arthern. *See* Ardern.
Asheburne, Joh., Assheburn, Ayssheburn, 213, 242, 315, 318, 351, 388, 389, 390, 416, 842.

Asheburne, Nic., 105, 106.
—— Rob., 6.
Asheby, Walt., Assheby, Ashebye, 40, 77, 80, 89, 126, 143, 154, 163, 178, 213, 242.
Ashewell, Joh., Asshewell, 125, 143, 152, 153, 160, 161, 180.
Askemare, Joh., 52.
Asshow, Katerina, Assho, 162, 179.
Astelene, Tho., Astlyn, Esterlen, Astelyn, Astleyn, Astlen, Astlelene, 602, 630, 631, 632, 634, 636, 638, 641, 642, 643, 647, 649, 650, 651, 652, 653, 654, 663, 665, 666, 667, 668, 676, 677, 679, 682, 684, 686, 688, 690, 691, 692, 694, 695, 696, 697, 701, 704, 706, 707, 711, 713, 714, 715, 717, 718, 720, 721, 722, 723, 724, 725, 726, 727, 728, 737, 738.
Astley, Felicia, 165.
Atkynse, Will., 761.
Atkynson, Will., 307, 313, 320, 321, 339, 352, 362, 373.
Attemer, Tho., 450.
Atterton, Hen., Adderton, Aderton, Adurton, Addurton, Atturton, Attourton, Adirton, 128, 155, 168, 175, 214, 240, 244, 246, 248, 269, 270, 271, 272, 277, 278, 280, 283, 284, 285, 293, 301, 302, 305.
—— Joh., 209, 214, 242, 247, 360.
—— Rob., 242, 247, 285, 286, 305, 312, 315, 317, 320, 321, 332, 333, 334, 335, 336, 338, 339, 343, 344, 347, 351, 352, 360, 361, 362, 364, 367, 370, 376, 378, 382, 385, 388, 389, 416, 419, 421, 423, 424, 431, 435, 436, 443, 473, 482, 485, 503, 513, 516, 518, 520, 521, 522, 524, 528, 532, 842.
—— Will., 128, 155, 167, 175, 351, 355, 363, 372.
Attilborgh, Johanna, Attilborugh, Attilburgh, Attylburgh, Attilbourgh, 88.
—— Will., 20, 22, 36, 37, 41, 50, 79.
Atwall, Alicia, Attewall, Attwell, Otewalle, 154, 178.
—— Joh., 79, 90, 126, 139, 162, 167.
Atwoode, Joh., Attewoode, Atwode Attewode, Awode, 82, 90, 129, 167, 176, 213, 221, 242.
—— Ric., 221, 266.
—— Rob., 377.

Name Index. 863

Aubem. *See* Aubenie.
Aubenie, Will., Aubem [*read* Aubeni].
  See also Daubeney, 129, 166.
Aubrey, Will., Awberey, Awbrey,
  Abrey. *See also* Dawberey, 156, 165,
  197, 212, 219, 238, 243, 246, 248,
  256, 269, 286, 315, 318.
Audeley, Sim., Awdeley, 164.
—— Will., 566.
Auger, Joh., Awger, 40, 82, 90, 129,
  143, 159, 166, 171.
Aunsell, Will., 318.
Austen, Ric., Awsten, Austeyn, Aws-
  tyn, Austyn, Aweston, 198, 204,
  213, 218, 219, 221, 230, 231, 232,
  235, 242, 243, 245, 246, 252, 254,
  255, 256, 259, 262, 266, 270, 271,
  272, 275, 276, 277, 278, 279, 280,
  283, 284, 285, 293, 296, 301, 302,
  304, 305, 306, 307, 310, 312, 316,
  317, 320, 321, 332, 333, 334, 335,
  336, 337, 338, 339, 343, 351, 352,
  360, 361, 362, 370, 372, 375, 376,
  378.
—— Tho., 238, 573.
—— Will., 573.

Babynton, Will., 67.
Bache, Tho., 248.
—— Will., 237.
Bacon, Tho., Bakon, 351, 636.
Badeley, Jas., 608.
Bagott, Joh., Bagot, Bagett, Bagotte,
  376.
—— Tho., 210, 352, 357, 360, 368,
  370, 371, 373, 376, 378, 390, 416,
  423, 424, 431, 443, 481, 483, 485,
  514, 520, 531, 532, 533, 539, 540,
  542, 543, 544, 547, 552, 553, 842.
—— Will., 17, 78, 125, 132, 421,
  566, 579.
Baguley, Ric., 736.
Baker, Ad., Baxster, 78, 87, 125.
—— Alen, 354.
—— Dav., 162, 180.
—— Ed., 479.
—— Hen., 167, 214, 241, 319, 363.
—— Hum., 831.
—— Joh., 78, 81, 82, 87, 89, 90,
  120, 125, 127, 128, 132, 139, 142,
  153, 161, 165, 166, 176, 209, 210,
  218, 219, 221, 222, 228, 230, 232,
  235, 240, 242, 245, 247, 248, 252,
  255, 256, 266, 270, 275, 278, 284,
  285, 296. 304, 638, 641, 842.

Baker, Joh., de Priory, 168.
—— Jas., 530.
—— Mat., 364.
—— Ric., 128, 156, 165, 166, 175,
  176, 179.
—— Rob., 81, 89, 90, 125, 128, 156,
  167, 174, 212, 432, 443, 478, 481,
  482, 520.
—— Rog., 534, 540.
—— Sim., 76, 153, 160, 180, 209,
  240.
—— Tho., 80, 89, 127, 153, 161,
  179.
—— Will., 89, 174, 240, 241, 244,
  250, 315, 318, 320, 321, 333, 335,
  337, 338, 339, 345, 347, 351, 352,
  362, 368, 371, 372, 375, 376, 378,
  382, 385, 389, 390, 416, 419, 747,
  842.
Balche, Nic., 250. *Read* Bache.
Ball, Hen., Balle, 162, 164, 179, 370,
  377, 391, 416, 421, 424, 431, 435,
  443, 481, 483, 485, 514.
—— Joh., 81, 89, 128, 156, 166, 174.
—— Rob., 81, 236, 248.
—— Rog., 89, 128, 156, 166, 174.
Ballsall, Joh., 80, 88.
Banburgh,——, Bamburgh, Baumburhg,
  Bambour, Bramburgh, Bamboro,
  429.
—— Chr., 317, 318.
—— Will., 53, 242, 336, 354, 376,
  414, 479, 482.
Banbury, Hen., Banbery, Banbere,
  128, 167, 214, 241, 244, 256, 269,
  285, 286, 343.
Banbroke, Ric., 482.
—— Tho., 542.
Bancroft, Tho., 482.
Bande, *see* Bond.
Banestur, Tho., 821.
Banwell, Tho., 637, 638, 643, 645,
  647, 654, 665, 666, 667, 668, 676,
  677, 682, 684, 686, 689, 691, 692,
  693, 694, 695, 696, 697, 700, 701,
  704, 706, 707, 711, 714, 715, 717,
  718, 720, 721, 722, 724, 726, 727,
  728, 737, 739, 740, 742, 746, 759,
  766, 767, 768.
—— Will., 601, 602, 604, **619**,
  631, 636, 638, 647, 650, 652, **653**,
  654, 665, 676, 679, 684, 693, **694**,
  695, 696, 697, 699, 700, 701, 704,
  706.
Bapthorp, Babtharpe, Rob., 61.

C. LEET BK. 3 L

Bapthorp, Will., 317, 815.
Barber, —, Barbur, Barbour, Burbur, 209.
—— Ed., 481, 483, 512, 514, 533, 542, 563, 571, 573, 581, 584, 598, 599, 600.
—— Elis, 165, 211, 236.
—— God., 39, 41, 48, 80, 89, 251, 842.
—— Hen., 252.
—— Hugo, 128, 156, 166, 174, 212, 244, 246, 256, 269.
—— Jacobus, 238.
—— Joh., 81, 129, 155, 164, 168, 175, 176, 177, 209, 214, 238.
—— Joh., atte Bulryng, 251.
—— Ranulph, 238, 252.
—— Ric., 153, 161, 179, 210, 212, 238, 239, 251, 377, 379, 479.
—— Ric., atte Gosford stulpes, 252.
—— Rob., 82, 90, 154, 163, 166, 178, 240.
—— Tho., 80, 88, 89, 154, 161, 164, 167, 239, 240, 241.
—— Will., 128, 163, 168, 176, 252, 553, 557, 562, 566, 571, 594, 598, 600, 602, 621.
Bardford, —, 167.
Bareboche, —, 82.
Barfote, Har., Barfete, 343, 377.
Barkeby, Joh., 156.
Barker, Alex., 82, 90, 163, 167, 176.
—— Hen., 210, 236, 249.
—— Joh., 840.
—— Ric., 239, 830, 831, 832.
—— Tho., 87, 161.
Barley, Joh., 211.
—— Rob., 164.
—— Will., 164, 177.
Barlowe, Rob., 574.
Barnard, Joh., Bernard, 80, 88, 127, 154, 164, 177.
Barnebroke, —, 531.
—— Ric., 212, 239, 365.
—— Will., 212, 239.
Barnesley, Rob., Barnsley, 154, 163, 178, 207, 213, 219, 242, 247.
Barnwell, Tho., 153, 179. *Read* Darnwell.
Baron, —, sen., 47.
—— Joh., 177, 352, 421, 435, 443, 478, 481, 483, 531, 556, 566.
—— Rad., 161.
—— Ric., 535, 566, 570, 579, 586.
—— Tho., 482, 514, 533, 540.

Barre, *read* Barro.
Barro, —, 90.
—— Joh., 180.
—— Nich., 81, 89, 127.
Barres, Joh., 167, 180.
Barrett, Edm., Berett, 352.
—— Joh., 80, 85, 88, 210.
—— Will., 82, 90.
Barton, Joh., 101, 210, 237, 247.
—— Laur., 241, 250.
—— Rob., 608.
—— Rog., 166.
—— Will., 22.
Bartram, Ric., 213, 242.
Barwell, Ric., 164, 177.
Baryngton, Will., 211, 237.
Basset, Joh., 164, 177.
Bassyngburn, Tho., Bassyngburne, Bassingburn, 81, 90, 128, 155, 168, 189.
Bate, Hen., 80, 88, 126.
—— Joh., 6.
—— Ric., 451.
—— Tho., 212.
—— Will., 40, 41, 82, 90, 129, 166, 167, 224, 842.
Bateman, —, 212, 535.
—— Rob., 543, 566.
—— Tho., 161, 184, 239, 249.
Bathe, *read* Bache.
Batter, Joh., 241.
Bawdewyn, Joh., 340.
Baxster. *See* Baker.
Bay, Will., 366.
Bayly, Jas., Baly, Bailly, Baylly, Bayle, Baille, Bally, Bale, Beilie, 363, 377, 421, 483, 512, 514, 528, 532.
—— Joh., 127, 156, 169, 178, 179, 210, 222, 237, 247, 251, 285, 286, 305, 307, 312, 315, 317, 320, 321, 333, 334, 335, 337, 338, 339, 343, 345, 351, 352.
—— Nic., 239.
—— Tho., 53, 80, 126, 154, 163, 166, 168, 175, 178, 213, 219, 242, 248, 337, 351, 352, 354, 357, 365, 377, 390, 403, 406, 419, 421, 424, 481, 482, 483, 485, 503, 513, 518, 520, 521, 522, 532, 533, 534, 535, 539, 540, 542, 543, 544, 547, 552, 553, 557, 563, 567, 571, 572, 579, 581, 582, 584, 585, 587, 588, 598, 599, 600, 601, 602, 603, 604, 605, 606, 619, 621, 623, 624, 625, 628.

Name Index. 865

Bayly, Will., 39, 41, 82, 87, 178, 183, 212, 239, 247, 250, 285, 318, 337, 339, 735, 736, 760, 788, 790, 796, 797, 800, 801, 803, 806, 809, 812.
—— Will., jun., 746.
Baynton, Joh., Beynton, 242, 249.
Bealson, Ric., 214.
Beaufitz, Ric., Bowfyse, 7.
—— Rob., 352, 483.
Beauchamp, Joh., Bechampe, Bechamp, Beachamp, 80, 85, 88, 126, 134, 139, 142, 143, 156, 160, 169, 177, 189, 210, 221, 237.
Beck, Tho., 768.
Bedemaker, Joh., 163.
Bedford, Tho., 39, 41, 48, 127.
—— Will., 20, 22, 36, 210, 236, 252.
Bedon, Ric., 155, 168, 176, 214, 241, 250, 256, 316, 318, 343, 352, 368, 377.
—— Will., 128, 167, 175, 214, 240, 250, 315, 318, 328, 329, 330, 331, 332, 343, 351.
Bedull, Joh., 351.
—— Joh., de Stychall, Styvechall, 403, 406.
Bedworth, Agnes, Bedwurthe, 321.
—— Joh., 250.
Bee, Nic., 248.
Beilie. See Bayly.
Beke, Laur., Beeke, 483, 530, 531, 535.
Bekynham, Tho., 351.
Belchier, Humf., 583.
Belgrave, Will., Bellgraue, 20, 22, 36, 37, 39, 40, 41, 42, 44, 54, 58, 79, 88, 107, 111, 114, 117, 120, 122, 126, 133, 134, 154, 163.
Belle, Will., 319.
Beller, Ric., 78, 87, 125.
Bellours, Ric., 46. (?) See Beller.
Belmon, Joh., 162.
Belper, Joh., 213.
Belston, Joh., 82, 90.
Benchis, Ric., 39.
Benduyle, Joh., Benefell, Benefeld, Benyfeld, Benyfold, 5.
—— Will., 242, 250, 356, 483.
Benet, Hen., 162, 213.
—— Joh., 37, 39, 41, 46, 60, 77, 80, 82, 111, 117, 126, 131, 163, 166, 842.
—— Rog., 105.
—— Will., 81, 128, 155, 176, 214, 241, 319.

Bentley, Joh., 163, 213, 242, 243, 248, 256, 269, 351, 376.
—— Will., 237, 250.
Berbroun. See Parbroun.
Bere, Joh., Beor, Beer, Bery, 127, 163, 177, 240, 365.
—— Reg., 214, 221, 226, 227, 228, 229, 232, 240, 245, 246, 250, 255, 256, 266, 267, 269, 271, 275, 277, 278, 279, 280, 283.
—— Ric., 81, 219.
—— Tho., 162, 180.
Berkeley, Sir Will., 369.
Berkeswell, Bened., 451.
Bernard. See Barnard.
Berrett. See Barrett.
Beryngton. See Byryngton.
Beryton, Ric., 480.
Betriche, Rob., 242.
Bett, Joh., Bette, Bet, Bete, 89, 127, 153, 155, 165, 174, 214, 240, 250, 285, 305, 306, 307, 310, 316, 317, 320, 321, 332, 333, 335, 337, 338, 339, 343, 345, 347, 351, 360, 361, 362, 364, 366, 370, 371, 375, 376, 377, 378, 382, 385, 387, 388.
—— Laur., 167.
—— Rob., 366.
—— Tho., 179, 251.
—— Will., 90, 125, 161, 167, 179.
Bettley, Will., Betley, Betteley, 37, 154, 162, 178, 228, 229, 238, 245, 266, 285, 307, 316, 317.
Beuer, Hugo, 82.
—— Ric., 88.
Beverley, Will., 154, 162.
Bevys, Rob., 428, 429, 438.
Bifeld. See Byfeld.
Billingsley, Rog., Byllyngesley, 540, 566.
Birches, Evan, Burches, Byrches, Byrche, 436.
—— Owen, 543.
—— Symkyn, 192, 195, 207, 212, 229, 238, 245, 259, 285, 310, 316, 317, 343, 360, 364, 390.
Birde, Hen., Brydde, Bryde, Bryd, Brid, Byrde, Bird, 37, 39, 41, 46, 60, 79, 88, 111, 127, 143, 156, 169, 178.
—— Johanna, 168.
—— Joh., 37, 42, 81, 86, 107, 128.
—— Ric., 128.
—— Tho., 156, 166, 210.
—— Will., 37, 39, 41, 44, 46, 60, 69, 79, 83, 85, 87, 91, 98, 102, 103, 107,

109, 111, 117, 120, 122, 126, 133, 134, 143, 144, 152, 154, 160, 162, 171, 172, 178, 184, 186, 187, 189, 195, 198, 207, 212, 217, 238, 336.
Birdlyme, Will., 598.
Biston, Ric., 129.
Bitter, Ed., 167.
—— Joh., 167.
Bixton. *See* Brixton.
Blackamour, Joh., Blakamour, Blackamoore, 154, 164, 177, 210.
Bladdurwyk, Rob., 3.
Bladsmyhth, Joh., Bladsmythe, 343, 352, 365.
Blake, Joh., 318.
—— Ric., 318.
Blakman, Joh., Blakeman, Blakemon, Blackmon, 39, 60, 77, 80, 85, 89, 102, 108, 120, 127, 131, 133, 134, 138, 143, 144, 151, 152, 155, 160, 164, 175, 183, 184, 211, 221.
—— Joh., jun., 164.
—— Margareta, 236.
Blakmere, Owyne, Blakemer, 687, 736, 760, 767, 768, 779, 780.
Blakenale, Joh., Blaknale, 165, 212.
—— Will., Blakenale, 212, 239, 248, 366.
Blakeney, Joh., 174.
Blakwall, Dan., [*read* Dav.] 579.
—— Dauid, 566, 599.
Blokkeswych, Joh., 318.
Blokley, Joh., 168, 176.
Blore, Hug., Bloure, Blour, Blowre, 706, 718, 737, 738, 740, 742, 746, 759, 766, 767, 768, 769, 770, 773, 778, 779, 782, 783, 789.
Blubery, Rob., Blewbere, Blewbery, Blowbere, Blebere, Blubere, Blebury, 249, 333, 336, 344, 351, 352, 356, 360, 361, 365, 370, 371, 376, 385, 389, 390, 416, 421, 423, 424, 473, 481, 513, 520, 843.
Blyburgh, Rob., 240, 313, 315, 318.
Bobynhull, Ric., 5.
Bocher, —, Bochar, 39.
—— Joh., 534.
—— Moricius, 81, 128, 246.
—— Nic., 168.
—— Rad., 128.
—— Ric., 209, 240, 249, 251.
—— Rob., 238.
—— Wal., 241, 313.
—— Will., 209, 240, 247, 285.
Bogett, Tho., [Bagett?] 354.

Boise. *See* Boys.
Boland, Hugh, Bolen, 479.
—— Joh., 318.
Bolat, Joh., Bowlat, Bollet, 725, 727, 735, 736, 781, 806.
Bolewyke, Will., 344, 351.
Bolter, Joh., 237.
Bolton, Will., 162, 165, 180, 210, 238, 249.
Bomye, Will., 161.
Bond, Joh., Bande, 351, 514, 609, 624, 628, 636, 637, 638, 641, 645, 647, 649, 650, 652, 653, 654, 666, 667, 670, 674, 675, 676, 677, 679, 682, 684, 686, 688, 691, 692, 693, 694, 695, 696, 697, 701, 704, 711.
—— Tho., 482, 528, 529, 544, 547, 563, 567, 581, 584, 585, 588, 592, 594, 595, 598, 599, 600, 601, 602, 603, 604, 605, 762.
—— Walt., 78, 87, 125, 153, 161, 183, 184, 209.
Bondy, Joh. Bandy, Bande, 81, 128, 155, 168, 175.
—— Johanna, 81, 89.
—— Rob, 82, 92, 129.
—— Will., 3, 17.
Boohghe, Hen., 179.
Booke, Will., 156.
Boote, Joh., Bote, 214, 543.
—— Joh., sen., 483.
Bordale, —, Bordall, 368, 503.
—— Joh., 79, 88, 126, 156, 169, 178, 210, 314, 343, 344, 351, 354, 370, 371, 376, 379, 422, 435, 481, 482, 513.
Bordemon, Al., 352.
—— Olyuer, 248.
Borewell, Law., 352, 357.
Borresley, Joh., 728, 736, 761.
Botell, Ric., 242, 251.
—— Tho., 354, 368, 371, 377, 379.
Boteler. *See* Butler.
Bothe, Joh., Boithe, 318, 365.
—— Tho., 651, 687.
Botoner, Ad., Bottoner, Bootoner, 5.
—— Joh., 3.
—— Ric., 37, 39, 60, 77, 81, 90, 102, 104, 107, 108, 112, 113, 114, 115, 116, 117, 122, 128, 130, 134, 137, 138, 140, 141, 143, 144, 150, 152, 154, 157, 159, 160, 163, 169, 171, 172, 184, 186, 187, 188, 189, 192, 193, 194, 195, 197, 198, 200, 201, 202, 204, 207, 214, 221, 227,

Name Index.

228, 229, 231, 232, 233, 235, 241, 243, 252, 254, 255, 256, 259, 266.
Botte, Joh., [Bette?] 168, 176, 214, 241, 249.
Boughton, Edw., 830, 831, 832.
Bowdon, Edm., 381.
Bowdy, Joh., 249.
Bowfyse. *See* Beaufitz.
Bowland, Will., [Boland?] 365.
Bowman, Will., 242, 252.
Bowne, Joh., 821.
—— Ral, 821, 830, 831, 832.
Bowterode, Joh., 164.
Bowton, Will., 17.
Bowyer, Alex., Bower, Bow3er, Bowyere, Boure, Bouer, Bowar, 164, 175.
—— Avericius, 237.
—— Galf., 211, 219, 236, 256, 314, 318.
—— Joh., 22, 36, 37, 39, 41, 44, 48, 54, 56, 58, 60, 62, 64, 69, 71, 73, 80, 83, 84, 85, 89, 98, 99, 102, 104, 106, 107, 108, 109, 111, 112, 113, 114, 115, 117, 120, 122, 127, 130, 132, 134, 137, 138, 140, 141, 143, 146, 238, 450.
—— Margeria, 155, 165, 175.
—— Reg., 155, 164, 175.
—— Ric., 318, 337, 343, 345, 357, 360, 365, 368, 370, 377, 379, 435, 482.
—— Rob., 571, 581, 582.
—— Tho., 153, 161, 209, 240, 246, 336, 481, 766.
—— Will., 67, 210, 318, 352, 360, 377, 503, 516.
Bowyes, Will., 561.
Boyden, Joh., 11.
Boys, Joh., Boise, Boyes, Boyse, 128.
—— Margery, 361.
—— Ric., 78, 87, 126, 139, 142, 154, 163, 178, 195, 197, 201, 202, 204, 207, 213, 217, 218, 219, 221, 226, 229, 230, 231, 232, 233, 235, 242, 243, 245, 246, 253, 254, 255, 256, 262, 263, 267, 268, 269, 270, 271, 272, 275, 276, 277, 278, 279, 280, 283, 284, 285, 293, 296, 302, 304, 305, 306, 307, 308, 310, 312, 313, 316, 317, 320, 321, 332, 333, 335, 336, 337.
Brabon, Alicia, Braban, 240.
—— Joh., 80, 125, 153, 160, 170, 209, 222, 228.
Brabson, Johanna, 154, 163, 178.
—— Joh., 79, 88, 138, 153, 163.
Bradbury, Joh., 586.
Bradley, Joh., 153, 162, 163, 168, 177, 178, 180, 213, 237, 242, 248.
—— Katerina, 177.
—— Rob., 88.
Bradmedow, Rob., Bredmedowe, Brodmedow, Brodmedew, 207, 213, 219, 222, 230, 235, 242, 243, 245, 247, 252, 253, 255, 256, 259, 260, 262, 266, 270, 271, 272, 276, 277, 279, 280, 283, 284, 285, 293, 296, 297, 301, 304, 305, 306, 307, 310, 311, 312, 313, 316, 317, 320, 321, 332, 333, 334, 335, 336, 337, 338, 339, 343, 344, 347, 351, 360, 361, 362, 363, 365, 367, 370, 371, 372, 373, 375, 376, 377, 382, 385, 416, 419, 421, 423, 424, 435, 482, 514, 518, 576.
—— Tho., 207, 213, 242, 246, 247, 256, 276, 278, 280, 285, 292, 293, 296, 301, 302, 305, 306, 307, 310, 312, 316, 317, 320, 321, 332, 333, 334, 335, 336, 337, 338, 339, 343, 344, 347, 351, 360, 361, 362, 367, 370, 371, 372, 375, 376, 377, 378, 382, 385, 387, 388, 389, 390, 416, 419, 421, 423, 424, 431, 435, 437, 443, 473, 474, 481, 482, 485, 503, 514, 516, 518, 520, 522, 524, 528, 530, 532, 533, 534, 539, 540, 843.
Bradmere, Will., 161, 179.
Bradshawe, Joh., 608.
Bradwell, Joh., 640.
Bramston, Joh., Brampton, Brampston, 37, 39, 42, 48, 80, 138, 140, 169, 188, 189, 195, 200.
Branche, Will., Brawnche, Braunch, 343, 354, 376, 421, 432, 481, 513.
Brase, Joh., Brasse, 88, 168, 175.
Brasier, Joh., 174, 176, 239, 241.
Braunston, Joh., 20, 43, 54, 58, 60, 69, 85, 89, 100, 101, 102, 103, 104, 105, 106, 108, 109, 111, 112, 115, 117, 119, 122, 127, 130, 134, 137, 138, 140, 141, 143, 144, 150, 151, 152, 155, 157, 159, 165, 171, 172, 175, 184, 186, 187, 189, 191, 192, 193, 194, 202, 207, 211, 236, 451, 452, 465, 469.
—— Joh., jun., 127, 165.
Brayleford, *read* Braylesford.
Braylesford, Joh., 162, 179.

Braylesford, Will., 352.
Braymere, Tho., 251.
Brayn, Joh., Brayne, 162, 178.
—— Tho., 239.
Braynesford, Hen., Braynsford, 687.
—— Joh., 608.
—— Tho., 608.
Braytoft, Joh., Braytofte, Braitofte, Bray-Tofte, Bray-toofte, 20, 22, 34, 36, 37, 39, 40, 42, 43, 44, 54, 57, 60, 62, 65, 68, 71, 73, 79, 82, 84, 85, 86, 87, 91, 98, 99, 101, 102, 103, 104, 106, 107, 109, 110, 111, 112, 113, 114, 115, 117, 119, 122, 126, 130, 131, 132, 134, 137, 138, 139, 140, 141, 143, 144, 146, 150, 151, 154, 159, 163, 169, 171, 172, 179, 184, 185, 186, 187, 188, 189, 191, 193, 194, 195, 197, 198, 231.
—— Ric., 53, 88, 127, 134, 143, 150, 152, 154, 157, 163, 169, 171, 178, 184, 186, 188, 189, 192, 193, 195, 197, 198, 200, 201, 202, 203, 205, 207, 208, 211, 214, 217, 218, 219, 220, 225, 226, 228, 229, 230, 231, 232, 233, 235, 236, 243, 246, 252, 253, 254, 255, 256, 259, 262, 266, 267, 270, 271, 275, 276, 277, 278, 279, 280, 283, 284, 285, 292, 296, 301, 302, 304, 305, 306, 307, 308, 310, 311, 312, 313, 316, 317, 320, 321, 322, 332, 333, 334, 335, 336, 337, 338, 339, 343, 344, 347, 351, 352, 360, 361, 362, 364, 365, 367, 368, 369, 370, 371, 372, 373, 375, 376, 377, 378, 382, 385, 387, 388, 389 390, 391, 416, 419, 423, 424, 431, 443, 473, 481, 482, 485, 489, 503, 504, 513, 516, 520, 521, 522, 524, 529, 532, 533, 539, 540, 541, 542, 543, 544, 547, 552, 553, 557, 563, 567, 571, 579, 581, 582, 584, 585, 587, 588, 593, 594, 598, 599, 600, 601, 602, 603.
—— Ric., sen., 533 843.
—— Ric., jun., 359, 370, 371, 375, 376, 378, 385, 387, 388, 389, 390, 409 411, 414, 415, 416, 419, 421, 423 424.
—— Will., 146, 154, 207, 212, 217, 218, 221, 222, 226, 228, 229, 230, 231, 232, 233, 235, 243, 245, 246, 252, 253, 254, 255, 256, 261, 266, 267, 270, 271, 276, 277, 278, 279, 280, 283, 284, 285, 296, 301, 302, 304, 305, 306, 307, 308, 310, 311, 318.
Bredon, ——, 363, 530.
—— Joh., 35, 88, 89, 97, 227, 228, 251, 315, 318, 365, 518, 556.
—— Rad., 80, 89, 108, 165, 175.
—— Tho., 53, 155, 168, 175, 214, 240, 241, 256, 541, 549, 553, 557, 579.
—— Will., 80, 127, 155, 165, 175, 211.
Brere, Joh., 81, 89, 127. 165.
Breres, Breers, Hen., 821, 830, 831, 832.
Bretford, ——, 363.
—— Rob., 355, 377, 482.
Brethe, Gibben, [? Brettbe] 562.
Breton, Alicia, Bretayn, Breten, 153, 161.
—— Joh., 45, 78, 99, 104, 115, 125, 132, 141.
Brett, Joh., Brette, 127, 165, 174.
—— Rog., 542, 561, 566.
Brettby, Joh.. Brettebe, 81, 89.
—— Tho., 562.
Breux, Hen., Brewes, 34, 36, 37, 39, 40, 41, 42, 44, 54, 57, 58, 60, 62, 65, 67, 68, 71, 81, 83, 84, 90, 91, 98, 99, 102, 104, 106, 107, 108, 109, 112, 113, 114, 115, 117, 452.
—— Joh., 87, 153, 184.
—— Margaret, 128, 155, 167.
Brewer, Elys, Bruer, Breuster, 541.
—— Gobett, (?) 179.
—— Joh., 125, 153, 161, 165, 179, 211, 213, 236, 238, 241.
—— Tho., 651, 706, 707, 717, 718, 721, 722, 723, 724, 725, 727, 728, 737, 738, 739, 740, 742, 746, 759, 767, 768, 769.
—— Will., 163.
Brid and Bryd. *See* Birde.
Brigeman, Bregeman, Ric., Brigman, 483, 517, 535, 541, 579.
Brigges, Gil., Brygges, Bregges, Bryg, 480.
—— Joh., 534.
—— Will., 541, 573, 579, 601, 602, 631, 633, 647.
Brikwode, Ric., 562.
Briscow, Alicia, Bristow, Brystowe, B[r]ystowe, Bryskowe, 211.
—— Ed., 479, 500, 501, 506, 509, 515.
—— Joh., 22, 34, 37, 39, 40, 42, 43, 44, 54, 57, 60, 62, 65, 68, 71, 80, 83, 84, 85, 89, 102, 104, 105,

Name Index.

109, 111, 113, 114, 116, 117, 119, 121, 122, 127, 130, 131, 132, 134, 137, 138, 139, 144, 151, 152, 155, 157, 159, 164, 169, 171, 172, 175, 179, 184, 185, 186, 187, 188, 189, 191, 193, 195, 197, 198, 200, 201, 202, 203, 204, 207, 208, 211, 213, 217, 218, 219, 220, 222, 226, 228, 229, 230, 231, 232, 235, 236, 243, 246, 252, 254, 349.
—— Ric., 164, 177, 541.
—— Tho., 146, 207, 210, 237, 247.
—— Will., 349, 350, 376, 378, 379, 380, 436, 439, 440, 471, 478, 483, 489, 490, 491, 494, 498, 499, 500, 501, 502, 505, 506, 507, 508, 509, 510, 515.
Bristoll, Ric., 482.
Bristowe. *See* Briscow.
Brixston, Joh., B[r]ixton, 560, 562.
Brodde, Agnes, Broode, 79, 87.
—— Rob., 20.
Brodmedowe. *See* Bradmedowe.
Brogreve, Edm., 81, 89, 126, 143, 154, 158, 163, 171, 178, 189, 195, 198, 201, 204, 207, 208, 210, 217, 218, 219, 221, 226, 227, 229, 230, 231, 232, 233, 235, 236, 246, 252, 253, 254, 255, 256, 259, 266, 267, 270, 271, 272, 275, 276, 277, 278, 279, 280, 283, 284, 285, 293, 296, 301, 302, 304, 305, 306, 307, 308, 310, 311, 312, 313, 316, 317, 320, 321, 322, 332, 333, 334, 335, 336, 337, 338, 339, 343, 344, 347, 351, 352, 360, 361, 362, 365, 367, 370, 371, 372, 373, 375, 376, 377, 378, 382, 385, 387, 388, 389, 390.
—— Ric., 280.
Brooke, —, Clerke of the markette; Broke, Brokes, 267.
—— Tho., 285, 317, 320, 321, 332, 336, 337, 339, 343, 344, 361, 364, 370.
—— Will., 37, 39, 41, 46, 60, 77, 80, 85, 88, 111, 126, 163, 169, 177, 210. 842.
Brokesby, Barth., 123.
Brome, Nyc. (Nic), 351, 357, 365, 371, 443, 473.
—— Will., 195.
Bromley, Chris., Bromeley, 746, 759, 766, 781, 789.
—— Jch., 579.
—— Ric., 154, 162, 164, 179, 212, 222, 238, 250, 256, 266, 319.

Bromley, Rog., 542, 586.
—— Will., 482, 535, 579,582,584,585.
Bromyche, Will., Bromwyche, Bromwiche, 81, 121, 128, 133, 155, 159, 160, 171, 175.
Browderer, Bart., Broderer, 210.
—— Watkyn, 354, 377.
Brown, Ad., Broun, Bron, 366.
—— Ed., 219.
—— Hen., 166, 583.
—— Joh., 44, 48, 60, 77, 81, 84, 85, 89, 91, 102, 103, 107, 111, 117, 120, 127, 146, 156, 162, 165, 166, 174, 176, 189, 211, 239, 319, 524, 525, 526, 541, 542, 573.
—— Nic., 163, 377, 423, 432, 481, 485, 503, 514, 518.
—— Rob., 155, 176.
—— Rog., 318, 337, 345, 352, 354, 368, 377, 483.
—— Tho., 80, 82, 89, 90, 127, 129, 133, 143, 155, 160, 164, 166, 174, 175, 176, 211, 212, 213, 236, 239, 242, 247, 248, 256, 266, 285, 318, 319, 451.
—— Wal., 214, 251, 318.
—— Will., 79, 80, 87, 126, 128, 152, 154, 163, 165, 171, 178, 184, 188, 189, 192, 193, 201, 204, 206, 207, 208, 209, 221, 222, 228, 229, 240.
Brownall, Tho., Brounale, 81, 89.
Brownhill, Edm., 780, 781.
Brvyngton. *Read* Brvynton.
Bryan, Eliz., Brian, Briant, 238.
—— Joh., 39, 41, 45, 60, 78, 87, 125, 143, 150, 152, 153, 154, 161, 163, 168, 171, 172, 177, 178, 179, 183, 184, 186, 189, 193, 194, 195, 197, 198, 200, 201, 202, 204, 206, 207, 208, 209, 217, 218, 219, 222, 235, 305.
Bryddesmere, Will., 120.
Bryghtmer, Joh., Bryghtmere, Bryhtmer, Brygtsmere, 39, 53, 81, 90, 128, 139, 142.
Brykhull, Katerina, 211.
Brykstocke, Alicia, Brykstook, Bristoke, 237.
—— Ric., 81, 128.
Brynklow, Hen., Brinklow, 79, 88.
Brynton, Will., ? Brvynton, 167, 248.
Brysaldon, Johanna, 165.
Brystowe. *See* Briscow.
Bug, Hen., Bugg, Bugge, 126, 163, 212, 238.

Bukbrig, Tho., 250.
Bukland, Joh., 561.
—— Will., 561.
Bulbek, Joh., 451,
—— Sim., 469.
Bulkeley, Joh., 166.
—— Reignold, 407.
—— Rob., 166, 174, 239, 248.
—— Will., 153, 162.
Bulker, Wal., 128, 156, 166, 174, 212.
Bullesdon, Joh., 163, 164.
Bullok, Joh., 165.
—— Ric., 174.
Bulwyk, Agnes, 175.
—— Dav., 167.
Bunbury, Nic., substituted for Bowyer, 175.
Bunsale, Tho., 161.
Burbage, —, 89, 156.
—— Joh., 79, 88, 127, 128, 156, 165, 169, 174, 178, 212.
—— Joh., jun., 146.
—— Ric., 174.
—— Will., 541, 546.
Burbury, Nic., 168.
Burden, Tho., Burdon, 631, 633, 634, 665, 666, 667, 690, 692, 693, 700, 704, 707, 711, 714, 717, 718, 721, 723, 724, 725, 728, 737, 739, 740, 759, 766, 767.
Burdet, Tho., 378.
Burdeux, —, Burdews, 237.
—— Joh., 250.
—— Tho., 203.
Burfrey, Ric., 162, 179, 212, 238.
Burges, Rob., 131, 160, 180, 183.
Burglen, Wlll., Burglym, 533, 535, 600.
Burley, Hen., Burghly, 421.
—— Tho., 237, 244, 247, 255, 318, 376.
—— Will., 480, 518.
Burman, Rob., 128.
Burne, Hen., Bryn, 690.
—— Joh., 81, 90, 166.
—— Rob., 168, 214, 222, 241, 251.
Burnell, Ric., 250.
—— Rob., 237, 250, 318, 333, 334, 339, 343, 345, 351, 360, 362, 365, 370, 371, 372, 375, 376, 416, 419, 421, 423, 424, 431, 435, 437, 443, 473, 481, 482, 513, 530, 532.
Burnes, Rog., 212, 239, 247, 256, 319.
Burnam, Joh., Burnham, 162, 179.
Burrowes, Edw., 821, 831.

Burton, David, 89, 127.
—— Johanna, 178.
—— Joh., 79, 88, 111, 126, 137, 138, 148, 149, 152, 154, 163, 192, 482.
—— Ric., 80.
—— Ric. de, 10.
—— Tho., 106.
Burwell, Lau., 377.
Burwey, Nic., Borwey, 549, 598, 604, 623, 625, 634, 636, 637, 638, 641, 642, 643, 645, 647, 651, 652, 653, 654, 665, 679, 687, 690, 721, 745.
—— Ric., 600, 631, 641, 642, 649, 651, 652, 653, 663, 665, 667, 676, 677, 682, 684, 686.
—— Rob., 382.
—— Tho., 162, 179.
Bushebury, Ric., Bussebury, 37, 39, 41, 44, 46, 60, 69, 77. 80, 85, 88, 102, 104, 107, 112, 113, 115, 116, 117, 120, 127, 132, 134, 137, 138, 140, 141, 143, 144, 150, 151, 152, 154, 157, 159, 164, 169, 171, 172, 177, 184, 185, 186, 187, 188, 189, 191, 192, 193, 194, 197.
Busteler, Sim., 81, 89, 128, 156, 165, 174, 212, 239, 250.
Busterd, Tho., Bustarde, 737, 780, 781.
Butler, Greg., Boteler, Boteller, 209, 240.
—— Hen., recorder, 266, 283, 284, 285, 296, 304, 305, 307, 310, 313, 316, 317, 320, 321, 322, 323, 333, 335, 337, 343, 344, 351, 352, 362, 364, 369, 370, 373, 382, 388, 409, 411, 423, 436, 443, 474, 481, 482, 485, 504, 513, 516, 518, 520, 521, 522, 526, 529, 530, 533.
—— Joh., 39, 129, 139, 142, 151, 152, 153, 155, 161, 168, 169, 171, 175, 177, 201, 210, 232, 237, 240, 246, 256, 266, 286, 436, 474, 483, 499, 503, 506, 515, 522, 528, 534, 535, 579, 593, 594, 598, 600, 602, 603, 624, 628, 629, 631, 634, 636, 637, 638, 641, 647, 651, 653, 665, 667, 676.
—— Ric., 840.
—— Rob., 128, 156, 166, 174, 212.
—— Rog., 160, 238.
—— Tho., 481. *Read* Hen.
—— Will., 168, 176, 213, 241, 557 570.
Butter, Johan, Buter, 585.

Name Index. 871

Butter, Joh., 480, 531, 585.
Butterley, Ric., 163.
Button, Tho., 161.
Buxston, Joh., Bucston, 352.
—— Will., 254.
Buyton, Joh., 87.
Byddell, Ric., Bydell, 82.
—— Will., 167, 213, 242, 251.
Byfeld, Johanna, Bifeld, 154, 162, 178.
—— Nic., 39, 41, 46, 60, 68, 79, 88, 91.
—— Ric., 126, 163, 178.
—— Rob., 20, 37, 39, 40, 41, 79, 88.
—— Will., 22, 36, 37, 39, 41, 42, 44, 58, 60, 68, 79, 83, 84, 87, 91, 98, 99, 102, 104, 107, 109, 110, 113, 114, 115, 117, 119, 126, 132, 134, 137, 138, 139, 140, 141, 143, 148.
Byg, Will., 161, 180.
Bykenhull, Rad., 241.
Bylston, Joh., Bilston, Bylton, 166, 168, 175, 213, 241, 248, 251.
—— Ric., 82, 90, 167, 213, 241, 248.
—— Ric., jun., 248.
—— Rog., 82, 90.
—— Will., 175, 210.
Byngham, Sir Ric., 336.
—— Dame Margaret, 336.
Bynley, Agnes, Byneley, 214, 241.
—— Joh., 168, 176, 214, 241, 250, 266, 285, 315.
—— Will., 41, 73, 81, 90, 128, 168, 176, 842.
Byram, Joh., Biram, Byrame, Byrome, 156, 201, 210, 222, 228, 230, 232, 237, 245, 246, 252, 253, 255, 256, 259, 260, 262, 266, 270, 272, 275, 276, 278, 279, 280, 283, 284, 285, 296, 301, 302, 304, 306, 307, 312, 316, 317.
Byrton, Tho., 237.
Byryngton, Will., Byrynton, Beryngton, 214, 240, 244, 285.
Bystowe, Ric., *read* Bristowe, 164.

Cade, Joh., Cadde, 168.
—— Ric., 155, 176.
Caladon, Will., 161.
Caldebek, Joh., Calbek, Caldbek, 316.
—— Rad., 242, 246, 285, 286, 313, 317, 321, 334, 336, 337, 338, 339, 344, 351, 352, 360, 361, 362, 365, 370, 372, 376, 378, 382, 385, 387, 514.
Caldon, Tho., 212.

Caldwell, Tho., 166.
Cale. *See* Gale.
Cambryge, Joh., Cambrige, Caumbyrge, Cambirge, Cambrig, 37, 39, 41, 59, 79, 88.
Camell, Joh., 180.
—— Tho., 540, 546, 566, 579.
Campion, Ric., Campyon, 479.
—— Tho., 343, 351, 358, 376.
Canley, Wal. de, 815.
—— Will., 14, 164, 211, 237.
Cannyng, Joh., 480.
Capmaker, Ric., 174.
Capper, —, Cappar, Cappe, 171.
—— Agnes, 209.
—— Galf., 166, 174, 236.
—— Joh., 80, 88, 127, 139, 142, 154, 164, 177, 211, 237.
—— Rad., 238.
—— Ric., 81, 89, 128, 166, 207.
—— Rob., 156, 480.
—— Tho., 211.
—— Will., 153, 161, 239, 479.
Carbonell, Tho., 127, 139, 142, 171, 211.
Carde, Ric., 175.
—— Tho., 129, 175.
Cardemaker, Joh., Carmaker, Cardmaker, 81, 127, 156, 168, 177.
—— Ric., 79, 88, 705.
—— Tho., 126.
Cardyff, —, Kardyffe, Cardyf, Kerdiffe, 214.
—— Ric., 166, 215, 240, 251.
—— Tho., 82, 90, 168, 214, 240.
—— Will., 237, 251, 352.
Cariour, Hugo, 168, 176.
Carles, Joh., 163.
Carre, Nic., 210.
Carreke, Joh., 239.
Carter, Hen., 154, 482, 540, 546, 579.
—— Joh., 79, 88, 125.
—— Rog., 239.
—— Tho., 39, 80, 85, 89, 129, 166, 842.
—— Will., 535, 566, 601.
Cartwryght, Hugo, 129, 166.
Carver. *See* Kerver.
Castell, —, 212.
—— Joh., 125, 153, 160, 237, 247, 344, 345, 352, 358, 365, 368, 377, 390, 424, 435, 473, 482, 485, 503, 513, 516, 518, 520, 522, 528, 533, 540, 599, 768, 769, 770.
—— Tho., 482.

Castell, Will., 556.
Castelton, —, 162.
—— Will., 153, 179, 210, 238.
Castron, Hen., 163.
Catesby, Joh., 379, 380, 440, 474.
—— Will., 474, 490.
Caton, Will., 479.
Catur, Joh., Cater, Catter, 119, 134, 153, 161, 179, 210, 226, 228, 229, 230, 231, 232, 235, 238, 247, 253, 255, 270, 272, 275, 279, 280, 283, 285, 293, 296, 304, 305, 306, 307, 310, 312, 320, 321, 335.
—— Tho., 164.
Cauldenall, Tho., 174.
Caunten, Joh., 421.
Caunter, Joh., 163. *See also* Chaunter.
Cawdrey, Ric., 242.
—— Tho., 241, 247.
Cawley, Joh., 450.
Cayche, Tho., 352.
Cayfeld, Will. de, 3.
Caytewayte, Ph., Kaytewayte, 241, 251.
Cerotte, Will., 452.
Cesyle, Cysyll. *See* Sessyle.
Chacombe, Joh., 79, 82, 88, 126, 154, 163, 167, 178, 210.
—— Ric., 213.
—— Tho., 82, 90.
Chadley, Joh., 212.
Chadurton, Hugo, 250.
Chakeman, Tho., 128.
Chaloner, Joh., 448.
—— Magote, 127.
Chambur, Joh., Chambre, Chambers, 79, 88, 127, 169, 240, 249, 377, 736, 773, 782, 788, 789, 794.
—— Rob., 584.
—— Rog., 542, 543, 544, 562, 563, 567, 571, 602, 604, 605, 606, 609, 619, 622, 623, 624, 625, 627, 628, 629, 630, 631, 633, 634, 636, 637, 638.
Chapell, Tho., 238.
Chapman, Joh., Chapmon, 162, 164.
—— Ric., 121, 133, 356, 363, 377, 391, 430, 483, 503, 514, 515, 539, 540, 572.
—— Rob., 79.
—— Rog., 213, 242, 248.
—— Tho., 160, 250, 269.
—— Will., 81, 90, 166.
Charite, Joh., 240, 246.
—— Ric., 214, 235, 240, 245, 246, 270.

Charlton, Pet. de, Charelton, 5.
—— Will., 79, 87, 120, 126, 133, 143, 146, 150, 154, 162, 179.
Chaturton, Joh., Chaterton, 127.
—— Wal., 154.
—— Will., 164, 177, 211, 237, 250.
Chaundeler, Editha, Chandeler, 214.
—— Joh., 39, 78, 87, 126.
—— Magott, 80.
—— Matill., 89.
—— Rad., 51, 81, 86, 90, 128, 144, 152, 155, 160, 167, 175.
—— Tho., 449.
—— Will., 242.
Chaunter, Joh., 178, 242.
Chausers, Tho., 73.
Chawderell, Will., Chauderell, 213, 247.
Chebsey, Joh., Chybsey, 248, 319.
Cherman, Joh., 518.
Chester, Joh., Chestur, 81, 89, 128, 156, 165, 174.
—— Tho., 167.
—— Will., 250.
Chesterfeld, Tho., 229.
Chetell, Will., 183.
Chetwyn, Joh., 46.
Chichester, Elizabeth, Chychestur, 241.
—— Ric., 129, 167, 176, 213.
Chiltern, Rob. de, 9.
Chircheman, Tho., Chyrchemon, Chichman, Churchman, Chourchman, 355, 365, 368, 377, 379, 390, 414, 416, 421, 424, 473, 482, 485, 513, 516, 518, 520, 522, 524, 528, 533, 542, 544, 547, 553, 557, 563, 567, 571, 579, 581, 582, 584, 585, 587, 588, 598, 599, 600, 601, 602, 603, 604, 605, 606, 609, 619, 621, 623, 624, 625, 627, 628, 629, 630, 631, 632, 633, 634, 636.
Chirk, Davy, Chyrke, 351, 365, 482, 566, 588.
Chiry, Joh., 166.
Chok, Ric., 327.
Cholley, Tho., 211, 236, 248.
Chubbok, Joh., 39, 79, 88.
Chybsey. *See* Chebsey.
Cleke, *read* Clerke.
Clement, Joh., 161, 237, 377.
—— Rad., 161.
—— Ric., 162, 180, 479.
Clerk, Hen., Clarke, Cleke, *read* Clerke, 163, 213, 242, 251.

Name Index.

Clerk, Joh., Clerke, Clarke, 20, 22, 37, 39, 41, 44, 46, 47, 50, 54, 58, 60, 68, 79, 83, 84, 85, 87, 91, 100, 102, 104, 106, 107, 111, 113, 114, 115, 117, 121, 122, 126, 130, 131, 132, 134, 137, 138, 140, 141, 142, 143, 144, 146, 150, 152, 154, 157, 159, 160, 162, 163, 169, 171, 172, 178, 184, 185, 186, 187, 188, 189, 192, 193, 194, 195, 197, 198, 200, 201, 202, 204, 206, 208, 212, 213, 217, 219, 221, 222, 226, 227, 229, 230, 232, 318, 382, 566, 579, 582, 586, 602, 603, 604, 607, 619, 621, 622, 624, 625, 627, 628, 629, 630, 631, 634, 636, 637, 638, 641, 642, 649, 650, 651, 652, 653, 662, 665, 666, 667, 668, 676, 677, 679, 682, 684, 686, 724, 725, 731, 736, 761.
—— Joh., de Michael, 42.
—— Joh., de Sticheall, 13, 47.
—— Ric., 5, 7, 129, 153, 162, 167, 169, 176, 178, 179, 202, 207, 208, 210, 211, 213, 217, 222, 226, 229, 230, 231, 232, 236, 238, 241, 242, 245, 246, 248, 251, 252, 253, 254, 256, 262, 266, 267, 270, 272, 276, 277, 279, 280, 284, 285, 286, 293, 296, 301, 302, 304, 305, 377, 518, 542, 553, 566, 570
—— Rob., 78, 87, 125, 153, 162, 180.
—— Tho , 166, 168, 241, 242, 250.
—— Walt., 80, 169.
—— Will., 79, 88, 127, 156, 169, 178, 202, 204, 210, 217, 219, 221, 228, 232, 235, 237, 240, 243, 245, 246, 247, 248, 252, 255, 256, 270.
Clerkesor, Pet., 343, 352, 354, 363, 365, 390, 414.
—— Ric., 479.
Cleybroke, Joh., Cleibrok, Cleibrooke, Claybroke, 166, 213, 242, 252.
—— Ric., 210.
—— Tho., 129, 166, 176, 213, 242, 252.
—— Will., 78, 87, 126, 131, 139, 142, 154, 162, 179, 183, 212, 239, 249.
Clifford. *See* Clyfford.
Clifton, Joh., 79, 88, 239, 252.
Clokmaker, Bernard, 238.
Close, Gef., Clowes, 663.
—— Ric. de la, 16.
—— Will., in the, 19.
Club, Joh., Clubb, 81, 89.
Clyff, Joh., 237, 246, 317, 318, 352, 365, 368, 377, 379, 421, 443, 482, 513, 534, 539.
Clyfford, Joh., Clifford, 180, 212, 238, 248, 376.
Clyston, Joh., 40, 128.
Cobbes, Will., 241, 246, 247.
Cobeler, Tho., 168.
Cockes, Joh., Cokes, Cokkes, Cokke, Kokkes, Kockes, Kockys, Koxe, Kox, Cock, Cookes, 162, 166, 209, 238, 564, 569.
—— Ric., 125, 153, 161, 166, 167, 209, 213, 222, 240, 241, 246, 248, 251, 256, 266, 285, 286, 315, 318, 337, 343, 344, 351, 357, 368, 377, 483.
—— Rob., 212.
—— Rog., 37, 39, 41, 46, 77, 80, 85, 133, 138, 143, 151, 152, 154, 164, 177, 842.
—— Tho., 39, 41, 79, 88, 153, 160, 166, 240, 246, 248, 266, 285, 286, 296, 305, 307, 312, 315, 317, 332.
—— Will., 6, 78, 125, 153, 160, 164, 209, 336, 343, 344, 351, 354, 360, 364, 368, 371, 373, 376, 378, 382, 385, 387, 390, 416, 421, 423, 424, 449.
Coke. *See* Cook.
Cokes, Cookes, Cokke. *See* Cockes.
Colam, Agnes, 165.
—— Joh., 318, 366.
—— Tho., 89.
Colas, Rob., 482, 540, 546.
—— Will., Tolas (?), 60, 78, 79, 87, 154, 842.
Colbrond, Egid., 174. *See also* Corbrond.
Colclow, Tho., Colchowe (?), Colclough, Colclohe, 236, 251, 318, 365.
Cole, Gal., Coole, Colle, 82.
—— Gerv., 129, 156, 165, 174, 198, 202, 207, 214, 217, 219, 221, 226, 228, 229, 230, 232, 233, 235, 241, 243, 245, 247, 253, 256, 259, 262, 272, 276, 277, 278, 279, 280, 283, 284, 301, 302, 305, 306, 310, 312, 318.
—— Joh., 233, 243.
—— Ric., 368.
—— Tho., 449.
—— Will., 352.
Colett, Alice, Colet, Collet, Collett, 705, 706.
—— Edw., 705, 706.
—— Eliz., 531.

Colett, Ric., 161, 209.
—— Tho., 240, 247, 266, 318, 351, 377.
Colgraue, Ric., 88.
Collshull, Edm., Colshull, Collyshull, 80, 85, 99, 106.
—— Joh., 41.
Colman, Joh., Colmon, 163, 480, 635.
—— Rob, 358, 371, 377, 423, 481, 483, 485, 514, 516, 528, 531, 532, 534, 538, 542, 543, 547, 553, 563, 567, 571, 581, 582, 587, 588, 598, 599, 604, 605, 606, 737, 738, 740, 780, 789, 793, 794, 798, 801, 806.
—— Tho., 80.
—— Will., 739, 740, 746, 750, 760.
Colmere, Tho., Colmer, 239, 247.
Cologne, Ric., 79, 163. *Read* Colgraue.
Colvyll, Will., 80, 88.
Coly, Joh., 177.
Colyn, Joh., 128, 765.
Colyns, Hen. (Har.), Collynse, Collins, Colens, 48, 81, 90, 318, 352, 368, 377, 390, 421, 424, 435, 443, 483, 514, 531, 587, 737, 806.
—— Joh., 127, 155, 163, 168, 175, 176, 178, 214, 241, 249, 302, 316, 318, 352.
—— Mat., 840.
—— Ric., 338, 339, 343, 347, 351, 352, 360, 362, 368, 372, 376, 378, 382, 385, 387, 390, 421, 424, 431, 435, 443, 473, 474, 481, 483, 485, 512, 514, 516, 518, 520, 521, 524, 528, 530, 532, 533, 534, 539, 540, 541, 542, 543, 547, 552, 553, 557, 563, 643, 736.
—— Ric., de Radford, 333.
—— Rob., 351.
—— Tho., 343, 351, 354, 365, 422, 432.
—— Will., 11, 48.
Combe, Abbot of, 378, 380.
Comber, Christiane, 449.
——Sir Joh., vicar of St. Michael's, 92.
Compton, Joh., 239.
—— Will., 249, 376, 390, 406.
Constantyne, Rog.. Costantyne, 175, 214, 237, 246, 377.
Conwey, Galf., Cunwey, 154.
—— Joh., 212, 239.
Cook, —, Coke, Cooke, 343.
—— Alicia, 240.
—— Hen., 81, 90, 128, 153, 162, 541.

Cook, Johanna, 168, 176.
—— Joh., 82, 251, 336, 352, 376, 414.
—— Laur., 20, 22, 36, 37, 39, 41, 42, 44, 47, 54, 58, 60, 61, 63, 64, 69, 70, 71, 73, 78, 83, 85, 86, 87, 91, 98, 99, 102, 104, 105, 106, 107, 108, 110, 111, 112, 114, 115, 117, 120, 121, 122, 125, 129, 130, 131, 134, 135, 136, 137, 138, 139, 140, 141, 143, 144, 147, 148, 149, 150, 151, 153, 157, 159, 160, 169, 171, 172, 184, 185, 186, 187, 188, 189, 191, 193, 194, 197, 198, 209, 518.
—— Nic., 167.
—— Ric., 53, 365, 377, 390, 414, 421, 424, 431, 435, 436, 443, 481, 482, 503, 514, 516, 520, 522, 528, 529, 532, 533, 534, 539, 540, 542, 543, 544, 547, 552, 553, 563, 567, 571, 579, 585, 588, 593, 594, 598, 599, 600, 601, 602, 603, 604, 605, 606, 609, 717.
—— Rob., 167, 365.
—— Rog., 127, 164, 177.
—— Tho., 80, 160, 212, 239, 826.
—— Will., 87, 641, 665, 667.
—— Will., de Charterhouse, 239.
Cookes. *See* Cockes.
Coper, Joh., Cope, Coppe, Coope, 176.
—— Ric., 485.
—— Will., 37, 125, 176.
Copsey, Joh., Copesey, 242, 247.
Corbet, Will., Corbett, Corbette, 160, 212, 238, 248, 286.
Corbrond, Egid., Corbronde, 128, 156, 165, 212, 239, 255.
Corby, —, 503.
—— Dauid, 5, 144.
—— Ric., 165.
—— Will., 126, 242, 247, 579.
Corell, Joh., 214.
Corkemaker, Tho., 365.
Corker, Bened., Corkar, 213, 248.
Cortnale, Alice, Cortenhall, Cortenhale, Cortenale, Cortonhale, 67.
—— Rob. de, 5.
—— Will., 111, 120, 126, 138, 154, 179.
Coruiser, Hugo, Coruyser, 126.
—— Joh., 162.
Coryour, Edw., Coriour, Coryer, 164, 177.
—— Joh., 168.
—— Ric., 163.
—— Rob., 210, 237.

Coryour, Tho., 87, 169.
Coston, Joh., 129.
Coteler, Galf., Coteller, Cuttyler, 164, 237.
—— Ric., 6.
—— Rob., 39.
—— Will., 6, 164.
Cotes, Tho., 721, 737.
Cotoner,[1] Hen., Cotener, 125, 134.
—— Johanna, 126.
—— Joh., 80.
—— Marg., 79.
Cotoner, Rad., 80, 88, 126, 169.
—— Ric., 153, 162, 178, 180.
—— Rob., 37, 39, 175.
—— Will., 163, 213, 251.
Cotton,[1] Hen., Coton, Cooten, Coten, 131, 153, 158, 161, 170.
—— Joh., 20, 34, 36, 37, 39, 40, 44, 45, 54, 57, 60, 65, 69, 76, 78, 83, 84, 87, 100, 102, 104, 105, 106, 109, 111, 112, 114, 117.
—— Rafe, 503.
—— Ric., 319.
—— Tho., 663.
—— Will., 242, 358, 377, 665, 695, 697, 701, 704, 706, 707, 711, 718, 720, 721, 727, 728, 730, 739, 740, 742, 746, 759, 760, 762, 766, 767, 768, 769, 770, 773, 778, 779.
Cotyngham, Joh., 366.
Couche, Ric., 248.
—— Steph., 81, 89.
—— Tho., 239.
Coucher, Joh., Cowcher, 168, 211, 238.
—— Ric., 236, 248.
—— Rob., 162.
—— Tho., 211, 249.
—— Will., 163, 178.
Couentre, Ric., 541.
Coundulme, Will., 451.
Cowper, Agnes, Couper, Coupar, Coupper, 163.
—— Hugo, 125, 153, 161, 179.
—— Joh., 82, 90, 165, 166, 167, 176, 212, 213, 239, 241, 242, 247, 252, 318, 351, 365, 377, 435, 436, 534, 542.
—— Ric., 80, 88, 127, 154, 164, 165, 175, 177, 238, 241.
—— Tho., 483.
—— Will., 5, 129, 166, 211, 213, 242.

[1] It is difficult to distinguish between these names in the MS.

Coyche, Ric., 366. (?) *See* Couche.
Coyte, Joh., 480.
—— Rob., 541.
Craas, Will., 6.
Craddock, Rauffe, 608.
Cragges, Joh., 739.
Crampe, Geruard, Crumpe, Crampp, 239, 247.
—— Joh., 211, 243, 268, 624, 628, 666, 667, 676, 677, 679, 682, 684, 686, 687, 688, 692, 695, 696, 697, 699, 700, 701, 704, 706, 707, 711, 713, 714, 715, 717, 720, 721, 722, 723, 724, 725, 727, 728, 738.
—— Will., 209, 238, 251, 286, 304, 317, 320, 321, 332, 333, 334, 376, 416, 424, 431, 435, 443, 481, 485, 503, 516, 518, 520, 530, 534, 740, 842.
Creke, Joh., Creeke, 78, 153, 162, 180.
Cressy, Joh., Cresse, 41, 78, 87, 120, 125, 133, 153, 162, 180, 842.
—— Rog., 161, 179.
——Will., 153.
Crofte, Joh., Croft, Croftes, Croftez, 212, 238, 318.
—— Sir Ric., 440.
—— Rob., 248.
—— Tho., of Pembrigg, 429.
Crofton, Rob., 242.
Cromcote, Joh., 828.
Cronesford, Joh., 163.
Crooke, Joh., Croke, Creeke (?), Crokez, 87, 125, 162, 229.
Crosby, Joh., Croseby, 126.
—— Ric., 35, 61, 69, 80, 97, 101, 112, 123.
—— Will., 377.
Crosse, Christian, Crose, Crosses, 125.
—— Hen., 563, 566, 583.
—— Joh., 39, 67, 79, 88, 127, 156, 169, 178, 210, 211, 222, 237, 242, 247, 251, 266, 365.
—— Joh. de, 3.
—— Rob., 344, 351, 355, 376, 382, 406, 422, 424, 443, 363, 482, 513, 515, 520, 521, 534.
—— Tho., 37, 79, 87, 117, 126, 137, 140, 143, 144, 154, 163, 171, 178.
—— Will., 22, 36, 37, 39, 41, 43, 44, 54, 58, 60, 62, 67, 68, 71, 72, 78, 79, 83, 84, 87, 88, 91, 98, 102, 104, 106, 107, 109, 111, 112, 113, 114, 115, 117, 126, 134, 137, 144, 163.

Crossely, Joh., Crosley, 541.
—— Katerina, 169.
—— Ric., 546, 583.
Crouche, Joh., 382.
Crowe, Joh., 352, 365, 377.
—— Will., 210, 237, 247, 352, 377.
Crudworth, Agnes, 154, 163, 178, 213, 242.
—— Joh., 5.
—— Rob., 166.
—— Will., 38, 40, 41, 42, 44, 51, 69, 73, 82, 83, 86, 90, 101, 102, 107, 110, 120, 132, 137, 138, 140.
Crulle, Joh., Crull, 236, 249, 314, 317, 318, 337, 354, 358, 362, 366, 376.
Crumpe. *See* Crampe.
Cull, Walt., 6.
Cumberford, Will., 379, 380.
Cunwey. *See* Conwey.
Curtes, Mat., Curteys, 209, 240, 251, 318, 376.
Curwayn, Joh., 451.
Cutt, Will., 129.
Cuttyler. *See* Coteler.

Dadynton, Ric., Dadyngton, 601.
—— Rob., 532, 534, 546, 604.
Dagette, Joh., Daget, 237, 246, 315, 317.
—— Will., 87, 163.
Dalawey, Hug , Dalawarr, 706, 718, 720, 722, 736, 738, 761.
Dalby, —, 214, 240.
—— Agnes, 81, 90.
—— Edm., 256, 285, 286.
—— Hen., 163, 178, 212, 218, 239, 252, 337, 352, 377, 382.
Dale, Rad. (Rauf.), 700, 701, 706, 707, 736, 737.
—— Will., 663, 687.
Dalton, Hen., 238, 249.
—— Joh., 177, 211, 237, 252.
Damas, Joh., 453, 466, 470.
—— Simon, 452, 466, 470.
Damport, Chr., Davenport, 840, 841.
—— Edm., 721, 760.
—— Edw., 766, 767, 768, 770, 773, 778, 779, 780, 781, 782, 788, 790, 793, 795, 796, 801, 806, 831.
—— Hen., 840.
Danby, Rob., 326.
Dandy, Rog., 6.
Dannam, Ric., 480.
Danyell, Rob., 39, 60, 76, 79, 81, 85, 87, 125.

Darby. *See* Derby.
Darlyng, —, Dorlyng, Derlyng, Dorling, 343.
—— Joh.. 343, 352, 354, 368, 377, 414, 421, 432, 481, 483, 514, 516, 520, 522, 528, 532, 533, 540, 542, 547, 552, 553, 561, 573, 585, 603, 604, 605, 606, 609, 619, 622, 624, 628, 629.
—— Tho.,' 414, 522.
Darsett, Will., Darset, Darsette, Derset, Dorsette, 81, 86, 90, 107, 121, 128, 133, 135, 138, 140, 141, 143, 147, 148, 149, 151, 152, 155, 160, 171, 176, 188, 189, 190, 214, 452.
Daugh, Tho., 562.
—— Will., 562.
Davenport. *See* Damport.
Daventry, Will., 166.
David, Joh., Dauid, 78, 87, 248.
Davy, Ad., 319.
—— Joh., 239, 242, 246, 247, 252, 352, 365, 377, 432, 482.
—— Lewes, 479.
—— Phil., 352.
—— Will., 541.
Daw, Joh., 212.
—— Tho., 39, 46, 79, 87, 98, 119, 125.
—— Will., 79, 88, 126, 153, 160, 180, 209, 213, 219, 222, 240, 242, 248, 275, 304, 307, 310, 312, 315, 317, 320, 333, 336, 337, 343, 344, 347, 351, 352, 360, 361, 362, 365, 367, 370, 371, 372, 376, 378.
Dawbeney, Ric., Dawbney, 237,
—— Will., 80, 88, 127, 154, 158, 164, 211.
Dawber, Rog., 653, 654, 665.
Dawberey, *read* Dawbeny.
Dawes, Hugo, 432, 540, 566, 579, 601, 607, 622, 628, 633, 634, 636, 637, 638, 641, 642, 643, 645, 647, 649, 650, 651, 652, 653, 654, 663, 665, 666, 667, 668, 676, 677.
—— Joh., 430, 483.
—— Ric., 390, 478, 514.
Dawson, Will., Dawsen, 605, 607, 622, 636, 650, 663, 665, 667, 668, 676, 677, 682, 686, 687, 688, 690, 691, 692, 693, 694, 695, 697, 699, 700.
Day. *See* Dey.
Dean, Ric., Dene, Deen, Deene, Deane, 38, 40, 68, 79, 84, 85, 87, 91, 100, 102, 104, 109, 111, 117, 122, 126,

130, 134, 135, 137, 138, 140, 141, 146, 147, 148, 149, 150, 152, 154, 157, 162, 172, 178, 193, 194, 198, 200, 201, 202, 204, 207, 208, 212, 217, 221, 222, 226, 227, 228, 230, 231, 232, 233, 235, 238, 243, 245, 246, 252, 254, 255, 256, 259, 262, 266, 267, 270, 272, 275, 277, 278, 279, 280, 283, 284, 285, 296, 301.
Defford, Rob., Defforde, Derford, 45, 76, 78, 120, 125, 133, 153, 161, 842.
—— Will., 214.
Deister, Ad., Deyster, Deisterer, 3, 20, 39, 41, 42, 44, 54, 81, 108, 121, 165. *See also* Hyton.
—— Ed., 153, 598.
—— Hen., 167.
—— Joh., 37, 39, 41, 44, 48, 77, 81, 84, 89. 98, 100, 102, 104, 107, 109, 111, 114, 117, 128, 130, 132, 134, 138, 141, 144, 150, 151, 152, 156, 161, 165, 171, 174, 184, 185, 187, 188, 189, 192, 200, 212, 214, 221, 227, 228, 239, 241, 250, 251, 335, 356, 365, 377, 430, 482, 483, 842.
—— Laur., 128.
—— Ric., 79, 88, 127, 156, 168, 177, 210, 237.
—— Rog., 78, 87.
—— Sim., 39, 78, 87, 125, 158, 160.
—— Tho., 176.
—— Will., 37, 39, 41, 45, 60, 76, 78, 87, 90, 125, 128, 131, 139, 142, 143, 154, 155, 159, 162, 168, 171, 174, 176, 183, 212, 214, 222, 239, 240, 241, 250, 256, 269, 437, 542, 543, 585, 598. *See also* Dyer.
Delamare, Joh., 167.
Denton, Joh., 479.
—— Will., 1.
Denyver, Rob., 167.
Derby, —, Darby, 222.
—— Joh., 79, 80, 87, 89, 126, 127, 153, 154, 160, 162, 165, 179, 211, 212, 238, 249, 266, 315, 371, 376.
—— Tho., 317.
Derlyng. *See* Darlyng.
Dernwell, Tho., Darnwell, 161, 184.
Dersett. *See* Darsett.
Deves, Een., Devyas, 806.
Dey, Joh., Day, Deye, 164, 175, 211, 214, 236, 240, 246, 280, 293, 297, 301, 304.

Dey, Tho., 177, 213, 242, 243, 247, 266, 269, 285.
—— Will., 81, 88, 90, 126, 128, 154, 155, 163, 168, 176, 178.
Di——. *See* Dy——.
Dicas, Kenelme, 440.
Digbye, Geo., Dygby, 830, 831, 832.
—— Sim., 626.
Diglyn, Tho., Diglyng, 728, 736, 737, 761, 768, 769, 770.
Dilcok, Edw., Dilcoke, Dilkok, Dylcok, Dilcocke, 168, 176, 214.
—— Hen., 5.
—— Joh., 20, 22, 37, 39, 41, 42, 60, 69, 78, 84, 85, 87, 98, 100, 102, 103, 111, 117, 122, 125, 137, 138, 140, 143, 150, 153, 161, 162, 171, 179.
—— Joh., sen., 41.
—— Nic., 238.
—— Will., 20, 22, 36, 41, 42, 44, 54, 58, 60, 68, 71, 81, 83, 84, 86, 90, 91, 99, 102, 103, 104, 105, 106, 107, 108, 109, 110, 111, 112, 113, 114, 115, 117, 122, 128, 130, 132, 134, 137, 138, 139, 140, 141, 143, 144, 147, 150, 151, 155.
Dillare, Will., 250.
Disher, Tho., 11.
Dixon, Joh., 604.
Dixsey, Wolston, 818.
Dodd, Ric., Dod, Dode, Dodde, 770.
—— Tho., 634, 636, 637, 649, 660, 667, 684, 687, 688, 690, 694, 697, 700, 701, 704, 706, 711, 714, 717, 718, 721, 722, 723, 724, 725, 726, 727, 728, 737.
Dodenale, Ric. de, 5.
Doff, Tho., 168. *See also* Dove.
Dokerell, —, 546.
Dokon, Tho., 168.
Dolfyn, Tho., 352.
Domina, (?), 238.
Donam, Rob., 239.
Doncastre, Joh., 449.
Donyngton, Will., Donnyngton, Donynton, 79, 88, 99, 126, 141, 146, 150, 152, 154, 156, 157, 158, 163, 171, 175, 178, 213, 214, 220, 241, 247, 335.
—— Will., (Recorder), 134, 154, 157, 163, 172, 202, 204, 218, 226, 228, 232, 234, 235.
—— (his pension), 236, 242.
Dorlyng. *See* Darlyng.
Dormesa, Joh., 167.

Dorset. *See* Darsett.
Doubrigge, Will., Dowbryge, Douebrigge, Dowbryg, 183, 210, 238, 249.
Doughty, Emma, Doughtye, Dowghty, Dohgty, 240.
—— Geuys, 352.
—— Joh., 38, 39, 41, 42, 51, 81, 84, 90, 109, 111, 112, 114, 115, 117, 122, 128, 130, 134, 135, 137, 140, 141, 143, 144, 150, 151, 152, 155, 157, 160, 167, 169, 175, 185, 186, 187, 188, 189, 192, 193, 194, 195, 197, 198, 200, 201, 202, 204, 214, 221, 227, 228.
—— Matillda, 450.
Douse, Joh., 213.
Dove, Joh., Dowve, Dowe, Douve, Dovue, Doue, Dovy, 351, 362, 364, 376, 390, 419, 421, 424, 432, 435, 436, 443, 473, 481, 485, 513, 516, 534, 540, 544, 547, 553, 557, 567, 571, 573, 575, 579, 581.
—— Tho., 82, 90, 176, 239, 314, 317, 318, 321, 332, 334, 335, 337, 338, 343, 345, 347, 351, 360, 361, 364, 367, 370, 371, 372, 375, 376, 378, 382, 385, 387, 390, 419, 541.
Downes, Hugo, 562.
—— Joh., 562.
Drake, Ric., 344, 352, 376, 422, 429, 482, 514, 549, 579.
—— Tho., 236.
Draper, —, 530.
—— Elias, 74.
—— Gal., 128, 163.
—— Guydo, 167.
—— Joh., 246, 247, 377, 409, 411.
—— Phil., 240, 247, 318, 365, 368, 377, 432, 482.
—— Ric., 365, 368.
—— Tho., 120, 127, 133, 152.
—— Will., 127, 154, 164, 177, 211, 237.
Drasse, Joh., 80. *Read* Brasse.
Draughton, Joh., 240, 248.
—— Tho., 78, 87.
Drave, Ric., 566.
Draycote, Hen., 3.
Drayton, Joh., 163.
Drewe, Ric., 576.
—— Will., 315, 351, 368, 376.
Drought, Ric., Drowht, Drowthe, Drowght, Drught, 155, 168, 175, 214, 240, 249, 314, 317, 318, 337, 344, 345, 352, 356, 358, 363, 377, 379, 390, 421, 430, 435, 474, 482, 485, 489, 501, 514.
—— Ric., sen., 249.
—— Tho., 828.
—— Will., 211.
Drover, Edm., Drouer, 82, 90, 129, 167, 176, 195, 200, 201, 202, 207, 208, 213, 217, 221, 242.
Dryffeld, Joh., 162.
Dubber, Gil., Dubbar, 162.
—— Ric., 6.
—— Rob., 212.
—— Will., 210, 237.
Duddesbury, Joh., Duddisbury, Duddesbure, 422, 443, 478, 481, 482, 514, 518, 520, 532, 533, 540, 543, 544, 547, 552, 563, 569, 572, 579, 585, 598, 603, 604, 605, 606, 609, 619, 621, 623, 624, 625, 627, 628, 629, 630, 631, 633, 634, 636, 637, 638, 641, 642, 645, 647, 649, 650, 651, 652, 653, 654, 662, 665, 666, 667, 668, 676, 677, 679, 682, 684.
Dudley, Johanna, Duddeley, Dudlay, 81, 89.
—— Joh., 546.
—— Nich. de, 3.
—— Ric. de, 6.
—— Tho., 806, 809, 812.
Duffield, Rad., 88, 126, 164, 177, 210
—— Ric., 212.
Dunmowe, doctour, 474.
Dwale, Joh., Dwall, 88, 482, 540 552, 553, 557, 563, 572, 579, 588, 599.
Dyer, Ad., Dier, Diere, 39, 41, 46, 60, 77, 79, 85, 88, 120, 127, 133, 143.
—— Johanna, 165, 175. *See also* Deister.
Dykar, Joh., Dyker, 248.
—— Lewes, 259, 260.
Dykons, Tho., Dicons, Dykens, Dykonnes, Dikons, 78, 87, 125, 153, 158, 162, 180, 210, 238, 248.
Dyngley, Will., 211, 237, 250.
Dyrham, Joh., Dirram, Byram (?), Deram, 81, 301.
—— Tho., 443, 468.
Dyssher, Juliana, 168.
Dyvet, Joh., Dyvette, Divett, 162, 179.
—— Ric., 79, 88, 126, 139, 142, 156, 168, 177, 207, 210, 221, 232, 235, 237, 245, 246, 247, 252, 256, 259, 260, 266, 268, 272, 276, 278, 279,

280, 283, 284, 285, 293, 296, 301, 304, 305, 306, 307, 310, 312, 316, 317, 320.
—— Tho., 79, 88, 128, 168.
—— Will., 129, 168, 175, 240, 250.
Eborall, Joh., Eburhale, 128, 155, 168, 175, 210, 219, 237, 244, 249, 269, 285, 286, 314, 317, 318.
Eburne, Eborne. *See* Eyburn.
Edmunde, Dav., 246, 248.
Ednam, Will., 154, 163, 178, 212.
Edward, Joh., Edwardes, 40, 82, 90, 166, 530, 812.
—— Nic., 79, 88, 168.
—— Ric., 343, 365.
—— Will., 241, 248, 351, 354, 365, 377.
Egeston, Joh., Egiston, 20, 22, 37, 39, 58, 60, 66, 68, 69, 77, 80, 89, 98, 100, 102, 104, 105, 107, 112, 115, 117, 134, 137, 138, 144, 150, 151, 165, 171. [? *See* Egynton.]
Eglee, Joh., 179.
Egleston, Joh., 162, 180.
Egull, Joh., Egle, 125, 153, 161, 210, 238, 248.
Egynton, Joh., 41, 84, 102, 109, 111, 122, 127, 155. [? *See* Egeston.]
—— Rob., 562.
—— Will., 562.
Eire. *See* Eyre.
Ekffurth, Will., 530.
Ekilsale. *See* Exsale.
Elage. *See* Illage.
Elcock, Agnes, Elcok, 14.
—— Joh., 14.
—— Tho., 238.
Elderbek, Joh., Eldurbek, Eldbek, Elderkeke, 162, 180, 183, 210, 238, 249.
—— Tho., 79, 87, 125, 131, 139, 142, 153, 158, 160, 161, 170, 179, 183, 184, 207, 209, 238, 249.
—— Tho., jun., 134.
Elford, Isabella, Ellford, 78.
—— Joh., 37.
Ellerton, Mat., Elerton, 59, 176.
Elmes, Joh., 172, 239.
Elton, Will., M.P. for Coventry, 1452, 313.
Elyot, —, Elyott, 167, 365.
—— Hugun, 368.
—— Will., 451.
Elys, Will., 351, 352, 360, 366, 368, 370, 376, 382, 385, 389, 419, 423, 424, 431, 435, 443, 481, 483, 485, 514, 516, 518.
Eme, Rob., 162, 178, 195, 207, 209, 219, 221, 238, 243, 246, 251, 256, 266, 268, 276, 277, 280, 284, 285, 286, 293, 297, 301, 304, 305, 306, 307, 310, 312, 316, 317, 320, 321, 332.
Emmott, —, Emmottes, Emettes, Emottes, 79.
—— Joh., 239, 344, 351, 360, 363, 368, 379, 385, 389, 390, 416, 435, 443, 481, 483, 485.
Empson, Ric., Emson (Sir Ric.), 547, 553, 563.
—— Tho., 622.
Enderby, Tho., Enderbie, Enderbye, 695, 696, 735, 736, 768, 769, 770, 773, 778.
Engillon, Joh., 251.
Erbere, [Arbury] Prior of, 378.
Erlle, Joh., 535.
Essex, Joh., Esex, 77, 81, 89, 111, 127, 142, 150, 151, 152, 156, 157, 165, 169, 174, 186, 187, 189, 192, 193, 195, 198, 200, 201, 202, 207, 208, 211, 217, 218, 219, 221, 222, 226, 229, 230, 232, 233, 235, 239, 243, 247, 250, 254, 255, 259, 262, 266, 267, 270, 271, 272, 276.
—— Ric., 164, 177, 210, 219, 237.
—— Tho., 815.
—— Will., of the Exchekur, 214.
Est, Sim., 81, 89, 842.
Esteldon, Rob. de, 3, 6.
Esterlen. *See* Astelene.
Esterton, Joh., 22, 37, 39, 40, 41, 42, 43, 44, 54, 55, 56, 58, 60, 62, 64, 67, 68, 70, 71, 73, 79, 83, 87, 99.
—— Nic., 168, 213.
—— Rob., 67.
Eston, Joh., Eiston, 141, 153, 161, 209, 240, 247, 364.
Ethorp, Tho., 242.
Eton, Tho., Etone, 167.
—— Walt., 78, 87, 125.
—— Will., 212.
Eue, Will., 125.
Eueryngham, Sir Tho., 426, 427, 428.
Everdon, Hen., Euerdon, 128, 168, 176.
—— Joh., 37, 39, 41, 42, 43, 44, 46, 54, 60, 66, 69, 73, 77, 79, 83, 84, 88, 97, 98, 101, 102, 104, 107, 111, 112, 113, 115, 117, 119, 121, 122, 126, 130, 131, 132, 134, 137,

138, 139, 140, 141, 143, 150, 152,
154, 157, 158, 159, 163, 169, 171,
172, 178, 180, 183, 185, 186, 187,
841.
—— Joh., jun., 146.
——Ric., 337, 345, 356, 360, 366, 368,
371, 406, 423, 424, 431, 435, 436,
483, 485, 502, 514.
—— Tho., 92, 377.
Evesham, And., Evysham, 78, 87, 125,
153, 161.
—— Johanna, 209, 240.
—— Joh., 78, 87, 125, 138, 153, 160,
162.
—— Margareta, 241.
Exsale, Joh., Ekilsale, 162, 214, 241.
Eyburn, Joh., Eburne, Eborne, Eyburne, 586, 604, 647, 677, 679, 684,
737, 761, 789, 793, 794.
—— Will., 821.
Eyre, Joh., Eire, Eyres, 81, 89, 128,
156, 165, 174, 178.

Fachaum, Rob., 451.
Fairfax, Rob., 212.
Fane, Laur., 711, 713.
Fareman, Joh., Feyremon, Feryremon, Fayreman, 240, 313, 318,
352.
—— Rob., 352, 391, 483, 517.
—— Tho., 242, 601, 624, 628.
Farmour, Jac., Fermour, 725, 726, 727,
728, 736, 737, 742.
Farre, Raffe, 366.
Farthe, Will., 365. *See* Ford.
Farwell, Ryc., 535.
Faseman, Will., 37, 42, 43, 44, 46, 54,
58, 60, 69, 79, 84, 87, 91, 98, 101.
Fawkes, Alicia, Faux, Falk, Falkes,
Fawcus, Fawcs, 177.
—— Joh., 177.
—— Rob., 214, 239, 244, 247, 256,
269, 286.
—— Tho., 183, 210, 213, 219, 237,
241, 249, 250, 286.
Fawkonbruge, Will., Fawconbrygg,
Fawconbrugge, 249, 319, 352.
Feld, Will., Felde, 129, 166, 176, 213.
Feldyng, Joh., Fildeng, 183, 239.
Felowys, Joh. a, 366.
Felse, Hugh, 608.
Fennes, Joh., 161.
Ferby, Joh., 240.
Fermon, Will., 162, 179.
Ferrers, —, de Groby, 123.

Ferrers, Tho., 507.
Ferres, Her., 327.
Fethy, Joh., 166.
Feythyng, Joh., Feithyng, 203.
Fildeng. *See* Feldyng.
Filippes. *See* Philips.
Fishepole, —, Fysshepole, 546.
—— Rob., 541.
Fisher, Hen., Fysher, Fyssher, 174,
212.
—— Joh., 80, 127, 168, 317, 336,
343, 344, 351, 354, 356, 360, 363,
364, 368, 370, 376, 377, 379, 387,
389, 390, 416, 419, 421, 424, 431,
435, 443, 473, 481, 482, 485, 503,
514, 518, 520, 521, 522, 626.
—— Margeria, 164.
—— Rob., 163, 178.
—— Will., 53, 212, 314, 352, 366,
379, 414, 483.
Fitzherbert, Ant., Fitzherberde, Fytherbert, 628, 631, 634, 635.
—— Joh., 408, 414, 415, 416, 783,
803, 805.
FiȝtRobert, Will., FithRobert, 139, 142.
Flawndurs, Tho., 6.
Flaxhale, Joh., 168.
—— Will., 240.
Flecher, Gal., Fletcher, 211.
—— Hen., 531.
—— Joh., 82, 211.
—— Ric., 164, 240, 344, 358, 482.
—— Rob., 89, 128, 155, 167, 175,
541.
—— Rog., 155, 165, 175.
—— Tho., 365, 482, 542.
—— Will., 238, 249, 352, 365, 377,
379, 414, 421, 481, 532, 540, 553,
563, 566, 579, 581, 584, 598.
Flekney, Will., Fleknay, Flekeney,
39, 41, 80, 88, 127, 154, 164, 177.
Fleshehewer, Tho., 53.
Flower, Gal., Floure, Flour, Flore, 20,
36, 37, 39, 41.
—— Will., 80, 163.
Floytour, Alicia, Flouter, 169.
——, Will., 162, 180, 210, 238.
Flynt, Elias, 518.
—— Joh., 211, 236, 317, 318, 357,
365, 368, 377, 482.
—— Ric., 155, 165, 175, 211, 219, 236,
244, 256, 269, 286, 318, 365.
—— Will., 482, 541.
Folkeshull, Joh., Folshull, Folshill,
Foxall, Foxhall, Foxhale, 78, 153,

Name Index. 881

161, 179, 184, 210, 212, 238, 239, 567, 711.
—— Joh., sen., 249.
—— Rad., 161, 184, 240, 249.
—— Ric., 432, 482, 566, 570, 579, 588, 602, 603, 604, 605, 607, 609, 619, 621, 622, 623, 624, 625, 629.
—— Tho., 563.
—— Tho., extra le New-yate, 249.
—— Vitalis de, 13, 815.
Follipoot, Joh., 126.
Folvile, Joh., Folvyle, Folvill, 82, 90, 129, 167, 176, 213, 242.
Forbur, Will., 212.
Ford, Hugo, Furd, Forte, Forth, Fourth, Foorde, 239, 250, 251.
—— Joh., 162, 178, 212.
—— Rob., 239, 251.
—— Tho., 251, 313, 318, 333, 336, 339, 343, 351, 360, 362, 366, 368, 371, 372, 375, 376, 378, 385, 389, 390, 416, 419, 421, 423, 431, 435, 443, 473, 481, 483, 503, 514, 518, 528, 532, 534, 540, 600, 602, 603, 605, 606, 607, 619, 622, 628, 629, 631, 633, 634, 636, 637, 638, 641, 642, 643, 645, 647.
—— Will., 242, 248, 377, 406, 481, 482, 514, 522, 542, 543, 563, 567, 572, 579, 581, 582, 584, 587, 598, 600, 601, 603, 604, 605, 606, 609, 619, 620.
Forest, ——, 167.
—— Joh., 88, 127, 155, 164, 175, 211, 236, 248.
—— Olyver, 736.
—— Rob., 366, 376.
Forget, Tho., 247.
Forman, Tho., 693.
Forster, Joh., Foster, 239, 249, 352, 366, 377, 483.
—— Will., 80, 89, 164, 781.
Forth. See Ford.
Foston, Ric., 209, 240.
Founder, Joh., 5.
Fovell, Hugh, 479.
Fox, Alicia, 164.
—— Rob., 479.
Foyden, Tho., 788, 789.
Fraiter, Joh., Frayter, 82, 90, 128.
Francis, Joh., Fraunses, Fraunces, 13, 14.
—— Will., 239, 449.
Franklen, Joh., Frankelen, Frankleyn, 44, 46, 60, 68, 77, 79, 84, 88, 91, 98, 102, 107, 111, 117, 122, 125, 127, 131, 143, 150, 152, 154, 156, 163, 165, 169, 180, 207, 209, 210, 219, 238, 246, 251, 255, 256, 262, 266, 267, 270, 278, 841.
—— Millesant, 178.
Frebern, Sim., 5.
Frekynton, Ed., 352.
Freman, ——, Fremon, 126.
—— Joh., 78, 80, 87, 90, 120, 125, 133, 143, 153, 158, 161, 162, 166, 178, 180, 211, 221, 226, 227, 228, 233, 235, 236, 245, 246, 252, 253, 254, 255, 256, 259, 262, 266, 267, 271, 272, 275, 276, 279, 280, 283, 284, 285, 293, 296, 301, 302, 304, 305, 306, 307, 310, 311, 312, 316, 317, 320, 352.
—— Katherina, 154.
—— Raffe, 344, 355, 358, 365, 478, 482, 534.
—— Ric., 127, 164.
—— Will., 79, 87.
Frenshe, Joh., French, 161, 422.
Frere, Joh., 319.
Frereby, Joh. de, Freyby, Fyreby, Frayby, 6.
—— Nic. de, 5.
—— Ric., 604, 619, 624, 629, 631, 634, 637, 638, 641, 647, 651, 653, 665, 667, 676.
—— Rog., 686.
Frisby, Will., Frisbye, Fryssby, Frysby, Fryssheby, 37, 39, 41, 44, 46, 68, 77, 79, 83, 84, 85, 88, 98, 102, 104, 107, 109, 111, 112, 113, 114, 115, 117, 126, 130, 134, 135, 137, 138, 140, 141, 143, 144, 147, 148, 149, 150, 152, 154, 157, 160, 163, 169, 178, 185, 186, 187, 188, 189, 192, 193, 194, 195, 197, 198, 200, 201, 202, 204, 206, 208, 213, 217, 219, 226, 227, 228, 229, 230, 231, 232, 242.
Frithe, Joh., Frythe, 90, 128, 155, 159, 167, 171, 175.
Frogette, Tho., 238.
Fryche, Joh., 81. See Frythe.
Frynes, Ric., ffreynes, 238, 247.
Frysley, Will., 20. ? See Frysby.
Fulbroke, Joh., 344.
Fuller, Tho., 249.
Fulnaby, Hen., 478, 546.
Fureneaux, Rob., 6.
Furnes, Ric., 169.

Fyge, Rob., 251.
Fyleng, Joh., 160.
Fynche, Joh., 148, 153, 161, 175, 201, 202, 211, 218, 226, 230, 232 235, 236, 246, 252, 255, 270, 276, 278, 280, 284.
—— Ric., 354, 357, 366, 377, 482.
Fyndon, —, jun., 167.
—— Joh., 167.
Fynyowes, Joh., [Fineux] 490, 498.
Fyppus, Joh., Fyppe, Fyppys, 371.
—— Will., 249, 351.
Fysche, Nic., 81.
—— Tho., 82.
Fysshepole. *See* Fishpole.

Gage, Ad., Gawge, Gavge, Gauge. 209, 240, 249.
—— Ezabell, 364.
—— Joh., 53, 242, 247, 269, 285, 286, 304, 305, 307, 310, 311, 312, 316, 317, 320, 321, 329, 332, 333, 335, 336, 337, 338, 339, 343, 344, 347, 351, 352, 360, 361, 362 365, 367, 370, 371, 372, 375, 376, 377, 378, 382, 385, 387, 388, 389, 390, 416, 419, 421, 423, 424, 435, 443, 473, 481, 482, 503, 514, 516, 518, 520, 521, 524, 528, 532, 533, 534, 539, 540, 541, 542, 543, 544, 547, 552, 553, 557, 563, 567, 571, 579, 581, 582, 584, 585, 587, 588, 598, 842.
Gale, Gillot de, Gales, (?) Cale. 449.
—— Joh., 78, 87, 126, 154, 162, 179, 212, 238.
—— Will., 78, 125, 153, 162, 170, 180.
Gamill, Joh., Gamil, Gamull, Gamyll, 79, 88, 125, 153, 162, 166.
—— Ric., 126.
—— Tho., 125.
—— Will., 82, 90.
Gardenere, Rob., Gardnere, Gardiner, Gardynour, Gardynor, 351, 358, 371, 390.
—— Tho., 244, 250, 269, 318, 337, 344, 352, 377, 686, 688, 693, 699, 701, 706, 707, 711, 713, 714, 715, 717, 718, 720, 721, 722, 723, 724, 726, 727, 728, 737, 738, 739, 740, 759, 766, 767, 768, 769, 770, 773, 778, 779, 780, 782, 783, 788, 789, 790, 793, 794, 795, 796, 798, 800, 801, 803, 806, 809, 811.
Garen, Will., 168.

Garett, —, Garette, 129.
Garett, Rob., 238, 249, 352, 376, 379.
—— Will, 167, 176.
Garnet, Joh., Garnett, 239, 247.
—— Tho., 211, 238, 248.
Gart, Joh., 3.
Garton, Johanne, 268.
—— Joh., 67, 126, 138, 143, 144, 145, 154, 160, 162, 179, 212, 222, 232, 233, 235, 238, 245, 246, 252, 253, 256, 259, 260, 266, 267, 268, 270, 271, 275, 276, 278, 279, 280, 283, 284, 285, 296, 301, 302, 304, 305, 306, 307, 310, 312, 316, 317, 320, 321, 332, 333, 334, 335, 336, 337, 338, 339, 343, 351, 360, 361, 362, 365, 370, 371, 372, 375, 376, 378.
—— Rad., Rafe, 20, 22, 36, 37, 39, 40, 41, 42, 44, 54, 60, 62, 67, 68, 79, 83, 84, 85, 88, 98, 99, 102, 104, 106, 107, 109, 111, 112, 113, 114, 115, 117, 119, 122, 126, 132, 134, 137, 146.
—— Ric., 164, 177, 534, 586.
—— Tho., 167.
Gascoyne, Johanna, Gesskyn, 128.
—— Joh., Gasquyne, 81, 90.
—— Tho., 356.
Gates, Tho., 573, 586.
Gayton, Will., 161.
Gefferey, Hen., 344, 354.
Gelam, —, 360.
Gelot, Joh., 155.
Gely, Joh., 663.
Gene, Ric., 248, 352.
George, Joh., Goorge, Jeorge, 80, 88, 127, 128, 139, 142, 154, 163, 178, 207, 213, 218, 221, 230.
—— Will., 89.
Gerles, Joh., 534. *Read* Gerves.
Gerveys, Joh., Gerves, 391, 414, 443, 481, 483, 514, 535, 579.
Gesskyn. *See* Gascoyne.
Gest, Geest, Joh., 517.
—— Tho., 176.
—— Will., 561.
Gey, Joh. [Dey ?], 155.
Gibbes, Joh., [Job *read* Joh.], Gybbes, 483, 543, 547, 552.
Gidlowe, Rob., Gydlowe, Gedlowe, Gydlow, 238, 251, 286, 315, 352, 354, 377.
Gilbert, Jas., Gylbert, Gilbard, Gylbard, Gylberd, 667, 668, 676, 695, 697, 701, 704, 706, 717, 718, 720,

721, 722, 723, 724, 725, 726, 727, 728, 737, 738, 739, 740, 742, 746, 759, 766, 767, 768, 769, 770, 773, 778, 779, 780, 781, 782, 783, 788, 789, 790.
—— Joh., 82, 127, 129, 156, 158, 160, 169, 171, 178 213, 242, 247, 600.
—— Maur., 725, 726, 727, 728, 761.
—— Tho., 161, 212, 239, 246, 252, 256, 266, 284, 285, 293, 296, 305
—— Will., 153, 178, 209, 240, 246, 255, 256, 267, 276, 283, 284, 285, 296, 301, 302, 304, 305, 310, 312.
Giller, Ant., Gyller, Gillar, 728.
—— Ric., 740, 765, 769, 770, 796, 800, 801, 803, 806, 809, 812.
Gilmyn, Joh., 480.
Giterner, Rad., 161.
Glasewright, Nic., 6.
Glasier, Hen., Glasyer, 88.
—— Nic., 237.
—— Patr., 163, 179.
—— Pet., 78, 87.
—— Will., 87, 126, 154, 162, 179.
Glastenbury, Joh., 165.
Glegg, Tho., 727.
Glenne, Tho., Glene, (?) Slenne, 111, 126, 154, 163, 178.
Glew, Ryc., 535, 546.
Gloucester, Rob., Gloucestre, Glouseter, Gloucestur, Glouceter, Gloucetur, 79, 88, 127, 156, 169, 178, 210, 237, 244, 246, 251, 256, 266, 280, 284, 285, 296.
—— Tho., 453.
—— Will., 252.
Glover, Hen., Glouer, 318.
—— Hug. (Huw.), 344, 352, 365, 377.
—— Jac., 163.
—— Joh., 212.
—— Ric., 167, 176, 213, 238, 241, 248.
—— Rog., 343, 376, 579.
—— Tho., 175.
—— Will., 210, 242.
Gobeler, Will., 165.
Gobett, —, 179.
—— Joh., 128.
Goddesley, Ric., Godesley, 36, 82, 86, 131, 169, 177.
Godeale, Tho., 6.
Goderiche, Arth., Gudrich, Goodrich, 725, 727, 737, 761, 767, 768, 769, 770, 773, 778, 779, 780.
—— Ric., 219.

Godfrey, Joh., Godefrey, Godfray, Godefroy, 239.
—— Margeria, 125, 153, 161, 179.
—— Ric., 168.
—— Tho., 164, 177.
Godknave, —, Good Knave, 343.
—— Joh., Godeknave, 241, 352, 369, 377.
Godlad, Will., Goodlade, Goodlad, Godelade, Godeladde, 53, 344, 357, 366, 391, 483, 514, 534.
Godson, Hen., 740, 746.
Godyng, Joh., 160.
Gold, Joh., Golde, Goolde, 82, 86, 90, 129, 152, 160, 166, 176, 189, 195, 197, 198, 200, 201, 202, 204, 213, 221, 228, 230, 232, 235, 241, 245, 247, 252, 255, 256, 262, 266, 270, 271, 275, 278, 280.
Goldman, Ric., 541.
Goldsmyth, Agnes, 166, 174.
—— Ed., 179.
—— Reg., 175.
—— Ric., 214, 237.
—— Rob., 531.
—— Tho., 80, 81, 88, 89, 108, 128, 155, 168, 175, 211, 214, 222, 228, 229, 237, 319, 365.
—— Will., 237.
Golofre, Christiana, Golofur, Goloffre, 125, 153, 161, 209, 240.
—— Eus., 161, 209, 240, 247, 256, 266, 285, 318.
—— Joh., 20, 21, 33, 34, 35, 37, 39, 40, 42, 44, 54, 56, 58, 60, 62, 65, 68, 71, 84, 85, 87, 91, 99, 102, 104, 107, 108, 109, 111, 117, 214, 241, 249.
—— Tho., 168.
Gomery, Rob., 129.
Goode, Joh., Gode, 89, 165, 175.
Goodeyere, Will., 250.
Goodwright, Joh., 80.
Goodwyn, Joh., 213.
Goose, Rog., Gose, 82, 90, 166.
Goote, Johanna, Got, 79, 88, 126, 135.
—— Joh., 20, 21, 36, 37, 39, 41, 42, 61, 115, 236, 279.
Goppeshyll, Tho., Gopeshyll, Gopesell, Gobsell, Gopsill, 631, 633, 677, 679, 684, 686, 687, 688, 690, 692, 693, 694, 695, 696, 697, 699, 700, 701, 704, 706, 707, 711, 713, 714, 715, 717, 718, 720, 721.
Gordon, Tho., 676.

Gore, Nich., Goor, Goore, 78, 87, 125, 152, 154, 164, 177.
Gosselyn, Joh., 812.
Gossnore, —, Gosnore, 126.
—— ffylippe (Ph.), 256, 286, 314, 317, 318.
—— Joh., 154, 163.
—— Katerina, 179.
Gough, Hugh, 540.
Grace, Joh., 96, 97.
Grasier, Ric., 80.
Grauncester, Will., Grauncestre, 169, 177.
Gravenour, Tho., 821.
Graystok, Geff., 365.
Gregory, (old) Gregorie, Gregorye, 7.
Gregory, Art., 816, note, 817, 831, note, 831.
—— Edm., 816, 831, note.
—— Hug., 700, 701, 706, 720, 721. 724, 725, 726.
—— Tho., 317, 701, 741, 780, 789, 794, 796, 800, 816, note.
Greme, Rob., 443. *Read* Grene.
Grene, Alice, Greene, 723.
—— Humf., 546, 579, 601, 602, 607, 623, 624, 630, 631, 633, 634, 636, 637, 638, 641, 643, 645, 647.
—— Jac., 242, 247.
—— Joh., 129, 166, 176, 240, 318, 557, 573, 687, 706, 714, 736, 760.
—— Nich., 79, 85, 88, 126, 155, 163, 175, 214.
—— Rad., 18, 19.
—— Ric., 238.
—— Rob. (Rob a Grene), 78, 87, 125, 153, 162, 180, 183, 352, 365, 474, 478, 481, 482, 490, 502, 513, 515, 516, 518, 520, 522, 528, 533, 534, 540, 542, 543, 544, 547, 552, 553, 559, 563, 567, 571, 574, 579, 581, 582, 584, 585, 587, 588, 598, 599, 600, 601, 602, 603, 604, 605, 606, 608, 620, 621, 623, 624, 625, 627, 628, 629, 630, 631, 632, 633, 634, 636, 637, 638, 640, 641, 642, 645, 649, 650, 651, 652, 653, 654, 662, 665, 666, 667, 668, 676, 677, 679, 682, 684, 686, 693, 696, 700, 701, 706, 711, 718, 721, 725, 728, 737, 746, 768, 770, 778.
—— Rob., jun., 676.
—— Tho., 6, 19, 20, 22, 36, 37, 39, 41, 42, 44, 54, 58, 60, 62, 68, 78, 81, 90, 105, 106, 129, 211, 239, 246, 247, 252, 256, 351, 436, 483, 563, 585, 598, 599.
—— Will,, 126, 154, 162, 164, 177.
Greneway, Tho., 250.
Grennowe, David, Greno, 495, 496, 504.
Grevile, Grivell, Sir F., 830, 831, 832, 833.
Grey, Hen., 601.
Griffith, Joh., 540, 561.
Groome, Tho., Grome, 87, 125.
Grove, Anna, Groue, Growe, 212.
—— Joh., 313, 316, 318, 336, 343, 351, 355, 360, 364, 368, 370, 376, 378, 388, 389, 390, 842.
—— Tho., 54, 429, 432, 481, 531, 553, 557, 570, 571, 581, 582, 598, 600, 601, 602, 603, 605, 607, 609, 621, 625, 628, 629, 630, 634, 636, 637, 638, 642, 643, 645, 647, 649, 650, 651, 652, 653, 654, 662, 665, 666, 667.
—— Will., 162, 178.
Grubber, Rob., 81, 90, 107, 128, 152, 155, 160, 167, 175, 185.
Gryme, Annes, 365.
—— Joh., 78, 87, 127, 143, 156, 169, 178, 207, 210, 221, 237, 244, 246, 247, 255, 256, 266, 267, 270, 271, 276, 277, 279, 280, 284, 285, 293, 296, 301, 302, 304, 305, 306, 307, 310, 312, 316, 317, 320, 321, 333, 334, 335, 336, 337, 344, 345, 351, 358, 362, 363, 365, 368, 369, 370, 376, 377, 387, 389, 390, 416, 419, 421, 431, 435, 473, 482, 513, 520, 542, 547, 553, 557, 563, 571, 579, 581, 582, 598.
—— Tho., 80, 88, 169, 178, 237, 247, 255, 314, 317, 337, 343, 345, 352, 357, 485.
—— Will., 5.
Grynder, Joh., Gryndar, 82, 90, 92, 93, 107, 121, 128, 129, 133, 143, 151, 152, 156, 160, 165, 174, 200, 201, 204, 207, 208, 211, 218, 219, 221, 222, 226, 227, 228, 229, 230, 231, 232, 233, 235, 239, 247, 253, 254, 256, 259, 262, 266, 270, 271, 272, 276, 277, 278.
—— Rob., 166.
Grysley, Tho., 252.
Gryve, Nic., 39, 79, 87, 126, 139, 142, 154, 162, 179.
Gudrich. *See* Goderiche.

Name Index.

Gurdeler, —, 3.
—— Ric., 238.
Gurdelsford, —, Gurdelford, Gurdelesford, 156.
—— Joh., 127, 165, 174.
Guye, Joh., Gye, 155, 214.
Gyam, Will., 249.
Gybons, Tho., 210, 239, 252.
Gylbert. *See* Gilbert.
Gyller. *See* Giller.
Gyllyng, Joh., Gillyng, 534, 543.
Gylmyn, —, 365. *See* Gilmyn.
Gylous, Tho., 218
Gylyon, Will., 168.
Gynne, Joh., 163, 178.
Gyttyns, Tho., 608.

Hache, Rob., 165.
Hadcokke, Will., 240. *See* Adcok.
Haddon, Joh., Hadon, 169, 432, 482, 533, 542, 544, 547, 563, 567, 579, 581, 584, 588, 598, 599, 601, 602, 603, 604, 605, 606, 609, 619, 620, 621, 623, 624, 625, 627, 628, 629, 630, 631, 633, 634, 636, 637, 638, 640, 641, 642, 645, 647, 649, 650, 651, 652, 653, 654, 662, 665.
—— Ric., 163.
—— Tho., 214, 241, 246, 247, 256, 266, 270, 271, 284.
—— Will., 209, 240, 250, 318, 478, 482, 514, 520, 532.
Hadley, Edm., Haddeley, 343, 351, 371, 376, 478, 481, 513, 533, 542, 566, 604, 607, 623.
—— Joh., 166, 174, 212, 221, 239, 246, 275, 278, 283, 285, 302, 305, 306, 307, 312, 315, 316, 317, 318, 320, 334, 336, 337, 339, 345, 347, 351, 352, 360, 361, 362, 370, 371, 372, 373, 375, 376, 378, 382, 387, 389, 390, 416, 421, 423, 431, 576, 753, 842.
—— Joh., "de Fletestrete," 321, 335, 338, 339, 343.
—— Joh., "de Welstrete," 320, 335, 339.
—— Rob., 409, 411, 752.
—— Tho., 478, 481, 483, 502, 514, 530.
Hakett, Tho., Hakette, Hagette, 210, 238, 251.
Hales, Cha., 831.
—— Joh., *ib.*
Haliday, Ric., Halyday, 237, 365.
—— Rob., 164, 236.

Hall, Deonysia, 240.
—— Hen., 483.
—— Joh., 90, 121, 128, 133, 139, 142, 143, 153, 155, 162, 168, 176, 209, 214, 219, 236, 238, 241, 250, 252, 315, 317, 334, 635.
—— Margett, 50, 78, 87.
—— Nyc., 360, 365, 368, 377, 390, 432, 443, 482, 514.
—— Tho., 209.
—— Will., 336.
Hallome, Joh., 14.
Haloughton, Will., Halloughton, 7, 482.
Halows, Hen., 247.
Halyngton, Will., 73.
Halywode, —, 167.
Hammond, Joh., Hamond, 166, 840.
—— Rob., 608.
—— Tho., 252.
—— Will., 212.
Hampton, Joh., 146, 155, 164, 167, 175, 176, 211, 236, 237, 250, 365.
—— Ric., 78, 87, 125, 156, 210, 237, 266.
—— Tho., 351, 360, 371, 406, 421.
Hancock, Will., 840.
Happeford, Joh., 20, 67.
—— Will., 80, 89, 127, 155, 164, 175.
Harberd, Ric., Harbard, 167.
—— Rob., 213, 241, 248.
Harborgh, Joh., Herburgh, Herborugh, Harborough, Harbourghe, Harburgh, Herdburgh, Herdeborgh, Hardborghe, 20, 22, 37, 39, 41, 42, 44, 54, 58, 60, 62, 69, 79, 81, 83, 84, 85, 88, 91, 120, 126, 133, 143, 156, 158, 168, 171, 213, 842.
—— Joh., jun., 39, 41.
—— Margareta, 154.
—— Matill, 163, 178.
—— Ric., 128, 155, 167, 175.
—— Will., 125, 143, 168.
Hardwaremon, Dav., 155.
Hardwen, Joh., Hardewyn, Hardwyn, Harwyn, Herdwen, 599, 601, 603, 604, 605, 606, 619, 624, 627, 628, 629, 630, 636, 637, 638, 641, 642, 645, 647, 649, 650, 651, 652, 653, 654, 662, 665, 666.
Hardwyke, Rob., Herdwyk, Herdwike, Herdewyk, 79, 81, 88, 126, 139, 142, 156, 158, 169, 171, 178.
—— Will., 128, 156, 166, 213, 241, 248.

Hardy, Rob., Herdie, Herdy, 337, 354, 421, 435, 478, 483, 514, 518, 520, 579.
—— Will., 421, 435, 481, 483, 503, 514, 515, 532, 533, 563, 566, 571, 579, 601, 602, 603, 605, 693, 694.
Hare, Joh., 164, 177, 211, 237.
—— Rob., 168.
Harfrey, Sim., 156, 169, 178.
Harley, Averey, 211.
Harewarde, Joh., Horwarde, Harewood, 80, 89.
—— Rob., 82, 90.
Harold, Nic., 166.
—— Will., 163.
Harper, Hugo, 248.
—— Tho., 163, 165, 179.
Harriesson, Row., 319.
Harrington, Sir Joh., Harryngton, 833.
—— 530.
Harry, Rob., Harre, 176.
—— Will., 608.
Harrys, Agnes, Harries, Harres, 81, 89.
—— Joh., 81, 128, 156, 161, 164, 165, 174, 184, 211, 218, 244, 252, 269, 535.
—— Margareta, 163, 179.
—— Ric., 647, 650, 676.
—— Tho., 20, 22, 39, 41, 46, 69, 77, 79, 162, 179.
—— Will., 160, 194, 209, 240, 247.
Harvye, Hugo, Hervie, Hervy, 778, 781, 790, 796, 800, 801, 806, 812.
—— Tho., 668, 669.
—— Will., 541.
Hasclyffe, Joh., Hastlyff, 81, 89, 127, 158, 165.
—— Tho., 156.
Hassale, Ric., Hassall, Harssall, 566, 579, 598, 599, 600, 602, 603, 604, 605, 609, 621, 622, 623, 625, 627, 629, 630, 631, 633, 634, 635, 636, 638, 641, 642, 643, 645, 647, 649, 650, 651, 652, 653, 654, 662, 665, 666, 667, 676, 679, 682, 684, 686, 688, 690, 691, 692, 693.
Hastyng, Joh., Hasteng, Hastynge, Hastynges, Hustyng, Hasting, 240, 249, 343, 351, 354, 360, 362, 364, 368, 372, 376, 390, 406.
—— Tho., 160, 183.
Hatter, Ric., 5.
Hauker, Will., 319.
Haw, Joh., 6.

Hawes, Will., 573.
Hawkeslowe, Joh., 176.
—— Tho., 166.
Hawkyns, Joh., Haukyns, Hawkyn, 78, 87, 125, 153, 154, 161, 163, 178, 179, 209, 210, 238, 248.
—— Sim., 319.
—— Tho., 817.
Hawnell, Rand., Hauenell, 87.
—— Tho., 344, 351, 355, 366, 368, 370, 371, 390, 482, 514.
Hawton, Joh., 163.
—— Ric., 797, 798.
Hay, Hen. dell, 3.
Haydon, Sir John, Heydon, 110.
—— Joh., jun., 81.
Hayes, Will., 176. *See* Heys.
Hayle, Isabel, Hayly, Haley, 162.
—— Joh., 82, 90, 168, 176, 212, 238.
—— Tho., 161.
Hayward, —, Heyward, 160.
—— Tho., 211.
Hazard, Joh., Hasard, 343, 351.
Hedde, —, his Wyfe, Hed, Hede, Heede, 532, 549.
—— Will., 351, 403, 406, 421, 424, 430, 435, 436, 437, 481, 483, 514, 576.
Heges, Hegges. *Read* Hoges.
Hegley, Chris., 482.
Heley, Will., 821, note.
Helony, Ric., Heleny, 3, 6, 451.
Hencote, Joh., 164, 177.
Hend, Hen., Hende, Hendy, 211, 237.
—— Ric., 81.
—— Will., 128, 155, 167, 175, 240, 249.
Hendman, Rob., Hendeman, Hendemon, 126, 139, 142, 154, 158, 163, 179.
Hensham, Ed., 212.
Henware, Joh., 167.
Herborugh, Herdburgh. *See* Harborgh.
Herdwen. *See* Hardwen.
Herdwyk. *See* Hardwyke.
Herford, Joh., [Hefford *read* Herford], Harforde, Hareford, 352, 737, 738, 740, 746, 765, 768, 770, 773, 778, 779, 780, 783, 788, 790, 793, 794, 795, 796, 797, 800, 803, 806, 809, 811, 821.
Hert, Rob., 79
Heryng, Joh., Herringe, Herryng, 483, 840.

Name Index.

Heryng, Ric., 629, 630, 631, 633, 652, 654, 665, 666, 667, 668, 676, 677, 682, 684, 686, 687, 688, 690, 691, 692, 693, 694, 695, 696, 697, 698, 700, 701, 704, 706, 707, 711, 713, 714, 717, 718, 721, 722, 723, 724, 725, 726, 727, 737, 738, 739, 740, 742, 746, 759, 766, 767.
—— Tho., 679, 693, 711, 713.
Hethe, Hen., 82, 90, 129, 176, 183, 184.
—— Ric., 351.
—— Will., Heth, 177, 541.
Hethull, Joh., Hethul, 79, 161.
Heton, Chris., 319.
Hewent, Will., 214.
Hewer, Joh., 128, 240. *See* Huewer.
Heydok, Gil., 422.
Heyman, Hen., 482.
Heyne, Greg., Heynes, Haynes, 343, 351.
—— Joh., 210, 242.
—— Nic., 573, 600, 602, 606, 621, 624, 625, 628, 629, 631, 634, 636, 637, 638, 641, 643, 645, 647, 650, 651, 653, 654, 663, 665, 666, 667, 688, 689, 690.
Heys, Will., Heyes, 126, 155, 168.
Heywoode, Joh., Heywode, 125, 162.
—— Nich., 78, 87, 125.
—— Rob., 213.
—— Will., 165.
Hi —. *See* Hy —.
Hiddesman, Ric., (Hykman ?), 322, 323, 327.
Hiklyng, Ric., Hikelyng, Hickeleng, Hicklyng, Hickelyng, 39, 48, 60, 69, 77, 80, 85, 89, 107, 120, 127.
Hill, Ad., Hulle, Hyll, 242, 247.
—— Baldw., 831.
—— Greg., 162, 180.
—— Hen., 82, 90, 167.
—— Joh., 80, 88, 127, 169, 177, 210, 237, 251, 319, 647, 649, 650, 686, 736, 761, 788.
—— Nich., 81, 90, 107, 128, 167, 534.
—— Rad., 155, 168, 176.
—— Tho., 241, 251, 483, 619, 620, 623, 624, 636, 647, 649, 651, 654, 663, 665, 666, 667, 668, 676.
—— Will., 128, 155, 176, 214, 241, 479.
Hinch, Nic., 161.
Hipstoones. *See* Ipstones.
Ho—, Ric., 90.

Hobbes, —, Hobbys, —, 87, 370.
—— Hen., 79, 87, 126, 154, 162, 178, 212, 238, 250.
—— Ric. 79, 126.
—— Tho., 210, 237, 246, 247, 266, 269, 285, 313, 314, 316, 317, 345, 351, 365, 368, 372, 376, 385.
Hobbons, Tho., 635.
Hobley, —, 581.
Hobson, Hopson, Jac., 679, 685.
—— Joh., 480.
—— Nic., 631, 633, 634, 794, 796, 761.
Hobyns, Joh., 557.
Hodson, Mayster, 366.
Hoges, Joh., Hogges, 128, 164, 165, 237, 251, 315.
Holbargh, Joh., 144.
Holbeche, Rog., 167.
Holbroke, Will., 18.
Holcote, Ed., Hulcote, Hulcottes, 390, 432, 443, 482, 514, 520, 522, 534, 542, 547, 552, 553, 563, 572, 581, 582, 584, 585, 588, 598, 600, 601, 602, 604, 605, 606, 609, 619, 621, 622, 623, 624, 625, 627, 628, 629, 630.
Holland, Joh., Holande, 81, 128.
—— Tho., 248.
Holme, Joh., 239.
—— Rob., 80, 89.
—— Will., 213, 242, 243, 269.
Holt, Hen., 81, 89, 128, 156, 165, 174.
—— Johanna, 164.
—— Joh., 156.
—— Ric., 79, 88, 164, 212, 239.
—— Will., 177.
Holy, Joh., 126, 160.
Holybrig, Tho., Holybryg, 155, 168, 175.
Holyes, Joh., 153.
—— Rog., 360.
Honey, Joh., Hony, 154, 162, 164, 178, 179, 211, 244, 266, 269, 285, 286, 365, 482.
—— Will., 365.
Hongerford. *See* Hungerford.
Honington, Joh. de, Honyngton, 13, 815.
—— Will., 452.
Honyburne, Joh., Honeyburn, 127, 156, 165, 174, 207, 212, 221, 239, 250, 256, 266, 275, 285, 304, 318.
Honyman, Rad., 89.
Hoode, Joh. of the, 167.

888   Name Index.

Hopkyns, Joh., Hopkeynes, 481, 631, 633, 634, 638, 641.
—— Nic., 809.
—— Rad. (Rauf.), 706, 707, 711, 735, 736, 760, 778, 779, 782, 788, 789, 796, 798, 800.
—— Ric., 796, 811.
—— Tho., 165.
—— Will., 354, 391, 403, 406, 421, 431, 483, 485, 514, 518, 520, 557, 571, 581, 582, 584, 585, 598, 600.
Hopton, Joh., 211, 251.
Hore, Alan, Hoore, 317.
—— Joh., 11.
Horley, Hug., 450.
Horne, Jacobus, 238.
—— Joh., 831.
—— Tho., 162.
Horneby, Hen., Hornby, 79, 88.
—— Joh., 20, 42, 61, 168, 179.
Horner, Will., 78.
Horram, Will., 211.
Horsley, ——, Horseley, Horselay, Horsseley, Hoursseley, 240.
—— Alex., 542, 543, 544, 566, 574.
—— Hen., 250.
—— Tho., 153, 160, 209, 249.
—— Will., 129, 166, 176, 183, 213, 219, 241, 246, 247, 286, 302, 304, 305, 310, 312, 313, 316, 317, 318, 320, 332, 334, 335, 336, 337, 339, 343, 345, 347, 351, 360, 361, 362, 366, 368, 370, 371, 372, 375, 378, 382, 385, 387, 389, 390, 416, 419, 421, 424, 431, 435, 443, 481, 483, 509, 514, 516, 517, 520, 521, 522, 524, 528, 530, 532, 533, 534.
Horswell, Joh., 453.
Hosier, Johanna, Hosyer, 126, 154, 163.
—— Joh., 80, 88, 158, 161, 238.
—— Rob., 162.
—— Tho., 127.
—— Will., 155, 168, 175, 214.
Hothoos, Will., 250.
Hoton, Joh., Hotton, 241, 247, 343, 345, 352, 362, 368, 370, 372, 375, 376, 378, 385, 419, 421, 423, 424, 473, 481, 483, 485, 503, 514, 516, 603, 842.
—— Tho., 238, 249.
Houlott, ——, 90.
Howdon, Joh., 165.
Howdy, Rob., 371.
Howe, Alex., Houe, 727.

Howe, Joh., 236.
Howton, Will., 59.
Hudson, Will., 483.
Huet, ——, Huett, Hewett, Huwett, Huwet, 343.
—— Joh., 81, 90, 128, 139, 142, 155, 168, 176, 214, 218, 318, 352, 354, 358, 363.
—— Ric., 47.
—— Rob., 241.
—— Will., 81, 90, 128, 155, 168, 176, 214, 241, 249, 328, 329, 330, 331, 332, 377, 406, 482, 514, 540, 566, 570, 578, 601.
Huewer, Joh., 175. See Hewer.
Hugford, Joh., 378, 381, 491.
—— Will., 378, 380, 381.
Hukyn, Joh., Hukyns, 351, 354, 376, 382.
Hull. See Hill.
Humberston, Auicia, Humburston, 240.
—— Will., 128, 129, 159, 167, 171, 176, 214.
Humfrey, Joh., 546, 566, 570, 579, 598, 602, 605, 607, 624, 625, 628, 629, 630, 631, 636, 637, 638, 641, 642, 643, 645, 647, 651, 652, 653, 662, 666, 667, 668, 676, 677, 679, 682, 684, 686, 688, 690, 691, 692, 693, 694, 695, 696, 697, 698, 700, 701, 704, 706, 707, 711.
—— Ric., 718, 720, 766, 767, 768, 770, 773.
Hungerford, Ric., Hongerford, 626.
—— Walt., 125.
Hunte, Ric., 573.
—— Rob., 541.
Huntley, Joh., 80, 88, 128, 154, 164, 177.
Hunton, Nic., 321.
Hurley, Joh., 37.
—— Will., 161.
Hurt, Ric., Hurte, 728, 737, 773, 778, 779, 781, 782, 783, 788, 789, 790, 793, 794, 795, 797, 798, 800, 806, 809, 811.
Hutchyns, ——, 829.
Hutgray, Joh., 368.
Huyron, Laur., Hyron, Yrn, 174, 212, 239, 248, 351, 376.
—— Will., 163, 242, 248.
Huyson, Laur., 166.
Hyde, Tho., 364, 481.
Hygreve, Joh., Higreve, 165, 175, 211, 236.

Hykkes, Joh., Hykes, Hykkys, Hickes, Hickkes, 663, 665, 667, 676, 677, 679, 682, 686, 687, 688, 690, 691, 692, 693, 694, 695, 696, 697, 699.
Hykman, Ric., Hiddesman, Hyddesman, 322, 323, 327, 541.
Hyllage. *See* Illage.
Hynde, Hen., Hinde, Hynd, 579, 586, 667, 715, 736, 768, 769, 779, 780, 781, 783, 788, 789, 796, 797, 798, 800.
—— Joh., 562.
—— Tho., 541, 562.
Hyndeman, Joh., 770, 778, 806.
—— Will., 801, 803, 811.
Hynkley, Tho., 212, 241.
Hynton, Will., 239.
Hyton, —, Hiton, Hy3ton, Huyton, Huyton, Highton, Heyton, 355.
—— Ad., 22, 36, 37, 40, 44, 58, 60, 61, 63, 67, 68, 69, 71, 73, 83, 84, 90, 98, 99, 105. *See* Deister.
—— Huwe, 371, 377, 390, 443, 482, 503, 509, 515, 520, 532, 547, 552, 563.
—— Isabella, 128, 157.
—— Ric., 166, 237.
—— Tho., 318, 343, 344, 357, 406, 483.
—— Will., 155, 157, 168, 176.

Illage, Alicia, Illedg, Elage, Hyllage, 88, 154, 164, 177. 210.
—— Jas., 840.
—— Joh., 236, 240, 280, 285, 302, 305, 306, 307, 312, 316, 317, 318, 320, 321, 333, 334, 335, 336, 337, 338, 339, 347, 351, 352, 365, 370, 371, 372, 373, 376, 378, 385.
—— Ric., 168, 175.
—— Tho., 82, 90, 107, 125, 139, 142, 153, 162, 180, 212, 246.
Illyot, Rob., 164.
Imayne, Joh., Ymayne, 155. 168, 176, 214, 241, 251, 318.
—— Ric., 128, 168.
Inge, Joh., 3.
—— Will., 78, 125.
Inglond, Joh., Ingland, 174, 212, 238.
Ingram, Tho., Inggram, Ingeram, 304, 305, 307, 310, 317, 320, 321, 333, 336, 337, 338, 339, 344, 347, 351, 352, 360, 362, 365, 367, 370, 372, 375, 376, 378, 382, 385, 387, 390, 416, 421, 843.
Ingre, Tho., 238.
Ingrewf, Rob., 164.
Inner, Joh., 248.
Insturley, Pet., 377.
Ipstones, Tho., Hipstoones, 213, 242, 247.
Iremonger, Rog., 165.
Iressheman, Will., 166.
Irysshe, Tho., Irisshe, 165, 174, 241, 248.
—— Will., Irysshe, 81, 89.
Isham, Joh., 493, 505.
Ismay, Ad., 209, 240.
Ive, Hen., Ives, 17.
—— Margeria, 155, 165, 175.
—— Ric., 693.
—— Tho., 39, 80 89, 127.
—— Will., 155, 164, 165, 175, 211, 236, 242, 247, 250, 314.
Iveley, Joh., 155, 168.

Jabet., Joh., Jabette, 164.
—— Tho., 241, 252.
Jacombe, Joh., Jacome, 90, 238.
—— Ric., 242, 247, 286.
Jakemon, Tho., Jakeman, 156, 158, 169, 171, 177, 210, 219, 237, 249, 256, 285, 315, 318, 321, 332, 365.
Jakson, Ric., Jackeson, 483, 502, 532, 542, 549, 567, 571, 584, 585, 594, 599, 601, 602, 603, 604, 605, 606, 609, 619, 620, 621, 623, 624, 625, 627, 628, 629.
—— Agn., 829.
—— Rob., 483, 553, 557, 566, 570.
—— Will., 541, 766.
Jamys, Joh., 89.
Janyns, Cecilia, 177.
—— Joh., 47, 80.
—— Sibell, 164.
Jatkyns, Margareta, 168.
Jekys, Rob., Jakys, Jekes, Jakes, (?) Jokys, 337, 344, 351, 355, 358, 365, 377, 390, 416, 419, 423, 424, 435, 443, 481, 482, 485, 503, 514, 516, 518, 520, 522, 528.
Jeorge. *See* George.
Jette, Joh., Jett, 637, 699, 700, 701 704, 706, 707, 714, 717, 718, 721, 722, 723, 726, 727, 728, 737, 739, 740, 746, 759, 766, 767, 768, 769, 770, 773, 778.
Jeynard, Joh., Jonarde, Joynarde, 770 773, 778.
John, Maur., (Mores), 422, 481, 483, 514, 534, 541, 566.

Johnson, Crysteffor, Joneson, Jhonson, 541.
—— Hugh, 602, 603.
—— Will., 210, 248.
Jones, —, Joones, Jonys, 239.
—— Joh., 126, 163.
—— Nic., 131, 164, 213, 241, 249.
—— Ric., 154.
—— Rob., 248, 318.
—— Tho., 239.
—— Tho., of Dedelone, 249.
—— Will., 80, 89, 127, 155, 162, 165, 178, 209, 236, 240, 248.
Jowderell, Will., Jewderell, Jawderell, Jawdrell, Jauderell, 238, 336, 343, 376, 406.
Joy, Agnes, 214.
—— Ric., Joye, 20, 22, 34, 36, 37, 39, 41, 42, 44, 56, 58, 60, 62, 68, 71, 73, 81, 83, 84, 86, 90, 99, 101, 102, 103, 105, 106, 109, 110, 111, 112, 113, 114, 117, 119, 122, 128, 130, 132, 134, 137, 138, 139, 140, 141, 143, 144, 150, 151, 155, 157, 159, 168, 169, 171, 172, 175, 184.
—— Tho., 80, 89, 127, 155, 165, 175, 211, 236, 248.
Joynour, Cuthbert, Joynor, Jeynour, Joyner, 700, 722, 723, 725, 726, 727, 728, 737, 738, 739, 740, 742, 746, 759, 765, 767, 768, 769, 770, 773, 778, 779, 780, 782, 783, 788, 789, 790, 793, 794, 795, 796, 798, 800, 801, 803, 806, 809, 811.
—— Joh., 80, 127, 169, 238, 770, 773, 778.
—— Raffe, 831.
—— Tho., 210, 237, 377.
—— Will., 714, 715, 717, 718, 769, 770, 773, 778, 779, 782, 783, 788, 789, 790, 793, 795, 797, 798, 805, 809, 811.
Joyster, Tho., 354. (?) See Just.
Julyans, Joh., Julians, 390, 430, 514, 542.
—— Ric., 156, 169, 177, 213.
Just, Tho., Juster, Inster (?), 365, 482, 535.

Kardyffe. See Cardyff.
Kay, Patric., 88, 127.
Kebull, Hen., Keble, Kebeelles, 53, 368, 371, 377, 414, 421, 424, 443, 481, 482, 485, 514, 518, 520, 521, 524, 525, 528, 532, 533, 534, 539, 540, 542, 547, 552, 553, 731.

Kebull, Joh. 82, 90, 129, 139, 142, 143, 167, 176, 209, 213, 240, 241, 246, 249.
—— Tho., 474, 524, 525, 526, 527, 528.
Keen, Tho., 479.
Kekwike, Tho., Kekewyke, 213, 242, 248.
Kele, Hen. de, 3.
—— Joh., 164.
Kelmestowe, Tho., Kelmstowe, 241, 247.
Kelow, Joh., 89.
Kelyngworth, Abbot of, 377, 380.
—— Tho., 605, 622, 647.
—— Will., 737.
Kemp, Tho., 138, 167.
—— Will., 82, 90, 129, 159, 167, 171, 176, 201, 213, 217, 221, 222, 226, 229, 230, 232, 233, 235, 242, 243, 245, 252, 253, 254, 255, 256, 259, 262, 266, 267, 270, 271, 272, 275, 276, 277, 278, 279, 280, 283, 284, 285, 293, 301, 302, 305, 306, 308, 310, 312, 316, 317, 320, 321, 322.
Kemsey, Nic., 631.
—— Ric., 629, 630, 633, 665, 666, 668, 676, 677.
—— Will., 636.
Kendale, Rob., 248.
Kent, Joh., 409, 411.
—— Nic., 211, 221, 236, 244, 251, 256, 266, 269, 285, 286, 318, 365, 377, 390.
—— Ric., 543.
Keresley, Ad. de, Kersley, 6.
—— Will., 51, 58, 90, 135.
Keriche, Nic., 212.
Kersyman, Ric., 166.
Kerver, Wal., Kervar, Keruer, Carver, 262.
—— Will., 41, 48, 63, 69, 73, 81, 83, 85, 89, 91, 99, 101, 102, 106, 107, 111, 114, 117, 119, 128, 130, 134, 137, 138, 140, 143, 144, 150, 151, 152, 156, 157, 159, 165, 169, 172, 174, 184, 185, 186, 187, 188, 189, 193, 194, 195, 197, 198, 200, 201, 202, 204, 206, 207, 208, 212, 217, 218, 219, 221, 222, 226, 227, 228, 229, 230, ‘231, 232, 233, 235, 239, 243, 245, 250, 252, 253, 254, 255, 256, 259, 266, 267, 270, 271, 272.
Kervyn, Kyrvyn, Hen., Kirvin, Kervyne, Kirvyn, Kirwyn, 821, 831.

Name Index. 891

Kervyn, Rob., 686, 687, 688, 693, 694 696 699, 701, 706, 707, 711, 713, 714, 717, 718, 720, 721, 724, 725, 726, 728, 732, 737.
—— Tho., 599, 740, 746, 801, 806, 809, 812.
Kevet, Tho., Keveit, Keyvett, Keyvet, Keivet, 711, 720, 736 740, 768, 769, 770, 773, 778, 779, 780, 782, 783, 788, 790, 794, 795, 796 798, 800, 801, 803, 806, 811.
Kirkebank, Joh., 164.
Kirkeland, Rob., 483, 542.
Kirtley, Tho., Kirteley, 162, 179.
Kirton, Clemens, 183.
Knede, Ric., 236.
Knott, Hen., Knot, Knotte, Knottes, 38, 39, 41, 77, 86, 90, 121, 133, 139, 142, 176, 194, 213, 241, 247.
Knyght, Joh., Knyghte, Kny3t, 78, 87, 160, 183, 351, 355, 358, 364, 371, 379, 406, 414, 481, 565.
—— Nic. 210.
—— Wik., 209, 240, 243, 248, 268, 315, 316, 318, 343, 344, 351, 356, 364, 368, 370, 373, 376, 378, 385.
Knyghtley, Edm., Knyghteley, Knightley, 693.
—— Hen., 518.
—— Joh., 165.
—— Ric., 126, 154, 163, 179, 212, 238, 251.
Knyttesford, Ric., 163, 178.
Kockes, Kokkes, Kox. *See* Cockes.
Kylby, Hen., 686.
—— Ric., 794, 795, 796.
Kyldraught, Tho., Kildraught, 162, 179.
Kyng, Ric., 78, 87, 352, 377, 421.
—— Rob., 125.
—— Will., 252.
Kyngeley, Rog., 162.
Kyngston, Joh., Kyngeston, 127, 155, 165, 175, 212.
Kynnesbury, Tho., 209.
Kyppyng, Wal., 164, 177.
Kyrke, Tho., Kirke, 146, 154, 163, 178, 247.
Kyrkeby, Joh., Kirkeby, 154, 163, 178, 250.
—— Tho., 319.
—— Will., 518, 542.
Kyrton, Tho., 87.
Kyrvale, Tho., Kirvall, Kirvyle, 211, 214, 483, 566.

Laborer, Edw., 165
—— Nic., 167.
Lacy, Joh., 125.
Lambard, Hen., 153.
—— Reg., 161.
—— Will., 209, 240.
Lancaster, Joh., Langcastell, 169, 177, 202, 240, 251.
—— Will., 168.
Lancroff, ——, 365.
Lare, Ric., 128, 155, 167, 175, 214, 240, 250.
Langestell, *read* Langcastell
Langham, Sim. de, 3.
Langley, Alic. de, 449.
—— Gal., 13.
Langton, Joh., Lancton, Launcton, 125, 153, 209, 240. 243, 248, 268.
—— Ric., 351, 365.
Lansdale, Ric., 482, 563, 566, 567. 570, 579, 599, 600. 601.
Lapworthe, Tho., 829.
Large, Pet., 448.
—— Phelipp., 241 247.
Laughton, Rob., 88.
Launcelen, Rob., 318.
Launde, Joh., Launder, 37, 40, 60, 79, 85 88, 103, 111, 117, 126, 130, 132, 168.
Laurence, Hugh, Larons, Laurans, 212, 239.
—— Joh., 240.
Lawe, Sim., 242
Lawton, Hugo, 676, 677, 692, 693, 694, 695, 696, 697, 699, 700 701, 704, 706, 707, 711, 713, 714, 715, 718, 720, 721, 722, 723, 724, 725, 726, 727, 728, 731, 737, 738, 739, 740, 742, 746, 765.
—— Joh., 721, 736, 742, 760
Lebbes, Joh., 179.
Leche, Rob., 246.
—— Tho., 155, 165, 175, 211, 236.
—— Will., 82, 90.
Ledes, Joh., 479.
Lee, Joh., a Lee, o' the Lee, Le, Ley, a Lie, 39. 76, 78, 79, 87, 120, 125, 126, 133, 134, 138, 140, 143, 144, 148, 149, 150, 152, 153, 154, 161, 162, 171, 172, 178, 179, 184, 185, 189, 195, 197, 198, 201, 202, 204, 207, 208, 210, 217, 218, 219, 222, 226, 227, 228, 229, 230, 231, 233, 235, 238, 242, 243, 251.
—— Nic., 239.

Lee, Ric., 53, 352, 355, 360, 365, 368, 377, 424, 431, 443, 481, 482, 485, 514, 516, 520, 522, 528, 532, 533, 534, 540, 542, 543, 544, 547, 552, 553, 557, 563, 567, 571, 579, 581, 582, 584, 585, 587, 588, 598, 599, 600, 601, 602, 603, 605, 606, 609, 619, 624, 628, 700, 701, 722, 723, 725, 726, 728, 737, 739, 740, 746, 759, 766, 767, 768, 770, 773, 778, 779, 780, 782, 788, 789, 790, 794, 795, 796, 797, 800, 801, 803, 806, 809, 812.
—— Rog., 531, 542, 619, 620, 621.
—— Tho., 641, 642, 643, 645.
Leeder, Joh., Leder, 20, 21, 22, 33, 34, 35, 36, 38, 40, 41, 42, 44, 55, 56, 57, 58, 60, 61, 62, 63, 64, 65, 67, 68, 69, 70, 71, 73, 78, 82, 83, 84, 85, 87, 98, 99, 102, 103, 104, 105, 107, 109, 119, 122, 126, 130, 132, 134, 137, 138, 139, 140, 143, 144, 150, 151, 154, 157, 162, 169, 187, 189, 191, 194, 195, 198, 200, 201, 202, 203, 204, 207, 208, 212, 217, 218, 219, 220, 222, 226, 227, 228, 229, 230, 231, 232, 233, 235, 238, 243, 245, 246, 252, 253, 254, 364.
—— Ric., Loder (?) 176, 214
Leeke, Joh., 635.
Legburn, —, 242, 248.
—— Will., 131, 144.
Lemyng, Joh., 566.
Lemynton, Rob., 164.
Lenton, —, 156.
—— Joh., 160.
—— Ric., 377.
—— Tho., 81, 89, 128, 165.
Lesyngham, —, Leysyngham, Lessyngham, 89.
—— Joh., 48.
—— Ric., 39.
—— Rog., 82, 129, 166, 176, 842.
—— Tho., 166.
Letherbarrowe, Rob., 821.
Letys, Joh., 546, 566.
Leuer, Ric., 80.
Levyng, Joh., 166.
Leycester, Will., Leicester, Lecestre, 78, 87, 815.
Leyghton, Tho., 168, 178.
Lichefield, Edw., Lychefeld, Lichefeld, 20, 39, 52, 81, 90, 149, 171, 189, 222.

Lichefield, Joh., 39, 40, 41, 51, 60, 77, 81, 90, 107, 114, 115, 117, 129, 138, 140, 141, 143, 150, 151, 152, 159, 166, 169, 176, 184, 185, 186, 188, 189, 197, 204, 206, 207, 213, 228, 242, 250, 266.
——— Joh., 842.
—— Mold, 59.
—— Will., 167.
Liston, Step. de, 815.
Litelton, Tho., recorder, Lytelton, Litulton, 234, 235, 246, 252, 263, 266, 270, 276, 278, 280.
Lock, Tho., 79.
Locker, Will., 818.
Locok, Hen., Lokok, 541.
—— Joh., 127, 154, 164, 171, 177, 210, 237, 248, 639, 651, 652, 653.
—— Will., 541.
Lodyngton, Rog. de, 6.
Logge, Will., 546.
Loke, Tho., 79, 88, 127, 156, 169, 178.
Lokier, —, de New-strete, Lokyer, 180.
—— Joh., 161, 168, 238.
—— Joh., de Mil-lone, 180.
—— Ric., 530, 546, 566.
—— Tho., 81.
—— Will., 160.
Lokkey, Joh., Lokhey, 237, 262, 335.
Lokyngton, Tho., Lokynton, 164, 177, 237.
London, Joh., 82, 155, 165, 175, 211, 236, 250.
Longshawe, Joh., 479, 541.
Lorde, Joh., 236, 249, 351, 365.
—— Ric., 167.
Lote, —, Loote, Lotte, 156.
—— Joh., 81, 89, 127, 156, 165, 174, 212, 239, 247, 256, 266, 285.
—— Rob., 212.
—— Tho., 210.
Louth, Hen., Louthe, Lowthe, Lothe, 163, 177, 248.
—— Joh., 80, 88, 156, 169, 177, 451.
Lovet, Tho., 474.
Lucy, Sir Tho., Lucie, 833.
—— Will., 491.
Ludlowe, Wal., 242.
—— Will., 248
Luff, Joh., Loff, 78, 87.
—— Ric., 5.
—— Will., 752.
Lusterley, —, Lysturley, Listerley, 194.

Name Index.

Lusterley. Joh., 39, 78, 87, 129, 134, 138, 150, 151, 152, 171, 176, 185, 186, 188, 189, 192, 193, 195, 198, 200, 201, 202, 204, 206, 207, 208, 213, 217, 218, 221, 222, 226, 228, 229, 230, 231, 232, 842.
—— Will., 167.
Lybard, Joh., Libard, 5.
—— Tho., 47, 351.
—— Will., 79. 87, 126.
Lye, Joh. a, 541.
—— Thurstanus, of the Lye, 236, 248.
Lyle, Will., 317.
Lyllyng, Ric., 145.
Lyllyngton, Joh., Lyllynton, 168. 176.
—— Margeria. 177.
—— Rog., 241, 251.
—— Tho., 81, 90, 128, 155, 168.
—— Will., 168.
Lyme, Joh., 138, 197.
Lyncoln, Agnes, 241.
—— Joh., 82, 90, 167, 176.
Lynd, Oliuer, 809.
Lyndsey, Rob., Lyndessey, Lynsey, 352, 390.
—— Step., 651, 653.
Lyney, Leo., 37.
Lyng, Ric., 237, 250.
Lyngvham, Hen., Lyngham, 782, 783, 806.
Lynne, Joh., le Lynne, Lynney, 127, 139, 142, 143, 155, 164, 175, 193, 195, 198, 201, 202, 204, 207, 211, 217, 219, 221, 222, 227, 228, 229, 230, 231, 233, 236, 315, 318, 453.
Lyons, Joh., Lyones, Lyonas, 154, 163, 178, 366.
—— Tho., 77, 80, 127, 164, 177, 211, 237, 248.
Lyrpole, Elizabeth, Lirpole, Lyrpull, Lirpull, 128, 168.
—— Joh., 80, 89, 105.
—— Ric., 168, 176.
—— Rob., 39, 41, 42, 44, 49, 51, 53, 77, 81, 90, 102, 107.
Lythe, Rob., 237.
—— Will., 164.
Lyuerey, Sampson, 248.

Machon, Ric., 177.
Madam, Will., Madame, 163, 238.
Magson, Will., 161.
Maidford, Joh., Maidforde, Maidtford, Mayford, Maydeford, 78, 87, 125, 153, 160, 210, 214, 238, 247, 285, 286.

Maidford, Tho., 125, 153, 162, 180, 240, 248, 329, 330, 406, 421, 423, 424, 431, 435, 436, 481, 483 485, 502, 503, 514, 518, 520, 532, 534, 540, 542, 544, 547, 552, 553, 563, 567, 571, 579, 581, 582, 584, 585, 588, 598, 599.
Makesey, Joh., 156, 179, 212.
Mallory —, Malory, 285.
—— Joh., 80. 88, 126, 154, 164, 165, 175 177, 210, 211, 219, 236, 250, 285, 318 483, 842.
—— Will., 250.
Maltby, Rog., 128.
Maltman, Agnes, 166.
—— Joh., 160.
Malyn, Will., 162.
Man, Joh. a, Aman, 318, 351, 377, 483.
Mannyng, Rob., 89.
Manton, Hugo, (Hugh.) Manten, 154, 158, 164, 177, 211, 236, 249, 263, 269.
—— Joh., 87, 125, 153, 161, 168, 184, 209, 214, 219, 240, 249, 318.
—— Will., 168.
Manston, Maunston, Joh., 82, 90.
—— Tho., 239, 246.
Mare, Pet. de la, 80, 88.
Marfood, Joh., 236.
Mariot, Will., 165, 175, 211, 236, 250.
Markeham, —, 326.
Marler, Hen., Marlere, Marlar, Marlowe, Merler, 351, 368, 370, 377, 388, 389, 390, 416, 419, 421, 423, 431, 443, 473, 483, 485, 503, 504, 512, 518, 520, 521, 522, 524, 525, 528, 530, 532, 533, 539, 542, 543, 544, 547, 553, 557, 561, 563, 567, 571, 581, 582, 584, 585, 587, 588, 598, 599, 600, 601, 602, 603, 604, 605, 606, 609, 619, 621, 622, 623, 624, 625 843.
—— Ric., 599, 603, 605, 619, 623, 624, 626, 628, 629, 630, 631, 632, 634, 636, 637, 638, 641, 642, 645, 647, 649, 650, 651, 652, 654, 662, 663, 664, 665, 667, 668, 676, 677, 679, 682, 686, 688, 690, 693, 694, 731.
—— Will., 707, 711, 714, 715, 717, 718, 721, 723, 724, 725, 728, 737.
Marlond, Rad., 319.
Marlowe. (?) See Marler.

Marnam, Emma, Marnarme, 128, 165.
—— Joh., 39, 41, 81, 89.
Marshall, —, Marchall, Marescall, 515.
—— Bened., 37, 39, 41, 44, 45, 60, 76, 78, 85, 87, 103, 107, 117, 120, 125, 132, 138, 143, 150, 153, 161.
—— Joh., 13, 161, 167, 168, 176, 249, 352, 364, 546, 578, 842.
—— Margerie, 450.
—— Ric., 67. — R., 815.
—— Tho., 6, 20, 250.
—— Will., 39, 41, 46, 80, 85, 127, 138, 139, 142, 161, 164, 179, 240, 249, 315, 318, 329, 330, 334, 335, 338, 339, 345, 352, 357, 366, 369, 370, 376, 409, 411, 416, 419, 421, 424, 431, 436, 443, 473, 483, 485, 503, 514, 516, 518, 520, 521, 522, 524, 528, 529, 530, 531, 532, 533, 842.
Marsharre, Joh., 365.
Marshe, Joh., Mershe, Mersche, Mersshe, 81, 89, 127, 142, 156, 165, 174, 211, 218, 221, 239, 244, 246, 248, 256, 285, 318, 329, 330.
—— Ric., 40, 82, 90, 95, 129, 842.
Marston, Joh., Merston, 39, 79, 88, 120, 126, 133, 138, 156, 168, 177, 210.
—— Tho., 162, 179.
Marton, Joh., 38, 164.
—— J. de, 1, 2, 3, 38.
Martyn, Will., Marten, 95, 128.
Mason, Hen., Masyn, 81, 89, 128, 214, 241, 249, 286, 316, 318, 344, 352, 365.
—— Joh., 365.
—— Ric., 161, 176.
—— Rob., 81, 90, 154, 158, 162, 170, 178, 214, 240, 246, 249, 371, 406, 422, 531, 542, 549.
—— Rog., 242, 250, 571, 581, 598.
—— Simon, 56, 57, 59, 163, 179.
—— Tho., 78, 87, 125, 139, 142, 153, 161, 163, 177, 209, 240, 249.
—— Will., 125, 155, 168, 175, 210, 214, 237, 241, 246, 249, 269, 285, 315, 317, 318, 337, 355, 360, 365, 368, 573.
Massey, Joh., 213.
Massyngham, Joh., Messyngham, 240, 247, 319.
Mathew, Joh., Mathewe, Mathowe, 82, 90, 166, 184, 249, 443, 482, 514, 516, 518, 520, 533, 544, 547, 552, 553, 557, 563, 567, 572, 581.

Matson, Her., 377.
Mawdeley, Gilb., 479.
Maxsey, Joh., 169.
Maxtok, Joh. de, Maxstock, 3, 6.
—— Prior of, 378.
May, Joh., Meie, 6.
—— Nyc., 352.
—— Tho., 543, 602.
Mayke, Tho., 239.
Maynard, Joh., Maynarde, Maynerd, 80, 89, 127, 139, 142, 143, 155, 164, 171, 175, 204, 211, 221, 236, 244, 246, 249, 256, 266, 285, 286, 318.
Mayowe, —, 541.
Maysbroke, Joh., 168.
Medburn, Joh., Metburn, 165, 175, 211.
Meke, Hugh, Meeke, 546.
—— Will., 128, 155, 168, 176.
Melody, Will., Melodye, 211, 236, 250, 352.
Melodyne, Will., 155, 165, 171, 175.
Melton, Agnes, Molton (?), Multon (?), 175.
—— Joh. de, 5, 76, 78, 80, 87, 125, 128, 153, 162, 164, 166, 167, 177, 180, 318.
—— Rob., 39, 88, 127, 248.
Menley, Joh., Meenley, 39, 81, 85, 89, 127, 156, 160, 165, 174, 229.
—— Leticia, 212, 239.
Mercer, Rad., 210.
Mereman, Chr., 686.
Merevale, Abbot of, 378, 380.
Merler. See Marler.
Meryhull, Will., Meriell, 352, 377, 482.
Meryngton, Hen., 240.
Mettley, —, 99.
—— Baldwin, 209, 240, 243, 268.
—— Nich., 77.
Metyngham, Joh., 282.
Michell. See Mychell.
Middelham, —, 90.
Milburn, Ric., Melburn, Mylburne, 39.
—— Rob., 34, 36, 37, 41, 42, 58, 60, 62, 64, 71, 73, 81, 84, 90, 91, 98, 99, 102, 103, 106, 107, 108, 109, 114, 115, 117, 119, 128, 130, 132, 134, 138, 143, 152, 155, 159, 167, 175.
Mildenhall, Ric., Mildenall, Mildnale, 78, 87, 125, 162, 247.

Name Index.

Miles. See Myles.
Mille, Her., Myll, 351, 406, 482, 535.
Miller, Tho., 250.
Milette, Joh., Milet, Millet, Mylet, 80, 156, 169, 177.
Milner, Alex., Mylner, Mulner, Milnar, 78, 87, 162, 179.
—— Hugo, 74, 166.
—— Joh., 81, 127, 155, 161, 167, 212.
—— Nich., 239.
—— Pet., 167, 176, 183, 184.
—— Rob., 165, 174.
—— Rog., 128, 164, 177, 211, 237, 248.
—— Tho., 238.
—— Will., 161, 251.
Milwarde, Elie, Mylleward, 19.
—— Tho., 161.
Mirifeld, Joh., Myrifelde, 236, 247.
Mirihurst, Will., 542.
Mohaut, Rog. de, 13.
Mokes, Joh., 144.
Moldriche, Joh., 6.
Molle, Gal., Mole, Moole, 161.
—— Joh., 81, 128, 133, 142, 156, 165, 174, 212.
—— Ric., 87, 125, 153, 160, 194, 209, 240, 248.
—— Will., 163, 248.
Mollesley, Humf., 579.
Montalt. See Mohaut.
Montgomery, Joh., Mongomery, 20, 38, 39, 44, 51, 77, 90, 100, 107, 842.
More, Moore, Joh., 126, 817, 818.
—— Nic., 162, 179.
—— Simon, 82, 90, 129, 156, 166, 174, 212.
—— Tho., 162, 179.
Moredok, Tho., Moradok, 566, 579.
Morell, Ric., 88, 127, 154, 158, 164, 171, 211.
Mores, ——, Morys, Morres, Morse, Mors, 167.
—— Dav., 166, 241.
—— Joh., 176, 213, 242, 256, 266, 307, 310, 312, 316, 317, 332, 333, 336, 337, 339, 345, 347, 351, 352, 360, 361, 362, 365, 370, 371, 372, 376, 378, 382, 385, 387, 390, 605, 622, 665, 667.
—— Rob., 155, 168, 176, 385.
—— Tho., 161, 250, 737, 746, 779.

Mores, Whaburley, 541.
Morewyk, Moric., 164.
Morgon, Tho., 242.
Morley, ——, 167.
—— Joh., 78, 87.
—— Will., 482, 535.
Morsby, Tho., 154, 163.
Morton, Tho., 165, 250.
—— Will., 250.
Moseley, Hum., Molsley, Moysley, 667, 668, 676, 688, 692.
—— Joh., 635, 714, 715, 717, 718, 770, 773.
—— Rob., 546.
Mosell, Tho., 601.
Mosse, Rob., 480.
Motte, Joh., Moote, 154, 158, 163, 171, 178.
Mountford, Sir Sym., Mountfort, Mownforth, 378, 380.
—— Tho., 240, 249.
—— Will., 123.
Mower, Tho., Mowyer, 365, 430, 482, 517.
Mowton, Editha, Moweton, 178.
—— Joh., 48, 59.
Mox, Will., 450.
Muklawe, Rog., Muklowe, 543, 566.
Mulner. See Milner.
Mure, Hen. de le, 145.
Mychell, Joh., Michell, Michel, Mechell, 20, 22, 36, 37, 39, 41, 42, 43, 44, 47, 54, 58, 60, 66, 67, 69, 71, 73, 79, 84, 85, 88, 91, 97, 98, 101, 102, 104, 106, 107, 109, 111, 112, 113, 114, 115, 117, 119, 126, 130, 132, 134, 137, 138, 140, 143, 144, 147, 149, 150, 151, 152, 154, 156, 159, 163, 172, 178, 184, 185, 186, 187, 188, 189, 190, 191, 193, 194, 195, 197, 198, 200, 201, 202, 204, 207, 213, 217, 218, 220, 226, 228, 230, 242, 246.
—— Ric., 366.
—— Tho., 238, 248, 377.
Myddelton, Will., 351, 369.
Mydnyght, Ric., 371.
Myles, Her., Myllys, Miles, 517.
—— Joh., 1, 821, 831.
—— Ric., 242.
—— Rob., 81, 128, 174, 638.
—— Sam., 837, 840.
—— Will., 161, 166.
Mynes, Joh., 421, 483.
Mynfold, Joh., 211.

Napton, And., 6.
—— Joh., 483.
—— Tho., 211, 237, 250, 285, 286, 315, 317, 318, 337, 343, 344, 352, 354, 360, 363, 366, 377, 379, 406, 514, 653, 679, 684, 715, 726, 761.
Nash, Joh., Nasshe, Naysshe, 518.
—— Ric., 163, 178.
—— Will., 319, 385, 388, 416, 419, 423, 424, 474, 503, 516, 522, 528, 532, 533, 534, 540, 542, 547, 553, 563, 571, 581.
Nassington, Tho. de, 3.
Naylston, Joh., 165.
Nedame, Joh., Nedam, 248, 352.
—— Sir Joh., 349.
Nedeler, Tho., 160.
Nele, Hen., Neele, 212.
—— Joh., 81, 82, 89, 90, 128, 155, 164, 165, 167, 175, 177, 210, 214, 237, 241, 248, 249, 256, 318, 352, 354, 371, 377, 406.
—— Tho., 318.
Nethermyll, Joh., Nethirmyll, Nethyrmyll, 780, 783, 788, 789, 793, 794, 795, 796, 803, 809, 831.
—— Jul., 634, 636, 637, 641, 642, 649, 651, 653, 654, 663, 665, 666, 667, 668, 676, 679, 682, 684, 686, 688, 690, 691, 693, 694, 695, 696, 697, 700, 701, 704, 705, 706, 707, 711, 713, 714, 715, 717, 718, 720, 721, 722, 723, 724, 725, 726.
Newell, *read* Neuell.
Neve, Joh., 161.
Nevell, Ric., Nevyle, Neuell, 364.
—— Rob., 209, 219, 222, 240, 246, 251, 256, 266, 318.
Newbold, Alicia, 211, 237.
Newby, Joh., Neuby, Nueby, 78, 87, 126.
Newman, Joh., Newmon, Neuman, 240, 241, 251, 356, 377, 391, 421, 483.
—— Tho., 351.
—— Will., 161.
Newport, Joh., Nuport, 128, 168, 176.
—— Will., 128, 168.
Newthorp, Tho., 248.
Newton, Hugo, Neuton, 161, 210, 250.
—— Joh., 248.
—— Reignald, 212.
—— Ric., 81, 89.
—— Rob., 49, 209.

Newton, Wal., 126, 162, 183.
—— Will., 82, 90, 129, 167, 176.
Niclyn, Ric., Niclyne, Nyclyne, Nyckelvn, 685, 696, 699, 700, 738, 766, 767, 768, 769, 770, 773, 778, 779, 782, 783, 788, 790, 793, 794, 797, 798, 800, 801, 803, 806, 809, 811.
Nicoll, Joh., Nicols, Nicolles, Niccolls, 162, 164, 241, 736.
—— Ric., 78.
—— Rob., 696.
—— Tho., 241, 831.
Nityngale, Nitynghale. *See* Nyhgtyngale.
Nix, Joh., 603.
Nores, Agnes, Norres, Norys, Nories, 163, 176, 178.
—— Johanna, 160.
—— Joh., 79, 88, 718, 720, 721.
—— Ric., 53, 351. 421, 473, 481, 482, 485, 489, 490, 501, 520, 553, 563, 579, 581, 582, 588, 599, 600, 601, 602, 603, 604, 605, 607, 619, 624, 628, 631.
—— Will., 213, 815.
Norfolke, Joh., Northfolk, 5.
—— Ric., 248, 579.
—— Wal., 127, 155, 165, 174, 212, 239, 246, 248, 256, 266.
Normanton, Joh., Normaton, 20, 37, 39, 79, 88, 107, 126, 138.
Northampton, Joh., 10, 81, 90, 126, 128, 155, 168, 176, 191, 214, 219, 241, 251, 286.
—— Will., 214, 241, 251, 318, 362, 369, 370, 376, 421, 435, 443, 481, 483, 514.
Northman, Joh., Northemon, 90, 155.
Northwood, Johanna, Northwode, Norwoode, Norwode, 37, 79, 88, 126, 134, 163, 178.
—— Joh., 41, 88, 126, 213, 221, 228, 242, 245, 254, 259, 266, 285, 316, 317.
Norton, Joh., 565, 573, 579, 588, 601.
—— Tho., 285, 352.
—— Will., 168, 176, 214, 241, 251, 696, 713, 720, 722, 737, 740, 742, 759, 766, 767, 768, 770, 773, 778, 779, 780, 781, 782, 783, 788, 789, 793, 794, 795, 796, 797, 798, 801, 806, 809, 811.
Norwiche, Tho., Norwyche, Norwhiche, Norwyc, 81, 90, 128, 154,

Name Index.

155, 162, 168, 175, 178, 212, 238, 249.
Notworthe, Joh., 352.
Nyclyne. *See* Niclyne.
Nyhgtyngale, Joh., Nityngale, Nitynghale, 352, 365, 377, 414.

Odard, Will., 10.
Oddon, Will., 541.
Oderyche, Joh., Oderiche, Orderiche, Orderyche, Osteriche, 127, 169, 178, 210, 219, 237, 247, 250, 285, 337.
—— Ric., 210, 242, 247, 351, 354, 365, 368, 371, 376, 406.
Odyngsels, Gerard, 511.
Okburn, Rog., 155.
Okeham, Elizabeth, Ookeam, Okam, Okcam, 80.
—— Tho., 214, 241, 248, 365.
—— Will., 6.
Okeley, Joh., Okley, 307, 564, 569.
Oky, Rog., 449, 453.
Okyn, Will., 80.
Oldbury, Joh., Oldebury, Oldbere, 238, 251, 318, 344, 351, 365, 377, 379.
Oldenhall, Joh., Oldenhale, 213, 236, 251.
Olyve, Joh., Olyffe, 80, 89, 210.
—— Will., 89.
Olyuer, Ric., 249.
Onfeld, Joh., 210.
—— Will., 184.
Onley, —, Oneley, Ooneley, 162.
—— Agnes, 212, 240.
—— Joh., 11, 20, 22, 37, 39, 41, 42, 44, 52, 58, 69, 80, 83, 89, 98, 100, 102, 103, 104, 106, 109, 111, 112, 113, 114, 115, 116, 117, 127, 130, 132, 134, 137, 138, 140, 141, 143, 144, 150, 151, 155, 157, 160, 164, 171, 172, 175, 184, 185, 238, 249, 305, 338.
—— Margeria, 164, 177.
—— Ric., 37, 39, 41, 42, 44, 54, 58, 60, 62, 69, 71, 73, 80, 83, 85, 89, 99.
—— Sir Rob., 53, 312, 320, 323, 333, 335, 339, 344, 345, 347, 352, 360, 361, 362, 363, 364, 368, 371, 373, 375, 376, 378, 382, 385, 387, 388, 389, 416, 419, 421, 423, 424, 435, 436, 443, 473, 481, 482, 489, 502, 503, 504, 511, 514, 516, 518, 520, 521, 522, 524, 526, 528, 529, 530, 532, 534, 539, 540, 541, 747, 842.
Onyon, Tho., 239.

Ookes, Rad., Okes, 128, 156, 166, 177.
Oone, Joh., 183.
Opton. *See* Upton.
Orme, Will., 239.
Orsley, Will., 249.
Orwell, Rob., 318.
Osbern, Ric., Osburn, Osbarne, Osborn, Osburne, Osberne, 89, 127, 139, 142, 154, 165, 175, 189, 194, 195, 207, 211, 217, 222, 226, 236, 247, 256.
—— Rog., 175.
—— Will., 126, 163.
Osgathorp, Will., 639.
Osteler, Rog., 127.
Ostynton, Joh., 352.
Oswestre, Rob., 248.
—— Rog., 244, 246, 266, 269, 286.
Otewalle. *See* Atwall.
Otley, Joh., Ottley, Otteley, 177.
—— Will., 21, 33, 79, 88, 156, 168, 177.
Oures, Joh. of, Owrys, 358.
—— Tho., 53, 352, 371, 377, 414, 421, 483, 530, 737, 739, 742, 761, 780, 781, 798, 800, 801.
Outered, Joh., Outerede, Owtrede, Owterede, 80, 89, 127, 155, 165.
—— Rob., 167.
Over, Hen., Ouer, 714, 722, 727, 728, 737, 738, 740, 746, 759, 769, 770, 773, 779, 781, 782, 783, 789, 790, 793, 794, 795, 796, 797, 798, 800, 803, 806, 811.
Overton, Nic., Ouerton, Ourton, 162, 179, 183, 210, 238.
—— Tho., 13.
—— Will., 583.
Owdeby, Tho., 163, 178.
Owen, Jasper, 765, 766.
Oxton, Will., Oxston, 43, 69, 98, 99, 102, 109, 114, 117, 122, 137, 140, 144, 150, 153, 162, 171, 179, 195, 196, 198, 201, 202, 218, 226, 230, 232, 235, 247, 252, 255, 270, 276, 278, 280, 284, 296, 304, 305.

Pace, Tho., Pase, 482, 543, 579.
Pachet, Joh., 483, 583, 619.
Padland, Joh., Padlond, Padlonde, 390, 406, 422, 430, 482, 513, 518, 520, 531, 532, 534, 542, 543, 547, 552, 553, 557, 563, 572, 581, 582, 584, 585, 587, 588, 598, 599, 600, 601, 602, 603, 604, 605, 606, 609, 619, 621, 623, 624, 625, 627, 628,

629, 630, 631, 632, 633, 634, 636,
637, 638, 640, 641, 642.
—— Tho., 482, 533, 543, 557, 563,
567, 572, 573, 579, 581, 582, 584,
585, 588, 598, 601, 602.
Pake, Joh., 153, 162, 180.
Pakstaf, Will., 6.
Palmer, Guy, Palmeer, 626.
—— Hen., 534.
—— Johanna, 82, 90, 167.
—— Joh., 242, 247.
—— Nich., 77, 79, 85, 88, 91, 107,
111, 120, 126, 133, 154, 158, 160,
163, 178, 213, 221, 242, 285.
—— Ric., 212, 239, 249.
—— Rog., 676, 694, 695, 700, 701,
704, 706, 711, 713, 714, 715, 717,
718, 721, 722, 723, 724, 725, 726,
727, 728, 737, 738, 739, 740, 742,
746, 759, 766, 767, 768, 769, 770,
773.
Palyngton, Will., 449.
Pape. *See* Pope.
Parbroun, Ric., Parbron, Parbronde,
Berbrom, Perbram, Perbrown, 142,
156, 169, 177, 210, 237, 257.
—— Tho., 219, 241, 246, 248, 266,
313, 316, 318.
Pardy, Joh., 318.
Parker, ——, Parkere, Perker, 546.
—— Alicia, 81, 168.
—— Joh., 20, 36, 37, 39, 41, 42, 44,
49, 54, 58, 60, 81, 83, 84, 90, 91, 99,
102, 107, 109, 112, 113, 115, 122,
128, 130, 132, 137, 138, 167, 798,
806.
—— Michell, 191.
—— Sim., 686, 704, 706, 707, 711,
715, 718, 721, 722, 723, 724, 726,
727, 728, 737, 738, 740, 742, 746,
759, 766, 767, 768, 769, 770, 773,
778, 779, 780, 781, 783, 788, 789,
790, 793, 794.
—— Tho., 164, 213, 238, 241, 247,
250, 314, 319, 333, 334, 338, 339,
351, 361, 362, 366, 368, 376.
—— Will., 679, 682, 821.
Parkyns. *See* Perkyns.
Parre, Hugo, Par, 239, 250.
Pars. *See* Pers.
Partriche, Anne, 705.
—— Phil., 705.
—— Will., 352.
Paslowe, Wal., 127, 154, 164, 177, 210.

Passant, Joh., 479.
Passynger, Joh., 128.
Pastey, Ric., 638.
Patage, Ric., 238.
Patch, Joh., Pache, 21, 453.
Patenmaker, Joh., 80, 156.
—— Will., 162.
Patrike, Ric., 237.
Patter, Joh., 250.
Paules, Gunter, 562.
Paunton, ——, Pawnton, 166.
—— Ric., 39.
—— Tho., 162, 179, 214, 238, 241,
243, 246, 249, 269, 315, 317, 318,
351.
Pavier, Rob., 179.
Payne, Joh., Payn, 540, 604.
—— Sym., 81, 128, 168, 171, 176.
—— Will., 318.
Paynell, Alicia, Peynell, 156, 165, 174.
—— Tho., 42, 44, 48, 54, 60, 69, 81,
84, 85, 89, 91, 98, 99, 102, 108, 109,
111, 112, 113, 114, 117, 120, 122,
124, 130, 131, 132, 133, 134, 135,
136, 137, 138, 139, 140, 143, 147.
—— Wyll., 53, 356, 358, 406, 481,
483, 512, 514.
Paynton, Tho., 175.
Peche, Joh., (?) Poche, 161, 184, 210,
238, 243, 249, 268.
—— Ric., 155, 165, 175, 242, 251.
Pedworth, Hugh, 480.
Pell, Edw., 800, 801, 803.
Pemberton, ——, 474.
Pen, Joh., 165.
Penson, Ric., 128, 155, 160, 168, 175,
214, 219, 228, 241, 246, 256.
Pepur, Rog., 212.
Perbroun. *See* Parbroun.
Percy, Ric., 564.
Pere, Joh., Peer, Perre, Pir, Piere,
Per, 80, 89, 165.
—— Will., 82, 128, 143, 156, 165,
174, 191, 192, 194, 195, 198, 201,
202, 204, 206, 207, 208, 214, 221,
222, 226, 227, 230, 231, 232, 233,
234, 235, 241, 243, 245, 247, 252,
253, 254, 255, 256, 259, 262, 266,
267, 270, 271, 272, 275, 277, 278,
279, 280, 283, 301, 302, 305, 306,
310, 316, 317, 320, 321, 332, 333,
334, 335, 336, 337, 338, 339, 343,
345, 347, 351, 352, 360, 361, 362,
366, 367, 370, 371, 372, 375, 376,

Name Index.

378, 382, 385, 387, 388, 390, 421, 463.
Perett, Joh., 128.
Perines, Nic., 174.
Perkes, Will., Parkes, 213, 242.
Perkyns, Hen., Parkyns, 541, 588, 623, 624, 630, 631, 633, 634, 636, 637, 638, 645, 647, 649, 650, 651, 652, 653, 654, 663, 665, 666, 667, 668, 676, 677, 679, 682, 686, 688, 690, 691, 692, 693, 694, 695.
—— Joh., 125, 153, 161, 179, 210, 242.
—— Rob., 704.
—— Tho., 213, 248.
—— Will., 579, 602, 628, 629, 631, 633, 634, 636, 637, 638, 641, 642.
Perpoynt, Joh., Perpoynte, 154, 163, 178, 207, 213, 242, 246, 248.
Pers, Joh., Purs, Pars, 127, 164, 177, 211, 248.
—— Wal., 160.
—— Will., 165, 204, 211, 319.
Persale, Har., Perseele, 337, 351, 354, 366, 377.
—— Rob., 164, 177, 211, 237, 252.
Persons, Ric., 249.
Persyvale, Joh., 177.
Perte, Will., Peerte (Percy?), 126, 154, 160, 163, 175.
Pery, Joh., Perey, Perry, 6, 365.
—— Tho., 363, 482.
Petchey, Ric., 352.
Peverell, Will., 162, 179, 239.
Pewterer, Johanna, Peuterer, 164, 175.
—— Joh., 41, 51, 81, 90, 112, 162, 174.
—— Ric., 175.
—— Rob., 164, 210.
—— Tho., 80, 88, 120, 126, 133, 155, 164, 169, 175, 177.
—— Will., 37, 41, 48, 80, 89, 107, 127.
Peynell. *See* Paynell.
Peyntour, —, of the New-strete, Peynter, 180.
—— Hen., 155, 599, 600, 601, 602, 603, 604, 605, 622, 629.
—— Joh., 586.
—— Margerie, 215.
—— Ric., 128, 155, 168, 251.
—— Tho., 79, 154, 162.
—— Will., 6.
Peyto, Hen., Peytoo, Peito, Peitoo, 20, 21, 35, 37, 39, 42, 43, 44, 54, 55, 56, 57, 60, 61, 62, 63, 64, 65, 66, 67, 68, 69, 70, 71, 79, 83, 85, 87, 99, 102, 103, 104, 105, 109, 110, 111, 112, 113, 114, 115, 117, 119, 122, 126, 130, 132, 134, 137, 138, 140, 141, 143, 144, 150, 151, 154, 159, 162, 169.
Philips, Elys, Phelippes, Phillippes, Filippes, Fillippes, Philippus, Phelippes, 483.
—— Geo., 684, 686, 700, 717, 718, 721, 722, 724, 725, 726, 728, 737, 738, 739, 740, 742, 746, 759, 767, 768, 769, 770, 773, 778, 779, 780, 781, 782, 783.
—— Johanna, 241.
—— Joh., 162, 179, 343, 351, 356, 377.
—— Ric., 80, 82, 88, 90, 108, 117, 121, 129, 133, 143, 159, 167, 171, 176, 183, 184, 213, 221.
—— Tho., 761, 778, 780.
—— Wyll., 351, 358.
Pigou, Joh., 164.
Pikstaff, Nic., Pykstaff, 164, 177.
Pinkston, Tho., 67.
Pinnok, Rob., Pynnock, Pynnok, 39, 41, 46, 76, 79, 842.
—— Stevyn, 541.
Pipe, —, 530.
Pisford, Joh., Pisfort, Pysford, 135, 242, 252, 285, 286, 314, 317, 318.
—— Ric., 82, 148, 167, 213, 242, 252.
—— Will., 483, 528, 529, 544, 552, 553, 557, 563, 579, 588, 600, 602, 603, 604, 605, 606, 609, 619, 620, 621, 625, 627, 628, 629, 630, 631, 633, 634, 636, 637, 638, 641, 642, 645, 647, 649, 650, 651, 652, 653.
Pittes, Tho., Pyttes, 482, 520, 522, 547.
Pixley, Joh., 840.
Plant, Tho., Plante, Plont, 53, 365, 406, 430, 483, 540, 570, 579.
Plasterer, Joh., 81, 89, 128, 156, 166, 174, 212.
Plesantyn, Joh., 601.
Plumer, Joh., Plomer, Plymer, Plymmer, 78, 87, 125, 126, 156, 161, 166, 169, 177, 185.
—— Ranulph, Raffe, 155, 162, 164, 175, 180, 210, 211, 236, 238, 315, 318, 365.
—— Ric., 78, 87, 125, 169, 178.

Plumer, Tho., 164, 175, 211, 236, 482, 543.
Plumpton, Joh., Plumton, Plompton, 250.
—— Ric., 351, 354, 362, 376, 414, 422, 481, 534, 540.
Pollard, Hugo, Pollar, Pollerd, (Huwe), 238, 243, 246, 268, 285, 315, 317, 318, 344, 351, 355, 356, 360, 371, 376.
Polle, Galf., 167.
—— Joh., 354, 363.
—— Tho., 364.
—— Will., 351.
Polton, Ric., 240.
Poole, Tho., 81.
Pope, Joh., Poope, Pape, 6, 50, 352, 406, 517, 534, 535, 566.
—— Ric., 212.
Porter, Ad., 450.
—— Baldwin, 650, 686, 693, 696, 700, 706, 711, 714, 718, 721, 725, 728, 737, 746, 768, 778, 780, 789, 794, 796, 800.
—— Joh., 153, 161, 179, 605, 619, 624, 629, 631, 634, 636, 637, 638, 641, 642, 647, 651, 653, 665, 667, 676.
—— Tho., 207.
—— Will., 41, 92.
Possell, Hochyn, 47.
Potager, Will., Poteger, Potynger, 81, 90, 128, 453.
Potell, Ric., Pootell, 313, 315, 316, 318.
—— Tho., 343, 478, 481, 483, 514, 530.
—— Will., 53, 543, 566, 579.
Potter, Tho., 840.
—— Will., 238, 246, 285.
Pova, Ric., Povey, Povie, 562, 594, 601, 641, 679, 684.
Poverete, Will., 212.
Power, Joh., Poweyr, 79, 88, 127, 156, 169, 178, 210, 237, 247.
—— Ric., 20, 22, 36, 37, 39, 41.
—— Tho., 88.
Powes, Joh., 167, 241, 252.
Powet, Will., 192.
Powle, Joh., 213.
Pratte, Joh., Prate, 82, 90, 482.
—— Ric., 242, 247.
—— Tho., 81, 89, 127, 165, 174.
—— Wal., 133.
—— Will., 37, 39, 41, 48, 77, 81, 85, 89, 107, 111, 127, 156, 165, 174, 566, 842.
Praty, Joh., Pratty, 146.
—— Rob., 60, 77, 80, 111, 120, 127, 133, 138, 143, 145, 154, 163, 178.
Prese, Ric., Preese, 236, 248.
—— Will., jun., 20.
Prentes, Christiana, Prentys, 238.
—— Joh., 41, 60, 62, 63, 76, 78, 85, 87, 102, 107, 109, 111, 114, 117, 122, 125, 130, 131, 134, 137, 138, 140, 141, 143, 144, 150, 152, 153, 157, 161, 168, 169, 172, 179, 184, 185, 186, 187, 188, 189, 192, 193, 194, 195, 197, 198, 200, 201, 202, 204, 206, 208, 210, 217, 219, 221, 222.
—— Tho., 80.
—— Will., 80, 88, 127, 155, 167, 175.
Prescote, Margeria, 165, 175.
Preston, Hen., 52, 80, 89.
—— Joh., 20, 160, 242, 247, 351, 365, 560.
—— Tho., 560.
Priest, Ric., Prist, Pryst, 15.
—— Tho., 337, 360.
Prikonshawe, Tho., 249.
Priory, Dav. de le, 168.
Prophet, Matillda, Profette, Profete 167, 241.
—— Reignald, 82.
—— Rog., 155, 164, 175.
Pryce, Tho., Pryse, 318.
—— Nich., 81.
Prynse, Hen., 166.
Pulteney, Ric., 421, 520.
Pulter, Ric., 128, 165, 175.
—— Tho., 377, 421, 430.
Pulton, Joh., Pultun, 481.
—— Ric., 247, 314, 318, 351, 352, 357, 364, 368, 370, 376, 382, 387, 390, 416, 424, 431, 435, 443, 481, 482, 485, 503, 513, 522, 532, 534, 843.
Purdon, Joh., 168.
—— Rob., 175.
Purs. *See* Pers.
Purser, Hugo, 237
Pynchard, Joh., Pyncherd, 118, 126, 210, 238.
Pynchbek, Joh., Pynchbek, Pynchebeke, Pinchebek, Pynchebekke, 22, 39, 41, 44, 48, 49, 69, 89, 98, 213, 242, 246, 247, 284, 285, 293, 305, 306, 307, 310, 312, 316, 317,

332, 333, 334, 336, 337, 338, 339, 343, 344, 347, 351, 352, 360, 362, 364, 367, 370, 371, 372, 375, 376, 377, 378, 383, 385.
Pynchbek, Will., 239, 246, 250, 256, 285, 286, 314, 343, 345, 351, 360, 363, 370, 377, 416.
Pynder, Joh., 161.
Pyne, Edw., 166.
—— Ric., 166.
Pynkyll, Joh., 365.
Pynley, Will. de, 12.
Pynne, Joh., 167.
—— Sim., 129.
Pynner, Agnes, 162.
—— Steph., 213.

Quynton, Marg., 829.

Raby, Will., 167.
Race, Reynold, 483.
Radburn, Will., Rodburn, 356, 363, 390, 391, 421, 430, 483.
Radcliff, Joh., Rad-Clyffe, Radclyf, 214.
—— Rog., 337.
—— Wyll., 81, 90, 128, 139, 142, 143, 155, 167, 175, 214, 219, 228, 240, 250.
Radeley, Joh., Radley, 126, 154, 163, 178, 210, 237, 248.
Rage, Joh., Ragge, 160, 209.
—— Ric., Ragge, 210, 238, 249, 376.
Raignold, Regnold. *See* Reynold.
Ralegh, Sir Ed., 626.
Randle, Ant., Randull, Rondull, Rondall, Randell, 831.
—— Hen., 40, 81, 90, 128, 143, 155, 168, 176, 214, 241.
—— Joh., 160.
—— Nic., 53, 214, 240, 315, 318, 344, 345, 352, 358, 368, 377, 443, 483, 514.
—— Will., 721, 722.
Ranke, Will., 382.
Rasche, Ric., 126, 213.
—— Rob., 249.
Rastell, Hen., Restell, 176, 211.
—— Isabel, 318, 365.
—— Joh., 605, 619.
—— Tho., 128, 156, 158, 165, 174, 201, 202, 204, 207, 211, 221, 236, 247, 256, 352, 370, 603, 604.
Ratlyffe, Rob., 829.
Raves, Tho., 286, 313, 316, 317, 333, 338, 351, 376.

Ravon, Joh., 212, 238, 251.
Rawlot, Will., 241.
Rawlyn, ——, Rawlyns, 366, 371, 377.
—— Will., 483.
Ray, Joh., Raye, 6, 40, 49, 60, 69, 79, 87, 107, 112, 126, 154, 162, 178.
—— Patricius, 79.
Raymond, Joh., 79, 88.
Rebull, *read* Kebull.
Recheford. *See* Rocheforde.
Rede, Elena, Reede, 164.
—— Reg., 81.
—— Ric., 166, 212, 251, 343, 352, 365, 366, 368, 377, 379.
—— Tho., 163.
—— Will., 164, 175.
Ree, Sir Rog., 369.
Reffus, Tho., 212.
Reper, Rob. *Read* Roper, 212.
Repyngton, Will., Repynton, 37, 79, 121, 126.
—— Will., auditor of the Duke of Bedford, 121.
Restall. *See* Rastell.
Reve, Joh., Rewe, Reives, Reves, 237, 250.
—— Rob., 213, 241.
—— Tho., 87, 153, 161, 184, 366, 663, 699.
Reynold, Johanne, Reynod, Regnold, Raignold, Raynold, Reynoldes, 535, 536.
—— Joh., 129, 213, 351, 357, 366.
—— Ric., 390, 406, 478, 535, 536, 542.
—— Will., 79, 88, 248, 430, 478, 483.
Reynolds, Hum., Reynoldes, 765, 788, 790, 795, 796, 800, 803.
—— Joh., 11, 90, 167, 176, 241, 242, 248, 252, 285, 478, 483, 512, 514, 533, 542.
—— Ric., 10. *See also* Reynold.
Reyuer, Tho., Reyner (?), Ryver, 39, 79, 84, 88, 107, 111, 117, 120, 126, 133, 134, 142, 143, 154, 163.
Richardson, Joh., 608.
—— Tho., 562.
—— Will., 166, 176.
Riconjay, Joh., Ryconjay, Ricongay Rycongey, 163, 211, 237, 250.
—— Tho., 89.
Ridell, Margeria, Ridale, 128.
—— Mart., 728, 736.
—— Maur., 737.
Ridware, Tho., 163.

Riley, Rieley. *See* Ryley.
Rise, Hugo, Ryse, Rice, 167.
—— Ric., 619, 622, 623, 624, 668, 676, 682, 686, 687, 688, 690, 693, 694, 695, 696, 697, 699, 701, 704, 706, 707, 708, 711, 713, 714.
Robartes, Joh., Robardes, Robertz, Roberdes, Robartys, Robert, 128, 242.
—— Mich., 788, 789.
—— Phil., 343, 351, 363, 365, 377, 390.
Robson, Math., Robbeson, 800, 803.
Roby, Tho., Robye, 343, 352, 354, 365, 371, 377. 414.
Robyns, Hen., 161.
—— Joh., 164.
—— Tho., 561.
Rocheforde, Joh., Rocheford, Recheford, 76, 78, 85, 87, 125, 131, 140, 150. 153, 160, 161, 170, 179, 180, 184, 198, 210, 222, 238, 249, 266, 284, 285.
—— Ric., 78, 87, 125, 153, 162, 183, 210, 238, 249.
—— Rob., 45.
—— Tho., 180.
Rodburn. *See* Radburn.
Rodes, Rob., Roodes, 212, 239, 250.
Rodley, Joh., 88.
Rogeley, Hugo, Rugeley, Rigeley, 39, 41, 44, 48, 63, 77, 81, 85, 89, 106, 107, 128, 165.
Rogers, Hen., Roger (Har.), 211, 237, 250, 314, 317, 351, 602, 609, 621, 625, 628, 630, 631, 636, 637, 638, 641, 649, 650, 651, 662.
—— Jas., 718, 728, 736, 738, 742, 759, 765, 767, 768, 769, 773, 779, 781, 788, 789, 790, 793, 794, 795, 796, 800, 803, 806, 809, 811, 821.
—— Joh., 308, 309.
—— Will., 693, 713, 715, 718, 720, 721, 722, 723, 724, 725, 727, 728, 737, 738, 739, 740, 742, 746, 766, 767, 768, 769, 770, 773, 778, 779, 780, 783, 788, 795.
Rogerson, Joh., 821.
Rokardyne, Will., Rocardyne, Wrokwarden, 432, 535, 566, 619, 624.
Rolf, Will., Rolfe, Rolff, 167, 213, 241, 249.
Rollesley, Joh., 319.
Rondaunt, Rob., de Stoke, Rondant, 403, 406.

Ronkorne, Will., 213, 248.
Ronton, Joh., Runton, Ronten, Rontten, Rounton, 39, 41, 44, 46, 60, 69, 77, 80, 85, 88, 98, 103, 107, 109, 111, 112, 114, 115, 117, 120, 122, 126, 132, 134, 137, 138, 140, 141, 143, 150, 152, 156, 157, 159, 169, 172, 177, 184, 185, 187, 189, 192, 194, 207, 210, 241.
—— Tho., 241, 249.
Rook, Joh., Rooke, 36, 81.
Rooper, Joh., Roper, 800, 801, 803.
—— Rob., 212, 239.
—— Will., 165.
Rose, Gal., 177, 250.
—— Joh., 365.
—— Will., 352, 406, 421, 430, 483, 534.
Rothe, ——, 66.
Rothewell, Joh., 248.
—— Will., 125, 160, 209.
Rouke, Joh., 240.
—— Rog., 164, 211, 236, 244, 269.
Rouncke, Will., 365.
Rowby, Tho., 249. *See* Roby.
Rowlett, Will., Rowlot, 214, 249.
Rowley, Joh., Rouley, Rewley, 81.
—— Tho., 629, 631, 636, 637, 638, 650, 653.
—— Will., 343, 354, 360, 365, 368, 371, 379, 390, 421, 424, 431, 436, 443, 481, 482, 485, 520, 522, 524, 528, 530, 533, 534, 540, 542, 543, 547, 552, 553, 557, 563, 567, 571, 579, 581, 582, 584, 598, 599, 600, 601, 602.
Rows, Ric., 165.
—— Tho., 451.
Royster, Tho., 371.
Ruffeld, Nic., 178.
Russell, Joh., 6.
—— Nic., 127, 154, 163, 237, 247.
—— Raffe, 478, 483.
—— Tho., 39, 540.
Russheton, Joh., 127, 163.
—— Ric., 241.
—— Will., 166, 242, 248.
Ruydyng, Joh., Rudyng, Ruddyng, Ridyng, 296, 304, 305, 307, 312, 318, 320, 321, 333.
—— Tho., 164.
—— Will., 690, 692, 736.
Ruyton, Joh., Ryton, 237, 284, 293, 296, 302, 305, 306, 307, 310, 311, 316, 317, 320, 321, 322, 323, 333,

334, 335, 336, 337, 338, 339, 343, 344, 347, 351, 352, 360, 361, 362, 365, 367, 370, 371, 372, 375, 376, 378, 382, 385, 387, 388, 389, 390, 416, 419, 421, 423, 424, 425, 426, 431, 435, 437, 443, 473, 474, 481, 483, 485, 503, 514.
Ruyton, Tho., 143, 144, 151, 154, 164, 177, 314, 343, 344, 377, 450.
Rydale, Joh., Ridale, 81, 89.
Ryder, Will., Ruyde, 155, 177.
Ryley, Alan, Ruyley, Riley, Reiley, Rieley, 601.
—— Hen., 479.
—— Tho., 711, 739, 779, 780, 783, 788, 811, 819.
Ryngley, Tho., Ryngeley, 239, 247.
—— Will., 214.
Ryngold, Joh., Ringold, Rynggold, 496, 531, 540.
—— Will., 535.
Rypon, Joh., Repyn, 164, 177.
Ryvell, Joh., Rivell, Revell, 79, 88, 111, 120, 126, 138, 154, 163.
—— Ric., 88, 126, 163.

Saburton, Joh., 89.
Sadler, —, Sadeler, 47, 318.
—— Joh., 176.
—— Katerina, 211, 236.
—— Nic., 155, 165, 175.
—— Ric., 89, 842.
—— Tho., 167.
Salbery, Rob., 377.
Salbruge, Tho., 351.
Sampson, —, Saumson, 239.
—— Hen., 543, 603.
—— Ric., 53, 318, 377, 430, 483.
—— Tho., 128, 166. *See also* Saunsom.
Sande, Joh., 161.
Sandes, Tho., 829.
Sandebroke, Joh., 794.
Sandon, Joh., 166.
—— Tho., 363.
Saunders, Edw., Sandurs, Saundurs, Saunder, Sawnders, Saundres, 764, 768, 770, 778, 780, 789, 794, 796, 800.
—— Joh., 156, 165, 566, 573, 582, 584, 585, 601, 606, 609, 619, 621, 623, 625, 627, 628, 629, 631, 633, 634, 636, 637, 638, 640, 641, 642, 643, 645, 647, 700, 713, 715, 718, 720, 724, 725, 726, 727, 728, 737, 738, 740, 746, 759, 766, 767, 768, 770, 773, 778, 779, 780, 781, 782, 783, 788, 789, 790, 793, 794, 795, 796, 797, 798, 800, 801, 806.
Saunders, Lawr., 343, 351, 360, 364, 368, 377, 424, 430, 431, 432, 433, 434, 435, 437, 439, 441, 442, 443, 447, 463, 464, 481, 483, 510, 511, 512, 513, 515, 520, 521, 530, 556, 557, 564, 567, 574, 575, 576, 577, 578, 579, 580.
—— Ric., 663, 821.
—— Tho., 482, 546, 736, 738, 739, 740, 798, 800, 806, 809, 812.
—— Tho., 737, 821, 829, 831.
—— Will., 46, 47, 153, 160, 211, 218, 229, 239, 245, 247, 252, 256, 266, 272, 276, 278, 279, 280, 283, 284, 293, 296, 301, 302, 305, 306, 307, 312, 316, 317, 320, 334, 336, 338, 339, 343, 344, 345, 347, 349, 351, 360, 362, 364, 367, 369, 370, 371, 372, 373, 375, 382, 385, 387, 388, 389, 390, 416, 419, 421, 423, 439, 444, 454, 471, 694, 715, 742, 759, 765, 767, 768, 769, 770, 773, 778, 779, 780, 781, 782, 783, 788, 789, 790, 795, 796, 797, 800, 801, 803, 806, 843.
Saunsom, Ric., Sansom, 352, 354, 357.
—— Tho., 174. *See also* Sampson.
Savage, Joh. [Savaye, *read* Savage], 166, 175, 180, 214, 238, 241, 250, 256, 285, 286, 296, 305, 306, 310, 312, 316, 317, 320.
—— Will., 129.
Saw, Will., 73.
Sawyer, Joh., 160.
—— Moric., 167.
—— Will., 167.
Saxton, Rob., Saxston, 39, 77, 80, 85, 120, 139, 842.
Sch —. *See* Sh —.
Schulton, Joh., 82.
Sconse, Tho., 736, 740, 742, 790, 793.
Scot, Johanna, Scotte, Skott, 163, 240.
—— Ric., 78, 87, 125, 153, 161, 195, 201, 202, 207, 209, 217, 222, 228, 231, 782, 783, 797, 801.
—— Sim., 483.
—— Tho., Skotte, 81, 89, 214, 221, 224, 228, 241, 246, 256.
Sedyngwode, Joh., 250.
Seele, Joh., Seill, 167, 720, 721, 724, 725, 726, 727, 728, 737.

Seman, Joh., Semon, Semans, Symondes (?), 315, 317, 337, 338, 339, 343, 345, 352, 360, 361, 362, 365, 370, 371, 376, 385, 387, 416, 419, 421, 424, 431, 435, 436, 443, 473, 481, 482, 485, 489, 502, 503, 504, 514, 516, 518, 520, 521, 522, 526.
—— Mistress, 530.
Semyng, Joh., Shemyng, Shemeng. Shemynges, Shemyn, 242, 251, 285, 314, 343, 351, 355, 360, 365, 371, 377, 514.
—— Ryc., 535, 566, 601.
Sencler, Joh., 480.
Sendell, Tho., 59.
Sengull, Joh., 319.
Seny, Rob., Seyne, Seynye, 676, 677, 699, 701, 706, 707, 711, 713, 714, 715, 717, 718, 720, 721, 722, 723, 724, 727, 728, 737, 738, 739, 740, 742, 746, 759, 766, 767, 768, 769, 773, 778.
—— Tho., 736, 780, 781.
Serjaunt, Jac., Seriaunt, 176.
—— Rob., 155, 168, 176.
Sessyle, Joh., Seysell, Sissell, Syssill, Sysell, Cysyll, Cesyle, 363, 432, 481, 483, 503, 514, 515, 518, 528, 532, 533, 540, 542, 547, 553, 563, 571, 581, 582, 588, 598, 600, 601, 602, 605, 619, 624.
Sethe, Ric., 80.
—— Will., 80. *See also* Shether.
Seuster, Agnes, Sewster, 162, 180.
Sewall, Hen., 840.
—— Ric., Sewell, Shewell, Sewald, 694, 696, 724, 726, 728, 737, 738, 739, 740, 742, 746, 766, 767, 768, 769, 770, 773, 778, 779, 782, 783, 788, 789, 790, 793, 794, 795, 796, 797, 798, 800, 801, 803, 806, 809, 812.
—— Ric., jun., 693, 790, 793, 794, 796, 801, 806.
—— Rob., 15, 17, 19, 48.
—— Will., 840.
Seward, Joh., 333, 334, 337, 351, 363, 365, 368.
—— Isabella, 79, 88.
Sewker, Tho., 167. *See also* Suker.
Sewyne, Joh., Seywyn, Sewen, Sewyn, Sewon, 81, 89, 127, 156, 165, 171, 174, 211, 218.
Sexten, Joh., 483.
Shade, Hugo, Shadd, Shad, Shadde, 222.

Shade, Joh., 87, 120, 125, 138, 139, 142, 152, 153, 162, 180, 209, 210, 219, 221, 228, 238, 246.
Sharman. *See* Sherman.
Sharp, Hen., 146.
—— Joh., 238, 248.
—— Ric., 39, 44, 60, 67, 68, 79, 84, 88, 91, 98, 100, 102, 106, 107, 109, 111, 112, 113, 114, 117, 119, 122, 126, 131, 132, 134, 137, 138, 140, 143, 144, 146, 148, 149, 150, 152, 154, 157, 159, 163, 171, 172, 178, 184, 185, 186, 187, 189, 191, 198, 202, 203, 206, 207, 213, 217, 218, 222, 226, 227, 228, 229, 230, 231, 232, 233, 242, 245, 246, 252, 253, 256, 262, 267, 300, 453, 467.
Shaw, Hen., 213, 242.
—— Hugo, 82, 129, 167, 176, 213.
—— Hugo, jun., 166.
—— Joh., 78, 212, 239, 365.
—— Ric., 495, 496, 504, 595.
—— Rob., 153, 161, 179.
—— Tho., 79, 88, 163, 166, 178, 251.
Shawbury, Rob., Shabury, Schawbury, 390, 406, 414, 430, 481, 483, 514, 540.
She ——. *See* Se ——.
Sheffeld, Pet., Shefeld, 81, 168, 175.
—— Sim., 6.
Sheldon, Joh., 78, 87, 125, 131, 138, 153, 160, 170, 175, 183, 184.
—— Joh., jun., 153, 160, 184, 209, 240, 249.
Shelley, Will., 635, 637, 638, 641, 642.
Shene, Tho., 364.
Shenston, Joh., 168.
Sheparde, Joh., 480.
Shepey, Joh., Shippey, Shyppey, 168, 365, 377, 422, 443, 482, 566.
—— Wyll., 355.
Sherde, Joh., 237.
Shergrynder, Joh., Sheregrynder, Shergryndar, 162, 179, 212.
Sherman, Ed., Sharman, Shermon, 126, 158, 162, 170, 178.
—— Johanna, 175.
—— Ph., 248.
—— Ric., 79, 153, 161, 174.
—— Rob., 164.
—— Tho., 162, 163, 178, 211.
Shether, Ric., Schether, 89.
—— Will., 127, 164.
Sheynton, Joh., 59.

Shilton, Joh., 166.
Shipley, Joh., Schipley, 453.
—— Rob., 11, 20.
Shippey. *See* Shepey.
Shipston, Rog., 126, 163.
—— Will., 239, 249, 318.
Shireff, Hugo, Shyryf, 177, 237.
Shirley, Joh., Shurley, Sherley, 239, 249, 318.
—— Will., 78, 87, 125, 153, 161, 179, 184, 215, 238.
Shirrerd, Phil., Sherrarde, Sherarde, 736, 737, 761, 778, 781.
Shirwode, Joh., Shurwode, Shyrwode, 255, 273, 318, 345, 483.
Shopes, Tho., 196.
Shore, Ric., Shor, 482, 586.
—— Will., 352, 360, 368, 370, 373, 375, 376, 378, 382, 385, 387, 409, 411, 416, 423, 424, 437, 443, 481, 483, 485, 503, 512, 514, 516, 518, 520, 521, 522, 524, 528, 529, 530, 532, 534, 539, 540, 541, 542, 543, 544, 547, 553, 557, 563, 571, 576, 581, 582, 584, 585, 587, 588, 598, 599, 600, 601, 602, 603, 604, 605, 606.
Shoteswell, ——, Priour, Shotteswell, Schotteswell, 463, 472.
—— Joh., 79, 88, 126, 163.
Shrouesbury, Joh., 248.
Shryve, Hugo, 210. *See* Shireff.
Shuffenall, Tho., 541.
Shukborgh, Rob., Shukborough, 153.
—— Will., 638.
Shultern, Shulton, Joh., de, 13, 815.
Shustock, Ric., Shustoke, Shurstooke, Shirstoke, Shistoke, 81, 89, 127, 156, 158, 165, 171, 174, 211.
—— Tho., 211, 239, 248.
Shutte, Joh., Shut, 503, 516, 518, 522, 529.
Sircok, Hen., Sircoke, Syrcok, Sircokke, Syrcok, 37, 41, 81, 90, 107, 119, 122, 127, 132, 134, 135, 136, 140, 141, 151, 152, 154, 160, 164, 172, 177, 184, 185, 188, 189, 193, 194, 195, 197, 198, 200, 201, 206, 207, 208, 211, 217, 218, 219, 222, 227, 228, 229, 230, 231, 233, 235, 237, 243, 245, 246, 253, 254, 256, 259, 262, 266, 267, 271, 272, 275, 276, 277, 278, 279, 280, 284, 285, 293, 296, 301, 302, 305, 317,
—— Joh., 39, 77, 79, 85, 88, 107, 126, 138, 143, 150, 156, 168, 177, 207, 210, 219, 221, 237, 247, 266.
Sircok, Joh., jun., 247.
Sissetur, Joh., Syssettur, Sircetur, Sirseter, 81, 89, 120, 127, 133, 142, 156, 165, 174.
Skarborgh, Joh., 20.
Skelton, Geo., Skylton, 608.
—— Tho., 239.
Skille, Hen., Skyll, Skylle, 78, 87, 125, 153, 160, 180, 239.
—— Joh., 79, 88, 126, 156, 169, 178, 210.
—— Rob., 154, 162, 178, 210, 237, 244, 250, 269.
Skinner, Elys, Skynner, 163.
—— Joh., 179, 238.
Sklatier, Rob., 34.
Slede, Will., 166.
Sloley, Will., 127.
Slough, Nic., 483, 565.
Slye, Rob., 128.
Smale, Ric., 169, 175, 210, 248.
Smallwood, Hum., Smalewood, Smallwod, 840.
—— Will., 809, 812.
Smert, Joh., Smerte, 355, 358.
Smyth, Agn., Smythe, Smith, 174.
—— Baldw., 213, 246.
—— Edw., 739.
—— Hen., 166, 576, 840.
—— Joh., 3, 139, 142, 166, 179, 180, 184, 237, 238, 241, 242, 247, 251, 260, 318, 336, 344, 345, 352, 355, 357, 360, 362, 364, 368, 371, 376, 377, 378, 379, 390, 414, 429, 479, 481, 482, 514, 518, 525, 526, 530, 540, 542, 546, 547, 557, 569, 570, 579, 582, 588, 604, 607, 631, 633, 638, 641.
—— Maude, 531.
—— Mores, 586.
—— Nich., 80, 89, 128, 155, 156, 166, 167, 174.
—— Rad., 166.
—— Ric., 126, 390, 421, 443, 474, 478, 480, 481, 485, 502, 513, 515, 516, 520, 528, 533, 534, 540, 543, 544, 552, 567, 571, 581, 585, 598, 609, 619, 620, 621, 625, 627, 628, 629, 630, 631, 633, 634, 636, 637, 638, 647, 649, 650, 651, 652, 653, 654, 662, 665, 737, 780, 781, 783, 798, 800, 806, 809, 830, 831, 832,
—— Rob., 53, 174, 209, 212, 239, 365,

424, 431, 436, 443, 478, 481, 482, 483, 513, 520, 522, 528, 532, 533, 534, 540, 542, 543, 547, 553, 693, 713.
Smyth, Rob., sen., 742.
—— Tho., 78, 81, 82, 87, 90, 125, 128, 153, 156, 160, 161, 166, 167, 179, 184, 209, 210, 233, 240, 249, 351, 414, 570, 603, 636, 637, 638, 641, 642, 643, 645, 647, 649, 650, 651, 652, 663, 665, 667, 668, 676, 677, 679, 682, 684, 686, 690, 691, 692, 694, 695, 697, 698, 701, 704, 706, 711, 713, 714, 715, 717, 718, 720, 721, 723, 724, 725, 726, 727, 728, 737, 739, 740, 746, 759, 766, 768, 770, 773, 778, 780.
—— Tho., jun., 711.
—— Tho., de Gosford-strete, 249.
—— Will., Smythe, 161, 167, 179, 209, 240, 247, 250, 478, 480, 482, 665, 676, 688, 690, 691, 693, 694, 695, 696, 697, 699, 700, 701, 704, 706, 707, 711, 715, 717, 718, 720, 721, 722, 723.
—— Will., of ffolsshull, 406.
Smythyar, Joh., Smythyer, Smythear, 447, 450, 461.
Snape, Alanus, 212, 241, 248.
Sneyd, Joh., Sneyde, Sneide, 788, 797, 798, 801.
Snodon, Hen., 608.
Solant, Will., Solans, Solond, 179, 212, 239.
Solyhull, Joh., Sohihull, Solsell, 53, 78, 87, 164.
Somer, Ric., Somur, 87, 125, 139, 153, 158, 161, 209, 240, 248.
Somerfelde, Joh., 696, 700.
Somerland, Joh., 699.
Sompton, Joh., 167.
Sorche, Tho., 127. [? Serche.]
Sore, Joh., 240.
Sothurnewode, Joh., 237.
Southam, Ric., 20, 22, 36, 38, 39, 41, 42, 44, 50, 54, 58, 60, 64, 67, 69, 70, 71, 73, 79, 82, 84, 90, 91, 98, 99, 102, 104, 105, 109, 111, 112, 113, 117, 119.
—— Ric., jun., 39, 41.
—— Rob., 134, 137, 138, 141, 143, 144, 146, 151, 152, 156, 159, 167, 171, 172, 176, 184, 186, 187, 188, 189, 193, 194, 195, 197, 198, 200, 201, 202, 204, 206, 208, 213, 217, 218, 219.

Southam, Will., 79, 87, 126, 154, 163, 179.
Sowle, Will., 167.
Sowre, Joh., 212.
Spake, Joh., 161, 183.
—— Ric., 242, 243, 246, 247, 255, 256, 266, 277, 278.
Spaldyng, Gilb., 449.
Span, Joh., 166. *See also* Sponne.
Sparke, Joh., Sparkes, 535, 761.
—— Ric., 262.
Sparrow, Joh., 566.
Sparrye, Ric., 783.
Speke, Guy, 736, 761, 789, 794, 796, 800.
Spencer, ——, Spenser, 531.
—— Hugh, 78, 125, 153, 160.
—— Johanna, 237.
—— Joh., 39, 60, 80, 120, 126, 133, 143, 150, 152, 156, 160, 169, 177, 185, 188, 189, 193, 194, 195, 197, 198, 201, 202, 204, 206, 207, 210, 211, 217, 221, 226, 227, 228, 229, 230, 236, 251.
—— Rob., 168.
—— Tho., 126, 154, 177, 210, 219, 236, 244, 251, 647, 686, 689, 690, 692, 693, 694, 695, 696, 697, 699, 700, 701, 706, 707, 711, 714, 717, 725, 728, 739, 740, 742, 746, 766, 767, 768, 769, 770, 773, 778, 779, 780, 782, 783, 788, 789, 790, 793, 794, 795.
—— Will., 80, 88, 127, 154, 156, 164, 166, 174, 177, 210, 212, 236, 239, 251, 286, 314, 317, 318, 371, 377.
Sperpoynt, Joh., 126.
Speyght, Ric., 561.
Spicer, Juliana, Spycer, Speycer, Spyser, 126.
—— Ric., 129, 155, 167, 168, 176, 213, 219, 241, 244, 247, 266, 269, 351, 573.
—— Tho., 213, 241, 248.
Sponer, Tho., Sponar, 166, 167.
—— Will., 252.
Sponne, Joh., Spon, Spone, 240, 249.
—— Tho., 665, 666, 667.
—— Will., 239.
Sporyour, Rob., Sporyar, Sporiour, 80, 88, 164, 177.
—— Tho., 46, 80, 88, 160.
—— Will., 241, 250.
Sprag, Joh., 560.
—— Will., 560.

Squyer, Joh., Swquyer, Squiar, Sqwyer, 209.
—— Tho., 237, 247, 314, 317, 318, 337, 338, 351, 365, 368, 370, 373, 376, 390.
Stafford, Alicia, 179.
—— Joh., sen., 39, 45, 60, 76, 78, 82, 85, 87, 90, 105, 120, 125, 129, 131, 132, 134, 138, 143, 150, 152, 153, 160, 167, 176, 180, 184, 207, 209, 213, 218, 219, 221, 222, 226, 227, 228, 229, 230, 231, 232, 233, 235, 240, 242, 245, 249, 252, 253, 254, 255, 256, 259, 262, 266, 267, 270, 271, 272, 275, 344, 376.
—— Joh., jun., 209, 240, 249.
—— Joh. de, 5.
—— Tho., 131, 166, 176, 184, 213, 249, 266, 285.
—— Will., 177, 249, 285, 286, 305, 307, 310, 312, 313, 316, 317, 320, 321, 323, 332, 333, 334, 335, 336, 337, 338, 339, 343, 344, 347, 351, 352, 358, 360, 362, 364, 367, 369, 370, 371, 375, 376, 377, 378, 382, 385, 387, 388, 389, 390, 409, 411, 414, 415, 416, 419, 842.
Staffordshire, —, Staffordshyr, 87.
—— Hen., 238, 314, 368, 371, 376, 390 406, 478, 481, 482, 514, 516.
—— Ric., 79, 126, 154, 162, 179, 212, 219, 238, 243, 249.
Stalow, Joh., 376.
Stalworth, Will., 452.
Stamford, Agnes, 87.
Stanbury, Joh., 163, 248.
Standiche, Tho., 89.
Stanlake, Ric., 82, 90.
Stanley, Joh., 127.
—— Rog., 210, 237, 252.
Stanlowe, Joh., 318, 354, 390, 432, 533, 535.
Stanniforde, Agnes, 78.
Stansfeld, Joh., Stanfeld, 153, 162, 180, 213, 241, 269.
—— Margareta, 167.
Stapulford, Tho., 248.
Starky, Jch., 88.
—— Rad., 163, 318.
—— Rog., 88.
Staunton, Joh., 82, 90, 514.
—— Wil., 38, 39, 41, 51, 82, 90, 117.
Stedeman, Will., 250.
Stele, Joh., 728, 760.

Stele, Rad., 319.
—— Will., 542.
Stere, Joh., 161.
Sterlyng, Ric., 209.
Stevons, Joh., Stephens, Stevyns, 313, 315, 316, 333, 335, 338, 339, 343, 347, 351, 352, 360, 361, 364, 369, 375, 376, 378.
—— Tho., 240.
—— Will., 369.
Stevenson, Hen., 222, 251.
—— Ric., 586.
—— Will., 608.
Steyne, Hugo, Stene, Steyn, 128, 156, 166, 174.
—— Rob., 352, 364, 421, 481, 533, 546.
—— Tho., 513.
Steynour, Joh., Steyner, 162, 179.
—— Moric., 129, 167, 176.
—— Tho., 78.
Steynton, Joh., 80, 88.
Stille, Joh., Styll, Style, Stile, Stylle, Stelle, 37, 39, 44, 51, 69, 77, 78, 81, 84, 86, 87, 90, 102, 107, 114, 115, 117, 125, 128, 132, 134, 137, 138, 140, 150, 151, 152, 155, 168, 169, 176, 214, 241, 841.
—— Ric., 48, 81, 89.
—— Will., 41.
Stirropp, Will., Styrope, Sterope, 718, 721, 736, 742, 761, 768, 780, 781, 783.
Stivechall, R. de, 12.
Stiward, Styward, Joh., 761.
—— Ric., 164.
Stocke, Will., 126.
Stockton, Benedict, Stokton, 164, 177, 204, 249.
—— Joh., 81, 82, 90, 167.
—— Rob., 81, 128.
—— Will., 81, 89, 128, 165.
Stodealf, —, 477.
Stoke, Joh., Stokes, 130, 143, 165, 167.
—— Nic., 161.
Stokes, Ric., Stokys, Stokkes, Stookes, 352, 363, 365, 368, 377, 422, 430, 482, 535.
—— Rob., 212, 238.
Stone, Ston, —, Stoone, 162.
—— Hen., 161.
—— Hugo, 89.
—— Joh., 166, 266.
—— Ric., 212, 252.
—— Tho., 78, 87, 125, 153, 161, 170, 209, 221, 228, 240, 247.

Stone, Will., 48, 49, 81, 89, 156, 166, 174, 179, 239.
Stoneley, Abbot of, Stonley, 378, 380.
—— Alex., 449.
—— Joh., 153, 162, 165, 174, 179, 184, 210.
—— Ric., 573.
—— Will., 39, 78, 87, 128, 155, 168, 176, 183.
Stonew, Tho., 219.
Storiour, Will., 251.
Stow, Joh. de, 5.
Straughton, Chris., 561.
—— Will., 561.
Straunge, Joh., Strange, Strawnge, 125, 131, 169, 177, 184, 209, 237, 278, 280, 285, 292, 296, 310, 312, 317, 339, 343, 351.
—— Tho., 81, 89, 128, 166, 174, 243, 268, 313, 343, 351, 355, 364, 368, 371, 376, 379, 390, 421.
Street, Gal., Strette, Strete, Streyte, 213.
—— Joh., 87, 210, 238, 248, 376.
—— Tho., 236, 248.
Strelley, Sir Rob., 380.
Stretford, Will., 175.
Stretton, Joh., 45, 60, 78, 85, 87, 125, 138, 142, 150, 153, 158, 161, 180.
—— Rob., 238, 251.
—— Tho., 160, 199, 240.
Strong, Joh., Stronge, 571, 581, 599, 600, 602, 603, 604, 609, 621, 623, 625, 627, 629, 630, 631, 632, 634, 636, 637, 638, 641, 642, 643, 645, 647, 649, 650, 651, 652, 653, 654, 665, 667, 668, 676, 677, 762, 765.
Stryngar, Tho., 248.
Sturdy, Rob., 165, 212.
—— Tho., 163.
—— Will., 160.
Styff, Rob., 156, 169, 178, 242.
Style, Stylle. See Stille.
Suker, Joh., Suger, 155.
—— Will., 214, 240.
Sulby, Tho., 129, 166, 176.
Sutton, Joh., Suetton, 78, 87, 125, 127, 153, 155, 162, 168, 170, 175, 180, 663.
—— Laur., 168.
—— Rog., 364, 390, 429, 478, 481, 513, 520, 522, 539, 540, 542, 563, 571, 623, 629.

Sutton, Tho. de, 3, 6.
Swalynton, Nic., 241, 251.
Swan, Humph., Swane, Swanne, Swayne, 146, 247, 318.
—— Joh., 207, 344, 355, 365, 368, 370, 377, 421, 424, 431, 435, 482, 485, 514, 520, 528, 532, 533, 534.
—— Tho., 79, 88, 126, 128, 143, 154, 155, 159, 163, 168, 176, 178, 214, 240, 241, 247.
—— Will., 37, 39, 46, 77, 79, 84, 88, 91, 102, 107, 111, 117, 120, 122, 126, 130, 131, 132, 134, 135, 136, 137, 138, 140, 141, 143, 150, 152, 154, 157, 159, 163, 169, 171, 172, 178, 180, 184, 185, 186, 187, 188, 189, 192, 193, 194, 195, 197, 198, 200, 201, 202, 204, 206, 207, 208, 213, 217, 219, 221, 222, 226, 228, 230, 231, 232, 233, 235, 242, 243, 245, 246, 247, 252, 253, 254, 255, 256, 259, 262, 266, 267, 270, 271, 272, 275, 276, 277, 278, 279, 280, 841.
Swanlond, ——, Swonland, 155.
—— Joh., 165.
—— Tho., 167, 175.
Swete, Ad., Swette, Suett, Swett, 39, 60, 79, 88, 98, 107, 111, 120, 126, 133, 139, 142, 143, 150, 152, 154, 157, 163, 169, 196.
—— Joan, 196.
—— Pet., 213.
Sweteng, Tho., 238.
Swettenham, Joh., Swetnam, Suettenham, Suetham, Swettnam, 211, 238, 246.
—— Raufe, 608.
—— Tho., 79, 88, 126, 134, 139, 142, 154, 163, 178, 187, 189, 197, 198, 200, 202, 204, 207, 213, 217, 228, 229, 230, 242, 247, 271, 573.
—— Will., 39.
Swettglade, Tho., Sweteglade, 210, 237, 247.
Swetton, Joh., 106.
Swift, Joh., Swyft, Swifte, 238.
—— Rob., 579, 768, 770, 778, 780, 789, 794, 796, 800.
—— Will., 210, 237, 251.
Swyllington, Rauff, Rad., 642, 651, 653, 665, 667, 676, 686, 688.
Swyndryver, Will., 212.
Syde, Tho., 812.

Symondes, Joh., Symiond, Symon, 81, 125, 153, 162, 203, 213, 241, 249.
Symson, Joh., 237, 249, 366.
Syngere, Joh., 352, 573.
—— Ric., 573.
Syvetare, Will., Syvekar, 168, 175.

Taberet, Rob., 482.
Takeby, Ric., 237. (?) *Read* Tokeby.
Talontes, Joh., Talont, Tallontes, Tallantes, 706, 711, 724, 726, 728, 737, 738, 739, 740, 746, 759, 762, 766, 767, 768, 769, 770, 778, 780, 781, 782, 783, 788, 789, 790, 793, 794, 795, 796, 797, 798, 800, 803, 806, 809, 811.
Tanner, Ric., 793.
Tasker, Rob., Taskar, 336, 344, 352, 363, 376, 379, 390, 422, 478, 513.
Tate, Joh., Tatte, 3, 22, 39, 48, 60, 83, 84, 89, 98, 120, 122, 127, 133, 134, 138, 143, 144, 151, 155, 158, 842.
—— Jos., 80.
—— Margareta, 238.
—— Tho., 128, 154, 163, 164, 170, 179, 210, 242, 246, 314, 337, 343, 351, 354, 360, 362, 366.
Taverner, Hen., Taunerer, Tauerner, 128, 168, 176.
—— Ric., 210, 237.
—— Will., 167.
Taylour, —, Tayler, Tailour, Taylliour, Tailler, Tayller, 163.
—— Alanus, 175.
—— Elias, Elys., 162, 165, 180.
—— Galf., 166.
—— Hen., 165, 212, 238, 248.
—— Joh., 161, 176, 239.
—— Nic., 167, 168, 240, 249.
—— Pet., 162, 180.
—— Ric., 161, 166, 179.
—— Rog., 82, 90, 129, 167, 176, 213, 240, 242.
—— Tho., 796, 797, 798, 800, 806.
—— Will., 174, 237, 252, 356, 368, 370, 371, 379, 388, 416, 419, 421, 423, 424, 431, 435, 436, 473, 481, 482, 485, 503, 514, 518, 520, 521, 522, 528, 533, 543, 544, 557, 567, 571, 579, 581, 584, 585, 588, 598, 599, 601, 602, 842.
Tebbe, Joh., 167, 176.
—— Tho., 167.
Tedde, Joh., 581.
—— Ric., 166, 176, 213.

Tedde, Rob., 566.
Tedyngworth, Joh., 161.
Temple, Clement, Tempull, 736.
—— Joh., 163.
Tenwynter, Ric., 693.
Tewe, Joh., 167.
—— Tho., 165, 174.
Tewkesbury, Ric., 481.
Teynton, Ric. de, 3.
Thed, Rob., Thede, 79, 88, 126, 154, 163, 171, 178.
Thirkell, Hen., Thirkyll, 721, 725, 728, 737, 740, 746, 768, 770, 778, 780.
Thomas, Lambert, 817, 818.
—— Ric., 184.
—— Rob., 125.
—— Tho., 153, 161, 179, 184.
—— Will., 179, 241, 248.
Thomason, Joh., Tomson, Thomson, Tomsone, Thompson, 251, 377, 724, 725, 793, 794, 796, 797, 798, 800, 801, 803, 806, 812.
—— Rauffe, 608.
—— Ric., 129, 166, 176, 210.
Thomlynson, Joh., 480, 543.
Thorn, Tho., 390.
Thornton, Joh., Thronton, 128, 166, 212, 237, 285.
—— Rog., 248.
—— Will., 82, 129.
Thorp, Joh., Thorpe, 168, 177, 227, 241, 248.
—— Rob., 319.
—— Tho., 79, 88, 127.
—— Will., 482.
Thressher, Joh., 542.
Threston, Tho., 180.
Throgmorton, Joh., 806.
Throwley, Joh., Throughley, Throweley, 371, 482, 535, 547, 552, 566, 579, 581, 582, 588, 598.
Thrumpton, Joh., Thrompton, 286, 314, 316, 317, 318, 320, 321, 334, 338, 345, 347, 351, 360, 361, 362, 365, 368, 370, 371, 372, 373, 375, 378, 385, 387, 416, 419, 421, 423, 424, 431, 435, 436, 443, 473, 474, 481, 482, 485, 503, 514, 515, 516, 518, 520, 521, 522, 524, 528, 530, 532, 533, 534, 539, 540, 541, 542, 543, 544, 547, 552, 553, 557, 563, 567, 571, 579, 581, 582, 584, 585, 587, 588, 590, 598, 599, 600, 842.
—— Rob., 315.

Thrustans, —, Thrustanus, 78, 87, 125, 153.
Thurston, Tho., Thruston, 125, 153, 158, 162.
Thymeler, Tho., 180.
Thystelton, Hen., Thysilton, Thistelton, Thestilton, 238.
—— Will., 337, 338, 339, 351, 357, 360, 365, 368, 370, 373, 377, 378, 382, 385, 389, 390, 416, 419, 421, 424, 431, 435, 443, 473, 482, 485, 503, 514, 516, 520, 522, 843.
Ti —. *See* Ty —.
Tibottes, Will., Tybbottes, 425, 531.
Tillett, Will., Tylet, Tyllet, Tyllottes, 280, 629, 630, 631, 634, 682, 684, 686, 687.
Tipler, Alice, 717.
Tirvile, Joh., Turvile, 162, 179.
—— Will., 239.
Todde, Joh., 546.
Toftes, Joh., Toft, 5.
—— Joh., jun., 161.
Togoode, Will., 252.
Tokeby, Ric., 169, 177, 210, 249, 256.
—— Tho., 79, 88, 128, 156, 165, 174, 212, 239, 248, 256.
Tolas, Will., Colas (?), 60, 78, 79, 87, 154, 163.
Toly, Ric., 209.
Tomkyns, Ric., 167.
Topclyff, Rob., Topclyffe, 302, 333, 334, 337, 339, 351, 352, 362, 369, 373, 385, 388, 390, 416, 419, 423, 424, 473, 483, 503, 514, 516, 518, 522, 528, 532, 533, 534, 540, 542, 547, 553, 563, 571, 582, 588, 598, 599, 600, 601, 602.
Toppe, Joh., Top, 252, 382.
—— Rob., 239, 252.
Torfote, Rob., Torsote (?), 251, 319.
Torsote, Rob., Torfote (?), 251, 319.
Tote, Joh., Toty, Totte, 315, 318, 344, 345, 351, 356, 365, 368, 377, 379, 403, 406, 482, 514.
—— Ric., 668, 676.
—— Tho., 647.
Tough, Tho., Towh, 162, 179, 212, 238, 246.
Touney, Joh., 573.
Towers, Joh., Toures, Tours, Towres, 532, 533, 534, 540, 542, 547, 553, 563, 571, 582, 588, 589, 599, 600, 601, 602.
—— Will., 638, 647, 649, 667, 676, 682, 684, 686, 687, 688, 690, 692, 673, 694, 695, 696, 697, 699, 700, 701, 704, 706, 707, 711, 713, 714, 715, 717.
Towker, Tho., 238.
Townnesyend, Hen., Townesynde, Townesende, 540.
—— Huw, 352.
—— Ric., 634, 636, 637, 665, 679, 690, 692, 693, 694, 695, 696, 697, 699, 700, 701, 704, 706, 707, 711, 714, 715, 717, 718, 720, 721, 722, 723, 724, 725, 726, 727, 728, 737, 738, 739, 740, 759, 766, 767, 768, 769, 770.
Travas, Joh., 209, 240.
Tredsyn, Hen., 161, 183, 238, 249.
Trentham, Ric., 80, 88.
Treves, Joh., 160.
Trowley, Joh., 377.
Trueman, Joh., Trewman, 176, 241.
—— Rob., 82, 90.
—— Will., 166, 213.
Trumper, Joh., Trumpere, 59.
—— Will., 566.
Trussell, Tho., Tressell, 667, 688, 690, 691.
Tryg, Walt., Trygg, Trig, 82, 90, 129, 166, 176, 213.
Tryske, Will., 167.
Turnour, —, Tournour, Tourner, Turner, Tornour, 239, 356, 818.
—— Joh., 240.
—— Ric., 351, 357, 368, 377, 391.
—— Rob., 239, 344, 815, 831.
—— Tho., sen., 78, 87, 126, 481, 483, 514, 516, 531, 533, 563, 571, 579, 601, 602, 606, 609, 623, 627, 628, 629, 633, 634, 636, 637, 638, 641, 642, 645, 647, 650.
—— Tho., jun., 600.
Turselyan, Joh., 364.
Turvey, Joh., 315, 317, 318.
Tuttebury, Will., Tuttbury, 167, 211, 239, 247.
Twenge, Joh., Twyng, 5.
—— Juliana, 78.
Twygge, Joh., Twyg, 352.
—— Ric., 164, 177.
Twys, Magister Joh., 229.
Tybeaudis, Will., 282.
Tyburton, Isabella, 165.
Tyder, Joh., 503.
Tygen, Galf., Tigon, Tygull, 165, 174, 212.

Tykell, Joh., 166.
Tyler, Joh., Tiler, Tylor, 480, 491, 492.
—— Math., 153, 161.
—— Perkyn, Pet., 78, 87.
—— Ric., 154, 162, 209, 218, 352.
—— Rob., Tyler, 78, 87.
—— Tho., Tiler, 126, 154, 158, 163, 170, 179, 212, 238, 251, 269, 285, 286, 315.
—— Will., 164, 177.
Tylleot, Tho., 541. (?) *See* Tillett.
Tylinge, Chr., 800, 801, 803.
Tyllesley, Joh., 318, 365.
Tylston, Joh., 608.
Tyndale, Will., 421, 423.
Typper, Hen., 169.
Typpyng, Pet., 781.
Typtoft, Joh., 73.
Tyrrel, Walt., Tirrell, Tyrell, 78, 87, 153, 162, 179, 209.
Tyrsethion, Joh., Tyrsitheon, 160, 240.
Tyrvyn, —, 212.

Vaghan, Sir Tho., 420, 426.
Vale, Will., of the Vale, 242, 246, 247.
Vauasour, Joh., 474.
Verdon, Ric., 5.
Vgan, Dav., 530.
Vikers, Rog., de Wykyn, 403, 406.
Virgyn, Eleanora le, 162.
Vlnere, Ric., 210.
Vmbem, Will., Vnbem, 82, 90.
Vndurwoode, Johanna, Vndurwod, Vnderwode, 126.
—— Joh., 79, 88, 143, 154, 163, 177.
—— Will., 736, 761, 767, 768, 779, 782.
Upton, Hen., Opton, Vpton, 79, 88.
—— Joh., 88, 126, 165, 237.
—— Sim., 126.
Vyell, Tho., 448.
Vynsent, Joh., 168, 176.

Wade, Chris, Waid, Wadde, Wayd, 690, 694, 704, 706, 707, 711, 714, 718, 721, 722, 724, 725, 726, 737, 738.
—— Joh., 78, 87, 153, 161, 179, 781, 789, 790, 796, 800, 803.
—— ffran, 809.
Wadley, Joh., 239.
Wadmore, Joh., Woodmer, 82, 90.

Wadylove, Will., 483.
Wait, Joh., Weyt, Weytt, 694, 706, 711, 714, 718, 721.
—— Ric., 59.
Wake, Joh., 238.
Wakefelde, Joh., 248.
—— Tho., 167.
Walcote, Will., 352, 354, 365.
Walden, Is., 840.
—— Rob., 789, 790, 794.
Waldyf, Joh., 167.
Wale, Ad., 238.
—— Will., 829.
Wales, Rog., Walles, Walees, 79, 88, 120, 127, 133, 142, 156, 166, 174, 212, 239, 634, 636, 637, 652, 654, 665, 666, 667, 668, 676, 677, 682, 686, 687, 688, 690, 691, 692, 693, 694, 695, 697, 699, 701, 705, 706, 707, 711, 713, 714, 715, 717, 718, 720, 721, 722, 723, 724, 725, 726, 727, 728, 731, 737, 738, 739, 740, 742, 746, 759.
Walford, Ric., Wallford, 81, 89, 120, 128, 166, 174, 212.
Walgrave, Johanna, Walgraue, Waldegraue, Wallgraue, 167.
—— Joh., 38, 39, 44, 52, 77, 86, 90, 103, 107, 108, 117, 129, 134, 143, 152, 176, 185, 195, 197, 198, 201, 202, 204, 208, 213, 217, 218, 219, 221, 222, 226, 227, 228, 229, 230, 231, 232, 235, 243, 245, 252, 253, 254, 255, 256, 262, 266, 267, 268, 270, 271, 272, 275, 276, 277, 278, 279, 280, 283, 284, 285, 293, 296, 301, 302, 304, 305, 306, 307, 308, 310, 311, 312, 316, 317.
—— Laur., 318, 321, 334, 337, 343, 345, 352, 358, 362, 372, 373, 375, 376, 385, 389, 483, 570, 626, 627,
—— Tho., 129, 139, 142, 166, 176. 213, 241, 242, 266, 285, 286.
Walkeden, Tho., 818. (?) Walkelen.
Walkelen, Walkleyne, Margareta, 162.
—— Ric., 39.
Walker, —, 368.
—— Hen., 40, 82, 86, 90, 129, 167, 582, 588, 598, 602, 619, 624, 631, 634, 637, 638, 641, 647, 651, 653.
—— Hugh, 480.
—— Isabell, 81, 89, 128.
—— Joh., 161, 166, 239, 250.
—— Rad., 314, 343, 369.
—— Ric., 45, 78, 87, 741.

Walker, Rob., 248.
—— Tho., 174, 211, 241, 249, 371, 429, 482.
—— Will., 81, 176, 239.
Wall, Ed., 573.
—— Hen., 619, 623, 624, 645, 647, 651, 652, 653, 654, 663, 665, 666, 667, 668, 676, 677, 679, 682, 684, 686, 688, 690, 691, 692, 694, 695, 696, 697, 698, 700, 701, 704, 706, 707, 711, 713, 714, 715, 717.
—— Joh., 81, 126, 152, 155, 175, 214, 240, 250, 737.
Walland, Joh., 781.
Waller, Tho., 450, 451.
Walley. See Whalley.
Walsale, —, 167.
—— Johanne, Wallsall, Walsale, 268.
—— Joh., 6.
—— Ric., 164.
—— Tho., 79, 87, 126, 154, 162, 178.
—— Will., 268.
Walsch. See Welsch.
Walton, Hen., 79, 88, 156, 169, 178.
—— Joh., 344.
—— Ric., 542.
—— Will., 164, 177.
Wamburn, Joh., 166, 203, 204, 212, 239, 248.
Wappenbury, Joh., Wiponbury, Wapunbury, 211.
—— Tho., 178. See also Wyponbury.
Ward, Joh., 81, 89, 127, 128, 155, 168, 176, 213, 781.
—— Tho., 164, 177, 237, 329, 355, 356, 357, 369, 409, 411, 483, 547, 552, 566, 604, 605, 624, 645, 653, 667, 686, 693.
—— Will., 126, 156, 168, 177, 204, 214, 663.
Wardelowe, Joh., Wardelove, 534, 535.
—— Tho., 481, 483, 514, 528, 531, 532, 542, 547, 553, 562, 567, 571, 603, 604, 606, 609, 619, 621.
Wardrope, Joh., Waredrop, Wardropp, Wardroper, 211, 239, 351, 377.
Wardyghter, Tho., 167.
Waren, Cris., Warene, Waryn, Waroun, 714, 718, 720, 727, 728, 737, 738, 739, 740, 742, 746, 759, 766, 767, 769, 770, 773, 778, 779, 780, 781, 782, 783, 788, 793, 794, 796, 798, 806, 809, 811.
—— Joh., 128, 156, 165.

Waren, Ric., 81, 89, 127, 166.
—— Tho., 128, 154, 162, 167, 176, 212, 213, 219, 238, 243, 256, 269, 285, 286, 315, 317, 336, 377, 541, 570, 602, 630, 631, 632, 636, 638, 641, 642, 643, 645, 647, 649, 651, 652, 654, 662, 664, 665, 667, 668, 676, 677, 679, 682, 684, 686, 688, 691, 692, 694, 695, 696, 697, 698, 700.
—— Will., 126.
Warmyngton, Hen., Warmynton, 161, 209, 240, 252.
—— Joh., 247.
—— Tho., 79, 88, 126, 133, 154, 160, 162, 179, 201, 202, 204, 207, 208, 212, 217, 218, 221, 226, 227, 228, 235, 238, 243, 245, 246, 253, 255, 256, 259, 262, 266, 267, 270, 271, 272, 275, 276, 277, 278, 279, 280, 283, 284, 285, 293, 296, 301, 302, 304, 305, 306, 307, 310, 312, 320, 321, 332.
Warnour, Ric., Warner, Warnar, 737, 742, 780, 782, 797, 806.
—— Tho., 80, 88, 214, 240, 316, 318, 414.
—— Will., 365, 482, 513.
Warrant, Joh., Warront, Warraunt, Warant, 37, 39, 40, 44, 58, 60, 67, 69, 79, 84, 88, 91, 98, 102, 106, 109, 111, 112, 114, 115, 117, 122, 126, 134, 137, 138, 140, 141, 147, 148, 149, 150, 152, 154, 159, 163, 169, 171, 172, 178, 184, 186, 187, 188, 189, 192, 193, 194, 195, 198, 201, 202, 204, 206, 207, 208, 213, 217, 226, 227, 228, 229, 230, 231, 232, 233, 235, 242, 243, 252, 255, 256, 259, 262, 266, 267, 270, 272, 275, 276, 277, 278, 279, 280, 283, 284.
Warwyke, Will., Warrwyk, Warrewyk, Warrewik, Warwyk, Warrewyke, 78, 87, 129, 167, 176, 213, 219, 222, 228, 230, 232, 235, 241, 243, 245, 247, 252, 253, 254.
Wastell, Tho., 164, 177.
Waterfall, Joh., 154, 163.
—— Ric., 164, 248.
Watford, —, 343.
—— Hen., 88, 126, 156, 168, 177, 210, 237, 247, 255, 256, 269, 285.
—— Joh., 127, 153, 161, 178.
Watres, Joh., 160.

Name Index.   913

Watstyd, Hen., 79.
Wattes, Joh., 352, 363.
—— Rob., 89, 161, 180.
Webbe, Wyll., 365, 530.
Wedon, Agnes, Weedon, 38, 81.
—— Johanna, 79, 88.
—— Rog. de, 6.
Wedurby, Joh., of Leycetur, 292.
Welbek, Joh., 241.
Weley, Ric., Welye, 180.
—— Will., 3.
Wellford, Hugo, Welford, Wallford, 161.
—— Joh., 37, 39, 41, 44, 45, 60, 67, 78, 84, 87, 102, 117, 128, 166, 176.
—— Ric., 81, 89, 128, 133, 156, 165, 174, 842.
—— Rob., 87.
Welles, Joh., Wellys, Wellis, 87, 88, 166.
—— Ric., 161, 163.
—— Rog., 126.
—— Tho., 153, 162, 178.
—— Wal., 212.
—— Will., Wellys, Welles, 79, 81, 89, 128, 156, 158, 165, 171, 174, 212.
Wellynton, Joh., Wellyngton, 81, 89, 128.
Welsch, Joh., Walsch, Walshe, Welsh, 483.
—— Rob., 653, 654, 663, 665.
—— Will., 81, 89.
Welsheman, Dav., Walsheman, 164.
—— Will., 449.
Welton, Ric., 6.
Went, Ric., 239, 250.
Wentbrygg, Hen., 20.
Weram, Johanna, 165.
West, Joh., Weste, Weist, 166, 696, 700, 736, 770, 779, 780.
—— Step., 540.
—— Wal., 608.
Westbury, Agnes, Westbere, 168, 175, 241.
—— Joh., 356, 522, 529, 531.
—— Will., 164.
Westley, Hen., Westeley, 164, 177.
—— Joh., 81, 89, 128, 156, 166, 174.
—— Ric., 641, 642, 643, 645.
—— Will., 169, 189, 210, 237, 286, 377, 778, 779, 780, 781, 783, 788, 789, 790, 793, 794, 795, 796, 797, 798, 800, 801, 803, 806, 809, 812.

Weston, Guy, Wyston, Wiston, Whiston, 175, 240, 246, 250, 256, 276, 279, 280, 284, 285, 393, 301, 304, 305, 306, 307, 310, 312, 316, 317. 320, 321, 334, 366.
—— Hen., 132, 160, 176.
—— Joh., 36, 44, 69, 71, 82, 90, 98, 99, 102, 110, 114, 117, 122, 123, 128, 141, 144, 155, 168, 176, 238.
—— Nyc., 351.
—— Pet., 20.
—— Rob., 51, 82, 90, 129, 166, 213, 241.
—— Rog., 480.
—— Will., 212.
Westron, Tho., Western, 238, 318.
Wether, Hen., Wethers, Wyther, 694.
—— Ric., 665, 666, 667, 682, 684, 686, 687, 692, 693, 695, 696, 697, 699, 701, 704, 706, 707, 711, 713, 714, 715, 717, 718, 720.
—— Tho., 700.
Wetoft, Joh., 168. *See also* Whittofte.
Weuer, Egid., Wever, (Wene?), (Wooner?), (Wouer?), 78.
—— Geo., 81.
—— Hen., (Wene?), 161.
—— Paul., 166.
—— Ric., (Wouer?), 81, 90, 155, 168, 176, 214, 241.
—— Ric., (Wooner?), 128.
—— Sampson, 166.
—— Tho., 125, 153, 160, 167, 175.
—— Tho., (Wene?), 161.
Whalley, Joh., Walley, 37, 44, 60, 69, 78, 83, 84, 85, 87, 91, 98, 102, 106, 109, 111, 114, 117, 122, 125, 130, 131, 134, 137, 138, 140, 143, 144, 150, 152, 153, 157, 161, 171, 172, 179, 184, 185, 186, 187, 188, 189, 192, 193, 195, 198, 200, 201, 202, 204, 208, 210, 238, 256, 259, 266, 267, 270, 271, 272, 275, 276, 277, 278, 279, 280, 283, 284, 285, 293, 296, 301, 302, 304, 305, 306, 307, 310, 312, 316, 317, 320.
Whamburn, Joh., 74.
Wharton, Cris., Whayton, 696, 713, 736, 761, 769.
Whetecroft, Tho., 165, 175.
Wheteley, Tho., Whaiteley, Whayteley, Wheyteley, Wheateley, 728, 778, 779, 780, 783, 788, 793, 794, 795, 796, 797, 800, 803, 809, 812.
Wheton, Joh., 337, 339.

Whirley, Joh., Wirley, Wyrley, 212, 242, 247.
—— Tho., 46, 60, 79, 84, 88, 111, 127, 134, 138, 140, 143, 144, 148, 149, 150, 152, 156, 169, 171, 172, 177, 186, 187, 189, 192, 193, 194, 195, 197, 198, 200, 201, 202, 204, 207, 208, 210, 217, 219, 221, 222, 227, 228, 229, 230, 232, 235, 237, 243, 245, 246, 252, 253, 254, 255, 259, 262, 266, 267, 270, 271, 272, 275, 276, 277, 279, 284.
Whitacre, Raignald, Whitacur, Whitaker, 89, 128.
—— Rob., 211, 239, 249.
Whitchurch, Will., 60.
White, Elizabeth, Whight, Whyte, Whit, 279.
—— Hug., 637.
—— Joh., 39, 81, 90, 128, 155, 164, 166, 177, 178, 213, 242, 251, 252, 319, 337, 365, 842.
—— Mat., 39, 68, 81, 89, 107, 111, 120, 133, 134, 137, 138, 141, 143, 151, 152, 156, 166, 174, 842.
—— Moric., 166.
—— Ric., 211, 212, 222, 236, 251, 561.
—— Tho., 128, 155, 168, 176, 214, 222, 228, 235, 241, 245, 250, 251, 256, 266, 270, 279, 318, 624, 628, 637, 641, 642, 649, 651, 652, 654, 663, 665, 666, 667, 668, 676, 677, 679, 686, 688, 690, 692.
—— Will., 176, 214, 239 241, 244, 246, 269, 333 366, 421, 443, 691.
Whiter, Will., 161.
Whitgreve, Joh., 422, 430, 482, 532.
Whithall, Randull, 479.
Whitehede, Joh., Whitehed, Whythed, 210, 237, 247, 482, 542, 566, 581, 582, 605, 606, 609, 623, 625, 627, 628, 629, 630, 631, 633, 634, 636, 637, 638.
—— Ric., 79, 88, 432.
Whithiford, Will., 90.
Whitley, Joh., Whettley (?), Wytley, 39, 79, 88, 126, 156, 168, 177, 210, 222.
Whitside, Tho., Whiteside, 127, 155, 164, 175, 211, 241.
Whittawer, Joh., 211.
—— Reg., 156, 165, 174.
Whittofte, Joh., Whittoft, 214, 241, 250.

Whytehals, Hug., 318.
Wi ——. See Wy ——.
Wicam, Will., Wycam, Wykam, Wykham, Wykan, Wickam, Wikame, Wicame, 601, 604, 605, 624, 628, 630, 634, 636, 637, 638, 641, 642, 643, 645, 647, 649, 650, 651, 652, 653, 654, 663, 665, 666, 668, 676, 679, 682, 684, 686, 688, 690, 691, 692, 693, 694, 695, 696, 697, 698, 700, 701, 704, 705, 706, 707, 711, 713, 714.
Widowe, Alicia, 166.
Wightman, Ric., 735, 736, 768, 769, 803, 805, 809, 812.
—— Will., 728.
Wigston, ——, Wygstan, Wigeston, Wygeston, 430.
—— Joh., 541, 542, 543, 547, 553, 557, 563, 571, 584, 587, 588, 598, 599, 600, 601.
—— Rog., 696, 700, 706, 711, 714, 718, 721, 725, 728, 737, 740, 746.
—— Will., Wygston, Wygeston, 53, 483, 566, 571, 579, 598, 606, 619, 622, 623, 625, 627.
Wilbye, Joh., 39.
Wilkyns, Joh., Wylkyns, 177, 210, 314, 351, 376.
—— Steph., 210.
—— Will., 40, 82, 90, 129, 166, 176.
Willaston, Will., 213.
Willcotys, Will., Wylcote, 164, 177.
Williams, Joh., Wyllyams, 239, 250.
—— Ric., 319.
Williamson, Rob., 573.
Willnale, Gal., Wyllnale, 60, 79, 88, 126.
—— Joh., 126, 166.
—— Rog., 152, 156, 160, 174.
Willmer, Pet., Wylmer, 821.
—— Tho., 653, 679, 684, 686, 689 692, 693, 695, 696, 697, 698, 704, 711, 713, 715, 717, 720, 721, 727, 728.
—— Will,, 828, 829.
Willowby, Agnes, Willouzby, Wilowby, Wyloughby, Wylouzby, 213.
—— Joh., 79, 88, 111, 117, 126, 134, 139, 140, 141, 143, 152, 154, 163.
Wilson, Ed., Wylson, 249, 351, 377, 379, 421.
—— Joh., 391.
—— Ric., 343, 344, 351, 363, 365, 377, 390, 533, 540, 546, 602, 607.

Wirdrawer, Clem., Wiredrawer, 164, 177.
—— Nic., 129, 155, 175.
Wirley. See Whirley.
Wirthyngton, Joh., Wirthynton, Wurthynton, Wyrthyngton, Worthyngton, Worthynton, 211, 236, 248, 269, 285, 286, 314, 317, 318.
Witham, Alan, Wytham. 252.
—— Joh., 154, 162, 179.
—— Tho., 177.
Withe, Mat., 128.
Withibrock, Joh. de, Withybroke, 5.
—— Rob., 89.
—— Will., 81, 89.
Withiforde, Will., Wythiford, 129, 166, 176, 213.
Wodcoke, Joh., Wodecok, 82, 90.
—— Tho., 129, 161, 167, 176, 179.
Wode, Humf., Wood, a Woode, o' the Wode, Wodde, 482, 514.
—— Joh., 125, 244, 252, 269, 542, 609, 622, 725, 728, 737, 740, 746.
—— Rafe, 482.
—— Ric., 214, 229, 232, 233, 243, 245, 246, 248, 253, 259, 262, 266, 267, 272, 276, 277, 278, 283, 284, 293, 296, 300, 301, 302, 304, 305, 306, 307, 311, 312, 313, 316, 317, 320, 321, 322, 332, 333, 334, 335, 337, 338, 339, 343, 344, 345, 347, 351, 352, 359, 360, 361, 365, 546, 570.
—— Rob. (Othewode), 240, 249, 318, 369, 371, 391, 478, 483, 514.
—— Rog., 517, 542, 543, 544, 549, 566, 594, 598, 601.
—— Tho., 390, 423, 424, 482.
—— Will., 368.
Wodecote, Joh., Wodcote, 166, 176, 213, 242, 252.
Wodeland, Joh., 314.
Wodeward, Hen., Wodward, Wadard, Wodard, 239.
—— Joh., 535.
—— Rob., 211, 236, 250.
—— Rog., 169.
—— Tho., 155, 156, 164, 175, 211, 222, 236, 247.
Wodnet, Joh., 566, 601.
Wodusbury, Will. de, 5.
Wolff, Rob., Wolfe, Wulf, 6.
—— Tho., Wolff, Wolfe, Wulf, 214, 240, 246, 247, 313, 316, 318, 337, 343, 363, 370, 377, 379.
—— Will., 3.

Wolman, Hug., Woleman, 6.
—— Will., 358.
Wolmere, Joh., Wolmer, 352, 377.
Wolpyner, Gal., Wolpynner, Woolpayner, Wulpyner, Wulpynne, 128, 155, 168, 176, 214, 241, 251, 318.
—— Joh., 377.
—— Tho., 351, 369.
Wolston, Guy, 474.
Worsley, Rauf., Worseley, 640, 687, 706.
—— Rob., 562.
Worstedman, Joh., 177.
Worthyngton. See Wirthyngton
Wotton, ——, Wutton, 162, 180.
—— Joh., 212, 483, 514.
Wright, Alex., Wryght, 3.
—— Chris., 153, 161.
—— Dav., 126, 161, 163.
—— Hen., 166, 168, 210, 237, 247
—— Hugo, 174.
—— Joh., 87, 125, 160, 166, 168.
—— Math., 81.
—— Rad., 212, 239, 249, 256, 318, 351.
—— Ric., 82, 90.
—— Rob., 82, 90, 167.
—— Sim., 166, 176.
—— Tho., 82.
—— Will., 126, 169, 177, 238, 241.
Wrobwardyn. (?) Read Wrokwarden, See Rocardyne.
Wulpyner, Wulpynne. See Wolpyner.
Wurthynton, Wyrthyngton. See Wirthyngton.
Wutton. See Wotton.
Wyche, Joh., Wiche, Whiche, 80, 127, 156, 169, 177.
—— Ric., 167.
Wydwell, Hen., 168.
Wygons, Ric., Wygens, 238, 249.
Wyke, Joh., 479.
—— Will., 541.
Wykesley, Rob., 238.
Wykyns, Steph., 422.
Wylde, Joh., Wilde, Wyldy, 78, 87, 125, 155, 158, 165, 171, 175, 211, 219, 236, 240, 247, 256, 266, 318, 344, 365, 368.
—— Ric., 360.
—— Rog., 318.
—— Rol., 794, 795, 796.
—— Will., 78, 168.
Wyldegrys, Isabella, Wildegrise, Wyldgrise, Wylgryse, Wilgrys,

Wilgres, Wyldegrice, Wylgrys, Wilgrisse, Wylgreys, Wilgris, Wilgrice, 240.
—— Joh., 146, 217, 218, 226, 229, 230, 232, 233, 235, 240, 243, 246, 252, 253, 254, 255, 262, 267, 269, 271, 276, 277, 279, 280, 283, 284, 285, 293, 296, 302, 304, 305, 306, 307, 308, 310, 311, 316, 317, 320, 321, 332, 333, 334, 335, 336, 337, 339, 343, 344, 345, 347, 351, 360, 361, 364, 367, 369, 370, 371, 372, 375, 376, 377, 378, 382, 385, 388, 389, 390, 394, 395, 416, 419, 421, 424, 443, 452, 469, 473, 474, 481, 498, 503, 504, 510, 513, 514, 515, 516, 518, 520, 521, 522, 524, 528, 529, 534, 539, 540, 541, 542, 543, 544, 547.
—— Ric., 488, 503.
—— Rob., 79, 88, 125, 163.
—— Tho., 20, 22, 36, 37, 39, 40, 41, 42, 44, 47, 54, 58, 60, 62, 64, 67, 69, 70, 71, 73, 74, 78, 82, 83, 86, 87, 91, 98, 99, 102, 103, 104, 105, 106, 107, 108, 109, 110, 111, 112, 113, 114, 115, 117, 119, 122, 125, 130, 131, 134, 137, 138, 139, 140, 141, 143, 144, 146, 150, 151, 153, 157, 159, 161, 169, 171, 172, 185, 186, 187, 188, 189, 191, 193, 194, 195, 197, 198, 200, 201, 202, 203, 204, 206, 207, 208 209, 217, 218, 219, 220, 222, 226, 227, 228, 229, 230, 469, 753.
Wylkes, Joh., 637, 638.
Wylot, Tho., Willott, 154, 162, 178, 212, 238, 248.
Wyly, Joh. de, Wilye, Willy, 3.
—— Ric., 161, 180.
—— Rog., 209.
Wymondeswold, Joh., Wymswold, Wymeswold, Wymswoold, Wymyswold, Wymynswold, 20, 42, 60, 80, 89.
—— Ric., 127, 155, 158, 164, 175, 207, 211, 236, 256, 285.

Wymondeswold, Will., 22, 37, 40, 50, 51, 52, 60, 61, 69, 77, 86, 92, 100, 106, 107, 108, 109, 115, 117, 121, 129, 133, 134, 137, 138, 143, 151, 160, 166, 171, 176.
Wynchestre, Tho., 162.
Wyndull, Tho., Wyndall, 236, 248.
Wynfeldon, Joh., 165.
Wyngode, Will., 167.
Wynhale, Johane, 531.
Wynnesdon, Joh., Wynsden, 212, 239, 366.
Wynwyke, Joh., Wynwyk, 168, 176.
Wyponbury, Joh., Wypenbury, 155, 165, 236, 247. See Wappenbury.
Wyresdale, Will., Wirisdale, 164, 211, 252.
Wyttoft, Joh., 175. See Whittofte.

Yale, Joh., ȝale, 211, 219, 236, 250, 286, 315, 318, 344, 345, 352, 368, 377, 379, 403, 406, 416.
Yate, Joh., ȝate, 76, 80, 89, 127, 154, 156, 158, 160, 162, 164, 169, 171, 179.
—— Ric., 179.
—— Tho., 608.
—— Will., 79, 87, 127.
Yemons, Tho., 251.
Yerdeley, Joh., Yardeley, 731.
—— Will., 81, 89.
Yerwell, Joh., 164.
Ymayne. See Imayne.
Yolyn, Rafe, 479.
Yorke, Tho., 87, 126, 143, 179.
Yong, Dav., Young, 165.
—— Joh., 79, 87, 127, 128, 155, 162, 164, 168, 171, 175, 178, 238, 250.
—— Laur., 579.
—— Tho., 327.
—— Will., 87, 166.
Yrelonde, Laur., 635.
Yrn. See Huyron.

ȝate, Will., 39, 41, 842. See Yate.

PLACE INDEX

Names of fields, streets, lanes, towns, hamlets, in the vicinity of the city and county of Coventry

Allesley, Allyslay, Alseley, 10, 15, 48, 430, 762, 823 ; -way, 49, 762.
Alltogeder-medow, 47.
Alsden-feld [? Earlsden], 48.
Alshawe, 10.
Alsorsaie, 12.
Anstey, Anstie, 354, 363, 539, 753, 827 ; *see also* Shire *in Subject Index;* -stakes, 827.
Aschaw, Asshewe, ? Assho, 48, 440, 511, 731.
Ashemore, Aschemore, 7, 10, 511 ; -feld, 51.
Asthull, Astill, 12, 749 ; *see also* Shire *in Subject Index ;* -grove, 265.
Astley, 15, 824.
Attilburgh-place, 202.

Babethorp-wast, 822.
Bablake, Babulake, 21, 157, 255, 287 ; *see also* Church *in Subject Index ;* -gate, 257, 260, 261, 262, 391; school at, 818–19.
Bagington, Baggington, Bakyngton, Bathekinton, 519, 815, : -mill, 12, 822; -weye, 510.
Bancroftes-lane, 766.
Bannefeld, 48.
Barkers-buttes, 576, 766 ; -grove, 823 ; -leys, 731, 823.
Barnacle-, Barwangle-, parke, yate, 826.
Barons-fyld, [? Barnes-feildes], 350, 500, 501, 507, 509 ; -lane, 104 ; -well, 277.
Bastell-gate, 463 ; -milne, 759.
Batemansacre, Botmansacre, Botemansacre, 4, 7, 10, 38, 51, 52, 731 ; Nether-, 762.
Bawdye-lane, 825.
Bayly-lane, 6, 37, 144, 255, 261, 267, 449, 451, 586 ; *see also* Ward *in Subject Index.*

Bedfordes-feldes, 50.
Bedworth, 16, 825 ; -heathe, 825; -way, *ib.*
Bell-orchard, 52.
Benitt-hedge, 9.
Bennettes-feild, 9, 11.
Biggyng, Bygyng, 45, 354, 540, 754 ; *see also* Shire *in Subject Index.*
Billynges-, Byllyng-, feld, feildes, 46, 336, 732.
Binley, Bynley, 46 ; -bridge, 821, 829 ; -milne -Dame, 829.
Birch-feild, 824.
Bishop-gate, -yate, -ȝate, 142, 196, 254, 345, 664, 763.
Bishopes-, Byschoppes-hay, 45, 46, 510, 576 ; -waste, 440.
Bishop-street, "Vicus Episcopi," 37, 108, 254, 259, 260, 417, 448, 451, 453 ; *see also* Ward *in Subject Index.*
Blackamoor, 16, 19.
Black Croft, 731.
Blaklane, 115.
Blaklow, 49.
Blakorchard, Blake Orchard, 49, 576, 841, note.
Boker-mill-lane, 7.
Botgrene, Botsgrene, 30, 52.
Bowyers -croft, 48.
Boyden-grove, 9.
Boyse waste, Boyswast, 16, 17, 19, 825 ; -meadow, *ib.*
Braysfeld, 48.
Bridgemeadowe, 815.
Broad Gate, Brade yaite, Brodyate, Brodeȝate, Broide-yate, "Lata Porta," 6, 37, 106, 108, 261, 392, 452, 466, 470, 586, 807 ; *see also* Ward *in Subject Index.*
Broad-well, Brodewell, 201, 277, 557, 570, 572, 663.
Broche-leys, 827.

Place Index.

Brodehocke, Brodwocke, 18, 439; -waste, 440, 510, 576.
Broke-feild, 823.
Browneshack, Brounshacke, 9, 10.
Brownes-lane, 9.
Bryches, Breches, 15, 16.
Bryghtmere-feld, 53.
Bulkington-waye, 825.
Bullryng, 83, 233, 780.
Burgess, 449.
Bushefeld-lane, 52.
Bushell-field, 9.
Butchery, Bochery, 58, 272, 741; Litel-, 233.

Callers Lane, 822.
Caludon, Calloudon, Caloughdon, Calwedon, 354, 539, 749, 753; *see also* Shire *in Subject Index;* -lane, 11; -well, 18.
Cancard Lane, 826.
Canley, 12, 265.
Cannoll Close, 822.
Catcroft-lane, 16, 825.
Catesby-lane, 361, 388, 417.
Chappell-feild, 826.
Charterhouse, 732; -leys, 439, 763.
Cheylesmore, Chelismore, Chellesmore, 108, 109, 325; -Court, 792; -gate, 261, 363, 712; -green, 48, 59, 262, 307, 338; leet of, 326; manor of, 322-8, 751, 752; officers of, 322, 324, 325; -park, 322, 507, 510.
Childrous-buttes, 576.
Chiltern-, Childern-, Chilter-, Chilterns-, leys, 7, 51, 439, 453, 467, 731.
Chirchadland, 510.
Clarkes-peice, 827.
Cobelyng-crofte, 7.
Cocks-, Cock-lane, 12, 822.
Combe-broke, 829; -pastures, 827.
Coningre, Conynger, 115, 829.
Cook-street, Coke-strete, 108, 417, 766; -gate, 33, 101, 259, 261, 447, 462, 563, 662, 664.
Corks-lane, *read* Cockslane.
Corley, 10, 14, 15, 823, 824; -broke, 16; -grove, 15, 824; -heye, 15; -wast, 18.
Corner-field, 731.
Cotes-wast, 46.
Coundon, Cowndull, Cowndulne, 7, 8-11, 14, 15, 48, 49, 823; *see also* Shire *in Subject Index;* -fields, 11;

-lane, 48, 51, 576; -way, 50; -wast, 824.
Cowe-lane, 792.
Cowles-ground, 829.
Crab-tre-feld, 47, 335, 761.
Crampy-feld, 51, 52.
Cristes-crofte, 115.
Cros-feld, 49.
Cross-cheaping, Crose-chepyng, 6, 37, 68, 104, 105, 289, 291, 389, 392, 393, 449, 452, 466, 470, 586, 590, 624, 761, 766, 793, 798; *see also* Ward *in Subject Index;* -ward, 826.
Crosse-holt, 826.
Crowe-nest, 827.
Crow-lane, 48.
Crow-mill, 208, 227, 634.
Curweyns-crofte, 49.

Danyell-, Daniell-field, 822; -grove, 46.
Deed-, Ded-lane, 50, 261, 765.
Deedmore-corner, 18.
Derne-yate, 30, 463; *see also* Bastell-gate.
Dilcockes-mill, 576, 763.
Dillotford in le Hale, 12.
Dog-lane, 259, 261.
Dounebroke, 16.
Doun-3ate, 16.
Dudmanneswell-felde, 50.
Dunstall, 826; -hill, *ib.*

Earl's-mill, Erle-myle, 108; -flod-yates, 140.
Earl-street, Yorle-streit, 5, 61, 386, 450, 586, 705, 761; *see also* Ward *in Subject Index.*
Erles-orchard, 144.
Eaton, Eton, Eyton, [Nuneaton], 17, 53; -way, 53.
Endemer, Endemore, 8, 18.
Exhall, Ecclesall, Ecleshall, Exhale, 15-17, 19, 51, 354, 540, 749, 753, 825; *see also* Shire *in Subject Index.*

Farthing-heye, 18.
Fillungley, Old, 1.
Fleete-street, 808.
Foleshill, Folkeshull, Folleshill, 16, 17-19, 51, 354, 540, 749, 753; *see also* Shire *in Subject Index.*
Four-pound-fields, 762 note.

Place Index.

Fowlesmere, 8.
Fremans-quarell, 191.
Friar-gate, -lane, see Grey-frere.
Frith-, Fryth-broke, 10 ; -feld, 48.
Fryres-garden, 345.
Fynford, 10, 11.
Fynham-ffieldes, 822.

Gallowe-, Gallows-tre-feild, 11, 14.
Geffrey-feild, 11.
Gibe-, Gybe-lane, 17, 19.
Goldy-crcfte, 49.
Goldynges-felde, 576.
Golofur-place, 261.
Goose-crcft, 732.
Gosford-, Goseford, Gosseford-gate, 227, 254, 261, 386, 457, 540 ; -green, 46, 100, 227, 346, 732 ; -street, 5, 37, 66, 149, 261, 449, 452, 453, 765 ; see also Ward in Subject Index.
Gowers-place, 202.
Grange-lane, 12 ; -peece, 822.
Grene-lane, 822.
Grey-frere-, Gray-fryre, -frer, -dunghill, 805 ; -gate, 30, 254, 261, 262, 348, 350, 425, 761 ; -lane, 6, 261, 360 ; -hospital, 628, note.
Guphill-, Guphul-, Guppylle-lane, 50, 440, 576, 823.

Hagthorne, 826 ; -waye, ib.
Hale, 12.
Hamond-feld, 48.
Hanging, 827.
Happisford-feild, 827.
Harnal, Harnale, Harnehall, Harehal, 11, 12, 254, 453, 467, 749, 754 ; see also Shire in Subject Index ; -bridge, 732 ; -field, 445, 459 ; -wast, 18.
Hasil-, Hasel-, Hasle-wood, 11, 18, 46, 53, 115, 263, 336, 440, 445, 455, 456.
Hay,- Hey-lane, 6, 261.
Henley, 11, 17, 18, 749 ; see also Shire in Subject Index ; -broke, 18.
Hethesale, Hethsall, Horsall, Hersall, [Hearsall], 46, 48, 49, 576, 731, 762, 823.
Heyne-lane [mod. Hen-], 15, 824,
Heytell, 828.
Hill-, Hul-, Hull-crosse, 50, 453, 732 ; -ffeld, 3, 48, 53, 540, 576 : Nether-, 813 ; Over-, ib. ;-lane, 7, 9, 10 ; -mill (Hulles Milne), 417, 663 763 ;

-myl-broke, 208 ; -myl-meadow, 51, 52, 53 ; -street, 449, 452, 762 ; -strete-yate, 58, 261, 662, 767 : Hullȝarde, 50.
Hobcroft, 11.
Holifast, Holynfast, 9, 10.
Holowe-wey-feild, 731.
Hoomestalles, 50.
Horewell, Horwell, 749, 754, 822, see also Shire in Subject Index ; -streame, 822.
Horlen, 826.
Howe, 17.
Hower-hyron, 822.
How-yate, 16, 825.
Hugland, 18.
Humfrey-holme, 827.

Jeffreyes-milne, 732.
Jordan-, Jurdan-well, 5, 37, 215, 217, 360, 622, 761, 765, 808 ; see also Ward in Subject Index.

Keresley, Kerusley, 14–15, 18, 48, 451, 452, 465, 469, 540, 742, 749, 753 ; see also Shire in Subject Index.
Kewe-ditche, 824.
Kinges-feildes, 732.

Lady-lane, 17.
Lazars-lane, 576.
Lebroke (?), 17.
Ledyat-lane, 15.
Leicestur-, Leycester-way, 51, 826.
Litel-graunpesfeld, Litle-Grauntpursfeild, 115, 762.
Litle-heath, 16.
Litle-park, Lytull-parke, 30, 37, 47, 96, 101, 260, 321, 351, 775, 790 : -street, 5, 196, 201, 217, 261, 277, 450, 622, 792 ; -gate, 30, 261, 386.
Litle-wast, 12, 13.
Locardes-lane, 18.
Long-croft, 4, 38, 46.
Long-forde, 827.
Ludlow-feld, -feildes, 46, 732.
Lufay-grene, 16, 825.
Lullehurst-lane, 18
Lychefeldys-feld, 49.

Madgeleys, 17, 19.
Marden-, Merdon-siche, 12, 822.
Margeries ffeild, 824.
Marl-felde, 49.
Maydons Mille, 576.

Maynerds-feild, 15.
Merstone waye, 16, 19.
Mich-graunpes-feld, 115.
Miles-medowe, 18.
Mil-hay, 50.
Mill-, Myl-lane, 5, 37, 261, 532.
Miry-, Myree-feild, 48, 440. 511, 576, 731 ; -hull-grove, 51.
Mordiffe, 17.
Mote-house, 823.
Muche-, Miche-, Myche-park, 47, 145, 351 ; -street, 5, 37, 196, 215, 261, 361, 450, '752, 765 ; -ward, 502 ; *see also* Ward *in Subject Index.*
Myriholt, 7.

New-feld, 46.
New-gate, Newe-yaite, Nu-yate, -ʒate, 30. 33, 47, 57, 113, 145, 345, 350, 375, 386, 440, 471, 513, 540, 576, 763, 775, 798.
Newe Rent, 664.
Newland, 15, 18, 489 ; -parke, 824.
New Street, 5.
Nightingale Lane, 822.
Norman place, 11.
Northbrocke, 9.
Nuneaton, Nuneeton, 46, 480 ; -way, 52.

Old-broke, 824.
Old-forlong, 826.
Ouerheye, 15.
Ounettes-forthe, -ford [? Quentesford], 8, 18, 53.

Pakes-croftes, 51, 52.
Palace-Yard, 811 note.
Palmer-lane, Palmers-lane, 157, 232.
Panyer, the, 393.
Paradise, Paradyse, 47, 351.
Parke-myll fforde, 47, 510.
Parsonnys-feld, 48.
Peggmyll, 510.
Pennymore, 53.
Penyfeildes, Penny-feld, 48, 731.
Pepur-lane, 261.
Percies-felde, 50.
Pere-tre-feld, 50.
Picardes-croft, 731.
Picardypere-field, 732.
Pit-feild, Pyt-feildes, 731, 761.
Pody-, Podyng-, Poody-, Puddinge-croft, 4, 38, 43. 48, 259, 261, 262, 800 ; -little, 761.

Pokebroke, 9.
Popyng-pitte, 389. *Read* Podyng-pitte.
Preistes-wood-end, 16, 19, 825.
Prestes-feld, 440.
Priors-feild, 9, 823 ; -orchard, 447, 462 ; -waste, 46, 350, 375, 439 note.
Priory, 196, 208, 229, 231, 233, 263, 445, 454 ; -gate, 662, 664, 759 ; -milne, 455, 759.
Pykedpere-crose, 53.
Pynley, 749, 754.

Quarell-feild, 732.
Quenes Crosse, 822.
Quetesforde, [? Que[n]tesford], 115.

Radford, 7-8, 51, 53 354, 453, 467, 539, 732, 749, 753, 762, 763 ; *see also* Shire *in Subject Index;* -mille, 576 ; -croft, 52 ; -way, 51, 52.
Rad-man Rowe, 827 ; -wall, *ib.*
Red-ditch, Redde-diche, 31, 59, 119, 186, 201, 202, 208, 227, 231, 360, 361, 609, 622, 702, 727.
Redeslowe, 18.
Rie-field, 731, 762.
Rodehall, 448.
Ropers-feilders, 762.
Rowdiche,-ditche, 16, 825.
Rowe of okes-feild, 762.
Ruydinges, 12, 17, 18.

Sacherscroft, 115.
Saint-, Seynt-Anne Grove, 47, 510 ; -Fraunces yait, 712, *see also* Grey-frere-gate ; -Johns-brige, -briges, 6, 663, 765, 800 ; -Nicholas-leys, 763 ; -street, 448, 451 ;-Osburn pole, 463.
Sandeley-grene, 12.
Sandipit-lane, Saynt put-lane, Seynt pit-lane, 8, 52.
Schocher-, Schochers-, -Skorchers-feld, 50 ;- -lane, 7, 10.
Sewall-pament, -pauement, 45, 46.
Shel-felde, 50.
Sherbourne river, Schirburn, Schyre-burn, Shirburn, Shurburn; 12, 46, 47, 107, 189, 208, 257, 347, 349, 440, 500, 501, 507, 509, 510, 513, 719, 800, 811.
Shilton, Shelton, Shulton, 354, 539,

749, 753, 826; *see also* Shire *in Subject Index*; -Asmedowe, 827; -Crosse, 826.
Shittcroft-corner, 19.
Sholder of mutton close, 732.
Shortley-feld, 335.
Shortt-croft 828.
Shottes-field, 7; -lane, 7, 9.
Shuckmore, Shokemore, ? Sugmore, 8, 731; -croft, 52.
Sidells, Sidoles, 16, 19.
Sidenhall-, Sydnall-, Sydenhall-yate 19; -wood, 16, 19, 825.
Sitcheford, 828.
Skynners-buttes, 513; -croft, 48.
Slepers-lane, 452, 466.
Smercote water-mill, 16, 824.
Smithford-, Smythford-brige, 108, 339; -street, 6, 37, 157, 288, 339, 450, 451, 453, 470; -ward, 586, *see also* Ward *in Subject Index*.
Somerlesow-, Somerlesue-, Somerles-buttes, 338, 762; -feld, 48; -lane, *ib.*
Sowe, Sow, 17, 354, 539, 754; *see also* Shire *in Subject Index*; -bridge, -broke, 828, 829; -feild, 827, 828; -lane, 46; -meare, 828; -wast, *ib.*
Spetelmore, 446, 459.
Spicerstoke, 699.
Spitelcroft, 115.
Spon, Spanne, Span, Spane, Spone, Sponne, "de Sponna," Spoone, 48; Barre, *see* gate; -bridge, 10, 307, 663; -broke, 48, 50, 800; -cross, 50; -ende, 762; -gate, 254, 570, 589, 792; -market, 338; -street, 6, 37, 257, 259, 262, 451, 453, 467, 586; *see also* Ward *in Subject Index.*
Stake-Crosse, 17.
Stapull-, Steple-croft, 52; -feld, 8, 52.
Steppyng-stones, 731; -ston-feild, 823.
Stivichall, Stichall. Stychall, Sty-cheall, Stynchall, Stevechall, 12–14, 47, 48, 354, 403, 540, 754, 775. 818, 822; *see also* Shire *in Subject Index;* -fields, 12; -hiron, -hurne, 4, 38, 440, 511, 576.
Stoke, Stooke, 11, 45, 354, 403, 540, 754; *see also* Shire *in Subject Index.*
Strip (the), Stripe, Stripp, 18, 731, 761.
Strypes, Stryppes, 440, 576.

Styffordhale, 452, 465, 469, 510, 513.
Swannes-crofte, Swannys-croofte, 46, 115; Great-, 763; Litle, -, *ib.*
Swannes-lane, 46.
Swannes-well, 53; -pole, 190, 446 459.
Sweyns-crofte, 53.

Thamley, 7.
Thiefstake, Theefestake, Thieffestake, 10; -feild, 9; -hedge, 824; pitis, 15, 824.
Thistell-feild, 731.
Turk-ffurlong, 827
Tutburie-waye, 826.

Wall-forlong, 45.
Walsiche-lane, 18.
Warche-lane, 16.
Wardense-feild, 732.
Warensdam, 9.
Warynges-milne, 732.
Washe-broke, 827.
Watton's-feild, 18.
Welle-croft, 453, 467.
Well-street, "Vicus Fontis," 41. 108, 194, 417, 448, 449, 451, 453, 467, 543; *see also* Ward *in Subject Index;* -gate, 272, 662; -ward, 502; -yard-gate, 446, 459.
Wemen-feld, 185.
Weston, 123 note, 742; *see also* Shire *in Subject Index;* -heye, 16.
Westorchard, 21, 27, 59, 105, 194, 231, 234, 261, 272, 452, 765; *see also* Ward *in Subject Index.*
Wethersfeild, 17.
Whaburley, 48, 731, 749, 754; -feldes, 50.
Whitchurch-place, 67.
Whit-frere-milne, 350, 759.
Whitley, 46, 47, 349, 350, 354, 380, 489, 540, 626, 749, 754, 763; *see also* Shire *in Subject Index ;* -brook, 380; -Crosse, 440, 507, 510; -mill, 510.
Whitmore, Whitemore, Whittemore, 8, 11, 444, 454, 458, 471; -feld, 52; -hege, *ib.*; -park, 7, 15, 18, 444, 445, 455.
Wolpit-lediat, 19.
Wolston, 123 note.
Wolues Crosse, 440.

Woodende, 749, 754.
Wood-lane, 17, 828.
Woodmilles-heye, 10.
Wybylyns-broke, 17.
Wyken, Wykyn, 13, 17, 45, 354, 403, 540, 749, 753; *see also* Shire *in Subject Index*; -feild, 828.
Wyllenhale, 480.
Wyndmyl-feld, 50.
Wynhall-bridge, 822.

INDEX

Places outside the vicinity of the county of Coventry

Abingdon, Abyndon, 367.
Ashbourne, Assheburn, 480.
Aston, *ib*.

Banbury, Banbery, 341 note, 346.
Barnet-field, 366.
Birmingham, Brymmyngham, 96.
Boston, 86, 610.
Bridgewater, Brugewater, 346.
Bristol, Bristoll, Bristow, 260, 527, 549-52, 592, 594-5, 599-600, 610.
Burford, 493.

Chepstow, Chapstowe, 346, 359.
Chard, Cherd, 366.
Chester, 610.
Coleshill, Collyshull, Colshull, 96, 298, 300, 313 note.
"Cowalker," 562.

Doncaster, Doncastyr, 329, 330, 358 note.
Dartmouth, Dortmouthe, 340, 358 note.
Durham, Dirrham, Duram, 346, 561.

Eccleshall, Eculsale, 300.
Exeter, 610.

Feckenham, ffekenham, 405.
Fotheringay, Foderinghey, 341.
Fulbrook, ffulbrooke, 103, 152.

Gloucester, 592, 594, 595.
Grantham, Grantam, 353, 355.
Greenwich, Grenewyche, 426, 537, 539, 717.

Hampton, *see* Southampton.
Harfleur, Harflete, 121, 122.

Hull, 427, 610.
Hunningham, Honyngham, 480, 515.

Isleworth, Thistellworthe, 819.

Kenilworth, Kellengworth, Kyllyngworth, 52, 265, 297, 298, 301, 550, 822.

Leicester, Leycestre, 112, 263, 292, 301.
London, 57, 60, 83, 86, 97, 99, 112, 129, 151, 266, 283, 313, 314, 315, 327, 342, 359, 369, 380, 458, 474, 477, 478, 497, 498, 499, 502, 503, 504, 515, 525, 526, 528, 549, 550, 579, 610, 818.
" Long Collyworth," 562.
Ludlow, 408, 429, 432, 433, 435, 442, 485, 488, 489, 490, 496, 498, 504, 506, 515.
Lynn, Lynne, 359.

Middleton, 628 note.

Nantwich, -wych, 562.
Newark, Newerk, 343.
Newcastle, Newcastell, 610.
Northampton, Norhampton, 308, 309, 323, 324.
Norwich, 610.
Nottingham, Notynham, 346, 356, 358, 561.

Oatlands, Otelandes, 830.

Pembroke [*read* Pembridge], Pembrigg, 429.

Reading, Reding, 304, 331, 492.
Richmond, Rychemount, 625

Place Index.

Rochdale, 480.
Rockingham, Rokyngham, 301.
Rothwell, Rowell, *ib.*
Rouen, Roan, 130.

St. Albans, Sent Albones, 282, 313.
St. Paul's, Powlys, 359, 625.
Sandwich, Sondwiche, 86.
Sharnford, 301.
Southampton, Hampton, 432, 499, 549, 550, 610, 821.
Stafford, 560.
Stamford, Stanford, 341, 353 note.
Stoneley, 561.
Stratford - on - Avon, Stretford super Avyn, 369.

Tewkesbury, 366 note.
Totternhoe, Totnowe, 562.

Walsall, 96.
Wappenbury, 480.
Warwick, Warrewick, 103, 391, 477, 480, 799, 817.
Wellingborough, Wendlyngborough, 561.
West Bromwich, 562.
Westminster, 118, 124, 310, 320, 354, 359, 375, 384, 405, 408, 409, 414, 415, 420, 422, 424, 476, 524, 536, 537, 625, 835.
Windsor, Wyndsore, 340, 428, 833.
Woodstock, Woodstok, 493, 496.
Wootton-sub - Edge, Wotton - vndur-Egge, 76.
Worcester, 367 note, 480, 490, 592, 594, 595, 610.

York, 316, 343, 346, 527, 610.

SUBJECT INDEX

Abergavenny, Lady, and the loan, xli. *See also* Bergavenny.
Accounts, 367–71; not rendered by officers, 295; chamberlains', 34, 42, 54–5, 57, 65–6, 99, 101, 109, 116, 135–6, 194, 504; mayor's, 56–7, 98–99, 117, 121–2, 501–3, 514–5, 529–32, 587–8, xlv; wardens', 22, 66–7, 97–8, 113, 134–5, 147–9.
"Agnus Dei," musical score of the, xii.
Alchemist, 422, 856.
Aldermen, 258, 420, 586, xxvi, note; to make a census, 783–4; and conduit, 607; and constables, 692; council-house of the mayor and, xxvi; mayor's brethren, to sit in the court, 604–5; to elect ale-tasters, 725, 726, to punish idle persons, 784; to make a list of inns, 785; to remedy abuses, 652–3; to search for beggars, evil doers or vagabonds, 539, 629, 652, 677; to make wells, 548.
Ale, assize of, *see* Assize; sale of, 169, 192; by retail, not to be combined with brewing, 801; —houses, increase of, 771; resort to, 786, 808, xxviii–ix; suspect, 652, 785;— tasters, 191, 541, 677, 678, 725, 726; —wives, excessive number of, 801. *See also* Brewers, Licensing.
"Algarbe," 24, 847.
Anne Boleyn, letter of, announcing birth of a princess, 716–7, xlix.
Apparel, 680–1.
Apprentices, barbers', 225; cappers', 573, 670–1, 673, 774, 778, 792; drapers' and mercers', 655; fines of, 655, 690–1; list of, 560–3; names of, to be entered, 560, 666–7; oath of, 553–4, 559, 560; payment of, 558–9, 567; number of, 670, 687, 774, 792; tanners', 641.
Archery, 661; shooting with long bows compulsory, 652, xxviii, note.
Armour, provision of, by crafts, 244–52, xlvi; worn by watch, 253.

Arms, delivered to the captains, 345; provision of, by crafts, 244–52. *See also* Weapons.
Arragon, King of, 410.
Arras, council of, 173.
Arthur, King, figure of, in pageants, 589–90; Prince, and local disputes, 592–3, 595; pageants of welcome for, 589–92.
Arundel, Earl of, (1) Joh. Fitzalan, 129, (2) Will., 298; (3) Tho., 610.
Assize of ale, 25; of bread, 23–4, 682, 711, 799; of brick, 767; of novel disseisin, 171; of various crafts under the (so-called) Statute of Winchester, 397–401; of water, 193, 335, 389, 634, 842–3; of wine, 24–5, 386.
Attorney, 34–5, 302.
Austria, Duke of, Maximilian, 428.

Bailiffs, bill against, 198; forbidden to farm issues, 141; oath of, 224; and sub-bailiffs, 293. *See* Sheriffs.
Bakers, 220; provide armour, 251; assize of, 397; of the city, 139; non-citizen, 24, 29, 139, 717, 740, 799; contumacy of, 519, xxxii; and horse bread, 29, 385, 683, 711–2; not to keep inns, 638; and the market, 223, 385, 518; the mayor's control of, 779; mayor appoints keeper of the craft of, 669, xxxvii.
Banester, Tho., town-clerk, Scribe Z, xvi.
Barbers provide armour, 251–2; rules of, 224–6; and Sunday shaving, 185, 226, xxxiv; and spiritual courts, xxxiv–v.
Barkers, provide armour, 252. *See also* Pageants, Tanners.
Barley, 695–6, 715, 799.
"Bastard," 24, 847.
Bath, Bishop of, 129.
Beale, Rob., clerk to the Privy Council, 858.

Subject Index.

Beauchamp, Lord, 298.
Beaufort, Cardinal, 173. *See also* Winchester, Bishop of.
Beaumont, Lord, 299.
Bedford, Duchess of, (1) Anne, 103, 104; (2) Jacquette, 152, 359; John, Duke of, in the French wars, 75; concerning loans to, 63, 121, xlvii; presents to, 103, 104, 152.
Beggars, in churches, 687; licensed, 677, xxix.
Benedictines, chapter of, at Coventry, 588–9, xxxvi.
Benevolence, 409–11; commissioners of, 412–3.
Bergavenny, Joan, Lady, 104; on the commission for a royal loan, 123. *See also* Abergavenny.
Berkeley, Lord, 828.
Berners, (1) Joh. Bourchier, Lord, 298; (2) Hen., 610.
Binley, leet at, xviii, note.
Bits, not to be thrown into the Broadwell, 277.
Bitters, 847; and the Broadwell, 201, 570; charges of, 793.
"Black Book," the, 464, 837, xiii, xv.
Booth, Lau., privy seal, 297.
Bosworth. *See* Richard III.
Boteler, Joh., Scribe B, xv, xvi. *See also* Town-clerk.
Bounds, the, 7–19, 571, 821–9, 843; triers of variances about, 382. *See also* Riding.
Bowling, against, by poor craftsmen, 656; in the street, 661–2.
Brakemen, 181, 182 and note, 183, 847–8.
Bredon, friar John, 35, 97; and the standard measures, 854; suit concerning, 228.
Brewers, 25, 111, 675; abuses of, 771; assize of, 397-8; not to use hops, 683; to brew when malt is dear, 637, 724; excessive numbers of, 771, 838; strangers and the calling of, 839. *See also* Ale, Licensing.
Brewsters' gild, 234, 623, 855.
Bridge, the, to be made, 157; grant to the, 191.
Briscow, Will., 349–50, 376–81, 440, 489–91, 494, 498–501, 505–10, xliii; aged men's verdict and the claim of, 349, 380–1, 490; bounds of land claimed by, 509–10; commons support the mayor in the dispute with, 376-7; riot caused by, 494; and the Prince's Council, 440, 490, 494, 501, 505–6; wilfulness of, in appealing to the common law, 499, 500.
Bristol, dispute between, and Coventry concerning tolls, 592, 594–5, 599–600.
Brittany, Duke of, 409.
Brokesby, Barth., 123.
Buckingham, Duchess of, 299; Duke of, 297, 299; at the "Angel," 308; bond of Joh. Rogers to, 309. *See also* Stafford, Earl of.
Bull-baiting, 58, 83.
Burgoyne, Rob., Sheriff of Warwickshire, 857.
Burgundy, Margaret, Duchess of, 359; Duke of, 359, 409.
Burleigh, Lord, 830.
Burton, Hum., town clerk, MSS. of, ix.
Butchers, 25–6, 32, 108, 556, 572, 623, 683, 715, 808; provide armour, 250-1; assize of, 398: craft of, 684–5, 739, 770, 797, 803, xxxvii, xxxviii; craft-keeper of, chosen by mayor, 669, xxxvii; non-citizen, 26, 780, 795, 797, 803, 807–8, xxxvii–viii; non-craftsman and retail trade, 689; refuse, disposal of, 43, 271–2, 389, li; rules of, inspected, 27; and wholesale trade, 338, 557–8. *See also* Hides, Scalding-house, Tallow.
Butter, regratry of, 361.
Butts, to be made, 196, 338, 572.

Cake-baker, and craft of bakers, 723.
Cakes, 697.
Calais, Calys, 130.
Caldecote, xvii, note.
Candles, sale of, reserved to certain butchers, 685; to chandlers, 632, 643, 651; out of the city, 648, 650, 651, 703; in the city, by strangers, 705, xxxix. *See* Prices.
Canterbury, Archbishop of, (1) Hen. Chicheley, 73; (2) Joh. Morton, 579.
Cappers, craft of, ruled by twelve, xl; and the cardmakers, 707–10; and piece-work, 773-4, 781, 792; rules of, 572–4, 670–3; and stolen yarn, 774. *See also* Apprentices, Church, Journeymen, Pageants, Searchers.
Caps, not to be made of cloth yarn,

729; flocking of, forbidden, 633, 645, 702. *See also* Searchers.
Cardmakers, provide armour, 251; and sadlers, painters and masons, 220; dispute among, 205–6; rules of, 205; associated with cappers, 707–10, 726. *See also* Pageants.
Cards, 182; playing-, 786.
Card-wiredrawers. *See* Wiredrawers.
Carpenters, craft of, allowed, 695, 806; contribute to coopers, 767; to tilers, 185; of the country, 807; fines of, 281; unemployed, 807; wages of, 21, 806–7. *See also* Pageants.
Cathedral of S. Mary, the, 448; the Lady Chapel of, 452; rents to the cellerar, pittancer, prior's treasury, and sacristan of, 448–53.
Census, of persons and store of food stuffs during dearth, 674–5; of inhabitants of wards, with reference to unemployment, 783–4.
Chains, for defence of streets, 257, 261.
Chamberlains, finances of, 333, 339, 347, 546; and the making of the fortifications, 33, 385–6; and the opening of the pastures at Lammas, 333–4; and the murage, xlv. *See also* Accounts, Office, Riding, Saunders, Lau.
Chandlers, 400, xxxix; bakers, fishmongers, shearmen and the calling of, 634, 651; craft of, to be formed, 643, 703; keepers of, 703; to be ruled by the mayor, 387; to serve the city sufficiently, 646; to contribute to the smiths, 547. *See also* Candles, Pageants, Prices.
Chapel, royal, dean of, 299; of S. Chad, 10; of S. Christopher, 376; of S. George, xxxiii; of S. Margaret at Gosford Green, *see* Hermitage; of S. Mary Magdalen, 570; of S. Thomas, or the cappers', *see* Church, S. Michael's.
Charcoals to be sold in lawful sacks, 766.
Charter, 100; of Edward, the Black Prince, 323, 325; of Joh. Garton's land, 144–6, 855; of Henry I, 323 and note; of Henry III, *ibid.*, of Henry VI, 266; payment for, 221; of Isabella, 325; of James I, xxiv; of Ranulf, 323.

Chester, or Coventry, Bishop of, (1) Will. Heyworth, 123; (2) Reg. Butler, 297; (3) Joh. Arundel, 592, 593, 594, 595; Ranulf, Earl of, 12, 323.
Cheylesmore, Court, 792; Jurisdiction of court of, dispute concerning, 323–8; manor of, 751; park of, arrest in, 322; steward of, 327. *See also* Edward IV, Leet.
Chimneys, wooden, forbidden, 549.
Church, affairs of, secular control of, xxx; bells, 335, 338, 585; clock, 335, 338, 522; daily service in, by priests of the crafts, 544–5, xxxi;— of S. John the Baptist at Bablake, 287; priests of, 264, 318;— of S. Michael, 460–1, 472; canopy over high altar in, 131–2; door of, verses on, 566; Henry VI attends mass at, 264–5; parish of, 12; porch of, and cloth market, 281; chapel of S. Thomas, or of the cappers in, 708, 726, xxxi note; vicar of, Dr. Hinton, 835; — of S. Nicholas, 8, 52; Trinity — 97; S. Mary's altar in, 52, 53; parish of, 8; Percy's chantry in, 50; vestments, 110.
Churchwardens, to give in their accounts, 296, xxxi; of S. Michael's Church, 110, 446, 460.
Churchyard, filth in, 23, 372; of S. Michael's Church, 185, 460, 472, 588, 759, 792; right to lop trees in, 446–7, 460; of S. Nicholas, 30; of Trinity, 759, 792.
Cirencester, Abbot of, 297.
Clarence, George, Duke of, intercedes for Coventry, 381; jewels of, in pledge, 381–2, 420–1, 855–6, xlviii; and the Earl of Warwick, 358, 359.
Clinton, Lord, 311.
Cloakbearer, 775.
Cloth, 633, 659; breadth of, 776; dyeing of, 698; length of, 188; making, searching and sealing of, 656–61, 687, 721–2, 724, 727; sale of, 100, 104, 281, 565; stretching of, 660–1; unsaleable, purchase of, 791. *See also* Walkers, Weavers.
Clothier, 689, 776–7.
Clothmakers, 181, 182; loans to poor, 658–9; and spinners, 640, 658.
"Cok-fytyng place," 196.
Common box, 600; keys of, to be kept

Subject Index. 927

by four elected commoners, **600–1**, xlv.
Common labour at fortifications, **258**; to cleanse the river, **227**.
Common, of pasture, in Hazelwood, **445, 456**.
Commons, **28, 45–54, 191, 729–37, 782–3**, xliii–iv; and butchers, **769, 792–3**; covenant concerning broken, **49**; enclosure of, **46, 47, 104, 375, 439–40, 576, 577, 633, 641, 679–80, 719–20, 729–37, 760–4**: as gardens, **50–1**; opening of, **115, 633, 692, 788–9, 843**; riots concerning, **350, 491–7, 504**; and the prior, **46, 350–1, 515**; stint of cattle on the, **438, 789**, xliv; surcharging of, **100, 340, 348, 438–9, 730**. See Briscow, Gild, Hospital, Saunders, Lau.
Conduit, **108, 157, 312, 338, 606**; keepers of the, **517**; locking up of, **208, 584**; obstructed, **105, 189–90**, repair of, **586**; regulations concerning water from, **232, 517, 548, 788, 808–9, 812**; tapping the, **21, 549**.
Constables, **42, 132, 137, 650, 782**; and arrests, **58**; names of, **421–2**.
Conyers, Lord, **610**.
Cooks, **26, 111, 220**; provide armour, **252**; assize of, **398–9**. See also Pageants.
Coopers' craft, **699**; contributes to carpenters', **306**, of the country, **272**. See also Pageants.
Cordeners, **681, 705**; assize of, **401**. See also Shoemakers.
Corn, **780**; forestalling of, **666**.
Cornwall, Dukes of, **747**, xix. See also Edward, the Black Prince.
Coroner, **701**; election of, **676**; fee of, **281**; oath of, **274–5**; jurisdiction of, extends through Cheylesmore, **325**; clerk of recognizance of debts, **275, 854**. See also Statute Merchant.
Corvisers, provide armour, **249**; dispute with weavers, **203–4**. See also Pageants, Shoemakers.
Council, the, xxiii–v; disobedience to, **647–8**; of the city and labour questions, **784**; common, **420, 681, 835–7**, xxv–vi, xxvii note; and the Forty-eight, **421**; Saunders and the, **564**; general, **31, 32**; grand, of mayor and aldermen, xxiv; the king's, **71–3, 297, 692**; mayor's,

C. LEET BK.

44, 69, 111, 183–4, 204, 205, 206–7, 485, 584, 587; orders of, **22–3, 33–4, 35**; secrecy of, **516**; weekly meeting of, **516, 571, 599**; the Prince of Wales', **487**; and local disputes, **440, 441, 511–2, 592, 593, 594, 595–8**; the Privy-, **830, 858**. See also Forty-eight.
Council-house, S. Mary Hall, **376, 379, 486, 587, 705**; election in, **620**; book of the leets in, **653**; body of the mayor and alderman, xxvii note.
Coundon, leet at, xviii note.
Court, **190, 224, 274, 548, 804, 853–4**; baron, of Cheylesmore, **325**; of the city, the fortnightly, the king's, of the mayor and bailiffs, the Portmanmote, **34, 59, 223, 294, 296, 322, 325, 548, 604–5, 699–700**; county, **274, 756**; spiritual, **303**, xxxiv; of Statute-Merchant, see Coroner; suit in a foreign, **20–1, 28, 118, 194, 281, 294, 581, 790**; jurisdiction of the city, with regard to the trial of rioters, **494, 495**. See also Leet, Session.
Courtesy of England, II, vii, **268**.
Coventry, derivation of, IV. vi; officers of, party in the treaty of the Princess Mary's marriage, **610**; seal of, **857**.
Cox, Captain, library of, li.
Crafts, apprentices of, **655–6**; by-laws of, copied in the Leet Book, xxxi, note; inspection of, **29, 32, 170, 418, 641, 645–6**; contributions of, to pageants, **555–6, 558**; and the corporation, xxxi–xli; and spiritual courts, **303**, xxxiv; exclusiveness of, xl; fines of, **222, 585, 623, 641, 646, 654–5, 690–1, 745**; localization of the, xlii, note; maintenance of mutual quarrels among, **27**; masters of, and the mayor, xxxvi–vii; membership of, compulsory, **724, 790–1**; and military equipment, **244–52, 582–3**; and municipal office, xxxii note, xlii note; oaths of, **418, 654**; oligarchy in, xl–xli; searchers of, xxxi; suppression of, butchers', xxxviii; dawbers', **653**; dyers', xxxv. See also Apprentices, Gilds, Journeymen, Pageants, Victuallers.

3 P

928 Subject Index.

Croft, James, 830.
Croftes, Ric. and Clarence, 855.
Cromwell, Crumwell, de, Lord, 73.
Cross, in Cross Cheaping, the, 55, 57, 68, 289, 775; fish sold near, 651.
Cuckstool, 59, 186, 188.
Curriers, assize of, 401; to work outside the walls, 302, 312.

Dacre, Lord, 610.
Danby, Lord Chief Justice, and the Cheylesmore dispute, 325, 326.
Dawbers, craft of the, and rough masons, suppressed, 653 ; wages of, 21, 806-7.
Deer-slaying forbidden, 27.
Derby, Earl of, 610.
Devonshire, Earl of, 130, 298.
Ditch, common, in the Cross Cheaping, inspection of, 622 ; town, cleansing of, 54, 254, 256, 258, 259-60, 261, 662 ; filth and nuisances in, 118, 130, 140, 628 ; making of, 121. *See also* Redditch, Sanitation.
Dogs, 361.
Doomsday, pageant of, 300.
Dragon and elephant, 857.
Drainage, xxviii, note.
Drapers, provide armour, 246-7 ; apprentices of, 655 ; assize of, 401 ; and municipal office, xxxii note, xlii note ; and the searching of cloth, 657. *See also* Pageants.
Drapery, the, 566, 567 : cloth, linen and mercery sold in, 100, 104, 223, 361, 565.
Ducks in the street, 27.
Dudley, Lord, 298, 325, 491.
Dunster, 856.
Durham, bailiff of, beheaded, 346, xlix ; Bishop of, 73.
Dye, deceitful, 698.
Dyers, 28, 31-2, xxxii, xxxiv-v ; craft of, provide armour, 247 ; and "blacklegs," xxxv ; not contributary to pageants, 556; oaths of, 418 ; ordinances of, *ibid.* ; organization of, attempt to crush, 697-8, 704, 714-5 ; reconstruction of, 795. *See also* Saunders, Lau

Earl's-half,—part, 752, xviii.
Edgcote Field, battle of, 346 note.
Edward the Confessor, figure of, in pageants, 287-8, 392.

Edward III, 746, 752.
Edward IV, and the alchemist, 422, 856; charter of confirmation of, 747-59 ; of pardon, 381, 383 ; and Cheylesmore dispute, 322-8 ; and Clarence's jewels, 420-1 ; at Coventry, 316, 326; flight of, 359, xlix; letters from, 314, 314-5, 315-6, 319-20, 322-3, 328-9, 330-1, 340, 341-2, 342-3, 345-6, 353-4, 373-5, 383-4 ; 402-5, 409-11, 413, 420 ; 422, 423-4, 425-6, 426-7, 428, 474-7, 492, 496, 499-500 ; from Prince Edward sent to, 366-7 ; and local troubles, 328-31, 492, 494, 496, 499-500 ; money demanded by, 403, 408, 409-13 ; at Nottingham, 358 ; oath of allegiance to, 367 ; franchises redeemed from, 369, 370-1, 388 ; at Stratford-on-Avon, 369 ; troops for, 317-8, 342-4, 353-4, 355-8, 369, 477-89, 505. *See also* March, Earl of.
Edward, the Black Prince, charter of, 323, 325 ; made Duke of Cornwall, 747.
Edward, Prince, of Wales (Edward V) 359, 407, 432, 436, 442, 492, 506, 509, xlviii ; council of, xlix ; letters to and from, concerning Briscow, Saunders, military and other matters, 428-9, 432-5, 441-2, 484-5, 486-7, 488, 489, 493, 493-6, 498, 501, 505-6 ; levy in name of, 477, 484, 505 ; livery of, for soldiers, 485 ; oath to, 394 ; reception of, 390-3. *See also* Council.
Edward, Prince of Wales, 288 ; marries Anne Neville, 358; letter from, 313, 366-7.
Egynton, John, dyer, xxxv.
Election, of searchers by cappers, 663 ; of a new chamberlain, 620 ; of clavers, 600-1 ; of officers, 22 *et passim;* of a recorder, 635-6, 642.
Elephant, " Olyvaunt," 657, 658, 677, 857.
Elizabeth, Queen (Woodville), 336, 393, 407-8 ; takes sanctuary, 359, gift of venison from, 405-6.
Elizabeth, Queen of Henry VII, buried at Westminster, 625.
Elizabeth, Queen, letter of, 819-21, 833.
Ely, Bishop of, 129.

Subject Index. 929

Empson, Sir Ric., *see* Recorder.
Enclosure of Little Heath, 13. See *also* Commons.
Essex, Earl of, (1) Hen. Bourchier, 610 ; (2) Rob. Devereux, 858.
Essoins permitted, 137.
Everyingham, Sir Harry, 313.
Exeter, Bishop of, 297, 324 ; *see also* York, Archbishop of ; Duke of, (1) Tho. Beaufort, 73 ; (2) Hen. Holfort, 297.

Fairfax, Sir Guy, 527.
Falconbridge, the Bastard, 358, xlix.
Fee-farm, of £50 a year, 62, 751, 793 and note, xix ; from the prior and convent, 751–2.
Feudal labour, boon-work at Finford, 10–11, xliii.
Fifteenths, collectors of, 120–1, *et passim* ; inhabitants not to collect, in the county, 197.
Finances, xliv–xlv ; scheme for bettering the city's, discussed by wards, 630.
Fines, for not obeying the mayor's summons, 31, 157, 170 ; in the mayor's accounts, 587. *See also* Crafts.
Fineux (ffyneux) Chief Justice, 579. *See also* Fynyowes *in* Name Index.
Fire, leather buckets for fear of, 549 ; —hooks, 414
Fish, cutting up of, 312., 635, 652 ; -hooks, 181 ; inspection of, 29, 646–7 ; in the market, 569, 646, 651, 800 ; share of bargain in, 193.
Fishers, 220 ; assize of, 398.
Fishmongers, orders concerning, 25 28, 276, 306, 383, 555, 632, 635, 680 ; provide armour, 250 ; assize of, 382 ; keeper of, chosen by mayor, 669 ; non-citizen, 29, 33 ; make no payment to pageants, 556.
Fitz Hugh, Lord, 73.
Fleet, Lau. Saunders in the, 580.
"Foreigns," competition and exclusion of, xxxvii. xxxviii, xxxix, xl ; sellers of oatmeal, 32 ; place in the market of, 59. *See also* Bakers, Butchers, Crafts, Hides, Victuallers, Walkers, Weavers, Yarn.
Forest iron, 745 and note.
Fortifications, building and repair of, 257–62, xlv–vi.

Forty-eight, the, 57, 102, 132, 227–8, 431, xxiii, xxiv, xxv, xxvi ; hear accounts, 54, 65, 66, 101, 117 ; or common council, 421–2 ; and the common lands, 633, 692 ; commoners, 42, 626, xxv, xxvi ; or mayor's council, 44, 69 ; confirm an ordinance, 159, 160 ; ordinances of, binding on all inhabitants, 157, 520 ; confirmed by the leet, 258 ; twelve of, a quorum, 228 ; to be sufficient men, 157.
Franchises, confiscation and redemption of, 369 note, 370.
Fullers, xxxi note, xl ; distinctive mark of, 338, 640 ; mill of, at Baginton, 12, 14 ; gild of the Nativity of, and tailors, *see* Gild. *See also* Walkers.

Games, unlawful, 271, 652.
Gaoler, 254 ; not to sell ale, 142 ; to attend on the mayor, 632 ; fees of, 632, 643–4, 645 ; and prisoners and condemned persons, 130, 184, 293, 644.
Gate-house at Bishop Street, 664.
Gates, 56, 57, 58, 188, 261, 262 ; to be locked at night, 254, 669.
Genoa, paper from, xi–xii.
Gild, 364, 369, 544 ; of S. Anne, *see* Journeymen ; of Corpus Christi, 563–4 ; master of, 267, 295 ; payments by, 59, 198, 532, 681, xliv, note ; and Stratford members, 1 ; to be united to the Trinity, 722–3 ; of S. George, *see* Journeymen ; of the Holy Cross, Stratford, 1 ; of the Nativity, xxxii, xxxiii ; of the Trinity, 130, 141, 262 ; and tenure of common lands as compensation for payment of the prior's ferm, 2–6, 20, 33, 38–40, xviii ; payments by, 59, 207, 221, 370, xliv : and the gate, 188 ; master of, 267, 295, 381, 414, 415, 503, 607, xxviii ; heads list of leet jurats, xxiii ; key-keeper, 22 ; question of precedence of, and the recorder, 521, 642.
Gilds, 294 ; craft, suppression of, xxxi and note ; Saunders, a brother of both, 578.
Girdle, "gurdel," 181, 184, 849.
Girdlemen, 181, 183, 849.

Girdlers, 705-6; provide armour, 247; and cappers, 699, 701.
Glastonbury, Abbot of, 297.
Gloucester, Abbot of, 297; Duchess of, 138; Duke of, (1) Humphrey, 57, 73, 111-12; and a loan, 83-90; and Lollardy, xlviii; present to, 137-8; (2) Richard, and the Scots, 475, 505, xlviii. *See also* Richard III.
Glovers, 220.
Godiva, "goode Eve," 567, 856-7.
Grace, the hermit, preaching of, 96-7.
Grafton, Ric., printer, li.
Granborough, leet at, xviii note.
Gravenor, Hen. and the musters, 858.
Greville, Sir Fulk, commissioner for musters, 858, xlvii.
Grey of Ruthin, Lord, 298.
Grocer, assize of a, 401.
Guns of brass from Bristol, 260, 262.
Gutter, the, from the "Peacock" to the West Orchard, 231, 234.

"Hakmen," 185.
Hall, or assembly, of discreet, worthy men, or commoners, summoned to decide municipal questions, 39-40, 138, 143, 220-1, 244-6, 256-7, 266, 285, 310, 351-2, 360, 376-7, 478, 481, 485, 626; according to wards, 5-6, 60-2, 62-3, 513-4, xxiv, xxv, xxvi.
Hall, S. Mary, 42, *et passim*; municipal business transacted in, 38-40, 131, 227, 229, 323, 485; municipal property deposited in, 214, 267, 383, 600; parochial business transacted in, 110; of S. Nicholas, or Corpus Christi, 66, 110. *See also* Councilhouse.
Hardwick, xviii note.
Harrington, Sir John, 858; commissioner for musters, xlvii.
Hastings, Lord, 426; hears of Cheylesmore dispute, 325; flees with Edward IV to Flanders, 359.
Hat-makers and mercers, 545.
Hatton, Sir Chr., 830, 832.
Hay, sale of, 399.
Hemp and flax, watering of, forbidden, 811.
Henry IV, loans to, 60, 62, 64, xlvii.
Henry V, Mayor Hornby and, xlviii

and note; loans to, 37-8, 61, 62, 67; present to, on his visit to Coventry, 34, 57, 59.
Henry VI, 289; and the charter, 265, 266, 747, 749, 753; letters from, 74-5, 282, 309; loans to, 76-83, 122-30; minstrels of, 121; pays his devotions to S. Michael, 264-5; presents to, 159, 264, 292; released from prison, 359; troops for and against, 282-3, 317; visits Coventry and neighbourhood, 159, 263-6, 297, 298, 299-300, 301.
Henry VII, death of, 625, xlix; letters from, 524, 535-6, 537, 538-9, 574; and dispute concerning tolls, 550; and Princess Mary's marriage, 610, 611, 612, 613, 615; present to, 529.
Henry VIII, coronation of, 625.
Herbert, (1) Cha. Somerset, Lord, 610; (2) Sir Ric., 346.
Hereford, Bishop of, 297, 299.
Hermitage, S. Margaret's chapel at Gosford Green, 100, 118, 227, 738, xxx, xxxi.
Herring, red, 382.
Hides, butchers and, 666; of the country to bring in, 795; purchase of, by country tanners, 689; sale of, 557, 581, 585, 649, 665, 689, 694, 718, 780, 782, 811, xxxvii-viii. *See also* Butchers, Tanners.
Historia Histrionica, x.
Holy-cake, the, 417, 669, 680, 739, xxx-i.
Honington, leet at, xvii, note.
Hornby, John, loans in time of, 42, 61. *See also* Henry V.
Hospital of St. John Baptist, 18, 190, 417, 459; dispute concerning common rights over property of, 570-1; master of, surcharges commons, 438.
Houses, ruinous, 386. *See also* Rebuilding.
Howard, (1) John, Lord, later Duke of Norfolk, 359; (2) Charles, Lord, 830.
Hungerford, Hongerford, Wal., treasurer, 73, 125.
Huntingdon, Earl of, 129.

Iklynton Collar, 70.
Innholder, assize of, 399. *See* Licensing, Morality.

Subject Index. 931

Ireland, Coventry on the thoroughfare to, 858.
Iron, forest, 745 ; abuses of workers in, 180–4 ; severance of crafts working in, 183–4. *See also* Breakmen, Girdlemen, Journeymen.
Ironmongers' horses, 108.
Isabella, Queen, and Coventry, 325, 853, xviii–xix.

James I and the Sacrament, letter concerning, 834–5, xlix.
Jesus Mass, 333, 662.
Jewels, for repayment of royal debts, purchased by the prior, 70. *See also* Clarence, Loans.
Jews, house of the, and the Exchequer, 752.
Journeymen, by-laws of, 656, 687 ; cappers', 573–4, 672–3, 693, 774 ; dyers', 694, 698, 714–5, xxxiv ; gilds of S. Anne and S. George, xxxiii–iv ; number of, unlimited, 687 ; and strangers' fines, 792 ; weavers', 91–6 ; of workers in iron, 183, 185 ; wiredrawers', provide armour, 249.
Jury, attempt to corrupt, punished, 372 ; discharge from serving on, 607. *See also* Leet.
Justices of the peace, 854 ; and wages, 21, xxiii note ; and the leet, 36, xxiii note ; inspection of the river by, 348 ; head list of jury of leet, xxiii ; and rebellious citizens, 569. *See also* Mayor, Sessions.

Katharine, queen of Henry V, visits Coventry, 34 ; minstrels of, 121.
"Kayage" at Bristol demanded, 599.
Kerseys, 661.
Kervyn, Hen., and the musters, 858.
Key-keepers, or clavers, 22 *et passim*.
King's Bench, Court of the, 854 ; indictments at, 121 ; local rioters to be tried by, 492.
"Kings of Cologne," 393.
Knights of the shire, 107, 854–5.

Lammas, *see* Ridings.
Latrinæ, 194, 202, 227, xlvi note. *See also* Sanitation.
Leather, to be sealed, 683–4 ; searching of, 277, 681, 712.
Leet, xvii–xxii ; court, affeerors of,

185–6 ; bills presented to, 3–4, 31, 35–6, 105, 115–6, 180–2, 189–90, 637–8, 638, 664, xx–xxii ; business of, concluded by the council, 661 ; by-laws of, xx–xxi, xxvii–xli; on bearing of weapons, xxv note, xxvii note ; observance of, to be enforced by aldermen, 652–3; of Cheylesmore, 325, xvii, xix ; derivation of, I. xi ; fines of, 187, 624, 661, 683, 804 ; judicial aspect of, xx ; jury of, 118–19, 182 [worthy men of], 186, 682, xxii–iv ; presentments to, 581, xx ; of the prior, 462, xvii–xviii ; procedure at, xix–xx.
Leet Book, the, xi–xvi ; scribes of, 845–6, xv–xvi.
Leicester, 855, xxiii ; Earl of, Rob. Dudley, 819, 830, 832.
Letherbarrow, Rob., and the musters, 858.
Licensing of ale-houses, 771, 781, 785, 801–2, 830.
Lighting of streets, 234, 777, xxviii.
Lincoln, xxiii note ; Bishop of (1) Joh. Chedworth, 297 ; (2) Will. Smith, president of the Prince's Council, 592, 593, 594, 595.
L'Isle, Edward Grey, Lord, 487.
Livery and cognizance of Prince of Wales, 487 ; illegal, 374 ; of mayors, aldermen and sheriffs, 648, 813 ; of sergeants, 718–9.
Loans, royal, 42, 121 ; repaid by grant for church vestments, 110 ; request for, 173, 122–4 ; security for repayment of, 83, 214, 215, 216. *See also* Bedford, Duke of; Clarence, Duke of ; Gloucester, Duke of ; Wards ; Warwick, Earl of.
Lollardy, xlviii. *See also* Gloucester, Grace.
London, and ale-silver, 855 ; bakers of, and the foreigner, xxxvii note : Bishop of (1) Joh. Kemp, 73 ; (2) Tho. Kemp, 297 ; (3) Tho. Savage, 579.
Lovel, Lord, 298.
Lucy, Sir Tho., commissioner for musters, 858, xlvii.

Mace borne by the mayor before the King and Queen, 263, 298. *See also* Sergeants.

passim; of wine, 24–5, 399, 797. *See also* Market, Mayor.
Prior, of Coventry, 63, 64, 70, 101, 104, 112. 116, 117, 122, 136, 299, 375–6, 425–6, 592–3, 595–8; and Friar Bredon, 228; and S. Michael's churchyard, 185; and the commons, 438, 447, 463–4; enclosures of, 46, 47, 350–1, 510; farmed by the mayor and community, 513, 515; Ric. Croseby, 35, 123; and the preaching of Grace, 97; Tho. Deram, complaint of, to the mayor and his brethren, 443–53, 468–73; reply to, 454–468; death of, 474; disputes between, and the city, 229, 474, 489–90; as feudal lord, 8, 10–11, 13–14, xliii; and the grammar school, 190, xxx; orchard of, 447; rector, 14; lord of the soil, 445, 456–7, 471: Joh. Shoteswell, and the city wall, 463, 472, xlvi. *See also* Gild, Murage.
Priory, gate of the, 263; Henry VI at, 264; interlude or mumming at, li, lii note; treasurer of, 13. *See also* Cathedral, Minster.
Procession, at the fair, 856; at Whitsuntide, 299. *See also* Ridings.
Proclamation, the, 192; of John Leeder, 23–33; date of, 845, xxv, note; made in tenements of different wards, 764–6.

Querns, mender of, 307.
Quoiters, against, 661.

Rastell, John, printer, li.
Rates, for the refuse cart, 21, 273, 552; vacant houses to be charged for, 543. *See also* Minstrels, Murage.
Reader, Will., and the Coventry MSS. ix.
Rebuilding of houses ordered, 199. 223, 765 note.
Recorder, 32; Hen. Boteler, 283; correspondence concerning the place of, 525–8, 537; death of, 537; ill-behaviour of, punished by grant of precedence to the master of the Trinity Gild, 520–1; illness of, 524; maintains the city's liberties against Edward IV, 324–6, 327–8; and Lau. Saunders, 437, 438, 439; of Bristol, 551, 599-600; Will.

Donyngton, appointed, 157; pension and *ex officio* councillorship for, 235–6; Sir Ric. Empson, 547; and Lau. Saunders, 575, 576; Tho. Empson shares office with, 622; fee and livery of, 113, 186, 681; Ant. Fitzherbert, *see* Errata III; appointed, 628; resigned, 635; Tho. Littelton, appointed, 235; greets Henry VI, 263–4; livery and fee of, 113, 186, 681; Edw. Saunders appointed, 764; Will. Shelley, appointed, 635; resigns, 642; Ralph Swyllington, appointed, and precedence of, decided, 642; released from residence, 688; Joh. Throgmorton, appointed, 806. *See also* Name Index under Knyghtley, Edm.; Weston, Joh.; Wigston, Rog.
Red-ditch, the, 59, 119, 360, 552, 609, 622, 653, 727, 728–9; inspection of, by the mayor and leet jury, 186; quarterly cleansing of, 702. *See also* Latrinæ.
Regratery, of brewers, 192, 771; of corn-dealers, 272, of fishmongers and others, 25; forbidden, 197, 401; and forestalling, 715, 795, xxxvi note.
Richard II, pageant figure of, 391.
Richard III, letter from, 523-4; field of (Bosworth), 531, 532, xlix, 1 note.
Riding, of armed watch on Midsummer and S. Peter's Eves, 220; bonfires and, 233; contribution to, by cappers and cardmakers, 709; disturbances at, 35–6; drinking by mayor and sheriffs before, 779; number reduced to one on Midsummer Eve, 791; smiths attend, 744; of the bounds, 33, 195, 197, 348, 622; of Corpus Christi, 220, 231; at Lammas to open up the commons, 565, 567, 843; on S. George's day, 589.
River, to be cleansed, 31, 100, 208, 227, 347–8, 586, 648, 719, 800, xxviii; defilement of, 29, 91, 107-8, 417, 445, 454–5, 631–2, 721; inspection of, 91, 108, 118, 119, 130, 190, 723; to be widened, 31, 170. *See also* Sanitation.
Rivers, Lady, 300; *see also* Bedford,

Subject Index.

Duchess of; (1) Ant.Woodville,Earl, 426, 484, 485, 498, 505; flies with Edward IV to Flanders, 359; letter to, from the mayor and his brethren, 486-7; (2) Ric. Woodville, Lord, 292, 300, 325; beheaded, 346.
Robin of Redesdale, 343; fight with, near Banbury, 346.
Rochester, Bishop of, (1) Joh. Langdon, 129; (2) Tho. Savage, 577, 579.
Roos, Lord, 298.
Rouen, Roan, 130.
Rutland, Edmund, Earl of, 308; attainted, 311.

Sacrament, the, and James I, 834-5.
Sadlers provide armour, 251. *See also* Cardmakers, Pageant.
S. Christian. play of, li note.
S. Edmundsbury, Abbot of, 297.
S. George, welcomes Edward, Prince of Wales, 393; and Arthur, Prince of Wales, 590-1. *See also* Riding.
S. John's, Clerkenwell, Prior of, 298.
S. Michael on Coventry seals, 857.
S. Osburg, or Osburn, pool of, 463; vigil of, 64.
Salisbury, Bishop of, 297; Ric. Neville, Earl of, 308, 311.
Salters, measures made for, 334.
Sanitation, xxviii and note, li and note; orders to promote, concerning cleansing of streets and ditches, and depositing of filth, 23, 43, 113, 170, 217, 272, 277, 388, 425, 587, 622, 624, 631, 668, 695, 775, 792, 810; concerning pollution of rivers and gutters by sweeping streets, especially during rain, 23, 30, 418, 804; concerning the maintenance of the cart for refuse, 21, 361, 552-3, xlv; rate for, and West-Orchard bridge, 234. *See also* Butchers, Rates, Red-ditch, River.
Saunders, Lau., 430-43, 510-2, 556-7, 574-80, xliii; and the Black Book, xiii; and the surcharging and enclosure of the commons, 437-40, 511-2, 575-6; deprived of his councillorship, and forbidden to ride at Lammas, 564; a dyer, xxxv; member of gilds at Stratford and Coventry, 578, 1; and the Prince of Wales's Council, 432, 440-3, 511-12; and the prior, 438, 447, 464; in prison, 431, 437, 442, 512, 557, 576, 580; and the recorder, 438, 439; appeals to the Bishop of Rochester, 576-7; his case tried at Ludlow and London, 441, 579-80; words of, to the mayor and populace, 556-7, 575; verses written by supporters of, 567, 577-8.
Saunders, Tho., and the musters, 858.
Savoy, Duchess of, 611.
Sawyers, wages of, 806.
Say, Lord, 359.
Scalding-house, 232, 271-2, 279.
School, at Bablake, bequest to, 818-9; donation to, 840-1; grammar --, 101, 118; and the prior, 190, xxx; and Lollardy, xxx note; and Trinity gild, *ibid.*
Scotland, Journey of Henry VII to, 582, 583.
Scots, expedition against, 505; Saunders put to ransom like one of the, 567.
Scraptoft, leet at, xviii note.
Scribes, 845-6, xiv-xvi.
Scrope, le, Lescrop, Lord, of Masham, 73.
Sea-coal, 339.
Seal, city, set on the cloth, 657, 721-2; 777; common, grants under, 40, 42, 73, 157; kept in a bag, 73; in a chest, 22, 218, xxvii note; mayor's, attached to a bond, 309. *See also* Elephant.
Sealer of cloth, 657, 687.
Searchers, of cappers, 645, 663; of cloth and caps, for non-citizen work, 704, 707; of cloth, to judge work of walkers and weavers, 639-40, 657-8, 659, 660; of cardmakers, 793-4; for flocks and thrums, 660; of leather, 277, 336, 681, 712; of tile and brick, 663; of the well and river, 663; of wool, 636, 687; for yarn, 774.
Segrave, John, Lord, 12.
Sergeant, 142, 196, 739; and the chamberlains, 629; and distress, 23; of the distress roll, 169-70, 623; maces of, 83, 298; mayor's 425, 517; to serve warrants without fees, 190. *See* Sub-bailiff.
"Serpentynes," 260.

936   Subject Index.

Sessions of the peace, 187, 190, 224, 274, 548, 854; quarter —, 802, 854 ; and recorder, 525.
Sewell, Hen., and the *Black Book*, xiii ; and the musters, 858.
Shakespeare, and provincial town life, l–li ; and local religious drama, lii ; and the Warwickshire musters, 857–8.
Sharp, Tho., and the Coventry MSS. ix–x.
Shearmen, 220 ; and tailors, provide armour, 248 ; gild of the Nativity of, *see* Gild. *See also* Pageants.
Sheep, complaint concerning, on the commons, by Saunders, 438–9 ; at fair time, 770.
Sheriffs, 751, 755–6, 756–8 ; certificate of, 269–70 ; charges of, 779 ; collection of fines by, 274, 294–5 ; fines levied on neglectful, 650 ; oath of, 273–4, 750, 756 ; office of, refusal to bear, 668–9 ; and outlaws, 303 ; promise to create, by Henry VI, 265 ; and single women, 568 ; and spinners, 271 ; and the sub-baillywick, 274. *See also* Bailiffs, Courts.
Shire, of Coventry, and elections, 854–5 ; taxes collected from, 406–7, 430, 534, *et passim* ; conversion of Coventry and hamlets into the, 748–59, xix; money for soldiers from, 354, 357, 363. *See also* Sheriffs.
Shoemakers, payment of, to tanners, 687–8. *See also* Corvisers, Pageant.
Shrewsbury, Countess of, the elder, 300 ; the younger, *ibid.;* Earl of, (1) Geo. Talbot, 610, (2) 830 ; (3) Joh. Talbot, 298, 359. *See also* Talbot.
Shuckborough, leet at, xviii note.
Skins, of cattle outside houses, 279.
Skinners provide armour, 251. *See also* Pageant.
Slaughter-house, 43.
Smallwood, Hen., and the musters, 858.
Smiths, 181–2 ; provide armour, 250 ; assize of, 401 ; and goldsmiths, 685–6 ; rules of, 743–6 ; twelve discreets among, 743, 744, 745, xli. *See also* Crafts, Pageants.
Snibston, Snypston, leet at, xvii note.

Somerset, Duke of, 297.
Southam, leet at, xvii note.
Sowe, leet at, xviii.
Spain, Charles, Prince of, 611, 613, 614, 615, 616, 617, 618.
Spicer, assize of a, 400.
Spinners, boycott of, if working for journeymen cappers, 672 ; to furnish a good character, 673 ; and truck wages, 658, 707 ; and weights of wool, 243, 255, 271, 640, 658, 707, 777, xli.
Sports, forms of, orders concerning hunting, hawking, deer-slaying, and dog-keeping, 27, 630, 666, 690 ; people of Coventry engage in, 446, 458.
Stafford, Earl of, (1) Humphrey, 112 ; 129 ; *see also* Buckingham ; (2) Henry, 298, 299 ; (3) Henry, Lord, 610 ; (4) Humphrey, Lord, of Suthwyck, beheaded, 346.
Stanley, Lord, 298, 359.
Star Chamber, Lau. Saunders tried in, 579.
Starkey, Sir Hum., recorder of London, 527.
Statute-merchant, coroner's court of, 275 ; or bond, for good behaviour, by the sureties of Lau. Saunders, 512–13.
Statute of Winchester, 395–401, 855.
Steward and apprentices, 560 ; book of the, 600. *See also* Town-Clerk.
Stivichall, fragment of a deed concerning, 815–17; copying of, in a scrivener's office, 817–18 ; leet at, xviii, note.
Strangers, examination of, before settlement permitted, 785, 812 ; to put in substantial sureties, 838–9 ; treatment of, 27 ; and victualling trades, 837–9.
Stratford and Coventry, connection between, xlix–l.
Strike, 141, 151, 852, 854 ; brazen, 151, 267, 276 note; of tree, 151, 267. *See also* Bredon, Measures, Weights.
Sub-bailiff, duties of, 425 ; and writs, 293. *See* Sergeant.
Sudely, Lord, 298.
Sunday, observance of, among crafts, xxxiv and note ; work enjoined on, to smiths, 185 ; forbidden on, to cappers and fletchers, 547, 640 ;

Subject Index. 937

drinking on, 739, 812. *See also* Barbers.
Surety, contumacious tanner and pewterer, under, 569 and note.
Surrey, Earl of, 610.
Swine, 27, 170, 200 ; and the commons, 348 ; orders concerning keeping of, and swine-sties, 217, 544, 652, 803 ; and the pound, 109, 199, 787 ; slaughter of, 43.
Swordbearer, fees of, 425.

Tailors, 220 ; and shearmen provide armour, 248 ; craft of, and walkers, separation of, 234 ; gild of the Nativity of, *see* Gild. *See also* Pageants.
Talbot, John, Lord, later Earl of Shrewsbury, 104 ; ransom for, 119–20, xlviii.
Tallow, butchers and sale of, 648, 650, 651, 705, 726, 739, 797, xxxix ; and shoe-makers, 683, 811. *See also* Prices.
Tanners, assize of, 400–1 ; fines of, 641, 655 ; and purchase of hides, xxxvii–viii. *See also* Butchers, Hides, Leather, Pageant, Surety.
Taverners, 24 ; assize of, 399–400 ; sell wine against ordinance, 157.
Taxation. *See* Fifteenths, Shire, Tenths, Wards.
Teasles, fullers', 640, 851.
Tenths, 403, 408, 414–16.
Thatch on buildings, 389.
Tilers, 220, 663 ; craft of, and tilers and coopers, 743 ; and carpenters, 767 ; and millers and wrights, dissolved, 798 ; and plumbers, separate occupations, 699, 702 ; and semi-tiles, 232, 279 ; wages of, 21, 806. *See also* Pageants.
Tiles, searching of, 188.
Tiplers, and sealed measures, 683, 713.
Tiptoft, Typtoft, Joh., 73. *See also* Worcester, Earl of.
Titchbourne "Crawl," 856.
Toll, dispute concerning, with Bristol, Gloucester, and Worcester, 549–52, 592, 594–5 ; determined by the recorders of Bristol and Coventry, 599–600 ; freedom from, of Coventry and Godiva, 567, 856–7 ; at Southampton, 302, 550.

Town clerk, 130 ; and apprentices, 553–4 ; Tho. Banester, xvi ; Symkyn Birches, 192 ; John Boteler, 474, 603, xv ; Baldwin Porter, 686, *et passim* ; Joh. Porter, elected, 605. *See also* Steward.
Town's-end, town-ends, cleansing of the, 334–5. *See* Sanitation.
Towton, Battle of, 315, 316.
Tremayle, Master, recorder of Bristol, 527.
Tripartite indenture, between Isabella, the prior, and the mayor, 444, 445, 454, 456, xviii–xix.
Tunstall, Sir John, at Whitsuntide procession, 299.
Turners and coupers of the country, 272.
Twelve, the, xxiii and note, xxiv, xxv.
Twenty-four, Council of, 323, 572 ; leet jury of, and electors, xxi–xxvi ; in other towns, xxiii ; overlook leet bills, 31.

Upholders, 191, 852.

Vagabonds, xxix ; search for, and expulsion of, 538–40, 568, 652, 658, 712 ; spread reports, 374.
Vaughan, Sir Rog., beheaded, 359 ; Sir Tho., the prince's chamberlain, 419, 420, 426, 855.
Victual, not to be bought by hucksters, 115.
Victuallers, 23–26, xxxv–vii ; offend against the assize, 386–7 ; and the leet jury, 682 ; mayor one of the, 738, 794 ; rules of, to be inspected, 27. *See also* Prices, Strangers.
Villeins, boon-work of, at Finford, 10–11.

Wages, assessment of, 21, 806–7, 810 ; average, 258 ; of cappers' journeymen, 574 ; of dawbers and masons, 653 ; of soldiers, 343, 354, 355, 356, 363, 366, xlvi ; truck —, 689, 707, 784–5.
Waits, badges and livery of, 200, 359 ; not to leave the city, 335 ; the quarterage of, 307 ; and the trumpet, 189.
Walkers, provide armour, 248–9 ; charges of, 659 ; and the length of cloth, 187–8 ; craft of, to be

formed, 782; master of, an inhabitant, 727; separated from the tailors, 234; mark of, 375; work of, to be done by residents, 659, 704–5, 707, 723, 724, xxxix note; workmanship of, 172, 640, 659. *See also* Fullers, Pageants, Searchers.
Walls, the city, 57, 142–3, 186, 261, 285, xlv–vi; cost of making, 136; to be inspected by the mayor, 284, 607, 628. *See also* Murage.
Walsingham, Sir Francis, 830.
Wanley, Hum., ix.
Wardens, 98, 115, 255; and obits, 67, xliv note; a two years' tenure of office, 606; overcharging of, forbidden, 546; and their tenements, overlooked, 516; and town rents, 58, 188, xliv. *See also* Accounts.
Wards, apportionment of money raised by, 321; for the conduit, 586; for the redemption of the franchises, 371; for loans and presents granted and collected according to, 37–8, 76–82, 85–6, 87–90, 125–9, 152–6, 160–9, 174–80, 209–14, 236–42, 286, 316–7, 336–7; for soldiers, 313–4, 315, 343–4, 354, 355–6, 356–7, 358, 362–3, 364–6, 478, 481–3; for taxation, 43, 120–1, 132–3, 139, 142, 158–9, 170–1, 243–4, 255, 268–9, 406, 429–30, 533–4, 534–5, 542–3, 546, 583–4, 741, 841–2; hall of the men of the, 5–6, 41, 151; *see also* Hall; captains of, for safeguard of the city, 344–5; men from each, assess murage, 119; give counsel concerning finance, 630; inspect the common lands, 730, 736–7, 760–1; let enclosed parts and collect rents, 733–5; population of, and store of foodstuffs, 674–5.
Warwick, Earl of, (1) Ric. Beauchamp, 73, 98; and loans, 74–5, 75–6, 123, xlviii; (2) Ambrose Dudley, 830, 832; (3) Ric. Neville, 308, 311, 324, 325, 420–1; intervenes in a city dispute, 332; keeps the city against Edward IV, 381; comes to Coventry in 1470, 358, xlix; in France, 358; and Henry VI, 359; letters from, 342; loan to, 364, xlviii; soldiers accompany, 317, 319, 364.

Wasperton, leet at, xvii.
Watch, 253, xxviii; armed, *see* Ridings; and constables, 712; and sergeants, 137; duty of keeping, from house to house, 738–9.
Watermarks on paper, xi–xii, xv.
Weapons, bearing of, order against, 28, 29, xxviii.
Weavers, 220, 796; provide armour, 247–8; assize of, 400; and breadth of cloth, 776; charges of, 660, 688–9; and clothiers, 776–7; and corvisers, quarrel between, 203–4; fines of, 93; and journeymen, 91–6; and number of looms, 92–3; municipal influence of, xlii note; wages of, not truck, 689; and woolwinding, 243: and workmanship, 638–9; work of, put out into the country, 639, 661, xxxix note; only to be given to members of the craft, 738; and yarn, 262, 639. *See also* Cloth, Pageants, Searchers.
Weights, 132, 133–4; assize of, according to the Statute of Winchester, 397; sealing of, 134, 843; and Stratford, xlix, 1 and notes. *See also* Measures, Strike.
Well, 375, 572; aldermen to make, 548.
Welles, Lord, (1) Leo, 298; (2) Ric. beheaded, 358.
Wenlock, Lord, 325.
Westmorland, Earl of, 73.
Whittawers, provide armour, 250; assize of, 401. *See also* Pageants.
Willoughby, Lord, 298.
Winchester, Bishop of, (1) Tho. (later Cardinal) Beaufort, 73; (2) Will. Waynflete, 297.
Wine, 386, 387; price of, 24, 797. *See also* Assize, Prices, Taverners.
Wire-drawers, 849; craft of, abuses of, 181, 182, 183; provide armour, 249; and the altar canopy, 131–2, 855, xiv; journeymen of, to work in their own houses, 115, 185.
Wirtel-maker, 852.
Women, in city life, xli and notes; as chandlers, 555; single, not to live alone, 545, 568, xxviii. *See also* Morality, Spinners.
Wood, size of a faggot of, 399; and the Friday market, 28, 648.

Subject Index. 939

Woodville, Sir Edw., 505 ; Sir John, beheaded at Gosford Green, 346.
Wool, to be clean, 636 ; custom for, 567 ; kinds of, 689 ; and the Friday market, 648 ; searcher of, 636 ; and the wool-hall, 192, 193, 787.
Worcester, xxvi note, xxvii note; Bishop of, (1) Joh. Alcock, 490 ; (2) Joh. Carpenter, 297 ; (3) Phil. Morgan, 73, 74, 75; assists in obtaining security for a loan, 83 ; Earl of, Tiptoft, 330 ; beheaded, 359 ; assigned to hear the Cheylesmore dispute, 326; with Edward IV, 324, 325.

Wright, James, makes first printed mention of the *Leet Book*, x–xi.
Wrights, provide armour, 252 ; craft of, dissolved, 798. *See also* Pageants.
Writs, return of, 224.

Yarn, 660 ; sale of, outside the city, 787, 791, xxxix.
York, xxvi note, xxxvii note ; Archbishop of, (1) Will. Booth, 297 ; (2) Geo. Neville, 359 ; Duke of, (1) Ric. father of Edw. IV, 129, 297, 308 ; (2) son of Edw. IV, kindness of the city to, mentioned by Elizabeth Woodville, 407.

County of Coventry,

IN 1841

Copy of Plan

EXHIBITED IN THE ACTION
OF THE CORPORATION
AGAINST
LYTHALL & OTHERS.

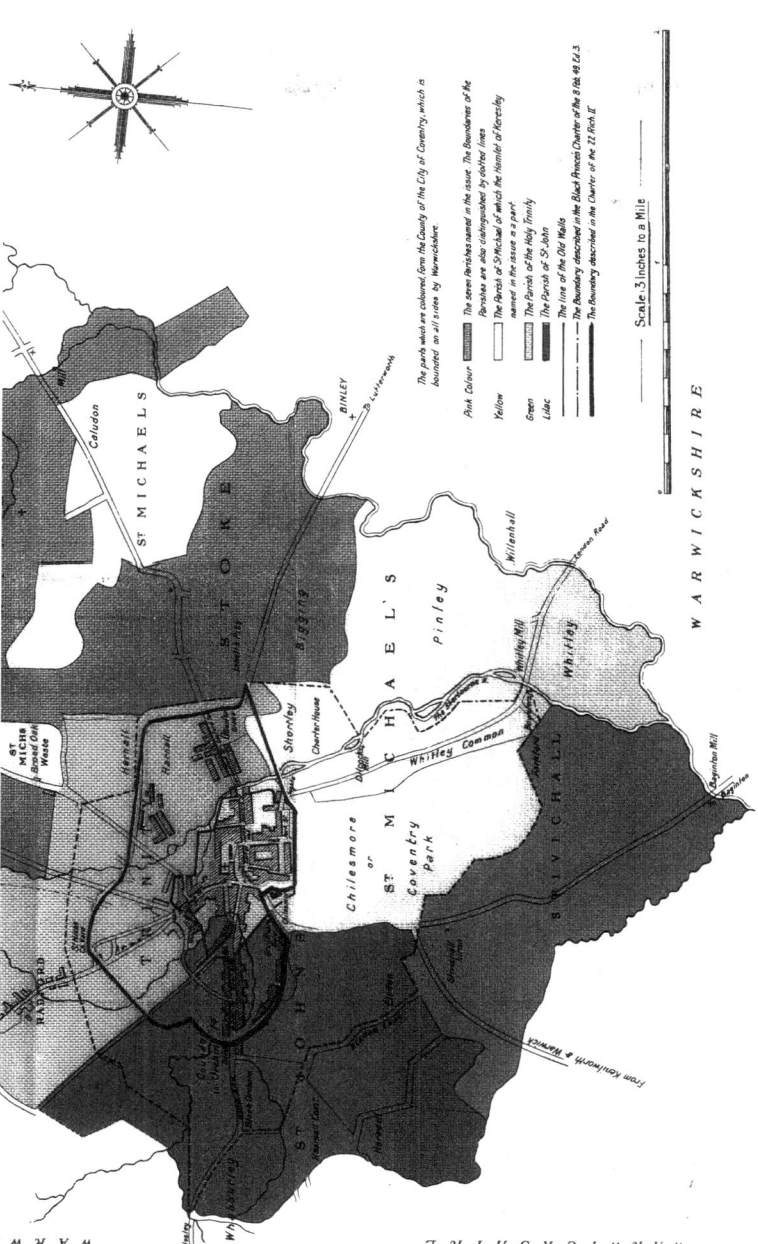

Printed and bound by CPI Group (UK) Ltd, Croydon, CR0 4YY